WEST ACADEMIC PUBLISHING'S LAW SCHOOL ADVISORY BOARD

CYBERSECURITY

AN INTERDISCIPLINARY PROBLEM

■ ■ ■

Derek E. Bambauer
University of Arizona College of Law
Professor of Law

Justin (Gus) Hurwitz
Nebraska College of Law
Associate Professor of Law
Menards Director of the Nebraska Governance & Technology Center

David Thaw
University of Pittsburgh School of Law
Associate Research Professor of Law
University of Pittsburgh School of Computing & Information
Assistant Research Professor of Computing & Information

Charlotte A. Tschider
Loyola University Chicago School of Law
Assistant Professor

AMERICAN CASEBOOK SERIES®

WEST ACADEMIC PUBLISHING

The publisher is not engaged in rendering legal or other professional advice, and this publication is not a substitute for the advice of an attorney. If you require legal or other expert advice, you should seek the services of a competent attorney or other professional.

444 Cedar Street, Suite 700
St. Paul, MN 55101
1-877-888-1330

Printed in the United States of America

ISBN: 978-1-64242-253-5

For Nadia, Dad, and Thinh, with love and gratitude.

—DB

For Smith & Coase, Epstein & Yoo, and Ma & Pa—
my intellectual, professional, and actual parents, respectively.
And Lynne, too, of course.

—GH

For my Dad, who taught me to believe anything is possible and who sacrificed his dreams to give me that chance; for my brother Steven, always a grounding force in my life (and who has Excellent Sports Taste); and for the love of my life, Carrie, who quite remarkably continues to put up with me (even if she makes Bad Sports Choices).

And in memory of John, whose friendship carried me through some of the darkest times.

—DT

To my parents: thank you for teaching me that all things should be done with excellence, curiosity, and kindness.

—CT

SUMMARY OF CONTENTS

TABLE OF CONTENTS

CYBERSECURITY

AN INTERDISCIPLINARY PROBLEM

INTRODUCTION

■ ■ ■

Cybersecurity is a concept that many people encounter in daily life, but to the uninitiated, it may seem intimidating. Terms like "hacking," "threat actor," "defense in depth," "incident response," "vulnerability assessment," and others often form the basics of conversations about cybersecurity problems. They inspire visions of battles fought through keyboards and screens—epic science fiction-inspired battles raging between defenders in "command centers" and attackers rapidly tapping keys from a secret, remote location while wearing black hoodies. And yet, when it comes to understanding and managing cybersecurity risk, nothing could be further from the truth. The activities involved in cybersecurity attack and defense tend to be unglamorous but remain vitally important to economic and national security.

The vocabulary used in public discourse is a key part of the problem. Prevalent vocabulary frames cybersecurity as a mostly technological problem, one to be "solved." This mindset arises, in part, from the historical linkages between the computer science subfields of cryptography and computer security. Cryptography is concerned primarily with intricate mathematical algorithms, and most cryptographic "problems" do have solutions. By contrast, as we discuss in this book, computer security presents a classic problem—but not a classic *math* problem, and not one with a classic solution.

Rather than debating the technical merits of, say, a specific encryption protocol, this book treats cybersecurity as a complex *risk management* problem that involves not only technical matters, but also administrative and physical, and business judgement and legal issues. In this regard, cybersecurity resembles many traditional risk management problems. Consider, for example, what good is a sophisticated lock on the front door if there is an open window next to it? Cybersecurity problems exhibit similar challenges. All the encryption, firewalls, password complexity requirements, and signature-based virus scanners in the world will provide little to no protection if someone unwittingly but voluntarily turns over their credentials via a phishing email. Sophisticated multi-factor authentication may be ineffective if physical tokens are themselves insecure. The cycle of new attacks countered by novel defense tools can proceed endlessly—never reaching a solution to the problem: where the system is actually secure.

That is to say, cybersecurity—generally, efforts to secure computer and computerized systems—is a risk management process. No usable system is *completely* secure.[1] (Yes, not even the one-time pads allegedly used in strategic arms control systems are perfect.[2]) We can never say we have reached a state of being "secure"—rather, security is a process, in which we are constantly making judgements and tradeoffs. This is true from technical, business, and legal perspectives.

Nothing is completely safe. Walking down the sidewalk or driving a car on a busy street are two highly dangerous activities compared to other methods of transportation. Yet people engage in these activities every day with little, if any, thought to the risks involved. Society has created collectively acceptable models to manage and allocate these risks, and to assign responsibilities for mitigating them. A similar process is not only the most effective way to think about cybersecurity problems, but indeed a *necessary* way—for there is not (and can never be) a solution that prevents all cybersecurity risk. This book explores these concepts as a foundation to help you learn to think about cybersecurity: the players, the risks, the technologies, and the types of questions involved. At the conclusion of this text, you should have developed a vocabulary and tool set for evaluating the effectiveness of various policy mechanisms for managing risk.

As we discuss in Chapter 1, we use the word "Problem" in our title advisedly. At one level this word connotes that as a field—and, too, this book—cybersecurity is more about problems than solutions. But even more, we use this in a Kuhnian sense, to connote that cybersecurity is not yet a field. Rather, it is a set of urgent issues that practitioners and researchers from myriad fields are working, not necessarily coherently, to understand. One of our goals with this book is to provide those working within each of these fields a vocabulary to work with others across those fields. The development of such a vocabulary is a first step towards the development of a new science—one that moves beyond struggling with problems to puzzling through solutions.

Cybersecurity, especially from a risk management perspective, exists at the intersection of three distinct fields: business, engineering, and law. This book is an attempt to do the impossible: to provide an interdisciplinary introduction to each of these three fields that is at once accessible to students and teachers from all of these fields but sophisticated enough to be useful to those from each of these fields. We apologize at the outset for the occasional glosses and simplifications that we must necessarily make in some of our discussion. As with all exercises in risk management, we

1 One of your casebook authors recalls a security conversation with a business leader who once said, "If we locked up the toilet paper, we wouldn't have anyone steal it, but we sure wouldn't sell very much toilet paper, either."

2 Why? Because the humans who must, eventually, evaluate or utilize those codes can themselves be compromised, however *unlikely* that may be.

have tried to not let the perfect be the enemy of the good—it is our hope that this text thread three needles sufficiently well to provide a useful introduction to the concepts from three distinct fields that are necessary to understand the issues that define cybersecurity as a new field.

This book would not have been possible without the support and assistance of many. We are each thankful to numerous classes of students at the Universities of Arizona, Nebraska, North Carolina, and Pittsburgh who have provided witting or, at times, unwitting help developing, testing, and debugging this book, as well as several colleagues at other schools who have used earlier iterations of these materials and provided helpful and thoughtful feedback on them. Each of us has specific individuals who have helped as we have worked on this project, including Kevin Adler, Sarah Mirs, Will Nelson, Vinnie Yasue, and professional friends and colleagues at various institutions, including (but surely not limited to) Mike Carroll, James Cooper, Oliver Day, Leslie Francis, Eric Goldman, Dan Hunter, Sasha Romanosky, Nathan Sales, Alan Trammell, Felix Wu, and Tal Zarsky. We also wish to thank Professor Joseph Kennedy who graciously "test-drove" multiple editions of this book for several years and provided invaluable feedback.

~ Bambauer, Hurwitz, Thaw & Tschider
Fall 2020

CHAPTER 1

WHAT IS (CYBER)SECURITY[1]?

■ ■ ■

Both technologists and lawyers have struggled to articulate what comprises cybersecurity—and what does not. Similarly, it can be challenging to differentiate cybersecurity from related terms such as data security, data protection, information security, and even privacy. This Chapter seeks to help you to begin to think conceptually about what cybersecurity is and is not. Without limits in our definition of the term, any legal question involving Internet technology could potentially be considered a cybersecurity problem. Cybersecurity spans a wide range of government and business functions and affects most sectors of the economy. We propose a formal definition for the term in Chapter 2, but for now, just consider what matters and what should be included in "cybersecurity."

A. INSECURITY IN THE WILD

We begin our introduction to the concept of (cyber)security with a series of examples. These scenarios are not intended to offer a formal definition of cybersecurity. Rather, they are selected incidents that meet two criteria: (1) the general consensus is they involve something called cybersecurity; and (2) they are of sufficient societal importance and impact to call for a policy response. Regardless of which substantive policy is ultimately applied by decisionmakers, these events matter.

1. CYBERSECURITY'S WILD HISTORY

We start with two historical anecdotes: what is likely the first compromise of a telegraph communications network, and the story of Lightning Ellsworth. Both of these anecdotes demonstrate that many of the themes of cybersecurity—and this book—can be disambiguated and stand separate from the newness of modern computer and communications technology.

The story of the Blanc brothers and the French mechanical telegraphs takes place in the 1790s:[2]

---

[1] We place "cyber" in parentheses because "security" as a field has long addressed many of the problems we examine in this text. However, the term "cybersecurity" reinforces internet connectivity as the source of many security problems.

[2] For more about this example, *see* Tom Standage, *The Crooked Timber of Humanity*, 1843 MAGAZINE (Oct. 5, 2017).

The world's first national data network was constructed in France during the 1790s. It was a mechanical telegraph system, consisting of chains of towers, each of which had a system of movable wooden arms on top. Different configurations of these arms corresponded to letters, numbers and other characters. Operators in each tower would adjust the arms to match the configuration of an adjacent tower, observed through a telescope, causing sequences of characters to ripple along the line. Messages could now be sent much faster than letters, whizzing from one end of France to the other in minutes. The network was reserved for government use but in 1834 two bankers, François and Joseph Blanc, devised a way to subvert it to their own ends.

As a human operated, mechanical, system, operators would occasionally make mistakes during transmission, sending the wrong character. To account for this, the "alphabet" for transmission included the equivalent of a backspace character. The Blanc brothers took advantage of this feature to secure financial gain. They were bond traders in Bordeaux, where most trades were based upon information sent from Paris by mail. This mail took several days to get from Paris to Bordeaux. The Blanc brothers bribed a mechanical telegraph operator to encode information about Paris market conditions into telegraph messages, using the "backspace" character to ensure that their messages would go unnoticed as anything other than innocuous errors.

Their treachery was discovered after a couple of years. Curiously, however, they avoided any legal consequences, by virtue of the fact that there were no laws on the books that made their conduct illegal.

The story of Lightning Ellsworth is similarly engaging.[3] This story involves the electromechanical telegraph—the precursor to the telephone—which relied on human operators to tap out messages, typically using Morse code, that were transmitted as electrical pulses over copper cables. Individual telegraph operators tended to have unique patterns in how they tapped own messages. This afforded some level of security: the recipient of a telegraph message could usually recognize the cadence of each tapped-out message, which gave some assurances as to its authenticity.

George Ellsworth was a Confederate telegraph operator who was able to use this element of security to his—and the Confederate army's—advantage. He had a remarkable ability to mimic the cadence of other telegraph operators. He would travel with forward units and, as they encountered Union telegraph wires (the Union army devoted substantial effort to building out a telegraph network to use for wartime

[3] Stephen Towne, *The Adventures of Lightning Ellsworth*, N.Y. TIMES (Dec. 12, 2012).

communications[4]) he would attach a small device to the wires that let him both listen in on transmissions and tap out transmissions of his own. Ellsworth's ability to intercept messages was useful, but not entirely unique. His ability to mimic the cadence of other operators, however, gave him the unique ability to send false messages, for instance providing false reports of Confederate troop movements to distract Union forces.

2. CYBERSECURITY'S WILD PRESENT

Turning to more contemporary examples, we begin with Target Corporation's 2013 data breach. Then, we will discuss incidents with Yahoo, Inc., Wyndham Hotels, and the federal government's Office of Personnel Management (OPM).

In 2013, Target Corporation experienced a major data breach: over 40 million customer records, including personal and credit card information, were stolen from its systems.[5] The attackers were able to install intrusion software on the Point-of-Sale (POS) systems—that is, the physical cash registers coupled with payment card readers—used for card payments in Target's retail stores. As the POS systems process customer transactions, this attacker software, named KAPTOXA, monitors the systems' memory for valuable information like credit card numbers. KAPTOXA records this information and sends the data to computers controlled by the attackers, from which the information is collected.

How were the attackers able to install this software on Target's POS systems? The intruders stole network credentials from a contracting company, Fazio Mechanical Services, that serviced one Target location's HVAC (Heating, Ventilating, and Air Conditioning) systems. The store's HVAC computer network was connected to a central network that processed POS data. Unbeknownst to Target and Fazio, Fazio's own systems had been compromised. This gave the attackers a foothold.

Once this foothold was established, the attackers discovered that Target had not divided its network into subnetworks, which is a standard security precaution. This enabled the attackers to access multiple systems, not just the air conditioning unites with which Fazio needed to interact. Once the attackers accessed the store's central network using Fazio's stolen credentials, they could control the individual POS systems. Moreover, they could also directly access the Target corporate network, which allowed

---

4 *See* Christopher Klein, *How Abraham Lincoln Used the Telegraph to Help Win the Civil War*, HISTORY.COM (Jul. 9, 2020).

5 Brian Krebs, *Inside Target Corp., Days After 2013 Breach*, KREBS ON SECURITY (Sept. 21, 2015), https://krebsonsecurity.com/2015/09/inside-target-corp-days-after-2013-breach/; Teri Radichel, *Case Study: Critical Controls that Could Have Prevented Target Breach*, SANS INSTITUTE (Aug. 5, 2014), https://www.sans.org/reading-room/whitepapers/casestudies/case-study-critical-controls-prevented-target-breach-35412; *Attacks on point-of-sales systems*, SYMANTEC (Nov. 20, 2014), https://www.symantec.com/content/dam/symantec/docs/white-papers/attacks-on-point-of-sale-systems-en.pdf.

them to communicate with all of the company's other retail facilities. In one account, cited by security researcher Brian Krebs, it may have been possible for an attacker to compromise a (computerized) deli meat scale in one store and to leverage that scale to control a POS system in another store. This account is likely a dramatization of what happened in this specific incident, but is not outside of the realm of the possible.

Two of the questions we will focus on in this text is: *what could the organization in question have done to prevent the breach? Legally, who, if anyone, should be liable for any resulting damage?* Without a doubt, Target's network had problems; the lack of segmentation between various network systems is usually unwise. However, we now live in a world where POS systems, HVAC systems, and even deli meat scales are nearly always computerized and networked. Once a determined adversary is in the network, it's very likely that they will be able to find a path from the HVAC system to the POS systems.

Besides Target and the attackers, who else might be liable? What about other entities or individuals within Target's computer ecosystem, perhaps those responsible for developing the POS system(s)? Or Fazio, the HVAC contractor, which experienced its own breach resulting in attackers gaining unauthorized access to Target's system? The question of who to blame is difficult largely because the cybersecurity ecosystem—the network of various systems, parties, rules, and enforcement mechanisms—is incredibly complicated. Whereas in a typical commercial transaction various risks may be apportioned between a half dozen parties, in the cybersecurity context, risks may be apportioned between ten times as many parties, or even more. Ultimately, the relationships among risks, parties, and liabilities are far less clear than in the offline context. Furthermore, from the facts reported, we have no idea how private agreements, such as using contracts, might have allocated these risks between the parties. For example, Fazio might have made contractual security commitments to keep Target's credentials secure that it ultimately did not fulfill. Or, Target might have agreed to ensure that the HVAC system was securely maintained, and separated from the larger corporate network. A third party responsible for Target's network security might have failed to install appropriate firewalls between systems to segment the network. Without more information, it is difficult to clearly identify who is responsible from a liability perspective.

Curiously, when a breach occurs, we often look at the organization that had the relationship with affected individuals to identify responsibility. And yet, cyberattackers broke the law, accessed the systems, and stole and resold Target customer credit card data, without any pre-existing relationships with the stores' customers. In traditional civil actions over physical harms (typically the domain of tort law), such as lawsuits against parking garages or storage facilities, liability does not clearly fall upon the facility operator in the event of a break-in. Physical structures generally are far less complex for analyzing liability than online systems. While this complexity might drive society to look immediately to the entity possessing the data, such as Target, the answer to the liability question is often far more complicated.

Target made mistakes, but many commentators argue that they had implemented reasonable security practices. Despite this, a number of lawsuits followed the breach, including breach of contract actions between banks that processed credit card transactions and the owners of those card brands (such as Mastercard or Visa), as well as customer tort actions. However, these lawsuits generally settled before trial, and thus without developing any significant case law that could guide future disputes.[6] The realities of litigating cybersecurity-related cases is another issue to which we will dedicate considerable attention because such lawsuits have proven very difficult to win. Notably, the Target breach was a one-time event. Target did not have a public history of security problems with its systems, and the attack that it experienced did not result from a failure to respond to prior incidents. Indeed, Target spent over $202 million remediating and managing the data breach, and after the breach, Target implemented extensive technology upgrades and bolstered its cybersecurity program. Many companies that experienced breaches during this period took similar post-incident steps.

There are many examples of firms whose security practices were lackluster, if not exceptionally poor. Yahoo! is perhaps the worst offender due to its repeated breaches: over three billion user accounts were compromised in the early 2010s, and Yahoo! experienced a breach again in 2016. After these breaches were made public, the New York Times published an article with the headline *Defending Against Hackers Took a Back Seat at Yahoo, Insiders Say*.[7] In addition to substantial legal costs, including settling a class-action consumer lawsuit for $117.5 million, Yahoo! experienced the first case of a sustained stock price decline.[8]

---

[6] Target has settled lawsuits with a wide range of plaintiffs. Jonathan Stempel & Nandita Bose, *Target in $39.4 million settlement with banks over data breach*, REUTERS (Dec. 2, 2015), https://www.reuters.com/article/us-target-breach-settlement/target-in-39-4-million-settlement-with-banks-over-data-breach-idUSKBN0TL20Y20151203; Kevin McCoy, *Target to pay $18.5M for 2013 data breach that affected 41 million consumers*, USA TODAY (May 23, 2017), https://www.usatoday.com/story/money/2017/05/23/target-pay-185m-2013-data-breach-affected-consumers/102063932/. In turn, in 2019, Target sued its insurance company to force it to reimburse costs of at least $74 million incurred in replacing credit cards due to the breach. Kavita Kumar, *Target sues insurer for up to $74 million in 2013 data breach costs*, STAR TRIBUNE (Nov. 19, 2019), https://www.startribune.com/target-sues-insurer-for-at-least-74-million-in-2013-data-breach-costs/565169292/.

[7] Nicole Perlroth & Vindo Goel, NEW YORK TIMES (Sept. 28, 2016), https://nyti.ms/2djkkel.

[8] *Here's How Much Yahoo Shares Are Dropping After Latest Hack Reveal*, FORTUNE (Dec. 15, 2016), https://fortune.com/2016/12/15/yahoo-shares-hack/.

Ultimately, Yahoo!'s security problems decreased its valuation by $350 million when it was acquired by Verizon in 2017.[9]

In other cases, firms have experienced repeated breaches and failed to respond to them. This was the case, as alleged by the Federal Trade Commission (FTC), with Wyndham Hotels. The FTC brought a regulatory enforcement action against Wyndham alleging unfair trade practices after hackers accessed Wyndham's systems on three separate occasions—and after Wyndham failed to address the underlying security problems. The Wyndham Hotel consent order, which memorialized the FTC and Wyndham's settlement, demonstrates how administrative agencies have the ability to impose cybersecurity program requirements:

> IT IS ORDERED that Hotels and Resorts shall, no later than the date of entry of this Order, establish and implement, and thereafter maintain, for twenty (20) years after entry of this Order, a comprehensive information security program that is reasonably designed to protect the security, confidentiality, and integrity of Cardholder Data that it collects or receives in the United States from or about consumers. Such program, the content and implementation of which must be fully documented in writing, shall consist of the following administrative, technical, and physical safeguards appropriate to Hotels and Resorts' size and complexity, the nature and scope of Hotels and Resorts' activities, and the sensitivity of the Cardholder Data at issue.[10]

The Wyndham settlement raises another theme that we will consider this semester: what is the role of the government, such as federal administrative agencies, in ensuring cybersecurity? There are a number of models for enforcing (and defining) legal rights. For example, individuals may bring suit based upon contract law or tort law (that is, the law of wrongful harms); shareholders may bring suit based on misbehavior of officers or directors of a company; regulatory agencies like the FTC can establish and enforce rules on behalf of consumers; and prosecutors can bring criminal actions against bad actors. In later chapters, we discuss each of these approaches in turn, including their relative benefits and challenges.

Another example suggests that we may want to be cautious about relying on government expertise for regulating cybersecurity. In 2015, hackers believed to be connected to the People's Republic of China accessed the sensitive personal information of about 22 million government employees stored by the Office of Personnel Management (OPM). This

---

[9] Jeremy Kirk, *Yahoo! Takes $350 Million Hit in Verizon Deal*, BANK INFO SECURITY (Feb. 22, 2017), https://www.bankinfosecurity.com/yahoo-takes-350-million-hit-in-verizon-deal-a-9736.

[10] Stipulated Order for Injunction, *Federal Trade Commission v. Wyndham Worldwide Corp.*, No. 2:13–CV–01887–ES–JAD (D.N.J. Dec. 11, 2015), https://www.ftc.gov/system/files/documents/cases/151211wyndhamstip.pdf, at 4–5.

information included comprehensive background forms on current and past government employees, including Social Security Numbers, residence history, family history, employment history, and further security clearance background check information. Hackers even accessed digital copies of fingerprints for 4.5 million employees, including active military and covert operations personnel. While not the largest data breach in recent history in terms of records, the breach of OPM's systems is surely one of the most devastating breaches in term of impact.

The OPM breach was also a result, at least in part, of poor security practices and failure to sufficiently respond to past security incidents. As reported by the House Committee on Oversight and Government Reform, attackers began exfiltrating data from OPM systems in July 2014—but were not detected until April 2015.[11] This followed years of reports citing substantial security problems. Since 2005, OPM's Inspector General had repeatedly raised concerns about the security of the agency's sensitive data. Surprisingly, the OPM breach involved two separate attackers. One was detected breaking into OPM's systems in March 2014, but was successfully locked out. While OPM technologists responded to the first attack, the second attacker was accessing the agency's systems using a different method. It took more than a year for OPM to find evidence of this second attacker.

3. CYBERSECURITY'S WILD WEST (OR, CYBERSECURITY IS HARD)

Despite these recent security problems, the federal government has some of the world's most sophisticated capabilities—both offensive and defensive. For example, organizations often contact the Federal Bureau of Investigations (FBI) after undergoing a cyberattack, especially when the attack is believed to originate in another country. In some situations, the FBI alerts private organizations when a data breach has come to the Bureau's attention through its own communication channels. Although the FBI does not overtly protect private organizations against cybersecurity attacks, the agency is an active partner in post-breach activities, such as by preserving evidence for later Department of Justice prosecutions.

---

[11] MAJORITY STAFF REPORT, THE OPM DATA BREACH: HOW THE GOVERNMENT JEOPARDIZED OUR NATIONAL SECURITY FOR MORE THAN A GENERATION (Sept. 7, 2016), https://republicans-oversight.house.gov/wp-content/uploads/2016/09/The-OPM-Data-Breach-How-the-Government-Jeopardized-Our-National-Security-for-More-than-a-Generation.pdf. This report was largely produced by the Republican majority of the House Committee on Oversight and Government. The Democratic minority on the committee also released a memorandum critical of the Republican majority's conclusions, placing blame for the compromise of OPM's systems on government contractors and raising concerns that the majority report constituted a partisan attack on OPM's Democratic-appointed leadership. DEMOCRATIC STAFF, MEMORANDUM RE COMMITTEE INVESTIGATION INTO THE OPM DATA BREACH (Sept. 6, 2016), https://oversight.house.gov/sites/democrats.oversight.house.gov/files/documents/2016-09-06.Democratic%20Memo%20on%20OPM%20Data%20Breach%20Investigation.pdf.

Multiple federal agencies have moved to regulate various aspects of cybersecurity, demonstrating the prevalence of and attention to problems with information technology security in recent years. This focuses generates an obvious question: if government entities are interested in cybersecurity, and have expertise to bring to bear, why do there continue to be so many cybersecurity problems?

The short answer is that it is remarkably difficult to design secure systems. Throughout this book, we will draw upon technical knowledge and business practices to describe these challenges, which help explain the complexity of regulating cybersecurity practices.

Consider three major recent security incidents that demonstrate the difficulty of doing cybersecurity well: the Heartbleed bug,[12] the Logjam bug,[13] and the DigiNotar attack.[14] All three of these incidents involve *encryption*. Generally stated, encryption is a way to mathematically transform intelligible data into unintelligible data. (The reverse process is called decryption.) Even if an attacker obtains encrypted data, they cannot read it. Under most state and federal laws, when an attacker accesses encrypted data elements but cannot decrypt them, there is no legal liability for the data breach—it is as though the attack did not occur. Practically speaking, the use of encryption does not eliminate the need for additional security techniques, such as limits on system access, but it reduces the overall risk of data loss or misuse. The combination of protective techniques used on a particular system or across a network provides cumulative security—what security professionals call "defense in depth."

Encryption remains, however, a critical part of most security strategies—albeit one of the most difficult parts to do well. Implementing encryption requires expertise, and designing encryption technologies is the realm of the most elite of these experts, so encryption-related incidents are truly remarkable.[15] The Heartbleed exploit was built upon a small flaw in the OpenSSL network security library—a piece of code that is at the heart of thousands of applications used by billions of people—that would allow

---

[12] *The Heartbleed Bug*, SYNOPSYS (June 3, 2020), http://heartbleed.com/.

[13] David Adrian et al., *Logjam Attack Proof of Concept Demonstrations*, https://weakdh.org/logjam.html.

[14] Hans Hoogarten et al., *Black Tulip Report of the investigation into the DigiNotar Certificate Authority breach*, FOX-IT (Aug. 13, 2012), https://www.researchgate.net/publication/269333601_Black_Tulip_Report_of_the_investigation_into_the_DigiNotar_Certificate_Authority_breach.

[15] It is worth noting that none of these incidents involved a fundamental mathematical flaw in the encryption algorithm (i.e., a scientific flaw) but rather a failure to implement that algorithm properly. These can be distinguished by analogy to a combination lock: a *fundamental mathematical* flaw in the algorithm is like a combination lock that opens when something other than the correct combination is entered (e.g., if the combination "0 - 0 - 0" always unlocked it, regardless of what the manufacturer or user set as the purported combination). By contrast, an *implementation flaw* is similar to a lock that makes a distinct noise when the dial is turned to the next correct number in the sequence of the correct combination, and thus revealing the combination.

anyone on the Internet to read memory from any computers affected by the bug. Logjam is a bug in the Apache web server's implementation of the Diffie-Hellman key exchange protocol—a fundamental encryption tool—that made it relatively easy to break the encryption of web traffic. In the DigiNotar attack, hackers were able to compromise DigiNotar, a firm responsible for issuing and verifying the encryption certificates used to identify trusted parties on the Internet. This incursion allowed attackers to pretend to be anyone they wanted to be online, including, for instance, Google, Microsoft, or Citibank.

The most remarkable thing about all three of these incidents is that they affected core aspects of the cybersecurity ecosystem. OpenSSL, the Apache web server, and certificate authorities like DigiNotar provide basic pieces of architecture that are essential for the security of the Internet. Further, these technologies have been designed, implemented, and maintained by elite experts. If they can't get things right, how are average security professionals, let alone typical users, supposed to secure and maintain their systems?

QUESTIONS

1. What harm do users experience due to cybersecurity incidents? What if hackers obtain personal information about you, but they never share it? Or if they obtain and use credit card information, but the credit card company refunds those charges? How about if a hacker installs software on your TV that is used to "mine" bitcoins or other cryptocurrency[16] while the television is turned off? What if a hacker installs a program on your new car that causes the horn to briefly honk once when you turn the car on?

2. Tarony Home recently experienced a security incident in which their systems were compromised in a way that resulted in substantial and concrete harm to thousands of individuals. Did Tarony Home have bad security?

3. Social media platforms developed in the United States, such as Twitter and Facebook, were instrumental in bringing about a change in governmental regimes in Egypt in 2011, sometimes referred to as the Egyptian Revolution. Russia attempted to influence the 2016 U.S. Presidential Election in part by releasing information and creating fake news content that circulated on social media platforms. How are these incidents similar? Different? From the perspective of Egypt's fallen government, are they the same or different?

4. Some of the citations supporting the examples discussed above are to reports and whitepapers written by private firms such as FireEye, Infoblox, the SANS Institute, Akamai, and Fox-IT. Many of these firms are security consultants—they are in the business of selling security services. How does this affect how you read these reports?

---

[16] Bitcoin, cryptocurrencies, and blockchain generally are discussed in [[chapter]]. For now, it suffices to say that "mining bitcoin" (or other cryptocurrencies) is the rough equivalent of "printing money" using computer processing power, albeit money that is highly volatile in value.

5. As mentioned above, the Democratic Party minority on the House Oversight and Government Reform Committee wrote a counter-report criticizing the report issued by the committee's Republican majority. How might this affect how you read these reports?

6. a) You are a junior associate at a law firm. One day, during your lunch break, you spend a few minutes playing online poker. Soon thereafter you become concerned that someone is accessing the files on your computer, which include hundreds of sensitive client documents.

b) You try to install a new program on your home computer, of which you are the only user, but you are unable to do so because you are out of hard drive space. After a few minutes investigating, you discover a large folder containing thousands of files—including what appears to be a collection of child pornography. The dates on many of the files are quite old, but others are very recent.

c) While booking airline tickets for a trip to visit your family over the holidays, you discover that if you enter information into the airline's web page in a certain way, it books your requested tickets but does not charge your credit card.

In each of a)–c), what security concerns do you see? Who has engaged in objectionable activity? Who is responsible for that activity? What does "responsible" mean?

B. ASSETS & THREATS: CENTRAL CYBERSECURITY CONCEPTS

The real reasons why security problems exist are twofold: first, there are many motivations for exploiting these problems, so there is always an adversary waiting eagerly for organizations to stumble. Intruders attack cybersystems with a wide range of motives: for fun, prestige, money, to harm one's competitors, for domestic political reasons (e.g., activism, political protest), for foreign political reasons, or out of sheer boredom and curiosity. Second, human nature means that even when intruders are not nefarious by intent, or motivated to cause damage, they are still human, and humans make mistakes. Poorly secured Internet-connected systems are vulnerable to human errors that impact data confidentiality, integrity, availability, safety, or privacy in unexpected ways.

Two critical concepts for understanding cybersecurity are assets and threats. An *asset* is anything of value to an individual or organization that might be targeted by attackers or be vulnerable to threats. Although in financial language, assets are items that can be reduced to a pecuniary sum, assets in cybersecurity parlance are physical or logical things of value, broadly construed.

For example, assets to an organization could include employees, physical offices, computer hardware, computer software, and intangible assets, such as intellectual property, trade secrets, proprietary information, or pure data. Assets can include personal physical property (moveable objects, such as computers or servers), physical real estate, people, and intangible property and data (what is stored in and transmitted between and within personal physical property). It is important to think broadly about assets, because assets are what an organization must protect, either because safeguards are required by law or because the organization seeks to preserve its financial investments or reputation.

Consider the Sony Pictures data breach of 2014. Attackers accessed Sony e-mail servers and released several internal e-mails to the public. These e-mails included embarrassing references to actors employed by Sony, damaging the reputation of the CEO and the company overall. Although sensitive personal information or trade secrets were not compromised, Sony would have preferred for these e-mails not to have become public. Assets in this case involved not only the e-mail server but also the contents of the messages. Organizations must identify which assets have value to the organization to make determinations about which cybersecurity protections a given asset requires and under what circumstances.

Many organizations implement a policy structure for internal cybersecurity requirements. This policy structure often includes a data classification regime or standard that categorizes data for purposes of specifying which cybersecurity requirements apply to particular data or system types. For example, sensitive personal information like biometric data might be required to be encrypted, while internal plans for marketing campaigns may not require encryption.

However, selecting the appropriate security approach has as much to do with the risks from potential threats as it does with the value of assets. Recall that without any attacker, human error, or natural disaster, assets would never need protection. Therefore, understanding the cybersecurity ecosystem means assessing both organizational or personal assets and who or what could compromise those assets. *Threats* are any potential event or action that may impact an asset negatively. Threats have three distinct aspects: the nature of their *relationship* to an organization, the *quality* of the threat source (or actual actor perpetuating the threat), and the *motivation* of the threat source. Understanding these differences helps an individual select an appropriate course of action for implementing a cybersecurity program and setting reasonable requirements.

The nature of the organizational *relationship* usually refers to the placement of the threat source. For example, threat sources are either internal or external to an organization—either part of the organization or outside it, such as a disgruntled employee (internal) and a foreign hacker (external). Further, the *quality* of a threat source may vary: threat sources may be people, or they may be a non-human events, such as a power surge or an "Act of God," like a tornado. Finally, *motivation* matters. "Acts of God," for example, have no motivation. Employees who might make an inadvertent error are not nefarious or disgruntled. And a hacking organization may be primarily motivated by money. Different motivations inform what to protect and under what conditions. For example, if potential threat sources are financially motivated, they are more likely to attack large volumes of sensitive data that may be sold on the Dark Web, and less likely to access an organization's maintenance records.

Attacks are threats in action—when a threat source undertakes an intentional, nefarious action to harm an organization. One type of attack that is usually purely financially motivated is a ransomware attack. Ransomware is where attackers deliver malware to a user, such as a link or an attachment in a phishing e-mail. After the user downloads the file or clicks on the link, the ransomware encrypts sensitive data on the user's computer, making it unusable, or held for "ransom," until the individual or an organization pays a specific sum. Attackers will only decrypt the data in exchange for payment, and frequently attackers threaten to destroy the data unless the payment is made within a prescribed number of hours or days. Targeted organizations that do not pay the ransom frequently cannot recover their data.

After the target individual or organization transfers money to the attacker (generally using cryptocurrency), the attacker provides them with a decryption key to recover the encrypted data. Many different organizations have been affected by ransomware, from large municipalities and healthcare organizations to law firms and other small businesses. The amount of money demanded is usually based on the data type, repository size, and importance, as well as the buying power of the organization. While an individual might only have to pay a few hundred dollars, law firms or other small businesses might have to pay in the hundreds of thousands, while large companies may have to pay millions.

For law students, it is worth noting that law firms have recently become important targets for attacks. Law firms have a poor history of cybersecurity and their computers often contain large amounts of sensitive and crucially important information from many clients. This makes them valuable targets. Attackers rarely care about harming the law firm. Rather, attackers care about using the information managed by the law firm for financial gain (e.g., insider trading[17]), to help an adverse legal party, or for political purposes (this is less common but, as the Panama Papers makes clear, is a real risk[18]).

---

[17] Nicole Hong & Robin Sidel, *Hackers Breach Law Firms, Including Cravath and Weil Gotshal*, WALL STREET JOURNAL (Mar. 29, 2016), http://www.wsj.com/articles/hackers-breach-cravath-swaine-other-big-law-firms-1459293504.

[18] *The Panama Papers: Exposing the Rogue Offshore Finance Industry*, INTERNATIONAL CONSORTIUM OF INVESTIGATIVE JOURNALISTS, https://panamapapers.icij.org/; Luke Harding, *What*

Another important attack motivation for hackers is to obtain control over systems that they will then use in their future activities. Sometimes hackers obtain control through graduated steps. During the Target data breach, for instance, the attackers first compromised an HVAC vendor. The credentials gained from the vendor provided an entry point into the rest of the Target network. Other times, the compromised system becomes a tool in the attacker's arsenal. On October 21, 2016, attackers used a network of roughly 100,000 compromised Internet-connected security cameras to launch a Distributed Denial of Service (DDoS) attack on Dyn, a company that provides Domain Name Server (DNS) and other infrastructure services to large parts of the Internet.

If DNS and other infrastructure services are interrupted, websites may not be available, impacting business and other operations. As a result of the Dyn attack, large parts of the Internet in the United States were inaccessible to users for much of the day. Importantly, this attack was facilitated using a network of several thousand compromised computers, yet these attackers had zero interest in "pwning"[19] individual computers with any motivation other than to create a network that could target Dyn.

In the following chapters, we will consider these and dozens of other examples as tools for looking at the issues highlighted above and many others.

QUESTIONS

1. Are you surprised by the wide variety of things that are considered assets? Without yet knowing details about security techniques, what do you think might be some of the differences between protecting a physical object, like a server, and protecting intangible data?

2. Organizations often begin the cybersecurity process by creating a "data flow diagram." What do you think the value of such a diagram might be? Using your internal home network, can you diagram how data flows from your device to your router, and to your ISP?

3. What are some of the differences among threat sources? Can you think of circumstances where internal threats might be a greater concern than outsider threats?

C. ("CYBER")SECURITY "LAW"?

"Cybersecurity law" lacks a clear definition; indeed, there is debate over whether such a field even exists. This may seem a problem for a class

---

are the Panama Papers? A guide to history's biggest data leak, THE GUARDIAN (Apr. 5, 2016), https://www.theguardian.com/news/2016/apr/03/what-you-need-to-know-about-the-panama-papers.

[19] *Pwning* (pronounced "own-ing") is the act of using a computer in an unauthorized manner to achieve specific goals related to the exercise of control, such as creating a DDoS attack network or encrypting a computer using ransomware.

that focuses on cybersecurity law and policy. Some also argue, at least partially in jest, that there is no such thing as cybersecurity policy, either. This glib assessment is, of course, not accurate, though it is correct to say that our approach to cybersecurity policy is in its infancy and that cybersecurity policy five years from now likely (hopefully!) will look very little like it does today.

To be sure, there are cybersecurity *laws*. There are also informal and "soft law" rules that apply today, such as norms, guidelines, best practices, and policies, some of which have been developed in response to cybersecurity concerns, and others of which were simply inherited from different contexts of varying relevance. There are also many practical cybersecurity concerns that lawyers face, from the cybersecurity issues that law firms confront as businesses, to the practical guidance a lawyer gives her clients about their security, to the new and unique ethical issues that draw upon existing norms and legal models, including the common law, statutory language, and administrative behavior.

Instead of surveying all cybersecurity *laws*, this book provides a wide base of knowledge and perspective about technology, cybersecurity principles, and legal principles that affect the field. Survey approaches can be useful in well-established fields or fields where studying the range of existing law is helpful to learn the deeper concepts that define the area. Neither of those is true of cybersecurity today. Therefore, we do not attempt to provide a comprehensive list of all legal regimes that could be considered cybersecurity laws. Rather, we offer examples and legal concepts.

Discussions of cybersecurity today recall the debate between Judge Frank Easterbrook and Professor Lawrence Lessig nearly two decades ago over whether there was value in studying cyberlaw. Judge Easterbrook argued that cyberlaw is akin to the "law of the horse," explaining that:

> Lots of cases deal with sales of horses; others deal with people kicked by horses; still more deal with the licensing and racing of horses, or with the care veterinarians give to horses, or with prizes at horse shows. Any effort to collect these strands into a course on "The Law of the Horse" is doomed to be shallow and to miss unifying principles. Teaching 100 percent of the cases on people kicked by horses will not convey the law of torts very well. Far better for most students—better, even, for those who plan to go into the horse trade—to take courses in property, torts, commercial transactions, and the like, adding to the diet of horse cases a smattering of transactions in cucumbers, cats, coal, and cribs. Only by putting the law of the horse in the context of broader

rules about commercial endeavors could one really understand the law about horses.[20]

Lessig responded that there was something different about cyberspace that made its study worthwhile. He explained:

> I agree that our aim should be courses that "illuminate the entire law," but unlike Easterbrook, I believe that there is an important general point that comes from thinking in particular about how law and cyberspace connect.
>
> This general point is about the limits on law as a regulator and about the techniques for escaping those limits. This escape, both in real space and in cyberspace, comes from recognizing the collection of tools that a society has at hand for affecting constraints upon behavior. . . . The choice among tools obviously depends upon their efficacy. But importantly, the choice will also raise a question about values. By working through these examples of law interacting with cyberspace, we will throw into relief a set of general questions about law's regulation outside of cyberspace.[21]

The past twenty years have delivered a mixed verdict in favor of Lessig. An important aspect of his argument is that the underlying characteristics of "real space" and cyberspace are somehow different.[22] This idea has not necessarily aged well: if anything, over the past decade the online and offline worlds have increasingly merged (a transition that has had important impacts on security), as a large portion of our personal and work lives have moved online. At the same time, the idea that there is something important to be learned about the law in general through the study of "cyberlaw" has proven quite sound.

Studying cybersecurity is the next step in the project Lessig articulated. When he began, the online and offline worlds were distinct. This made study of their differences valuable, both for the specific rules that govern conduct in each and for understanding the law generally. But today these worlds are colliding. That merger creates new risks for the offline world.

What makes cybersecurity *cyber* instead of just *security*? Adding the cyber prefix to just about anything is, of course, a common trope. It is a

---

[20] Frank H. Easterbrook, *Cyberspace and the Law of the Horse,* 1996 UNIVERSITY OF CHICAGO LEGAL FORUM 207 (1996).

[21] Lawrence Lessig, *The Law of the Horse: What Cyberlaw Might Teach,* 113 Harvard Law Review 501 (1999).

[22] The core thesis of much of Lessig's work is that "code is law"—in cyberspace, rules that govern how individuals interact are defined by the computer code that creates the cyberspace. Because cyberspace may be subject to the equivalent of different physical laws than the real world, we should expect that conduct online will be different from—and properly subject to different rules from—conduct offline.

largely meaningless way of modernizing otherwise stale content for the modern world. Anytime you take something that you already do offline and start doing it online, you're "cybering"—you're doing something new and exciting! Or so you think. More accurately, or, perhaps, more cynically, you're just using a computer to do whatever you were doing before. More often than not, adding the cyber prefix to an activity illustrates a lack of understanding about the internet and its pervasive nature.

But in the context of security, the "cyber" component really is doing something important.[23] Security is about managing risk: identifying threats, assessing exposure to harm from or vulnerability to those threats, and finding ways to avoid, reduce, or absorb that risk. When conduct moves from the real world to cyberspace, whole new classes of threats and vulnerabilities come into play. Cybersecurity is not merely "security in cyberspace." It's the study of how and why the transition to cyberspace changes the risk calculus, and how to respond to these changes.

Cybersecurity law is a young field. In 2011, Professor Joseph S. Nye Jr. compared the state of cybersecurity policy to that of nuclear policy in the 1950s:[24]

> Political leaders and analysts are only beginning to come to terms with this transformative technology. Until now, the issue of cyber security has largely been the domain of computer experts and specialists. When the Internet was created 40 years ago, this small community was like a virtual village of people who knew each other, and they designed an open system with little attention to security. While the Internet is not new, the commercial Web is less than two decades old, and it has exploded from a few million users in the early 1990s to some two billion users today. This burgeoning interdependence has created great opportunities and great vulnerabilities, which strategists do not yet fully comprehend. As Gen Michael Hayden, former director of the CIA says, "Rarely has something been so important and so talked about with less clarity and less apparent understanding [than cyber security]. . . . I have sat in very small group meetings in Washington . . . unable (along with my colleagues) to decide on a

---

[23] Perhaps the best criticism of the term cybersecurity is that it focuses attention on the technological, computer, and network components of the ecosystem, distracting from other equally important components. For instance, and as we will see throughout this book, physical security and operational security are critically important to a good cybersecurity posture. As explained by Professor Andrea Matwyshyn, "[r]eferring to all of information security, particularly in private sector contexts, as 'cybersecurity' is technically incorrect." Andrea M. Matwyshyn, *Hacking Speech: Informational Speech and the First Amendment*, 107 NORTHWESTER UNIVERSITY LAW REVIEW 795, 817 n.99 (2013). Matwyshyn describes this misnomer as ignoring the aspects of physical security inherent in "holistic" protection of data maintained by an enterprise. *Id.*

[24] *Nuclear Lessons for Cyber Security?*, 5 STRATEGIC STUDIES QUARTERLY 18 (2011), https://dash.harvard.edu/bitstream/handle/1/8052146/Nye-NuclearLessons.pdf.

> course of action because we lacked a clear picture of the long-term legal and policy implications of *any* decision we might make."
>
> Governments learn slowly from knowledge, study, and experience, and learning occurs internationally when new knowledge gradually redefines the content of national interests and leads to new policies. For example, the United States and the Soviet Union took decades to learn how to adapt and respond to the prior revolution in military affairs—nuclear technology after 1945. As we try to make sense of our halting responses to the current cyber revolution, are there any lessons we can learn from our responses to the prior technological transformation? In comparison to the nuclear revolution in military affairs, strategic studies of the cyber domain are chronologically equivalent to 1960 but conceptually more equivalent to 1950. Analysts are still not clear about the lessons of offense, defense, deterrence, escalation, norms, arms control, or how they fit together into a national strategy.

Nuclear policy is an interesting point of comparison as we begin to discuss the challenges in an inherently adversarial system. Although physical risks can be used to better understand the nature of cybersecurity risks, the physical environment differs, at least in part, from the unique challenges of cyberspace.

QUESTIONS

1. How is the "real world" different from cyberspace? What does it mean for someone to violate your security online versus offline?

2. Based on what you read above and otherwise know about nuclear technology, how is cybersecurity similar to and different from nuclear security?

3. How do law and technology relate to one another when it comes to studying and practicing cybersecurity? What does it mean to "practice cybersecurity"?

D. A NOTE ON TERMINOLOGY AND NAVIGATING THIS TEXT

Cybersecurity is a field with a great deal of specialized terminology with technical meaning. We, unapologetically, eschew much of this specialized meaning. We do so particularly where terminology is territory, where adherents to a particular usage insist upon technical accuracy because the term has a precise meaning to them rather than because it has a generally useful meaning. We do use terms that are necessary to communicate certain concepts within cybersecurity.

We take this approach with some reluctance and out of necessity. Meaningful discussion of cybersecurity as a distinct field requires bringing together multiple constituencies, often from across disciplines. This is not possible unless each constituency acquiesces to speak some common vulgar tongue.

Some perspective on our approach is captured in the excerpt below. This is a portion of Peiter Zatko's address at DEFCON 21 in 2013.[25] Zatko is better known as Mudge, one of the founding members of the L0pht,[26] a famous hacker think tank formed in 1992, and a member of the hacker group Cult of the Dead Cow. In 2010, Mudge "went legit," accepting a position with the Department of Defense (DoD) overseeing cybersecurity research at the Defense Advanced Research Projects Agency DARPA). In this excerpt, Mudge discusses the clash of cultures, language, purpose, and generally understanding between the DoD and the hacking community:

PEITER ZATKO A/K/A MUDGE, UNEXPECTED STORIES FROM A HACKER INSIDE THE GOVERNMENT

DEFCON 21 (2012)

I remember Anonymous from way back. I mean—Anonymous—I use it as like, you know a proper noun, but obviously we're all familiar, and it's much more. It's kind of a movement, a thought, it's more ephemeral than that. And when I remember them, they were going after Scientology, and RIAA and there was all the 4chans with the soap opera stuff going on. And at some point, their scope or the target expanded to include the government. And general wisdom was that the triggering event was the DoD's response to Wikileaks and [Chelsea] Manning, etc. But the way I saw it, there was actually something else that was a bit more subtle that folks hadn't realized.

So, in 2011, the DoD released the strategy for operating in cyberspace. There was some very minor backlash to some of the wording initially, I think there was an initial small leaked version of it that went out and it was followed by a later one. But there was some more specific backlash and chatter in the hacker researcher community. The strategy stated that the DoD was going to treat cyberspace as a domain to conduct operations in. And it appeared kind of modeled off of outer space, you know, treating space as—these are "DoDish words"—a domain. And there were some confused conversations going, "Oh, why is anybody upset if the treat cyberspace as a domain, there wasn't that much upset with treating space [as a domain,] and you know, nobody lives in cyberspace," which you could kind of only hear inside the government, a statement like that. Because if you think about it, you know, we all live in cyberspace. And the hacker

[25] A recording available at https://www.youtube.com/watch?v=TSR-b9yuTbM. This excerpt starts at approximately the 11:30 mark.

[26] For some introduction to the L0pht, including to Mudge, and their groundbreaking testimony before the United States Congress in 1998, *see* Craig Timberg, *A Disaster Foretold—And Ignored: L0pht's Warnings about the Internet Drew Notice but Little Action*, WASHINGTON POST (June 22, 2015).

researcher community made it—you know, made cyberspace—(I'm really not a fan of that word)—made the Internet an online our homes well before the government and everybody else kind made it just where they always lived and did everything in.

So if you send a message that that's somebody's back yard and that you're going to militarize and prep for war in somebody's backyard, that can sound really scary, and it can galvanize folks to respond. One of the problems was there was not an understanding as to who the message was actually intended for. So in addition to treating it as a domain, they said something else, which was, and in response to—and I'm paraphrasing—and in response to hacks, we'll consider responding with kinetic force.

So, if you don't actually specifically call out who the recipient of the message is, everybody reading it thinks it's directed to them. I read it. I thought it was directed to me. And I'm going like, you know, "What the heck?" You know, I joke, my buddy and I replace his, you know, the HTML, the main Web page, and that' considered a hack, and all of a sudden I've got somebody launching a Patriot missile at me? I mean, this makes no sense. What level of hack? Because if we look at like CFAA response, maybe they actually thing a Patriot missile is the right thing for defacing a Web site. I don't know. And none of these are the right questions. Because I'm not the intended audience. But of course, I'm reading it as if I was. And of course, the logical next question is, wait, do they understand how attribution works? Because, you know, what if I do it, you know, bouncing through an ally? What if I do it from within the U.S.? Are they going to kinetically respond against themselves? I mean, this is. . .

You kind of go, ok, wait. Back up. If the message were directed to, let's say, other countries, other. . . somebody in specific that's got a significant power that they say, look, we're talking about critical infrastructure, or something of that nature, if you turn off the lights in New York, we will probably be able to figure out who you are, because you're not a small little hacker defacing Web sites, and maybe there is attribution in place that we could respond to. That would have been an entirely different sort of message, and I wouldn't have read it as the whole like, wow, if I get root on something in my own system, is the Government going to shoot me? Which is just silly. But I wasn't the only person who read it that way. And it's nice having been in this field and in the hacker researcher community for, jeez going on almost 25 years. Actually, over 25 years. And some folks were sending me, they're like "Hey, have you seen what's going on in the chat rooms?" And there were some folks who were claiming affiliation of claiming support of Anonymous that were going "Hey, have you read this? Look who's trying to prep for war in our back yards. Do they even understand how attribution works? This is bullshit. If they think they can find me, it's on. Let's go."

And the next thing you know, there are a couple websites defaced, and they ended in .gov. Now, this is where it gets kind of funky. Defacing a website is kind of a message. It's a little warning shot. But that's in a language that govies don't know. So the govies didn't get the message, as far as, you know, what I saw. So here's the initial strategy for operating in cyberspace that goes out, probably directed to somebody else, but by poor messaging, is misinterpreted by a group. The group responds, fires a warning shot. The warning shot isn't understood. It's like, "Hey, what are these vagabonds doing? Look at the little street punks or whatever. They're not somebody who actually has a message that we should actually engage in." And it's just this little cascading effect.

So, that is kind of unfortunately where I saw, you know, the expanding of scope and a lot of misunderstandings. I'm not saying the two groups should be friends. And I'm not saying one group is good and one group is bad. But when you send a message out into the world, and this is for both groups: you really need to make sure it's understandable by all the parties that are going to receive it. You can't assume it's just going to be read by the person you had in mind. With all love and respect, there is one very obvious commonality between the hacker researcher group and the government, and it's that they can be very arrogant and expect that everybody will speak their own language and that they don't have to speak anybody else's. And I think that's a really common mistake.

So the recommendation for the government from my vantage point on both sides is: figure out how your messages are going to be received by the more general populace of cyberspace, because we all live there now. This is actually a great opportunity for diplomacy. You can kind of think of it like the Lost City of Atlantis. Because cyberspace kind of took the world, I think, the world by surprise. Obviously it hasn't been around that long. So what if Atlantis just popped back up, and there was an advanced, very technically capable group of people there? You wouldn't sit there and ignore them. You wouldn't taunt them. You wouldn't attack them. You'd probably actually try and understand them and figure out how messaging to somebody else might be interpreted to them. You might even try to figure out where you guys already see things eye to eye, and where you have differences.

So, my recommendations to the citizens of cyberspace is: keep in mind that the government and in particular, the DoD, has very specific focuses and goals. And they often only see things from their own point of view. Because they're really focused on doing that job. And when you read things that appear to be a message directed to you or your community, coming from an unlikely source, you should question whether or not the message is actually intended for you, or if it's just intended for somebody else and really poorly worded. And if you still think a response is necessary, you really need to think about the message that you're sending, to make sure that you don't make the same mistake in return.

Mudge identifies a critical challenge for cybersecurity as a field: a lack of common terminology. As is clear from his account, the emphasis there must be on the word *common*. Many individuals in many fields are working from many perspectives on things that can be called cybersecurity. But these myriad perspectives do not share a common understanding or language for the field, and sometimes describe similar things in different terms and different things in similar terms.

This lack of a *common* terminology explains in part our unapologetic if reluctant approach to terminology. Anything else would be impossible—we would necessarily be cabined into a single perspective, to the exclusion and marginalization of other perspectives. That would run directly contrary to the interdisciplinary ambitious of this book.

But there is another, more fundamental, reason that we eschew the language of any particular perspective on cybersecurity. Many fields claim cybersecurity as their own. DoD and the National Security community stake a claim to cybersecurity; engineers stake a claim to it; the business community has a claim to it as well; and, of course, lawyers claim all as their own as well. It is our perspective, and hope, that cybersecurity is coming into its own as a field—and that this book contributes to that development.

At the same time, we are not prescriptive about our choice of language, instead opting for a dialect that blends the terminology and perspective of these various constituent fields. This choice, too, is deliberate, because cybersecurity has not yet emerged as its own field. Rather, to successfully work in cybersecurity's broad domain, you should have some fluency across its constituent fields. From this perspective, our dialect is intended to familiarize readers with the terminology that one is likely to encounter in these various field. That is, regardless your own background, you should have some fluency in the language that engineers, business professionals, and lawyers use when discussing cybersecurity.

Dan Geer, one of the leading thinkers in this field, offered some relevant reflections that bear on our thinking about the language of cybersecurity, and the bearing that language has on cybersecurity as a field:[27]

---

[27] A recording, and text, of Geer's talk is available at https://www.usenix.org/conference/satcpi15/meeting-program/presentation/geer.

DAN GEER, *T.S. KUHN REVISITED*

NSF, Secure and Trustworthy Cyberspace
Principal Investigators' Meeting (2015)

"Does a field make progress because it is a science, or is it a science because it makes progress?"

As you know, I chose for my topic today a re-visitation of T.S.Kuhn's landmark work, *The Structure of Scientific Revolutions*. I rather suspect many of you have read it, and, if so, most probably as an assigned reading in your preparation for a career in science. It was published in 1962 by the University of Chicago as a volume in the International Encyclopaedia of Unified Science, a project that was never, in fact, completed. [. . .]

Kuhn's book, which he consistently refers to as an essay, is basically about what science is, based on the observables of what science does and has done. Between him, his supporters and his critics, many noted philosophers, and others, what science *is* is to this day unsettled at its core. Perhaps that is why both Kuhn's supporters and his critics agree on one thing: There is no algorithm to science. [. . .]

Biases aside, the time has come to read Kuhn's essay in the context of cybersecurity. He begins and ends with what is a circular idea, that a scientific community is defined by what beliefs practitioners share, and what beliefs practitioners share defines what community they are in. This is, in fact, instructive as no science begins in mature form, but rather any new science will begin in much more modest circumstances where, in fact, there is nothing approaching a consensus in any sense of the word, that, early on, consensus is not even a concept. As such, part of becoming a mature science is the development of a broad consensus about the core concerns of that branch of knowledge.

Kuhn's word for the collections of exemplars of good science was "paradigm," a word whose meaning today is all but entirely Kuhn's . . . .

But what is a "paradigm" and why do we want one? As Kuhn puts it, "[Paradigms] are the source of the methods, the problem field, and the standards of solution accepted by any mature scientific community at any given time." Kuhn's book and the two decade long back and forth between Kuhn and philosophers notwithstanding, the simplest version is that a paradigm is all the things that a scientist can assume that his or her colleagues will congenially understand about their common work without explicitly explaining them or arguing them from first principles again and again.

Several authors besides Kuhn have adopted that idea to explain the proliferation of jargon as being something that markedly improves the efficiency of communication between practitioners who do, in fact, share a paradigm, who share a set of techniques, trainings, and world view in common. As Kuhn said, "Although it is customary, and is surely proper to deplore the widening gulf that separates the professional scientist from his colleagues in other fields, too little attention is paid to the essential relationship between that gulf and the mechanisms intrinsic to scientific advance." In other words, impenetrable jargon between scientists sharing a paradigm is a side-effect of that sharing, and a tool of efficiency because it insulates science from society.

But, I hear you say, any field from poetry to American history to macroeconomics can have an impenetrable jargon, does that make those fields sciences? Clearly not, and here is where Kuhn's paradigm construct is central. In a science, the shared paradigm is universal whereas in the humanities, say, there are always competing schools of thought that are unlikely ever to sign some unifying intellectual peace treaty. As Kuhn would have it, a paradigm—a shared framework for how the world works—is the engine for creating the kinds of puzzles that individual scientists are able to solve if they work hard enough, the paradigm creates general agreement amongst those who hold it as to where further research is needed. When a body of scientists is asked "Where should research go next?" the answer will be the same as to the question "Where is research going?" because the shared paradigm makes it so. And note that I used Kuhn's word, "puzzles," rather than "problems." Kuhn is at some pains to make clear that a scientist doing science is solving the puzzles that the paradigm leaves open to solution. He or she is not solving problems in the vernacular sense of the word "problem." [. . .]

It is both the conceit and concern of this book that there is, or at least should be, an interdisciplinary field of cybersecurity. This is reflected in the subtitle of this book: "An interdisciplinary problem." As Geer suggests, there is a distinction between the puzzles that drive the work of an established science and the problems that drive a yet-inchoate field. We believe that there is a common set of issues to be addressed by an interdisciplinary cohort of researchers, practitioners, and policymakers, sharing a common language to puzzle through something called cybersecurity.[28]

---

[28] Those familiar with Kuhn's work, or who read the entirety of the address from which Geer's excerpt above comes, will be familiar with the idea that crises are the force that drive the development of new paradigms. Crises result, for Kuhn, where existing paradigms encounter "puzzles" that they lack the vocabulary to address—that is, problems, not puzzles. This failure of existing paradigms forces a refactoring of fields, to develop a new vocabulary that is capable of rendering these newly incomprehensible problems into comprehensible puzzles.

The language of "crisis" may be dramatic to describe the formation of a new scientific field. At the same time, the challenges posed by cybersecurity to nearly every aspect of modern life and society, and the failures of any current field to address these challenges in a consistent, timely, or predictable way, suggest that it may well be fair to describe the current state of the field as a crisis.

CHAPTER 2

SECURITY, PRIVACY, & "SECURITY VS. PRIVACY"

■ ■ ■

In this chapter, we further explore the meaning of cybersecurity, offering a more formal definition. We also consider the closely related topic of privacy, and the relationship between cybersecurity and privacy. Although cybersecurity ('security') and privacy both have data in common, they satisfy different aims and ultimately are managed quite differently both in law and policy. In particular, security is *referential*, while privacy is typically more static. Security is referential because good or reasonable security depends on any number of things, including the amount of data transmitted or stored, the category of data being protected, the overall system architecture, and even what type of organization collects, manages, or stores data. Privacy, however, focuses on one category of data—personal information—and because poor privacy practices can result in direct injury to an individual person, privacy practices can often be applied regardless of the size of the firm or type of systems involved. In this chapter, consider how you might explain to General Counsel of an organization some of the similarities and differences between the security and privacy fields.

A. DEFINING CYBERSECURITY, AS RISK

Security is a subject of longstanding and intensive study. It is a very well-developed discipline. In fact, it is so well-developed that there are numerous definitions of "security." At the broadest, dictionary-definition, level, security roughly means "safe from harm." Something is secure if it is safe from harm, and the process of securing something is the process of making it safe from harm.

At the other end of the definitional spectrum, many of security's subfields have more specialized definitions of security. For instance, the field of computer security focuses on ensuring the confidentiality, integrity, and availability (CIA) of information. This definition, frequently referred to as the CIA model, is so formalized that it has even been codified in some cybersecurity-related laws:

> (3) The term "information security" means protecting information and information systems from unauthorized access, use, disclosure, disruption, modification, or destruction in order to provide—

(A) integrity, which means guarding against improper information modification or destruction, and includes ensuring information nonrepudiation and authenticity;

(B) confidentiality, which means preserving authorized restrictions on access and disclosure, including means for protecting personal privacy and proprietary information; and

(C) availability, which means ensuring timely and reliable access to and use of information.[1]

The purpose of defining CIA in this way is to describe security as more than a confidentiality problem. Historically, security may have been viewed as a way to prevent unauthorized access or sharing of personal information or proprietary information (such as trade secrets); integrity and availability illustrate the necessity of accurate information. Modern life now depends on computers working as expected; for example, if airplane flight management systems were unavailable, serious issues affecting human health and productivity would result. For health care organizations, if diagnostic information is available but is inaccurate (for example, if known allergies are incorrect), patients could die. A manufacturing company that no longer can operate due to cyberattack could lose millions of dollars per day. To be sure, security is not only about protecting personal information or solely about its confidentiality.

To study cybersecurity problems, we must have a common language with which to examine problems. As noted at the end of the last chapter, "cybersecurity," and all of its associated terminology, may mean very different things to different parts of the security ecosystem. The CIA model may be a useful start, but it is far too reductive. Rather, it is better suited to theoretical proof and formal analysis than to addressing an interdisciplinary problem. To develop an effective interdisciplinary definition, we look to the goals of "security" which are common across many disciplines—recall the basic dictionary definition of "safe from harm." Somewhere between the dictionary-definition level of generality and the specialized-model level of specificity we find a good starting point for defining security. If we are fundamentally safe from harm—that is, secure—we do not care about security. Security only has meaning as a concept in relief, or when we are not secure. At the same time, when harm is fundamentally certain in all instances, security is irrelevant. We care about security, in other words, when we are exposed to *possibility but not certainty* of harm—i.e., *the risk of harm*. Security is about risk. In fact, we cannot discuss any of the topics related to security throughout this text without referencing the concept of risk and risk management.

---

[1] Federal Information Security Modernization Act, codified at 44 U.S.C. § 3551.

Risk comes in many forms. At a high level, we can divide it into two categories: stochastic and adversarial. *Stochastic risks* are those that are outside anyone's direct control. Stochastic risks are sometimes called "known unknown" risks, meaning that although we know they will happen, it is nearly impossible to predict exactly when with any degree of accuracy. They are often probabilistic and can be modeled but are generally not controlled.[2] There is a chance that a meteor will hit Earth tomorrow; or that there will be a storm that will interfere with your plans; or that someone will run a red light and hit your car. There also is a chance someone in an organization may just make an honest mistake (e.g., a "finger flub"). In legal terms, we generally think of this sort of risk in terms of tort law, the law of negligence and accidents. In less technical terms, this is the realm of "shit happens."

In contrast, *adversarial risks* result from deliberate conduct. Someone may steal your car or pick a fight with you. Someone may steal your wallet, or hack into your bank account and steal your money electronically. Someone may interrupt a presentation that you are giving, spread harmful rumors about you, or share your private information. Someone may do *something* intentionally that causes harm to you.

Stochastic and adversarial risks have similar characteristics. The risk results from a combination of some instrumentality that is capable of causing us harm. In security, we refer to the instrumentality as a *threat*, the origin of the threat (such as a person) as the *threat source*, and its ability to effectuate harm for a specific target as a *vulnerability*. Vulnerabilities can be understood by adopting the perspective that anything can be hacked, pwned, or destroyed, just like anything of value. A security practitioner's goal is to make it appropriately difficult to do so, keeping in mind the likelihood of a stochastic risk occurring or the potential motivation of adversaries achieving their respective ends.

Risks are impossible to completely mitigate, remediate, or avoid. The meteor that may hit us, the car that may run the red light, the thief who may steal our wallets—these are all threat sources. We may reduce our risk by avoiding or removing them. For instance, you can reduce the chances of a car accident by driving in less congested areas or at less congested times or using cars with cameras and sensors; you can reduce the chance of being pick-pocketed by storing your credit cards in unexpected places. The destruction of civilization by a meteor impact, injury or damage to our cars if hit by another driver, loss of our wallet if pick-pocketed, damage to our reputation if someone spreads rumors—these are vulnerabilities. We may also reduce risk by reducing or eliminating the

---

[2] As we discuss below, some stochastic risks can be mitigated. In this context mitigation is not "control" of the threat, but rather management of the probability it will impact a given target.

harms that result from a threat: building cities that may survive a meteor impact.

The relationship between risk, threat, and vulnerability is as follows: when a threat is capable of exploiting a vulnerability, there is risk.[3] In the cyber domain, we are primarily, though not exclusively, concerned with adversarial risk, because it is possible to mitigate, remediate, or avoid. As captured by Whitfield Diffie (one of the inventors of modern encryption) in a keynote at a 2002 computer security conference, in the computer context, security is about the "prevention of adverse consequences from illegitimate acts of human beings."[4] Although this definition does not account for non-adversarial risk that might nevertheless result in CIA impacts, it does illustrate the preventative function of security practices.

Because the cyber domain has been constructed by humans, for use by humans in human terms, there are comparatively few non-human threats. And, due to the nature of the cyber domain, risk is largely correlated. This means that if a vulnerability affects one person, it likely also affects many others; for example, a threat actor who can harm one person or organization can likely cause harm to millions of people or many organizations. In this regard, large-scale systemic adversarial risk (e.g., millions of accounts being compromised or individuals' data exposed due to ransomware) tends to occur with higher probability than large-scale systemic stochastic risks (e.g., a massive weather event shutting down entire geographic regions[5]).[6]

Another aspect of adversarial risk is that threats can be reduced both by eliminating the vulnerability and by making the target less attractive. Attackers, for example, do not attack systems for no reason: they are motivated to accomplish one or more objectives. The primary objective is successfully compromising a system, which means exploiting a vulnerability. If you can reduce or eliminate vulnerabilities, you therefore also reduce the incentive that adversaries have to attack a system (their motivation, at least for that particular system), and therefore you reduce threats.

A great way to think about this concept is home security. If someone really wants to break into your home, they will find a way. Each security measure you take to protect the contents of your home increases the difficulty of breaking into your home. Installing a security system,

---

[3] This relationship is often seen with a third factor, impact or consequences, included (e.g., RISK=THREAT × VULNERABILITY × IMPACT). This will be discussed in the Chapter 6 discussion of the Risk Management Framework.

[4] *Secure from What?* 27; LOGIN: 57 (Dec. 2002), https://www.usenix.org/system/files/login/articles/1791-salus.pdf.

[5] But, note, that these *do happen*, and poor planning can lead to the worldwide grounding of all flights of an airline. *See, e.g.*, https://money.cnn.com/2017/04/10/news/companies/delta-meltdown-what-went-wrong/index.html.

[6] [For a contrary view, see Linus Torvalds's argument that security flaws are merely bugs.]

especially cameras, enables you to respond quickly and contact the police or to piece together what happened. The door lock is considered a *preventative control*, or a measure used to reduce the probability of a threat source successfully accomplishing a goal. The security camera, when used to determine what occurred in the past is a *detective control*.

Controls are used to reduce the risk of a threat source successfully exploiting a vulnerability. When controls are non-existent or insufficient given the motivation of the threat source and the seriousness of the vulnerability, the threat source will be successful in accomplishing their goals. When the threat source successfully exploits the vulnerability, a risk is *realized*, and it is no longer just a threat: it becomes an incident, or the compromise of some asset, whether that asset is physical (a server) or logical (data). Under some circumstances, incidents may be considered data breaches. We will discuss the relationship between controls, risk, and incident throughout the rest of this book. For now, it is important to understand that controls are the primary means of changing the degree of adversarial risk, and that controls may be mandated by law or employed to reduce risk or organization.

One example of controls that are designed to prevent compromise are complex passwords, or passwords that adhere to any number of rules: elimination of passwords that have been previously used, use of special characters, numbers, varied capitalization, password length, and elimination of password parts that spell words that can be looked up in a dictionary. Over the past decade, the idea that complex passwords are necessary for good security has become ingrained in our collective consciousness. The idea is intuitively appealing: it is far easier to guess a simple password (e.g., "Password") than it is to guess a complex password (e.g., "la0oO0;;$sBanan4slug%"). This suggests that simple passwords are riskier than complex passwords. And, at some level this is true: truly simple passwords are truly insecure. But once you get beyond a reasonable level of complexity (e.g., an eight-character password with both numbers are letters in it), increases in complexity do little to decrease risk. In fact, they may increase risk.[7]

To understand this, we need only think about risk in terms of threat and vulnerability. What is the threat model under which someone would be trying to guess your password? In all likelihood, the threat source, the attacker, is either attempting an "online" attack—entering passwords one by one into an actual login form (or using software that tries one after the other)—or an "offline" attack—where the attacker has obtained a copy of your encrypted password and are attempting to compromise it on their own

[7] In Spring 2017 the U.S. National Institute of Standards and Technology somewhat quietly reversed its nearly two decade position that security improved continuously with increased password complexity. Shortly after that publication, the author of the original standard published a rather "unquiet" mea culpa in the Wall Street Journal, lamenting the years of authentication disarray resulting from the original NIST password complexity standard he authored. See *id.*

computer. In either case, the vulnerability is not the complexity of your password.

For online attacks, the vulnerability is the login form: it should not allow anyone to enter more than a small number of incorrect passwords (commonly, three) without implementing some form of countermeasure (e.g., requiring a 30-minute wait before another attempt is allowed or requiring an administrator to unlock your login). For offline attacks, if the attacker is able to obtain passwords, the vulnerability isn't the complexity of your password, it's that the attacker was able to break in to the system containing the passwords, that the password was not encrypted, or your password was guessable using other automated resources, as in a dictionary or rainbow attack.[8] Your password is like money in a bank: the risk facing money in a bank isn't that someone may steal it, it's that someone may break into the bank. If the attacker is able to break into the password equivalent of the bank, there are bigger problems than the complexity of any given user's password. Complex passwords are only one control in a full ecosystem of controls, and in the discussion that follows, you will consider whether they are an effective one.

On the other hand, overly complicated passwords lead to behavior that can create new vulnerabilities. The most common example is the ubiquitous post-it note: when passwords become too complex or numerous for people to remember, people write them down. At that point, you have created a new vulnerability that anyone with physical access to your computer (the threats) is able to exploit. Perhaps even more problematic, a focus on password complexity encourages users to adopt complex, difficult-to-remember, passwords—and this, in turn, encourages them to reuse those same complex passwords for various accounts. As a consequence, if any one of those accounts is compromised, all of their accounts are effectively compromised. It turns out that it is far more secure to use medium complexity, yet unique passwords for each account than to use a smaller number of more complex passwords. The unfortunate focus on complex passwords results in attention paid to the wrong threats and creates new vulnerabilities, resulting in an increase in risk.

This example—one likely familiar to readers across multiple disciplines—highlights the importance of understanding cybersecurity as risk. If the end goal is to minimize harm (or more precisely, the probability of harm), one must first determine what is the probability that such harm will result, and what are the threats and vulnerabilities that determine this probability. Further, in addition to probability, one must also consider the impact if a threat source exploits a vulnerability. As we will discuss in relation to managing and prioritizing risk, a useful equation that

[8] There is another vulnerability that is implicated here: if the user has *reused* the same password on multiple sites, compromising one password compromises multiple passwords. While complex passwords may offer minimal security over non-trivially simple passwords, using meaningfully unique passwords across accounts does meaningfully reduce risk.

cybersecurity practitioners use is PROBABILITY × IMPACT = RISK. Sometimes this risk, when explained as a numerical result, may be tied to expected financial losses.

For example, if an organization manages a database full of sensitive data that could be damaging to individuals and the organization overall (inherently high in impact if exploited), but the same organization implements several controls that reduce the *probability* of vulnerability exploit, the resulting *risk* should be low. Probability of exploit exists as an extension of potential threats that might target an asset and controls implemented specific to vulnerabilities within that asset. Impact usually represents inherent aspects of an asset, such as data classification, number of records or data volumes, or criticality of the asset (e.g., whether an asset is central to business operations).

Focusing solely on either threats or vulnerabilities or on just a few of either category may, as in the passwords example, result in a failure to mitigate risk. This can be because other threats or vulnerabilities are overlooked, or because new ones are created. Either way, the result is the same—a narrow focus obscures the fundamental goal of security, to increase "safety from harm" by mitigating risk through effective application of layered controls.

Thus, for the purposes of studying cybersecurity as an interdisciplinary problem, we begin by defining cybersecurity as the risk a system faces and the methods employed to manage, mitigate, remediate, or avoid that risk.[9] This is not a complete or detailed definition, and certainly there are limitations similar to the CIA model and other traditional definitions of computer security. Unlike the CIA model and many other definitions, however, understanding cybersecurity as risk allows for a far more robust discussion of cybersecurity, especially as it relates to business, policy, and legal decisions. Indeed, that is exactly the purpose of the next several chapters of this book.

B. DEFINING CYBERSECURITY, AS PROCESS

The discussion in the previous section of cybersecurity as risk management captures one of the central themes of this book. As an interdisciplinary topic, those coming at the topic from legal and business perspectives are likely most naturally attuned to thinking in terms of risk management.

A closely related perspective, which may be more natural but is ultimately very similar, views security as a process. This perspective may

[9] We will discuss the concept of a system as a type of asset in much greater detail in Chapter 5. In this context, the term "system" refers to the generic term system (describing an interoperating set of elements)—not just a "technological" system.

be more familiar to those coming at the topic from an engineering perspective, or from the compliance side of the business or legal world.

The idea of security as process is captured by a simple phrase: "secure is a verb, not a noun." A system is not secure; data is not secure, a protocol or algorithm is not secure. Rather, security is an ongoing process with no defined endpoint. There are multiple reasons for this. First, as discussed above, security is an adversarial process. Threat actors will always be looking for vulnerabilities that can be exploited to compromise a system. This is particularly true because, even if a system *could* be perfectly secured, from a risk management perspective, it rarely makes sense to incur the expense of fully securing that system. Rather, a reasonable approach to security will invest in security in proportion to the likely magnitude of harms that could result from that system being compromised. But threat actors, ever innovative, will constantly be working to reduce their costs of compromising systems, constantly pushing those working to secure their systems to invest in greater care.

Second, the complexity of computers, software, and networks, is such that vulnerabilities are likely always to exist. As discussed in 5 and 8, the complexity (in the technical sense) of these systems is such that they cannot ever be demonstrably proven to be "secure." What's more, and third, even if a system could be demonstrated to be secure, the moment it changed, or its operating environment changed, or any of the dozens or hundreds or thousands of dependencies incorporated into the system's design changed, it would no longer be secure.

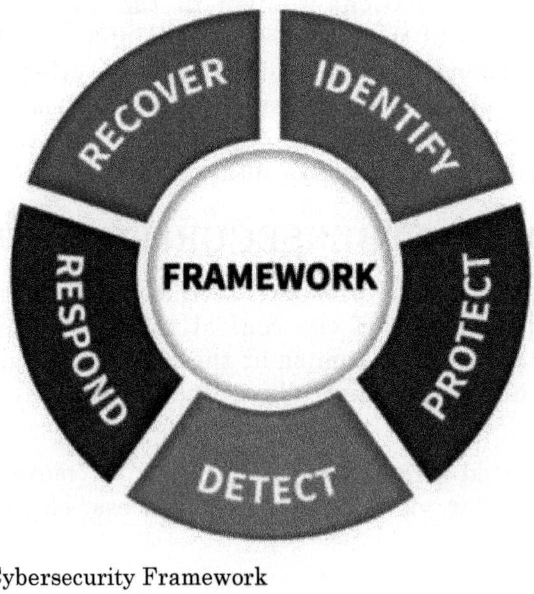

Figure 1: NIST Cybersecurity Framework

The NIST Cybersecurity Framework, discussed in more detail in Chapter 11, is one high-level framework for cybersecurity that effectively captures this idea of "security as process." At its broadest scope, the NIST Cybersecurity Framework is an iterative, 5-stage process. The process starts by identifying the assets or systems to be protected, then putting in place systems to protect them; then working to detect compromises; then responding to any compromises that happen to discontinue them and mitigate their effects; and finally recovering from those compromises, for instance by restoring lost data or notifying effected users.

But built in to each stage of this process is the idea that each stage provides feedback into each prior stage. So working to protect assets that have been identified for protection will generally inform an organization's understanding of those assets that need protection. Efforts to detect compromises will inform how the organization protects those assets. Responding to compromises will inform the organization's approach to detection. That is, this is an ongoing process.

The NIST Cybersecurity Framework was developed primarily to be used by the federal government to guide the security of federal information systems as required by the Federal Information Systems Management Act, Federal Information Systems Modernization Act, and various Executive Orders.[10] It should be emphasized that the NIST Cybersecurity Framework is both only one of many frameworks and approaches to security, and is itself only a high level description of hundreds of detailed security control processes.[11]

C. PRIVACY (IS NOT SECURITY)

Before proceeding to Chapter 3, where we take our first deep dive into the concept of cybersecurity-as-risk, one important distinction is appropriate: privacy. Privacy and security have been conflated throughout history, as one might expect—if security is being "safe from harm," and if privacy includes avoiding harms to private activities and personal dignity, it is easy to see how the two could be confused. Consider the classic example of privacy as "freedom from trespass": security measures deter trespassers, and trespass into a person's home could compromise the occupants' privacy, so surely security and privacy must be related concepts. In recent decades, this confusion has been imported into the "cybersecurity" space through a variety of technological, legal/regulatory, and scholarly mechanisms.

---

[10] For more information, see https://www.nist.gov/cyberframework/framework.

[11] Collectively, these controls are known as the Security and Privacy Controls for Federal Information Systems and Organizations, and are documented in NIST Special Publication 800–53, *available at* https://nvlpubs.nist.gov/nistpubs/SpecialPublications/NIST.SP.800-53r5.pdf. While the purpose of this book is not to provide detailed background on specific security frameworks, it may interest many readers to peruse SP 800-53 to get a sense of its structure, language, level of detail, and overall approach.

Privacy and security are related yet fundamentally distinct ideas. In this section and the next, we consider the concept of privacy and how it relates to security. We first examine what is privacy (Section B), then proceed to distinguish it from security (Section C). Readers should take care to develop a thorough understanding of this distinction.

By first understanding the foundations of privacy, we build a framework for distinguishing security and privacy questions from one another. As you read the following excerpts, please keep in mind that most of the overlap between privacy and security is related to information privacy, in particular the presence of personal information as data requiring protection. Where natural crossover exists is where information about an individual, such as protected health information, sensitive personal information, biometric data, or purchasing habits, is stored or transmitted by an organization. For these data types, cybersecurity is integral to maintaining privacy.

However, the roots of privacy law are much broader than their crossover. Privacy law is reflected in both the common law and civil rights. The most historically important article on common law privacy in the American tradition was written by Samuel Warren and Louis Brandeis in 1890.[12] Warren and Brandeis were prompted to write this article is response to the advent of the camera. It was the era of yellow journalism, when many newspapers were driven by rumor and sensationalism—and the camera was fuel to that fire, allowing (in Warren and Brandeis's view) the press to capture and circulate intimate and private details of individuals lives with photographic detail.

WARREN AND BRANDEIS, *THE RIGHT TO PRIVACY*

4 HARV. L. REV. 193 (1890)

That the individual shall have full protection in person and in property is a principle as old as the common law; but it has been found necessary from time to time to define anew the exact nature and extent of such protection. Political, social, and economic changes entail the recognition of new rights, and the common law, in its eternal youth, grows to meet the new demands of society. Thus, in very early times, the law gave a remedy only for physical interference with life and property, for trespasses *vi et armis*. Then the "right to life" served only to protect the subject from battery in its various forms; liberty meant freedom from actual restraint;

[12] It is a question of history where privacy emerged, legally, at least with respect to commercial enterprises, although it is likely connected to common law rules of fiduciary responsibility and confidentiality. The civil rights perspective in privacy in the United States is often an extension of the Fourth Amendment, wherein individual privacy, especially privacy of the bodily person, is central to a democratic society. It should be noted that historical perspectives in the United States are not duplicated internationally. To date, most countries in the world have included references to informational privacy within their respective constitutions, although the U.S. Constitution does not explicitly reference privacy anywhere.

and the right to property secured to the individual his lands and his cattle. Later, there came a recognition of man's spiritual nature, of his feelings and his intellect. Gradually the scope of these legal rights broadened; and now the right to life has come to mean the right to enjoy life,—the right to be let alone; the right to liberty secures the exercise of extensive civil privileges; and the term "property" has grown to comprise every form of possession—intangible, as well as tangible.

Thus, with the recognition of the legal value of sensations, the protection against actual bodily injury was extended to prohibit mere attempts to do such injury; that is, the putting another in fear of such injury. From the action of battery grew that of assault. [The authors describe other ways in which the law expanded from protecting concrete harms to protecting cognate intangible harm.] From corporeal property arose the incorporeal rights issuing out of it; and then there opened the wide realm of intangible property, in the products and processes of the mind, as works of literature and art, goodwill, trade secrets, and trademarks.

This development of the law was inevitable. The intense intellectual and emotional life, and the heightening of sensations which came with the advance of civilization, made it clear to men that only a part of the pain, pleasure, and profit of life lay in physical things. Thoughts, emotions, and sensations demanded legal recognition, and the beautiful capacity for growth which characterizes the common law enabled the judges to afford the requisite protection, without the interposition of the legislature.

Recent inventions and business methods call attention to the next step which must be taken for the protection of the person, and for securing to the individual what Judge Cooley calls the right "to be let alone." Instantaneous photographs and newspaper enterprise have invaded the sacred precincts of private and domestic life; and numerous mechanical devices threaten to make good the prediction that "what is whispered in the closet shall be proclaimed from the house-tops." For years there has been a feeling that the law must afford some remedy for the unauthorized circulation of portraits of private persons; and the evil of invasion of privacy by the newspapers, long keenly felt, has been but recently discussed by an able writer. The alleged facts of a somewhat notorious case brought before an inferior tribunal in New York a few months ago, directly involved the consideration of the right of circulating portraits; and the question whether our law will recognize and protect the right to privacy in this and in other respects must soon come before our courts for consideration.

Of the desirability—indeed of the necessity—of some such protection, there can, it is believed, be no doubt. The press is overstepping in every direction the obvious bounds of propriety and of decency. Gossip is no longer the resource of the idle and of the vicious, but has become a trade, which is pursued with industry as well as effrontery. To satisfy a prurient taste the details of sexual relations are spread broadcast in the columns of the daily papers. To occupy the indolent, column upon column is filled with idle gossip, which can only be procured by intrusion upon the domestic circle. The intensity and complexity of life, attendant upon advancing civilization, have rendered necessary some retreat from the world, and man, under the refining influence of culture, has become more sensitive to publicity, so that solitude and privacy have become more essential to the individual; but modern enterprise and invention have, through invasions upon his privacy, subjected him to mental pain and distress, far greater than could be inflicted by mere bodily injury. Nor is the harm wrought by such invasions confined to the suffering of those who may be the subjects of journalistic or other enterprise. In this, as in other branches of commerce, the supply creates the demand. Each crop of unseemly gossip, thus harvested, becomes the seed of more, and, in direct proportion to its circulation, results in the lowering of social standards and of morality. Even gossip apparently harmless, when widely and persistently circulated, is potent for evil. It both belittles and perverts. It belittles by inverting the relative importance of things, thus dwarfing the thoughts and aspirations of a people. When personal gossip attains the dignity of print, and crowds the space available for matters of real interest to the community, what wonder that the ignorant and thoughtless mistake its relative importance. Easy of comprehension, appealing to that weak side of human nature which is never wholly cast down by the misfortunes and frailties of our neighbors, no one can be surprised that it usurps the place of interest in brains capable of other things. Triviality destroys at once robustness of thought and delicacy of feeling. No enthusiasm can flourish, no generous impulse can survive under its blighting influence.

It is our purpose to consider whether the existing law affords a principle which can properly be invoked to protect the privacy of the individual; and, if it does, what the nature and extent of such protection is.

[. . .]

The common law secures to each individual the right of determining, ordinarily, to what extent his thoughts, sentiments, and emotions shall be communicated to others. Under our system of government, he can never be compelled to express them (except when upon the witness stand); and even if he has chosen to give them expression, he generally retains the power to fix the limits of the publicity which shall be given them. The existence of this right does not depend upon the particular method of expression adopted. It is immaterial whether it be by word or by signs, in painting, by sculpture, or in music. Neither does the existence of the right depend upon the nature or value of the thought or emotions, nor upon the excellence of the means of expression. The same protection is accorded to a casual letter or an entry in a diary and to the most valuable poem or essay, to a botch or daub and to a masterpiece. In every such case the individual is entitled to decide whether that which is his shall be given to the public. No other has the right to publish his productions in any form, without his consent. This right is wholly independent of the material on which, the thought, sentiment, or emotions is expressed. It may exist independently of any corporeal being, as in words spoken, a song sung, a drama acted. Or if expressed on any material, as in a poem in writing, the author may have parted with the paper, without forfeiting any proprietary right in the composition itself. The right is lost only when the author himself communicates his production to the public,—in other words, publishes it. It is entirely independent of the copyright laws, and their extension into the domain of art. The aim of those statutes is to secure to the author, composer, or artist the entire profits arising from publication; but the common-law protection enables him to control absolutely the act of publication, and in the exercise of his own discretion, to decide whether there shall be any publication at all. The statutory right is of no value, unless there is a publication; the common-law right is lost as soon as there is a publication.

[. . .]

The belief that the idea of property in its narrow sense was the basis of the protection of unpublished manuscripts led an able court to refuse, in several cases, injunctions against the publication of private letters, on the ground that "letters not possessing the attributes of literary compositions are not property entitled to protection;" and that it was "evident the plaintiff could not have considered the letters as of any value whatever as literary productions, for a letter cannot be considered of value to the author which he never would consent to have published." But those decisions have not been followed, and it may not be considered settled that the protection afforded by the common law to the author of any writing is entirely independent of its pecuniary value, its intrinsic merits, or of any intention to publish the same and, of course, also, wholly independent of the material, if any, upon which, or the mode in which, the thought or sentiment was expressed.

Although the courts have asserted that they rested their decisions on the narrow grounds of protection to property, yet there are recognitions of a more liberal doctrine. Thus in the case of Prince Albert v. Strange, already referred to, the opinions of both the Vice-Chancellor and of the Lord Chancellor, on appeal, show a more or less clearly defined perception of a principle broader than those which were mainly discussed, and on which they both place their chief reliance. Vice-Chancellor Knight Bruce referred to publishing of a man that he had "written to particular persons or on particular subjects" as an instance of possibly injurious disclosures as to private matters, that the courts would in a proper case prevent; yet it is difficult to perceive how, in such a case, any right of privacy, in the narrow sense, would be drawn in question, or why, if such a publication would be restrained when it threatened to expose the victim not merely to sarcasm, but to ruin, it should not equally be enjoined, if it threatened to embitter his life. To deprive a man of the potential profits to be realized by publishing a catalogue of his gems cannot per se be a wrong to him. The possibility of future profits is not a right of property which the law ordinarily recognizes; it must, therefore, be an infraction of other rights which constitutes the wrongful act, and that infraction is equally wrongful, whether its results are to forestall the profits that the individual himself might secure by giving the matter a publicity obnoxious to him, or to gain an advantage at the expense of his mental pain and suffering. If the fiction of property in a narrow sense must be preserved, it is still true that the end accomplished by the gossip-monger is attained by the use of that which is another's, the facts relating to his private life, which he has seen fit to keep private. Lord Cottenham stated that a man "is that which is exclusively his," and cited with approval the opinion of Lord Eldon, as reported in a manuscript note of the case of Wyatt v. Wilson, in 1820, respecting an engraving of George the Third during his illness, to the effect that "if one of the late king's physicians had kept a diary of what he heard and saw, the court would not, in the king's lifetime, have permitted him to print and publish it; "and Lord Cottenham declared, in respect to the acts of the defendants in the case before him, that "privacy is the right invaded." But if privacy is once recognized as a right entitled to legal protection, the interposition of the courts cannot depend on the particular nature of the injuries resulting.

These considerations lead to the conclusion that the protection afforded to thoughts, sentiments, and emotions, expressed through the medium of writing or of the arts, so far as it consists in preventing publication, is merely an instance of the enforcement of the more general right of the individual to be let alone. It is like the right not to be assaulted or beaten, the right not to be imprisoned, the right not to be maliciously prosecuted, the right not to be defamed. In each of these rights, as indeed in all other rights recognized by the law, there inheres the quality of being owned or possessed—and (as that is the distinguishing attribute of property) there may some propriety in speaking of those rights as property. But, obviously, they bear little resemblance to what is ordinarily comprehended under that term. The principle which protects personal writings and all other personal productions, not against theft and physical appropriation, but against publication in any form, is in reality not the principle of private property, but that of an inviolate personality.

More than a century after Warren & Brandeis' foundational privacy article, the meaning and importance of privacy is still hotly debated. Indeed, with the development of computers and the Internet—and especially the development of mobile devices—these concerns are far more important today than they have ever been before. Understanding "privacy" therefore requires more than the mere concept of a right to "be let alone," but rather a robust framework for evaluating the types of harms one might experience as "privacy" violations. It is important to note that these harms not only are contextual to the individual, but they are also *inherently normative* in nature—they are only "harms" because we decide they are harms. As we will discuss in 2.C: Privacy and Security below, the same is not necessarily true for cybersecurity.

In the following excerpt, Daniel J. Solove proposes a taxonomy for evaluating and understanding privacy harms. As you review this excerpt, consider the extent to which the outlined harms overlap with, interact with, or are orthogonal to cybersecurity.

DANIEL J. SOLOVE, *A TAXONOMY OF PRIVACY*

154 U. PA. L. REV. 477 (2006)

Privacy is a concept in disarray. Nobody can articulate what it means. As one commentator has observed, privacy suffers from "an embarrassment of meanings." Privacy is far too vague a concept to guide adjudication and lawmaking, as abstract incantations of the importance of "privacy" do not fare well when pitted against more concretely stated countervailing interests.

In 1960, the famous torts scholar William Prosser attempted to make sense of the landscape of privacy law by identifying four different interests. But Prosser focused only on tort law, and the law of information privacy is significantly more vast and complex, extending to Fourth Amendment law, the constitutional right to information privacy, evidentiary privileges, dozens of federal privacy statutes, and hundreds of state statutes. Moreover, Prosser wrote over 40 years ago, and new technologies have given rise to a panoply of new privacy harms [. . .]

Often, privacy problems are merely stated in knee-jerk form: "That violates my privacy!" When we contemplate an invasion of privacy—such as having our personal information gathered by companies in databases—we instinctively recoil. Many discussions of privacy appeal to people's fears and anxieties. What commentators often fail to do, however, is translate those instincts into a reasoned, well-articulated account of why privacy problems are harmful. When people claim that privacy should be protected, it is unclear precisely what they mean. This lack of clarity creates a difficulty when making policy or resolving a case because lawmakers and judges cannot easily articulate the privacy harm. The interests on the other side—free speech, efficient consumer transactions, and security—are often much more readily articulated. Courts and policymakers frequently struggle in recognizing privacy interests, and when this occurs, cases are dismissed or laws are not passed. The result is that privacy is not balanced against countervailing interests.

Abstract incantations of "privacy" are not nuanced enough to capture the problems involved. The 9/11 Commission Report, for example, recommends that, as government agencies engage in greater information sharing with each other and with businesses, they should "safeguard the privacy of individuals about whom information is shared." But what does safeguarding "privacy" mean? Without an understanding of what the privacy problems are, how can privacy be addressed in a meaningful way?

Many commentators have spoken of privacy as a unitary concept with a uniform value, which is unvarying across different situations. In contrast, I have argued that privacy violations involve a variety of types of harmful or problematic activities. Consider the following examples of activities typically referred to as privacy violations:

- A newspaper reports the name of a rape victim.
- Reporters deceitfully gain entry to a person's home and secretly photograph and record the person.
- New X-ray devices can see through people's clothing, amounting to what some call a "virtual strip-search."
- The government uses a thermal sensor device to detect heat patterns in a person's home.
- A company markets a list of five million elderly incontinent women.
- Despite promising not to sell its members' personal information to others, a company does so anyway.

These violations are clearly not the same. Despite the wide-ranging body of law addressing privacy issues today, commentators often lament the law's inability to adequately protect privacy. Courts and policymakers frequently have a singular view of privacy in mind when they assess whether or not an activity violates privacy. As a result, they either conflate distinct privacy problems despite significant differences or fail to recognize a problem entirely. Privacy problems are frequently misconstrued or inconsistently recognized in the law. The concept of "privacy" is far too vague to guide adjudication and lawmaking. How can privacy be addressed in a manner that is non-reductive and contextual, yet simultaneously useful in deciding cases and making sense of the multitude of privacy problems we face?

In this Article, I provide a framework for how the legal system can come to a better understanding of privacy. I aim to develop a taxonomy that focuses more specifically on the different kinds of activities that impinge upon privacy. I endeavor to shift focus away from the vague term "privacy" and toward the specific activities that pose privacy problems. Although various attempts at explicating the meaning of "privacy" have been made, few have attempted to identify privacy problems in a comprehensive and concrete manner. The most famous attempt was undertaken in 1960 by the legendary torts scholar William Prosser. He discerned four types of harmful activities redressed under the rubric of privacy:

1. Intrusion upon the plaintiff's seclusion or solitude, or into his private affairs.
2. Public disclosure of embarrassing private facts about the plaintiff.
3. Publicity which places the plaintiff in a false light in the public eye.
4. Appropriation, for the defendant's advantage, of the plaintiff's name or likeness.

Prosser's great contribution was to synthesize the cases that emerged from Samuel Warren and Louis Brandeis's famous law review article, "The Right to Privacy."

However, Prosser focused only on tort law. American privacy law is significantly more vast and complex, extending beyond torts to the constitutional "right to privacy," Fourth Amendment law, evidentiary privileges, dozens of federal privacy statutes, and hundreds of state privacy statutes. The Freedom of Information Act contains two exemptions to protect against an "unwarranted invasion of personal privacy." Numerous state public records laws also contain privacy exemptions. Many state constitutions contain provisions explicitly providing for a right to privacy.

Moreover, Prosser wrote over forty years ago, before the breathtaking rise of the Information Age. New technologies have given rise to a panoply of different privacy problems, and many of them do not readily fit into Prosser's four categories. Therefore, a new taxonomy to address privacy violations for contemporary times is sorely needed.

The taxonomy I develop is an attempt to identify and understand the different kinds of socially recognized privacy violations, one that hopefully will enable courts and policymakers to better balance privacy against countervailing interests. The purpose of this taxonomy is to aid in the development of the law that addresses privacy. Although the primary focus will be on the law, this taxonomy is not simply an attempt to catalog existing laws, as was Prosser's purpose. Rather, it is an attempt to understand various privacy harms and problems that have achieved a significant degree of social recognition. I will frequently use the law as a source for determining what privacy violations society recognizes. However, my aim is not simply to take stock of where the law currently stands today, but to provide a useful framework for its future development.

The Taxonomy

Privacy cannot be understood independently from society. As sociologist Barrington Moore aptly observes, "the need for privacy is a socially created need. Without society there would be no need for privacy." Society is fraught with conflict and friction. Individuals, institutions, and governments can all engage in activities that have problematic effects on the lives of others.

Privacy is the relief from a range of kinds of social friction. It enables people to engage in worthwhile activities in ways that they would otherwise find difficult or impossible. Of course, privacy is not freedom from all forms of social friction; rather, it is protection from a cluster of related activities that impinge upon people in related ways. This taxonomy attempts to identify and organize these problematic activities. These activities often are not inherently problematic or harmful. If a person consents to most of these activities, there is no privacy violation. Thus, if a couple invites another to watch them have sex, this observation would not constitute a privacy violation. Without consent, however, it most often would.

Of course, declaring that an activity is harmful or problematic does not automatically imply that there should be legal redress, since there may be valid reasons why the law should not get involved or why countervailing interests should prevail. As Anita Allen argues, there are certainly times when people should be held accountable for their private activities. The purpose of this taxonomy is not to argue that the law should or should not protect against certain activities that affect privacy. Rather, the goal is simply to define the activities and explain why and how they can cause trouble. The question of when and how the law should regulate can only be answered in each specific context in which the question arises. But attempts to answer this question are increasingly suffering because of confusion about defining the troublesome activities that fall under the rubric of privacy. This taxonomy will aid us in analyzing various privacy problems so the law can better address them and balance them with opposing interests.

In devising a taxonomy, there are many different ways to go about carving up the landscape. I focus on the activities that invade privacy. The purpose of the taxonomy is to assist the legal system in grappling with the concept of privacy. Since the goal of the law is to have privacy protections that best prevent and redress particular problems, we need to first understand the problems in order to evaluate the effectiveness of the protections.

Therefore, my focus is on activities that create problems. I aim to show that these activities differ significantly yet share many commonalities. Privacy is too complicated a concept to be boiled down to a single essence. Attempts to find such an essence often end up being too broad and vague, with little usefulness in addressing concrete issues. Elsewhere, I have argued that privacy is best understood as a family resemblance concept. As philosopher Ludwig Wittgenstein explained, certain things may not share one common characteristic, but they nevertheless are "related to one another in many different ways." Wittgenstein analogized to members of a family, who generally share some traits with each other (eye color, height, facial structure, hair color, etc.), although they may not have one common trait. There is, however, "a complicated network of similarities overlapping and criss-crossing."

The term "privacy" is an umbrella term, referring to a wide and disparate group of related things. The use of such a broad term is helpful in some contexts yet quite unhelpful in others. Consider, for example, the term "animal." "Animal" refers to a large group of organisms—there are mammals, birds, reptiles, fish, and so on. Within each of these groups are sub-groups. For some purposes, using the term "animal" will suffice. Suppose Sue asks Bob, "How many animals are in the zoo?" Bob does not need to know anything more specific in order to answer this question. The use of the term "animal" in this sentence will be perfectly clear in most contexts. Now suppose Sue wants Bob to bring her a dog. She will not get very far by saying, "Bring me an animal." Rather, she will specify the kind of animal she wants. Even saying "dog" probably will not be adequate, since Sue probably wants a specific kind of dog. As with the term "animal," there are many times when using the general term "privacy" will work well. But there are times where more specificity is required. Using the general term "privacy" can result in the conflation of different kinds of problems and can lead to understandings of the meaning of "privacy" that distract courts and policymakers from addressing the issues before them.

The taxonomy demonstrates that there are connections between different harms and problems. It is no accident that various problems are referred to as privacy violations; they bear substantial similarities to each other. But we also must recognize where they diverge. The goal is to define more precisely what the problem is in each context—how it is unique, how it differs from other problems, and how it is related to other types of privacy problems.

Often these problems involve harms to individuals. Certain kinds of harm, such as physical injuries, are very easy to articulate and understand. A privacy violation presents a more difficult case. Warren and Brandeis spoke of privacy as an incorporeal rather than a physical injury. They noted that the law was beginning to recognize nonphysical harms and that "modern enterprise and invention have, through invasions upon [a person's] privacy, subjected him to mental pain and distress, far greater than could be inflicted by mere bodily injury." Privacy, contended the authors, involves "injury to the feelings."

The harms Warren and Brandeis spoke of are dignitary harms. The classic example of such a harm is reputational injury. As Warren and Brandeis noted, defamation law has long recognized and redressed this kind of injury that lowered people in the esteem of others. But as Warren and Brandeis understood, and as this taxonomy will demonstrate, there are other kinds of dignitary harm beyond reputational injury. These are the harms of incivility, lack of respect, or causing emotional angst. At the time Warren and Brandeis wrote, they were concerned that such dignitary harms might strike some as too ethereal to be legally cognizable. Their project aimed to demonstrate that these were genuine harms that were legally cognizable. And they succeeded, as Prosser emphatically demonstrated in 1960 by collecting hundreds of cases.

There is another, more modern kind of privacy problem that does not readily fit with this dignitary understanding of harm. These problems are more structural in nature. I refer to them as "architectural" problems. They involve less the overt insult or reputational harm to a person and more the creation of the risk that a person might be harmed in the future. They are akin, in many ways, to environmental harms or pollution. In the taxonomy, two kinds of architectural issues emerge most often. First is the enhancement of the risk that a harm will occur. Activities involving a person's information, for example, might create a greater risk of that person being victimized by identity theft or fraud. Such risk-enhancing activities increase the chances of the individual suffering dignitary harms as well as monetary or physical harms. Second, a particular activity can upset the balance of social or institutional power in undesirable ways. A particular individual may not be harmed directly, but this balance of power can affect that person's life. The classic example is law enforcement officials having too much power, which can alter the way people engage in their activities. People's behavior might be chilled, making them less likely to attend political rallies or criticize popular views. Surveillance can also have these effects. This kind of harm is often referred to as a "chilling effect." Imbalances in power can also be risk enhancing, in that they increase the risk of abuses of power.

When we speak of these activities, we often focus on how they affect an individual's life. This does not mean that privacy is an individualistic right. Philosopher John Dewey astutely argued that individual rights need not be justified as the immutable possessions of individuals; instead, they are instrumental in light of "the contribution they make to the welfare of the community." Employing a similar insight, several scholars contend that privacy is "constitutive" of society. Constitutive privacy understands privacy harms as extending beyond the "mental pain and distress" caused to particular individuals; privacy harms affect the nature of society and impede individual activities that contribute to the greater social good. Spiros Simitis recognizes that "privacy considerations no longer arise out of particular individual problems; rather, they express conflicts affecting everyone." Robert Post contends that the tort of invasion of privacy "safeguards rules of civility that in some significant measure constitute both individuals and community." The theory of constitutive privacy has been further developed by Julie Cohen and Paul Schwartz, who both argue that privacy is a constitutive element of a civil society.

In the taxonomy that follows, there are four basic groups of harmful activities: (1) information collection, (2) information processing, (3) information dissemination, and (4) invasion. Each of these groups consists of different related subgroups of harmful activities.

I have arranged these groups around a model that begins with the data subject—the individual whose life is most directly affected by the activities classified in the taxonomy. From that individual, various entities (other people, businesses, and the government) collect information. The collection of this information itself can constitute a harmful activity. Not all information collection is harmful, but certain kinds of collection can be. Those that collect the data (the "data holders") then process it—they store it, combine it, manipulate it, search it, and use it. I label these activities as "information processing." The next step is "information dissemination," in which the data holders transfer the information to others or release the information. The general progression from information collection to processing to dissemination is the data moving further away from the control of the individual. The last grouping of activities is "invasions," which involve impingements directly on the individual. Instead of the progression away from the individual, invasions progress toward the individual and do not necessarily involve information.

Solove's taxonomy is largely chronological—it classifies privacy harms primarily as a function of the stage of information flow at which they occur. This type of classification fits well with the normative, socially constructed view of privacy in which privacy harms are defined as such through a social or political process, as opposed to an inherent or mathematical one. For the purposes of this Chapter (and indeed, this book), we do not suggest whether such a view is correct, only that frequently law, policy, and scholarship embrace such a view.

1. WHICH, NATURALLY, BEGS THE QUESTION—WHAT IF OTHER SOCIETIES VIEW OR CONSTRUCT PRIVACY DIFFERENTLY?

In the excerpt below, James Q. Whitman considered the meaning of privacy through a comparative international lens, focusing on the United States and continental Europe. Because privacy results from normative determination, countries have different social values and different views of the role of privacy. In brief, some scholars argue that the traditional U.S. view has developed under a theme of the state as a necessary institution that must be restrained, and the market is the primary instrumentality for resolving questions of choice. Conversely, the traditional EU view has developed under a theme of the state as the primary instrumentality for resolving questions of choice by protecting consumers, and the market as a necessary institution that must be restrained. As you read the following excerpt from Professor Whitman, consider how these contrasting views of the role of the state might affect transatlantic perceptions of privacy.[13]

JAMES Q. WHITMAN, *THE TWO WESTERN CULTURES OF PRIVACY*

113 YALE L.J. 1151 (2004)

I. A Transatlantic Clash

In every corner of the Western world, writers proclaim "privacy" as a supremely important human good, as a value somehow at the core of what makes life worth living. Without our privacy, we lose "our very integrity as persons," Charles Fried declared over thirty-five years ago. Many others have since agreed that privacy is somehow fundamental to our "personhood." It is a commonplace, moreover, that our privacy is peculiarly menaced by the evolution of modern society, with its burgeoning technologies of surveillance and inquiry. Commentators paint this menace in very dark colors: Invasions of our privacy are said to portend a society of "horror," to "injure [us] in [our] very humanity," or even to threaten "totalitarianism," and the establishment of law protecting privacy is accordingly declared to be a matter of fundamental rights. It is the rare privacy advocate who resists citing Orwell when describing these dangers.

At the same time, honest advocates of privacy protections are forced to admit that the concept of privacy is embarrassingly difficult to define. "[N]obody," writes Judith Jarvis Thomson dryly, "seems to have any very clear idea what [it] is." Not every author is as skeptical as Thomson, but many of them feel obliged to concede that privacy, fundamentally important though it may be, is an unusually slippery concept. In particular, the sense of what must be kept "private," of what must be hidden before the eyes of others, seems to differ strangely from society to society. This is a point that is frequently made by citing the literature of ethnography, which tells us that there are some societies in which people cheerfully defecate in full view of others, and at least a few in which the same is true of having sex. But the same point can be made by citing a large historical literature, which shows how remarkably ideas of privacy have shifted and mutated over time. Anyone who wants a vivid example can visit the ruins of Ephesus, where the modern tourist can set himself down on one of numerous ancient toilet seats in a public hall where well-to-do Ephesians

---

[13] *See also* Pierluigi Perri and David Thaw, *Ancient Worries and Modern Fears: Different Roots and Common Effects of U.S. and EU Privacy Regulation*, 49 CONN. L. REV. 713 (2017), https://ssrn.com/abstract=2596382.

gathered to commune, two thousand years ago, as they collectively emptied their bowels.

If privacy is a universal human need that gives rise to a fundamental human right, why does it take such disconcertingly diverse forms? This is a hard problem for privacy advocates who want to talk about the values of "personhood," harder than they typically acknowledge. It is a hard problem because of the way they usually try to make their case: Overwhelmingly, privacy advocates rely on what moral philosophers call "intuitionist" arguments. In their crude form, these sorts of arguments suppose that human beings have a direct, intuitive grasp of right and wrong—an intuitive grasp that can guide us in our ordinary ethical decisionmaking. Privacy advocates evidently suppose the same thing. Thus, the typical privacy article rests its case precisely on an appeal to its reader's intuitions and anxieties about the evils of privacy violations. Imagine invasions of your privacy, the argument runs. Do they not seem like violations of your very personhood? Since violations of privacy seem intuitively horrible to everybody, the argument continues, safeguarding privacy must be a legal imperative, just as safeguarding property or contract is a legal imperative. Indeed, privacy matters so much to us that laws protecting it must be a basic element of human rights.

This kind of argument can certainly make a powerful impression on first reading, since it is true that we can all imagine some violation of our privacy that seems very horrible. This is especially so when the writings in question are composed by scholars with a real literary gift, like Fried. Nevertheless, no matter how anxiety-inducing it may be to read these authors, their arguments only carry real weight if it is true that the intuitions they evoke are shared by all human beings. Yet all the evidence seems to suggest that human intuitions and anxieties about privacy differ. We do not need to refer to the practices of exotic ancient or modern cultures to demonstrate as much: It is true even as between the familiar societies of the modern West. In fact, we are in the midst of significant privacy conflicts between the United States and the countries of Western Europe—conflicts that reflect unmistakable differences in sensibilities about what ought to be kept "private."

To the Europeans, indeed, it often seems obvious that Americans do not understand the imperative demands of privacy at all. The Monica Lewinsky investigation, in particular, with its numerous and lewd disclosures, led many Europeans to that conclusion. But the Lewinsky business is not the only example: There are plenty of other aspects of American life that seem to Europeans to prove the same thing. Let me offer a variety of examples from France and Germany, two countries that have been my focus in recent research, and that are my focus in this Article as well. Some of the things that bother French and German observers involve what Americans will think of as trivialities of everyday behavior. For example, visitors from both countries are taken aback by the ill-bred way in which Americans talk about themselves. As a French article warns visitors to the United States, America is a place where strangers suddenly share information with you about their "private activities" in a way that is "difficult to imagine" for northern Europeans or Asians. Americans have a particularly embarrassing habit, continental Europeans believe, of talking about salaries. It is "normal in America," an Internet site informs German tourists, for your host at dinner to ask "not just how much you earn, but even what your net worth is"—topics ordinarily quite off-limits under the rules of European etiquette. Talking about salaries is not quite like defecating in public, but it can seem very off-putting to many Europeans nevertheless.

But it is not just a matter of the boorish American lack of privacy etiquette. It is also a matter of American law. Continental law is avidly protective of many kinds of "privacy" in many realms of life, whether the issue is consumer data, credit reporting, workplace privacy, discovery in civil litigation, the dissemination of nude images on the Internet, or shielding criminal offenders from public exposure. To people accustomed to the continental way of doing things, American law seems to tolerate relentless and brutal violations of privacy in all these areas of law. I have seen Europeans grow visibly angry, for example, when they learn about routine American practices like credit reporting. How, they ask, can merchants be permitted access to the entire credit history of customers who have never defaulted on their debts? Is it not obvious that this is a violation of privacy and personhood, which must be prohibited by law?

[. . .]

For sensitive Europeans, indeed, a tour through American law may be an experience something like a visit to the latrines of Ephesus. Correspondingly, it has become common for Europeans to maintain that they respect a "fundamental right to privacy" that is either weak or wholly absent in the "cultural context" of the United States. Here, Europeans point with pride to Article 8 of the European Convention on Human Rights, which protects "the right to respect for private and family life," and to the European Union's new Charter of Fundamental Rights, which demonstratively features articles on both "Respect for Private and Family Life" and "Protection of Personal Data." By the standards of those great documents, American privacy law seems, from the European point of view, simply to have "failed."

But it is not just that Europeans resent and distrust the American approach to privacy: The reverse is also true. Anyone who has lived in the United States knows that Americans can be just as obsessively attached to their "privacy" as Europeans, sometimes defending it by resort to firearms. As for American law, it too is obsessed with privacy. Indeed, some of the most violently controversial American social issues are conceived of as privacy matters. This has been true of abortion for thirty years. With the Supreme Court's decision in Lawrence v. Texas, it is now true of homosexuality as well. It is simply false to say that privacy doesn't matter to Americans.

In fact, let us make no mistake about it: When it comes to privacy, there are plenty of European practices that seem intuitively objectionable to Americans. Some of these have to do with seemingly minor aspects of the anthropology of everyday life, most especially involving nudity. If the Europeans are puzzled by the ill-bred way in which Americans casually talk about themselves, Americans are puzzled by the ill-bred way in which Europeans casually take off their clothes. Phenomena like public nudity in the parks of German cities are particularly baffling to Americans, but so are phenomena like the presence of female attendants in men's washrooms. It is genital nudity that Americans find most bizarre: One's genitalia are "privates" in the full sense of the word in America, and one does not ordinarily expose them in public, and certainly not before the opposite sex. Even breasts are supposed to be kept covered in the United States—as the occasional female European tourist has discovered, when arrested (or even jailed!) for sunbathing topless on an American beach. ("Those Americans are Out of their Minds!" howls a headline from a Swiss tabloid reporting one such incident from Florida.) Even American advertising, which doesn't stop at much, doesn't show bare breasts.

Public nudity may seem little more than a curiosity (though we shall see that it raises revealing problems in the European law of privacy). But here again, it is not just a matter of norms of everyday behavior; it is a matter of law. There are numerous aspects of European law that can seem not only ridiculous, but somewhat shocking to Americans. For example, continental governments assert the authority to decide what names parents will be permitted to give their children—a practice affirmed by the European Court of Human Rights as recently as 1996. This is an application of state power that Americans will view with complete astonishment, as a manifest violation of proper norms of the protection of privacy and personhood. How can the state tell you what you are allowed to call your baby? Nor does it end there: In Germany, everybody must be formally registered with the police at all times. In both Germany and France, inspectors have the power to arrive at your door to investigate whether you have an unlicensed television. Evidence that Americans would regard as illegally seized is routinely considered in continental adjudication. In France and Germany, according to a recent study, telephones are tapped at ten to thirty times the rate they are tapped in the United States—and in the Netherlands and Italy, at 130 to 150 times the rate. All of this will make many an American snigger at the claim that Europeans have a superior grasp of privacy. What kind of "privacy" is there, Americans will ask, in countries where people prance around naked out of doors while allowing the state to keep tabs on their whereabouts, convict them on the basis of unfair police investigations, peer into their living rooms, tap their phones, and even dictate what names they can give to their babies?

Evidently, Americans and continental Europeans perceive privacy differently. Privacy advocates sometimes try to downplay these differences. The felt need for privacy, they insist, is in fact universal, and the only real difference is that American protections are the product of piecemeal legislation, less systematically developed than European protections as yet, but nevertheless evolving in a European direction. There is certainly some truth in this: There are indeed important resemblances between the systems on either side of the Atlantic. Any proper account of comparative privacy law will have to explain many similarities as well as many differences.

Nevertheless, when all is said and done, it is impossible to ignore the fact that Americans and Europeans are, as the Americans would put it, coming from different places. At least as far as the law goes, we do not seem to possess general "human" intuitions about the "horror" of privacy violations. We possess something more complicated than that: We possess American intuitions—or, as the case may be, Dutch, Italian, French, or German intuitions. We must make some effort to explain this fact before we start proclaiming universal norms of privacy protection. In particular, we will not do justice to our transatlantic conflicts if we begin by declaring that American privacy law has "failed" while European privacy law has "succeeded." That is hogwash. What we must acknowledge, instead, is that there are, on the two sides of the Atlantic, two different cultures of privacy, which are home to different intuitive sensibilities, and which have produced two significantly different laws of privacy.

II. Dignity Versus Liberty

So why do these sensibilities differ? Why is it that French people won't talk about their salaries, but will take off their bikini tops? Why is it that Americans comply with court discovery orders that open essentially all of their documents for inspection, but refuse to carry identity cards? Why is it that Europeans tolerate state meddling in their choice of baby names? Why is it that Americans submit to extensive credit reporting without rebelling?

These are not questions we can answer by assuming that all human beings share the same raw intuitions about privacy. We do not have the same intuitions, as anybody who has lived in more than one country ought to know. What we typically have is something else: We have intuitions that are shaped by the prevailing legal and social values of the societies in which we live. In particular, we have, if I may use a clumsy phrase, juridified intuitions—intuitions that reflect our knowledge of, and commitment to, the basic legal values of our culture.

Indeed, to get a handle on our transatlantic privacy conflicts, we must begin by recognizing that continental European and American sensibilities about privacy grow out of much larger and much older differences over basic legal values, rooted in much larger and much older differences in social and political traditions. The fundamental contrast, in my view, is not difficult to identify. In one form or another, it is a contrast that has been noticed by observers of the transatlantic scene for a century. It is the contrast between two conceptions of privacy most recently distinguished by Robert Post: between privacy as an aspect of dignity and privacy as an aspect of liberty.

Continental privacy protections are, at their core, a form of protection of a right to respect and personal dignity. The core continental privacy rights are rights to one's image, name, and reputation, and what Germans call the right to informational self-determination—the right to control the sorts of information disclosed about oneself. These are closely linked forms of the same basic right: They are all rights to control your public image—rights to guarantee that people see you the way you want to be seen. They are, as it were, rights to be shielded against unwanted public exposure—to be spared embarrassment or humiliation. The prime enemy of our privacy, according to this continental conception, is the media, which always threatens to broadcast unsavory information about us in ways that endanger our public dignity. But of course, this concern does not end with media exposure. Any other agent that gathers and disseminates information can also pose such dangers. In its focus on shielding us from public indignity, the continental conception is typical of the continental legal world much more broadly: On the Continent, the protection of personal dignity has been a consuming concern for many generations.

By contrast, America, in this as in so many things, is much more oriented toward values of liberty, and especially liberty against the state. At its conceptual core, the American right to privacy still takes much the form that it took in the eighteenth century: It is the right to freedom from intrusions by the state, especially in one's own home. The prime danger, from the American point of view, is that "the sanctity of [our] home [s]," in the words of a leading nineteenth-century Supreme Court opinion on privacy, will be breached by government actors. American anxieties thus focus comparatively little on the media. Instead, they tend to be anxieties about maintaining a kind of private sovereignty within our own walls.

Such is the contrast that lies at the base of our divergent sensibilities about what counts as a "privacy" violation. On the one hand, we have an Old World in which it seems fundamentally important not to lose public face; on the other, a New World in which it seems fundamentally important to preserve the home as a citadel of individual sovereignty. What Europeans miss in Americans is a sense of the demands of public face; indeed, Europeans have been denouncing American law on that ground since at least 1903. When Americans seem to continental Europeans to violate norms of privacy, it is because they seem to display an embarrassing lack of concern for public dignity—whether the issue is the public indignity inflicted upon Monica Lewinsky by the media, or the self-inflicted indignity of an American who boasts about his salary. Conversely, when continental Europeans seem to Americans to violate norms of privacy, it is because they seem to show a supine lack of resistance to invasions of the realm of private sovereignty whose main citadel is the home—whether the issue is wiretapping or baby names. The question of public nudity presents the contrast in piquant form. To the continental way of seeing things, what matters is the right to control your public image—and that right may include the right to present yourself proudly nude, if you so choose. To the American mind, by contrast, what matters is sovereignty within one's own home; and people who have shucked the protection of clothing are like people who have shucked the protection of the walls of their homes, only more so. They are people who have surrendered any "reasonable expectation of privacy."

As you have seen in the previous excerpts, privacy is a broad concept that extends to a variety of different circumstances, both physical and informational. Further, privacy tends to be represented in different respects under the law, due to its normative nature. In line with embracing the free market, the U.S. has favored a sectoral model for informational privacy, focusing on areas of more risk, such as activities involving financial and health data, or more socially vulnerable individuals, like children. In the European Economic Area and beyond, the dominant information privacy model has been omnibus, or creating a floor informational privacy protection model for all individuals and organizations.

The primary differences between informational privacy and cybersecurity are that they have different relative goals: privacy protects natural persons whereas cybersecurity protects natural persons and organizations (*See* Figure 1). For example, privacy might require certain steps are taken with respect to personal information, such as an "access request," wherein an individual requests information stored by an organization about them for purposes of inspecting, correcting, or transferring data to a new organization. These are not cybersecurity concerns. Although cybersecurity controls seek to manage risk to a wider variety of data types, a strong cybersecurity program is essential to manage risk to personal information and to advance privacy goals.

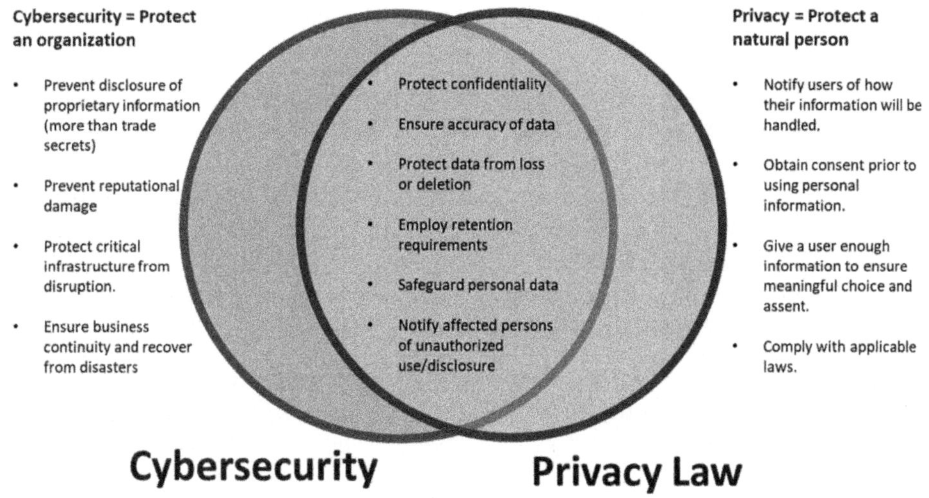

Figure 1: Cybersecurity v. Privacy Law

In coming chapters, we will reference privacy where it is useful for discussing cybersecurity concepts, but the scope of cybersecurity is both inclusive and exclusive of privacy concepts.

QUESTIONS

1. Is the right to privacy described by Warren & Brandeis a dignitary or a liberty right?

2. How might Warren & Brandeis describe the relationship between "security" and "privacy"? Do you think they would view this relationship similarly in contemporary society as they would have in 1890?

3. Against whom and what does the European-style dignity-based right to privacy protect? Against whom and what does the American-style liberty-based right to privacy protect? Stated differently, for each side of the Atlantic, who is the "feared surveiller?"

4. Under each of these understandings, what rights does an individual have to control the use that a third party makes of information that the individual voluntarily disclosed? Of information that the individual did not voluntarily disclose?

D. PRIVACY AND SECURITY

In law, "privacy" and "security" often are viewed as two highly similar concepts both in legal privacy practice and in privacy research. In engineering and science, "privacy" and "security" are similarly viewed as highly related concepts, albeit with different formal mathematical definitions. And indeed, these two concepts certainly are related. However, both the legal and the technical approaches described above miss key points regarding the relationship between the concepts of "privacy" and "security."

We consider the relationship between these concepts through a series of essays written by your casebook authors. In the first, Professor Hurwitz discusses (U.S.) consumer perceptions of the two concepts. In the second, Professor Bambauer examines the conflation of the two terms within legal scholarship with regard to their degree of normativity. In the third, Professor Thaw categorizes the myriad terms which have evolved in the privacy, cybersecurity, and data protection spaces along Bambauer's continuum and according to their respective areas of law.

In the following excerpt, Professor Hurwitz explains the differences between privacy and security, framing his discussion in terms of consumer concerns about each.

GUS HURWITZ, *PRIVACY AND CYBERSECURITY ARE NOT THE SAME, AND AMERICANS CARE FAR MORE ABOUT CYBERSECURITY*

American Enterprise Institute Study (July 2016)

Introduction

A recent analysis published by the National Telecommunications and Information Administration (NTIA)[14] discusses data showing "that Americans are increasingly concerned about online security and privacy" and that "these concerns are prompting some Americans to limit their online activity." . . . Press coverage almost uniformly framed discussion of these data in terms of privacy concerns, to the exclusion of security concerns. Even those articles that mentioned the security side of the NTIA data treated security concerns as comparable to privacy concerns.

But the NTIA data show something quite different than suggested by press coverage. They show that two to three times as many American Internet users are concerned about online security as are concerned about online privacy. Or stated another way, the NTIA data show that a majority of users are concerned about security, but that a majority do not identify privacy as a major concern.

[. . .]

The NTIA Data

The data presented by the NTIA are based on data collected in July 2015 as part of the Computer and Internet Use Supplement to the Census Bureau's Current Population Survey (CPS). The Census Bureau conducts

---

[14] Rafi Goldberg, *Lack of Trust in Internet Privacy and Security May Deter Economic and Other Online Activities*, US Department of Commerce, National Telecommunications and Information Administration (NTIA), May 13, 2016, https://www.ntia.doc.gov/blog/2016/lack-trust-internet-privacy-and-security-may-deter-economic-and-other-online-activities.

this supplement to the CPS and collects responses to NTIA-designed questions relating to Internet use from 53,000 households.

> [The NTIA data report that about] 63 percent of households reported being concerned about identity theft, and 45 percent reported concern about credit card or banking fraud. (Respondents were free to report as many concerns as they had.) Both of these concerns are security related.

The next three categories of responses reported in the NTIA data would generally be classified as privacy related: data collection by online services, loss of control of personal data, and government data collection. Unlike the previous two categories, which relate to unknown actors accessing information without authorization (that is, stealing it), these categories generally relate to known parties collecting and using information that they are authorized to access (that is, without the need to break into a computer system to obtain it). Under each of these categories, the NTIA data shows 23 percent, 22 percent, and 18 percent of Internet users reporting major concerns about each of these privacy harms.

This substantial gap between privacy- and security-related concerns suggests a number of things. First, Internet users recognize a difference between the two types of harms. Second, they are far more concerned about security-related concerns than privacy-related concerns. Third, the majority of users simply do not identify privacy-related issues as "major" concerns.

[. . .]

Privacy and Security are Distinct Fields

Although the story that the NTIA data tells is one in which Internet users are substantially more concerned about security than privacy, most popular coverage disproportionately focuses on privacy-related concerns. This is both unsurprising and problematic.

It is unsurprising because discussion of privacy and security tends to conflate the two issues into a single set of concerns. We see this perhaps most starkly in discussions of encryption, which typically are framed in terms of a tradeoff between privacy and security, suggesting that these are two sides of a single coin. And if we approach these two issues from the perspective of user autonomy and control over their information, then indeed privacy and security both implicate the same set of concerns.

But while privacy and security both raise related concerns they are, fundamentally, different issues. At its core, privacy is about how one person uses information lawfully obtained about or from another person—including what it means for such information to be lawfully obtained. Contemporary privacy discussions are difficult because technology is changing social understandings about what it means for information to be "lawfully obtained." Online tracking, drones, and police surveillance, for instance, are all generally done in accordance with established law—these raise important privacy issues because many people believe that the laws governing these activities are outdated and should be changed.

Security, on the other hand, relates to information unlawfully obtained about or from other parties. While the underlying concern—how information about one party is used by another—is similar, security presents different issues that need to be thought about and, ultimately, addressed differently. In security, for instance, a key concern is typically how or whether information about one party was obtained by another party—in privacy we are concerned with how or whether that information was used, not with how it was obtained.

Professor Bambauer draws a similar distinction between privacy and security concerns. The excerpt below further develops this distinction and considers various approaches that the law may take to each—contract, tort, and criminal—and how those may apply differently to privacy versus security. We will return to these different approaches and consider them in greater detail throughout this book.

DEREK BAMBAUER, *PRIVACY VS. SECURITY*

103 J. CRIM. L. & CRIMINOLOGY 667 (2013)

I. Privacy Versus Security

Acxiom is one of the world's foremost data mining companies. The company's databases contain information on over half a billion consumers, with an average of 1,500 transactions or data points per consumer. It processes one billion such records each day. Each consumer receives a unique numeric identifier, allowing Acxiom to track and classify them by location, credit card usage history, and even interests. Acxiom earns over a billion dollars annually by selling this data to companies that want to market their wares more effectively. If Big Data has an epicenter, it is likely located in Conway, Arkansas, where Acxiom's server farm can be found.

Even giants make mistakes. In February 2003, Acxiom provided a defense contractor with the Social Security numbers of passengers who flew on JetBlue flights. The contractor used one of those Social Security numbers in a PowerPoint presentation, and that passenger's information quickly became public. The disclosure led to intense criticism of the company and to a complaint to the Federal Trade Commission.

And, in 2002 and 2003, hackers penetrated Acxiom's computers, accessing records on millions of American consumers. Acxiom failed to detect the breaches; rather, the attacks were noticed first by local law enforcement and then by the Federal Bureau of Investigation (FBI). Indeed, in the 2003 case, Acxiom had no idea its systems had been compromised until a Cincinnati sheriff turned up compact discs filled with the company's records while searching the home of a systems administrator for a marketing firm. It was only while the FBI was investigating the case that agents stumbled upon a second group of hackers who had broken into Acxiom's server three times the prior year. The Cincinnati systems administrator captured the sensitive data while it was being transferred via File Transfer Protocol (FTP), without encryption, from a server outside Acxiom's firewall—the equivalent, in security terms, of writing it on a postcard sent through regular mail.

Thus, Acxiom exposed sensitive consumer data three times—once through a deliberate choice and twice through incompetence. Privacy advocates were outraged in each instance. This Article argues, though, that these cases—the disclosure, and the hacks—should be treated differently. The disclosure is a privacy problem, and the hacks are a security problem. While legal scholars tend to conflate privacy and security, they are distinct concerns. Privacy establishes a normative framework for deciding who should legitimately have the capability to access and alter information. Security implements those choices. A counterintuitive consequence of this distinction is that law should punish security failures more readily and harshly than privacy ones. Incompetence is worse than malice.

Security, in contrast to privacy, is the set of technological mechanisms (including, at times, physical ones) that mediates requests for access or control. If someone wants access to your online banking site, he needs your username, password, and personal identification number (your credentials). The security of your online banking is determined by the software on the bank's server and by who knows your credentials. If someone wants access to your paper health records, they need physical access to your physician's file room. The security of your health records is determined by the physical configuration of the office and by who holds a copy of the key to it. As a privacy matter, you might want only your doctor and her medical staff to have access to your records. As a security matter, the office's cleaning staff might have a key that lets them into the file room.

The differences between privacy and security matter. Security defines which privacy choices can be implemented. For example, if your entire electronic medical record is secured by a single mechanism (such as a password), it is not possible to enforce selective access, so that your dermatologist can see information about your sunscreen use but not about your antidepressant use. And privacy dictates how security's options should be implemented, the circumstances under which they are appropriate, and the directions in which they ought to develop.

II. Privacy

At base, privacy issues are arguments about values. Privacy debates are some of the most contentious in information law. Scholars and courts disagree about virtually everything: the theoretical bases and contours of privacy rights; the relative merits of free-expression rights versus privacy; the risks posed by de-identified data; the virtues of a "right to be forgotten"; and the benefits of ad-supported media versus Internet users' interests in not being tracked online. What makes these debates so important, and heated, is that they embody a clash between values and policies that have legitimate claims for our attention.

The answers to those arguments can rarely be resolved empirically; rather, they depend upon one's prior normative commitments.

[. . .]

[Privacy] is about clashing interests and values, and about the difficult task of choosing among them. Shifts in privacy rules nearly always burden some stakeholders while benefiting others. Rule configurations are justified by recourse to value frameworks: efficiency, distributive justice, or religious prohibitions. And these configurations describe how privacy ought to function. Security, by contrast, describes how privacy does function.

III. Security

Security implements privacy's choices. Security determines who actually can access, use, and alter data. When security settings permit an actor without a legitimate claim to data to engage in one of these activities, we do not view that fact as altering the normative calculus. The actor's moral claim does not change. The access or use is simply error. . . . Security's debates are more cold-blooded and technical—they are about relative informational advantages, the ability to bear costs, and the magnitude and probability of harm. Like precautions against civil harms (the domain of tort law), security measures exist along a continuum. Perfection is generally unattainable or unaffordable. Where there are normative choices—such as who should bear residual risk—they tend to be more deeply buried, or subsumed in utilitarian methodologies.

Formally, then, security is agnostic about how privacy rules dictate selection of who may interact with data. The capability to access or alter data can be granted to all users or none, it can be added or revoked, and it can even be bifurcated. A particular technology may provide for more or less robust, granular, or transparent choices for security. That limits how effectively security can implement privacy. It does not, however, challenge the legitimacy of privacy choices in selecting the desired end state.

Privacy determines who ought to be able to access, use, and alter information. It justifies these choices with reference to larger values—

values that compete for priority and attention. Security implements that set of choices. . . .

IV. Keep 'Em Separated

Paying attention to the distinction between privacy and security has important consequences. At a theoretical level, it concentrates attention on issues where normative models differ versus instances that demonstrate failures of implementation. To borrow an example from computer science researcher Christopher Soghoian, whether the California company Biofilm should ask for, and then retain, customers' e-mail addresses as the price of a sample of the personal lubricant Astroglide is a privacy question. It was a security problem when Biofilm accidentally made those addresses available on its Web server. When customers submitted their information to Biofilm, both parties wanted to keep that data between them. Customers gained no benefit from the inadvertent disclosure. And Biofilm's goals did not change—it did not release the information in pursuit of greater revenue or more targeted marketing. It was simply a mistake.

From a utilitarian perspective, privacy issues are a zero-sum game. If firms can track users' activities on their own websites (and perhaps other ones) and retain that data, they gain relative to a "do-not-track" regime where they cannot do so. Users' gains are inversely correlated: they benefit more from a regime where they can elect to reveal information to websites versus one where they cannot. Security issues, by contrast, result in an outcome that is worse for both sides. After the breach above, Biofilm is worse off, and its consumers are worse off. That difference between security and privacy has important ramifications for regulation.

At a practical level, this approach suggests that when disputes involve security flaws, rather than privacy debates, courts should permit liability at a much lower threshold of harm and fault or blameworthiness. Security might be conceptualized as akin to a contractual bargain between those who supply data and those who hold it. And contract, unlike tort, is a doctrine of strict liability. Courts do not care whether a breaching party is blameworthy, or whether the harm resulting from a breach is weighty or small. Merely showing breach is sufficient.

Alternatively, one might envision security within tort law's framework. Firms could be held to owe a duty to the subjects of the information they possess, or even to society generally, to securely store and handle data. Security failures could be evaluated under strict liability (firms bear the entire cost of the harm their insecurity creates), under a negligence standard (firms only bear costs when they have failed to meet some criterion for security), or both (such as strict liability for data leaks and negligence for hacking). Tort law may be preferable since it offers the possibility of compensating those harmed by security failures, even if only nominally, and of imposing greater deterrence ex ante through the threat of punitive damages.

Finally, one might approach security from the perspective of criminal law, by conditioning liability upon a blameworthy mental state. As with scienter in tort, the level of *mens rea* could be reduced, such as to negligence, or even eliminated, as with strict liability. And as with strict liability crimes generally, security failures might be punished without the traditional requirement of blameworthiness because these violations are seen as less morally culpable. Security breaches will less typically involve situations where the defendant benefits directly. Society is more likely to condemn actions where a defendant gains from his crimes than where his benefit may be minimal (the cost of some precautions not taken) or even negative (such as market harm from breaches). Thus, security failures generally leave everyone involved (except for the attacker) worse off. Privacy failures, by contrast, typically involve a transfer of utility between parties: if Biofilm sold the e-mail addresses rather than losing them, it would be enriched, and the Astroglide samplers would be worse off. Thus, privacy disputes involve courts or regulators deciding whether such transfers should be sanctioned. Security problems destroy utility. Society should have less hesitation about imposing liability for actions (or inactions) that only reduce utility.

[. . .]

V. Conclusion

Security and privacy can, and should, be treated as distinct concerns. Privacy discourse involves difficult normative decisions about competing claims to legitimate access to, use of, and alteration of information. It is about selecting among different philosophies and choosing how various rights and entitlements ought to be ordered. Security implements those choices—it mediates between information and privacy selections. Importantly, this approach argues that security failings should be penalized more readily, and more heavily, than privacy ones, because there are no competing moral claims to resolve and because security flaws make all parties worse off.

Professor Bambauer wrote his piece *Security Versus Privacy* in 2012 (published in 2013). Curiously, in the seven years (as of January 2020) since then, little attention has been paid to the distinctions between privacy and security as such. If anything, during those 7 years (a lifetime in "internet years"), the distinctions between privacy and security have become even further blurred, particularly with the introduction of additional terms such as "data protection," "cybercrime," and "cyberwarfare" into the public and scholarly discourse.

In response to this confusion, Professor Thaw has articulated a framework for understanding these terms within the context of their respective areas (or "tools") of law—the criminal law, the regulation and the administrative state, international law, and private law. This framework, applied to a "normativity spectrum" based on Bambauer's distinctions between privacy and security, aims to create an operationally functional vocabulary for cross-disciplinary discourse around topics related to cybersecurity.

DAVID THAW, *DISAMBIGUATING "CYBER"*

Working Paper (2019)

Cybersecurity is perhaps one of the most poorly-defined and "overloaded" professional terms-of-art in contemporary society. Heavily used by popular media, policymakers, business leaders, professionals, and academics, it evokes images of technical systems, adversaries, criminals, foreign actors, and surveillance issues. Which is precisely the problem—this single sentence identifies 25 simple permutations of potential meanings for the terms, without even opening the door to the more complex issues. Terms emerging from these meanings include privacy, cybercrime, cyber warfare, data protection, computer security, and numerous other related sub-topics. Some of these terms are used interchangeably, and all are poorly-defined across disciplinary, political, and sectoral silos.

Effective discourse about a topic requires a common language for description of the topic. This Essay tackles the challenges inherent in our widespread yet overloaded use of the term cybersecurity. It proposes disambiguating the term across two metrics: 1) normative versus objective questions; and 2) the areas and tool of law and policy implicated. Building on Professor Derek Bambauer's proposal that "security implements privacy," this framework presents a robust set of distinctions among the oft-confused terms associated with cybersecurity. The robustness of these distinctions arises from their clear distinctions from the perspective of legal theory, while accommodating many professional communities-of-practice extant usage of those terms. Stated more simply—this approach creates a common language for discussing complex "cyber" problems.

Professor Bambauer distinguishes the concepts of "privacy" and "security" primarily on their degree of normativity. (Curiously, this distinction has not received much direct attention since his writing.) He describes privacy as primarily a normative exercise, making political choices regarding the arrangement of power and control over information. Security, by contrast, merely implements those decisions—it is an objective exercise measured by how well it gives effect to normative choices, rather than imbuing normative choices itself. "Security" and "privacy," however, are not the only terms with which we must contend.

The normativity/objectivity distinction can be extended to address the myriad cyber-related terms which have become mainstream in the years since Bambauer's original work developing the distinction into a spectrum. Such a spectrum would, by default, run from pure "privacy" choices (most normative) to pure "security" decisions (most objective). Creating this spectrum, however, first requires some additional definitional precision, and second requires an additional metric to help distinguish similar terms. The first takes on the challenge of defining "security," and the second employs basic legal theory to distinguish terms based on the areas and tools of law they engage.

Basic Terminology—Defining Security

Since the source of ambiguity arises from interactions with the term—and technology—of "cyber" systems, an initial step to create an operational definition of "cyber" is required. The term "cyber" is perhaps (ironically) the easier term for which to create an operational definition. Professor Gus Hurwitz proposes that the taking of any traditional activity "online"—such that it is conducted or becomes part of an internetworked environment—properly implicates the term "cyber." While not a mathematically complete definition, I argue that an operational definition is superior for the purposes of disambiguating conflating terms.

The term "security" poses a greater challenge. Substantial varying definitions exist within the available literature, including definitions from computer science, information technology, international relations, contract law, criminal law, engineering, business, and many other fields. Generally speaking, each of these respective definitions is context-specific and focuses narrowly on a precise problem within its respective discipline. Such an approach is useful for understanding particular problems, but no one such definition of this nature is likely to prove useful for defining a broad concept which spans multiple disciplines. Rather, an approach which identifies commonality—or more specifically common purpose—better forms an operationally-useful definition for understanding the concept of "security" within the context of discussions about cyber- and other internetworking-enabled technologies.

Generally-speaking, the various definitions of security concern themselves with some form of managing risk. Risk management across each of these fields seeks to achieve a relatively common goal—avoidance of undesired operational outcomes. Thus security concerns itself with the degree to which "desired" or "predicted" system states can be maintained under operational conditions. Somewhat oversimplified, security is concerned with the degree to which things operate as expected.

This definition is operationally-useful for two important reasons. First, it accords extremely well with the objectives of risk management. It can be evaluated empirically and objectively, is well-suited to root-cause analysis, and (generally) can easily map costs onto particular operational deviations. This is essential for risk management activities, which at their core involve cost-benefit tradeoffs as a mechanism for determining the deployment of mitigative measures. Second, the definition makes security an operational question—one capable of being evaluated and implemented objectively.

This is both *operationally* and *normatively* desirable because it makes the evaluation of operational success more straightforward (unclouded by normative differences) and because it makes the process of debating critical normative questions (e.g., surveillance) more focused on the underlying political values and goals and less complicated by implementation challenges.[15]

QUESTIONS

1. Consider the descriptions of "normative" (Bambauer) & "social understandings" (Hurwitz). From your brief read of these excerpts, how do you think these concepts might apply to the world of cybersecurity? Can you think of the ways in which certain countries or populations might view cybersecurity?

2. Based on Professor Thaw's articulation of the differences between cybersecurity and privacy, how might you explain these concepts to a work colleague with no experience in data or technology?

3. What do you think the difference is between a normative and an objective perspective? How might you describe this using layman's terms? Name one or two examples of how you think this might play out for privacy law versus security decisions.

4. Describe how you think risk might be an extension of threats and vulnerabilities. What is one example of a threat and a vulnerability for an e-mail system? For a social networking app? For a hospital record? For each of these assets, which general controls someone might someone implement to reduce the likelihood of the risk being realized and an incident occurring?

[15] Implementation challenges are, I suggest, a very poor proxy for normative decision-making. To be sure, some implementation challenges are effective barriers (we do not yet have the technology to dispose of waste in the vastness of galactic space, or to migrate to other worlds should our global environment fail). Generally speaking, however, implementations are not elements of an underlying normative debate, but rather a *factor to be weighed* in determining the policy outcome once a normative framework first has been reached. For example, scarcity of water does not determine what we *should* do with water. We must first decide how we value water and its uses, and then once decided, we can evaluate what to do under the conditions of available water and other related factors. Conflating the two risks conflating an underlying normative framework (the degree to which we value water) with an input to a policy decision (the *current*—but critically, not *inherent*—quantity of available water and conservation/re-use methods).

CHAPTER 3

A BASIC INTRODUCTION TO CYBERSECURITY RISK

■ ■ ■

The concept of risk is ever-present in any organization, whether public to private entities. At their root, risks are negative situations that have some probability of occurring, and they usually are not possible to completely avoid. The goal with all risks is to make a calculated risk—that is, to know what the potential risks are—and *decide* that the costs to eliminate, minimize, or avoid the risk outweigh the impact, financial or otherwise, if the risk is realized (or occurs). Most organizational leaders understand one key concept as it pertains to organizational decision-making: the benefits of neutralizing the risk must outweigh the known or potential costs. Often, as in highly competitive industries, without risk, there is no reward.

Aside from common business adages like "without risk, there is no reward," the concept of risk is usually prospective at least to some extent. Consider the following example: a corporation is considering opening new stores in a new market, such as a new country, in a geographic expansion. Without considering the specific cybersecurity risks, what business risks might that business face? In this case, a business might want to assess potential financial implications to understand whether consumers might buy from these stores, where the competition is located, how to differentiate these stores in the market, or how to get product to stores in a new geographic area. The business might assess whether the taxes in this new area might influence the pricing for specific products, and whether the expected profit margin will recoup investments, and, if so, when or whether it makes sense to lease or purchase property for the stores.

Often, organizations consider practical business risks without considering legal, or "compliance," risks. *Compliance* is the activity of an organization making calculated, legal risk-based decisions in its everyday operations. Compliance departments within organizations think about risk as *legal risk*, but several other departments consider risk as part of their everyday responsibilities. In the example above, a corporate compliance department might assess the new expansion from the perspective of legal risk, specifically which new laws might apply in the new market. For example, operating stores in a new geography might mean new environmental standards, such as implementing new chemical disposal procedures, or installing alternative energy sources. It might mean different or more frequent financial disclosures or new competitive relationships. The same business might have to navigate new import requirements for certain types of goods it intends to sell in its stores, and the business may need to be exceedingly careful in its dealings with local government entities to arrange shipments or obtain approval for certain licenses.

However, for all organizations, risks are multi-faceted and not only legal in nature. Generally, there are four kinds of risks all organizations face, and it is these types of risks, to varying degrees, that inform which decisions should be made: financial risk, operational risk, legal risk, and reputational risk. Technology-related risks may fall into one or multiple categories. It is important to learn about each type of risk because analyzing a cybersecurity scenario requires an expert (in law, business, or technology) to think about different impacts. In fact, most systems analyzed will pose a combination of these types of risks to an organization. You will have an opportunity to analyze scenarios considering these risk types throughout the book and at the end of this chapter.

A. RISK TYPES

The first risk type is financial risk. *Financial risk* is risk related to direct money losses. These losses could be due to financial overextension, such as failure to anticipate certain types of risks in a new investment, e.g.: purchase of real property that requires more repairs than expected, a bad stock pick, unanticipated costs when a crucial piece of property in a factory breaks down, or compromised trade secrets. Financial risk, however, can also be related to cybersecurity. For example, when a data breach occurs, often significant costs result from forensic services to identify the cause of the breach, certified mail notification to consumers, external legal counsel and media consultants, credit monitoring services, and costs to remediate the vulnerabilities that caused the breach. Financial risks are directly financial in nature, rather than indirect losses related to other risk types, such as operational risks, legal risks, or reputational risks. Certainly, anything can be "financial" at some level, but this risk type focuses on direct financial risks.

The second risk type is operational risk. *Operational risks* are risk that impact an organization's ability to conduct business or perform desired and required functions. An example of an operational risk in the cybersecurity context, for example, would be a cyberattack that prevented employees from working, such as a server failure or a ransomware attack. It might also impact operations if data are incorrect, such as incorrect raw material orders, electronic health record data switched between patients, or increased velocity levels for a nuclear reactor.

The third risk type is reputational risk. *Reputational risk* is intangible risk related to reputational damage. Reputational damage tends to be more speculative and is tied to factors like reduced sales, foot traffic, stock price, and *going concern*, or that an organization has the resources to operate effectively. When a publicized incident occurs, such as a large-scale data breach, the reputation of the organization is harmed. For example, if a data breach occurs and a publicly traded company did not alert the Board of Directors or its shareholders, shareholders may sell their stock, resulting in lower stock prices.[1]

Reputational risks also complicate organizations from operating effectively as a for-profit entity. For example, a highly publicized data breach could discourage some shareholders from buying stock from a company, especially if this is not their first data breach. In the Target Corporation data breach, sales, especially credit card sales, slowed substantially in the first few months after the publicized data breach, which was during the "black" period, or when sales move from the "red" (loss) to "black" (gain), or "Black Friday." As most retailers make up for losses during the year after Black Friday, the biggest sales day of the year, experiencing a data breach around this time damaged Target's reputation, resulting in depressed sales and stock price dips.

The fourth risk type is *legal risk*. As described above, legal risk ties to specific legal requirements established in statute or through the common law. For example, the Health Insurance Portability and Accountability Act of 1996 (HIPAA) includes a Security Rule, which establishes, albeit at a high level, specific security requirements for certain HIPAA-defined organizations. If an organization does not implement one of these requirements and, for example, an unauthorized person accesses a patient record, certain obligations are triggered. If the Office for Civil Rights (OCR), a division of the Department of Health and Human Services, charged with responding to incidents of non-compliance with HIPAA, determines an organization has failed to comply, they may choose to fine the organization.

At the state level, state attorneys general and sector-specific departments enforce statutes, as well. Under California's SB-327 of 2018, dubbed the Internet of Things (IoT) Security Law, Internet-connected devices must implement "a reasonable security feature . . . appropriate to the nature and function of the device." If a company does not implement reasonable security features for its IoT device, California's Attorney General can prosecute and fine.

---

[1] Several studies have been conducted regarding stock price after a data breach. While the results are somewhat inconclusive, for most publicly traded corporations, stock price bounces back after a period of time following the data breach. The exception to this is for repeat data breaches. Some studies have suggested that repeat data breaches have a higher impact on overall stock price. D. Schatz & R. Bashroush, *The impact of repeated data breach events on organisations' market value*, 24 INFORMATION AND COMPUTER SECURITY 73–92 (2016), https://doi.org/10.1108/ICS-03-2014-0020.

All states have passed data breach notification laws, which may require implementation of security programs. Often, these laws permit the state's Attorney General to fine organizations, rather than provide for private rights of action by individuals. It should be noted that data breach notification statutes are one of the areas of substantial overlap between privacy law and cybersecurity law.[2]

CHARLOTTE A. TSCHIDER, *EXPERIMENTING WITH PRIVACY: DRIVING EFFICIENCY THROUGH A STATE-INFORMED FEDERAL DATA BREACH NOTIFICATION AND DATA PROTECTION LAW*

18 TUL. J. TECH. & INTELL. PROP. 45 (2015)

While early adoption of data breach notification statutes did not include data protection requirements, such as employing reasonable security procedures or limiting data retention timeframes, this trend has changed significantly in the past three years. Today, 55% of all data breach statutes passed since 2005 include multiple data protection requirements, and 14% have at least one. Since 2012, nine of thirteen statutes passed have multiple data protection requirements . . .

Penalties and private action illustrate the push and pull between Attorney General suits and associated penalties with a consumer's right to recover for injury sustained. Across all statutes, a wide variety of penalties are imposed, and often no penalty amount is specified. The wide variety of penalties shows the significantly divergent status of data breach notification statutes: incorporation of data breach notification statutes into existing consumer fraud statutes versus creation of data breach notification-specific penalties for noncompliance. Private action likewise occupies the spectrum of options. While before 2013 only 17% of statutes permitted a private right of action, this figure has increased in recent revisions. Most statutes specifically limit rights to the Attorney General's prosecutorial power.

This prosecutorial power usually results in settlement at the state level including a fine. When assessing legal risk, these fines are the potential cost of a legal risk being *realized*, that is, when a risk is no longer a probability but has actually occurred, and a fine or some other legal cost results. In cybersecurity, a realized risk is called an *incident*. Notably, because each of these risk types can exist for technology, cybersecurity risk can be evaluated from the perspective of each risk type. Most internet-

---

[2] Because most state laws exist to enforce state residents' health and public safety, most state laws implicating cybersecurity practices are actually privacy laws, designed to protect residents' personal information. Most of the time, state laws do not protect organizations from themselves by requiring cybersecurity practices when there is no impact on actual people.

connected systems will pose a combination of these risk types. *See* Figure 1 below illustrating the four types of risk.

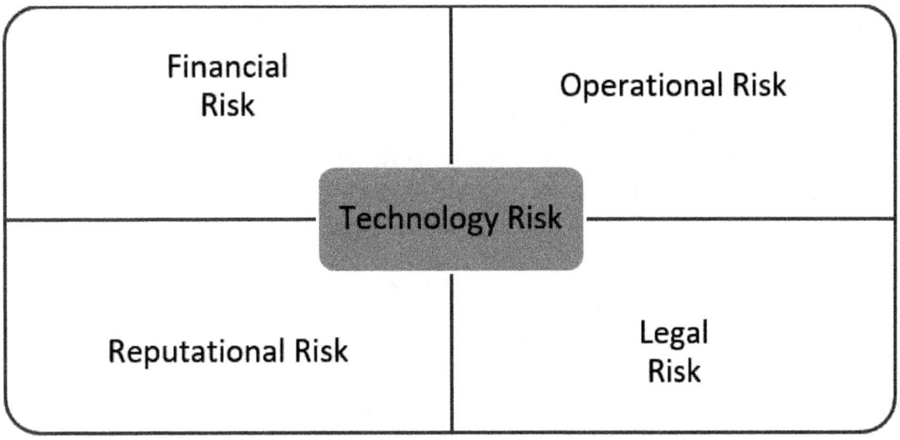

Figure 1: Risk Types

Another example of legal risk is related to compliance behaviors not established by statute but established by administrative agency behavior. The Federal Trade Commission (FTC) is charged, under Section 5 of the FTC Act of 1913, with protecting consumers from "unfair *or* deceptive trade practices." As we will explore later in this book, several key decisions established that the FTC can prosecute organizations for unfair or deceptive trade practices with respect to a company's privacy and cybersecurity practices. However, the FTC has not established any specific rules related to cybersecurity, except where the FTC has extended statutory protections to cover gaps in statutory applicability.[3] Although administrative agencies do adjudicate some cases in their respective administrative courts, most frequently the FTC reaches settlement with organizations before pursuing court action. These settlements, called consent agreements, consent orders, or consent decrees, are common both for the FTC at the federal level and for state attorneys general at the state level. In both cases, the FTC or state attorneys general may fine an organization for their behavior as part of these settlements, which are publicly disclosed.

There is some significance to consent agreements as quasi-legal or *soft law*: although no legally enforceable rules exist, settlements do provide some predictive instruction as to the issues the FTC (and other administrative agencies) will likely prosecute. They do not, however, establish a true common law in the way contract, tort, corporate, and property law have developed. Settlements may at least indicate the types

[3] The FTC has extended the HIPAA data breach notification to all organizations handling personally identifiable health data and has also clarified the definition of a "financial institution" for the Gramm-Leach-Bliley Act's Safeguards Rule.

of behavior deemed unacceptable from the perspective of an administrative agency. Consider the following two alternative perspectives of FTC decision-making from Daniel J. Solove & Woodrow Hartzog and a response from one of this book's author's, Justin (Gus) Hurwitz. Please note that these pieces may reference privacy cases, but their subject is the FTC's approach to regulation of both privacy and data security cases.

DANIEL J. SOLOVE & WOODROW HARTZOG, *THE FTC AND THE NEW COMMON LAW OF PRIVACY*

114 COLUM. L. REV. 583 (2011)

Although the FTC's privacy cases nearly all consist of complaints and settlements, they are in many respects the functional equivalent of common law. While the analogy to traditional common law has its limits, it is nonetheless a useful frame to understand the FTC's privacy jurisprudence. Common law is a form of Anglo-American law that is characterized by incremental development through judicial decisions in a series of concrete cases. The decisions serve as precedent—judges aim to decide cases consistently with previous decisions. In the most traditional form of common law, judges develop the legal rules. Much of Anglo-American tort law, contract law, property law, and criminal law emerged through this process. Many parts of these bodies of law were later codified into statutes, especially criminal law, which today in the United States is almost entirely statutory.

There is also another form of common law that emerges through the interpretation of constitutions and statutes. Although judges do not create the initial rules, their decisions on the meaning of those rules have precedential effect and become essential to the interpretation of the rules. Indeed, the meaning of many provisions of constitutional and statutory law cannot be understood simply by looking to their text—the body of judicial decisions offering a gloss on those provisions is an essential component that must be consulted. The key factor that makes it imperative to consult these judicial decisions when interpreting constitutional or statutory text is the fact that the decisions have precedential weight.

FTC privacy settlements technically lack precedential force for other companies. The FTC is not strictly required to be consistent, but the FTC has demonstrated a commitment to remaining consistent in practice. As will be discussed, new complaints and settlement orders do not stray far from previous ones. Instead, the FTC incrementally develops this body of law in a stable way. Practitioners look to FTC settlements as though they have precedential weight. The result is that lawyers consult and analyze these settlements in much the same way as they do judicial decisions. This Part will demonstrate how the FTC privacy settlements serve as the functional equivalent to a body of common law.

1. FTC Settlements.—Although the FTC has specific rulemaking authority under COPPA and GLBA, for Section 5 enforcement—one of the largest areas of its jurisprudence—the FTC has only Magnuson-Moss rulemaking authority, which is so procedurally burdensome that it is largely ineffective. The FTC must rely heavily on its settlements to signal the basic rules that it wants companies to follow. Indeed, this is how courts create rules in the common law. Because courts cannot legislate, they craft rules in judicial decisions, which remain in effect for future cases by way of precedent. When the FTC issues a settlement, it typically issues a complaint and settlement document simultaneously, and these are publicized on the FTC's website. Among privacy law practitioners, FTC settlements are major news and generate significant attention.

Why are these settlements akin to common law? First, they are publicized, and the FTC follows them. Accordingly, they have a kind of precedential value, and they serve as a useful way to predict future FTC activity. Chris Wolf notes that "consent orders have immediate nationwide impact (to the extent they affect behavior) unlike in the litigation context, where there can be a split of authority on what is or is not prohibited conduct." Additionally, every state has adopted some form of a consumer protection statute, often called "[L]ittle FTC Acts," many of which explicitly look to FTC interpretations of overlapping concepts to guide enforcement.

Second, FTC settlements are viewed by the community of privacy practitioners as having precedential weight. Privacy lawyers routinely use FTC settlements to advise companies about how to avoid triggering FTC enforcement. For example, Wolf notes that when counseling clients, he frequently references activities that triggered FTC actions. Many firms that counsel clients on privacy matters routinely post and disseminate information about recent FTC settlements on their blogs. Addressing the precedential value of FTC settlements, David Vladeck states:

> "It is not uncommon for lawyers representing respondents in agency proceedings—investigations and then formal complaints—to cite prior complaints or orders (consent or litigated) as "precedent" as to what constitutes an unfair or deceptive trade practice. And I think that practice makes sense. Complaints do signal the agency's view of the applicable law, and do inform regulated parties as to the agency's view of how the law applies to a discrete and identified set of facts. So it seems entirely appropriate that counsel would rely on them to draw inferences about the correctness, or fairness, of the agency's position in an investigation and contested action" [. . .]

FTC settlements are thus like the common law because they are treated in practice like the common law. The orders are publicized with the intent that practitioners rely upon them, and practitioners do so. The FTC's intent is just part of the equation, for the common law effect of FTC settlements rests heavily upon how they are received by the companies they regulate and the community of practitioners that advises these companies.

Of course, settlements are not equal to judicial decisions. Unlike judicial decisions, where other stakeholders are able to be heard through amicus briefs, FTC settlements have no such process. FTC investigations of companies are often secret and only announced when the settlement has been issued. As Wolf observes, "Unlike in litigation, the adversarial process and . . . role of the tribunal is quite limited as companies frequently enter into consent orders to avoid publicity, and thus agree that there has been enough of a case made to settle (even though in litigation, they might be able to prove otherwise)." Nevertheless, the FTC does have a comment period where other stakeholders can be heard before the settlements are finalized. Commissioners vote on settlement orders and often write concurring and dissenting statements to reflect their view on an action. The Commission also sends direct letters to those who comment on the proposed orders addressing their concerns. This is similar in effect to an appellate court's handling of particular issues in a case and the ability of interested parties to voice support and concern, and highlight various interests through amicus briefs.

Settlements need not be as binding on future cases as judicial decisions to reflect aspects of the common law. While there is no well-established doctrine of precedent for settlements, the FTC has been relatively consistent in its privacy jurisprudence. Although the FTC rarely explicitly cites settlement orders in later, separate settlement orders, Levin states that while she was at the FTC, "[i]n a new action, internal memoranda accompanying proposed pleadings would typically cite to the Bureau and the Commission prior complaints or consent orders as precedent for bringing the action against a proposed respondent." The FTC has referenced previous consent orders in statements that accompany final orders. For example, in a letter to commenter Sidley Austin, LLP as part of In re Sears Holdings Management Corp., the FTC referenced two prior consent orders that were similar to the current one to demonstrate consistency. Indeed, the FTC settlements are rarely inconsistent with each other. There have been hardly any noted instances of inconsistency, despite a sizeable number of practitioner commentators who have analyzed FTC cases.

Precedent is largely a practice that is held together by custom and norms. Of course, appellate courts can reverse lower courts, and this prospect serves to reinforce precedent. The FTC settlements do not appear to be any less consistent than bodies of case law. According to Joel Winston, who served as associate director for DPIP from 2000 to 2011 and whose career at the FTC spanned more than thirty years, although "[a]s a general matter, the Commission doesn't cite consents as legal precedent in formal adjudicatory proceedings," the FTC and its staff "often blur the lines between consents and adjudicated orders in citing cases as precedent. This may come up in consent negotiations, speeches, and other informal communications."

Winston notes that consent decrees are often "designed" to "have a huge impact on other businesses in the same industry or that use similar practices" because the FTC "must be strategic in bringing its cases, since it doesn't have the resources to pursue more than a relatively small fraction of law violators." Thus, "the cases are designed to send a message to others similarly situated."

Winston notes that in his current role as a privacy lawyer in private practice, he has been "surprised at how intense the level of scrutiny is both by the business community and the private bar." He goes on to observe:

> "They seem to analyze literally every word of the complaint and order in search of hidden messages; in particular many of the law firms with FTC practices put out client alerts whenever the FTC issues a settlement that include highly detailed analyses of the pleadings and predictions on what they might portend for the future."

In some ways, settlements might have good features that judicial decisions lack. A settlement is mutually agreed upon by both the FTC and the defendant, so it represents a workable compromise. Judicial decisions need not reach this compromise point. The benefit of reaching a compromise is that the doctrines emerging from these compromises are likely to be workable for at least several key stakeholders, whereas there is no such guarantee with judicial decisions, which can be entirely unworkable or unsatisfactory to any stakeholder.

On the other hand, the company brokering the compromise might not be representative of all stakeholders or even of a majority of stakeholders. The compromise might be workable for that company and others of a similar size and structure, but might not be as workable for other companies. In fact, there is a risk that the FTC could bully small companies with limited resources in order to collaterally attack larger organizations through the consent decree process. While this risk is present, the fact that the FTC has pursued the largest and most popular players in the internet space suggests that the agency has not behaved in this manner.

Regardless of the desirability of a body of doctrines crafted from settlements, this is the body of doctrine that exists in the domain of privacy regulation, and in practice it functions similarly to common law.

The doctrines in the FTC settlements should be studied like a body of common law as adaptive, iterative, and increasingly determinative. Doing so demonstrates that there is order to what might appear chaotic. It shows that there is predictability and clear doctrinal development in this body of regulation. Viewing the FTC settlements as a common law evolutionary process also provides a perspective in the debate over how specific FTC privacy jurisprudence must be. As will be discussed below, standards that might have initially seemed vague are becoming more specific over time.

2. *FTC Reports and Materials.*—In addition to settlement agreements, the FTC has created a form of "soft law" that consists of guidelines, press releases, workshops, and white papers. In the past two years alone, the FTC has issued reports on the proper use of facial recognition technologies, privacy disclosures on mobile applications, mobile applications for children, and a sweeping report entitled Protecting Consumer Privacy in an Era of Rapid Change, which summarizes the FTC's current and future approach to privacy regulation centered on privacy by design, simplified choice for businesses and consumers, and greater transparency.

These materials are purportedly offered by the FTC as guides, yet the FTC has never clearly articulated which parts of its recommendations are mandatory and which parts are simply best practices. Many have criticized this lack of clarity because they feel compelled to be overly cautious to avoid running afoul of opaquely defined boundaries.

Nevertheless, because these materials serve to illuminate the FTC's philosophy and approach, as well as its interpretation of Section 5, these materials have weight. They may not be exactly akin to advisory opinions, but they can come quite close. Companies take the guidance in these materials seriously. In some cases, statements in these materials can become almost like rules.

Perhaps the best analogue to this soft law is dicta in judicial opinions. The FTC materials do not have the same force and effect of a settlement; they are merely statements by the FTC about how it interprets its regulatory authority and Section 5, and how it might choose to enforce in the future. The FTC might change course or not enforce in that manner. The FTC might attempt an enforcement but be challenged by a company in court. Thus, FTC materials do not appear to be as strongly precedential as settlements, but they create incentives for companies to comply, and thus serve as a softer kind of rule.

Vladeck, former director of the Bureau of Consumer Protection, said that there is a key difference between the best practices the FTC proposes for guidance purposes and the standards it uses "to measure unreasonableness or unfairness in enforcement cases." For the cases it brings, the FTC "look[s] at the company's conduct and see[s] to what extent it measures up to industry standards writ large." When determining best practices for guidance purposes, the FTC arrives at these "through deep and ongoing engagement with all stakeholders, and reference to the statutes the agency enforces."

Contrast this excerpt with Professor Hurwitz's response:

JUSTIN (GUS) HURWITZ, *DATA SECURITY AND THE FTC'S UNCOMMON LAW*

101 IOWA L. REV. 955 (2014)

Once we move beyond the superficial understanding of the common law as being merely a series of semi-precedential decisions, it becomes difficult to maintain an analogy of the FTC's approach to the common law. Most fundamentally, the FTC is not operating in a domain of convergence; it is operating in a domain of modal policies [. . .]

The FTC is not an independent adjudicator; it is a party to the enforcement actions it brings. And instead of taking and deciding whatever cases come to it, it has discretion to choose what cases it hears. Those familiar with the FTC's process describe this as a benefit because it allows the Commission to use its case-selection prerogative to guide the development of the law. Whatever the benefits of such an approach, it is a clear departure from the common law. Although in some cases, firms and individuals may be able to initiate their own action against the FTC, it is unlikely that the FTC will take action in close cases—those in which we would say there is a case or controversy—when it can instead choose only to bring those cases that are most likely to advance its policy goals.

While this may be advantageous to the FTC as it works to craft the rules that it wants to develop, such benefit accrues to the agency in its capacity as a rule-maker, not as a rule-enforcer. As discussed above, the common law approach works well where adjudicators hear a large number of cases that present issues at the margins of existing law. Indeed, easy cases may well make bad law. Where the FTC selects cases that allow it to shape the broad contours of the law, it is misusing the adjudicatory mechanism. Decisions that result from such a process will be overbroad, because they are made without the benefit of facts that would tend to be considered more seriously in a legislative or notice & comment rulemaking process.

The contrast between this approach and that of a common law court is stark. Courts decide cases because they must, and in rendering decisions, they are careful to address only the relevant issues and do so narrowly. This is a central theme that cuts to the heart of the argument in favor of the FTC's approach: Agencies, unlike courts, can engage in quasi-legislative rulemaking. Recall that in Chenery II the Court started its analysis by saying that "[s]ince the Commission, unlike a court, does have the ability to make new law prospectively through the exercise of its rule-making powers, it has less reason to rely upon ad hoc adjudication to formulate new standards of conduct."

With the agency wearing the hats of both litigant and adjudicator, it is also unsurprising that the Commission has an unprecedented success rate in its adjudications. This is well documented in recent literature: Until 2014, the FTC's complaint counsel (administrative prosecutor) hadn't lost a case adjudicated before the Commission (on appeal from the Administrative Law Judge) in nearly 20 years. And, when one excludes cases in which the full Commission dismissed some claims, that winning streak goes back 30 years. This outstanding success rate is particularly remarkable given that FTC matters initially prosecuted before the Commission are more, not less, likely to be overturned by the courts of appeal than FTC matters initially prosecuted in district court. This plain fact runs in the face of justifying deference to administrative agencies because of their supposedly greater expertise.

These statistics raise clear questions about the FTC's impartiality as adjudicator, an important difference between the FTC's "common law" and judicial common law. They also highlight another important difference. The parties have more of a substantial reason to settle the cases due to the money and time costs of litigating a case before the Commission. In addition, the parties face reputational damage if an FTC complaint does get adjudicated. Settlement offers the opportunity to resolve complaints with minimal publicity as well as saving time and money.

But as discussed above, development of the common law is a positive externality that results from private litigants having an incentive to see cases through to decision. Where this is not the case, parties' private incentives do not align with the public development of the law. While the various public documents relating to an FTC enforcement action may provide some understanding of FTC policy, it is disingenuous to describe the resulting policy in common-law terms.

The FTC's "common law" analogy also fails on multiplicity grounds. Multiplicity—especially of different adjudicators deciding similar cases—helps adjudicators find the margins along which the law needs to develop and to identify the directions in which it may develop. The FTC's approach—especially where the Commission proceeds by identifying high-impact cases that address broad issues—assumes the conclusion. Unlike the common law, the Commission begins knowing the direction in which it wants the law to develop, and selects cases that allow it to proceed along this path. This robs the Commission of the benefit offered by hearing many perspectives, and it robs the public of the better policies that such perspectives would allow the Commission to craft.

A final difference between the Commission's approach and that of the common law is that there is no reason to believe that the Commission's jurisprudence will be stable over time. Administrative agencies are not bound by principles of stare decisis. They are largely free to change their policies, even to create direct conflicts with prior policies. Indeed, agencies are even free to adopt policies that contradict previous judicial constructions of their statutes. The primary constraint is that whatever policy they adopt must reasonably be within the ambit of the agency's statutory authority. Simply stated: Stare decisis does not constrain administrative decision-making.

Many of the commentators who have discussed the Commission's "common law" approach have recognized this, at least to some extent. They respond to concerns such as these by saying that the Commission has approached its development of the law with an eye to consistency. While this may be historically true, it is a leap to compare 10–15 years of consistency from the FTC with the common law's hundreds of years of consistency. Institutional leadership changes, and tomorrow's leaders are not bound by either the procedural or substantive values of today's leaders. The Commission has been developing these areas of law under the stewardship of only three Chairs, and only recently has the Commission begun thinking of itself as operating in a common-law-like manner. The FTC would not be the first agency whose jurisprudence become untethered from stable precedent, oscillating to match the political preference of whichever President appoints its chair. Indeed, looking at the closing letters offered by the Commission in its data security investigations, it is apparent that the Commission is providing parties significantly less guidance under the stewardship of Chairwoman Ramirez than it did previously.

Administrative agencies, whether specially designated to enforce a statute or with more general jurisdiction like the FTC, are not the only sources of legal risk. When a specific statute permits a civil right of action, it means that individual people, companies, or shareholders may recover. The California Consumer Protection Act of 2018 (CCPA), AB-375, while not specifying security controls that must be implemented, does provide a private right of action for consumers, for reasons including the following:

> . . .nonencrypted or nonredacted personal information . . . is subject to unauthorized access and exfiltration, theft, or disclosure as a violation of the duty to implement and maintain reasonable security procedures and practices appropriate to the nature of the information to protect the personal information may institute a civil action . . .

The risk of private action under the CCPA, as well as fines allocated under the Attorney General's "Consumer Privacy Fund," for example, would qualify as legal risks.

The common law itself may also apply to cybersecurity risks. A shareholder derivative lawsuit, where the shareholders of a publicly traded company, representing the best interests of the company, sue the directors or executive management of a company for not implementing appropriate mechanisms to protect the value of the company. One example of a cybersecurity-related shareholder derivative lawsuit is if directors or executive management forego implementing a technical security program or investing in security for critical assets, only to experience a data breach. Tort, specifically negligence or negligence per se actions, might also be the source of legal risk, which will be discussed later in this book.

Contracts actions between business entities may also be the source of legal risk. A technology services company, for example, may be required to implement certain security controls with respect to important assets for their business customers. If the organization does not implement these security controls and the business customer experiences a loss, such as due to a data breach, the court may award damages. Take, for example, an organization providing technology software for a business customer in the financial services field. If this organization has committed to encrypt certain financial information and a data breach occurs, the business customer may successfully sue for breach of contract and may recover for some or all of the data breach cost.

The financial services customer could be fined under the Gramm-Leach-Bliley Act, which mandates reasonable security controls for banking data, or under Regulation S-P, which mandates the same for financial services firms, like investment companies. The financial services customer may also have to pay for data-breach-related costs as previously discussed. In this case, the customer will likely sue the technology software company for breach of contract if the contract mandated the company to encrypt this data or implement other security controls.

QUESTIONS

1. Name and explain the four risk types. Why do you think most organizations think of risk in four types? Can you explain how each of these risk types might be posed for a cybersecurity risk?

2. What is the difference between compliance and risk? What are the sources of legal risk as you understand them from the text?

3. Why might an organization take a risk-based, rather than a compliance, approach to cybersecurity?

4. Consider Professors Solove and Hartzog's position on the FTC versus Professor Hurwitz's. Knowing what you know now, do you think the FTC's consent agreements with organizations operate like the common law? How might the FTC's agreements nevertheless shape an organization's perception of legal risk?

B. RISK GOVERNANCE

As you have read, organizations of all kinds, public and private, are subject to four risk types. Of course, most organizations are faced with these four types of risk as they apply to any number of different risks, not just those that pertain to cybersecurity. And organizations must determine how to appropriately allocate their resources to mitigate, remediate, or avoid these risks at a cumulative level. The Director of a government agency or non-profit organization, the Chief Executive Officer (CEO) of a publicly traded company, or the President of small, closely held business, all must consider all potential risks to them. Business risks, including cybersecurity risks, and organizations must make a calculated decision about when, where, and in what amount to allocate resources, including people and money. Of course, typically there are constraints, such as funding cycles that have already allocated funds in a specific way, or funds dedicated to other purposes.

For these reasons, boards of directors for businesses and non-profit organizations and oversight committees for government agencies advise these organizations on how these resources should be allocated given the goals and risks an organization faces. For this reason, some organizations, such as publicly traded companies have appointed a Chief Risk Officer (CRO), created an Enterprise Risk Management (ERM) program, or have an in-house audit, or *assurance*, function. Although these roles and teams are distinct (and will be discussed in more detail in later chapters), they all are situated to provide advisory services to executive leadership and directors with their organization. It should be noted that these functions are usually performed separately from pure compliance functions, which focus primarily on legal risk. Instead, these functions review global risk, or situations an organization faces considering all four types of legal risk.

For smaller organizations, this function might be performed by an external body, such as an external auditor, or identified by leadership and aggregated. It is crucial to remember that risk is multi-faceted, and often there are competing priorities an organization must consider when making investment decisions. Consider a manufacturing company that must prioritize a variety of different risks: aging manufacturing equipment, crumbling premises, investments to compete in a new market, unsupported supply chain software, or important systems without appropriate security controls. Each of these scenarios poses a variety of different risks, and this company's leadership will need to determine how to allocate resources to address each of these risks.

The act of determining how to allocate resources and what to do about a particular risk posed is called *risk decisioning*. With respect to cybersecurity risks, available risk decisions include: remediate, mitigate, avoid, transfer, or accept risk. Risk remediation is the act of completely eradicating, or closing, the risk. This means that after remediation has been completed, no risk remains. Risk mitigation is the act of reducing risk in some measurable way. Risk mitigation leaves remaining, or *residual,* risk, but typically the act of risk mitigation reduces risk to a lower, more acceptable level. Risk avoidance is foregoing some opportunity or direction completely; this usually applies to scenarios where a direction or investment is prospective, rather than currently implemented. An example of risk avoidance is when an organization opts not to choose a particular service provider because they cannot agree to minimum security controls or deciding not to scale a proof-of-concept app because it isn't protected with enough security controls.

Risk transfer is the act of transferring risk to a third party to offset potential costs. The primary method of risk transfer is through cybersecurity insurance. Also known as cyberliability or cyberrisk insurance, these policies offset potential cybersecurity risks by covering expenses associated with incidents and data breaches resulting from threats exploiting system vulnerabilities. In order to qualify for such insurance coverage, organizations may be required to complete an assessment of their risk profile to ascertain whether insurance is available, and if so, what the premiums should be. Certain types of vulnerabilities, however, may be unavailable for insurance coverage, and often insurance companies resist paying out for these claims, for example looking for inaccuracies in information previously provided. Another model for risk transfer involves transferring risk to a third-party service provider. Unfortunately, in both of these cases, not all risks are extinguished. For example, operational, legal, and reputational risks may not be completely transferred, although the insurance company may provide financial coverage for incident or data breach costs.

Finally, risk acceptance is the act of accepting a risk without mitigating it. Although risk acceptance is a viable risk decision, it does not reduce risk in any way. However, it may be used in circumstances when risk mitigation or remediation is too expensive, impractical, or the risk itself is low. For example, if the cost to remediate a database by encrypting it is a million dollars, but the database will be replaced in a year, it may not make much sense to remediate the system.

However, the act of accepting risk is not as simple as just deciding to accept risk. When an organization accepts risk, it should be accepted according to a prescribed governance model that ensures the appropriate level of management accepts each identified risk. Governance models couple an action that may be taken, such as mitigation, remediation, or acceptance decisions with a corresponding decisional level. If a risk has been reviewed, and it has been rated as extremely risky to the organization overall, for example being a known vulnerability that may lead to a multi-million-dollar data breach, it may not be appropriate for a lower-level employee to decide to accept the risk and not to remediate.

Many organizations treat risk acceptance as a separate process, called an *exception* or *variance* process, because usually accepting a known risk means that the organization is not following its internal security requirements. Therefore, when a department or individual is requesting risk acceptance, they are essentially requesting a time period, perhaps indefinitely, to deviate from the organizationally mandated policy and required security controls.

Because of the nature of receiving an exception from organizational policy, sometimes organizations establish a risk governance board or committee consisting of representatives from key departments to ensure the risk profile of the requested exception is fully explored. Due to the multi-faceted nature of risk, sometimes the members of the committee consist of the Chief Financial Officer (CFO) or similar finance leader, the Chief Information Officer (CIO) or similar Information Technology (IT) leader, a communications or public relations leader, General Counsel (legal), the Chief Information Security Officer (CISO—usually the individual accountable for the security program), the Chief Privacy Officer or Chief Compliance Officer, and the executive leader over the applicable business or functional area where the risk has been identified, such as Marketing or Human Resources. In other cases, key leaders may be designated to make the decision, such as the CIO and General Counsel in combination.

QUESTIONS

1. Name and explain the five possible decisions that can be made about a risk. What might be the relative benefits to each decision type?

2. Why might you want to include multiple leaders across an organization in risk decisioning or to review proposed decisions for higher risk situations?

3. Why might a higher risk require a higher level of review by leadership? Do you think that exceptions should receive even more scrutiny? Why or why not?

4. Can you think of the relative benefits of knowing versus not knowing about certain risks? If you were an administrative agency, how might you respond differently to an organization that knows it has risks and accepts most of them versus an organization that has not identified risks at all?

C. RISK ASSESSMENT AND RISK RATING

Now that you have learned the different risk perspectives and which decisions might be made about risk, you might be asking how risk is actually determined. While hypothetically a risk may come to the attention of a department at any time, risks have typically been identified through one of three primary processes: risk assessment, vulnerability assessment, and incident response. Each of these processes is a part of a *risk management program*. A risk management program is a systematic approach to managing risk for an organization. In order to manage risk, an organization needs to have a common and repeatable set of controls and processes in place. We will discuss how a risk management program is organized and operates in more detail later in this book, but for now, it will be useful for you to think about how an organization might discover potential risks.

Risks are identified through assessment, or the process of reviewing a given asset, such as a system, using a repeatable set of controls. Controls are derived from legal and industry requirements and are framed in a Yes or No format, for example: "encrypts all sensitive personal information in transit over the open Internet." A risk analyst uses a control set applicable to the asset being evaluated to assess the asset. Some assets are more critical operationally, more valuable financially, or storing more sensitive data, and therefore require more stringent controls. The controls framework determines which controls apply and when, so that an analyst can effectively assess the right requirements in a given scenario and determine if risk remains. *See* Figure 2 for a visual explaining the risk assessment process at a high level. Note the role of risk decisioning in this process.

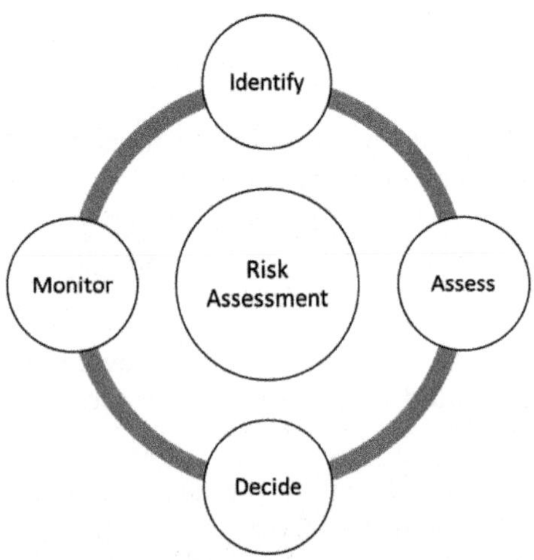

1. Determine what is of value to your organization.
2. Determine what requirements apply.
3. Assess if the requirements have been applied.
4. Make a decision about what to do and do it.
5. Monitor progress on decisions made.
6. Ensure follow-through.
7. Repeat.

Figure 2: Risk Assessment Process

Consider electronic health record-keeping. Electronic health records are often used as the central source of truth for a hospital system or multiple health systems to understand the history and status of their patients. These records include very sensitive data, such as a patient's HIV status, disabilities, sexual behaviors, mental conditions, or even religious observance that might expose the patient to discrimination. Further, health records are very valuable to hackers who might sell these records on the open market, as this data can be used for insurance fraud. Finally, without correct and available electronic health records, hospital systems would fail to provide effective treatment to their patients. In this case, it is likely that the control set would mandate that when electronic health record information is transmitted over the open Internet that it be encrypted using an industry standard protocol because attackers who might want to use the data for nefarious purposes or profit would likely seek to interrupt, change, or steal data from these systems. A control set in this case, then, is designed to anticipate likely threats in a routine way: by requiring certain requirements be implemented for certain types of systems, collectively the risk of exploit is reduced significantly. Application of a control effectively closes a known vulnerability from the perspective of the organization and renders the risk nearly zero.

Risks result from an assessment when a control is not in place for a given asset, exposing a vulnerability. For example, if sensitive medical data are not encrypted in transmission, as required by the control, attackers could intercept data, a "man-in-the-middle attack," change or scramble data as it is being transmitted by rearranging or changing the order of files transmitted, or stop the transmission altogether. When no control is in place, a risk results because unencrypted, highly valuable data transmitted over the open Internet increases the probability a threat source will exploit a vulnerability in that asset.

"Vulnerability" may be used generally to represent any technical issue that exposes an asset to a threat. We also note that new vulnerabilities may appear as attackers become more knowledgeable or sophisticated. For example, some vulnerabilities have already been exploited by the time an organization becomes aware of them. Vulnerabilities like these, usually related to application or server code, may require code fixes or updates. For example, Microsoft Corporation launches updates and code fixes at least once per month, which organizations then must evaluate and apply without causing outages or other functionality issues with the applicable systems.

A vulnerability need not be remediated unless a threat will exploit it or the security community expects a vulnerability to be exploited in the near future. For this reason, we often express risk as an extension of threat and vulnerability, or RISK = THREAT × VULNERABILITY. Although not necessarily used mathematically, it demonstrates that both a threat and a vulnerability are needed for a risk to result. There are a variety of scenarios where the data or the systems have no value to a hacker. Compare electronic medical records with a system storing publicly aggregated data that is used for marketing purposes. Although that system could be very useful for a company, it might be easy to recompile the aggregated data from other systems if the system is unavailable. And it is unlikely that hackers would go to the effort of breaking into a system to steal public data, even if it is of some use to the company. In this example, the threats are very limited.

In the electronic medical record example, perhaps the organization has applied all or most of the required controls for the medical record system, including encrypting the data in transit. In this case, few if any vulnerabilities exist, which means that although the threats might be numerous, the risk might be reduced to a very low level. Of course, controls are only one part of an effective risk management system because they are designed to be inflexible and codify strong security practices. However, for some assets, a specific control may be extraneous or a poor fit for that particular asset's security design. For example, whether or not to encrypt some databases, or even which encryption algorithm to use, can be a hotly debated subject amongst engineering teams.

When the data are not particularly sensitive and an organization significantly limits access to these data, encryption may not be especially appropriate, even if a control requires it. In this example, the likelihood of a threat exploiting a vulnerability to cause some negative impact may be relatively small. Although the assessment might flag a risk, the existence of *compensating controls*, or controls that partially reduce the risk that are already in place (such as limited access and storage on a self-managed server that is properly segregated on the internal network), means that the resulting risk rating would likely be low. The key take-away is that although security controls may be framed as required and inflexible, the risk of a situation may not demand it.

An equation often used for determining the severity of risks is RISK (RATING) = PROBABILITY (LIKELIHOOD) × IMPACT. This equation is used practically to consider what the level of risk actually is when a control has not been applied to an asset. Usually this equation is not used quantitatively, that is plugging in an actual number, primarily because the likelihood of a threat exploiting a vulnerability for a particular organization is difficult to numerically define. Further, impact is difficult to determine in a highly predictive manner for each of the four types of risk (e.g., we do not know, yet, to what degree the California Attorney General intends to prosecute IoT security issues, or how many private rights of action might result from CCPA violations related to security). Most of the time, organizations ask a small group of security experts to conduct regular rating meetings to calibrate risk across an organization, and it benefits these experts to consider the types of impacts from the four different perspectives (operational, financial, legal, and reputational). Although risk ratings may not be objectively verifiable, they should be internally calibrated for purposes of remediation prioritization, the key purpose of risk ratings. See Figure 3 for a simple example of how organizations might plot potential issues for an asset for purposes of remediation planning activities.

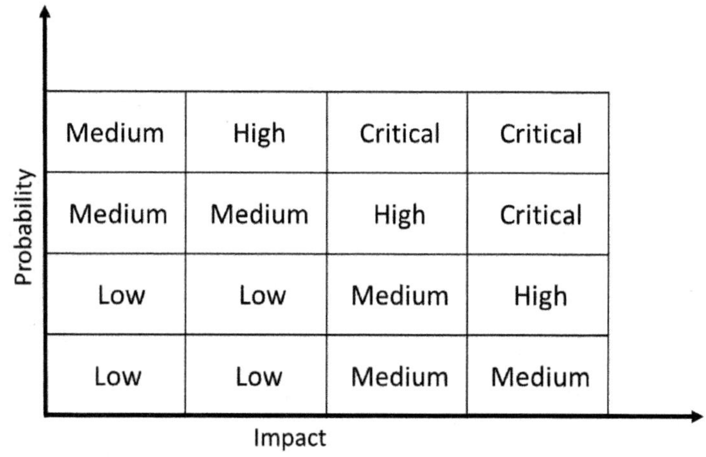

Figure 3: Risk Prioritization

Remediation prioritization is a key part of any risk management program because, as described earlier in this chapter, organizations have limited resources and competing risk priorities outside cybersecurity risks. Prioritizing risk is essential for any organization to effectively reduce global risk to the organization overall. A third, "z" quadrant to Figure 3 is the ease of remediation, or effort. Organizations are often faced with limited budgets and specific planning requirements for any spending, so an effort to prioritize different remediation activities on a specific timeline is often desirable.

A risk-based conception of cybersecurity explains why some technologies and situations may demand certain security controls, whereas other technologies and situations may not. Understanding both the different facets of risk and learning how to prioritize them within an organization helps to determine where resources should be spent most effectively. Without a useful risk discourse, organizations either may overinvest or underinvest in cybersecurity.

QUESTIONS

1. How might you explain the equation RISK = THREAT × VULNERABILITY in layman's terms to an executive or director of a government organization?

2. Risk management is an extension of both preventative measures likely to reduce vulnerabilities *and* regular updates and code changes as new vulnerabilities emerge. How would you expect these processes to be distinct and separate?

3. What are the four steps in a risk assessment? Why are controls so important for purposes of a risk assessment? What are the two main sources of controls?

4. Why might you expect any organization needs to rate identified risks? How might you ensure that risk is consistently rated within an organization? How might risk rating and corresponding decisions be useful from a legal perspective?

CHAPTER 4

THE CYBERSECURITY ECOSYSTEM

■ ■ ■

In this chapter we delve into the "ecosystem" of cybersecurity. Understanding cybersecurity solely as a technical field (even as an interdisciplinary one) fails to capture important parts of the picture depicting the interconnected world in which we live and transact business. In our discussion of adversarial risk, we examine the motivations of various actors in the ecosystem. Those motivations play an important part of understanding how to think about, manage, and mitigate adversarial risk. In our discussion of stochastic risk, we examine how such risks may include human forces—human error, for example, makes up a very significant portion of threats associated with stochastic risk.

We start by considering the different types of attackers and their motivations. We then look at the rest of the security ecosystem, which comprises far more than merely targets. Important participants in this ecosystem include individual and institutional users, developers designing and selling software and network-connected devices, independent contractors designing and implementing systems on behalf of third parties, and firms that provide network infrastructure, among others.

We also introduce a set of high-level guidance for how one may think about securing systems. At one level, this guidance is the nuts-and-bolts practical takeaway from this text: if you leave it without a basic understanding of these ideas . . . well, both you and we have failed. But this introduction is also only the starting point, setting the stage for material discussed in the next chapter, in which we will consider that nature, utility, and design of security guidance and frameworks.

As we proceed through this chapter there are some basic terms with which you will become familiar:

- *System*—a combination of individuals, entities, devices, networks, physical objects or entities, biological objects or entities, energy, or other factors that interact and interoperate in a given manner to produce results. A common example of a computer system is a basic arithmetic calculator. A common example of a biological system is an animal or plant. Common examples of physical systems are roads (constructed) or weather storms (naturally occurring).[1]

- *Actors*—individuals, entities, or systems who participate in and have impact upon the cybersecurity ecosystem.
- *Individuals*—natural persons[2] who participate in the cybersecurity ecosystem.
- *Entities*—organizations, usually comprising at least one individual,[3] which participate as actors in the cybersecurity ecosystem.
- *Users*—individuals or entities who (volitionally) make use of, participate in, or otherwise interact with a system.
- *Adversaries*—individuals or entities, bearing some type of intent, who engage in volitional acts that create threats posing risk to systems.
- *Attackers*—adversaries actually engaged in the process of attempting to compromise targets.
- *Defenders*—individuals or entities actively engaged in attempting to mitigate risks to targets.
- *Targets*—systems, individuals, or entities bearing some risk of security compromise.

A. HACKERS AND ATTACKERS

Identifying the adversary is critical in any defensive exercise. Cybersecurity presents a particularly challenging task in this regard because the "adversary" comprises perhaps the most diverse set of permutations of motivations, skill sets, allegiances, and methods of any adversarial/defensive relationship in the history of security analysis. At a high level, the many-to-many relationships created by a fully internetworked world create bigger and more complex problems than previously considered.

Some background is useful in understanding the varied terminology used when describing attackers. First, the term "attacker" is a generic term

---

[1] We discuss the concept of a system as a type of asset in much greater detail in Chapter 5. In this context, the term "system" refers to the generic meaning of the term (describing an interoperating set of elements), not just a "technological" system.

[2] Note that while we avoid the use of the term "person" in this taxonomy, in most contexts the law defines a "person" to *include* various types of business organizations (juridical persons). We attempt to avoid this ambiguity by using the term "individuals" and having it refer only to natural persons, which is how the term is defined by a majority of jurisdictions worldwide.

[3] But note that entities may not comprise individuals. This could be either because they comprise "strong artificial intelligence" agents (far less common), for example IBM's Watson; or because they comprise autonomous non-intelligent actors, for example Distributed Autonomous Organizations (DAO's) enabled by blockchain or other distributed verification technologies (DVTs).

used to describe any party which seeks to gain unauthorized access to a system and/or to disrupt or alter the activities, functions, or data of that system without authorization. There is a robust debate regarding the legal definition of the term "authorization" within the context of the Computer Fraud and Abuse Act, which we will discuss later in this text. Authorization in the present context is different from that debate: here, we simply use it descriptively to identify whether adversarial actions constitute "attacks." Put simply, if an adversarial action (e.g., altering or accessing data) is unauthorized, it constitutes an attack.

The term "hacker" is vastly ill-defined in modern discourse, although it does have a rather precise etymology. It comes from a sub-culture of early computer users in the 1980s and 1990s who engaged in modifications to common codebases (e.g., rewriting computer software), most commonly by extracting and reassembling pieces of code from various programs. Hence the term "hacking"—such modifications often were quite literally the result of hacking up code.

"Defenders" is a simple yet confusing term. The formal definition at the beginning of this chapter is relatively straightforward—a defender is someone who actively defends. But understanding who actually is "actively engaged in attempting to mitigate risks to targets" in a practical context is much more difficult. For example, consider the hospital which implements a set of technical and administrative practices such that medical device systems are "locked" after the treating medical personnel complete their activity and leave the room. A key part of this process is the affirmative step of the personnel to "lock" the device when finished, so it does not remain "unlocked" during the timeout period. This is a classic security measure found in many hospitals to prevent patients or other unauthorized personnel, who frequently must be left unattended in the presence of medical information systems or other computationally controlled medical devices, from accessing or operating those devices. This is important not only to patient privacy, but also to patient safety.

Medical personnel generally are not cybersecurity personnel—indeed, many medical professionals possess very little, if any, training in computing and information systems.[4] And yet they are following a protocol which makes them take an "active" step in defending such systems. The same analysis would be true of non-technological personnel implementing a "clean desk" policy in the workplace, or using a VPN when connecting remotely to their organizations' systems. Are these examples of defenders, or just users? *Why might this distinction matter?*

The terms adversary, attacker, and hacker are used indiscriminately in contemporary cybersecurity discourse, often with little attention to the important nuance distinguishing them. The misappropriation of the term

[4] This is a contemporary statement as of 2020. Depending on which experts' opinions one trusts, this may or may not substantially change over the next 5–10 years.

hacker is instructive here. Modern attackers are often viewed by defenders as including anyone who played any (witting) role in the compromise of a system.[5] This would, for example, include the computer programmer who discovered a flaw in an information system and distributed knowledge of that flaw. And, indeed, that person is arguably a "hacker" in the classic definition of the word.[6]

But what if that person was a security researcher who reported the vulnerability to the National Vulnerability Database, whose work was assigned a Common Vulnerabilities and Exposures (CVE) number, and who actively advocated for organizations to "patch" (install code which mitigates) that vulnerability? It would certainly seem odd to call this person an "adversary"—one might argue they are better described as a defender! But what if that person found the vulnerability by reverse engineering code without permission? What if they only disclosed it to facilitate patching in exchange for compensation? As you can see, this question is far from simple. As we will discuss later, this distinction can matter a great deal in the context of examining how to mitigate risks through incentives management—in this particular context, for example, through the use of the criminal law as a general deterrent.

Drawing clear distinctions in the cybersecurity ecosystem is quite hard. Yet, as you will come to see while working through this text), those distinctions matter! As you read further about the potential motivations of attackers, consider the extent to which motivations—potential *mens rea,* as we say in criminal law—provide critical context to shaping rules governing conduct in the cybersecurity ecosystem.

QUESTIONS

1. How might you describe the difference between "hackers" and "attackers?" Can you think of situations where an attacker may not be a hacker?

2. What are the potential attackers of a database containing financial information? What are their respective motives for attacking this database?

B. ATTACKER MOTIVATIONS

It is important to distinguish "attacker motivations" from "thinking like an attacker." The former refers to the incentives that drive individuals or organizations to engage in adversarial actions. The latter, as discussed in later in Section 4.D.2: Thinking like an attacker, is the method or means

---

[5] For more information on perceptions of adversaries, see Joseph Kennedy and David Thaw, *Monstrous Hackers* (forthcoming 2020).

[6] An alternative term from that time period might be "cracker", however, this was debate as to whether status as a "cracker" required someone affirmative to attempt to compromise systems, or just to discover methods of doing so.

by which adversaries think about *executing* their attacks. This section focuses on the former.

Entire books cover the concept of attacker motivations, and those books focus only on one or a few subsets of attackers. It is quite impossible to discuss all potential motivations, philosophy, and psychology of those parties who engage in cyberattacks. A modest classification, however, is useful to help new students of cybersecurity understand the spectrum of attacker sophistication and the most common motivations.

Consider the following excepts. The first excerpt is commonly referred to as the "Hacker's Manifesto," published in the hacker-focused magazine Phrack, in 1986. The second excerpt is by David Thaw, in which he offers a classification of hackers based upon their incentives and sophistication. In the third excerpt, Gus Hurwitz discussed a similar classification offered by Steve Bellovin.

"THE HACKER MANIFESTO"

Or The Conscience of a Hacker
Phrack Magazine (January 1986)[7]

=-=

The following was written shortly after my arrest. . .
\/\The Conscience of a Hacker/\/

by

+++The Mentor+++

Written on January 8, 1986

=-=

Another one got caught today, it's all over the papers. "Teenager Arrested in Computer Crime Scandal", "Hacker Arrested after Bank Tampering". . .

Damn kids. They're all alike. [. . .]

I'm in junior high or high school. I've listened to teachers explain for the fifteenth time how to reduce a fraction. I understand it. "No, Ms. Smith, I didn't show my work. I did it in my head. . ."

Damn kid. Probably copied it. They're all alike.

I made a discovery today. I found a computer. Wait a second, this is cool. It does what I want it to. If it makes a mistake, it's because I screwed it up. Not because it doesn't like me. . .

Or feels threatened by me. . .

Or thinks I'm a smart ass. . .

---

[7] A full copy of The Hackers Manifesto, is available at http://phrack.org/issues/7/3.html. It was written in 1986 by Loyd Blankenship, who has since had a long and successful career.

Or doesn't like teaching and shouldn't be here. . .

Damn kid. All he does is play games. They're all alike.

And then it happened. . . a door opened to a world. . . rushing through the phone line like heroin through an addict's veins, an electronic pulse is sent out, a refuge from the day-to-day incompetencies is sought. . . a board is found.

"This is it. . . this is where I belong. . ." [. . .]

This is our world now. . . the world of the electron and the switch, the beauty of the baud. We make use of a service already existing without paying for what could be dirt-cheap if it wasn't run by profiteering gluttons, and you call us criminals. We explore. . . and you call us criminals. We seek after knowledge. . . and you call us criminals. We exist without skin color, without nationality, without religious bias. . . and you call us criminals. You build atomic bombs, you wage wars, you murder, cheat, and lie to us and try to make us believe it's for our own good, yet we're the criminals.

Yes, I am a criminal. My crime is that of curiosity. My crime is that of judging people by what they say and think, not what they look like. My crime is that of outsmarting you, something that you will never forgive me for.

I am a hacker, and this is my manifesto. You may stop this individual, but you can't stop us all. . . after all, we're all alike.

+++The Mentor+++

The Hacker's Manifesto was published in 1986 and has since been regarded as a defining text of the Hacker Ethic, both in popular and hacker culture. It featured prominently, for instance, in the 1995 film Hackers, and was also visible in Mark Zuckerberg's fictional dorm room in the movie The Social Network. In "hacker culture," one would be hard pressed to find a hacker (or even a computer enthusiast who came of age in the 1990s) who is not at least passingly familiar with it.

Over 30 years later, a hacker known as TheHackerGiraffe reportedly hacked over 50,000 printers around the world, using them to print messages encouraging their owners to subscribe to YouTube user PewDiePie's YouTube channel.[8] Shortly after this incident, TheHackerGiraffe, realizing his conduct potentially exposed him to serious criminal liability and expecting the hammer of consequences to come down upon him, apparently posted the following public message:

[8] *See, e.g.*, A.J. Dellinger, *Hacker hijacks 50,000 printers to tell people to subscribe to PewDiePie*, ENGADGET (Nov. 30, 2018), https://www.engadget.com/2018-11-30-pewdiepie-printer-hack-thehackergiraffe.html.

PUBLIC MESSAGE FROM THEHACKERGIRAFFE

https://pastebin.com/raw/pfX5p4ze (Nov. 2018)

So, here we are. At the endgame. I'm sorry for leaving so suddenly, and I'm sorry for all of you who expected more tutorials, guides, or anything. I can't do this. It may not look like it, but the constant pressure of being afraid of being caught and prosecuted has been keeping me up and giving me all kinds of fears and panic attacks.

I just wanted to inform people of their vulnerable devices while supporting a YouTuber I liked. I never meant any hard, nor did I ever have any ill intentions. I'm sorry if anything I've done has made you feel under attack or threatened.

Most of all, I'm sorry to the people who supported me on Patreon. I didn't want to leave like this, you deserve more for your money, and I'm truly sorry that I've failed to meet your demands and my promises when it comes to the guides.

@pewdiepie, I love your content man, keep on going.

I guess there is a lesson to be learned here, don't fly too close to the sun and then act like you don't know you'll get burned. Well, here I am, burned and roasted, awaiting my maybe-coming end. I thank you all, thank you all so much for the past month. It's been amazing to see all of you who wanted to learn hacking/cybersecurity. Please do push on, don't give up! Stay safe, stay legal, and most of all, be civil.

What will I do now? Probably suffer from this horrible panic for the next few days before I completely lose my mind until either my end comes or this all flies over and I'll probably never touch a computer again.

I hope I'm overreacting and this is all in my head, I really do hope so.

Peace out guys,

TheHackerGiraffe

Contrast the accounts of the Hacker's Manifesto and TheHackerGiraffe with that presented by Professors Thaw and Hurwitz below.

DAVID THAW, *CRIMINALIZING HACKING, NOT DATING*

103 J. CRIM. L. & CRIMINOLOGY 101 (2013)[9]

[This Section describes a crime "ecosystem" that has emerged comprising modern variations on [the 1980s hacker and crackers] and some views on the motivations of various elements of that ecosystem.]

---

[9] First published by the *Journal of Criminal Law and Criminology*, Volume 103, Issue 03.

[. . .]

In the early 2000s, Finnish scholar Pekka Himanen authored a qualitative work describing three motivations for so-called "hackers." In this work, Professor Himanen describes three motivations for hackers: a "work ethic," a "money ethic," and a "nethic." The first motivation contrasts what Himanen calls the traditional Protestant work ethic of work as a means of sustenance with the "hacker work ethic" in which technologically inclined individuals are motivated by the "intrinsic interest" and "playful explorations" in which the accomplishment of the work is itself the reward sought. The second motivation attempts to build on the first, casting hackers' view toward financial gain as disjunctive from traditional capitalism, focusing on a desire to achieve only that level of financial gain necessary to achieve individual independence after which one derives fulfillment from accomplishment, rather than a strictly increasing measure of fulfillment as a function of wealth accrual. Finally, the third motivation asserts that hackers adopt certain social norms in their online interactions, norms that may override other motivations or serve as primary motivations. Himanen gives freedom of expression and personal privacy as two leading examples of such norms.

Himanen's work may be (perhaps rightly) criticized as relying too heavily on philosophical and political economic analysis and too weakly on empirical evidence, particularly in addressing a question ripe for qualitative analysis. Nonetheless, its analysis provides a useful link in drawing the connection between [1980s hackers] . . . and the modern cybercrime ecosystem proposed in this section. [These] technologically sophisticated youth[,] driven primarily by Himanen's first motivation[,] . . . might later develop into financially motivated criminals [seeking] . . . the financial independence depicted by Himanen's second motivation. [T]he hacker's desire for financial independence . . . suggests individuals who highly value that independence. While resorting to computer-based fraud, theft, and other crimes might seem less likely in the Internet boom days during which Himanen's work was written . . . such activities follow quite logically as the demand for [computer] skills . . . diminished following [the economic downturns of the early 2000s]. And indeed, what limited data is available on the subject reveals that many with such skills have resorted to participation in computer-based criminal activity over the past several years. Nor have the capacities of these would-be criminals and the potential market for such activities gone unnoticed by organized crime.

The modern result is what I describe as a "cybercrime ecosystem," in which participants are stratified along levels of technical sophistication, access to the most recent data on and methods for compromising computer systems, and degree of sensitivity of target computer systems. The teenage youths hacking the Pentagon of Rep. Hughes's day are not so much gone as supplanted or captured by organized activity in an interconnected world where computer exploits are commoditized and access to large-scale attack networks (Botnets) are controlled by a smaller set of more sophisticated gatekeepers.

Security Vulnerabilities and the "Cybercrime Ecosystem"

The activities of financially motivated hackers or organizations, and to some extent politically motivated hackers or organizations, rely heavily on the availability of cybersecurity vulnerabilities. Colloquially known within the industry as "exploits," these vulnerabilities are aspects of computer systems that provide a potential attacker the ability to engage the target computer system in activities for which it was not intended or which the administrators of that system have attempted to prohibit by technical means.

[. . .]

Cybersecurity vulnerabilities can be modeled in a lifecycle from initial discovery to final commoditization. The emergence of vulnerabilities can best be described primarily as a process of discovery by scientists rather than one of creation by hackers. Technologists study information systems to determine unanticipated ways in which those systems can be manipulated to deviate from their normal operation. The methods for causing such deviations are vulnerabilities that can be activated or "exploited" to exercise (unauthorized) control over the system. This process of discovery, which often focuses on technical vulnerabilities but may also include administrative or physical vulnerabilities, is the first stage in the vulnerability lifecycle.

While some vulnerabilities may be widely distributed soon after discovery, most follow a lifecycle of distribution commensurate with their ability to be exploited for strategic, financial, or social gain. Potential for strategic gain focuses on incentives for organizations or state actors to target specific assets. Generally these assets are targeted to enable political, military, or economic goals, and the targets are not fungible. Potential for financial gain creates incentives for individuals and organizations to exploit vulnerabilities that may allow them to engage in fraud, identity theft, and other financial crimes that can be executed through or substantially facilitated by unauthorized access to information systems. Unlike with strategic incentives, financially motivated attackers generally view targets as commodities—any target capable of resulting in a "fraud conversion" is as valuable as any other such target. Social gain follows a separate pattern, under which actors—primarily individuals—seek to elevate their standing within social groups by gaining unauthorized access to information systems.

These three categories collectively suggest the incentive structures that result in the vulnerability lifecycle. The lifecycle models the emergence of cybersecurity threats from advanced, recently discovered attacks to highly commoditized, well-known vulnerabilities for which readily accessible solutions exist. Strategic incentives drive the first stage in the vulnerability lifecycle. This "innovation" occurs when strategically oriented entities identify or fund the identification of "new" vulnerabilities. Such entities consistently need to identify new vulnerabilities because their incentives are based around the idea of finding the crack in the wall of a specific target, rather than any wall with a known (but unrepaired) breach. Consider, for example, the case of the car thief. Most car thieves are unconcerned with getting any one person's specific car, but rather focus on ensuring they get any (acceptable) car. Hence the advice about easily circumventable security devices—if you can slow down the thief enough to make it not worth their while compared to the next car, the thief will move on to that next car. In contrast, the high-end or specialty-order car thief—the one from the movie *Gone in 60 Seconds* who takes orders for specific cars—will need to be able to circumvent all the security devices for that one, specially modified, 1966 Ford Mustang. And so it goes with information-security incentives: if the attacker is strategically motivated, he will need to identify every possible vulnerability to ensure he can deface the Arizona State Police website, not just the website of any random police department. Thus these goals drive the identification of new vulnerabilities, whether by members of the organizations or governments engaged in strategic actions themselves or by those entities contracting the services of skilled technologists.

Once developed, these vulnerabilities create a "secondary market" through which strategically oriented entities can "fund" their future operations (or, perhaps, derive secondary "social" benefits in the case of politically-motivated organizations like LulzSec). This "commercialization" of threats forms the second stage in the vulnerability lifecycle, when financially motivated organizations "purchase" newly developed vulnerabilities after initial use but before those vulnerabilities become widely known. The key difference for financially motivated entities lies in the lifecycle stage at which they operate. While most financial fraud efforts do not require targeting a specific entity, such as a given bank, they do require overcoming leading-edge security—financial institutions, historically aware of their attractiveness as targets, are likely to repair vulnerabilities before those compromises become well-known. For organized criminal enterprises to profit from attacks on more fortified financial institutions, therefore, those enterprises must be able to exploit vulnerabilities sufficiently early in the lifecycle that enough targets have not yet patched the vulnerability.

The final stage in the vulnerability lifecycle (historically at least) is driven by the desire for social gain. Colloquially termed "script-kiddies," attackers in this category are concerned with elevating their social standing by compromising any information system. This elevation of social standing can take many forms, ranging from simple praise and admiration of peers to literal gain from identity theft and (disorganized) fraud. Unlike in the case of commercialized vulnerabilities, socially motivated attackers generally are completely nonspecific as to what class of system they attack, and are unconcerned with compromising only systems that are likely to employ more current and/or advanced defensive procedures. Thus, compromising these systems becomes a matter of identifying any system that does not maintain up-to-date security, an easy task in the contemporary security environment. The transfer mechanism from commercialized vulnerabilities to fully commoditized vulnerabilities is not specifically clear, but the transfer incentives can partially be defined by the limited term of usefulness for commercialized vulnerabilities discussed above. Once a commercialized vulnerability becomes sufficiently well-known that it no longer is likely to yield a financial return, maintaining the relative "secrecy" of that vulnerability no longer confers an advantage on financially motivated attackers and their incentives to keep it secret—and force their constituent members to do the same—drop accordingly.

Finally, it is worth noting that certain activities, variously titled "hacktivism," may be somewhat orthogonal to the ecosystem described in this Section. . . . hacktivists have many incentives for their activities, some of which may be fully independent of (and perhaps opposite to) financial gain. . . .

Professor Thaw's article suggests two potential criteria for generally classifying attackers. First, a spectrum of sophistication ranging from the most sophisticated (usually state-sponsored) development of new methods to the most commoditized techniques commonly available to anyone with an Internet connection and for which adequate defenses generally are publicly available. The motivations within this spectrum can vary, but generally range from macroeconomic financial or political motivations for more sophisticated attackers to petty crime (economically motivated or otherwise), thrill, and individual self-validation for less sophisticated attackers.

Second, attackers at any point on this spectrum may have other—often orthogonal—motivations which drive their actions. A sophisticated attacker who developers original "zero-day" attacks, for example, may do so not for macroeconomic impact nor major political gain, but rather for personal pecuniary goals. Conversely, a less sophisticated attacker (e.g., U.S. Army Private Chelsea Manning) using commodity methods may have goals with global political implications. Professor Thaw's analysis of the literature describing and evolution of attacker motivations suggestions that this is a rapidly changing sociological phenomenon and formal categorical classification may be premature. A simple descriptive classification may be useful, however, for understanding some of the more common sets of attacker motivations. These include direct financial gain, macroeconomic financial impact, personal political motivation, global or national political action, and personal self-edification.

This framework suggests a two-dimensional matrix which may be helpful to understanding the range of attacker motivations. It is critically important that, while a useful tool, matrices like this run the risk of being overly reductive and fooling us into thinking that people's emotions and motivations can be grouped into nice boxes. But, as the old economics saying goes, "all models are wrong, some are useful."

	Commodity Actor	**Individual Technical Expertise**	**Organized Crime**	**State Actors**
Financial	*Running Metasploit to gather financial account info*	*Using a combination of multiple tools, including some self-developed tools and pretexting, to gain access to target(s) financial accounts*	*Deploying large-scale, coordinated attacks both against individuals and institutions, designed to leverage vulnerabilities at scale to extract money from accounts or transactions*	*Covert attempts to introduce instability into the financial system(s) of target nations*
Political	*Running commoditized social media bots*	*Running a "troll farm"*	*Attempting to influence the outcome of elections*	*Covert attempts to interfere with the elections of target nation(s)*[10]

[10] This is further discussed under the Special Case of Election Hacking later in this chapter.

Individual Emotional Fulfillment	*Running Metasploit to gain access to local law enforcement websites*	*Using a combination of multiples tools, including some self-developed tools and pretexting, to gain access to high-security government systems or files*	*A multi-pronged attack aimed at taking down a particular law enforcement agency*	*(generally N/A)*
Individual Emotional Angst	*Installing spyware to track the activities of or learn about a romantic interest*	*Advanced cyberstalking, revenge porn campaigns, and other coordinated efforts to undermine or destroy an individual's or entity's reputation*	*A sophisticated attack designed to result in the escape from custody of a high-value member of the organization*	*(generally N/A)*

Table 1: Adversarial Motivation

The top axis indicates the level of technological and strategic sophistication of the actor, from least sophisticated at the left to most sophisticated on the right. Often, more sophisticated actors will enlist the aid of (wittingly or otherwise) less sophisticated actors.

Perhaps most importantly, consider how these different motivations may affect risk management. Putting aside the technological distinctions among the categories—of which there are many!—the ways in which a defender would approach risk mitigation strategies will vary widely depending on whether the primary threats they face are financially-motivated or politically motivated. All defenders face serious scarcity problems in resource allocation,[11] and efficiently allocating resources to best manage risk requires understanding these motivations.

Another classification of hackers and their motivations is discussed in the following excerpt:

---

[11] This is functionally true for all potential defenders, with the possible (and somewhat uninteresting) example of strategic weapons control systems. This example is often described as largely uninteresting because the level of resources deployed by declared nuclear powers to ensure no unlawful deployment of strategic arms occurs often is more than sufficient to eliminate scarcity issues, leaving only design challenges and level of scientific and technological sophistication.

JUSTIN (GUS) HURWITZ, *RESPONSE TO MCGEVERAN'S THE DUTY OF DATA SECURITY: NOT THE OBJECTIVE DUTY HE WANTS, MAYBE THE SUBJECTIVE DUTY WE NEED*

103 MN. L. REV. HEADNOTES 139 (2019)

The question not asked: Why does the Duty of Data Security Matter?

The greatest failing of the academic and regulatory discussion about data security is its failure to consider why liability for data security failings matters. This question is predicate to questions about what the duty to secure data should be. Rather, the trajectory of discussion about the duty to secure data has progressed in a less thoughtful, more legalistic manner: Data breaches occur resulting in harm to the owners of whatever data was compromised; liability is the legal remedy to that harm. Under our standard theories of remedies, imposing liability both makes the harmed parties whole *ex post* and creates incentives *ex ante* for data custodians to invest in precautions to protect data from future compromise.

But this is not how things play out in the data security context. What constitutes "reasonable" data security is so indeterminate that the vast majority of firms have little ability to invest in precautions prudently. To be sure, there are "worst practices" that may reasonably be the basis for liability; and large firms may be sufficiently sophisticated and well-resourced to be considered sophisticated security actors. But for the majority of firms, liability for a data security incident is purely random. And, it turns out, that in terms of incentives this is the worst of all possible worlds: for these firms either a strict liability or a no liability rule would be far superior to a "reasonableness" standard—for both the firms and general data security practices.

A. Hackers Gonna Hack. But Why?

The starting point for understanding what a duty for data security should be is understanding what that duty is responding to. Security compromises occur in an adversarial setting; a compromise means that a third party has been able to access information stored on a data custodian's systems without authorization. The duty of data security, therefore, is not about ensuring that that custodian keeps data in a locked box. Every locked box has vulnerabilities and in the adversarial cybersecurity setting threat actors and others are constantly searching for new vulnerabilities and new ways to exploit known vulnerabilities. The duty of data security, therefore, is more akin to keeping apace of advancements in the field of cybersecurity, of constantly monitoring, updating, testing, and replacing the locked box that data is secured into.

We can better understand what this duty should entail by looking at who these threat actors are—including what their motivations are. Steven Bellovin categorizes threat actors along two dimensions, as seen in Figure

1. One dimension measures the skill of the attacker; the other measures the extent to which the attacker focuses on a specific target. From this, he identifies four categories of attackers.

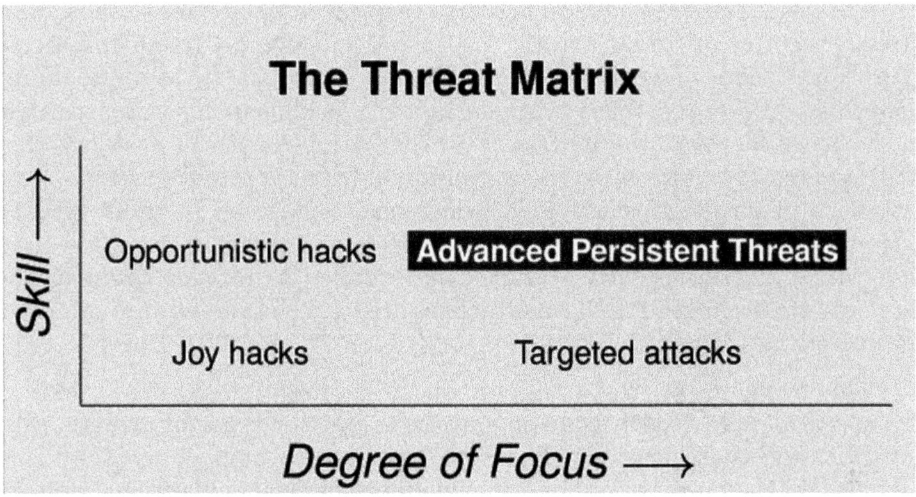

Figure 1: Steven Bellovin's Threat Matrix

First are "Joy Hackers," who are neither sophisticated nor focused, but rather attack firms on an ad hoc basis where they opportunity arises, using the tools in their existing skill set. Their motivation is, as the name suggests, the sheer joy of hacking. These individuals generally represent the threat model of the 1990s, when there were far fewer systems connected to the Internet and less thought was given to securing them at all. They do not need to seek out targets or develop innovative ways into the systems of whatever targets they find. Rather, they have enough sophistication to recognize obvious vulnerabilities as they happen upon them and exploit them on an ad hoc basis for little reason other than "because they can."

Moving to the right on Figure 1, "Targeted attacks" are low-skill attacks that target a specific firm or individual. These attacks are the realm of the CFAA, Wiretap Act, and Stored Communications Act and generally involve acquaintances, employees, or romantic partners—they also generally involve scenarios where attackers have some level of access to their target's facilities and devices. Importantly, these threat actors are generally not motivated simply by a desire to access their targets' data or systems, but rather view that access as instrumental to some other purpose. Moving up from there, "Advanced Persistent Threats" ("APTs") are skilled, well-resourced, focused actors. This is the realm of state-actors. APTs generally are focused on valuable targets—sometimes they target a specific firm, other times they spread exploits widely to see what valuable targets they can identify. Once they identify a target, they employ a sophisticated range of tools to get a foothold into the target's systems—they then slowly move laterally through the target's networks and deliberatively and carefully engage in whatever malfeasance they intend. These attacks typically go undetected for months.

The reasonableness of a firm's data security is irrelevant to these first three categories of threat actors. A firm whose systems are compromised by a "Joy Hacker" has per se unreasonable security. Or, to state things somewhat differently, these systems' security is objectively unreasonable. In the other corner of the matrix, if an APT targets a firm's systems, that APT is going to compromise them. Similarly with targeted attacks—these attackers generally already have some level of access to their target's systems and the damage caused by their efforts is different in nature than that which a data security standard is intended to protect against. The legal system's response to these attackers is better channeled through more specific statutes like the CFAA.

This brings us to "Opportunistic hacks"—those undertaken by skilled threat actors who do not focus on specific targets or types of targets. Like Joy Hackers, these actors will compromise whatever systems they can. Like APTs they are constantly developing new tools, both to identify potential targets and to create new ways in to those targets' systems.

Opportunistic attackers are the broadest category of threats actors. They likely are the most dangerous and the most difficult category of attackers for most firms to deal with. This category includes everything from ransomware to cryptojacking, from attacks designed to do nothing more than passively measure the "size" of the Internet to cripple it. This category includes everything from phishing attacks spread randomly by e-mail, to ad-injection attacks delivered when victims go to compromised websites, and brute force scanning attacks that actively probe every IP address on the Internet looking for vulnerable targets. Other categories of attackers (especially APTs) may use some of these same techniques—but opportunistic attackers deploy them indiscriminately and at scale

These attacks are also the most likely to harm consumers. Unlike APTs (generally motivated by geopolitical interests), targeted attacks (generally motivated by individualized interests), and joy hacks (generally motivated by the sheer joy of the hack), opportunistic hackers are generally interested in exploiting large numbers of systems for personal gain. This may mean stealing CPU time to mine cryptocurrency, it may mean assembling massive botnets that can be sold for DDoS attacks, or it may mean stealing consumer data to sell on the dark web. These motivations mean both that Opportunistic Hackers are more likely to cause consumer harm than other types of attackers and that they have resources to invest in developing and implementing new attacks.

If there is to be a meaningful duty of data security, it should be tailored to protecting systems against Opportunistic Hackers. Unlike Bellovin's other categories of threats, the duty of data security is a lever that may meaningfully calibrate the precautions that firms take against these attackers.

QUESTIONS

1. Who are hackers? Does reading the Hacker's Manifesto and TheHackerGiraffe's apology affect your perception of these individuals?

2. Why do hackers hack? What are their motivations? Do The Mentor and TheHackerGiraffe have the same motivations? Are their motivations intrinsically good or bad?

3. How different are hackers from "ordinary" people?

1. THE SPECIAL CASE OF ELECTION HACKING

Election hacking is an incredibly complex subject, a full treatment of which is outside the scope of this text. There are a few aspects of this example, however, which are distinctive from traditional cybersecurity threats, attacker motivations, and the nature of the democratic election process. In short, the intersection of free elections, protections against government regulation of political speech, and the non-deterministic nature of influence operations designed to affect voter choice presents a fundamentally different challenge in cybersecurity—one not seen, possibly ever, before.

The following excerpts from Professor David Thaw's article *From Russia With Love* describe the nature of those challenges and offer thoughts on why they may need to be considered separately. Or, at least, why they represent an intersection of many of the aspects above in a way that discussion suggests otherwise might not occur. As you read through the excerpt, consider what are the core issues which make this problem different from other cybersecurity problems.

DAVID THAW, *FROM RUSSIA WITH LOVE*

Working Paper (2021)

I. Influencing Elections

The 2016 U.S. federal election drew substantial attention to the question of foreign interference in national elections. While hardly the first such instance of foreign interference in a national election, several factors distinguished the 2016 case as a "first of its kind". The political polarization of the parties and the candidates in the Presidential election, the vastly different policy directions the U.S. was likely to follow under each electoral outcome, the scope and scale of the U.S. domestic and foreign policy influence distinguishes this result from any other contemporary example. When combined with the narrow effective margin of victory, the net result elevates the question of foreign influence to a level not previously experienced in contemporary history.

A substantial portion of this attention focuses on the related concepts variously described as election "hacking," "meddling," "interference," or other similar terms. This Article will refer to the problems posed by these related terms simply as "election interference". This term does not yet have a widely-accepted formal definition, but has been used extensively by government officials, public figures, and the media of record to describe variations on electronic or "cyber" activities designed to alter the outcome of an election. While an energizing term, whose imagery aligns well to a "cyber" oriented view of contemporary society, this term is both technologically misleading and frames a distorted view of the fundamental legal questions confronting foreign influence on elections.

Unlawful efforts to alter the results of elections generally come in two forms: (1) efforts to "alter" official voting records ("Election Hacking"); and (2) efforts to "persuade" individuals how to vote ("Influence Operations). Within each group, under current U.S. law, there generally are two primary "attack surfaces"—vote choices and voting ability (registration/ turnout). Efforts to alter voter records are best understood as Election Hacking because they are targeted at the election infrastructure itself, in an attempt to compromise or otherwise interfere with the normal operation of those systems. Efforts to persuade individuals how or whether to vote are best understood as Influence Operations because they are independent of election infrastructure, and focus on influencing voter behavior.

This Article focuses primarily on Influence Operations. It argues that extant legal systems and technological solutions are capable of producing a combination of deterrent, mitigation, and redress mechanisms which are sufficient (if technologically challenging) to manage the risks of Election Hacking. Influence Operations, by contrast, are technologically difficult to mitigate (and impossible to prevent). Furthermore, legal mechanisms for mitigation and deterrence of Influence Operations are constitutionally problematic, and ex-post legal redress is effectively impossible.

This Part begins with a brief discussion of what should be called "Election Hacking"—those activities involving Changing Information—and a discussion of why that category of problems, while vitally important, presents a different set of questions than those posed by the types of Influence Operations which are the focus of this Article. This typology distinguishes the types of activities involved in election interference and frames the discussion of deterrence, mitigation, redressability problems for Influence Operations in Part III and IV.

I.A. Election Hacking

Election Hacking can be a misleading term. It evokes imagery of using technological means to compromise or otherwise alter information or systems. This Article argues therefore that Election Hacking is better understood as a specific subset of unlawful election interference dealing with threats to election infrastructure and records, and distinguishes these activities from attempts to influence voter behavior. Section I.B., "Influence Operations", deals with those methods designed to alter how or whether an individual exercises their lawful voting choice. Election Hacking, by contrast, is not concerned with voter persuasion. Put simply—Influence Operations are not "Election Hacking."

I.A.1 Altering Recorded Votes

Perhaps the most easily-recognized form of electoral interference is the concept of altering recorded votes. This category encompasses a wide variety of actions, all of which result in some alteration of ballots or counts of votes resulting, or otherwise cause a vote count result which does not match voters' actual choices. The most common colloquial example of this is the vision of foreign adversaries remotely connecting to and altering the results tally in electronic voting systems. However, it is important to note both that: (1) "remote" connections are not the only attack vector; and (2) the voting machines on which individuals cast their ballots are not the only attack surface. The collective system responsible for recording, transmitting, aggregating, and storing election results comprises the attack surface, and provides many opportunities for administrative, technical, and physical attacks.

The concept of altering recorded votes is not new in principle and the example of "ballot box stuffing" dates back decades, if not centuries. Physical methods like this, some of which have were employed in the 2018 federal midterm elections, essentially seek to achieve the same goals as do "cyber election hacking" methods. Cyber methods, however, introduce a new dimension to the process of changing vote records—the ability to execute large-scale attacks, with low marginal cost to scale, and the ability to force defenders to engage in substantially higher expenditures to mitigate risk than otherwise would be the case with physical balloting systems.

The result is something akin to a "Cyber Space Race," not dissimilar from that found in traditional attacker-defender cybersecurity adversarial models, in which unlawful actors compete against State and Federal "defenders" to achieve the ability to modify election data. Much scholarship and scientific research has examined these problems, and the results are promising, if daunting.

. . . . First, this work suggests that most of the present vulnerabilities in election systems can be addressed, and that ongoing mitigation strategies can substantially reduce the risk of future compromise. Second, to the extent that some attacks are successful, notwithstanding mitigation efforts, the impact of the external operations to alter votes ("hacking") is redressable . . . . In this key respect of redressability, "Election Hacking" threats related to vote alteration are substantially different from Influence Operations in that they are manageable through legal and technological solutions which do not necessarily conflict with other constitutional and fundamental principles of representative government. In addition to the plausibility of significant mitigation through technological measures, post-election redress measures not only are available, but are not a new challenge and indeed have been invoked and utilized before.

I.A.2. Altering Voter Registration

This category encompasses the breadth of actions designed to alter the ability or "authorization" of an individual to vote, such that they either are unable to vote or such that the process of casting their vote is more difficult. . . [the challenges relevant to this section, and accompanying analysis, are similar as those in Altering Recorded Votes.]

I.B. Influence Operations

Influence Operations also are a subset of unlawful election interference. Unlike Election Hacking, however, Influence Operations focus on persuading individuals either *how* to vote or *whether* to vote. Influence Operations present a problematic scenario for deterrence and mitigation efforts because political speech is at the core of such activities.

Perhaps even more troubling, they present a currently-unsolvable problem for redress. In the presence of Influence Operations—even ones which can be properly criminalized or otherwise declared unlawful—the *result* of those activities causes an individual to vote differently or change whether or not they vote at all. In either case, however, *the individual has lawfully made the choice how and whether to vote.* Under current law, therefore, no authority would have a proper legal basis for failing to certify an election result. Indeed, solutions declaring individual votes "invalid" because a lawfully-registered voter had been "influenced"—even if by a foreign adversary—may themselves commit the very acts those solutions seek to prevent. If the polity is the ultimate source of political authority and legitimacy, then what other authority than "the people" could be empowered to determine an individual's vote not to have been of their own free will? And what mechanism other than voting could the polity have for expressing such a preference regarding the validity of an election?

Political solutions *may* remain—in a Presidential election, for example, via the Electoral College in jurisdictions without "faithless elector" prohibitions. Legal redress would be precluded, however, because voters' choices were not frustrated—they just were *persuaded* to do something differently. Part II discusses this problem in more detail, and Parts III and IV explore the solution space to mitigate the risks of Influence Operations.

Understanding the threat to democratic elections through unlawful Influence Operations is critical. It not only was a subject of substantial activity in the U.S. Intelligence Community during the years 2016 – 2020, but it also creates a deeply problematic situation where two different core principles of representative democracy are placed at odds with one another. One the one hand, free political speech is a core tenet of democracy. Political campaigning—*persuasive* messaging—is the quintessential example of protected political speech. On the other hand, the right of each individual to participate equally and free of coercion in democracy also is a core value, and this arguably includes freedom from influence the government has prohibited (e.g., physical coercion, foreign influence, etc.) This Section explores the nature and character of Influence Operations and lays groundwork for understanding the challenges of balancing the competing values inherent in representative democracies.

I.B.1. Influencing Voter Ballot Choices

The concept of influencing voter ballot choices is, perhaps, the most problematic category of electoral interference. It does not involve modifying election data or compromising election infrastructure. Rather, it seeks to influence a voters' decision-making processes through persuasion, usually by promoting false, misleading, divisive, or emotionally-charged political messaging. The goal of this activity is to interfere with the outcome of an election by *persuading a voter to vote differently.*

This persuasion-based approach is precisely the problem—it is incredibly difficult to distinguish from a different category: core political speech. Consider, for example, a Presidential debate. The core function of such an event is, through the candidates' discussion and debate of policy matters and other political issues, to help voters make decisions regarding whom they wish to vote for. The challenging question inherent in this category, then, is how we can create an articulable delineation between lawful and unlawful activity.

Parts II and III of this Article discuss the problem in greater detail and explore the limits of technological and legal solutions. Part IV explores potential solutions possible notwithstanding the substantial challenges presented by the conflicting democratic values raised by Influence Operations.

I.B.2. Influencing Voter Turnout

The concept of influencing voter turnout bears many similarities to influencing voter ballot choices but has categorical distinctions which are important to understanding how legal frameworks can address the set of such activities generally considered to be inconsistent with democratic or republican governance. At its core, this category also is about influencing voter decision-making choices. Unlike influencing ballot choices, however, influencing voter *turnout* need not employ measures related to political or any other potentially-protected speech.

Voter turnout is affected by a wide variety of factors. These factors extend far beyond mere levels of satisfaction with the available candidates or interest in the listed ballot measures. Logistical factors including transportation, weather, family and professional obligations all have been shown substantially to impact voter turnout, particularly for the archetypical marginal or "undecided" voter. Less-motivated voters, for example, may be deterred from voting in the presence of inclement weather or transportation difficulties. There is also some evidence that such voters might also be deterred in national elections following early polling reports indicative that their candidate of choice may lose (or, for that matter win) the national election regardless of their vote. In a world increasingly relying upon modern information services for up-to-the-second information regarding weather, traffic, and electoral results, the ability to insert false information into common information services may be sufficient to alter the choices of voters to vote at all in key districts statistically-likely to vote in a certain direction such that the outcome of an election can be influenced by a foreign or other potentially-unlawful actor. Unlike the third category above, however, such "false" information likely would not fall under any form of protected speech and furthermore likely would be capable of being (if not already) criminalized under other existing laws such as fraud and computer crime statutes.

While this Article generally treats the persuasion-oriented aspects of these two categories as facing the same set of problems, the distinctions identified above are considered separately as "corner-cases" because the availability both of technological and of legal solutions are different for a variety of reasons . . . .

An entire book could be dedicated to answering the important questions posed by the recent election interference issues. For the purposes of this textbook, however, it is important that readers grasp the difficulties of the problem and the degree to which this special case in the cybersecurity ecosystem illustrates well a fundamental problem of cybersecurity. Complex threats may have few straightforward or simple solutions.

QUESTIONS

1. How might you identify potential motivations for a given adversary?

2. What does Professor Thaw's analysis suggest about the degree to which Influence Operations in the context of election interference are a unique problem in cybersecurity? What might make it not true? What solutions could exist? What tensions would those solutions create?

C. THE OVERALL SECURITY ECOSYSTEM

Most attention in cybersecurity is focused on attackers. But there are many other actors in the cybersecurity ecosystem, ranging from defenders and users at one end, to third-party users and other systems in the middle, to attackers at the other. Political entities, economic arrangements, businesses, societal organization, and other macro-level institutions make up important elements of the global infrastructure within which information systems—and therefore security—operate across the globe and across society.

The excerpt below describes the scope of this ecosystem and considers some of the competing and conflicting incentives facings its various constituencies.

JUSTIN (GUS) HURWITZ, *CYBERENSURING SECURITY*

49 U. CONN. L. REV. 1495 (2017)

I.C. The Multiplicity of Actors

The technical difficulties of designing secure computer systems are dramatically compounded by the sheer number of actors in the security ecosystem. It is useful to identify these actors here, before discussing how their (often conflicting) incentives further complicate computer security.

On one far side of the web, we have "users"—those who actually use a (possibly) secure system. Even this basic unit of the ecosystem is more complicated than one would expect. "Users" can refer to the consumer end-users of a piece of software, such as Microsoft Windows. In a firm, users may refer to the employees of the firm who use software purchased or designed by the firm. The firm itself may be said to be the user of software purchased by use by its employees, or even of software that it designed (or bespoke software designed by a contractor). And, of course, the firms' customers are "users" of services offered by the firm, which may or may not rely upon systems designed or implemented by third parties.

Those third parties may be firms such as Microsoft, Apple, or Google. They could also be vendors that sell turnkey solutions, designed by themselves or by others. They may be contractors, who design bespoke systems. Or they may be "integrators," who integrate various platforms designed by third parties with a firm's own systems. Connecting all of these systems are various Internet-based entities. This includes the ISPs that connect firms to the Internet, or a firm's customers to the firm's servers and services. It also includes cloud-based services, which often host information.

All of these relationships quickly explode into a complex network of relationships and dependencies—or, in more legalistic terms, reliance interests, duties, and potential liabilities. Consider a firm storing its customers' information on a cloud storage service that it integrated into its back-end systems (running Microsoft Windows) using proprietary software written by a contractor that relies on the API provided by both Microsoft and the cloud provider. If the proprietary software leaks the customers' confidential information due to a previously-unknown problem with how Microsoft's API interacts with the cloud provider's API, who is liable?

Now let's add in to this mix cyber-physical systems and Internet of Things devices: your modern, Internet-connected car, with literally hundreds of networked computers running a range of software—including location-aware software that automatically turns your HVAC system to energy-saving mode when you leave the house and unlock your front door when you get home. Some of the software running on your car's computers is commercial software, some of it was developed internally by the car manufacturer's own software development team (made up mostly of software engineers who couldn't get jobs in Silicon Valley . . .), and some of it is "open source software" that has been developed over the years by an army of hundreds or thousands of anonymous volunteers whose commitment to the quality of the software only runs as deep as their possibly transient interest in working on open source projects as a way to learn the basics of computer programming.

This multiplicity of actors makes establishing cybersecurity responsibility difficult. Each of the actors has some legitimate argument that at least some of the others bears responsibility almost any cyber-incident. Software was poorly designed or integrated; systems were improperly implemented or managed by firms or their contractors; ISPs should have detected harmful activity by malicious actors and informed their targets or cut off access; firms failed to train or monitor their employees, or employees failed to comply with established procedure; customers chose to work with unknown firms that had unknown or poor security practices, or firms failed to have satisfactory security practices. The response to any security incident will invariably be to assign blame to any number of other parties.

It is notable that responsibility for security breaches is rarely meaningfully attributed to the parties that are actually responsible: the attackers behind the cyber-incident. This is a nod to the practical reality that it is often impossible to identify the attackers, that it would typically be almost impossible to bring suit against the attackers if it were possible to identify them, and that even then one would be unlikely to recover meaningful damages from them. Amazingly enough . . . even if you could find the attacker. . . it would be very difficult to establish the legal elements required to be awarded damages against them. For instance, given the multiplicity of actors and difficulties of designing secure systems, it can be difficult, if not impossible, to establish causation and (especially) harm. As a result, it often makes more sense to seek legal recourse against one of the many intermediary actors, even when they were not in a meaningful position to prevent a given harm. This is the canonical case of the data breach, where damages (when they are sought) are almost always sought against the firm that experienced the data breach and are almost never sought against the actual parties that caused the breach (either as attackers or for having designed or implemented insecure systems).

[. . .]

I.D. The Multiplicity of (conflicting) Incentives

Each of the myriad actors in the cybersecurity ecosystem faces their own incentives in deciding how—or whether—to respond to security concerns. While each would likely benefit from an improved cybersecurity ecosystem, none has strong incentives to invest substantially in such benefits. And many, in fact, have incentives to adopt bad security practices.

Perhaps the most important set of incentives echoes the fundamental trade-offs between security and usability. . . Both users and those designing software and other computer systems are generally willing to forego security for greater usability and performance. This results in large part from the difficulty of holding designers liable for defective software—the threat of legal liability would of course be a powerful incentive for firms to improve their products' security. This is further exacerbated by firms' ability to attribute fault for security incidents to others in the security ecosystem—including attributing fault to users themselves. This reduces firms' ability (or need) to compete along a security dimension—especially when consumers are often more responsive to the usability and short-term cost dimensions. And there is reason to argue that users do, in fact, bear some responsibility for the poor state of the cybersecurity ecosystem: despite professed fears about the collection and use of sensitive data, and widespread concern about cybersecurity, consumers very readily engage in conduct online that exposes them to risks. This is surely, in some part, a reflection of putatively irrational decisionmaking by consumers. It is also, to some extent, a form of rational ignorance: consumers are not security experts, they do not have the time or knowledge necessary to evaluate most firms' security practices, and they reasonably believe that the law will protect them should they be harmed by malfeasing firms—so it is eminently reasonable for consumers to engage in what appears to be ordinary online activities.

Similarly, firms that make use of third party systems in their broader business—that is, the vast majority of firms—face poor security incentives. Most security incidents target firms' customers' information, such that the firms themselves are unlikely to experience any loss from an attack—unless, that is, the fact of the attack becomes public, in which case a firm may face substantial reputational harms and may also bear some direct costs from responding to the attack. In other words, the incentive for most firms is to invest in very basic security—only enough to secure their systems from casual attackers—and otherwise pay no attention to security. These incentives were arguably even worse before the recent, and relatively widespread, adoption of state data breach notification laws—laws that require firms to notify affected consumers of data breaches that may affect their (the consumers') data. Before the adoption of such laws, firms often faced no incentive to disclose, or even to respond to, a data breach, and faced incentives to keep the fact of the breach secret. But even following adoption of these laws, firms still do not face substantial incentives to adopt strong security practices. This is in part because there is still little likelihood that a firm will be held liable for damages resulting from a data breach. More tragically, this is also largely because consumers have become inured to data breaches, such that the reputational harm to a firm of a data breach is much less today than it was even two or three years ago.

Perhaps the worst incentives are faced by the cybersecurity industry itself. Estimates vary, but the size of the cybersecurity "market"—comprising firms that specialize in various aspects of cybersecurity, from systems design, to consulting, to incident response and litigation—is currently pegged at somewhere around $75–100 billion. This amount is expected to grow to $150–170 billion by 2020, a growth rate significantly exceeding that of other parts of the economy. In other words, the status quo is working well for this industry. Its participants have little reason to improve the state of the cybersecurity ecosystem. Indeed, they may have incentives to foment concern and fear, or even to facilitate attacks and other cyber-incidents.

What accounts for the scope of the cybersecurity ecosystem? At an abstract level, the answer that we have already given is "the cyber": as products and services turn from being built around physical, tangible items to being implemented on networked computers in human-defined code, the scale of participants in the ecosystem grows. Part of this is a reflection of an increased number of physical components: the computers on which these systems run and the networks connecting those computers. The network interconnection these networks afford promotes mutually desired interaction between parties while also providing an avenue for potential attackers and potential targets to gain access to these interactions.

The more important trend, however, may well be that of "software eating the world." What we think of as computers and networks are, in a very real way, all reducible to software. As we will discuss in Chapter 7, software presents a range of formal security problems. The most fundamental of these problems is that any software beyond a trivial level of complexity generally cannot be proven not to contain errors, and software errors can often be exploited by an attacker to compromise a system. Beyond this, software is almost never designed in a monolithic way. Rather, complex programs are broken down into many simpler subroutines called modules, each of which received information from and passes information to other modules via programming interfaces. Each of these interfaces is a potential vulnerability: any module that doesn't properly filter or process information being passed to it can potentially be corrupted and made to behave in an unanticipated manner.

These issues will be discussed in more detail in Chapter 7. As we consider the extent of the cybersecurity ecosystem, the key takeaway is that as systems are increasingly implemented in software, the extent of potential vulnerabilities multiples. And software is likely to continue to "eat the world" unabated:

MARC ANDREESEN, *WHY SOFTWARE IS EATING THE WORLD*

WALL STREET JOURNAL (Aug 20, 2011).[12]

More and more major businesses and industries are being run on software and delivered as online services—from movies to agriculture to national defense. Many of the winners are Silicon Valley-style entrepreneurial technology companies that are invading and overturning established industry structures. Over the next 10 years, I expect many more industries to be disrupted by software, with new world-beating Silicon Valley companies doing the disruption in more cases than not.

Why is this happening now?

Six decades into the computer revolution, four decades since the invention of the microprocessor, and two decades into the rise of the modern Internet, all of the technology required to transform industries through software finally works and can be widely delivered at global scale.

Over two billion people now use the broadband Internet, up from perhaps 50 million a decade ago, when I was at Netscape, the company I co-founded. In the next 10 years, I expect at least five billion people worldwide to own smartphones, giving every individual with such a phone instant access to the full power of the Internet, every moment of every day.

On the back end, software programming tools and Internet-based services make it easy to launch new global software-powered start-ups in many industries—without the need to invest in new infrastructure and train new employees. In 2000, when my partner Ben Horowitz was CEO of the first cloud computing company, Loudcloud, the cost of a customer running a basic Internet application was approximately $150,000 a month. Running that same application today in Amazon's cloud costs about $1,500 a month.

---

[12] Marc Andreesen was the founder of Netscape, the first vendor of a commercial web browser, and today is one of the most prominent and influential venture capitalists and thought leaders in Silicon Valley.

With lower start-up costs and a vastly expanded market for online services, the result is a global economy that for the first time will be fully digitally wired—the dream of every cyber-visionary of the early 1990s, finally delivered, a full generation later.

QUESTIONS

1. What changes have you seen in your life in terms of technical complexity? Is anything automated now that used to require more effort?

2. When you think about the technology changes you've identified, do you think those technologies have increased the likelihood of attackers targeting that system? What might their motivations be?

D. THE "SECURITY MINDSET"

Understanding how to think about the problem of security is, like with any academic or professional discipline, a core element of understanding and succeeding in that discipline. While security is hardly a new concept, the introduction of all things cyber-the Internet, mobile devices, sensors, and brain-computing interfaces, changes certain aspects of how we must *think* about security. This Chapter begins to introduce this mode of thinking, beginning with basic scientific principles and moving into discussions of "attackers" and "defenders" both in traditional and "cyber" spaces.

Law students spend their first year of law school learning to "think like a lawyer." Engineering students spend their first semesters of school learning to "think like an engineer." Our next few chapters are a brief introduction to, to borrow a term from Steve Bellovin, "thinking security"—understanding how someone deeply immersed in the practice of security sees the world.

The security mindset is both frighteningly simple and impossibly complex. The initial challenge of security is identifying risks—threats and vulnerabilities. When you are thinking security, you see threats and vulnerabilities everywhere. (Think back to our earlier discussion of how defenders perceive attackers!) You quickly realize that the greatest threat you face, and your greatest vulnerability, is people who are better at thinking security than you are—people who see vulnerabilities that you do not. This quickly gives way to a game of "cat and mouse." The goal of the attacker is to know something about the target's system that the target does not know—to identify one vulnerability that the target did not recognize.

This chapter introduces the security mindset: how do cybersecurity experts think about cybersecurity, how do attackers think about cybersecurity, how should potential targets think about security, and the futility of everyone not thinking about security enough. The next chapter provides a deeper dive into the psychology and motivations of attackers (and "hackers"), maps out the cybersecurity ecosystem in greater detail, and offers a simple menu of best practices that potential targets should bear in mind when securing their systems. This is followed by a deeper dive into these "best practices," considering, comparing, and contrasting, various sorts of approaches to security and security frameworks.

1. THE SCIENCE OF CYBERSECURITY

We begin our discussion of the "security mindset" with basic scientific principles. One of the most fundamental elements of any discipline is the method by which it establishes "truth" or, alternatively, what "proof" it requires to accept something as "true" or "false". In law, a body of doctrine has evolved around the law of evidence. In most engineering and science disciplines, we have a scientific method that achieves this.[13] All of these various approaches have at their core this fundamental concept: how do we collectively represent something as "correct" to society. *Cybersecurity today lacks such a science.*

To be clear, cybersecurity is distinct from the subfields of computer science such as computer security, network security, cryptology, and cryptanalysis. Each of these fields has formal methods of proof for theory and, to some extent, empirical approaches for evaluating observed evidence. There are many other subfields that have such approaches as well. However, the broader concept of cybersecurity—the integration of the "full" question of ensuring system operation—lacks such a unifying theme.

An initial response to this challenge might be to say that if each of the constituent disciplines has such methods of proof, then the aggregated problem of "cybersecurity" should require for each element within it the contextually-appropriate method of proof. Even assuming that each constituent discipline has such a method, this response still is deficient. It requires two conditions, both of which are false: 1) that the constituent disciplines' methods of proof are compatible; and 2) that the questions do not traverse sub-disciplines in a manner which requires a single "method of proof" be applied because a single question is being evaluated across sub-disciplines.

Both these conditions are false. The incompatibility of disciplinary methods is fairly straightforward: a normative position regarding what "should" be the case about the *degree* of mass surveillance is incompatible with a question which seeks to evaluate what is the most prevalent malware on the Internet by reading public Internet traffic. From a *scientific* standpoint, this conflates normative opinion with objective

[13] For those interested, the social sciences tend largely to follow the models proposed in science and engineering, and the humanities have their own methods of critical scholarly evaluation, which vary by discipline. The creative disciplines, such as art and music, are likely (and very appropriate) an exception to this approach.

inquiry. To be sure, both are important but cannot be combined into a single method without consideration of their interaction.

The second, and perhaps more critical point is that the most challenging questions of cybersecurity traverse sub-disciplines! Consider again the problem of password complexity. A mathematical proof of the difficulty of brute-force guessing a password is, within cryptanalysis, a quite-correct method of evaluating password "strength." And indeed, when a password is used as a "seed" to generate an encryption key (e.g., with a password to a file or the passcode for an iPhone) this is a critical part of the analysis. However, in the context of authentication interfaces—like your basic login screen—such an analysis is woefully incomplete. It fails to consider the larger questions such as "what is the goal of the authentication interface" and "what other methods to avoid unauthorized access can the system/interface include?"

Thus, we need a method for determining what constitutes "proof" within cybersecurity, and that method must be more than the mere sum of the methods of cybersecurity's constituent sub-disciplines. Stated differently, we need a science of cybersecurity.

But wait: don't we already have such a method? Don't cybersecurity experts tell us things about "what works" and "what are risks" and doesn't the law integrate these into compliance requirements? Well, yes, both of the latter are true—however this does not necessarily mean that it constitutes a scientific method. Medicine is particularly informative here as an example.

Snake oil, an oft-repeated derogatory term, quite literally was widely sold as a medical treatment through the United States and other parts of the world through the 1800s and even into the early 1900s.[14] The efficacy of snake oil subsequently was evaluated by the government, determined through ineffective at curing any medical ailments, and snake oil sales were precluded for this purpose. The question becomes "h*ow* was this inefficacy proven?" The answer lies within the scientific approach adopted by allopathic, osteopathic, and other forms of "evidence-based medicine." These approaches to the treatment of illness and injury require the demonstration of empirically valid results before the acceptance of an approach is considered a valid method of treatment or prophylaxis. This is how the disciplines of medicine have solved the "snake oil problem" and the reason we can trust in the practice of physicians. It is not because they are "authorities;" it is because their training is based on methods which have been demonstrated to be supported by empirically-valid scientific evidence.

Cybersecurity, to be sure, has evidence. Earlier in this text, we examined a few cybersecurity incidents, such as the Target breach, and examined published post-mortem analyses to determine what failed. These

---

[14] For an interesting recap of this history, see https://en.wikipedia.org/wiki/Snake_oil.

analyses suggest potential future improvements. Likewise, much attention is paid within the fields of computer security and network security to empirical analysis of network traffic in attempts to characterize the nature of attacks on systems. But not all evidence is empirically valid.

In brief, there are three critical elements to empirical validity: 1) internal validity; 2) external validity; and 3) construct validity. Internal validity asks the question of whether evidence demonstrates a causal relationship, or only a correlational one. External validity asks whether evidence generalizes to other contexts and examples. Construct validity asks whether the evidence presented supports the conclusions drawn from that evidence. The use of only post-incident analysis and network traffic analysis fails all three tests.

Post-incident analysis suffers from severe selection bias, meaning that the only incidents that become public knowledge are examined broadly. If you only evaluate incidents in which *you have detected* a failure, you ignore: 1) incidents in which a failure occurred but you did not detect it; 2) incidents in which an attacker attempted to compromise a system but failed; and 3) incidents in which an attacker made a choice not to attack a system. All of these examples matter, compromising internal validity. Network traffic analysis, if done correctly, does overcome this problem to some extent. However, network traffic, by definition, is only a portion of system activity. It fails both external validity (it may not generalize under different system conditions) and construct validity (the conclusions may not result from the evaluated variable, even though they are causal, because the causal characteristics are dependent on something else: he activity on the systems).

Therefore, there is a strong need for a more rigorous "science" of cybersecurity.

While cybersecurity may yet lack the rigor or formality of a science, this has not kept it from being the subject of methodological study. The excerpts below discuss various ways that those who study and think about cybersecurity have approached the field. This is not a complete taxonomy of the research tools and methodologies that cybersecurity researchers have used. Notably absent is detailed discussion of tools from economics (which would generally fall under what Mulligan & Schneider call the Doctrine of Managing Risk), but it captures the overall range of methodologies.

MULLIGAN & SCHNEIDER, *DOCTRINE FOR CYBERSECURITY*

140 DAEDALUS 70 (2011)

2 Cybersecurity Doctrines: Past and Present

The advent of time-sharing in the 1960's meant that computations on behalf of multiple users were interleaved on a single computer. Each user's computation and data thus had to be protected from misbehavior by programs being run by other users. Confronted by a problem born of technology, engineers of early time-sharing systems sought solutions in technology. Therefore, the focus of early cybersecurity doctrine was on developing new technology. Societal values could be and were ignored, because users of these early computing systems had shared values which meant those values would be respected without explicit discussion.

Technological solutions for creating the needed isolation were beyond our capabilities, especially when users could be motivated and capable adversaries bent on disrupting another user's computation or stealing information. Improved technology, however, is not the only way to solve problems that technology has created, and subsequent cybersecurity doctrines focused on policy to leverage those technological solutions that were at hand. These doctrines too were unsuccessful. But had they succeeded, they ultimately would have been inadequate because the problem was changing.

Computer systems were becoming pervasive, which had two broad consequences. First, the information technology sector became a significant economic force. Concerns about freedom to innovate and success in the marketplace come with this first consequence. The second consequence was that computer systems increasingly touched the lives of ordinary people, as citizens whose records were stored electronically, and as workers who used information technology to be more efficient. Eventually, computer networks and the web were created; they changed how people shopped, communicated, socialized and engaged in politics. As a consequence, privacy and other societal values grew in importance. The requirement for a cybersecurity doctrine to take account of societal values became crucial.

Because their effectiveness has been limited, it is instructive to review the three doctrines that have dominated cybersecurity thinking for the past 50 years—the doctrines of prevention, risk management, and deterrence through accountability. In particular, by analyzing the measures these doctrines propose, we might hope to gain insights into properties that cause measures to be effective.

Doctrine of Prevention. The goal of this doctrine is systems that are completely free of vulnerabilities. Absent vulnerabilities, attacks are not possible, so the resulting system is secure.

Such *absolute cybersecurity* is worthwhile but unlikely ever to be achieved. For systems that incorporate humans as users and operators, we would need some way to prevent social engineering and intentional insider-malfeasance. Prevention, here, requires overcoming the frailty of humans, which is likely to involve more than technology.

If we ignore humans in a system then the problem is different but not easier. Software systems today are just too large and complicated to be verified using formal logics. Researchers, assisted by computers, have been able to devise formal proofs for small systems (i.e., under 10,000 lines of code), and software producers regularly employ automated checking for relatively simple properties of code and for analyzing specifications. Techniques are also being explored that reduce the size of code bases for certain key systems, because a smaller code base is more amenable to formal verification. But revolutionary advances are needed before formal verification could be used to verify the entire code base found today on a desktop system or server, yet that would be necessary for implementing the Doctrine of Prevention.

System testing is the obvious alternative for gaining assurance that a system has no vulnerabilities. Tests, however, only can reveal the presence of vulnerabilities—not their absence. Exhaustive testing would be necessary for demonstrating the absence of vulnerabilities, and the amount of work involved here is prohibitive even for small components, much less for large systems.

Formal proofs and testing are necessarily relative to some expectations about what the system must do and the environments in which the system will operate. So we must discharge the Doctrine of Prevention relative to some expectations, which is tantamount to establishing the absence of vulnerabilities only if certain assumptions hold. Unfortunately, assumptions about the environment that hold one day might subsequently be invalidated. Attacks evolve in sophistication in response to better defenses. And threats emerge to exploit new opportunities for disruption that are created when cyberspace provides access to new forms of value. So a system that was once considered secure might not remain so for very long.

In light of this dynamic, expectations about the environment must be periodically revisited and, if necessary, revised. Thus the Doctrine of Prevention involves a recurring expense. That recurring expense is inconsistent with the business model employed by many of today's software providers, which favors reuse and extension of existing hardware and software in order to lower the cost of producing new systems.

Doctrine of Risk Management. Absolute cybersecurity is not affordable but, fortunately, it is also not needed for most systems. The Doctrine of Risk Management responds by stipulating a more modest goal—that investments in security reduce expected losses from attacks. To adopt this doctrine is to admit that all vulnerabilities are not equal; one should focus only on vulnerabilities whose exploitation is (i) sufficiently likely by the perceived threats and (ii) could enable system compromises that are expensive (by some cost measure). In contrast to the Doctrine of Prevention, the more modest goal of defending a smaller body of code against a more restricted set of threats is likely within our capabilities.

Moreover, to maintain that steady state, fewer assumptions about the environment would have to be revisited periodically.

In theory, the Doctrine of Risk Management seems quite sensible. But the lack of information about vulnerabilities, incidents, and attendant losses makes actual risk calculations difficult. Companies and individuals do not know how to value (i) confidentiality of information, (ii) integrity of information, or (iii) the pain of dealing with recovery from an attack's effects (e.g., bad credit ratings). And these costs seem to vary tremendously. Also, people have difficulty reasoning about extremely low-probability events. Finally, investment incentives are missing when costs are borne by third parties, materialize only well after the breach occurs, and causation is difficult to discern much less prove.

Accurate information about threats and attacks may not be publicly available because those with that knowledge fear tarnishing their reputations or compromising their intelligence methods and/or sources. Even were that information available, deployment of replacement systems and upgrades changes the uses to which systems are being put and alters the set of vulnerabilities, which in turn can lead to the creation of new attacks. These differences mean that the past is not a good predictor of the future. As a consequence, actuarial models cannot be constructed, so insurance to transfer risk is impossible to price in a way that ensures profits to the policy underwriter.

Were there some way to analyze a system mechanically and obtain a quantity that indicates just how secure that system is, then we could have a basis for assessing what is gained from specific investments made in support of cybersecurity. But today such cybersecurity metrics do not exist. Quantities derived entirely from empirical observations also don't work for justifying investments. The absence of detected system compromises could indicate that investments in defenses worked, attacks haven't been attempted, or the compromise escaped notice (e.g., theft of confidential information). So whether or not prior security investments were well targeted is impossible to know, leaving security professionals to justify investments based solely on non-events.

Approaches based on risk management are further confounded by externalities that derive from the emergent nature of cybersecurity in networks. Individuals and entities here can neither fully reap the benefit of their security investment nor entirely control their vulnerability through investments. For example, a single compromised system anywhere in a network can serve as a launching point for attacks on other systems connected to that network. So local investment in defenses not only provides local benefits but also benefits others; and under-investment in defenses elsewhere in the network could facilitate local harms. Absent coordination, the only logical strategy would be to invest in insurance (were it available), because here an entity can reap the entire benefit of that investment. However, this strategy does nothing to improve security and, as noted above, viable long-term business models for insurance do not exist today.

The situation for risk management is not completely bleak, though. In the policy arena, state security breach notification laws can be viewed as a risk management intervention. Significant costs are incurred to notify individuals and to manage the adverse publicity surrounding reportable breaches. These potential costs act as a proxy for the costs of security failures to customers, forcing companies to internalize previously externalized risks of security failures. The price tag on breaches also means that these laws have created a set of data to use in risk and return on investment calculations. However, the laws focus on only a narrow set of breaches and, as a result, might artificially skew the focus of investments.

Doctrine of Deterrence Through Accountability. This doctrine is concerned with treating attacks as crimes, and it therefore focuses on infrastructure to perform forensics, identify perpetrators, and prosecute them. We deter attacks by increasing the chances that perpetrators will be found and prosecuted. Implementations of this doctrine require strong authentication technologies and surveillance of network activity. Robust forms of user identity allow us to overcome the loose binding that exists today between individuals and machines.

Absent an effective means for retribution, this doctrine has no teeth and fails. And efforts to punish perpetrators of cyber-attacks are not always feasible in today's global environment. Attribution of actions by machines to individuals is complicated, agreement about illegality is illusive, and cross-border enforcement requires more cooperation than is likely to emerge between important constellations of nations. Recent attacks against U.S. and other systems suggest that we cannot ignore non-nation state actors that engage in terrorism and large-scale financial crimes. The very features that make the internet a profitable environment for criminals—world-wide reach, connectedness, neutral treatment of packets, and weak binding of machines to individuals—make it difficult for law enforcement to identify and catch them, while other features of the international landscape make it difficult to bring them to justice.

There are also conceptual obstacles that limit the effectiveness of the doctrine. First, this doctrine is punitive. Like most criminal law, it is aimed primarily at punishing with expectations of producing both general and specific deterrence. This does little to keep networks up and running when they are under siege nor does it prompt proactive security investments. Second, the doctrine could require individuals to sacrifice privacy and, in the extreme, abandon the possibility of anonymity and the protections for freedom of speech and association it affords.

Nevertheless, many attacks are indeed criminals plying their trade, and it makes good sense that criminal activity in cyberspace face the risk of retribution that we employ to deter criminal activity in the physical world. The Doctrine of Deterrence Through Accountability thus brings value here. But in cyberspace, unlike in the physical world, terrorists or state actors are difficult to distinguish from common criminals. Deterrence through accountability is not necessarily effective against these trans-national threats. Other doctrine is also required.

Professors Mulligan and Schneider approach these issues from the lenses of computer and information science. Professor Nathan Sales, writing from a purely legal perspective, further discusses the concepts that Mulligan and Schneider identify as "Deterrence through Accountability." His approach, which highlights the importance of law enforcement and the law of armed conflict, highlights various questions about how these bodies of law operate in the cyber context. We will return to these questions in later chapters.

SALES, *REGULATING CYBER-SECURITY*

7 NW. U. L. REV. 1503 (2013)

II. Cyber-security Frameworks, Conventional and Unconventional

[. . .]

A. The Conventional Approaches: Law Enforcement and Armed Conflict

Scholars typically use a pair of analytical frameworks to understand cyber-attacks: criminal law and the law of armed conflict. Consider the former first. Broadly speaking, the criminal law seeks to protect people from unjustified acts of violence against their persons or property. The criminal law pursues this objective by imposing sanctions, such as incarceration, on those adjudged to have violated the law. These penalties will punish those who have transgressed society's moral code (retribution), dissuade the perpetrator or others from committing similar offenses in the future (specific or general deterrence), isolate the dangerous perpetrator from society (incapacitation), or teach the misguided perpetrator the error of his ways (rehabilitation). Cyber-attacks fit into this conceptual framework fairly comfortably. A person who hacks into another's computer may have thereby violated any number of laws, such as the federal Computer Fraud and Abuse Act. Society regards this sort of conduct as sufficiently blameworthy that it proscribes it and subjects those who engage in it to criminal penalties of varying severity.

Scholars who approach cyber-security from a law enforcement perspective focus on the "whodunit" questions. Who was responsible for launching this particular attack? Was it an individual hacker or a larger criminal enterprise? This framework also emphasizes jurisdictional questions. Which courts properly may exercise subject matter jurisdiction over a given cyber-attack? State courts, federal courts, or perhaps international tribunals? Should jurisdiction be determined by the location of the target? By the location of the attacker? By the location in which the effects of the attack are felt? Should cyber-attacks be subject to universal jurisdiction—the notion that a court may try certain crimes regardless of where in the world they occurred? How might courts gain personal jurisdiction over those suspected of committing the attack, especially if they are overseas? Do existing extradition treaties cover the range of offenses that cyber-criminals might commit? Should the United States negotiate new bilateral agreements with key international partners, such as our European allies, or with countries in which cyber-attacks are likely to originate, such as China and Russia? Or should there be a multilateral global convention on cyber-crime, one that will facilitate extradition of suspects from their home countries to the states in which they will stand trial for their alleged crimes?

The law enforcement framework also emphasizes punishment and deterrence. Certain economic theories of criminal law posit that a person's willingness to commit crimes is a function of the expected penalty for that activity—i.e., the sanction for the particular offense discounted by the probability that the person will get caught. The greater the sanction, and the greater the likelihood of detection and punishment, the less likely a person will choose to commit that crime. The question then becomes what should be done to increase the deterrent effect of laws that proscribe various cyber-intrusions. Should the penalties for violating these statutes be increased? Should society invest more resources in detecting cyber-crime, thereby increasing the probability that perpetrators will be caught and punished? Or should lawmakers pursue "cost deterrence," the objective of which is to increase the costs one must incur to perpetrate cyber-crime?

The second conventional approach regards cyber-attacks from the standpoint of the law of armed conflict (LOAC). The LOAC, also known as international humanitarian law (IHL), is a body of international law that regulates a state's ability to use force in several ways. First, it sets forth the circumstances in which a state lawfully may engage in armed conflict—the jus ad bellum regulations. For instance, the United Nations Charter forbids signatories "from the threat or use of force against the territorial integrity or political independence of any state," but also recognizes an inherent right to use force in self-defense against an "armed attack." Second, the LOAC regulates what kinds of force may be used during an authorized armed conflict—the jus in bello regulations. For instance, a state may not deliberately kill civilians or destroy civilian infrastructure (the "distinction" or "discrimination" principle), may not inadvertently inflict harm on civilian populations and structures that is disproportionate to the importance of the military objective ("proportionality"), and may not cause more harm to legitimate targets than is needed to achieve the military objective ("necessity").

Scholars who see cyber-security as an armed conflict problem typically focus on determining who was responsible for a particular attack. Was this attack launched by a state or an international terrorist organization, in which case the LOAC may permit some form of military retaliation? Or was it carried out by criminals, in which case the distinction principle likely would rule out a military response? If the attacker was in fact a state or terrorist group, which one? Was it China, or maybe Russia, or perhaps North Korea? Or was it al Qaeda, or al Qaeda in the Arabian Peninsula, or Hezbollah? Until the identity of the assailant is known, it will be unclear against whom to retaliate—or whether retaliation is lawful at all.

Another set of important questions concerns how to characterize a cyber-incident. Is a given intrusion espionage or an attack? It can be quite difficult to answer that question because the steps an intruder would take to steal information often are identical to the steps it would take to bring down a system. If the intrusion is properly understood as an attack, does it rise to the level of an "armed attack" that triggers the right of self-defense? Should these questions be resolved with an "instrument-based" test, which counts a cyber-intrusion as an armed attack when it causes harms that previously could have been caused only by a kinetic attack? Or a less demanding "effects-" or "consequence-based" test, which counts a cyber-intrusion as an armed attack when it has a sufficiently harmful effect on the targeted state? Or an even less demanding "intent" test, which counts a cyber-intrusion as an armed attack whenever it evinces a hostile intent, regardless of whether it causes actual damage? The LOAC approach also addresses possible responses. When a nation suffers a cyber-attack, is it limited to responding with a cyber-intrusion of its own? Or may a victim retaliate by launching a kinetic attack? How severe must the cyber-attack be before a kinetic response would be justified?

Other problems for the LOAC arise from the fact that much of the world's critical infrastructure is dual use—it serves a state's civilian population but the state's political leadership and armed forces also rely upon it. In the United States, for instance, civilian networks carry up to 98% of the federal government's communications traffic, including 95% of defense-related traffic. When, if ever, may a combatant direct a cyber-attack at an adversary's dual-use infrastructure? Finally, the LOAC focuses on deterrence. Given the differences between cyber-conflicts and kinetic ones, how can a state dissuade its adversaries from committing cyber-attacks? Key differences include the difficulty in determining who was responsible for a given intrusion, the possibility that a retaliatory cyber-strike might end up harming innocent third parties more than the actual assailant, and the fact that different nations are more or less dependent on cyber-infrastructure and therefore have more or less to lose from an exchange of cyber-weapons.

A central problem for both the law enforcement and armed conflict approaches to cyber-security is determining the identity of the assailant. Attribution is extraordinarily difficult; the challenges are "staggering" and "[n]o one has come close to solving" them. The problem is inherent in the basic architecture of the Internet. The Internet's TCP/IP protocol was designed to move packets of data as efficiently as possible; it is utterly unconcerned with who sent them. As such, it is fairly easy for attackers to obscure their true identities by routing their intrusions through a series of dispersed intermediary computers. These attribution difficulties can severely frustrate the law enforcement and armed conflict approaches to cyber-security.

In the excerpt below, Ross Anderson and Tyler Moore discuss the use of economic analysis in the study of security. In recent years economics has come to the fore as one of the most powerful tools for both studying and thinking about how to implement security.

ANDERSON & MOORE, *INFORMATION SECURITY: WHERE COMPUTER SCIENCE, ECONOMICS AND PSYCHOLOGY MEET*

367 PHILOSOPHICAL TRANSACTIONS OF THE ROYAL SOCIETY A 2717 (2009)

1. Introduction

As the Internet has grown, system engineers have realized that security failure is caused at least as often by bad incentives as by bad design. Indeed, the former often explain the latter. Systems are particularly prone to failure when the person operating them does not suffer the full costs of failure. Things also break when system users have conflicting interests, or even just no real reason to cooperate. Thus, while security engineers used to worry about malicious outsiders, the greatest concern now is selfish insiders. As a result, the tools of game theory and microeconomic theory are becoming just as important to the security engineer as the mathematics of cryptography.

We review recent results and live research challenges in the economics of information security. Our goal is to present several promising applications of economic ideas to practical information security problems. We first consider misaligned incentives in the design and deployment of computer systems. Next, we study the impact of externalities: network insecurity is somewhat similar to air pollution or traffic congestion, in that people who connect insecure machines to the Internet do not bear the full consequences of their actions. Asymmetric information presents further problems. Insecure software dominates the market for the simple reason that most users cannot distinguish it from secure software; thus, risks cannot be managed better until we can get better measurements, both of the raw risks and the effects of various countermeasures.

Finally, a recent growth area is the application of ideas from the boundary between economics and psychology. These ideas provide many useful insights into problems ranging from the ease with which computer users are deceived by fake websites, through why many people say they value privacy yet act otherwise when online, to societal misperceptions of risk. Why is it, for example, that most people care too little about online security and privacy, yet overreact to terrorism?

2. Misaligned incentives

One of the observations that sparked interest in information security economics came from banking. In the United States, banks are more liable for the costs of card fraud, as consumer protection law is stronger than in Britain. So one might expect that UK banks would spend less on security and fraud than US banks, but the reverse turned out to be the case (Anderson 1994). How could this be? It appears to have been what economists call a moral hazard effect: UK bank staff knew that customer complaints would be stonewalled, so they became lazy and careless. This led to an avalanche of fraud.

Varian (2000) made a similar key observation about the antivirus software market. People did not spend as much on protecting their computers as they might have. Why not? At that time, a typical virus payload was a service-denial attack against the website of a company such as Microsoft. Although a rational consumer might well spend $20 to prevent a virus from trashing his hard disk, he might not do so just to prevent an attack on someone else.

Lawyers have long known that liability should be assigned to whoever can best manage the risk. Yet online risks tend to be allocated poorly, resulting in privacy failures and regulatory tussles. For instance, medical records systems are bought by hospital directors and insurance companies, whose interests in cost control and research conflict with the patients' interests in privacy. Another example was documented by Bohm et al. (2000): banks used the move from branch to online banking to shift the liability rules in their favour and against customers.

The realization that incentive failures were important, and getting steadily worse, helped spark a research programme in information security economics (Anderson 2001). Researchers found they could use many established microeconomic models. For example, in a Nobel prize-winning work, Akerlof (1970) kicked off the study of asymmetric information. He imagined a town in which 50 good used cars (worth $2000 each) are for sale, along with 50 'lemons' (worth $1000 each). The sellers know the difference, but the buyers do not. What will be the market-clearing price?

One might initially think $1500, but at that price no one with a good car will offer it for sale, so the market price will quickly end up near $1000. Akerlof's 'market for lemons' explains why so many information security products are poor: buyers are unwilling to pay a premium for quality they cannot measure. This has led to various certification schemes that try to signal product quality to buyers.

As well as hidden information, there can be a problem with hidden action. Such problems arise when two parties wish to transact, but one of them can take unobservable actions that affect the outcome. The classic example comes from insurance, where the policyholder may behave recklessly. Hidden information and hidden action can be used to classify computer security problems (Moore 2005). Routers can quietly drop selected packets or falsify responses to routing requests; nodes can redirect network traffic to eavesdrop on conversations; and players in file-sharing systems can hide whether they are sharing with others, and thus 'free-ride' rather than help to sustain the system.

Once this is understood, designers can structure interactions to minimize hidden action or make it easier to enforce contracts. For example, early peer-to-peer systems forced users to cooperate with random other users, while more modern designs have the effect of clustering users by affinity, so that users help to defend other users with similar preferences. This leads to greater solidarity and makes systems more robust (Danezis & Anderson 2005). This model also sheds light on the more general problem of the trade-offs between diversity and solidarity—for example, whether the growing diversity of modern societies is in tension with the solidarity on which welfare systems are founded (Goodhart 2004).

3. Security as an externality

Economists use the term externality to describe the side effects of transactions; these can be positive (as with scientific research) or negative (as with environmental pollution). Externalities were already well known in crime prevention. Ayres & Levitt (1997) analysed the Lojack car-theft prevention system and found that once a threshold of car owners in a city had installed it, auto theft plummeted, as the stolen car trade became too hazardous. Camp & Wolfram (2000) built on this to analyse information security vulnerabilities as negative externalities, such as air pollution: someone who connects an insecure PC to the Internet does not face the full economic costs of that, any more than someone burning a coal fire. They proposed trading vulnerability credits in the same way as carbon credits.

A particularly important example in the information industries is the network externality: the more people use a service akin to voice over Internet protocol (VOIP), the more people there are to talk to, and so the value of the service scales more rapidly than the number of users. Similarly, the more people use a platform such as Windows, the more firms write software for it, and the more valuable it becomes. These effects—

together with the high fixed and low marginal costs of information goods, and the lock-in that comes from controlling interoperability—lead to the information industries having many dominant-firm markets, in which the winner takes all.

Curiously, this explains why many IT platforms and services are initially designed to be insecure. A firm trying to build a network monopoly must appeal not just to its customers, but also to its complementers, such as the software developers in the case of an operating system. Complicated access controls would make the developers' lives harder, and thus are generally avoided in the early stages. Later, once the platform vendor has established dominance, it will introduce excessive security in order to lock its customers in tightly (Anderson 2001). This pattern has been seen again and again, in mainframe, PC and mobile phone markets.

A different set of externalities can be found when we analyse security investment, as protection often depends on the efforts of many other principles. An interesting model, due to Varian (2004), is to consider whether defence depends on the efforts of the laziest defender, or of the most valiant defender, or on the sum total of all the defenders.

Consider a medieval city. If the main threat is a siege, and each family is responsible for maintaining and guarding one stretch of the wall, then the city will depend on the efforts of the laziest family. If disputes are settled by single combat between champions, then it depends on the strength and courage of its most valiant knight. But if wars are a matter of attrition, then the critical factor is the sum of all the citizens' efforts. Of these, sum-of-efforts is the most efficient, best effort is next and least effort gives the least defence of all.

System reliability is a mix of these. A critical vulnerability may be introduced by the most careless programmer; whether it is found prior to deployment depends on the sum of all the testers' efforts; and whether a deployed vulnerability leads to an actual attack may depend on the skill of the security architect, who designed the system's structure and interfaces. So a software company should hire fewer but better programmers, more testers and the best security architect it can find.

Other researchers have modelled interdependent risk. An influential paper by Kunreuther & Heal (2003) noted that security investments can be strategic complements: an individual taking protective measures creates positive externalities for others that may discourage their own investment. This has implications far beyond information security. An apartment owner who installs a sprinkler system can make his neighbours less likely to do the same, and people thinking whether to vaccinate their children may choose to free ride off the herd immunity instead. The Kunreuther-Heal model shows that several widely varying equilibria are possible, from complete adoption to total refusal, depending on the levels of coordination between principals.

There are further implications for technology adoption. A number of core Internet protocols, such as DNS and routing, are known to be insecure. Better protocols exist (DNSSEC and S-BGP), but the challenge is to get them adopted, and quite a lot of users may have to adopt a new protocol before it becomes economic for people to switch. There is a useful model, by Katz & Shapiro (1985), which analyses how network externalities influence the adoption of technology: they lead to the classical S-shaped curve, in which slow early uptake gives way to rapid deployment once the number of users reaches some threshold. Two security protocols that have already been widely deployed, SSH and IPsec, overcame the bootstrapping problem by providing adopting firms with internal benefits, thus reducing the size of the threshold to less than the size of the larger firms. Thus, adoption could proceed one firm at a time. Fax machines got deployed this way: companies initially bought them to connect their own offices.

QUESTIONS

1. What elements comprise questions of "cybersecurity"? Are we asking about a single computer, about a network perimeter, about multiple computers, or something else?

2. Using Mulligan & Schneider's terminology, does the Doctrine of Prevention focus on threats, vulnerabilities, or both? What about the Doctrine of Risk Management? The Doctrine of Deterrence through Accountability?

3. Both Mulligan & Schneider and Anderson & Moore discuss the concept of "externalities." What is an externality and why are the relevant to cybersecurity?

4. Sales discusses the challenges of attribution and ways in which the technical design of the Internet conflict with the goals of cybersecurity. How do these concerns relate to the Doctrine of Prevention and the discussion of the science of cybersecurity that preceded these excerpts? (We will discuss these technological issues in depth in later chapters.)

5. Those with a legal background may note with some surprise that both Mulligan & Schneider and Sales discuss deterrence through the criminal law but do not discuss civil liability. As we will discuss in later chapters, civil liability has historically played a surprisingly small role in cybersecurity, a feature that is likely to change in coming years.

2. THINKING LIKE AN ATTACKER

Understanding how to think about security requires understanding how attackers think. Attackers, or more broadly, threats,[15] drive the need for security. Thus, security should be attuned to the mindset and goals of attackers. It is easy when designing any construct—a building, a wall, or

[15] While we focus in this Section largely on "attackers" as autonomous entities, remember that a "threat" could include *anything* which disrupts normal operation of a system—such as a natural, economic, or political disaster.

an information system—to think about it in terms of "emotional defense"—those things that *feel* strong). But such approaches misunderstand *risks* to the building or system—those risks lie in the ways in which attackers or other threats can *misuse* aspects of that construct.

Most people use the words "use" and "utilize" interchangeably. More precisely, they utilize the word "utilize" when they mean to use the word "use." This is because utilize has a more particular meaning than use, connoting the use of something other than for its intended purpose.[16]

From a grammatical perspective, the distinction between "use" and "utilize" is generally regarded as anachronistic. It is, however, productive to utilize the distinction to capture what it is to think like an attacker. Attackers see the world differently from the rest of us. Where most people see a "thing," attackers see a "system of components interacting to be a thing"—each of those components is a possible vulnerability, as is each of the connections by which the components interact. Where most people see a security guard as a tool for keeping unwanted people out of a building, attackers see a security guard as someone who can be utilized to let them into the building. Where most people see a password prompt as a door that keeps users out of a system, the attacker sees something that can be utilized to learn about the system, to slow down the system, or to attempt to compromise the system.

Or, to flip this around, attackers understand that using security devices doesn't necessarily provide security. A classic example of this is a story from World War II: Nazi soldiers needed to secure a vault filled with treasure, so they replaced the door with a nearly indestructible steel door. When the Allies found the vault, they found an impenetrable door set in an old brick wall. The door was secure, but the wall was not. The door was "used" for its proper purpose—but it was used in a way that provided no meaningful security. This is, of course, analogous to the example of complex passwords from the previous chapter: in most systems, the vulnerability is not an insufficiently complex password, it's some other component of the system that provides access to the password subsystem.

Consider as other examples of this same phenomenon the following two images:

[16] See *Fowler's;* OED 2d.

Figure 1: Cars avoiding a security guard rail

Figure 2: Bike locked to a short, open pole

Both figures tell a similar story: a device intended to provide security was used in a way that provided none. A vehicle gate was placed in a road at a point where cars could easily drive around it; a bicycle was locked to a short pole with a "U" lock that could easily be slid over the top of the pole.

These are simple examples, but to the attacker they are ubiquitous. Users who do not understand the system they are trying to secure rely on security products—or devices that are supposed to provide security. The attacker need only understand the system slightly better than her target in order to follow these security devices back to a point from which they can be utilized to find a vulnerability. If you do not understand the system at least as well as the attacker, whatever you do to secure the system can easily become a roadmap for the attacker to compromise the system.

Thinking outside the box. Attackers tend to be people who look at systems differently than the rest of us. They think "outside the box." Or, more precisely, they see the box as part of the system.

In the 1930s, psychologist Karl Duncker was studying how people solve problems. He conducted an experiment in which he presented subjects with a relatively simple task: he gave them a candle, a box of thumb tacks, and a book of matches, along with the instruction that they were to use these items to affix the lit candle to the wall. Most subjects took between 5–10 minutes[17] to come up with a workable solution to this problem.

The materials subjects were given are depicted in the picture below. Take a moment to think about how you would solve this problem.

Figure 3: Initial presentation of candle problem

A second group of subjects were given the exact same materials, presented in a slightly different way, as depicted on the next page.

[17] Karl Duncker, *On problem solving*, Psychological monographs 58 (1945).

Compared to the first group, these subjects took, on average, less than half as long to come up with a workable way to affix the lit candle to the wall.

What is the difference between the presentation of the problem in Figures 3 and 4? In Figure 4, the thumb tacks have been placed on the table, sitting next to the box that they were in in Figure 3. The best way to affix the candle to the wall is to use the box as a platform, use the tacks to affix the box to the wall, and then place the candle in the box. The key to recognizing this solution is to recognize that the box of thumb tacks in a system made up of two components (the thumb tacks and the box) and that each of those components can be used separately. The box itself can be utilized for a purpose other than holding the thumb tacks.

Figure 4: Alternative presentation of candle problem

The attacker looks for ways that a system can be broken into components; and that each of those components can, in turn, be broken into more components; and, in turn, ways that each of those components can be utilized in way that bypass the security of the system. Duncker's experiment shows how hard this can be.

Seeing the unseen. Let us look at another example. During World War II the allies had a serious problem: German anti-aircraft guns were shooting down too many of their bombers. In order to reduce the number of planes they were losing, the allies needed add more armor to the underside of the bombers. But every pound of armor added reduced both their speed (making them easier targets) and range (making them less effective weapons). The allies knew that they could only afford to add additional armor to the most sensitive areas of the plane, but they did not know where that was.

To answer this question, they turned to what data they had available: they examined planes that had returned from missions to see where they were taking damage. The idea was simple: because all of the planes were similar, it was likely that the planes that returned from missions were taking similar damage to those that were not returning from missions. Therefore, they could use the returned planes as maps for where to add armor. A copy of the diagram showing where these returning planes showed damage is in Figure 5.

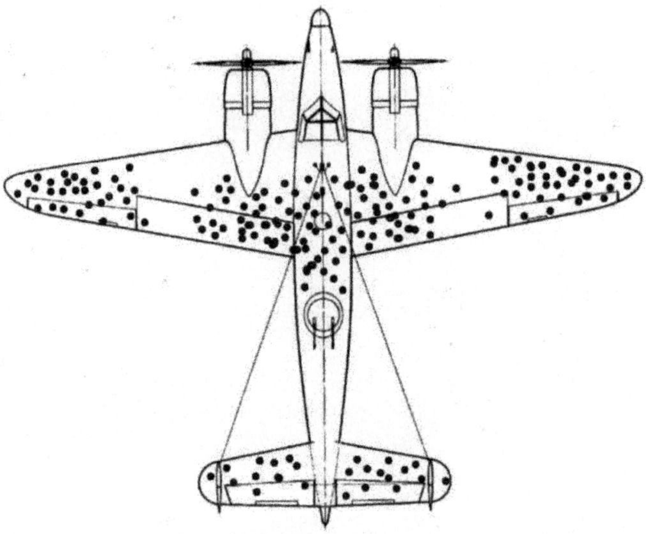

Figure 5: Diagram showing taken by WWII bombers returning to base

This logic was both exactly right and exactly wrong. The plane that returned from missions *could* be used as a map for where to add armor—but that armor should be added to the areas where the returned planes showed no damage, not to the areas where they did show damage. This critical observation was made by American statistician Abraham Wald, who recognized that, while both the planes that returned and did not return from missions were largely the same, the differed in one key respect: the planes that did not return did not return, so they were excluded from the data set. The planes that returned therefore were not representative of all planes, so could not be used to identify where all planes were taking damage. Rather, they told Wald where planes could afford to take damage and still be able to safely return to base. The damage that brought down planes that did not return, therefore, must be to parts of the planes that were undamaged on the planes that safely returned. Wald's recommendation was as effective as it was simple: add armor to the areas of planes that were undamaged after missions.

As with the box of thumb tacks, the way the system is presented focuses attention to certain components and to certain features of those components. If you are looking for where to put armor to prevent damage to planes, you are naturally going to look to where planes are taking damage. If you are looking to keep adversaries out of your vault, you are going to install a strong door to that vault. If you are looking to prevent your bike from being stolen, you are going to lock your bike to an immovable object. But in each of these cases, you are responding to the shadow of a vulnerability; you are using a tool that is designed to provide security without realizing that merely using it isn't enough. The attacker sees these components, how each works on its own and how each works together.

Knowing what counts. And the attacker looks for the subtlest ways that components of the system relate to one another. Consider the prisoners' hats problem: in order to reduce overcrowding at his prison, the warden has devised a sadistic way to reduce the prison population. He is going to place a red hat or blue on each prisoner's head, and then force the prisoner to call out "red" or "blue." If the called out color does not match the color of the hat on the prisoner's head (or the prisoner says anything other than "red" or "blue"), he is shot dead. But the warden is going to do this in an orderly way, having the prisoners line up front-to-back, such that each prisoner can see all of the prisoners in front of him, and then start at the back of the line and proceed forward. Being the sadist that he is, the warden tells his prisoners of this plan the night before, giving them the opportunity to fret over and discuss their coming abuse.

To what extent will the warden's plan reduce the prison's over-crowded population?

As a first approximation, most people will guess that half of the prisoners will die. There is a 50/50 chance that the hat on any prisoner's head is red or blue, so there is a 50/50 chance that the prisoner will correctly guess the color of the hat on his head. Like the allied bombers, on first blush there does not appear to be any connection between the prisoners. And even though each prisoner can see those who will lined up in front of him, and therefore will know the color of the hats on each one's head, each prisoner can also say only one word, "red" or "blue," such that there is little if any ability for the prisoners to communicate between one another.

But that one bit (literally) of information that the prisoners can communicate between one another is actually a huge amount of information. Using it, the prisoners can ensure that no more than one of them will die, and that that one will have a 50/50 chance of surviving. To do this, they all need only agree that the first prisoner forced to call out his hat color will count the number of red hats on the other prisoners' heads and, if that number is odd say "red" and if it is even say "blue." The next prisoner need only count how many red hats are in front of him and compare whether that is an even or odd number to what the first prisoner said to know the color of his hat. Each successive prisoner can then know precisely the color of hat on his or her head.

This classic logic puzzle is a nice example of how attackers approach problems. They identify what tools are available to them and think about how each can be used, both for its intended purpose and for some other purpose. And they identify ways into a system that match those available tools. In the case of the prisoners, there was only one tool: the ability of each prisoner to call out "red" or "blue." But this tool provided the prisoners with the ability to share an incredibly valuable piece of information: whether the number of red hats was even or odd.

No matter how complicated a system, very small quantities of information can be incredibly important. Indeed, the more complicated a system, with more components and more connections between components, the more likely it can be that very small pieces of information are critically important to the overall operation of the system. Two probes that humans have sent to Mars have crashed because a single number in millions of lines of carefully scrutinized code was incorrect. Numerous security flaws in sensitive computer code result from code that calculates the length of a string of text with the command "strlen(variable)" instead of "strlen(variable)+1"; from code that accidentally uses = instead of == (that is, a single equal sign instead of a double equal sign); and from code that uses double quotation marks where it should have used single quotation marks (e.g., "instead of').[18]

---

[18] In the first pages of *The Hacker Crackdown*, Bruce Sterling recounts a story that manifests an error similar to this example:

> On January 15, 1990, AT&T's long-distance telephone switching system crashed.
>
> This was a strange, dire, huge event. Sixty thousand people lost their telephone service completely. During the nine long hours of frantic effort that it took to restore service, some seventy million telephone calls went uncompleted.
>
> Losses of service, known as "outages" in the telco trade, are a known and accepted hazard of the telephone business. Hurricanes hit, and phone cables get snapped by the thousands. Earthquakes wrench through buried fiber-optic lines. Switching stations catch fire and burn to the ground. These things do happen. There are contingency plans for them, and decades of experience in dealing with them. But the Crash of January 15 was unprecedented. It was unbelievably huge, and it occurred for no apparent physical reason. [. . .]
>
> As it happened, the problem itself—the problem per se—took this form. A piece of telco software had been written in C language, a standard language of the telco field. Within the C software was a long "do. . . while" construct. The "do. . . while" construct contained a "switch" statement. The "switch" statement contained an "if" clause. The "if" clause contained a "break." The "break" was supposed to "break" the "if clause." Instead, the "break" broke the "switch" statement.

The entire long-distance telephone network had been brought down by a single, nearly imperceptible, bug, in a single piece of code. Importantly, from the computers' perspective, the code was *not* buggy. It was perfectly coherent. But by virtue of a single errant command, the coding equivalent of a misplaced comma—a mistake that can completely change the meaning of a sentence but that authors make every day—the entire network was compromised.

Each of these simple coding mistakes are the equivalent of the bike locked to the short pole. The programmer writes it expecting it to do something, and in most cases it will operate precisely as the programmer anticipates. It isn't until someone who is looking for mistakes such as theses comes around that functional code will become insecure code. The attacker thinks in these terms. The attacker sees computer code that likely has includes a "strcpy( )" function, and recognizes it as a possible way into a system. The attacker sees the overall system and knows what components like comprise that system, how they fit together, how they are commonly misused, and how those misuses allow one component of the system to be utilized to obtain unauthorized access to other components of the system.

Consider the following pseudocode that describes a function that a bank may use to transfer balances between accounts.

```
Obtain source_account
Obtain dest_account
Obtain amount_to_transfer
Obtain balance_in_source_account
If (balance_in_source_account < amount_to_transfer)
    Return Error(insufficient_funds)
Else
    Transfer(amount_to_transfer, source_account, dest_account)
    Return Success
```

It is reasonably clear what this code is supposed to do: it starts by getting the source and destination accounts and the amount of money to be transferred between them, it makes sure that there is a sufficient about of money in the source account to cover the transfer, and if there is it executes the transfer.

This code does exactly what a person would do, or at least what a person would think that they are doing. But there is a very important, very simple, very serious mistake in this code. What happens if the user requests to transfer a negative amount? This is implicit in how a human bank teller would carry out a transfer: they would see the negative number and refuse to process the request. But computers aren't that smart. Unless the programmer has a deeper understanding of how the system actually works, she may write code that doesn't make sure the transfer request is a positive value. And, indeed, this could well never be a problem, because most people do not try to transfer negative amounts of money between bank accounts. It won't be until someone more conniving comes along—an attacker—and, seeing a prompt that lets them enter negative numbers, tries to transfer a negative amount that this mistake will be discovered.[19]

3. THINKING LIKE A TARGET

Just as thinking from the perspective of an attacker is important, likewise thinking from the perspective of a *target* is important. Note that we use thinking like a *target* as opposed to thinking like a *defender*. Why is this? Recall that at the beginning of Section 3.2 we alluded to the differences between emotional security and responding to actual threats. This Section now explores how "targets"—those responsible for defending systems—can connect the ways attackers think (and other threats) to their own responsive, defensive thinking.

How should a potential target respond to the threat of attack? We will consider best practices for securing systems in later chapters. It is worth considering here the defense mentality—or, how to think like a potential target.

The first thing to understand is that *you are a target*. Even if you don't think you are a target, and even if you don't have anything of value to any particular attacker, the nature of cyberattacks today is such that anyone online is a target. If you were to monitor your home Internet connection for possible attacks, you would likely discover an attacker attempting to compromise your home network at least once every few minutes. Today, many attacks are autonomous, distributed, and random. The goal of these attacks is to identify vulnerable systems: once those systems are identified, attackers will think about how to use them. Or, the vulnerability itself may tell the attacker how to the system may be used.

The next step is to stop "thinking about security." There is a difference between "thinking about security" and "thinking security." Thinking about security leads to a search for solutions—the cyber-equivalents of bike locks and steel doors. Unless your understanding of how these tools work is at least as sophisticated at those attacking your systems, they are more likely to give a false sense of security. This is not to say that you should not use such tools. But they should be neither the starting point nor the focus of your security considerations.

Rather, you should understand that your systems are going to be attacked, that some of those attacks will be successful, and that you will therefore incur some losses as a result. Once you understand this, your approach to defense changes. Once you stop focusing on keeping attackers out, you can focus instead on how they are likely to get in. This tells you what systems to monitor, which systems have greater (and lesser) risk

---

[19] Lest this example seem too outlandish, consider that Citibank was recently fined $7 million by the SEC for a comparable coding error (a failure to properly check ranges for branch ID numbers) that went undetected in its code for 15 years, from 1999 to 2014. See https://www.sec.gov/litigation/admin/2016/34-78291.pdf.

exposure, and how to match different systems to different functions based upon those functions' importance or sensitivity. We will operationalize this in later chapters—for now, what is important is to realize this shift in thinking that this approach entails.

This shift in mentality isn't just a more effective response to attackers: it's a more effective way to use systems. It is well understood, for instance, that there is a tradeoff between usability and security. The more security controls that you put in place to try to prevent security incidents or to reduce risk, the more burdensome it becomes to actually use the underlying systems. As you can see in Figure 5, in the extreme case, perfect security almost necessarily renders systems unusable (unless you have a way to secure the human actors interfacing with the system, the system is necessarily unusable).

Figure 5: Dilbert cartoon

We can actually go a step further than this: perfectly secure systems aren't just unusable, but they are in fact insecure. This is because users—desiring, as they do, to use the system—will find ways to circumvent the security that is in place. Requiring users to use too-complex passwords causes users to write them down on post-it notes. Designing doors that cannot be unlocked, so that you need a key to open them, results in users propping them open. Making it difficult for users to actually use secure storage systems (e.g., backed-up and encrypted network attached storage) will cause users to store data locally. Making it difficult to securely access systems from off-site will encourage users wanting to work from off-site to bring sensitive information home.[20]

There is another reason that this mentality is a more effective way to use systems: maintaining constant vigilance is an exhausting exercise in paranoia. Unless you are well-resourced and operating as part of a sophisticated, dedicated, security team, the paranoia required for effective security is simply not healthy.

---

[20] For further reading, *see* Whitten & Tygar, *Why Johnny Can't Encrypt,* PROCEEDINGS OF THE 8TH CONFERENCE ON USENIX SECURITY SYMPOSIUM (1999).

INTERVIEW: HACKER OPSEC WITH THE GRUGQ

Blogs of War (November 10, 2013)

John Little [Interviewer]: You blog and have given conference presentations on Hacker OPSEC. You started doing this before the recent NSA revelations [by Edward Snowden about pervasive data collection by the U.S. government] (and the general hysteria surrounding intelligence collection) but you were already warning hackers that states had superseded them as the internet's apex predator. In just a couple of years we've moved from the seeming invincibility of LulzSec, to high profile busts, and now onto serious concerns being raised about the every aspect of the internet's architecture, security models, and tools. Rock solid OPSEC is a refuge but maintaining it for long periods of time under significant pressure is very difficult. The deck is obviously stacked against anyone trying to evade state surveillance or prosecution so where do freedom fighters and those with less noble intentions go from here?

The Grugq: You raise a number of interesting points. I'll ramble on about them in a moment, but before that I'd like to clarify for your readers a bit about where I am coming from. Firstly, I am not a "privacy advocate", I am an information security researcher. My career in information security has been mostly focused around denial and deception at the technical level.

Recently, however, I became aware that this "fetishizing the technology" approach is simply not effective in the real world. So I turned to studying clandestine skills used in espionage and by illicit groups, such as narcotics cartels and terrorist groups. The tradecraft of these clandestine organizations is what I am trying to extract, inject with hacker growth hormone, and then teach to those who need real security: journalists; executives traveling to adversarial environments; silly kids making stupid life altering mistakes, etc.

The media has actually expressed a lot of interesting in improving their security posture, and I am engaged in helping some journalists develop good OPSEC habits. Or at least, learn what those habits would be, so they have some idea of what to aspire to. There is a strange intransigence with some who reject improved security with the line: "but we're not criminals! Why do we need this?" Well, the only answer I have is that OPSEC is prophylactic, you might not need it now, but when you do, you can't activate it retroactively. As I phrased it in my "The Ten Hack Commandments"—be proactively paranoid, it doesn't work retroactively.

So, that's how I've arrived at hacker tradecraft, and where I'm trying to take it. On to the issues you've raised about good OPSEC and living a clandestine life.

The stress of the clandestine lifestyle is something that people tend to gloss over all too easily. This is an observation that comes up frequently in the literature about terrorist groups, espionage agents, and revolutionaries. There are a lot of compound issues which combine to make this sort of "good OPSEC" lifestyle very unhealthy for the human mind:

1. Isolation
2. Compartmentation of the ego
3. Paranoia related stress

Isolation provides the strongest security, and all good security involves a significant investment in maintaining a low profile, "going underground", "off the grid", etc. This means that the clandestine operative has reduced visibility over the social and political landscape, and their telemetry will suffer. Degraded telemetry means they will be unable to self-correct and reorient to what is happening around them. If they are part of a cell, a group of operatives in communal isolation, they will tend to self reinforce their ideology. Effectively radicalizing and distancing themselves further from the mainstream norms of society. This additional isolation can create a feedback loop.

If the operative isn't living a completely isolated clandestine lifestyle in their Unabomber cabin, they will have to isolate parts of their individual selves to compartment the different aspects of their lives. There will be their normal public life, the one face they show to the world, and also a sharded ego with their clandestine life. Maintaining strict compartmentation of the mind is stressful, the sharded individual will be a sum less than the total of the parts.

As if that wasn't enough, there is the constant fear of discovery, that the clandestine cover will be stripped away by the adversary. This leaves the operative constantly fretting about the small details of each clandestine operational activity. Coupled with the compartmentalization of the self, the operative also has to stress about each non-operational activity, will this seemingly innocent action be the trigger that brings it all crashing down?

Seriously, maintaining a strong security posture for prolonged periods of time is an extremely stressful and difficult act. Operatives working for the intelligence agencies have a significantly easier time of it than those on the other side of the protection of the state: e.g., their agents; hackers; terrorists, and narcos. The "legal" operatives have peers that they can confide in and unwind with thanks to the protections of the nation state. The true clandestine agents must be guarded with their peers, the public and the adversary. Any peer might be an informant, either now or in the future. Opening up and being friendly with their peers is part of what lead to the unraveling of the lulzsec hacker group. [. . .]

John Little: There is a significant amount of paranoia circulating in hacker and activist communities right now. How much of it is justified? More importantly, how should people go about conducting a realistic personal risk assessment before they start piling on layer after layer of

OPSEC? How can they strike that balance between the tedium and isolation and security that is "good enough"?

The Grugq: There is certainly a great deal of paranoia, some of it justified, some of it unjustified, and some of it misdirected. I think it is important to remember that paranoia is unhealthy, it is paralyzing, it is divisive, and it is harmful to operational effectiveness. The goal to aim for is caution. Allowing the adversary to inflict paranoia on you, or your group, gives them an easy psychological operation "win." So let's drop the paranoia and figure out what security precautions we must take in order to operate safely and effectively.

As you bring up, the core to effective security is performing a risk assessment, deciding what information is most important to protect, and then developing mitigation strategies to safe guard that information. There are books and manuals that go into this in great depth, so I won't spend a lot of time on the details.

A risk assessment should focus on the most high impact items first. To determine this, you list your adversaries and group them by intent and capability. So the NSA would have a very high capability, but probably has a low intent of targeting you. Then you make a list of information about your secrets, what you are trying to protect, and group that based on the negative impact it would have if it were in the hands of an opponent. The most damaging information must be protected from the likely and the most capable adversaries.

QUESTIONS

1. How would you describe "thinking about security" versus "thinking security?" Why is "thinking security" a more effective model for implementing cybersecurity?

2. The hacker mindset includes breaking apart technology, finding gaps in process, even misleading people to fulfill some goal. The concept of "security in depth" is designed to implement a security architecture that promotes layered security. How might security in depth counter static thinking about security?

4. THE BUSINESS OF CYBERSECURITY

The interview with the Grugq excerpted above captures one aspect of the isolation and mental toll required to maintain a state of defensive security. On the other side of the table, those engaged in the business of attacking—and it is increasingly a business, especially outside of the realm of national security and nation-state actors—is similarly droll.

Consider the following excerpt, which reflects, and builds on, the discussions throughout this chapter:

BEN COLLIER, RICHARD CLAYTON, ALICE HUTCHINGS, AND DANIEL R. THOMAS, *CYBERCRIME IS (OFTEN) BORING: MAINTAINING THE INFRASTRUCTURE OF CYBERCRIME ECONOMIES*

WEIS (2020)

2. Tools and skills: the mainstream view of cybercrime

The typically-conceived picture of cybercrime actors in the research literature from the 1990s onwards has focused on the idea of the 'hacker'. Indeed, much criminological scholarship has used the terms hacking and cybercrime interchangeably. We much prefer to separate these terms, with 'hacking' a set of practices and cultural sensibilities relating to obscure tinkering, technological exploration, engagement in law-making around technology, the creation of novel 'rebel infrastructures', political tool-breaking, and civil disobedience. These activities, although often portrayed as 'deviant', are not necessarily illegal. In contrast, many of the illegal online activities which constitute cybercrime require little technical creativity or skill, and have tenuous links to the rich subculture which surrounds hacking. Much cybercrime scholarship elides the broader aspects of 'hacking', and as a result, the portrayal of those who commit cybercrime as hackers has impacted how cybercrime has been understood by researchers and policymakers. We believe this conflation of the two communities has contributed to romanticised notions of the capabilities, the skills and some of the motivations of those who take part in cybercrime.

[. . .]

In terms of organisation, the 'classic' model of cybercrime communities has moved from a 1980's view that cybercrime is committed by highly-skilled individual actors (demonised as 'superusers') to a more top-down, or concentric, view of large subcultures of 'script kiddies' clustered around small numbers of genuinely skilled individuals. Cultural capital in the underground hacker scene is still very much linked to the cultivation of technical prowess (sometimes known as '1337' or 'elite' status). A (very) small core of actors actually develop exploits, a slightly wider group package up, monetise and distribute them, a large group of 'skids' use these packages and scripts, and yet larger groups (who aren't really technical at all) coalesce at the edges of these communities, purchasing services, running scams, performing other kinds of work (such as graphic design) and reselling products.

This has been described in previous criminological research as the 'cyber kill-chain'. These communities have existed in a range of different online spaces, which have proven fruitful sites for criminological research. Over time, driven by technological change, these online cybercrime spaces have moved from dial-up bulletin boards and IRC channels to web-based cybercrime forums, to open chat channels on Discord and Telegram, with actors maintaining a presence on social media channels such as Facebook and Twitter. While actors in these communities are perceived as responsible for high volume, low value/harm crimes, these are punctuated by small specialised groups or teams (who occasionally have links to state security services) who perform low volume, high harm attacks.

A wide set of motivations have been posited to explain participation in cybercrime economies. These revolve around the pursuit of profit, subcultural acclaim, social capital, and political goals. The perceived profits to be made may be an illusion created by overestimating the amount of cybercrime or aspirational (much as drug dealers tend to live with their parents). Importantly, these motivations are extended to include factors that are neither economic nor acquisitive—that persist regardless of failure, outlay, or risk. It is clear from the extensive literature on the (often non-criminal) computer hacker culture that many take part in these activities primarily for the enjoyment and excitement of the process of re-purposing, experimenting with, and building computer systems and—when combined with political activism—society. The motivations of those in hacker subcultures, for example, have been extensively studied by anthropologists, sociologists, and criminologists, and these (as will become clear) yield important insights for understanding these behaviours.

However, there is one important aspect that has been largely neglected in prior research. This undue focus on excitement, glamour, and prestige comes at the expense of understanding the dull and tedious nature of much of the work in which these actors are engaged. Most previous criminological research that has explored boredom and anomie have framed them as an initiator for crime, particularly functionalist and subcultural accounts of involvement in illicit economies, which frame crime as an exciting diversion from work or adolescence within the tedium of capitalist societies. Some work within cyber-criminology has explicitly used this to explain involvement in cybercrime communities. Conversely, we argue that as these illicit economies have grown and become more formalised, so has much of the work involved become equally rote and tedious—the underground equivalent of an office job. While prior research has not examined in detail the boring, tedious and mundane aspects of cybercrime, Meyer's (1989) classic work on the social organisation of underground bulletin board systems noted:

> Pirated commercial software is very rare; any programs that are available are usually noncopyrighted specialized programs used to automate the more mundane aspects of phreaking or hacking.

Cybercrime communities effectively provide a tool/skill-sharing economy, where skill-sharing takes place through creation of tools, scripts, and methods which are packaged up and can be used by others with lower levels of technical skill, or through directly contracting services through one-to-one agreements. Entry to these communities is no longer limited to those with technical skill, but now allows in those with the resources to purchase services, sometimes on a subscription basis. While they may sound glamorous, providing these cybercrime services require the same levels of boring, routine work as is needed for many non-criminal enterprises, such as system administration, design, maintenance, customer service, patching, bug-fixing, account-keeping, responding to sales queries, and so on. In the following section, we discuss this service economy in more depth.

QUESTIONS

1. This excerpt describes an increasingly organized, business-like, culture in which "hacking" (in the pejorative sense) has taken on the characteristics of a "boring" office job. What has contributed to this transition? Why would someone take an entry-level job as a hacker?

2. Who do these hackers work for? Other hackers? Non-hackers interested in the offensive hacking services they offer?

3. Compare this excerpt to those from The Hackers's Manifesto and TheHackerGiraffe, and Steve Bellovin's "Threat Matrix," all discussed earlier in this chapter. Do these tell complementary stories about who hackers are and why they do what they do?

CHAPTER 5

TECHNICAL FOUNDATIONS

■ ■ ■

This Chapter covers some foundational material regarding the theory and design of computing (and, therefore, computers and information systems). It is not designed to make non-technical readers "experts" nor to provide a comprehensive overview of relevant foundational topics for cybersecurity. Rather, the purpose is to introduce readers to foundational aspects of computing which *govern* modern computing systems—with an eye to helping readers understand the capabilities and limits of those systems.

A. COMPUTERS

Engineering is about understanding and designing systems, and efficiently designing and implementing systems subject to constraints. Computer science is, in this vein, a "pure" engineering field—or, if you will, an engineering science—in that the constraints under which problems are engineered are often those that are endogenous, or specific and internal to the problems, as opposed to those externally imposed. What this means will be considered in more detail in the discussion of computability, below. We start with discussion of the canonical problem of computer science: searching and sorting, which helps frame one of the most important—if not the defining—characteristics of computer science.

1. SEARCHING & SORTING—COMPLEXITY

At a fundamental level, a computer is quite literally what the root of its name suggests—a device which completes math problems by computation. In the case of binary computing (which comprises the overwhelming majority of extant computing technologies as of 2020), this is exactly one type of math—binary arithmetic—which essentially is adding and subtracting "1s" and "0s".

A common question for non-engineers at this point is—how do 1s and 0s make an app appear on my screen? This is a very important question, not so much for understanding how binary arithmetic can be extended to conduct advanced linear algebra, vector graphics, and therefore a fancy user interface, but rather because it tells us something important about understanding how computers work: *they do math.*

The faster and more efficient a computer can solve math problems, therefore, the "more" it can do. Humans do something similar. We also break down much of what we do into "math"—we just use much more complicated math, often involving proxies we have difficulty describing with language. (Remember the last time you tried to give someone directions to your home?)

The challenge comes with trying to do math of increasing scale. Vastly oversimplified, the more a computer program (or, in modern parlance, an "app") must do, the more "math" needs to happen. On its face, this seems fairly straightforward—if you want to design an app to give directions for a geographic area twice as large, you need twice as much computing power, right? Well, not quite. Searching and sorting (which really are specific instances of one another) don't scale linearly. Consider a very simple example. How long, or how many "moves", does it take to arrange in ascending order a line of balls numbered 1 through 100?

The most basic human approach would be simply to scan the line one ball at a time, move that ball to its correct "slot", and then do the same for the next unsorted ball. In the best case, this takes 100 operations—examining each ball, seeing that it is already in its correct slot, and moving on to the next one. Of course, the best case is uninteresting, because we live in a world of averages.

The average case is much worse. In the average case, you need to move each ball approximately half the length of the list. This means that each ball needs "*n* divided by 2" (n/2) operations to get it into its correct slot—one "operation" for each "move" from the incorrect slot to the correct slot. This then must be done n times—once for each number. This means the whole list takes (n/2)*n (or $n^2/2$) operations to sort.

For the moment (unless you love math), don't worry about the proof. But do think about the implication: sorting 100 numbers takes about 5,000 operations. How long does it take to sort 200 numbers? ***20,000 operations***. Doubling the problem size results in a problem that takes four times as long to solve. Doubling the size of the list again (to 400 numbers), sorting would require an average of 80,000 operations; and again to 800 numbers, sorting would require an average of 320,000 operations. Increasing the size of the list by a factor of 8 has increased the average time it takes to sort the list by a factor of 64.

Sorting—and many similar problems—is characterized by diseconomies of scale. When the increase in scale (colloquially, "size") of a problem causes the processing or management of that problem to become less efficient *faster* than the rate at which the size increases, that's a diseconomy of scale. You may have heard of economies of scale, in which the addition of the next item to a problem "costs" less in processing or management than did the addition of the previous item. This is the opposite.

Again, think back to things humans do, like solving puzzles. If it takes someone eight hours to complete a 500-piece puzzle, how long will it take for them to complete a 1000-piece puzzle? The intuitive answer is twice as long (16 hours). In practice, however, it will take closer to four times as long. This is a result of diseconomies of scale. Individuals who have developed sophisticated ways to put puzzles together may be able to reduce the time that it takes for them to solve a puzzle—but even the most skilled puzzle solver will always take more than twice as long to solve a puzzle of one size compared to another of similar difficulty that is half that size.

This means that, for computers, bigger and more complex problems are exponentially more difficult and time-consuming than you might expect. Advanced systems, such as artificial intelligence applications, therefore require substantial and often distributed architectures to power them. Further, this means that security controls for certain systems may 1) be difficult to implement and 2) may affect system performance. Encryption, as you will read about later in this chapter, often is a high-complexity and expensive implementation that simultaneously affects system efficiency. It is important to keep these concepts in mind, as the incentives for an engineer building a system might be different than for a security practitioner recommending a course of action. Although security is not the enemy of efficiency, their differing goals may complicate decisions related to systems when technology, business, and legal perspectives are considered.

For example, the process of encrypting or decrypting data to be used in some application may take time. Some systems store certain frequently used data, such as the results of a query, in a type of temporary storage (often called a *cache*). This helps make future queries, such as a request for the same report, more efficient. If encryption is needed, however, data cannot be stored in cache for easy retrieval because the benefits of the easy-to-access cache would be reduced or eliminated by the cost of encryption and decryption each time the cache is accessed. Although security controls like encryption will be useful in many cases, in other cases such controls may be expensive to implement and cause other technology challenges.

2. COMPUTABILITY AND COMPUTERS

Researchers have been studying algorithms since well before the advent of the modern computer. Discussion of the modern theory of algorithms generally starts with a puzzle posed by a German mathematician David Hilbert in 1900: he asked his colleagues whether it was possible to develop a step-by-step process (that is, an algorithm, though he did not use that term) to solve a certain type of mathematical problem. At the time no such process was known, and the purpose of his posing the question was to encourage people to try to develop such a method.

Over the following decades, mathematicians intensively studied the general question of how to develop algorithms to solve such problems. In general, this work proceeded by developing specific algorithms to solve specific problems. Over time, mathematicians began to realize that these algorithms tended to share common features in how they were specified. This observation eventually gave way to an insight known as the *Church-Turing Thesis*, named after papers published by Alonzo Church and Alan Turning (both in 1936). Roughly stated the Church-Turing Thesis is that there are some problems that have solutions that can be implemented through a formally specified series of steps (that is, an "algorithm").

This is a *very* abstract concept, but it is also very powerful. It leads to two fundamental conclusions. First, if you understand how to do all of the formally specified steps that any given algorithm may use, then you can implement *any* algorithm. Alan Turing's greatest claim to fame is that he imagined that it was possible to design a machine that is capable of implementing all such steps. Such a machine was called a Universal Turing Machine. In theory, such a machine would be able to execute *any* algorithm that could be developed. Today we call these computers. Prior to Turing, each problem was believed to potentially unique, having a unique approach to being solved. Turing told us that every problem that could be solved would be solved in a general way. Instead of needing to have one machine to solve each problem, we could have one machine that can solves all solvable problems.

Second, the Church-Turing Thesis tells us that some problems cannot be solved by algorithms.

That may seem like a simple proposition—of course there are some things that a computer cannot do! But it gives rise to a fascinatingly complex question: *what problems cannot be solved by an algorithm*? Indeed, using the tools developed by Turing, it was eventually proven that the question posed by David Hilbert in 1900 is one such problem: researchers spent over 70 years trying to provide a solution to Hilbert's problem before someone proved definitively that the "solution" was that there is no solution.

3. ALGORITHMS

As described in Section 5.A.1, computers are so-called because they compute. But computers must have some instructions for *how* to compute. Computers make decisions based on *code*, or instructions created by a human programmer. Code may instruct a computer to make a decision using computer logic, or "if X, then Y" statements. For example, the code may direct the computer "if user clicks on 'Submit' button, log their information in the database as submitted and display the 'Success' page." Because human language is designed to communicate complex ideas, including symbols, attitudes, tone, and a variety of other intonations (including artistic expression). Human language is, to some degree, ornamental, symbolic, representative, and inefficient. Computer code gives instructions to a computer using language the computer can read that is more efficient. However, computers cannot read all code. Code types are a type of language, and if the computer has not been designed with that code in mind or does not store any short-hand indices that will help the computer translate, it will not be able to compute. For example, software written for a Mac will generally not run (without changes or through an emulator) on a Windows-based system.

Algorithms, in their most simplistic form, are mathematical equations that are integrated in code. An algorithm calculates a result and the code gives instructions. These determinations are as simple as adding together the product cost on Amazon with the tax amount for a final amount to charge a customer, or as complex as making a recommendation of what product a specific customer should buy based on other customers' buying habits.

This is not a textbook on algorithms, or how to implement them. But it does help to *understand* them, what they are, and what they do. The examples of sorting a line of balls or doing a puzzle are examples of algorithms—admittedly very rudimentary ones. Many readers of this text probably already are thinking "but wait, I can do puzzles or sort balls MUCH faster than that!" Such instincts are correct. As you read through this section, remember that your goal is not to understand all the methods of formal proof nor to understand all the technical details of these aspects of mathematics. (While doing so will pay dividends later, as noted in the concluding paragraph, it is not a requirement.) What you *should* take away is an understanding of the depth of how difficult certain problems are, and just how much more difficult some problems are than others. The puzzle completion and ball sorting examples are excellent illustrations of this.

How does this happen? Are humans simply faster than computers? Not quite. What humans are doing is simply an adaptation of more efficient algorithms. Consider again how you assemble a puzzle. Many adages say "start with the corners" or "start with the edges." This not by accident! There is mathematical truth in those adages—they are simply more efficient algorithms (specifically, they're various modifications of tree structures and the merge-sort algorithm).

Let's consider the task of sorting a list or 100 numbers: a sorting algorithm is a series of steps that you can write out explaining how to accomplish this task. For example:

1. Start with a list of 100 numbers.
2. Find the smallest number in that list and move it to the end of the "result list" (the result list now has 1 number in it; and the list to be sorted has 99 numbers in it).
3. Repeat step #2 until to list to be sorted is empty.

This roughly mimics the approach that most people would take to sorting a list of numbers (imagine sorting a deck of cards, or a list of numbers written on a piece of paper).

Importantly, we can fairly precisely calculate how long it will take to perform this task: You need to go through a list of 100 numbers, then a list of 99 numbers, then a list of 98 numbers, then a list of 97 numbers, each time searching for the smallest number in the list. Adding all of these numbers up until there are no more numbers left in the list, you will need to effectively go through 5050 (the sum of 100+99+98+. . .3+2+1) items. (Compare this to the discussion in the previous section, where we said that sorting in this way takes about $n^2/2$ operations: 5050 is approximately equal to $100^2/2$.)

This three-step process for sorting numbers listed above is a prototypical algorithm. Algorithms are precisely specified processes for accomplishing some task—often for using or transforming an input and returning some output. A sorting algorithm takes a list of unsorted numbers, sorts them, and returns the sorted list. A simpler algorithm might provide the average value of a list of numbers. A more complex algorithm might take several months of weather observations and use them to identify the next several days of weather. The key is that each of these tasks is accomplished by a precisely specified set of instructions.

The fundamental goal of computer science is to figure out how to algorithmically accomplish various tasks, and then how to do so most efficiently. We will return to the first of these goals (how to algorithmically accomplish goals) below.

The number of instructions that it takes for a given algorithm to complete its task is referred to as its "complexity." In computer science "complexity" is an important term of art: there are formal methods for measuring and expressing the complexity of various algorithms. For instance, the sorting algorithm above has complexity of $O(N^2)$, which means that sorting a set of N inputs takes approximately N^2 "instructions." This notation is referred to "Big-O" notation, which refers to measuring the "Order of magnitude" of an algorithm's complexity.

We don't actually care how long a given "instruction" takes or how it is defined. What we care about is how the number of instructions required for the algorithm to complete changes as the size (N) of the input increases. This is because we generally use computers so solve "large-N problems"—

that is, problems using very large input sets. We don't need computers to search or sort lists of 10 or 100 numbers; we use them to search of sort lists of thousands or millions or billions of numbers. Complexity doesn't matter when we're using a computer to tell us the temperature outside (that is, to read the temperature from a single thermometer (N=1)); it matters when we're using computers to use a billion temperature readings from 1000 thermometers taking measurements 1000 times a day over a three-year period to predict weather trends (N=1,000,000,000).

It is possible, for instance, to implement a sorting algorithm with $O(N^2)$ complexity (as we did above), with O(N log(N)) complexity (described below), or even $O(2^N)$ complexity (which we will not describe). The $O(N^2)$ algorithm would take approximately 35,000,000 times as long to sort a list of one billion numbers as an O(N*log(N)) algorithm would. An $O(2^N)$ algorithm would take billions of times longer than that.

Can we improve our $O(N^2)$ sorting algorithm? You bet! To see one of many ways how, let's start by noting something about a related algorithm: "merging" two lists of a total of N pre-sorted numbers can be complete in O(N) time. The algorithm to do this is straightforward: start with the first number in each input list and move the smallest one to the output list; repeat until both lists are empty. The limitation on this "merge" algorithm is that it requires the input lists to be sorted. But here's the trick: an input list of a single number is always "sorted" (that is if you sort the input list of "1", the return list will be "1").

We can use this to turn a "merge" function into a "sort" function. Break the input list of N numbers into N/2 lists each with only two numbers in them, and merge each of those two numbers into N/2 sorted lists of numbers; then combine those N/2 lists of sorted numbers into N/4 pairs and merge them together. Each pass through this algorithm has an overall complexity of O(N), and you will need to complete a total of $\log_2 N$ passes. For those who are not mathematically inclined, you need only know that $\log_2 N$ is dramatically smaller than N, especially for large values of N. For a list of 16 numbers, this "merge sort" requires 4 complete passes through this list of numbers being sorted; for a list of 30, 5 passes; a list of 250 numbers requires 8 passes; a list of 1,000,000 numbers requires 20 passes, and a list of 4,000,000,000 numbers requires only 32 passes to completely sort. Adding in the O(N) cost of the merge function, Table 1 below compares the time required to complete a merge sort and the original sort function described above:

N	O(N)	O(log N)	Original Sort ($O(N^2)$)	Merge Sort (O(N log N) N))
16	16	4	256	64
32	32	5	1024	160
250	250	8	62500	2000

. . .	. . .	. . .	. . .	. . .
1,000,000	1,000,000	20	1,000,000,000,000	20,000,000
1,000,000,000	1,000,000,000	30	1,000,000,000,000,000,000	30,000,000,000
4,000,000,000	4,000,000,000	32	16,000,000,000,000,000,000	128,000,000,000

Table 1: Comparison of number of operations required for bubble vs. merge sorting

The complete operation of a merge sort of a list with 16 numbers in it is depicted in the figure below:

Input:	84	23	23	63	38	43	57	90	12	43	11	78	32	34	78	39
Pass 1:	23	84	23	63	38	43	57	90	12	43	11	78	32	34	39	78
Pass 2:	23	23	63	84	38	43	57	90	11	12	43	78	32	34	39	78
Pass 3:	23	23	38	43	57	63	84	90	11	12	32	34	39	43	78	78
Pass 4:	11	12	23	23	34	34	38	39	43	43	57	63	78	78	84	90

Table 2: Merge Sort Complete Operation

Do not worry if the details of the merge sort do not make sense to you. While it will pay dividends to spend some time trying to understand it, it is not our goal to teach you the details of any specific algorithm. Rather, our goals at this point are more modest: to demonstrate the importance and challenges of efficiently designing algorithms, to introduce you to some of the terminology of complexity, and to show how difficult and counterintuitive algorithm design can be. Who would have ever thought that an efficient "sort" algorithm could be built using nothing but a series of "merge" algorithms?

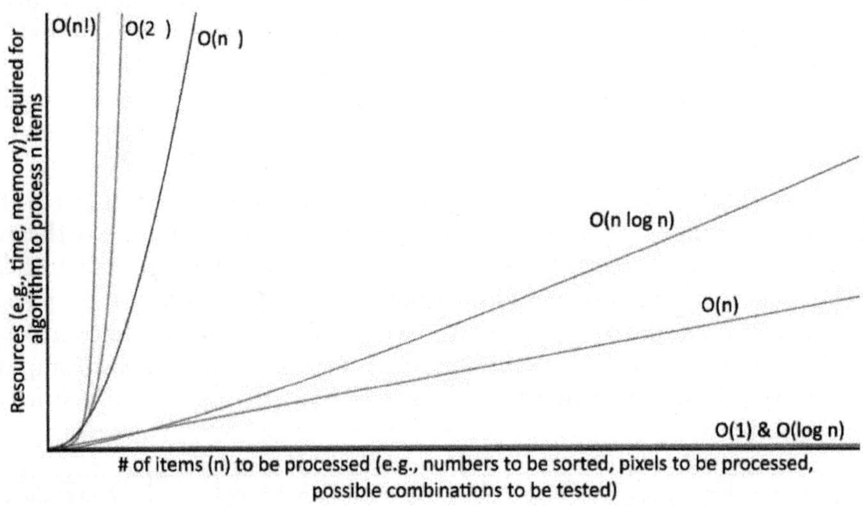

Figure 1: Operation Complexit

QUESTIONS

1. Why might you expect algorithms, and overall complexity, to matter for cybersecurity?

2. Why do you think it is "hard" to build programs/apps (i.e., to "solve problems with computers")?

3. What do you anticipate some differences might be between the goals of building efficient systems and building secure systems?

4. THE HALTING PROBLEM

Perhaps the most surprising—and, for cybersecurity, important—example of the challenge of complexity is found in the "halting problem." The halting problem is a fairly theoretical concept, so if you are not scientifically inclined, please bear with us. The halting problem explains why we cannot simply "invent" silver bullet cybersecurity software that will identify and find all vulnerabilities in a program. In fact, it's more than not knowing how to build such a program. *It is actually impossible to do so.*

The goal of the halting problem is to determine whether any given algorithm (or computer program) will ever finish running (that is, "halt"). It turns out that one cannot write a generalized algorithm to test whether other algorithms will ever finish running.

Consider the flowing algorithm:

```
variable x=1
while x is greater than zero
    x=x+1
exit
```

Will this algorithm ever reach the exit instruction? It is straightforward to walk through it and see that it will not: it will get stuck in an "infinite loop," repeatedly and indefinitely incrementing the variable x by one.

But while it is reasonably easy for a human to recognize that this is what will happen, Turing demonstrated that it is actually impossible to write a single program that will recognize all problems such as this![62] Rather, Turing proved that, in the general case, the best that you can do is prove that *some* algorithms that may halt will halt, and you can only do this by testing every possible configuration of the algorithm to see if it does in fact halt in each configuration.

Why does it matter whether we can prove whether any give program can halt? Halting is a specific, objectively identifiable, conclusion for a program to reach. **If we are unable to be sure that any given program will halt, we are consequentially unable to tell whether that program will or will not reach any other result**. Will a sorting algorithm ever return a sorted list? If it does, will that list, in fact, be sorted? For specific algorithms we may be able to design algorithm-specific tests. But there is no general-purpose way to test any given algorithm.

To turn to a security-related example, will an algorithm designed to password-protect a file actually protect that file? The halting problem tells us that we cannot prove that such an algorithm necessarily works! This means, simply, that it is impossible to prove that a system is secure. In a defensive security example, will an algorithm ever cause "damage" to a system? The halting problem tells us that we cannot use an automated process to prove whether a new piece of code will terminate, and therefore we cannot determine whether it will "do any damage" before it halts. (By the way, this is why detecting malware is so hard!)

What's more, even if we can determine that an algorithm does not work as intended, it may be exceptionally difficult to determine where or what the problem is. This is in part because algorithms can easily be very complicated, running thousands of even millions of instructions; and it is in part because all of those instructions are interrelated, both to themselves and to the computer that they run on. A trivial-seeming change in one part of a program can have very substantial effects in other parts of the program.

This is perhaps best seen by example. To start, consider how may lines of computer code we encounter every day. The F-22 fighter's control computers have 1.7 million lines of code; a Boeing 787's computers have 14 million lines of code; the Linux operating system has well over 16 million lines of code; recent Windows operating systems have over 45 million lines of code; and many modern luxury cars have over 150 million lines of code. In principle, a trivial error can lead the entire system to fail or, worse, to operate, but operate incorrectly.

Consider the following real-life examples:

- In 2014, a security researcher discovered a bug in a program called Bash. The bug, called "Shellshock", had existed since 1989—25 years—and could be exploited by any user on the system in order to obtain administrative privileges. This program is a basic part of most Unix-based operating systems, and has been since the mid-1980s. Tens of millions of computers, including most servers running the majority of web sites and critical infrastructure, were affected by this bug.
- Swiss trains must not have exactly 256 axles, because that will cause the computers that manage the tracks to fail to recognize the presence of a train.
- In December 2016 the FAA issued an airworthiness directive for the Boeing 787, requiring operators to reboot the plane at

least once every 22 days. This was in response to an undetected problem in the 787's flight control modules (that is, computers) that could cause all three of the computers that manage the plane's aerodynamics to reboot simultaneously. This was actually the second time the FAA issued an airworthiness directive requiring operators to periodically reboot their airplanes: in 2015 it was discovered that the 787 could lose all power if its computers had been running continuously for 248 days.

- Over a 15-year period, a programming error caused Citibank's computer systems to miscategorize 26,810 transactions, resulting in them not being reported to the SEC.
- In 1983 the Soviet Union almost launched a world-ending nuclear strike against the United States after a Soviet computer system mis-identified sunlight reflecting being reflected by clouds over the United States as a launch of US missiles against the Soviet Union.

5. MODULARITY

The ability of organizations to manage a larger complex system in smaller, self-contained pieces, is called modularization. A variety of technologies are designed to be modularized, including computers. For example, if your brake pads are worn down on your vehicle, you don't rebuild the entire vehicle. You just replace the brake pads with the appropriately sized replacement. To evaluate all patients and their history might be useful in some circumstances, but not necessarily when the individual presents symptoms of a standard cold. A modularized computer system achieves many of the same goals. Below, Christopher Yoo will discuss the role of modularity in more detail.

CHRISTOPHER YOO, *MODULARITY THEORY AND INTERNET REGULATION*

2016 U. ILL. L. REV. 1 (2016)

I. Introduction

Recent debates over Internet policy have proceeded from the premise that the Internet's success has stemmed in large part from its architecture and that this architecture must be preserved if that success is to continue. The current debate over network neutrality provides an apt illustration of these dynamics. The Open Internet Order that the D.C. Circuit struck down in January 2014 lauded how the network "architecture enables innovators to create and offer new applications and services without needing approval from any controlling entity, be it a network provider, equipment manufacturer, industry body, or government agency," which in turn permits "new technologies to be developed and distributed by a broad range of sources, not just by the companies that operate the network." Although the details of the revised Open Internet Order currently pending before the Federal Communications Commission has not yet been released, most expect that the new order will follow the same line of reasoning.

Commentators generally agree that modularity, the partitioning of a system into subsystems that are structurally independent but work together, represents one of the key architectural principles around which the Internet was designed and to which it owes much of its success. Computer scientists almost universally discuss modularity almost exclusively in laudatory terms and rightfully so. The shift to modularity played a critical role in triggering the explosion in computer technology since the mid-1960s. Indeed, as will be subsequently discussed at greater length, it represents the primary mechanism for making complex systems tractable. Furthermore, the current modular architecture has proven incredibly resilient and robust over a period spanning several decades.

That said, recognizing that modularity provides substantial benefits still leaves a host of questions unanswered. For example, is modularity always the best choice? If not, under what circumstances is modularity optimal and suboptimal? The absence of such a theory overlooks the fact that "neither modular designs nor interdependent designs are inherently superior." On the contrary, engineering principles recognize that no one architecture does everything well and thus, that every architecture necessarily involves tradeoffs. Assessments about the relative merits of particular modular schemes require evaluating the forces resting on each side of this balance in any particular context.

Moreover, even when modularity is desirable, there are many possible ways to modularize a system. Any designer of a modular system must decide how many modules to create, which design elements should be assigned to each module, where the interfaces between modules should be located, and how the interfaces between the modules should be configured. Identification of those determinants allows policymakers to create a dynamic theory of architectural design by asking an equally important question: how does one recognize the conditions under which a modular architecture should change?

Unfortunately, the considerations underlying these decisions remain poorly understood. As one commentator has noted, "the design tradeoffs inherent in abstracting from physical resources are rarely acknowledged in the computing literature." Other commentators similarly observed that "there is little systematic research on how decision makers partition designs into modules and what . . . the risks [are] of partitioning incorrectly." As a result, the literature tends to treat modular architectures as immutable artifacts without providing any heuristics to help determine when change might be beneficial.

[. . .]

II. Modularity Theory Basics

Any assessment of whether a particular modular regime is socially desirable necessarily depends on having some theoretical framework for understanding why modularity exists and what benefits it provides.

A. Near Decomposition as a Solution to Complexity

The special challenges associated with developing complex systems are well illustrated by an anecdote related by Frederick Brooks in his celebrated book, The Mythical Man Month, which documents IBM's efforts to design System/360, the first fully modular family of computer systems. Consistent with the prevailing conventional wisdom that everyone working on a project should have access to all of the available information about the project, the managers of the System/360 team insisted that every programmer maintain a formal workbook documenting all of the other parts of the system. After only six months, the workbook was more than five feet thick and required one hundred and fifty pages of updates every day. This led to Brooks' famous observation that adding more people sometimes slows down projects instead of speeding them up. This results from the communication cost associated with keeping more people informed possibly exceeding the potential advantages of more man-hours and a greater division of labor.

The classic solution to this problem is implicit in Herbert Simon's landmark analysis of complex systems. Simon suggested that one of the best ways to reduce complexity is to decompose the overall system into a series of subsystems in which interactions within subsystems are relatively frequent and stronger, while interactions between subsystems are relatively rare and weaker. This allows subsystems to operate largely independently of one another in the short run, but to integrate into a larger complex system over the long run. Such a system would only be nearly decomposable rather than completely decomposable, as the fact that all of the subsystems were part of a larger system meant that some inter-connections between subsystems would necessarily remain. That said, interactions among subsystems would remain relatively weak, but nonnegligible.

Near decomposition of complex systems yields a number of advantages. As an initial matter, it makes complex systems easier to describe and comprehend. By creating a larger number of intermediate forms that can constitute building blocks for the larger system, near decomposition permits experimentation to occur on a smaller scale instead of with the system as a whole. The existence of stable intermediate forms also allows complex systems to evolve more rapidly.

A related insight emerges from the field of software engineering, which has modeled complex tasks into a series of abstract sequential processes.

Subdividing a larger process into a series of smaller subprocesses greatly facilitated software engineers' ability to verify the accuracy of the system by allowing them to test portions of the overall system in isolation. Similarly, design scholars have turned to near decomposition to deal with complexity of designs by organizing tasks into groups that are "interlinked, yet sufficiently free of one another to adjust independently in a feasible amount of time."

B. Interdependencies as a Determinant of Module Boundaries

To say that complex systems are more easily analyzed and developed if broken down into smaller subcomponents does not provide much information about how such a decomposition should be implemented. Consistent with Simon's observation that interactions should be frequent and strong within subsystems and rare and weak across subsystems, Carliss Baldwin and Kim Clark argue that the key to understanding the "points of natural division" between the elements of a modular architecture is task interdependencies. System architects must group tasks that have strong interdependencies with each other inside the same protomodule, and then must "systematically . . . sever all dependencies known to exist across the protomodules." This implies that a well-designed module is "a unit whose structural elements are powerfully connected among themselves and relatively weakly connected to elements in other units." The boundaries between modules are located at the "thin crossing points" where interdependencies are the thinnest. Design theorist Christopher Alexander similarly advocated including variables whose interactions are very rich within the same subset, thereby permitting the subsets to act relatively independently. Organizational theorist James Thompson advocated grouping reciprocally interdependent tasks together and relying on key positions to serve as bridges to other groups.

Encapsulating highly interdependent tasks within the same module also reduces the costs of communication and coordination by reducing the need for cross-boundary communication, with cheaper cross-group communication leading to a larger number of modules.

The initial modular design must be based on the architect's expertise. Establishing these basic design rules has the effect of privileging certain parameters and "declaring certain parts of the design space to be out of bounds." No matter how well system architects believe they understand the systems they are designing, they cannot fully understand the way the various components interact with one another until they gain experience with the system by experimenting with different solutions. If done badly, the proposed modularization can cause the system to perform suboptimally or may require a redesign of the architecture. In the worst case scenario, the interdependencies cannot be solved without redesigning the basic architecture, in which case the modularization will fail.

This means that modular systems are never designed in a vacuum. Redesigns of current modular systems are framed by the existing modularization. Even with respect to new modularizations, they must respond and adjust to the initial design proposed by the architect, which, because of the lack of perfect prescience, typically includes some interdependencies that the architect did not foresee. The recursive and restricted nature of this adjustment process means that modularization emerges more through a process of "improvisation, bricolage, and drift" than from "planification and control."

C. Interface Design and the Role of Abstraction and Hidden Information

Dividing a production process into blocks of interdependent processes is only one step in modularizing a system. In addition, the architects must structure the interactions between the modules. To do this, each module must be reduced to an abstraction, which is a simplification of reality "that suppresses details of elements that do not affect how [modules] use, are used by, relate to, or interact with other elements."

Once a system architect predetermines how the modules will interact with one another, the architect must ensure that the programmers working on each module refrain from introducing new interdependencies that fall outside of the design. Individual programmers who have access to all of the information about the entire system will be tempted to use that information to improve the performance of the module on which they are working. The problem, according to David Parnas' seminal work, is that doing so can "disastrously increase the connectivity of the system" by introducing connections between modules that violate the goal of keeping the intermodule interdependencies to a minimum.

Parnas identified an ingenious way to ensure that the architect retains control over the overall structure. Instead of making all of the design information available to everyone, Parnas argued that architects could maintain the architecture's integrity by maintaining strict control over the distribution of information across the system. Specifically, architects could carefully design the interfaces connecting modules so that they include only the information associated with the interdependencies that other modules were permitted to take into account and to withhold information about the module's inner working from the other modules. Information included in the interface is part of the visible information shared between modules; design parameters not included in the interface are part of the hidden information.

Hiding information about the highly interdependent tasks that are supposed to be encapsulated within modules makes those tasks opaque to other modules and thus prevents them from creating interconnections with those tasks that fall outside the architectural design. This permits other modules to treat every other module as a "black box," which greatly reduces communication costs. After the computer science community criticized Parnas' proposal as "radical" and unworkable, Parnas took it upon himself to validate the concept by undertaking a real-world implementation of it.

Interfaces thus establish the fundamental assumptions that the various modules in a system make about one another and predetermine the manner in which the modules will interact. As such, decisions about what information to include in module interfaces thus represent critical architectural choices that must be made deliberately. As one noted modularity theorist pointed out, "Managers should understand that component interfaces are not minor technical details to be left to the engineering staff. Rather, interfaces will determine the range of strategic flexibilities the company will have to configure its products and adapt its processes in the future." In other words, interface design determines the functionality of the system. Moreover, the points of interactions cannot be dealt with in an ad hoc manner. Instead, they must be maintained throughout the architecture in a consistent and systematic way.

Limiting the number of interdependencies that pass between modules and the number of states associated with those interdependencies of which other modules have to take account simplifies the complexity of the system. For example, interdependencies sometimes form a circuit that loops back onto itself, such as occurs when task A depends on the design of task B, which depends on the design of task C, which recursively depends on the design of task A. When this occurs, the only way to determine the effect of the interdependencies is to cycle through a series of iterations until the design converges on a solution. If the design architecture does not limit the number of interdependencies, system designers must test every possible combination of interdependencies, which can lead to a "combinatorial explosion of system variants" if left uncabined. Modularity reduces the number of cycles required by narrowing and predetermining the universe of potentially relevant interdependencies and states.

[. . .]

E. Testing and Integration

Another essential element of any modular design is a means for testing and system integration. Because any initial modular design is necessarily incomplete, the architects of any modular system must provide some way to ensure that the system is functioning properly and that each module is functioning in accordance with the overall design. Indeed, such tests constitute a necessary precondition to distributed production systems in which different modules are produced by different firms. In the words of Baldwin and Clark, "The testable, verifiable dimensions of the module are the foundation that supports arm's length-contracts and market transactions." Indeed, "without tests, there is no way to know what is being bought and sold."

The need to test each possible state one module can occupy against every possible combination of states that other modules can occupy represents what Baldwin and Clark have called the "Achilles' heel of modular designs." Without modularity, this problem would have been far worse. Dijkstra's seminal analysis concluded that under integrated, nonmodular architectures, "the number of 'relevant states' would have exploded to such a height that exhaustive testing would have been an illusion." The failure to limit the number of ways different components can interact with one another leads to a "combinatorial explosion of system variants."

If the only available tests operate at the system level, architects cannot escape the combinatorial explosion of states that must be tested against one another. Thus, when system-level tests are the only option, designers inevitably tend towards unmodularized, integrated designs and low levels of experimentation. The exponential nature of the combinatorial explosion means that this problem cannot be overcome simply by making system-level testing more rapid and less expensive.

The situation is quite different when tests can be conducted on individual modules. Restricting the number of interdependencies and the number of states associated with those interdependencies that other parts of the system must take into account dramatically reduces the number of combinations that must be tested. Module-level testing permits the evaluation of individual modules against the module metrics inherent in the design rather than the entire universe of possible combinations. Later studies have confirmed this insight, showing that the cost of testing grows sublinearly with the number of physical elements for modular architectures, whereas the cost of testing grows exponentially for integrated architectures.

The presence of robust module-level testing is thus a necessary precondition for any modular system in which different firms produce different components. Indeed, the ability to verify that each module is working as envisioned by the architecture is a necessary condition to third-party, distributed production of modular components. Over time, new design rules are created to address the out-of-module interdependencies revealed by the testing. Eventually, the design rules may become so complete that testing and system integration can be conducted by the module designers and end users or may even disappear. At this point, the architects will have modularized themselves out of a job.

III. The Benefits of Modularity

It is widely recognized that modular architectures provide a number of benefits. Dividing the overall system into a series of subsystems makes complexity more manageable. It accelerates innovation by allowing experiments on different parts of the system to proceed in parallel. It facilitates the division of labor across different work groups and firms. It increases value by allowing the postponement of key technical decisions. Lastly, it promotes flexibility by allowing individual modules to be changed without disturbing the other parts of the complex system.

A. Making Complexity More Manageable

Breaking down complex systems into subparts helps make them more manageable. As an initial matter, partitioning a large system into smaller modules divides the larger task into subtasks "small enough to be fully comprehend[ed] by a single individual." In this manner, modularity allows architects to work on individual modules in isolation without having to grapple with the architecture as a whole. Conversely, an architect can understand the overall system without having to understand the details of every module.

Moreover, the fact that the design architecture predetermines the relationships between modules makes the elements and functions of complex systems easier to describe and understand. One needs to know only the design rules defining the interactions with adjacent modules. The details of the interactions contained within modules can be ignored without losing any relevant information. Moreover, reducing the total number of interdependencies and organizing them in systematic, predictable ways yields particularly strong benefits in reducing the cost of testing programs.

QUESTIONS

1. Based on your basic learning about computers in this chapter, what challenges might you expect to face when making decisions about security in complex technologies?

2. Professor Yoo describes the relationship between modules and the bigger complex system. What do you think some of the practical challenges might be for preventing exploitation if systems are managed as modules rather than systems?

3. Every computer system is different, and from a business or legal perspective, you likely will not have the time to understand any particular system in detail. Practically speaking, how might you begin to understand a given system so that you can anticipate potential issues?

B. NETWORKS

This section introduces the concept of networks, building on the concept of modularity introduced in section 5.A.5. The approach taken is different from typical approaches to introducing these concepts to law and policy-focused audiences. The approach taken here is "bottom-up," starting with the architecture and history of networks, and using that to explain the development initially of packet-switching architectures and then the Internet. This stands in contrast to more common approaches that focus first on explaining the functionality of the Internet (a specific example of a network), including concepts such as IP addresses, and using exposition of the Internet as a specific example to illustrate more general concepts. As you read this section, consider what each of complexity and modularity might suggest regarding why your authors made the choice to use this "bottom-up" structure to explaining networks.

1. MODULES AND NETWORKS

The previous section introduced the idea of modularity to reduce the complexity of a computer system. The idea of modularity is also important to understanding networks.

At the risk of providing a circular definition, a network is a system of interconnected modules, and the critical aspect of a network is its connections between otherwise independent modules. Every module performs three basic functions: it receives inputs, it processes those inputs according to rules contained within the module, and it provides some output as a result of that processing. One module's output, however, can be connected to the input of another module, so this means that information or data coming from the output can be transmitted to another module and vice-versa. A set of modules connected together and working as a system is a network of modules.

Thus, we can think of the earlier merge sort example as a network of interconnected merge modules. Each merge module takes (as input) two lists of pre-sorted numbers and merges them (processes the inputs) into a single list of sorted numbers (which becomes the output). The merge sort works by connecting two merges of two numbers each to one merge of four numbers; then two merges of four numbers are connected with a merge of eight numbers; and two merges of eight numbers are connected on a merge of 16 numbers; et cetera. That is, the merge sort is a system of interconnected merge modules.

Modules and networks need not be made up of algorithms. For instance, a computer's keyboard is a modular device that converts key-strokes to electrical signals that are sent as inputs to a hardware component in your computer; that component receives those inputs and sends output signals to computer memory and to the CPU to alert it that keys have been pressed; the CPU then sends a signal to a program running on the computer to inform it that keystrokes are ready to be read from memory. Each of those components is a module.

As discussed in the last chapter, modular approaches to designing computer algorithms are powerful way to address concerns about complexity and computability. Modularity has other, more pragmatic, advantages as well. Because modules operate independent of one another, so long as each module adheres to a common protocol for communicating with other modules, modules can be substituted for one another. One model keyboard can be substituted for another model keyboard without needing to change the rest of the system. Software designed for one CPU module can run on any CPU module. Or different software modules can all run on a single CPU.

QUESTIONS

1. What new security risks to modularity create? Are these threats of vulnerabilities?

2. Does modularity create new opportunities to reduce risk?

3. What is the opposite of modularity? Are there security risks or advantages to avoiding modularity?

2. EARLY COMPUTERS AND NETWORKS

a. Computers

It is natural, especially given the modern, highly integrated, state of computers, to think of a "computer" as a single unit. In reality, every computer is a system of interconnected modules. A typical computer may include a display, non-volatile memory ("long term" storage like a "hard disk"), a processing unit, a keyboard, and a mouse. Each of these is a distinct module, interconnected with the other modules. In the case of a desktop computer, users can typically substitute any number of keyboards, mice, monitors, or other peripherals, interconnecting them to the processing unit. Even in more tightly integrated systems like laptops, phones, or tablets, these components are distinct, if often permanently attached or integrated.

The "processing unit" is also highly modularized, even in modern computers. If you open up a modern computer, you will find dozens of chips interconnected on a circuit board. Each of those chips is a module, performing a certain set of functions and interconnected with other chips performing their own functions. You are likely to find, for instance, a CPU (the main, or "central," processing unit) chip, chips for RAM, a chip responsible for video, one or more chips that handle networking, a chip that interconnects to the hard drive and other media—among other chips. Collectively, these chips are all interconnected into a network, allowing them to function collectively as a single computer.

Even the CPU is a highly interconnected network of discrete modules. If you were to peel away the plastic packaging surrounding the actual microchip that makes up a CPU and looked at that chip under a powerful microscope, you would be able to identify dozens of discrete modules: microcode, arithmetic logic units, cache memory, instruction pipelines, and many others. Today these components, each of which requires billions of transistors electrochemically etched into small wafers of silicon, are all part of a single integrated circuit.[1]

About fifteen years ago, a typical computer may have had nearly as many transistors and components, but these were spread out over an entire computer motherboard (about a square foot, compared to a square centimeter today). About thirty years ago, a typical computer would have been about the same size, but only had tens, or maybe hundreds, of millions of transistors.

Those computers, where all of the electronics were small and integrated enough to fit in a single case on or next to a desk, were called microcomputers. Their predecessors were larger. So-called minicomputers, which were state of the art in the 1970s, were typically comparable in size to a refrigerator. And *their* predecessors, what were once simply called computers and with the advent of minicomputers later were called mainframes, would fill rooms.

Mainframes and minicomputers did not have "central" processing units in the way that we think of CPUs in modern computers. In modern computers, the various modular functions all fit onto a single integrated circuit (IC) the size of a fingernail. In mainframes and minicomputers, these functions would be spread across several individual circuit boards contained in a large chassis (the refrigerator-sized box) and would all be interconnected via what is called a backplane—a switchboard for their boards. Larger systems would make up multiple separate chasses spanning several backplanes, and interconnected with bundles of cables.

At the time, the various components of these (mainframe and mini-) computers did not, at least in principle, need to be in a single room. Within the tolerances of the electrical requirements of the equipment (longer cables have greater resistance so both generate more heat and require greater voltages), a mainframe or minicomputer's RAM, hard drive, or output device (e.g., monitor or printer) could be in a different room or even building than the rest of the computer. Query how different this is from using a cloud-based storage service to store files on a computer today.

b. Multi-User Computers and Terminals

By the early 1960s, computers were being used for a range of purposes, primarily by government and academic institutions and increasingly for

---

[1] The first integrated circuit was developed in 1958 by Jack St. Clair Kilby, an engineer working for Texas Instruments. This circuit places a small number of electronic components—transistors and capacitors—on a small circuit board that could then be treated as a discrete component. The modern integrated circuit is generally traced to Intel's release of the 4004 microprocessor in 1971 (though another engineer, Gilbert Hyatt filed a patent for a similar integrated circuit in 1970). The 4004 microprocessor fit approximately 2250 transistors on a silicon wafer roughly the size of a finger nail. For an account of the development of the 4004 by the engineer most responsible for its design, *see* Federico Faggin, *The Making of the First Microprocessor*, 1 IEEE SOLID-STATE CIRCUITS MAGAZINE 8 (2009).

commercial applications. But they were exceptionally large and expensive. To maximize the opportunity for researchers to make use of them, and to maximize the value of these exceptionally expensive resources, these systems were increasingly designed as multi-user systems. Multi-user systems were designed so that multiple users could access the systems at the same time and could sometimes (and as technology continued to develop, always) run programs on the computers at the same time.

One of the ways that users would access these systems was through terminals. To a modern user, a "terminal" would appear to be nothing more than a keyboard and monitor. A terminal, however, is a little more complicated and is, in fact, somewhat closer to a very basic computer than to just a monitor and keyboard. With modern monitors and keyboards, the processing of what keys are being typed or images to display occurs on the computer: if you type a combination of keys (e.g., CTRL-F), the computer interprets that series of keys and turns it into a command, or the computer renders an image to display on the monitor and sends signals to the monitor that contain that image. A terminal, on the other hand sends and receives strings of text to and from the computer (see Figure 2). So, most importantly, the computer can only send text (not graphics) to the display and the display contains its own circuitry that is responsible for turning that text into signals that are then displayed on the screen. (This was largely due to technical limitations at the time.)

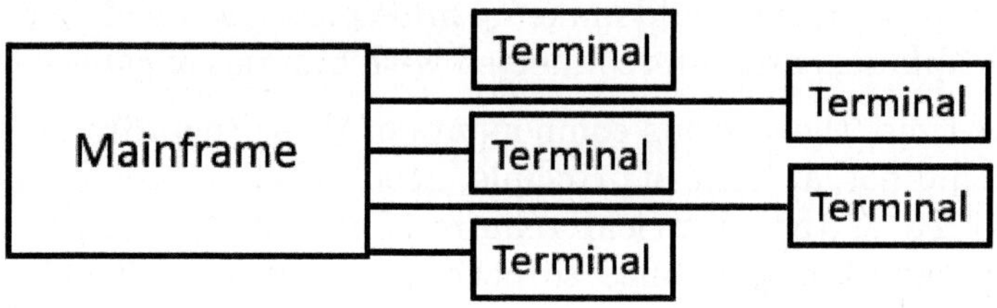

Figure 3: Mainframe Terminals

Because the logic for displaying the text being sent from the computer was hosted on the terminal, not the computer, terminals did not necessarily need to be installed in close proximity to the computer to which they were attached. Even a modern monitor, connected by a high-quality HDMI cable, needs to be within 15–20 feet of the computer to which it is attached in order to properly display the signal that it is receiving. (Recall that electrical signals degrade over distance.) But a terminal connected to a mainframe or minicomputer in the late 1960s could be in a separate room or even a separate building. Large mainframe systems could have dozens or even hundreds of terminals connected to them, spread across an entire research campus.

The ability to remotely connect terminals to a mainframe computer was pushed to its limits by a pair of researchers, Marill & Roberts, in 1965, when the connected a terminal located at MIT in Massachusetts to a mainframe computer located in California.[2] They obviously did not do this by running a long cable from Massachusetts to California. Rather, they connected their terminal in Massachusetts to the telephone network and used the telephone network to connect to the computer in California. This was the first example of what is today called a "wide area network"—and was arguably the origin of the modern concept of computer networking.

The key challenge that Marill & Roberts had to overcome was that the electrical connection between a terminal and mainframe—the interface by which these modules were interconnected—was different than that used to transmit signals between two telephones. This means that terminals could not be *directly* interfaced with a mainframe via the telephone network. Rather, Marill & Roberts used a device called a modem (a combination of the words MODulator/DEModulator) to translate the signals (i.e., modulate them) from the computer or terminal into signals that the telephone network transmit and then to translate those signals back (i.e., demodulate them) to signals with which the terminal and computer can interface (*see* Figure 1). We still use (much more sophisticated) modems today to translate signals from service providers into what can be interpreted by a router, and they are usually designed by the type of signal received.

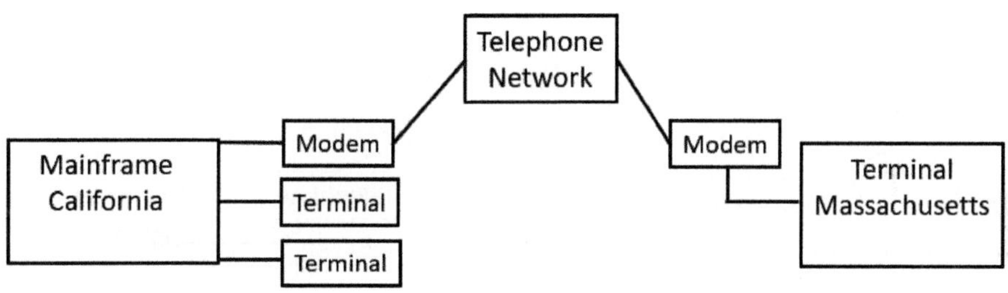

Figure 4: Communications Networks

The cross-country connection that Marill & Roberts established demonstrates a number of important concepts of modern communications networks.

Perhaps most important, the network is transparent from the perspective of the nodes communicating across it (in this case, that is, the terminal and mainframe). From the mainframe's perspective, it is directly connected to the terminal, and vice versa. There is nothing operationally different about how the mainframe communicates with this terminal and any other terminal, despite this terminal's being located several thousand miles away. (Note: in modern networking, operational differences, e.g., latency, can exist, however the complex "layered" approach to network

[2] Thomas Marill and Lawrence G. Roberts, *Toward a Cooperative Network of Time-Shared Computers*, Proceedings AFIPS Fall Joint Computer Conference 425 (1966).

management can control for these differences so they are largely invisible to the average end user. We discuss layering next.)

This is accomplished through a concept known as layering. This concept is simple but very powerful: interconnected modules do not care (or even necessarily know) what happens to information being sent between modules so long as it is received at its destination in the same form as it was sent. This means that communications between any two modules, regardless of how they are intended to be transmitted, can always be translated into another means of transmission without affecting the operation of the original two modules.[3] So long as this process is transparent to the modules (i.e., the signal is received by one modules exactly as it was transmitted from the other), this translation process should not affect the modules. It will always appear to the modules themselves that they are communicating with each other, as though directly interconnected.

In other words, from the perspective of the mainframe and terminal, each of the connections below are the functionally the same—in each case the mainframe and terminal appear to be directly connecting with each other. And, in principle, any number of additional layers could be inserted into this system, or alternatives swapped in, without any effect on the other layers.

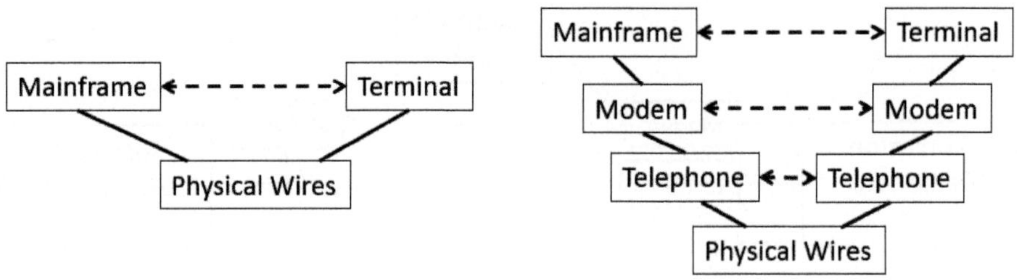

Figure 5: Layered Connections

A related concept is that these are "end-to-end" networks. In an end-to-end network, nodes at each end of the network (or at each layer of the network) appear to be communicating directly with each other. The rest of the network, at layers above and below the layer at which these "end" nodes are communicating with each other, is transparent from the perspective of these end nodes. (Note: each node is an "end" node from its own perspective, but is not necessarily an "end" from the user perspective—this is precisely what layering accomplishes.)

---

[3] One important limitation on this is that this translation process can't break the communications requirements between the modules. For instance, if the modules require near-immediate communications because they are engaged in high-speed processing (such as between a CPU and RAM), they likely would not operate well if placed at opposite sides of the country.

This implies several important considerations. First, nodes at any given layer *only* communicate with each other—they *do not* communicate with other layers of the network. Second, nodes at any given layer cannot expect any particular guarantees about the quality or even successful completion of communications between them. For instance, it is possible that background noise could cause errors to be introduced in the telephone-based communications between the mainframe and terminal—it is up to the mainframe & terminal (or the users thereof) to be cognizant of such errors.

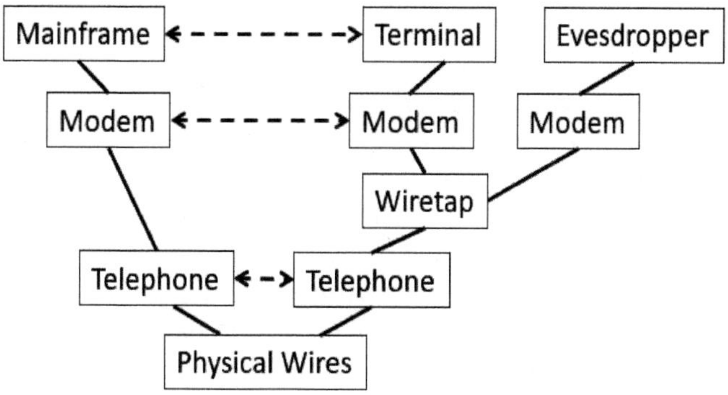

Figure 6: End-to-end Network

Third, an end-to-end network is inherently untrustworthy. It is possible, for instance, that any layer could be compromised by an attacker two could be surreptitiously monitoring, or even altering, communications. Or an attacker could even insert an additional layer into the communications channel, as below. Because the nodes at any given layer are presumed not to have visibility into any other layers, in an end-to-end network it is the responsibility of the nodes at each layer to be cognizant of and to take precautions against such concerns.

Importantly, not all networks are end-to-end or amenable to layering. For instance the myriad components that make up a computer—the CPU, memory, networking and video chips, and other components, are generally designed such that each is dependent on the precise operational characteristics of the others. Layering these components would break these dependencies and leave the components in uncertain (and likely non-functional) operational states.

But while not all networks have these characteristics, many, including the Internet and almost all communications networks do have these powerful concepts which are essential to our modern information society.

3. PACKET SWITCHING

a. The Need for Packet Switching

Marill & Robert's experiment to connect a terminal to a mainframe via the telephone network was a remarkable and important achievement. But it was also primarily a proof-of-concept and not a particularly practical way of interfacing with computers at the time. Indeed, the purpose behind their experiment was not to allow users to remotely access distant computers—it was to demonstrate that it would be possible for distant computers themselves to be remotely networked together so that multiple computers could function as a "cooperative network" to solve problems more effectively than a single computer could.

Practically, the approach taken by Marill & Roberts has important limitations.[4] Most important, the telephone network is designed for relatively long, sustained, periods of communication—that is, telephone calls. Generally, people spend the majority of their time while on a telephone call speaking. Even if much of the time in absolute terms is technically non-communicative (taking breaths, pausing between words, using filler words like "ah" and "um"), the majority of the time of the call would be characterized as "conversation." Communications with or between computers, on the other hand, is short and bursty, not long and sustained like a telephone conversation. When sitting at a computer terminal, for instance, a user is likely to type a small number of short commands and then receiving a screen of text in response; the user will then read that text, possibly think for a while, and then send more short commands. Even active terminal users spend only a small portion of their time actually sending commands to a remote computer. And at the same time, it generally does not make sense to go through the process of establishing a new connection to, and logging into an account on, a distant computer for each command you send. Rather, a user is more likely to let a terminal sit idle when not in use, only logging out of a given session once all work is completed.

These concerns are immediately compounded when you translate this to a multi-user computer. Remember that terminals were developed so that tens or even hundreds of users could simultaneously be connected to a mainframe or minicomputer, using that computer over the course of a day. It doesn't make sense to replicate this, in terms of technical architecture or economic cost, using the telephone-based model. If, for instance, a typical terminal is only sending or receiving data at a rate sufficient to saturate

[4] These limitations are particularly significant in the context of remote terminal access, where one user is remotely accessing the distant computer. The more general application that they were envisioning was not implemented as they envisioned, instead being overtaken by the development of packet-switched networking (as described presently). Their work, however, helped to set the stage for packet-switched networking.

1/50th of a telephone line's data capacity, it would make more sense to find a way for 50 users to share a single telephone line than for 50 users to connect to the remote computer using 50 separate phone lines.

The solution to this concern was the development of packet-switched networks.[5] The telephone network is a circuit-switched network, meaning that telephone switches establish a dedicated circuit or communications channel between two endpoints for the duration of the communication.[6] This is suitable for long, sustained, communications like telephone calls. Packet-switching, which routes messages in "chunks" over any valid available path, is better suited to computer-based communications, where most communications are short and bursty and there is a benefit to an "always-on" connection (e.g., so that you don't need to establish a new dedicated connection to the remote computer for each communications).

In a packet-switched network, each computer established a single connection to "the network." Packets destined for any computer on that network are sent to "the network," where they bounce around and find their way to the intended destination computer (more on that in a bit). So instead of having 50 terminals making 50 long-distance phone calls to a remote mainframe, those 50 terminals would make 50 local calls to the network, the mainframe would also be connected to the network, and that way the

---

[5] Readers playing close attention to the dates and familiar with the history of packet switching and the Internet may reasonably challenge the chronology being reported here: the initial concept of packet switching is generally attributed to Paul Baran Donald Davies (working independently) in 1962 and 1965, as well as more theoretically abstract (but equally foundational) work by Leonhard Kleinrock in 1961—before Marill & Robert's experiment was conducted. Baran & Kleinrock's work was undertaken through the Department of Defense and was influential within the Advanced Research Projects Agency (ARPA)'s Information Processing Techniques Office. Roberts & Marill's work was conducted under contract with this Office, with the purpose of demonstrating in initial viability of packet-based computer-to-computer communications. Prior to that point (and even after it) there was substantial belief within the communications research community—and especially among circuit-switched network researchers at Bell Labs—that packet-based communications was too unreliable to provide the basis for a useful communications network. The history recounted above focuses Marill & Robert's work because it crystalizes the technical architecture and need for packet-based communications so is logically antecedent to (and intuitively easier to understand) the development of packet switching, even if chronologically it was the theory of packet switching that drove Marril & Robert's applied work. It also bears some note that while Marill & Robert's is regarded as the first wide area network connection between computers. Computers had long used digital connections modulated with modems over telephone lines to communicate with remote devices. The best known example of this is the Air Force's SAGE system, which created a network of radar stations surrounding the United States to monitor objects entering its air space. This system made extensive use of dedicated telephone circuits to connect remote radar systems with regional monitoring facilities. These connections, however, were generally only used for single-direction communications and were not used for direct computer-to-computer communications. Finally, on that last note it is work recognizing that Marill & Robert's work actually directly connected to computers—not, as discussed above, a computer and a remote terminal. To the contrary, a special program was written to run on each computer to emulate the behavior of a terminal on either side of the telephone connection—an additional layer of detail that both does not affect the analysis offered above and in fact makes their work more impressive than it already is.

[6] For much of the history of the telephone network, until the advent of the transistor and then digital transmission in the 1960s, most telephone calls were completed by establishing a dedicated electrical circuit between telephones, hence the term circuit-switching.

terminals would be able to communicate with the mainframe as though they were directly connected to it.

This architecture allows for something else important: these 50 terminals will now be able to communicate with each other. So that one connection to the network now allows each terminal to communicate with the 50 other nodes on the network instead of just with the mainframe.

Graphically, this is frequently represented as a cloud. We can also represent it as a layered network. Contemporary readers may guess (correctly) that the "Modem" and "Telephone" layers in this layered diagram could be replaced by any number of communications technologies, from cable modems or fiber optics to mobile devices or satellites.[7]

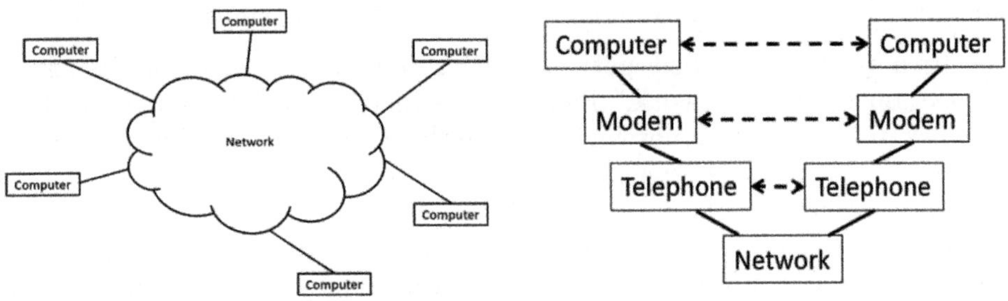

Figure 7: Cloud and Layered Network

The theory of "packet switching" is captured by its name. First, data to be sent over the network is broken up into packets. These packets are then sent out to other computers that are part of the network. Each computer that receives a packet looks at the packet's intended destination and sends it along to another computer that is incrementally closer to that destination. This process of routing data through the network is called "switching," and is metaphorically similar to throwing a switch to change which track a train is on. Engineers refer to this process of establishing connections or routing traffic as switching, and the locations at which such routing is done as switches.) As the packets reach their destination, they are typically reassembled in order and the original message is reconstructed.

The concept of the packet is relatively straightforward, even if implementation of working packet switching networks is exceptionally difficult. If you were, for example, physically sending a final paper to your advisor, and it was too big to fit in one envelope, you might use multiple envelopes. Depending on how sensitive the contents, you might label the envelopes differently or use a different closure method. The most important

7 Indeed, in a moment of technical humor, Internet engineers have even developed formal standards allowing for computers to connect to the Internet using carrier pigeon or smoke signals.

thing, however, is that the packets arrived within a reasonable period of time, to the right person, in the right order.

At the most basic level, like its physical counterpart, any information that can be represented in digital form and can be transmitted over a packet switched network. An audio file, for instance, may be represented as a string of 24 million 1s and 0s (assuming a three megabyte file and 8 bits to a byte). To packetize that data, you need only break it up into appropriately-sized blocks (typically about 1000 bytes) and then to send that those packets out to the network in a way that the network will be able to direct them to their destination and the destination will be able to reassembled them in order.

The hard part is figuring out what extra data to include to make sure the packet can get to and be used by its destination. We start by separating the packet into two parts: the header and the payload. The payload is the 1000-byte chunk of data that we're trying to send to the destination. The header is the extra information that we're going to add to the packet to get it there.

Most packet headers will include at minimum a few basic pieces of information: the identification of the sender and recipient, a sequence number for the packet (which the destination will use to reassemble the payloads in order), and the size of the payload. The identification of the sender and recipient are generally referred to as addresses. Every network has a system for assigning devices on it an address. The most familiar network addressing system today is the Internet Protocol address (IP address), used on the Internet. Taking this as an example, each computer on the Internet is given a unique number, represented as four separate three-digit numbers between 0 and 255 and separated by dots: for example, 192.168.123.213 is an IP address.[8]

It is relatively straightforward to understand how this information is sufficient to allow for the switches in packet switching network to deliver packets to the destination and for the destination to reassemble those packets in a usable order.[9] Think of the address like a postal mail address (discussed further below). When a postal carrier, post office, regional processing center, national transit operator, etc. receives an envelope, it looks at the address and determines what is the next step to get that particular envelope closer to its destination. IP switched networks, and more specifically the "switches" (sometimes colloquially called "routers") in

[8] The IP address is actually a single 32-bit number. The *aaa.bbb.ccc.ddd* notation breaks that single 32-bit number into four separate 8-bit numbers. Computers use the 32-bit number, but it is easier for humans to work with four small numbers than one large numbers—especially, as will be discussed with switching, since these numbers are also used to identify different networks and subnetworks.

[9] Indeed, not all of this information is even needed. As an exercise, it is worth considering what the minimum amount of header data is and the reasons that more data may be desirable.

the network have the same type of knowledge and perform similar operations.

Most packets, however, contain more information. For instance, packets typically contain something called a checksum that, in its simplest form, is the number you get when you treat each byte in a packet as number and add them all up. The checksum is a simple way to ensure that packets have not been altered while in transit—the sender and recipient can both quickly calculate the checksum for each packet and know that it should always match. Packets may also have other information in the header, such as the type of data being sent, whether the packet is being used by the computers to coordinate their communications or instead contains substantive information being sent by users, and other diagnostic information to ensure that the packets are arriving correctly and to coordinate how to resend packets when problems occur.

Much of this additional information needs to be included with most packets to ensure the useful operation of the network. Packet switched networks are generally built on the end-to-end principle discussed above. This means that they do not guarantee any particular measure of reliability or quality of service. As such, it is up to the senders and recipients of packets to ensure that they lower layers of the network are reliably transferring data, or to either detect problems that may occur in that transmission or not be beholden to transmission errors. The great challenge of developing packet networks—the path that Marill & Robert's first demonstration network set researchers upon—was to develop a protocol that would allow reliable packet-based transmission of data between computers over networks that could not be presumed to be (and in fact were assumed not to be) reliable. In other words, *unlike* a postal service, packet-switched networks operate over public, layered networks where the ultimate sender and receiver *cannot assume everyone is part of the same organization*. Thus, as a result, packet-switched networks must implement the types of techniques discussed here to ensure delivery.

b. Putting the Switching in Packet Switching

The packet part of packet switching is relatively intuitive. It can be fairly analogized to the postal system: you break a large message up into lots of pieces that will each fit in an envelope, put them in an envelope with an address and sequence number of the outside, and hand them off to the post office. Eventually they are delivered and the recipient can put all of the pieces back together. Switching is the harder part of the concept to understand—just like the postal service's delivery network as vast and complicated. At some level it is reasonable to accept a high-level "cloud" understanding over how packet switched networks get packets from sender to receiver: they are handed off to one computer in the cloud and then bounce around until they reach their destination. A somewhat more nuanced understanding, however, is useful, especially for understanding the security implications of packet-switched networks.

The switching part of packet switching networks is carried out by special computers called switches or routers. These computers are unique in that they have multiple network connections. Unlike a typical networked computer, which is only connected to a single network, switches are connected to two or, more often, three or more networks—this means that they have the ability (indeed, the necessity) to transfer packets between networks.

In a packet-switched network, most computers that users use have a single network interface that connects them to a switch and, perhaps, other computers on the local network. When that computer needs to send a packet to a computer that is not on the local network, that packet is sent to the switch. The switch consults a database stored on the switch called a routing table. This table tells the switch to which of the various networks it is connected any given packet should be routed. An example network, along with the routing table for each switch on the network, is depicted below in Figure 8:

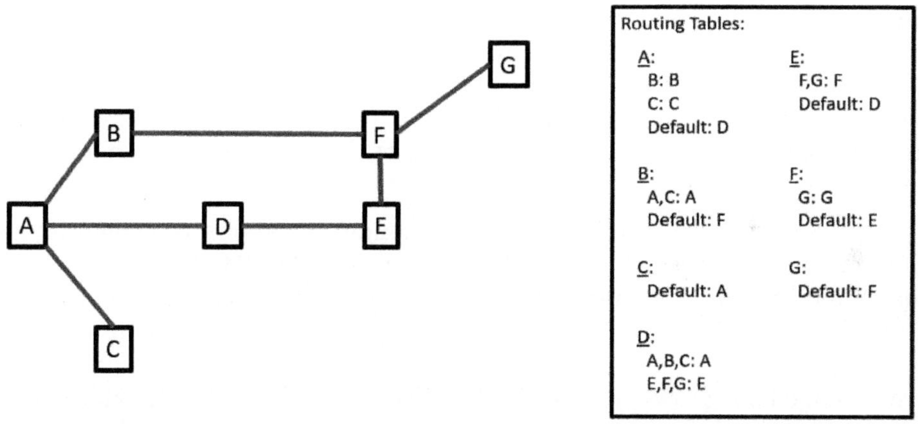

Figure 8: Network Switches

In this hypothetical network, the letter in each box represents a switch that connects a separate local network to the wider area network. So, for instance, computers on network A are connected directly by switch A to networks B, C, and D. And switch A's routing table tells the switch that packets destined for network B should be sent to switch B, packets destined for network C should be sent to switch C, and any other packets should be sent to switch D.

There are a few things to note about this network. First, most of the networks have a "default" route. In this example, only switch D has a routing table that doesn't include a "default" route. Networks like D (in this example) are sometimes called backbone or Tier 1 networks, meaning that they do not need to rely on other networks to route their traffic. Networks that do have a "default" route are said to have a "transit" relationship with their default-route provider. Most networks rely on transit providers for access to the Internet.

Next, due to this relationship, it isn't necessary that that any given network have more than a very limited understanding of the overall architecture of the network. The switch for network C, for instance, need not know anything other than "send all packets not intended for my own network to switch A." Even switch D—the "backbone" switch in this network—only has direct connections to networks A and E; while it knows that it should send packets destined for network G to switch E, it doesn't need to know whether network G is connected to network E, F, or for that matter, network B.

In principle, any given packet-switched network could be structured so that any given switch knows more or less about the overall architecture of the network. As the predominant example of a packet switched network, the Internet is instructive: changes to the connections that make up the Internet are completely decentralized, and each network connected to the Internet is, in principle, completely autonomous from every other network on the Internet. Network G, for instance, could subdivide itself into multiple networks—it wouldn't need to get permission from, or even notify, anyone in order to make such a change. All of the routing logic would be implemented in switch G to ensure that packets would still get to their intended destinations.

On the Internet, each of these independent systems is known as an Autonomous System (AS). As of 2018, there are over 84,000 AS networks that make up the Internet. While not a necessary or core aspect of how switching works in packet switched networks, it is useful to note that, as the Internet has grown in size and complexity, how these routing tables are managed has grown as well. Since 1994, most of the routing tables have been maintained through an automated protocol known as the Border Gateway Protocol (BGP). BGP allows for routing changes to be automatically propagated through the routing network.

One final aspect of the how packets are routed through a packet switched network is that the routing tables are not necessarily designed for technical efficiency. Rather, routing agreements are more often business arrangements, and packets may be routed based upon any number of characteristics—not just based upon destination. For instance, in the example above the connection between networks B and F could be much faster than routing packets across network B's backbone—but it may also be more expensive. In such a case, it is possible that the switch for network A would be configured to send certain high priority traffic to switch B for faster delivery across the network, but that lower-priority traffic would be routed across network D. Or, it is possible that a given network will raise its prices (for any number of reasons) which will result in traffic being routed through other networks.

4. THE INTERNET

Communications between modules requires some form of networking; and between physically remote modules requires some reasonably sophisticated form of networking. The ultimate value of a network, as in networking in human life, is to create a connection and share information. As in human networks, sometimes certain modules require input from another module to make a complete decision. For example, if you buy a product on Amazon, the Amazon Website needs to create a private connection to your bank or credit card company to charge the funds needed to pay for the product. In this case, the Website and your bank or credit card company account listing are the two modules exchanging information for purposes of executing a specific task (like buying dog food).[10]

In these cases, information is transmitted between modules that are connected over an internal network, or a network where the modules and the connection between them are maintained by a private organization, or over an external network, sometimes called a public network. The public network usually involves connectivity between private modules, each on their own private networks. For example, for you to receive an e-mail in your inbox, which is displayed on your computer at your home, the organization maintaining an e-mail account, such as your college university needs to have connectivity where an individual with an e-mail at a different organization can connect their e-mail server with your university's server. Further, to see it displayed on your computer, your computer must connect through your wireless network connection where you live or work to your university's server to see the e-mail displayed on your computer. Each of these connections in the example above occur over a public network, or the Internet. However, many organizations have a variety of modules that communicate where it is undesirable to share information over the Internet. Modules are *networked* when they are set-up to connect to other modules.

Over the Internet, this is accomplished by IP—the Internet Protocol. IP is protocol for connecting independent networks together (where the term 'internet' originated), without any centralized control, and creates consistent procedure for sharing and viewing information over the Internet. The basic design of IP is simple because it was an experimental solution to an engineering problem to be used within a closed community. However, it does not employ standard security approaches. For example,

---

[10] E-commerce purchases actually involve a complex number of connections between banks, credit card brands, payment processors, and others, but this example is designed to demonstrate a basic information sharing function of a network.

the protocol does not provide any confidentiality of the data transferred, including who sent or received it. IP does not encrypt any data in transit, verify who sent the information, who received it, and IP does not validate that it reached the correct destination. For these reasons, Internet connectivity is considered "public" and, without appropriate controls, is inherently vulnerable to attackers.[11]

We will be talking much more about the Internet and IP as we explore different modes of attack, but for now, keep in mind that the Internet poses a variety of additional security problems that are unique to open or public systems, whereas internal networks, or organizational *intranet* are under some control by organizations. As you will see, both networks and their respective modules are vulnerable to certain threats. However, effective security controls differ depending on the network and system evaluated.

C. IDENTITY, AUTHENTICATION, AND ENCRYPTION

Our discussion earlier in this chapter of modularity and networking introduced the problems of authentication and identity: The Internet does not provide any mechanism ensure the authenticity of any given party's identity. Or, as the common meme goes, "On the Internet, nobody knows you're a dog." The discussion in that chapter suggested that this is the result of design decisions—that the engineers developing the Internet Protocol either deliberately or inadvertently omitted incorporating a concept of "identity" into the Internet architecture. At one level this is true: the Internet was designed to be a network for interconnecting any number of independent, autonomous, networks to one another. It turns out that it is exceptionally difficult to design a network that is not centrally controlled but that also supports a concept of identity.[12]

Because the engineers who developed the Internet Protocol designed the network expressly not to be centrally controlled, the network that they designed necessarily forwent strong authentication and identity protocols. Rather, authentication and identity were concepts that had to be developed over time and layered on top of the existing Internet architecture. This section considers the development of these technologies.

---

[11] Remember that the purpose of the protocol is to facilitate *internetworking*, i.e., the interoperation of separate networks as a single communications system. What might be some of the tradeoffs involved with incorporating security measures into an internetworking protocol? How effective would such security measures be? Why?

[12] Prior to the development of blockchain technologies, very few examples of decentralized networks with successful federated identity existed. Blockchain technologies solve this only in part, and not (yet) in a way generally applicable to the present question of an internetworked communications system. *See generally* Deborah Gerhardt and David Thaw, *Bot Contracts*, 62 ARIZ. L. REV (forthcoming 2021).

1. IDENTITY

Authenticating one's identity online is difficult because the Internet is informationally sparse: one generally only has a few pieces of information that can be used to authenticate their counterparties. In the most classic case, all that is required for a user to prove that she is who she claims to be is a valid username and password. If an unauthorized third party obtains that information, he can readily assume the identity of the real user.

Similarly, when a user establishes an internet connection to some other party on the Internet, they have no way to be sure that that party is who it purports to be. When you direct your web browser to a bank's web page, you have no way of knowing if the page that displays is being sent by that bank or is instead a forgery.[13]

One of the classic types of online attacks takes advantage of the inability of both the party initiating and the party responding to a connection to authenticate one another. This attack, diagramed below, is known as a "man-in-the-middle" (MITM) attack. In an MITM attack, the attacker (Mallory) is able to interpose itself between the two communicating parties (Alice and Bob). To the party initiating the communication (Alice) Mitchel pretends to be the responding party (Bob). It then uses the information provided by Alice to initiate its own connection to Bob, pretending to be Alice.

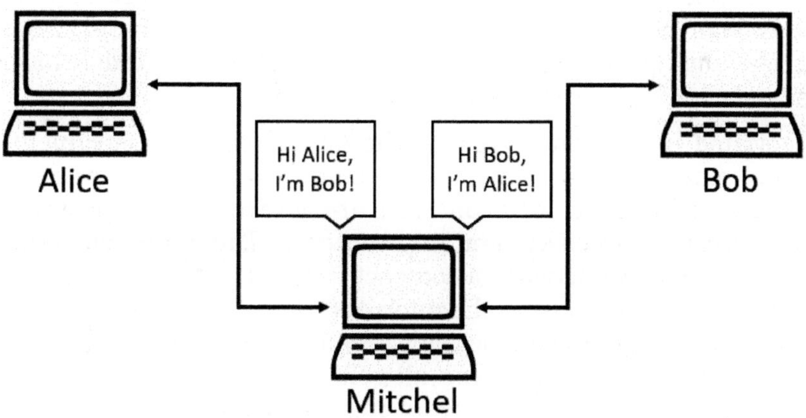

Figure 9: A Man-in-the-Middle Attack

Compare this to the physical world: when you go to a physical branch of a bank, there are a number of factors implicitly authenticating both you

[13] More precisely, you have no way of knowing whether it is authentic or a forgery *without relying on authentication mechanisms* that have been layered on top of the standard Internet Protocols.

to the bank and the bank to you. You are recorded on a number of cameras. The bank teller can see you and tell if you are acting unusually. You may be asked for your ID. A picture of you or your signature may be displayed on the teller's computer screen. Most bank tellers are trained to engage in small talk to solicit information that further verifies your identity. Reversing the relationship, there is a great deal of information authenticating the bank to you: it is in a building that looks like a bank, with tellers and customers. It is also located where you expect it to be, both based on your own recollection and the other proximate buildings.

The physical world, in other words, is information-rich from an authentication standpoint compared to the information-sparse online world. The problem of authenticating identity is not, however, unique to the online world. There are a number of legal tools, for instance, that are used for authentication. We most often see these used in information-sparse or high-risk situations.

The most obvious examples of authentication in the legal context arises in the law of evidence, which has specific rules relating to how evidence is admitted for consideration by a court. A photograph, for instance, cannot be admitted unless the party seeking its admission can establish what it is a photograph of, the circumstances under which it was taken, how it came to be in the possession of the party seeking its admission, etc.

As another example from the legal context, the law often requires registration of individuals, property, or businesses that others may seek to accurately identify. Cars have license plates to identify them. Property boundaries and ownership are recorded in public records. Licensed professionals are registered in public databases.

Negotiated instruments (that is, checks and similar instruments for exchanging money) are governed by a complex set of rules intended to ensure their authenticity. And contracts are governed by their own set of rules intended to address authenticity concerns. The parol evidence rule, for instance, prevents parties to a contract from introducing evidence from outside the contract to assist in the interpretation of the contract. This rule exists in part to avoid authentication problems: it encourages parties to incorporate and sufficiently define all relevant terms into the text of a contract. Because parties to a contract dispute generally don't contest the authenticity of the underlying contract, this rule helps to keep courts out of messy questions about the authenticity (as well as veracity, accuracy, and meaning) of the myriad extrinsic documents that parties would likely turn to in the course of litigation.

2. AUTHENTICATION

Authentication is slightly but critically different from identity. Authentication refers to the process (or result) of verifying that someone is who they claim to be. Identity is the claim itself. Authentication does not "grant" privileges—identity does. But to *establish* identity, a principal first must be authenticated. These two work hand-in-hand, but must be understood individually to understand security.

In the previous section, we referred to username and password as the most classic means of authenticating online, what we call one-factor authentication, because the only factor is what you know (your ID and password). This suggests a subtle, but important, change in how one usually thinks about usernames and passwords. Usernames and especially passwords are generally thought of as tools to keep unauthorized users from accessing a system. In modern security practice, they are more precisely understood as tools for authenticating users who are authorized to access a system.

This may seem like a trivial difference—keeping unauthorized users out vs. allowing authorized users in—but it suggests an important conceptual change in how we think about authentication. Thinking in terms of "who to keep out" tends to focus attention on the strength of the factors than an attacker may seek to compromise (e.g., password complexity). Thinking in terms of "who to let in," on the other hand, tends to focus attention on how we can identify authorized users.

There are three commonly recognized "authentication factors," described in the excerpt below. These are different, unrelated, types to information that can be used to identify an individual.

> NIST Special Publication 800-63-2, Electronic Authentication Guideline
>
> The classic paradigm for authentication systems identifies three factors as the cornerstone of authentication:
>
> - Something you know (for example, a password)
> - Something you have (for example, an ID badge or a cryptographic key)
> - Something you are (for example, a fingerprint or other biometric data)
>
> Multi-factor authentication refers to the use of more than one of the factors listed above. The strength of authentication systems is largely determined by the number of factors incorporated by the system. Implementations that use two factors are considered to be stronger than those that use only one factor; systems that incorporate all three factors are stronger than systems that only incorporate two of the factors.

Systems that rely on a username and password to authenticate a user actually only rely on a single authentication factor: something the user knows (the username and password). Indeed, even a system that requires a user to answer 100 detailed questions about his life is only based upon a single authentication factor.

The advantage of a multi-factor approach to authentication is that each factor presents a different attack surface that is subject to different vulnerabilities. A user can disclose things that he knows to an attacker. A user generally cannot, however, give an attacker a copy of this thumbprint or of his hair color.[14] An attacker may be able to kidnap a user and use his thumbprint to disengage a biometric lock. But the attacker then still needs to obtain the user's username, password, or other "things he knows" information. And the same analysis applies for using "something the user has" as an authentication factor, and generally this will be a device or physical token that was designed in a way that makes it difficult to copy or counterfeit.

3. ENCRYPTION

It turns out that one of the best solutions to the problem of authentication is encryption. This is somewhat counterintuitive. Encryption is generally understood as being a way to keep information secret. One uses encryption, for instance, to ensure that an attacker who obtains a copy of sensitive but encrypted information is unable to make use of that information, or to ensure that an unauthorized third party (such as a man-in-the-middle) that intercepts (encrypted) information is unable to make use of that information. This function, called confidentiality, is important and useful.

But if we invert our understanding of how encryption works, recognizing that only parties that know how to decrypt encrypted information are able to access it, we see that encryption can also be used for authentication purposes: if Alice sends a message to a third party encrypted in a way that only Bob knows how to decrypt, Alice can be confident that any counterparty who can decrypt that message must be Bob.

We discuss how encryption works and can be used below.

This discussion is, at times, moderately technical (with some limited mathematic discussion). But a basic understanding of how encryption works is important to understanding modern security—this includes an understanding of symmetric, asymmetric, and public key encryption.

---

[14] Importantly, however, a password can be changed if it is breached. Biometric data is (generally) unchangeable. It is also worth noting that since *all* authentication credentials must be reduced to data in order for a digital computer to process them, they are replicable as a *theoretical* matter. Currently, replicating one's retina for an optical scan is quite difficult, as is replicating the physical tokens employed by the U.S. Government (Common Access Cards, or "CACs"). However, there is no reason to believe that technological advances will not develop retina or fingerprint duplication technology that can be *practically* deployed (and, indeed, both technologies exist in theoretical design already). Physical tokens can, of course, be upgraded to resist technological circumvention—they are not generally immutable as are most biometric traits.

For instance, the implementation guidance for the Federal Information Security Management Act (FISMA), Gram-Leach-Bliley Act (GLBA), Health Insurance Portability & Accountability Act (HIPAA), and Sarbanes-Oxley Act (SOX) all require familiarity with encryption. Various National Security legislation and guidance expressly requires compliance with encryption mandates. Adherence to the NIST Framework, discussed previously, requires an understanding of encryption solutions. Industry standards, such as PCI-DSS, FINRA, and CobiT require use, or at least proper consideration of, encryption. And a number of state data security and breach notification laws expressly or impliedly require the appropriate use of encryption. In each of these cases, compliance requires at least a modestly sophisticated understanding of various forms of encryption.

The excerpt below provides a general overview of how what encryption is and how encryption works. It is followed by discussion of how public key, asymmetric key, encryption is used to implement a robust authentication ecosystem—called the Public Key Infrastructure—on the modern Internet.

GUS HURWITZ, *UNDERSTANDING ENCRYPTION: NO LONGER JUST ABOUT SENDING SECRET MESSAGES*

TechPolicyDaily (Oct 21, 2105)

Encryption is a key aspect of cybersecurity. Indeed, it is hard to have a meaningful conversation about cybersecurity without an understanding of what encryption is and how it works. Unfortunately, encryption is a complicated concept which many people don't understand all that well. Indeed, as explained here, encryption's most important function probably isn't that it lets us keep information secret from prying eyes—in the modern setting, encryption serves the more important role of identity verification.

What is encryption?

Before diving into how modern encryption has uses far beyond keeping secrets, let's briefly recap the basic mechanics of how encryption works. Encryption is the art of hiding information in plain sight. The classic setup involves two people, Alice and Bob, who wish to send secret messages to one another—but whose efforts are made difficult by their nemesis, eavesdropping Eve.

In order to send messages between each other, Alice and Bob need a way to encode messages that will be difficult for Eve to decode. For instance, Alice and Bob could agree to encode messages by shifting each letter one place to the left in the alphabet (e.g., "A" becomes "B," "B" becomes "C," etc.). Assuming that Alice and Bob have some way to agree on how far to shift each letter when encoding a message, they can be reasonably sure Eve won't be able to decode their messages. We can give names to three parts of this process: the "plaintext" is the message that

Alice wants to send to Bob; the "cyphertext" is the encoded message that is actually sent (and which Eve is able to see); and the "cypher" is the way that Alice and Bob have agreed on to transform the plaintext to cyphertext and back again.

The clever reader may see two problems with this method of encryption. First, it assumes that Alice and Bob are able to agree on a cypher without Eve overhearing what the cypher is. We'll return to that in a moment. The second problem is that if Alice and Bob agree on a simple cypher (e.g., "2," meaning "shift each letter 2 characters to the right") it is relatively easy for Eve to reverse-engineer the cypher. This is because some letters appear more frequently than others (for instance, in English, the letter "E" appears most often, followed by "T" and then "A"). Eve need only count how often each letter appears in the cyphertext, and she will have a good chance of being able to decode it. This approach to breaking encryption—counting the frequency of various letters' appearances—is called "frequency analysis."

The solution to [the frequency analysis attack] is surprisingly simple: instead of using the same cypher for each letter, Alice and Bob agree on a cypher made up of a series of random numbers (ideally one that is longer than the plaintext message). Because each letter is independently encoded, frequency analysis is no longer an effective attack.

So, if Alice wants to send Bob the message "TOO MANY SECRETS," which has 14 letters, they would start by agreeing on a cypher with at least 14 random numbers in it. Alice would then add each number to its corresponding letter (wrapping back around to "A" if she goes past "Z") to generate the cyphertext. The cyphertext, which would look something like "IWPDBTISLAYTJS," can then be sent to Bob (and Eve). Bob can decode the cyphertext because he knows the cypher; Eve has only a string of random letters that she will be helpless to decode—because the letters are randomly distributed, she will be unable to decode them.

Public key encryption

Above, we brushed past the question of how Alice and Bob agree upon a good cypher. That seems like a pretty big problem! If Alice and Bob are able to send a secret cypher between them without Eve overhearing, then surely they could also send any message they want, no?

In the early days of encryption—roughly from the time of Caesar through the Second World War—encryption relied on cyphers known as one-time pads. A one-time pad is little more than a really long random number agreed upon by Alice and Bob in advance. This approach to encryption is useful if Alice and Bob know in advance that they are going to be sending encrypted messages between each other. For instance, General Alice can give Commander Bob a book of one-time pads (called a codebook) with one for each day of a mission. Each day, Alice and Bob will be able to communicate secretly using that day's codes.

In the years following the Second World War, mathematicians developed a new way of communicating cyphers. The key insight in this field of mathematics is that some functions are very easy to calculate in one direction, but very difficult to reverse. For instance, it is relatively easy to multiply two large prime numbers (let's call them x and y) to get a third number z; but if I give you z it is relatively hard to figure out x and y. The key word here is "relatively": computationally it is actually quite easy to find x and y; but it will take a long time—more precisely, it will take a lot longer than it took to multiply x and y to get z. So, if calculating z takes a computer 1 second, it may take 10 days to calculate x and y; if it takes 10 seconds to calculate z, finding x and y may take 10 years.

Using this insight, mathematicians realized that Alice and Bob could pretty easily generate large secret numbers that could be used as cyphers. To roughly describe the process, first, each picks a large prime number, which they keep secret. Then Alice sends Bob another large prime number (which Eve may intercept). Both multiply this public number by their secret numbers, and exchange the results; they then multiply the exchanged results by their secret numbers. At the end of this process, Alice and Bob have both calculated the same number, which they can use as a cypher to encrypt messages. Importantly, Eve has all of the pieces needed to calculate this number, too—but doing so would require her to reverse part of the process that Alice and Bob used, and that would take a very long time.

This process roughly describes an approach known as the Diffie-Hellman protocol, after the mathematicians who figured it out. It is a key part of almost all modern encryption. If implemented correctly, it will guarantee that Alice and Bob can send secret messages that Eve will, practically speaking, never be able to decode. Again, the key words there are "practically speaking"—Eve has all the information required to decode Alice and Bob's messages. It will just take her a long time. And, if Alice and Bob are worried, they can make it arbitrarily harder for Eve to decode the message by using larger prime numbers. By using numbers that take only a few seconds longer to multiply together, Alice and Bob can literally add years to the time it will take Eve to reverse the process.

Encryption is about more than secrets

It is unsurprising that people generally think the primary use of encryption is to keep information secret (that is, to encrypt information). But modern encryption technologies have another, arguably more important, use: they allow us to verify the source of information being sent over the Internet. In other words, encryption can be used to verify that information sent to your bank is actually going to your bank, or that a software update to your computer's operating system is actually being sent by Microsoft or Apple.

To understand this, we need to return to the mathematics of how encryption works. The method of encryption described above used the same cypher to encrypt and decrypt messages sent between Alice and Bob. Alice uses the cypher to encode the plaintext, and Bob reverses the process to decode the cyphertext. This is called symmetric key encryption.

Using some slightly more sophisticated mathematics (which actually date to the 18th century mathematician Euler) allows for asymmetric key encryption. In asymmetric key encryption we have two separate keys, one for encrypting messages and one for decrypting messages. This means that Alice can encrypt a message that only Bob can read—indeed, once the message is encrypted, not even Alice can decode it! In fact, if Bob shares his encryption key, anyone can encode messages that only he can decrypt.

This may seem like a useless technology. Using Diffie-Hellman, Alice and Bob can already send each other secret messages. Secret is already secret—asymmetric encryption doesn't let Alice and Bob's secret messages be more secret.

Asymmetric key encryption, it turns out, solves a different problem. Think back to how Alice and Bob use Diffie-Hellman to establish a private key: they start by exchanging a few large prime numbers. But how does Alice know that she's sending those numbers to Bob? And how does Bob know that he's sending his prime numbers to Alice? Unless they have established a pre-determined way of identifying each other, they have no way of verifying that each is who they claim to be—and the need to rely on pre-determined information returns us to the age of one-time pads!

Indeed, this reveals an even more fundamental problem with any form of impersonal communications. Unless Alice and Bob are able to share their one-time pad in a direct, face-to-face exchange, they will never be able to trust that it is not a forgery. This may not have been a problem for General Alice sharing codebooks with a few dozen trusted Commander Bobs during wartime. But the story is entirely different in our modern economy: billions of Internet users almost never have personal interactions with any of the millions of websites with which they are likely to interact in the course of their online lives.

Modern encryption really isn't about secrets

Asymmetric key encryption gives us a solution to this problem, in the form of "chains of trust." If Alice has Bob's public key, she can encode messages that she is confident only Bob can decode. For instance, if Alice were a customer of Bank Bob, Alice could use Bob's public key to send her username and password, at which point both Alice and Bob could be confident that they were each who they claimed to be—at which point they could use ordinary private key encryption to communicate.

But how does Alice get Bob's public key? This is where the "chain of trust" comes in. Bob's key is kept by an online repository of public keys known as a "certificate authority"—these are service that sell and maintain encryption keys for whomever may need them. When Alice tells her web browser to go to Bob's web page, her web browser contacts the certificate authority to get Bob's public key. In order to do so securely, the web browser comes pre-installed with the public keys for various certificate authorities (otherwise your web browser would face the same problem that Alice and Bob have!). And, to make sure that your web browser hasn't been tampered with, when you install (or update) it, your operating system may use a public key to verify that the web browser is authentic.

So one public key can be used to verify another public key, which can be used to verify another public key. So long as there is a trusted public key at the start of the chain—such as one embedded in your operating system or web browser, which you purchase or install from trusted sources—Alice can trust that Bob is who he says he is.

This process has nothing to do with the ordinary understanding of "encryption." When we started, our concern was allowing Alice and Bob to communicate secretly despite eavesdropping Eve listening in on their conversation. But asymmetric key encryption isn't about protecting against Eve—it's about ensuring that Alice and Bob are who they say they are. Asymmetric key encryption can also be used to protect against Eve—but that problem is really much simpler than verifying the identities of the endpoints.

It really cannot be understated how important this technology is for the Internet. Every online interaction is indirect and intermediated. Without public key encryption, there is simply no way to trust that anyone or anything online is who or what it claims to be.

The security-minded reader may recognize a problem with how a bank or Microsoft would use public key encryption to authenticate their customers: public key encryption assumes that the parties have a way to securely share public keys. But this requires that the parties can authenticate one another! If they can't do this, then a man-in-the-middle attack is, once again, possible. In other words, who will authenticate the authenticators?

The answer, referred to as a "chain of trust" in the excerpt above, is something known as a "Public Key Infrastructure" (PKI). PKI relies on a trust third party known as a Certificate Authority (CA) to manage public keys. When a customer attempts, for instance, to log into their bank's web page, their computer requests the bank's public key from a certificate authority instead of from the bank itself. This prevents a fraudulent bank website from distributing a fraudulent public key.

But that, alone, is not enough! A sophisticated attacker could, in principle, compromise both the bank and the certificate authority. Or, more realistically, a sophisticated attacker could engage in a man-in-the-middle attack against *both* the bank and the certificate authority—if an attacker is in a position to pretend to be one, she is likely also in a position to be the other. To ensure against this type of attack, the certificate authority *also* uses public key encryption to protect its own communications. This, of course, requires that the user's computer has a copy of the certificate authority's public key. How does the user's computer get a copy of this key? Most modern operating systems and web browsers are distributed with a set of public keys for common certificate authorities pre-programmed in.

At some level, PKI assumes a trustworthy, unauthenticated, interaction. Whomever installs the operating system on your computer, or provides you with a copy of the operating system to be installed on your computer, has to be trustworthy. Assuming that this is the case, your operating system can securely connect to a certificate authority to ensure that software it installs—such as a web browser—is authentic; that web browser can then connect to a certificate authority to ensure that websites that users visit are authentic.[15]

4. ENCRYPTION IS NOT SECURITY

A final note is necessary in this discussion of encryption: encryption is none of synonymous with, a complete approach to, or a substitution for security. In practice, encryption draws an undue, and disruptive, amount of attention. This is in part because encryption is more difficult than it is important (and it is important). It is in part because many security incidents are made worse by lack, or improper use, of encryption. And it is in part because use and legality of encryption is an exceptionally political topic, and many within the cybersecurity community carry implicit and entrenched political beliefs that cause them to conflate their political advocacy for encryption with their understanding of good security practices.

Encryption is undoubtedly an important component of a complete security environment. In practice, however, overemphasis on encryption tends to distract from other equally-important aspects of security. We saw this play out in the 2000s and early 2010s with state data and security breach notification laws that require or incentivize use of encryption have led CISOs to adopt an approach to security. CISOs often deployed

---

[15] Importantly, and troublingly, computer manufacturers are not always trustworthy. For instance, in 2015 it was discovered that Lenovo was installing software called Superfish on its PCs that compromised the PKI. Lenovo did this so that they could inject ads into its customers' web browsing sessions. But the compromised infrastructure allowed for third parties to perform man-in-the-middle attacks against Lenovo customers. *See Man-in-the-Middle Attacks on Lenovo Computers*, https://www.schneier.com/blog/archives/2015/02/man-in-the-midd_7.html.

responses in which "the security investment is moved essentially to crypto. Just encrypt as much as you can. Whatever it takes, just encrypt it. If it moves, encrypt it. If it stays there, encrypt it."[16]

As discussed in the excerpts below, too much focus on encryption is problematic. Generally, a small amount of (well-implemented) encryption goes a long way. As with our discussion of password complexity, most security incidents involving encryption (as with passwords) result not because the encryption wasn't strong enough, but because of problems in the systems surrounding the encryption implementation (the "cryptosystem").

BRUCE SCHNEIER, *SECURITY PITFALLS IN CRYPTOGRAPHY*

INFORMATION MANAGEMENT & COMPUTER SECURITY (1998)

Magazine articles like to describe cryptography products in terms of algorithms and key length. Algorithms make good sound bites: they can be explained in a few words and they're easy to compare with one another. "128-bit keys mean good security." "Triple-DES means good security." "40-bit keys mean weak security." "2048-bit RSA is better than 1024-bit RSA."

But reality isn't that simple. Longer keys don't always mean more security. Compare the cryptographic algorithm to the lock on your front door. Most door locks have four metal pins, each of which can be in one of ten positions. A key sets the pins in a particular configuration. If the key aligns them all correctly, then the lock opens. So there are only 10,000 possible keys, and a burglar willing to try all 10,000 is guaranteed to break into your house. But an improved lock with ten pins, making 10 billion possible keys, probably won't make your house more secure. Burglars don't try every possible key (a brute-force attack); most aren't even clever enough to pick the lock (a cryptographic attack against the algorithm). They smash windows, kick in doors, disguise themselves as policemen, or rob keyholders at gunpoint. One ring of art thieves in California defeated home security systems by taking a chainsaw to the house walls. Better locks don't help against these attacks.

Strong cryptography is very powerful when it is done right, but it is not a panacea. Focusing on the cryptographic algorithms while ignoring other aspects of security is like defending your house not by building a fence around it, but by putting an immense stake into the ground and hoping that the adversary runs right into it. Smart attackers will just go around the algorithms.

Counterpane has spent years designing, analyzing, and breaking cryptographic systems. While we do research on published algorithms and protocols, most of our work examines actual products. We've designed and

---

[16] David Thaw, *The Efficacy of Cybersecurity Regulation*, 30 GA. ST. U. L. REV. 287, 321 (2014).

analyzed systems that protect privacy, ensure confidentiality, provide fairness, and facilitate commerce. We've worked with software, stand-alone hardware, and everything in between. We've broken our share of algorithms, but we can almost always find attacks that bypass the algorithms altogether. We don't have to try every possible key, or even find flaws in the algorithms. We exploit errors in design, errors in implementation, and errors in installation. Sometimes we invent a new trick to break a system, but most of the time we exploit the same old mistakes that designers make over and over again.

[Schneier goes on to discuss various ways that he has seen cryptography-based security systems fail, including: Attacks Against Cryptographic Designs, Attacks Against Implementations, Attacks Against Passwords, Attacks Against Hardware, Attacks Against Trust Models, Attacks on the Users, Attacks Against Failure Recovery, Attacks Against the Cryptography.]

[. . .]

Attack Prevention vs. Attack Detection

Most cryptographic systems rely on prevention as their sole means of defense: the cryptography keeps people from cheating, lying, abusing, or whatever. Defense should never be that narrow. A strong system also tries to detect abuse and to contain the effects of any attack. One of our fundamental design principles is that sooner or later, every system will be successfully attacked, probably in a completely unexpected way and with unexpected consequences. It is important to be able to detect such an attack, and then to contain the attack to ensure it does minimal damage.

More importantly, once the attack is detected, the system needs to recover: generate and promulgate a new key pair, update the protocol and invalidate the old one, remove an untrusted node from the system, etc. Unfortunately, many systems don't collect enough data to provide an audit trail, or fail to protect the data against modification. Counterpane has done considerable work in securing audit logs in electronic commerce systems, mostly in response to system designs that could fail completely in the event of a successful attack. These systems have to do more than detect an attack: they must also be able to produce evidence that can convince a judge and jury of guilt.

Building Secure Cryptographic Systems

Security designers occupy what Prussian general Carl von Clausewitz calls "the position of the interior." A good security product must defend against every possible attack, even attacks that haven't been invented yet. Attackers, on the other hand, only need to find one security flaw in order to defeat the system. And they can cheat. They can collude, conspire, and wait for technology to give them additional tools. They can attack the system in ways the system designer never thought of.

Building a secure cryptographic system is easy to do badly, and very difficult to do well. Unfortunately, most people can't tell the difference. In other areas of computer science, functionality serves to differentiate the good from the bad: a good compression algorithm will work better than a bad one; a bad compression program will look worse in feature-comparison charts. Cryptography is different. Just because an encryption program works doesn't mean it is secure. What happens with most products is that someone reads *Applied Cryptography*, chooses an algorithm and protocol, tests it to make sure it works, and thinks he's done. He's not. Functionality does not equal quality, and no amount of beta testing will ever reveal a security flaw. Too many products are merely "buzzword compliant"; they use secure cryptography, but they are not secure.

As Bruce Schneier described above, it is tremendously difficult to design secure cryptographic systems. Encryption is not a silver bullet; it requires the same care, attention, and design as other security practices. In the following excerpt, Professor Ross Anderson describes how attacks take place.

ROSS ANDERSON, *WHY CRYPTOSYSTEMS FAIL*

106 WIRELESS PERSONAL COMMUNICATION 85 (1993)

1. Introduction

Cryptology, the science of code and cipher systems, is used by governments, banks and other organisations to keep information secure. It is a complex subject, and its national security overtones may invest it with a certain amount of glamour, but we should never forget that information security is at heart an engineering problem. The hardware and software products which are designed to solve it should in principle be judged in the same way as any other products: by their cost and effectiveness.

However, the practice of cryptology differs from, say, that of aeronautical engineering in a rather striking way: there is almost no public feedback about how cryptographic systems fail.

When an aircraft crashes, it is front page news. Teams of investigators rush to the scene, and the subsequent enquiries are conducted by experts from organisations with a wide range of interests—the carrier, the insurer, the manufacturer, the airline pilots' union, and the local aviation authority. Their findings are examined by journalists and politicians, discussed in pilots' messes, and passed on by flying instructors.

In short, the flying community has a strong and institutionalised learning mechanism. This is perhaps the main reason why, despite the inherent hazards of flying in large aircraft, which are maintained and piloted by fallible human beings, at hundreds of miles an hour through congested airspace, in bad weather and at night, the risk of being killed on an air journey is only about one in a million.

In the crypto community, on the other hand, there is no such learning mechanism. The history of the subject shows the same mistakes being made over and over again; in particular, poor management of codebooks and cipher machine procedures enabled many communication networks to be broken. Kahn relates, for example, that Norway's rapid fall in the second world war was largely due to the fact that the British Royal Navy's codes had been solved by the German Beobachtungsdienst—using exactly the same techniques that the Royal Navy's own 'Room 40' had used against Germany in the previous war.

Since World War II a curtain of silence has descended on government use of cryptography. This is not surprising, given not just the cold war, but also the reluctance of bureaucrats (in whatever organisation) to admit their failures. But it does put the cryptosystem designer at a severe disadvantage compared with engineers working in other disciplines; the post-war years are precisely the period in which modern cryptographic systems have been developed and brought into use. It is as if accident reports were only published for piston-engined aircraft, and the causes of all jet aircraft crashes were kept a state secret.

2. Automatic Teller Machines

To discover out how modern cryptosystems are vulnerable in practice, we have to study their use elsewhere. After government, the next biggest application is in banking, and evolved to protect automatic teller machines (ATMs) from fraud.

[. . .]

3. How ATM Fraud Takes Place

We will start with some simple examples which indicate the variety of frauds that can be carried out without any great technical sophistication, and the bank operating procedures which let them happen.

[. . .]

3.2. More complex attacks

The frauds which we have described so far have all been due to fairly simple errors of implementation and operation. Security researchers have tended to consider such blunders uninteresting, and have therefore concentrated on attacks which exploit more subtle technical weaknesses. Banking systems have a number of these weaknesses too.

Although high-tech attacks on banking systems are rare, they are of interest from the public policy point of view, as government initiatives such as the EC's Information Technology Security Evaluation Criteria [ITSEC] aim to develop a pool of evaluated products which have been certified free of known technical loopholes.

The basic assumptions behind this program are that implementation and operation will be essentially error-free, and that attackers will possess the technical skills which are available in a government signals security agency. It would therefore seem to be more relevant to military than civilian systems, although we will have more to say on this later.

[. . .]

4. The Wider Implications

As we have seen, security equipment designers and government evaluators have both concentrated on technical weaknesses, such as poor encryption algorithms and operating systems which could be vulnerable to trojan horse attacks. Banking systems do indeed have their share of such loopholes, but they do not seem to have contributed in any significant way to the crime figures.

The attacks which actually happened were made possible because the banks did not use the available products properly; due to lack of expertise, they made basic errors in system design, application programming and administration.

In short, the threat model was completely wrong. How could this have happened?

4.1. Why the threat model was wrong

During the 1980's, there was an industry wide consensus on the threat model, which was reinforced at conferences and in the literature. Designers concentrated on what could possibly happen rather than on what was likely to happen, and assumed that criminals would have the expertise, and use the techniques, of a government signals agency. More seriously, they assumed that implementers at customer sites would have either the expertise to design and build secure systems using the components they sold, or the common sense to call in competent consultants to help. This was just not the case.

So why were both the threat and the customers' abilities so badly misjudged?

The first error may be largely due to an uncritical acceptance of the conventional military wisdom of the 1970's. When ATMs were developed and a need for cryptographic expertise became apparent, companies imported this expertise from the government sector. The military model stressed secrecy, so secrecy of the PIN was made the cornerstone of the ATM system: technical efforts were directed towards ensuring it, and business and legal strategies were predicated on its being achieved. It may also be relevant that the early systems had only limited networking, and so the security design was established well before ATM networks acquired their present size and complexity.

Nowadays, however, it is clear that ATM security involves a number of goals, including controlling internal fraud, preventing external fraud, and arbitrating disputes fairly, even when the customer's home bank and the ATM raising the debit are in different countries. This was just not understood in the 1970's; and the need for fair arbitration in particular seems to have been completely ignored.

The second error was probably due to fairly straightforward human factors. Many organisations have no computer security team at all, and those that do have a hard time finding it a home within the administrative structure. The internal audit department, for example, will resist being given any line management tasks, while the programming staff dislike anyone whose role seems to be making their job more difficult.

[. . .]

Finally we come to the "consultants" most banks buy their consultancy services from a small number of well known firms, and value an "air of certainty and quality" over technical credentials. Many of these firms pretend to expertise which they do not possess, and cryptology is a field in which it is virtually impossible for an outsider to tell an expert from a charlatan. The author has seen a report on the security of a national ATM network switch, where the inspector (from an eminent firm of chartered accountants) completely failed to understand what encryption was, and under the heading of communications security remarked that the junction box was well enough locked up to keep vagrants out!

[. . .]

5. A New Security Paradigm?

As more people become aware of the shortcomings of traditional approaches to computer security, the need for new paradigms gets raised from time to time. In fact, there are now workshops on the topic, and an increasing number of journal papers make some kind of reference to it.

It is clear from our work that, to be effective, this change must bring about a change of focus. Instead of worrying about what might possibly go wrong, we need to make a systematic study of what is likely to; and it seems that the core security business will shift from building and selling "evaluated" products to an engineering discipline concerned with quality control processes within the client organisation.

QUESTIONS

1. Why isn't the Diffie-Hellman approach to encryption sufficient to allow two parties to communicate with one another in confidence?

2. How can a bank use public key encryption to allow a customer to securely log into its website, providing assurance to the customer that the website she is communicating with is, in fact, her bank? How can a company like Microsoft use public key encryption to distribute security updates to its software, assuring its customers that those patches are authentic?

CHAPTER 6

LEGAL FOUNDATIONS

■ ■ ■

The law takes many forms and serves many purposes. Perhaps the most common understanding of the law is that it is a formal system of rules that proscribes and punishes bad conduct. Under this understanding, the law is logically coherent and serves as a form of specification for how one should and should not behave and includes legal sanctions implying a sense of moral disapprobation for violative behavior. To break the law is to do something objectively wrong, and the consequence of doing something wrong is not merely a punishment but moral judgement.[1]

While parts of the law do bear these characteristics, for the most part the law serves very different purposes. Chief among these[2]—and of particular importance for cybersecurity—the law works to modify individual behavior to encourage desirable behavior and to discourage undesirable behavior. And, because it is often unclear before the fact (to use legal jargon, *ex ante*) whether a given behavior is or is not desirable, legal rules are rarely prescriptive. Rather, they are structured to encourage parties to consider how their conduct will likely affect others.

As we will see in this chapter, this gives rise to a system that is very different from one based in formal rules and moral judgement. Rather than formal rules, legal principles more often than not are more akin to rules of thumb that encourage reasonable behavior and cooperation between parties. And legal sanctions are rarely about expressing moral judgement. Rather, they are more often about compensating parties harmed by innocent mistakes, not to punish the mistaken party but to encourage future parties to avoid making similar mistakes.

This Chapter covers some foundational material regarding legal theory, structures, and policymaking. It is not designed to make the legal layperson an expert in law or policy, nor is it designed to provide an introduction to political science (U.S. or otherwise). Rather, the purpose is to introduce readers to legal principles that are needed to understand contemporary cybersecurity challenges. Much like Chapter 5: Technical

---

1 Although largely outside the scope of this discussion, the concept of "moral judgement" is more commonly found in the context of violations of criminal law (as opposed to failure to conform with requirements of private law, such as breaching a contract). This distinction won't play a significant role in this chapter, but you may encounter it in discussions with others about the role of "cybercrime" laws.

2 The law also serves various other important purposes, such as instilling and supporting values of justice and implementing socially, economically, and politically desirable policies.

Foundations, the purpose is to draw readers' attention to the capabilities and limits of legal systems. It starts with a discussion of key legal principles, then discusses where the law comes from, and concludes with a discussion of how the law is enforced.

This Chapter is written for readers who have little or no background in law or political science beyond that contained in secondary education, and thus may be repetitive for some students with extensive backgrounds in those areas. For readers with greater familiarity with these foundational principles, Part B of this chapter may nonetheless be useful to review. Many of the ideas introduced in this chapter will be further developed or used in Chapters 8 and 10.

A. LEGAL STRUCTURES

The United States legal system consists of a layered model of legal requirements. In the following sections, you will explore the different U.S. approaches, including laws made by federal and state representative democracy, legal constructs created through judicial decision-making, and administrative law and executive actions. The U.S. approach to republican governance at both the federal and state level creates a unique legal model (and potential legal policy options) as you consider how cybersecurity issues might become legal issues.

1. STRUCTURE OF (REPRESENTATIVE REPUBLICAN) GOVERNMENT

The concept of democratic[3] governance implies that the ultimate source of authority for government is the "polity." The polity is a term describing the people who agree to form and be subject to a government. In this regard, a government can be regarded, in part, as an agreement among a set of people: citizens. By being a citizen, one agrees to abide by the obligations of the government. It is important to note a distinction here, between a citizen who is a member of the polity and an individual who is subject to the laws. While all citizens are subject to the laws, not all persons subject to the laws of a given government are citizens.

This isn't as complicated as it sounds! When you travel to another jurisdiction (i.e., another country), you are subject to the laws of that country, even though you are not a citizen of that country and therefore not

[3] A note on terminology—"democratic" here means a government given legitimacy by the agreement of, and periodic formation through action of, its people. This is—importantly—different than a "democracy", which is a type of government in which individual persons vote on most legislative actions of the government. The United States is *not* a democracy at the national level; rather it is a representative republic. No U.S. states are pure democracies—all have legislatures with plenary policymaking authority—although several states (e.g., California, Texas, and Connecticut) have aspects of a democracy through their "ballot initiative" process for taking legislative action through majority vote of the citizenry. Also note—the use of the terms "republican," "democratic," or derivatives thereof do not in any usage here refer to the similarly-named political parties, but rather the concepts of governance.

a member of its polity entitled to influence the choice of government in that country. This also may mean that you are not afforded the same protection or rights as in your home country. As you may recall from the privacy discussion at the beginning of this book, the main distinction between the United States and the European Economic Area (EEA) is that the United States does not view privacy as a civil right, while the EEA does. Yet data about an individual may be easily transferred to, shared with, or duplicated in another geographic location that will not recognize these rights. Keep this distinction in the back of your mind, because it may matter when thinking later about the extraterritorial application of certain cybersecurity laws. This is a common question in a world where *technological presence* and *geographic presence* do not match one another.[4]

If power then flows from people who have agreed to form, and therefore be subject to, a government, how is that government constituted? As the eponymous name suggests, this is precisely what is a Constitution. It is an agreement among people to form a "legitimate" government: one in which all persons are governed by their "consent".[5] A Constitution is the highest authority among published, black-letter law. It specifies not only the structure of the institutions to which governmental powers are allocated, but also which powers are granted[6] and which powers are expressly prohibited.[7]

Modern republican democracies share a fundamental principle of "separation of powers" in which the authority granted by the people to the government is divided into three "branches" of government which exercise separate functions of that power and are, to some degree, "set against" one another with the incentives to restrain and "check" the power of the others.

In the United States, the Commonwealth Nations,[8] and most other European and East Asian[9] democratic nations, three divisions of government apply: a legislature, an executive, and a judiciary. The legislature holds the primary policymaking authority within a government and generally is responsible for making decisions about what "should" be

[4] Indeed, it is much worse than a mere mismatch, as was the case in commerce-by-postal-mail—one might argue that the "physics" of the Internet are essentially orthogonal to the two-dimensional "physics" of Westphalian-style national borders.

[5] Note that, as a practical matter, consent is implicit—not express—among almost all modern democratic governments. This is because very few people alive at the time modern Constitutions were adopted still are alive today, with the possible exception (but interesting corner case) of democratic-style governments established in former Soviet republics.

[6] E.g., the exclusive power for the U.S. federal government to engage in and conduct the foreign policy of the United States.

[7] E.g., the restriction on the power of the U.S. federal government to limit the free exercise of speech, religion, or assembly (subject to certain exceptions).

[8] Nations descending from the British Commonwealth, including for example Canada, Australia, and the British Virgin Islands.

[9] For the purposes of this textbook, consider the People's Republic of China to be a special case to which this discussion generally does not apply.

the case (predominantly through writing laws). The executive is responsible for implementing the policy decisions of a legislature, and in many nations (including the U.S.) has primary policymaking authority in the areas of foreign policy and military command. The judiciary is responsible for interpreting the actions and rules of the other branches. As put simply by Chief Justice Marshall in *Marbury v. Madison*, it is the primary job of the judiciary "to say what the law is."

This three-branch design, however, still has many variations among it. The most common variation speaks to the method by which the chief executive is chosen by direct election,[10] proxy-direct election,[11] or by the legislature.[12] Variations on election by the citizens generally are called "presidential" systems and variations on selections by the legislature generally are called "parliamentary" systems. In the United States, both the Federal government and all states' governments use a Presidential model, where the chief executive is selected by the citizens,[13] not the legislature. Other, less common variations include a role for the legislature in the judicial appeals process,[14] role(s) for the President in the legislative process,[15] and allocations of executive power between "career" officials and elected ministers in parliamentary systems.

While this basic three-part structure can be found in the design of most western governments, it is uniquely explicit in the American constitutional design. The Constitution of the United States delineates three co-equal branches of government: in Article I, the Legislature; in Article II, the Executive; and in Article III, the Judiciary. In broad strokes, each of these branches is subject to being checked and balanced by each of the others. Thus, the Executive branch (headed by the President) generally can only engage in conduct authorized by the Legislature,[16] subject to review by the Judiciary. Laws enacted by the Legislature generally can only be enforced by the Executive Branch, and both are subject to review by the Judiciary. The Judiciary generally can only enforce laws created by the Legislature,

---

[10] E.g., the Republic of Korea (South Korea) and the French Republic (France).

[11] E.g., the United States (through the Electoral College).

[12] E.g., the United Kingdom, Germany, and Australia.

[13] The federal chief executive—the President of the United States of America—is selected by a proxy election, through the Electoral College. For the purposes of this book, this distinction from direct election generally will not be relevant.

[14] E.g., the former structure of the United Kingdom under which the House of Lords—the Upper House of Parliament—also served as a court-of-last-resort for certain appeals from the judiciary. This was restructured into a Supreme Court of the United Kingdom by the Constitutional Reform Act 2005 § 23, which took effect in 2009.

[15] E.g., in the United States, the President has plenary power to initiate (but not finalize) treaties with foreign nations (which have the force of law provided they do not conflict with other valid legislation), and can disapprove of legislation but is subject to override by a supermajority of the Congress.

[16] With some limited exceptions, for example the command of the military and the conduct of foreign policy, areas where the President has constitutional authority to act unilaterally or sharing power with, but not requiring the prior permission of, the Congress.

and where matters of the state are at issue, these cases must be brought by an agent of the Executive.

Perhaps the most important question to understand regarding the structure of government is *why* we have this three-branch design. It is, to be sure, extremely *inefficient*. But that is also by design—the same inefficiencies which often frustrate us are the very ones essential to preserving our liberties.

The most famous discussion of the structure of American government and the centrality to of it these concepts of a separation of powers and checks balances between them, is offered in Federalist 47, excerpted below:

FEDERALIST NO. 47, *THE PARTICULAR STRUCTURE OF THE NEW GOVERNMENT AND THE DISTRIBUTION OF POWER AMONG ITS DIFFERENT PARTS*

(February 1, 1788)

To the People of the State of New York:

HAVING reviewed the general form of the proposed government and the general mass of power allotted to it, I proceed to examine the particular structure of this government, and the distribution of this mass of power among its constituent parts. One of the principal objections inculcated by the more respectable adversaries to the Constitution, is its supposed violation of the political maxim, that the legislative, executive, and judiciary departments ought to be separate and distinct. In the structure of the federal government, no regard, it is said, seems to have been paid to this essential precaution in favor of liberty. The several departments of power are distributed and blended in such a manner as at once to destroy all symmetry and beauty of form, and to expose some of the essential parts of the edifice to the danger of being crushed by the disproportionate weight of other parts. No political truth is certainly of greater intrinsic value, or is stamped with the authority of more enlightened patrons of liberty, than that on which the objection is founded.

The accumulation of all powers, legislative, executive, and judiciary, in the same hands, whether of one, a few, or many, and whether hereditary, self-appointed, or elective, may justly be pronounced the very definition of tyranny. Were the federal Constitution, therefore, really chargeable with the accumulation of power, or with a mixture of powers, having a dangerous tendency to such an accumulation, no further arguments would be necessary to inspire a universal reprobation of the system. I persuade myself, however, that it will be made apparent to every one, that the charge cannot be supported, and that the maxim on which it relies has been totally misconceived and misapplied. In order to form correct ideas on this important subject, it will be proper to investigate the sense in which the preservation of liberty requires that the three great departments of power should be separate and distinct. The oracle who is always consulted and cited on this subject is the celebrated Montesquieu. If he be not the author of this invaluable precept in the science of politics, he has the merit at least of displaying and recommending it most effectually to the attention of mankind. Let us endeavor, in the first place, to ascertain his meaning on this point. The British Constitution was to Montesquieu what Homer has been to the didactic writers on epic poetry. As the latter have considered the work of the immortal bard as the perfect model from which the principles and rules of the epic art were to be drawn, and by which all similar works were to be judged, so this great political critic appears to have viewed the Constitution of England as the standard, or to use his own expression, as the mirror of political liberty; and to have delivered, in the form of elementary truths, the several characteristic principles of that particular system. That we may be sure, then, not to mistake his meaning in this case, let us recur to the source from which the maxim was drawn.

On the slightest view of the British Constitution, we must perceive that the legislative, executive, and judiciary departments are by no means totally separate and distinct from each other. The executive magistrate forms an integral part of the legislative authority. He alone has the prerogative of making treaties with foreign sovereigns, which, when made, have, under certain limitations, the force of legislative acts. All the members of the judiciary department are appointed by him, can be removed by him on the address of the two Houses of Parliament, and form, when he pleases to consult them, one of his constitutional councils. One branch of the legislative department forms also a great constitutional council to the executive chief, as, on another hand, it is the sole depositary of judicial power in cases of impeachment, and is invested with the supreme appellate jurisdiction in all other cases. The judges, again, are so far connected with the legislative department as often to attend and participate in its deliberations, though not admitted to a legislative vote. From these facts, by which Montesquieu was guided, it may clearly be inferred that, in saying "There can be no liberty where the legislative and executive powers are united in the same person, or body of magistrates," or, "if the power of judging be not separated from the legislative and executive powers," he did not mean that these departments ought to have no PARTIAL AGENCY in, or no CONTROL over, the acts of each other. His meaning, as his own words import, and still more conclusively as illustrated by the example in his eye, can amount to no more than this, that where the WHOLE power of one department is exercised by the same hands which possess the WHOLE power of another department, the fundamental principles of a free constitution are subverted. This would have been the case in the constitution examined by him, if the king, who is the sole executive magistrate, had possessed also the complete legislative power, or the supreme administration of justice; or if the entire legislative body had possessed the supreme judiciary, or the supreme executive authority.

This, however, is not among the vices of that constitution. The magistrate in whom the whole executive power resides cannot of himself make a law, though he can put a negative on every law; nor administer justice in person, though he has the appointment of those who do administer it. The judges can exercise no executive prerogative, though they are shoots from the executive stock; nor any legislative function, though they may be advised with by the legislative councils. The entire legislature can perform no judiciary act, though by the joint act of two of its branches the judges may be removed from their offices, and though one of its branches is possessed of the judicial power in the last resort. The entire legislature, again, can exercise no executive prerogative, though one of its branches constitutes the supreme executive magistracy, and another, on the impeachment of a third, can try and condemn all the subordinate officers in the executive department. The reasons on which Montesquieu grounds his maxim are a further demonstration of his meaning. "When the legislative and executive powers are united in the same person or body," says he, "there can be no liberty, because apprehensions may arise lest THE SAME monarch or senate should ENACT tyrannical laws to EXECUTE them in a tyrannical manner." Again: "Were the power of judging joined with the legislative, the life and liberty of the subject would be exposed to arbitrary control, for THE JUDGE would then be THE LEGISLATOR. Were it joined to the executive power, THE JUDGE might behave with all the violence of AN OPPRESSOR." Some of these reasons are more fully explained in other passages; but briefly stated as they are here, they sufficiently establish the meaning which we have put on this celebrated maxim of this celebrated author.

[The rest of Federalist 47 goes on to look at the constitutions of several (pre-United States) American states, to argue that none of them fully separates the powers of their respective branches of government]

QUESTIONS

1. How would you describe the American legal system to someone who does not live in the United States?

2. How might you expect the law might attempt to regulate cybersecurity behaviors, given this brief introduction to the legal system?

2. STRUCTURE OF LAW

As we discuss in Section 6.A.1, there are many possible structures for democratic representative republics. Arrangements regarding the concentration of policymaking and executive power—which occupy much of our discussion thus far—are not the only important distinctions in understanding how the law functions. The authority to *interpret* and *apply* the law is equally important. In any form of government, some entity must be responsible for deciding in each individual circumstance how the law is applied to a given set of facts. In nearly all modern democratic societies, this power is allocated to the judicial body, with some limited assistance from the executive branch.[17] Thus a critical question becomes—if an interpretation of the law is made by a judicial body, to what extent is that interpretation binding on future such interpretations and/or on future actions by executive or the legislature?

The answer to this question, which addresses the issue of *stare decisis* or precedent, is the key distinction between what are known as "common law" jurisdictions (e.g., the U.S. and UK) and what are known as "civil code" jurisdictions (e.g., Germany and France). In civil code jurisdictions, the decisions of a court generally have limited future impact and are not considered "binding" interpretations of the law. In common law jurisdictions, the opposite is true—making the decisions of courts effectively become a "part" of the "law" in the sense that if they interpret a law or regulation a given way, generally that court (and all courts inferior to it) must follow that interpretation of it—even if they later disagree with it.[18] Additionally, at least some courts act as "constitutional courts"—bodies with the authority to interpret the constitutional validity of laws, regulations, or other acts by the legislature or the executive—and potentially invalidate those laws, regulations, or acts.

This distinction may sound highly theoretical, and the province of political theorists and jurisprudence scholars. Yet nothing could be further from the truth; it is *deeply* important both to the average citizen and to the average business. Why? *Because in a common law system, the "law" effectively includes court decisions!* For an individual or a business to understand and comply with the law, they have to know not just what the statutes and regulations say but also how the courts have interpreted the meaning of the statutory language. This is a significant burden, and indeed highlights an important part of the role of attorneys as advisors in common law jurisdictions.

---

[17] In some—usually non-criminal—circumstances, the initial authority for a decision may be vested in the executive official who is also responsible for *administering* the law which must be interpreted. For example, when a person files their individual Federal income tax return, administrative personnel within the Internal Revenue Service review—and make decisions—regarding the validity of that return. Judicial review, while ultimately available, does not occur until many, many stages later in the process of "adjudicating" the validity of a return.

[18] While technically speaking, a court may subsequently overrule itself, the concept of *stare decisis* ("that which is decided should stay decided") deeply frowns upon this practice. In the United States, for example, the number of times the U.S. Supreme Court has overruled itself are few and far between. Of relevant note, even the famed case of *Brown v. Board of Education*—in which the Court "reversed" the holding in *Plessy v. Ferguson* and did away with the concept of "separate but equal" in racial segregation)—was *not* actually a reversal. Rather, the Court determined that the *core facts had changed* such that the basis upon which the "separate but equal" holding applied no longer was applicable, and thus even if separate could (in theory) be equal, the nature of the world was that in practice it could not be, thus violating the 14th Amendment of the U.S. Constitution. *See* Irwin Chemerinsky, CONSTITUTIONAL LAW (4th ed.)(2013). In common law systems, reversals are indeed rare.

From an engineering standpoint, this concept is a little bit like how engineers are required to know not just the technical specifications of a component, but also how it performs as a practical matter "in the wild." From a business standpoint, this is a little bit like how businesses must understand not just what their financial models and customer feedback tell them, but also how to interpret how overall market trends historically suggest when those models or feedback might be wrong.[19] Of course, neither analogy is perfect, but they provide some insight regarding the challenges of looking beyond the primary rules of the road and understanding those rules in context.

In the cybersecurity context, this is particularly important because many laws and regulations use terms like "reasonable security" or describe general rather than technologically-specific practices. Those terms almost certainly will be interpreted by courts in relation to specific entities or industry sectors, and have already been subject to substantial agency interpretation. Thus just knowing that one must develop methods to address perimeter security may not be enough; a healthcare organization subject to HIPAA must also be aware of what constitutes a reasonable security plan for perimeter security given the size, scope, and capabilities of their organization.

Of course, as one might expect, few (if any) jurisdictions adopt this distinction so rigidly.[20] As a practical matter, it is perhaps better to describe modern jurisdictions as either following a common law "tradition" or being more influenced by the common law rather than following a civil code "tradition" (or being more civil code "influenced"). Thus, is it important to spend some time discussing the finer details of each to understand how they might balance against one another within any given jurisdiction.

a. Legislative Choices ("Black-Letter Law")

Legislative choices are, quite literally, eponymous: they are policy decisions made by the legislature. As noted below, in some cases these may be delegated to administrative agencies. This is likely the portion of the law with which most people are familiar. Legislatures write the laws in democracies, right?

---

19 *See, e.g.*, Hayden Christensen, THE INNOVATOR'S DILEMMA (1997).

20 The United States, for example, has moved increasingly in the direction of adopting some civil code aspects as courts have abolished some "common law" practices, particularly in the criminal law. Additionally, as administrative agencies in the U.S. increasingly promulgate and interpret their own regulations and as courts defer to those interpretations, one might argue the judicial common law is being partially displaced by an agency-promulgated "civil code" of sorts.

One may also compare and contrast, for example, the Republic of Korea (South Korea), which historically was a classic civil code jurisdiction modeled heavily after the German system. In recent years, however, the influence of common law-trained lawyers returning to Korea and working with the judiciary (particularly the Supreme Court) has, according to some scholars, influenced the Court to act more as a constitutional court creating and applying precedent.

Well, it both is and is not that simple. This is in large part due to the complexities of modern society. In the early 1800s, when the United States was a fledgling nation, it was a comparatively simple matter to write a rule for whether or not a document filing deadline was met: a document either was delivered by hand or mail by the date or it was not. Why might that be different now? Well, for starters, we have to figure out what might actually be considered a document. Consider the example of a voter registration deadline. Delivery of a physical paper copy of the document by hand to the proper official before close of business almost certainly satisfies this requirement in every jurisdiction today. What about by postal mail? Does it have to be sent ("postmarked") by a certain date, or received by that date? What about electronic delivery? If electronic delivery is used, what is considered a "document?" Is it a web form, an Adobe Portable Document Format (PDF) file, a Microsoft Word (DOC) file, or something else? By what electronic delivery method (public Internet email, web upload, etc.) must the "document" be sent? Who decides? What happens if there is a system error? Who bears the burden of such error? How is this determined?

This is just one simple example. Think about all the ways in which electronic commerce is used. Now try to write rules that handle each and every potential case and corner case. Remember our discussion of complexity in Chapter 5? If solving a puzzle that is twice as large takes far more than twice the amount of time, think about how designing rules for an exponentially more complex society might be a daunting task.

The result, simply put, is that legislatures simply cannot write all the rules that handle every case. And indeed, legislatures know this. In all jurisdictions, they can "delegate" some of this responsibility to administrative agencies, which may in turn promulgate regulations to "fill in the gaps" of more generally worded statutes adopted by the legislatures. Often such agencies employ technical experts in the relevant field being regulated (e.g., in securities law, the U.S. Securities and Exchange Commission promulgates regulations applicable to the sale of publicly-traded stocks and other securities), but administrative agencies, in varying degrees, receive at least some direction from the state or federal executive branch (state governor or President of the United States). This means that the interpretation may not be static, making compliance with such laws difficult.

Additionally, in common law jurisdictions, legislatures may deliberately draft more flexible statutes with the expectation that the courts will interpret those statutes in the context of new and unpredictable circumstances which arise. This is particularly common in consumer protection, where nearly all states have some form of a statutory prohibition on "unfair or deceptive" trade practices, but where some or all of the definition of what constitutes "unfair or deceptive" is left up to the courts of that state to decide.

b. Interpretive Doctrine ("Common Law")

This issue of complexity brings us to the concept of interpretive doctrine, or the *common law*. It is important to note, however, that the concept of the common law predates not only the societal complexities brought respectively by the Industrial Revolution and the Information Revolution, but also predates the United States itself. In the United Kingdom, for example, the determinations of the courts became part of the law to which individuals were held to account well before the U.S. was established. This was particularly true in criminal law and tort law (the law of private liability). When courts decided cases and interpreted what was expected of individuals, those decisions became part of the law going forward even though they were never written into a statute by the Parliament. Indeed, much of early U.S. law was imported from this system in the UK, and it was not until much later that legislatures in U.S. states began formally to incorporate this "common law" into published statutes.

Interpretive doctrine is not limited to the actions of courts. In modern society, it also includes the actions of federal (and sometimes state) administrative agencies. This "agency common law" may be express or implicit—the legislature may write a law affirmatively telling an agency to make and follow its own interpretations, or it may give an agency the authority to make interpretations of the law, and the agency may elect by practice to apply those interpretations to future determinations, holding parties to the standards of those prior determinations. As you may remember from Chapter 3's FTC "common law" debate, the propriety of this "implicit" delegation (at least in cybersecurity) is a hotly debated topic. While there is less disagreement about the propriety of express delegation, because it results from legislative deliberation, scholars of administrative law do still debate whether administrative interpretation is appropriate.

What does this all mean for understanding how the law functions? First, it is important to understand that the law rarely, if ever, ends at the black-letter rules written in a Constitution and in the statutes passed by a legislature. In nations like the U.S., it does not even end with regulations written by administrative agencies designed to "fill in the technical gaps" about which the legislature is not an expert. It also includes the law of the decisions made by courts, and sometimes agencies, that have precedential authority on future actions by those courts or agencies.

In some respects, this concept of common law is beneficial because it gives organizations flexibility in their approach to cybersecurity. Cybersecurity is, as you have seen in previous Chapters, a complex topic and a highly technical one. These characteristics make it difficult to write rules that will account for all current situations, let alone for all situations which may arise in the future. In other respects, however, it may be detrimental in the sense that it could make it more difficult for organizations to determine in advance what specific requirements may avoid regulatory liability. In later chapters, we will examine this comparison in the context of existing cybersecurity laws. For now, consider how these potential benefits and detriments might interact with the effectiveness of cybersecurity law.

3. SOURCES OF LAW

In the previous sections, we reviewed and discussed the origins of governmental and legal authority, and the types of legal structures that those governments can employ. In this section, we dive deeper into the ways in which rules are made by each authority under a common law system. Some of this material may seem repetitive—that is by design. We are compressing many years' of education into a single chapter, and the repetition is designed to ensure that each statement has adequate context to help readers follow.

a. Constitutional Choices

Each representative democracy has some form of a constitution—a supreme document which establishes, empowers, and limits the functions of its government. We have discussed the concept of Constitutions earlier in our discussion of the structure of government. As a source of law, it is considered the highest authority, with which all other acts of government must comply and to which all other rules are subordinate. In the United States, the Constitution has an express clause to this effect (the "Supremacy Clause"). As a result, no provision in the Constitution cannot be overridden by the legislature, the President, by any State, or by any interpretation of the courts.[21] Constitutions generally specify procedures by which they can be amended, whether for structural reasons (e.g., changes to the design of government) or substantive reasons (e.g., the creation of rights, or prohibition of certain government actions). The process of amendment ultimately requires approval by the citizens, whether directly (as in the case of many U.S. states' amendment processes) or by the citizens' directly elected representatives (as in the case of amendment of the U.S. Constitution).

b. Statutes

Generally, a constitution empowers a legislative body to enact laws. These laws are generally codified in written form and are the "rules" of the nation, but must be consistent with the commands in the constitution. It is the role of the judiciary to evaluate those laws and determine whether any given action is consistent with them.

---

[21] Note, however, as discussed elsewhere, that certain U.S. federal courts have the power to *interpret* the Constitution. Since constitutional principles often are general, this interpretation can have quite powerful effect when done by a nation's highest court (e.g., the U.S. Supreme Court), as this power could result in the invalidation of legislation or of a Presidential action.

This latter function, at least in common-law jurisdictions (e.g., the U.S. and the UK), creates a second "body of rules" colloquially known as the "common law" or "judge-made law." As arbiters of disputes, the courts are responsible for issuing final binding judgments regarding compliance with the law. In the course of doing so, it often becomes necessary for the courts to interpret the meaning of a law when the actions in question are not precisely addressed by the text of the law. This may be the case, for instance, when a given law doesn't address a specific type of action. In such cases, judges are said to be "gap-filling." Or it may be the case when a given law contains ambiguous terms.

The ability to interpret statutes gives common-law judges a great deal of power. Most statutes leave some room for interpretation—some gaps or ambiguity—that effectively give the judges interpreting those laws the ability to make law.

There are, however, limits on a judge's power to make law, both as a matter of judicial custom and under the U.S. Constitution. A central principle of the common law tradition is *stare decisis*, which holds that decisions of the courts should remain stable except under extraordinary circumstances. Where one judge interprets a statute in one way, other judges are reluctant to adopt a contrary interpretation. Because common-law judges almost universally abide by this principle, their interpretations of the law tend to create a stable body of judicial interpretation. This body of law is referred to as the "common law." As each court interprets a statute, that interpretation becomes part of the statutory meaning until overturned by a higher appellate court or until the law is modified by the legislature.

The virtues of this approach to law-making come into focus if we consider how it will play out over time. Judges that make "good" decisions—interpreting laws in ways that tend to benefit many and harm few—are unlikely to see future litigants challenging their interpretations of the law. On the other hand, when judges interpret the law in ways that are, on balance, less beneficial to society, litigants are more likely to challenge previous judicial interpretations. Even in the face of *stare decisis*, bad rules will eventually give way to better rules as judges continue to review them. The common-law approach is inherently evolutionary, with good interpretations of the law tending to stand the test of time and bad interpretations tending to be repeatedly challenged until giving way to better interpretations.

Another important aspect of the common law approach to law-making is that judges are barred from deciding which laws to review (and, therefore, to interpret or otherwise change). The United States Constitution limits federal courts to hearing cases in which there is an active "case or controversy," and most states impose similar limitations upon their judges. The "case or controversy" requirement means that judges can only hear cases that are brought by litigants, and those litigants must have something at stake in the litigation (or "standing" to bring suit). Neither judges nor individual citizens are free to bring a lawsuit challenging a law simply because they disagree with it. They must wait until they are actually harmed, either by the law or by another party violating the law.

This requirement further ensures that judges' interpretations tend to improve over time. A law that does not produce "cases or controversies" is unlikely to need review: if no one is harmed by the law, it may be superfluous, but it's hard to say the law is "bad." On the other hand, requiring that parties to litigation have experienced actual harm ensures that they have "skin in the game"—that they have strong motivations to zealously argue their positions before the court and to ensure that judges have sufficient information, representing as many perspectives as possible, to inform their making the best possible interpretation of the law.

DEREK BAMBAUER, *RULES, STANDARDS, AND GEEKS*

5 BROOK. J. CORP. FIN. & COM. L. 49 (2010)

When it comes to regulating technology, the age-old debate between rules and standards tilts heavily towards standards. Rules, for all their clarity, are seen as slow-changing tools in industries characterized by dynamism. They are also viewed as being both under- and over-inclusive, and in prizing form—one means of achieving a desired result—over substance—the result itself. Moreover, setting legal rules for technology risks creating lock-in, which may cement a given technology in place. In short, standards—particularly standards that look to industry best practices—are lauded as the best means for governing code through law.

This Article, though, argues that rules are preferable for regulating data security, at least under certain conditions. In part, this is so because data security typically focuses on controlling the wrong set of events. Security is often preoccupied with regulating access to data—in particular, with preventing unauthorized access. Yet, strangely, unauthorized access is ubiquitous. Employees lose laptops, hackers breach corporate databases, and information is inadvertently e-mailed or posted to the public Internet. This Article argues that preventing data breaches is not only the wrong goal for regulators, it is an impossible one. Complex systems design theory shows that accidents are inevitable. Thus, instead of seeking to prevent crashes, policymakers should concentrate on enabling us to walk away from them. The focus should be on airbags, not anti-lock brakes. Regulation should seek to allow data to "degrade gracefully," mitigating the harm that occurs when a breach (inevitably) happens.

Such regulatory methods are optimally framed as rules under three conditions. First, minimal compliance—meeting only the letter of the law—is sufficient to avoid most harm. Second, rules should be relatively impervious to decay in efficacy over time; technological change, such as increased CPU speeds, should not immediately undermine a rule's preventive impact. Furthermore, compliance with a rule should be easy and inexpensive to evaluate. In addition, rules are likely to be helpful where error costs from standards are high; where if an entity's judgment about data security is wrong, there is significant risk of harm or risk of significant harm. Finally, this argument has implications for how compliance should be assessed. When regulation is clear and low-cost, it creates an excellent case for a per se negligence rule, or, in other words, a regime of strict liability for failure to comply with the rule. This Article thus addresses not the desirability of regulation—when data security should be mandated—but rather how to structure that regulation once it is deemed worthwhile.

The debate about framing legal commands as rules or as standards is a venerable one. Scholars have addressed the dichotomy in contexts from real property rights to patent law to antitrust. The merits and shortcomings of each approach have been analyzed from a variety of theoretical perspectives. Rules offer clearer signals to those whose behavior is constrained; they help both regulated and regulators assess compliance more cheaply and easily. In addition, they may prevent abuse by conferring less discretion on regulators. However, rules are often underinclusive—failing to cover behavior that should fall within their ambit, or failing to prevent risks they are designed to address—or over-inclusive—imposing burdens on unrelated actors or activities. Standards, by contrast, are more readily adapted to complex or changing situations, but often at the price of predictability and cost.

The discussion becomes more complex when we recognize that the distinction is continuous rather than binary. Standards can be rule-like, and rules standards-like. Consider two security mandates: "encrypt," and "follow industry best practice for securing data." The former looks like a rule, and the latter like a standard. However, "encrypt" could be seen as a standard: the command specifies a method, but leaves the implementation entirely up to the regulated entity. Encryption has been used since the days of Mary, Queen of Scots; its modes range from simple (and simply cracked) transposition ciphers to elliptic curve cryptography. Even a more specific command like "encrypt using asymmetric key cryptography" can be met with a variety of responses. The RSA, ElGamal, and DSS key techniques all meet the criterion, but have important differences among them. Thus, a rule can be transformed into a standard by altering the level of specificity.

Similarly, "follow industry best practice for securing data" could be a rule. If, for example, the industry has standardized on the use of SSL (Secure Sockets Layer) to safeguard sensitive data while it is being communicated over a network, that best practice standard effectively becomes a rule: "use SSL." Thus, even if an alternative technique were demonstrated to be functionally equivalent, it would not comply with the standard, even though standards are typically viewed as ends-driven and not means-driven. In short, the line between rules and standards blurs, particularly as a rule's command becomes more general.

[. . .]

I. THE VIRTUES OF STANDARDS

Technology changes quickly; law, slowly. Most commentators favor standards when dealing with technological regulation of issues such as security, for at least five reasons.

First, standards allow regulated entities to comply in a more cost-efficient fashion than rules. Requiring a particular technology or approach may be unnecessarily expensive, especially where infrastructures differ significantly, where there are a range of alternatives, or where the endpoint can be achieved without applying technology in some situations. Rules can limit creativity in achieving regulators' goals.

Second, standards can be less vulnerable to obsolescence. Rule-based specifications may decay quickly when technology changes rapidly. This either undercuts the efficacy of regulation, or forces frequent updates to it. The Clipper Chip controversy of the mid-1990s provides a potent example; regulation that mandated use of one particular encryption technique might well have undercut the deployment of e-commerce and other advances dependent on data security.

Third, standards can minimize the ill-effects of information asymmetry regarding technology. Regulators may not know what technologies are cutting-edge or appropriate or unnecessarily costly. Standards can wrap in expertise from regulated entities while meeting regulatory goals.

Fourth, standards may deal better with interoperability concerns. Most organizations have heterogeneous information technology environments for a variety of reasons: mergers, legacy systems, customer demands, and so forth. Regulations that specify a particular technology, or method of compliance, may make demands that are impossible or inapposite. For example, Deutsche Bank used the IBM operating system OS/2 long after most other customers had migrated to Microsoft Windows or a UNIX platform. Thus, requirements tied to Windows (for example, using the NTFS file system) or to software only available for that operating system would have forced Deutsche Bank into a costly migration, or to fall out of compliance. In contrast, a standard that specifies its goal, but is technology agnostic, allows entities with a range of infrastructures to comply adequately.

Finally, selecting one technology for regulatory compliance risks producing market-making effects. Regulation may confer success, or at least widespread adoption, on a single product or company—a problem that worsens if the technology is sub-optimal. For example, the memory chip manufacturer Rambus was able to influence the industry group JEDEC (Joint Electron Device Engineering Counsel) to adopt, as part of its standard for SDRAM (Synchronous Dynamic Random Access Memory), technology over which Rambus held patent rights. (Indeed, Rambus actually amended its pending patent applications to conform better to the JEDEC technology.) This led to lawsuits against Rambus for fraud, and to an initial Federal Trade Commission (FTC, or Commission) finding that the company had engaged in antitrust violations (under Section 2 of the Sherman Act). However, Rambus emerged unscathed from both the suits and the FTC investigation. Similarly, a legal mandate to incorporate a particular technology could create market power for that technology's owner, particularly if the technology were protected by intellectual property rights such as a patent. Thus, a rule may entrench a single technology into a powerful if not unassailable market position.

[. . .]

II. THE VIRTUES OF RULES

Arguing for rules in technological regulation is an uphill climb: they can become obsolete rapidly, may increase costs by forcing entities to comply in a highly specific fashion, and may be both over- and underinclusive. Yet, this Article argues that rules are preferable to standards when at least three conditions hold: sufficient minima, slow or low decay, and inexpensive verification.

First, a rule is helpful when the specified level of data security—effectively, a minimum—suffices in most or all circumstances. One example would be to mandate that transmission of data take place over a connection protected by 128-bit SSL. SSL certificates are widely and cheaply available, and root certificates are built into all major browsers. Currently, 128-bit SSL traffic is proof against brute-force decryption attacks even when adversaries use clusters or supercomputers. Thus, 128-bit encryption is strong enough to protect data in communication, even if institutions do not take additional measures, such as protecting against eavesdropping.

A corollary is that rules may be helpful where the impact of a data breach is high, and where the specified technology raises the cost to an attacker or discoverer of captured information. One example here is hard drive encryption. Stories of lost laptops, backup tapes, and USB drives are legion. Here, rules serve not to prevent loss—indeed, hard drive encryption is only useful after the loss has taken place—but to reduce its effects. Similarly, a rule mandating logging of access to sensitive data cannot prevent an employee from copying down customer account information displayed on a computer monitor, but can aid an institution to detect what has been revealed in the breach, and perhaps to minimize its spread. This condition requires that the rule specify protection that is good enough in most or all cases.

Second, rules work well when they need not be frequently updated—in other words, when they decay slowly. This reduces the administrative cost of the rule, and allows it to retain effectiveness over time. 128-bit encryption, for example, will likely suffice against brute-force attacks for at least ten years, given current rates of advance in CPU clock cycles and parallelization. To take another encryption case study, DES (Data Encryption Standard) was adopted as a Federal Information Processing Standard in 1976. It remained impervious to commercial-level decryption (as opposed to governmental attacks) until the late 1990s. A technology specifying rule that remains effective for over twenty years is relatively low-cost to update and relatively impervious to decay.

Finally, rules are particularly effective when monitoring is low-cost and accurate. An ongoing problem with data security breaches is the causation of downstream harm. For example, if a bank suffers a data spill, and its customers later suffer identity theft, is there a causal connection to the spill? Courts have largely interpreted the causation requirements built into tort law to exempt data owners or storehouses from liability. This may result in insufficient incentives to take precautions. A rule, for example, that requires data holders to encrypt data usefully serves as a bright-line negligence test—especially when compliance is relatively low-cost. Holding institutions responsible for downstream consequences of harms related to the spilled information provides strong incentives to comply with the rule—including that liability can be avoided entirely (under the current doctrine) simply through encryption. Concerns about over-deterrence, or excessive investment in precautions, are minimized (if not eliminated) where the entity can avoid liability relatively simply and cheaply, and where errors in adjudication are unlikely. When a rule is effective, both initially and over time, and where regulators can assess compliance cheaply and with confidence, a rule is likely to be superior to a standard in specifying technological measures for data security. Thus, data security rules can helpfully act as a forcing device that reduces the level of harm from breaches.

CONCLUSION

The default assumption for regulating information technology is that standards are not only the superior choice; they are nearly the only choice. This is because scholars and policymakers have focused on the wrong problem: they seek to prevent data spills, rather than to mitigate their impact. Rules can helpfully reduce the effects of a breach. For technology, rules are preferable when they can specify a minimum level of protection that is relatively effective against most risks or attacks; where obsolescence occurs slowly; and where monitoring the rule's implementation is relatively low-cost and accurate. Standards are not always superior, nor are they always inferior—instead, the preferred embodiment of regulation varies with the characteristics of the technological problem at issue. While application design is best governed by standards, due to the critical role of process, the transport and storage of data, along with identification of access to information, are best dealt with via rules. This Article questions the prevailing consensus in favor of standards for regulating technology, and also seeks to create testable predictions about when rules will work better. In short, I argue sometimes geeks require rules, not standards.

c. Administrative Law and Regulations ("Agency Choices")

Modern societal complexity has challenged some of the traditional assumptions of the tripartite system of government. The presumption that it is the province of the legislature to make every individual policy decision, for example, may be unworkable in a modern society of vast economic, geographic, and population scale and one of substantial and ever-increasing technological complexity. How, for example, could even 535 members of Congress possibly maintain all the expertise necessary to understand all of nuclear power, global macroeconomics, transportation engineering, cybersecurity, medicine, and agriculture?

Ultimately, sometimes legislature must seek help from the other branches of government. Regardless of whether one finds this approach appropriate, it is the reality of modern society in the United States and many other countries that the legislatures have created agencies to assist them in the administration of the law. These agencies are responsible for developing expertise, making recommendations on technical matters, and—to some extent—exercising quasi-legislative and quasi-judicial powers by writing regulations that fill in regulatory gaps. Administrative agencies also make preliminary adjudicatory decisions regarding the enforcement of those regulations.

The concept of an agency is not expressly contemplated by the Constitution. The Constitution does, however, provide for the appointment of officers: principal officers, who are appointed by the President with the consent of the Senate, and inferior officers, who may be appointed by principal officers or other government officials. These officers are "agents" of the Executive branch, authorized to act on behalf of the President to carry out the laws enacted by Congress. An agency is an organization created by Congressional legislation that is given specific grants of legal power through that legislation by Congress. The Federal Trade Commission, for instance, was created by the Federal Trade Commission Act Of 1913. It is led by five principal officers appointed by the President; and it is charged with taking action against business that engage in unfair methods of competition or unfair or deceptive act or practices. The Department of Homeland Security was created by the Homeland Security Act of 2002 and is headed by the Secretary of Homeland Security and a number of Deputy- and Undersecretaries.

Agencies have no power other than that which is conferred to them by Congress. This power is conferred to them by legislation (generally referred to as the agency's "enabling" or "organic" statute). These statutes may give agencies precise instructions (e.g., on an annual basis, prepare and publish a report documenting the state of competition in telecommunications markets). Other times, they grant an agency some form of power and authorize the agency to exercise that power. Such authorization generally comes in one of two forms: adjudication or rulemaking. The Federal Trade Commission, for instance, is authorized to take action to proscribe unfair methods of competition. In exercising this power, the agency can bring an adjudicatory (that is, trial-like) enforcement action against a firm that the agency believes is engaging in an unfair method of competition, or it can go through a special procedure known as "rulemaking" to issue law-like rules that define different types of conduct that the agency believes constitute "unfair methods of competition."

Agencies can be controversial, because they often combine both executive and judicial authority—that is, in some ways they can violate separation of powers principles.[22] That is, agencies often have the ability both to bring adjudicatory actions to enforce the law and also to use rulemaking proceedings to say what the law is.

Despite this apparent violation of separation of powers principles, courts have generally found that agencies do not violate the Constitution. There are three key reasons for this, one each corresponding to the power of each branch of government. First, agencies are not authorized to exercise any powers not conferred upon them by Congress through the agency's enabling statute. Second, the officials who head each agency must, at minimum, be appointed by the President, and therefore are subject to at least some modicum of executive control. And third, any action undertaken by an agency is subject to review by the courts, to ensure that it does not violate either the Constitution or the agency's organic statute.

QUESTIONS

1. Why do we have agencies?
2. What do agencies do and how are they created?
3. What limits are there on the conduct of agencies?

d. Judicial Interpretation ("Common Law")

We have discussed the concept of the common law generally at some length. This section provides detail regarding its authority, and practical function. Stated differently, assuming that "common law" exists as such:

[22] This is particularly true with agencies that are "independent" from the President. These are agencies where Congress has specified that the President cannot "remove" (that is, fire) the officers that head the agency if the disagree with the President's policies.

from where does its authority come, and how does that interact with other "sources" of law?

The common law, as we have seen, is the collective set of judicial decisions interpreting the Constitution, statutes, and, to a lesser extent,) administrative regulations. Recall that the role of the judiciary is to enforce the law. Specifically, the judiciary is expected to arbitrate disagreements and instruct officers to *force* or *compel* compliance when necessary. In this regard, obviously, judicial decisions are binding on the parties to a dispute, and this is generally true in all modern democratic governments.

But the nature of a common law jurisdiction is that judicial decisions establish *precedent*. This again is the idea that a decision involving a set of facts, requiring an interpretation of the meaning of the law, will be binding on similar disputes in the future requiring interpretation of that law. Thus, in effect, the interpretation *becomes part of the law*.

Quite obviously, however, the judiciary does not have the power to make law. So how do we reconcile this? How do we determine the "precedence"[23] to which to assign the common law? In short, there are two orders of precedence to consider: (1) the relationship between judicial interpretation and other sources of law; and (2) the relation among judicial interpretations by different courts.

As to the first, the formula is fairly simple: the interpretation carries the same weight of authority as does the law the court is interpreting. If a court interprets the Constitution, it has the same weight as does the Constitution. Likewise, if a court interprets a legislative statute, it has the same weight of authority as would that law. Given the role of the courts is to adjudicate disputes and enforce the law, this make sense. But what if the legislature or the executive doesn't like the outcome?

In the case of interpretation of the Constitution, both the legislature and the executive have no ordinary powers by which to respond. The court has interpreted the Constitution, and all parts of the government are bound by the Constitution. If the legislature, the executive, or their constituents (the polity) don't like those interpretations, their recourse is to amend the Constitution.

In the case of interpretation of a legislative statute, the interpretation has the same force as the statute. Thus, for example, the executive would be bound by that interpretation, even if the executive does not like it. The legislature, however, has other options. Because the legislature writes the law, if it does not like the way a court interprets it, it can simply change the law! (The legislative process, of course, is not so simple—particularly in a two-party political system—but the design is.)

---

[23] Referring to the order of priority, as opposed to the jurisprudential term "precedent", which refers to a principle established in common law by judicial decision.

Lastly, it is worth noting that courts do sometimes interpret the rules promulgated by the executive, including both rules made through administrative agencies and by the President. Although interpretation of agency regulations is less common (courts generally defer to the agency's interpretation of their own regulations[24]). Interpretation of Executive Orders in modern times is even more rare (usually only when the President is not a party to the action), in large part because Congress has created a public administration system in which most executive action is carried out by agencies. When courts do engage in such interpretation, the affected agency (or the President) generally can simply rescind, modify, and or promulgate a new regulation or Order, provided the proper Constitutional and statutory requirements are followed. Additionally, of course, the legislature could override the court's decision by passing new legislation.

This brings us to the second question: what happens when different courts reach different conclusions? The formula here again is simple in theory, albeit more difficult to predict in practice. Essentially, there are two questions: what happens when two courts of the same level conflict, and what happens when two courts at different levels conflict?

The answer to the latter is very simple—the Constitution and U.S. federal law assign a priority order to the courts. The U.S. Supreme Court is the highest judicial authority, both on Federal law and on questions of state law involving the U.S. Constitution. The Supreme Court's interpretative word is final, without exception, for the courts subordinate to its binding authority. The federal courts have a set of intermediate appellate courts, the U.S. Courts of Appeals, which are organized into twelve courts by geographic area and one specialized court. Finally, the courts of first instance (or the trial courts) are referred to as the District Courts and also are assigned geographically. Each state has at least one (and in some cases several) U.S. District Courts. Several states and/or territories[25] comprise each "circuit" for the Courts of Appeals. The jurisdiction of the U.S. Supreme Court lies over the entirety of the jurisdiction of the United States.

Because the United States has a dual, federated form of government, courts similarly are federated. State courts hear state cases, while federal courts hear interstate cases, cases related to federal law, and controversies

---

[24] There is a rich debate in U.S. administrative law, both among scholars and in the judiciary, as to whether such deference *should* be commonplace. *See, e.g., Christopher v. SmithKlineBeecham*, 567 U.S. 142, 158 (2012) noting that "[courts'] practice of deferring to an agency's interpretation of its own ambiguous regulations undoubtedly has important advantages, but this practice also creates a risk that agencies will promulgate vague and open-ended regulations that they can later interpret as they see fit, thereby frustrat[ing] the notice and predictability purposes of rulemaking . . . ." (internal citations and quotation marks omitted).

[25] Except in the case of the U.S. Court of Appeals for the District of Columbia Circuit, which comprises solely the nation's capitol—the (relatively) geographically tiny District of Columbia. Ironically, this court—because of its jurisdiction over the actions of nearly all federal agencies—is one of the most influential Courts of Appeals.

involving people or actions implicating more than one state. State court cases, when appealed, will ultimately be determined by the Supreme Court of the state. These determinations are binding for all lower courts in that state but generally are not binding with respect to any other state.[26]

Federal courts are organized by district, or a group of states. Each state has at least one District Court, where more populated states may have several district courts organized by geographic region within that state, such as the Eastern District of New York. District Court decisions may be appealed to the Circuit within which the District lies, which includes multiple districts.[27] For example, the Second Circuit includes the states of Connecticut, New York, and Vermont. Any appeal from a District Court in one of these states will be heard by the Second Circuit. Any appeal from a Second Circuit decision goes to the U.S. Supreme Court. Decisions from one district court are not binding with respect to any other district court, and decisions from one circuit court are not binding with respect to any other circuit court.

In the case of a conflict between a lower and a higher court, the higher court's interpretation always prevails. In the case of a conflict between two District Courts[28] within the same Circuit, the Court of Appeals for that Circuit[29] usually will resolve the issue. Until such resolution, the decisions of each District Court generally are binding within each respective court's geographic jurisdiction, and the District Court, for purposes of creating consistency in application of the law will try to act in line with its previous decisions, or *precedent*. For disputes between Circuit Courts—until and unless the U.S. Supreme Court resolves the "Circuit split"—the interpretations of each Circuit are binding within their geographical jurisdiction. "Circuit splits" are a somewhat more interesting circumstance because appeals are a matter of right to the Circuit Courts—all parties are generally always entitled to appeal—and thus few splits among District Courts go unresolved. Appeals to the U.S. Supreme Court are almost always discretionary, however, and statistically speaking are very rarely granted. Thus disagreements among the Circuit Courts—so-called Circuit splits—may go unresolved for years.

Lastly, we must return to the question of what happens when a court's decisions are inconsistent: when a subsequent sitting of a court fails to follow the interpretation of an earlier sitting of the same court (with

[26] When a state confronts a "new" question, it often will look to other states with similar laws to see how those states' highest courts ruled on the issue. While not binding, this often can be fairly "persuasive" authority, particularly in the case of very similar laws.

[27] With one notable exception—the U.S. Court of Appeals for the District of Columbia Circuit hears appeals from only one federal district—the U.S. District Court for the District of Columbia. Nonetheless, this remains one of the most influential federal appellate courts, as it reviews a disproportionate high percentage of actions involving the federal government.

[28] E.g., between a U.S. District Court in New York City and one in Hartford, CT.

[29] In this example, the Court of Appeals for the Second Circuit, which includes New York, Connecticut, and Vermont.

different judges) on the same question of law (for example if the Second Circuit in 2020 did not follow a Second Circuit decision from 1990). This implicates the principle of *stare decisis*, the idea that judicial decisions should remain settled. It is a fundamental principle of the common law—because if decisions could change frequently, the concept of the common law would provide very poor notice to people of what the law required of them. (Incidentally, such poor notice might violate the U.S. Constitution, particularly in the context of criminal law.) But what happens if a subsequent court decides that the earlier decision was truly incorrect?

The answer is that, while extraordinarily rare, the subsequent court decision would become the new answer in the common law. Again, recall as discussed earlier, that courts "overruling" themselves—as opposed to *distinguishing* the facts of the newer case from the older case—are quite rare as courts do seek to create consistency. Those "factual distinctions" may often have the *effect* of feeling like a decision was overruled, but strictly speaking, that is not correct.

QUESTIONS

1. Which approach to developing law—statutes created by legislatures or common-law rules developed over time—seems a better approach to developing rules related to cybersecurity?

2. Do you think judges are well-positioned to determine what reasonable cybersecurity might be in a given context? Why or why not?

e. Agency Interpretation ("Regulatory Adjudications and the "(Un)Common Law")

Lastly, it is worth noting that in addition to promulgating regulations, as discussed above, administrative agencies often will find themselves responsible for interpreting either their own regulations or the statutes which establish their authority. This is a complicated area of law, and not one which you need understand fully. However, a substantial portion of cybersecurity rules come from administrative agencies, and so it is important to be familiar with the fact that these agencies, acting with quasi-judicial power delegated to them by Congress, *do have the authority to interpret laws and regulations*. These interpretations are usually subject to review by the courts, however in most cases the court will defer to the agency's interpretation as long as it is "reasonable."[30]

---

[30] As noted earlier, there is some debate surrounding whether courts should defer to agencies interpretations of their own regulations. When an agency interprets a *law* that it has been charged by Congress with administering (i.e., Congress has declared them the "expert" on the subject), courts will almost always defer to an agency's reasonable interpretation of that law. *See Chevron U.S.A., Inc. v. Natural Resources Defense Council, Inc.*, 467 U.S. 837 (1984). Some scholarly debate exists as to the propriety of the so-called *Chevron* doctrine, however it remains binding precedent as of 2020.

For example, the Department of Health and Human Services, as the principal administrative agency overseeing human health interprets laws like the Health Insurance Portability and Accountability Act (HIPAA) and the Food, Drug, and Cosmetics Act (FDCA). They also propose certain rules that further specify how to comply through the Code of Federal Regulations (CFR), which are the set of legal volumes where administrative agency rules are housed. The CFR is a great example of how agencies may pass certainly requirements that have the binding force of law but nevertheless have not been explicitly determined by Congress.[31]

B. LEGAL PRINCIPLES

The next part of this chapter undertakes an ambitious project: to provide a concise but sufficient introduction to basic legal principles. In other words, to give non-lawyers a sense, over the course of a couple dozen pages, of what it is to "think like a lawyer." This, of course, is a fraught endeavor (though no moreso than the last chapter's efforts to introduce non-engineers or computer scientists to many foundational concepts from those fields).

Of course, this chapter does not provide a comprehensive introduction to legal theory. Rather, like Chapter 5 does for engineering principles, our present goal is to introduce legal principles important to understanding the law of cybersecurity, and to use those topics to provide a broader sense of how lawyers generally think about problem solving. These ideas are recurrent throughout the rest of this book. Chapters 8 and 10 will build on them in specific detail. More generally, a framing theme throughout this book is to think of cybersecurity as an exercise in risk management—and for this reason the primary area of law that we focus on is tort law.

Tort law is the law of wrongs or harms—those familiar with other languages may recognize the word tort as meaning "to harm," and the etymology traces to the medieval Latin tortum ("wrong, injustice") or Latin torquēre ("to twist"). This area of law addresses straightforward harms, such as battery, trespass, and theft (that is, harm where one person harms another). But it also covers the law of negligence or, generally, the law of accidents. Negligence law considers who is liable when accidents happen. A basic principle of this area of the law is simply that: accidents happen. The law recognizes that some level of accidents are unavoidable—as with security, where there is no such thing as a "secure" system, there is no such thing as an accident-free world—and that it doesn't always make sense to impose liability on an individual who has caused an accident. Rather, there are cases where it makes sense to place the burden on others to avoid being

[31] Without going into too much detail, under the Administrative Procedure Act, which regulates the behavior of agencies, administrative agency rules are subject to a public notice and comment period, wherein the general public or affected individuals may weigh in on proposed rules. Although agencies are not bound by these comments, agencies must consider them.

harmed, or to let injuries fall as they may such that each party to an accident bears its respective costs.

Our discussion starts with an excerpt from Oliver Wendel Holmes's famous essay, *The Path of the Law*, to focus on the question of the primary mechanism of the law (imposing liability on those who break it) and the purposes of that mechanism. It then turns to the field of law & economics to consider in more detail how the liability mechanism works—in particular, how we may think about *who* should bear the burden of avoiding harms. It should be noted and acknowledged that the perspective offered here is that of law & economics (a branch of legal theory that uses economic analysis to understand the structure of legal institutions). This is not the only school of legal though that can bear on these questions, and is not without some amount of controversy. Nonetheless, over the past half century this school of thought has been uniquely important and effective at elucidating the ideas that we discuss—and the economic methodology is similarly important to cybersecurity as a field. The final portion of this discussion adds an additional turn, introducing yet another branch of tort law, products liability (which is governed by the tort of strict liability). This discussion rounds out our introduction to tort law and legal theory and, again, adds an additional perspective on issues relevant to cybersecurity.

1. THE MECHANISM AND PURPOSE OF THE LAW

OLIVER WENDEL HOLMES, *THE PATH OF THE LAW*

10 Harv. L. Rev. 457 (1897)

When we study law we are not studying a mystery but a well known profession. We are studying what we shall want in order to appear before judges, or to advise people in such a way as to keep them out of court. The reason why it is a profession, why people will pay lawyers to argue for them or to advise them, is that in societies like ours the command of the public force is intrusted to the judges in certain cases, and the whole power of the state will be put forth, if necessary, to carry out their judgments and decrees. People want to know under what circumstances and how far they will run the risk of coming against what is so much stronger than themselves, and hence it becomes a business to find out when this danger is to be feared. The object of our study, then, is prediction, the prediction of the incidence of the public force through the instrumentality of the courts. [. . .]

I wish, if I can, to lay down some first principles for the study of this body of dogma or systematized prediction which we call the law, for men who want to use it as the instrument of their business to enable them to prophesy in their turn, and, as bearing upon the study, I wish to point out an ideal which as yet our law has not attained.

The first thing for a business-like understanding of the matter is to understand its limits, and therefore I think it desirable at once to point out and dispel a confusion between morality and law, which sometimes rises to the height of conscious theory, and more often and indeed constantly is making trouble in detail without reaching the point of consciousness. You can see very plainly that a bad man has as much reason as a good one for wishing to avoid an encounter with the public force, and therefore you can see the practical importance of the distinction between morality and law. A man who cares nothing for an ethical rule which is believed and practised by his neighbors is likely nevertheless to care a good deal to avoid being made to pay money, and will want to keep out of jail if he can.

I take it for granted that no hearer of mine will misinterpret what I have to say as the language of cynicism. The law is the witness and external deposit of our moral life. Its history is the history of the moral development of the race. The practice of it, in spite of popular jests, tends to make good citizens and good men. When I emphasize the difference between law and morals I do so with reference to a single end, that of learning and understanding the law. For that purpose you must definitely master its specific marks, and it is for that that I ask you for the moment to imagine yourselves indifferent to other and greater things.

I do not say that there is not a wider point of view from which the distinction between law and morals becomes of secondary or no importance, as all mathematical distinctions vanish in presence of the infinite. But I do say that that distinction is of the first importance for the object which we are here to consider,—a right study and mastery of the law as a business with well understood limits, a body of dogma enclosed within definite lines. I have just shown the practical reason for saying so. If you want to know the law and nothing else, you must look at it as a bad man, who cares only for the material consequences which such knowledge enables him to predict, not as a good one, who finds his reasons for conduct, whether inside the law or outside of it, in the vaguer sanctions of conscience. The theoretical importance of the distinction is no less, if you would reason on your subject aright. The law is full of phraseology drawn from morals, and by the mere force of language continually invites us to pass from one domain to the other without perceiving it, as we are sure to do unless we have the boundary constantly before our minds. The law talks about rights, and duties, and malice, and intent, and negligence, and so forth, and nothing is easier, or, I may say, more common in legal reasoning, than to take these words in their moral sense, at some stage of the argument, and so to drop into fallacy. For instance, when we speak of the rights of man in a moral sense, we mean to mark the limits of interference with individual freedom which we think are prescribed by conscience, or by our ideal, however reached. Yet it is certain that many laws have been enforced in the past, and it is likely that some are enforced now, which are condemned by the most enlightened opinion of the time, or which at all events pass the limit of interference as many consciences would draw it. Manifestly, therefore, nothing but confusion of thought can result from assuming that the rights of man in a moral sense are equally rights in the sense of the Constitution and the law. No doubt simple and extreme cases can be put of imaginable laws which the statute making power would not dare to enact, even in the absence of written constitutional prohibitions, because the community would rise in rebellion and fight; and this gives some plausibility to the proposition that the law, if not a part of morality, is limited by it. But this limit of power is not coextensive with any system of morals. For the most part it falls far within the lines of any such system, and in some cases may extend beyond them, for reasons drawn from the habits of a particular people at a particular time. I once heard the late Professor Agassiz say that a German population would rise if you added two cents to the price of a glass of beer. A statute in such a case would be empty words, not because it was wrong, but because it could not be enforced. No one will deny that wrong statutes can be and are enforced, and we should not all agree as to which were the wrong ones.

The confusion with which I am dealing besets confessedly legal conceptions. Take the fundamental question, What constitutes the law? You will find some text writers telling you that it is something different from what is decided by the courts of Massachusetts or England, that it is a system of reason, that it is a deduction from principles of ethics or admitted axioms or what not, which may or may not coincide with the decisions. But if we take the view of our friend the bad man we shall find that he does not care two straws for the axioms or deductions, but that he does want to know what the Massachusetts or English courts are likely to do in fact. I am much of his mind. The prophecies of what the courts will do in fact, and nothing more pretentious, are what I mean by the law.

Take again a notion which as popularly understood is the widest conception which the law contains;—the notion of legal duty, to which already I have referred. We fill the word with all the content which we draw from morals. But what does it mean to a bad man? Mainly, and in the first place, a prophecy that if he does certain things he will be subjected to disagreeable consequences by way of imprisonment or compulsory payment of money. But from his point of view, what is the difference between being fined and being taxed a certain sum for doing a certain thing? That his point of view is the test of legal principles is shown by the many discussions which have arisen in the courts on the very question whether a given statutory liability is a penalty or a tax. On the answer to this question depends the decision whether conduct is legally wrong or right, and also whether a man is under compulsion or free. Leaving the criminal law on one side, what is the difference between the liability under the mill acts or statutes authorizing a taking by eminent domain and the liability for what we call a wrongful conversion of property where restoration is out of the question? In both cases the party taking another man's property has to pay its fair value as assessed by a jury, and no more. What significance is there in calling one taking right and another wrong from the point of view of the law? It does not matter, so far as the given consequence, the compulsory payment, is concerned, whether the act to which it is attached is described in terms of praise or in terms of blame, or whether the law purports to prohibit it or to allow it. If it matters at all, still speaking from the bad man's point of view, it must be because in one case and not in the other some further disadvantages, or at least some further consequences, are attached to the act by the law. [. . .]

I mentioned, as other examples of the use by the law of words drawn from morals, malice, intent, and negligence. It is enough to take malice as it is used in the law of civil liability for wrongs,—what we lawyers call the law of torts,—to show you that it means something different in law from what it means in morals, and also to show how the difference has been obscured by giving to principles which have little or nothing to do with each other the same name. Three hundred years ago a parson preached a sermon and told a story out of Fox's Book of Martyrs of a man who had assisted at the torture of one of the saints, and afterward died, suffering compensatory inward torment. It happened that Fox was wrong. The man was alive and chanced to hear the sermon, and thereupon he sued the parson. Chief Justice Wray instructed the jury that the defendant was not liable, because the story was told innocently, without malice. He took malice in the moral sense, as importing a malevolent motive. But nowadays no one doubts that a man may be liable, without any malevolent motive at all, for false statements manifestly calculated to inflict temporal damage. In stating the case in pleading, we still should call the defendant's conduct malicious; but, in my opinion at least, the word means nothing about motives, or even about the defendant's attitude toward the future, but only signifies that the tendency of his conduct under the known circumstances was very plainly to cause the plaintiff temporal harm. [. . .]

This is not the time to work out a theory in detail, or to answer many obvious doubts and questions which are suggested by these general views. I know of none which are not easy to answer, but what I am trying to do now is only by a series of hints to throw some light on the narrow path of legal doctrine, and upon two pitfalls which, as it seems to me, lie perilously near to it. Of the first of these I have said enough. I hope that my illustrations have shown the danger, both to speculation and to practice, of confounding morality with law, and the trap which legal language lays for us on that side of our way. For my own part, I often doubt whether it would not be a gain if every word of moral significance could be banished from the law altogether, and other words adopted which should convey legal ideas uncolored by anything outside the law. We should lose the fossil records of a good deal of history and the majesty got from ethical associations, but by ridding ourselves of an unnecessary confusion we should gain very much in the clearness of our thought. [. . .]

So much for the limits of the law. The next thing which I wish to consider is what are the forces which determine its content and its growth. [. . .]

The fallacy to which I refer is the notion that the only force at work in the development of the law is logic. In the broadest sense, indeed, that notion would be true. The postulate on which we think about the universe is that there is a fixed quantitative relation between every phenomenon and its antecedents and consequents. . . . So in the broadest sense it is true that the law is a logical development, like everything else. The danger of which I speak is not the admission that the principles governing other phenomena also govern the law, but the notion that a given system, ours, for instance, can be worked out like mathematics from some general axioms of conduct. [. . .]

This mode of thinking is entirely natural. The training of lawyers is a training in logic. The processes of analogy, discrimination, and deduction are those in which they are most at home. The language of judicial decision is mainly the language of logic. And the logical method and form flatter that longing for certainty and for repose which is in every human mind. But certainty generally is illusion, and repose is not the destiny of man. Behind the logical form lies a judgment as to the relative worth and importance of competing legislative grounds, often an inarticulate and unconscious judgment, it is true, and yet the very root and nerve of the whole proceeding. You can give any conclusion a logical form. You always can imply a condition in a contract. But why do you imply it? It is because of some belief as to the practice of the community or of a class, or because of some opinion as to policy, or, in short, because of some attitude of yours upon a matter not capable of exact quantitative measurement, and therefore not capable of founding exact logical conclusions. Such matters really are battle grounds where the means do not exist for determinations that shall be good for all time, and where the decision can do no more than embody the preference of a given body in a given time and place. We do not realize how large a part of our law is open to reconsideration upon a slight change in the habit of the public mind. No concrete proposition is self evident, no matter how ready we may be to accept it, not even Mr. Herbert Spencer's Every man has a right to do what he wills, provided he interferes not with a like right on the part of his neighbors. [. . .]

Our law of torts comes from the old days of isolated, ungeneralized wrongs, assaults, slanders, and the like, where the damages might be taken to lie where they fell by legal judgment. But the torts with which our courts are kept busy to-day are mainly the incidents of certain well known businesses. They are injuries to person or property by railroads, factories, and the like. The liability for them is estimated, and sooner or later goes into the price paid by the public. The public really pays the damages, and the question of liability, if pressed far enough, is really the question how far it is desirable that the public should insure the safety of those whose work it uses. [. . .]

QUESTIONS

1. How does Holmes explain the purpose of the assigning liability in this excerpt? Under this view, what is the purpose of the law?

2. Generally, Holmes argues that liability is not about moral judgement. Is this true for all areas or types of law?

3. Holmes also argues that law has not developed through a system of logic. What does he mean by this? That the law is not logical? That it is not internally consistent? That it is not capable of internal consistency? Is the law subject to the halting problem?

2. WHO BEARS THE BURDEN OF AVOIDING HARM

In 1960, Nobel Economist Ronald Coase published *The Problem of Social Cost*, which went on to be one of the most influential articles ever published in the canon of law. Coase challenged long held conceptions about how the law addressed "social costs"—that is, costs that interactions between individuals to secure private benefits impose on society as a whole—and in so doing upended how the law thinks about the regulation of private action that imposes costs on third parties.

Coase's contribution is often characterized as the "Coase Theorem." Its origin and importance is discussed in the following excerpt.

GUS HURWITZ, *THE TECHNOLOGICAL PROBLEM OF SOCIAL COST*

Working Paper (2019)

The so-called "Coase Theorem" is the idea that gave rise to the modern law and economics movement, and is one of the most important ideas in modern legal theory. The idea was developed in his 1960 article *The Problem of Social Cost*, as part of his exploration of externalities (that is, social costs, or costs imposed on society by private conduct). Prior to Coase, the common understanding of externalities was that they could be best corrected by the government through the imposition of taxes (in the case of negative externalities) or subsidies (in the case of positive externalities). Taxing socially-costly conduct would reduce the amount of that conduct, and subsidizing socially positive conduct would produce more of it.

The classic example is that of a factory producing air pollution that is harmful to a neighboring community. The government would address this negative externality by taxing the factory. Either the factory would respond by reducing the amount of pollution that it produces, or the taxes can be used to compensate those harmed by the pollution.

Coase was not satisfied by this solution. As an initial matter, he did not understand how the government—the entity tasked with imposing such taxes—would know how much pollution was the socially optimal amount. More fundamentally, Coase was concerned that the taxation/subsidy mechanism responded only to a symptom of the underlying problem (a potentially sub-optimal amount of pollution) without any understanding of the underlying cause of the problem. For Coase, the interesting question was the cause of the underlying problem—why is there a sub-optimal amount of pollution. That was the starting point from which one had to undertake any solution.

Coase's realization was that the cause of the problem of social cost was the inability of those causing harmful conduct and those harmed by that conduct to bargain over that harm. They couldn't negotiate *ex ante* or take action against one another *ex post*—the factory, for instance, couldn't negotiate with every homeowner affected by its pollution, and not every homeowner affected by its pollution could sue the factory. If, counterfactually, all parties affected by conduct could bargain with one another, there would be no problem of social cost. If, for instance, the factory was harming the homeowners, the homeowners would be able to pay the factory to reduce its pollution output—and conversely, if the factory was engaged in socially valuable commerce (that is, making a lot of money), it would be able to compensate the homeowners for any harm so that it could continue polluting.

The only thing keeping homeowners and the factory from bargaining like this, Coase realized, was what he called "transaction costs"—the costs of gathering information (e.g., who is causing harm to whom, and the value of that harm to both parties), the costs of contacting and bargaining with those parties, and the cost of monitoring and enforcing any agreement between those parties. In other words, the "problem of social cost" was really a "problem of transaction costs." In a world without transaction costs, there would be no social costs, because every party affected by conduct could bargain over that conduct. If clean air were more valuable to the homeowners than the ability to pollute the air was to the factory, the factory would reduce its pollution output; and conversely.

From this comes two remarkable conclusions. The first is that in the absence of transaction costs, the legal rules protecting rights do not matter. If the factory has the legal right to pollute, it will only use that right if it values generating pollution more than the homeowners value their clean air—otherwise, the homeowners will pay the factory owner not to make use of her right to pollute. And conversely, if the homeowners have a right to clean air, they will only use that right if the factory owner is unwilling to pay them to forego enforcement of the right. In other words, no matter whether the right protects the factory or the homeowners, the factory will pollute the air if it is socially valuable for it to do so, and it will not if it is not socially valuable to do so.

But Coase also recognized that transaction costs are prevalent—indeed, high transaction costs are the norm. So, while we may be able to say that in the absence of transaction costs the legal rule does not matter, the more important conclusion from Coase's work is that *because transaction costs are high, the legal rule matters a great deal.*

This idea—the "Coase Theorem"—fundamentally changes legal theory. At a regulatory level, the prior model, in which the government determined the socially optimal level of various conduct and used taxes and subsidies to achieve that level of conduct, was out. In its stead came the Coasean idea that the role of law and government was to minimize transaction costs in order to maximize the ability of individuals to engage one another in voluntary exchange.

The Coase Theorem is also descriptively powerful. It gives meaning to the concept of "law" that was—amazingly—previously absent. Prior to Coase, law was just, or conduct was right, because it was sanctioned by the government and political process. The "socially optimal" level of conduct was however much that the heads of society said was optimal. Following Coase, the "socially optimal" level of conduct was to be determined by the values of the individual members of society affected by that conduct, aggregated by a market mechanism.

The implications of Coase's ideas have echoed through the past several generations of legal scholars—first cabined within the "law and economics" subfield, but today a foundational part of legal theory.

As an illustrative example, perhaps the most seminal of this work—its importance overshadowed only by Coase's own work—is Melamed & Calabresi's analysis different types of liability rules. Melamed and Calabresi built on Coase's recognition that the prevalence of transaction costs means that legal rules matter a great deal, asking how different types and incidences of transaction costs affect the design of legal rules. For instance, they recognized that where parties are well-positioned to negotiate with one another (that is, transaction costs are low), the law should rely on the parties' own negotiations in assessing damages; but where parties are not in a position to negotiate with one another (that is, transaction costs are high), the law should rely instead on a third-party, such as a judge or jury, to determine damages. Similarly, they use the concept of transaction costs to consider which party a legal rule should protect—whether, that is one party should need to "get permission" to engage in conduct that may harm another party, or whether the burden should be on that other party to protect itself from harmful conduct.

While Coase's work was initially focused on "social costs"—what today we would call externalities)—its implications quickly reshaped for more than government regulation of externalities. Over the course of the following 30 years, nearly every aspect of every legal institution was evaluated through a Coasean lens. Almost every private law institution, the rules of contract, property, and tort (that is, the law of accidents and other harms) that govern how individuals interact with one another was given a Coasean understanding.

GUIDO CALABRESI & A. DOUGLAS MELAMED, *PROPERTY RULES, LIABILITY RULES, AND INALIENABILITY: ONE VIEW OF THE CATHEDRAL*

85 HARV. L. REV. 1089 (1972)

Recently it has been argued that on certain assumptions, usually termed the absence of transaction costs, Pareto optimality or economic efficiency will occur regardless of the initial entitlement. For this to hold, "no transaction costs" must be understood extremely broadly as involving both perfect knowledge and the absence of any impediments or costs of negotiating. Negotiation costs include, for example, the cost of excluding would-be freeloaders from the fruits of market bargains. In such a frictionless society, transactions would occur until no one could be made better off as a result of further transactions without making someone else worse off. This, we would suggest, is a necessary, indeed a tautological, result of the definitions of Pareto optimality and of transaction costs which we have given.

[. . .]

All this suggests why distributions of wealth may affect a society's choice of entitlements. It does not suggest why economic efficiency should affect the choice, if we assume an absence of any transaction costs. But no one makes an assumption of no transaction costs in practice. Like the physicist's assumption of no friction or Say's law in macro-economics, the assumption of no transaction costs may be a useful starting point, a device which helps us see how, as different elements which may be termed transaction costs become important, the goal of economic efficiency starts to prefer one allocation of entitlements over another.

Since one of us has written at length on how in the presence of various types of transaction costs a society would go about deciding on a set of entitlements in the field of accident law, it is enough to say here: (i) that economic efficiency standing alone would dictate that set of entitlements which favors knowledgeable choices between social benefits and the social costs of obtaining them, and between social costs and the social costs of avoiding them; (2) that this implies, in the absence of certainty as to whether a benefit is worth its costs to society, that the cost should be put on the party or activity best located to make such a cost-benefit analysis;

(3) that in particular contexts like accidents or pollution this suggests putting costs on the party or activity which can most cheaply avoid them; (4) that in the absence of certainty as to who that party or activity is, the costs should be put on the party or activity which can with the lowest transaction costs act in the market to correct an error in entitlements by inducing the party who can avoid social costs most cheaply to do so; and (5) that since we are in an area where by hypothesis markets do not work perfectly—there are transaction costs—a decision will often have to be made on whether market transactions or collective fiat is most likely to bring us closer to the Pareto optimal result the "perfect" market would reach.

Complex though this summary may suggest the entitlement choice to be, in practice the criteria it represents will frequently indicate which allocations of entitlements are most likely to lead to optimal market judgments between having an extra car or taking a train, getting an extra cabbage and spending less time working in the hot sun, and having more widgets and breathing the pollution that widget production implies.

Calabresi & Melamed's article is one of very few that approaches Coase's article in significance. In the excerpt above they summarize a legal principle derived by Calabresi in earlier work, that of the "least cost avoider."[32] As explained in the excerpt above, "in the absence of certainty as to whether a benefit is worth its costs to society, the cost [of avoiding inefficient costs to society] should be put on the party or activity best located to make such a cost-benefit analysis; [and] in particular contexts like accidents or pollution this suggests putting costs on the party or activity which can most cheaply avoid them."

Under this paradigm, liability, that is, legal punishment, is assessed on the party to an activity that is in the best position to avoid undesirable harms both to himself and to other parties. No part of this assessment carries a sense of fault or moral judgement. For example, one common legal principle, the "last clear chance" doctrine, says that whichever party has the last clear chance to prevent an accident from happening is required to take advantage of that opportunity, regardless of whether they are responsible for the accident or are even likely to be affected by it. A party engaging in reckless behavior may be deemed to have "assumed the risk" of harm resulting from that behavior even if whatever harm results is from the negligence of another party.

---

[32] This concept was most formally developed by Calabresi in The Costs of Accidents: A Legal and Economic Analysis (Yale 1970). Calabresi & Melamed's 1972 paper's main contribution was its explication of two distinct forms of remedy that can be used to compensate parties that have been harmed by other individuals: property and liability rules.

The law may even assign liability to an absent party, as in the case of the doctrine of necessity, which allows a party to trespass on private property in order to avoid imminent danger, on the grounds that the owner of that property would be in the best position to help the endangered party avoid that harm by allowing her onto his property. This least cost avoider principle plays out in other areas of the law, as well. For instance, in contract law, ambiguities in poorly drafted contracts are interpreted against whomever drafted the contract because it was that person who had the greatest control over the language used.

Another way of understanding the approach of focusing on the "least cost avoider" is that the law, under the Coasean model, is concerned with creating incentives for a socially efficient level of activity. If I derive a great deal of enjoyment from driving recklessly, but my reckless driving is likely to cause harm to others, the law wants to discourage that activity. If I have the opportunity to take affirmative steps that help others to avoid harm to themselves and can do so at little or no cost to myself, the law wants to encourage that activity. "Liability" is the lever by which the law modifies individual behavior to encourage socially-desirable outcomes.

With this in mind, the following excerpt offers a further exploration of the how the law modifies individual behavior. As you read these materials, try to understand the difference between "negligence" rules (under which a party is "liable" for harms only if he was behaving negligently), "strict liability" rules (under which a party is liable for harms no matter whether she was behaving negligently), and insurance.

The concepts of strict liability and insurance have been applied to the cyber context in interesting ways.

QUESTIONS

1. How does the understanding of law offered by Coase relate to that offered by Holmes? What does the Coasean (and Calabresian) view add to our understanding of the purposes and function of the law?

2. What are transaction costs? What are externalities? Why are they important to the law?

3. Under either the Coasean or Holmesian view, is the purpose of the law to eliminate all risk?

4. Do Calabresi and Melamed share Holmes's view about the purposes of the law?

5. What, if anything, does Holmes tell us about who should bear liability when accidents or injuries occur? What does Coase tell us? What to Calabresi and Melamed tell us?

3. A MORE DIRECT APPROACH: ASSIGNING LIABILITY WITH STRICT LIABILITY

It has long been the case that it is difficult to successfully sue the developer of software for harms that result from the operation of that software. The excerpt below explains some of the reasons for this and considers how liability for these harms may be established. Alongside the legal theory of negligence, which has been our focus so far, it also considers products liability as a source of liability for defective software. It again bears noting that later chapters will get into a somewhat greater level of detail about the application of these legal theories. In particular, Chapter 10 will discuss the elements of negligence claims (a breach of a duty that causes harm, discussed in Part II of the excerpt below) and compares those elements to other theories of tort liability.

MICHAEL SCOTT, *TORT LIABILITY FOR VENDORS OF INSECURE SOFTWARE: HAS THE TIME FINALLY COME?*

67 MD. L. REV. 425 (2008)

I. INTRODUCTION

Software vulnerabilities cost businesses and consumers tens of billions of dollars each year. Every day brings news of freshly discovered security flaws in major software products. While Microsoft, due to its prominence in the operating system market, gets the brunt of the criticism for these flaws, there are many other companies whose software is also targeted for security-related complaints. Yet, software vendors have traditionally refused to take responsibility for the security of their software, and have used various risk allocation provisions of the Uniform Commercial Code (U.C.C.) to shift the risk of insecure software to the licensee. There were a few early cases in which licensees sought to have courts hold vendors liable for distributing defective software. These cases were unsuccessful.

[. . .]

Why aren't software vendors being held liable for distributing insecure code? Why haven't current laws regarding negligence, product liability, and/or professional malpractice been applied to the developers of insecure software? Is this situation likely to change? These questions and others are explored in this Article.

C. Is Software a Good or a Service?

Whether software is a good or a service is a critical question when examining whether software should be the subject of product liability or professional malpractice claims. That issue was hotly debated in the 1980s in the context of Article 2 of the U.C.C.

Article 2 applies by its own terms only to transactions in goods. The term goods means "all things [including specially manufactured goods] that are movable at the time of identification to a contract for sale." To determine whether the U.C.C. applies to a particular computer transaction, it is necessary first to ascertain whether goods are involved.

Computer hardware, as a movable object, is clearly a good and thus subject to the provisions of Article 2. Although hardware transactions often involve incidental services, such as installation, training, and maintenance, the presence of such services does not impair application of the U.C.C. Transactions involving primarily personal services, however, such as those for maintenance, training, and support, are often held not to be goods, and thus not to fall within the U.C.C. Some courts, however, have been willing to apply the U.C.C. when a service contract also includes the sale of goods. As the amount of goods involved in a service contract increases, the likelihood that the U.C.C. will be applied increases as well.

Major software transactions may involve the provision of both tangible property (e.g., the media on which the software is stored, documentation) and services (e.g., customization, installation, training, maintenance, support). The services inherent in off-the-shelf software that is bundled with hardware are generally considered incidental to the goods aspect of the transaction, and the entire contract is deemed controlled by the U.C.C.

The same is generally true for bundled, custom software: "Although the ideas or concepts involved in the custom designed software remained [the seller's] intellectual property, [the buyer] was purchasing the product of those concepts. That product required efforts to produce, but it was a product nevertheless and, though intangible, is more readily characterized as 'goods' than 'services.' "

As a result, most contracts involving bundled software, either off-the-shelf or custom, fall within Article 2. There is still a split of opinion on whether unbundled (standalone) software qualifies as a good because of its dominant service aspect, although the majority of cases have held that the transaction is one for goods, governed by the U.C.C.

II. APPLYING NEGLIGENCE LAW TO INSECURE SOFTWARE

"[M]any experts have suggested the use of tort law as a model for computer-related cases." Indeed, some argue that those who develop software and computer systems are in the best position to take action to prevent security breaches, and that the imposition of liability on developers will motivate them to create more secure software.

There have been a number of class action suits filed against software vendors and software users for breaches of security, particularly where such breaches have exposed consumers' personal and financial data to criminals who, in turn, have used the data for identity theft and other financial crimes. "Such plaintiffs may allege that vendors were negligent in their production or design of computer security systems, including . . . their coding of security and encryption software." However, while negligence law is an attractive tool to use against software vendors who distribute insecure software, it has some critical limitations.

First, to state a claim for negligence, a plaintiff must plead and prove that: (1) the software vendor owed a duty to the plaintiff; (2) the vendor breached its duty; (3) the breach of duty was a cause-infact of the plaintiff's injury; (4) the breach was a proximate cause of the plaintiff's injury; and (5) the plaintiff suffered compensable damages as a result of that breach. Each of these elements creates challenges for a plaintiff seeking to hold a vendor liable for insecure software.

[The author walks through the challenges of establishing each of these.]

[. . .]

III. APPLYING [STRICT] PRODUCT LIABILITY LAW TO INSECURE SOFTWARE

Under product liability law, liability is imposed on the theory that "[t]he costs of damaging events due to defectively dangerous products can best be borne by the enterprisers who make and sell these products." For the plaintiff, there are many advantages to a product liability claim over a breach of contract claim. The two most important benefits are (i) no privity of contract is required for recovery, and (ii) contractual disclaimers and limitations are not enforceable.

The Restatement (Second) of Torts Section 402A sets forth the elements of a claim for strict product liability:

> (1) One who sells any product in a defective condition unreasonably dangerous to the user or consumer or to his property is subject to liability for physical harm thereby caused to the ultimate user or consumer, or to his property, if (a) the seller is engaged in the business of selling such a product, and (b) it is expected to and does reach the user or consumer without substantial change in the condition in which it is sold.
>
> (2) The rule stated in Subsection (1) applies although (a) the seller has exercised all possible care in the preparation and sale of his product, and (b) the user or consumer has not bought the product from or entered into any contractual relation with the seller.

The doctrine applies to "any product sold in the condition, or substantially the same condition, in which it is expected to reach the ultimate user or consumer." Under Section 402A, the seller would be subject to strict liability "even though he has exercised all possible care in the preparation and sale of the product."

> It is not a question of fault but simply a determination of how society wishes to assess certain costs that arise from the creation and distribution of products in a complex technological society in

> which the consumer thereof is unable to protect himself against certain product defects.

However, the mere fact that a security device fails to protect the victim in a particular situation does not necessarily establish that the product was unreasonably dangerous.

The Restatement (Third) of Torts: Product Liability reformulated product liability law by redefining product defectiveness:

> "A product:
>
> (a) contains a manufacturing defect when the product departs from its intended design even though all possible care was exercised in the preparation and marketing of the product;
>
> (b) is defective in design when the foreseeable risks of harm posed by the product could have been reduced or avoided by the adoption of a reasonable alternative design by the seller or other distributor, or a predecessor in the commercial chain of distribution, and the omission of the alternative design renders the product not reasonably safe; . . . ."

Due care (negligence analysis) is explicitly excluded from this definition—it is a strict liability analysis. It requires a determination of the "intended design" and a comparison of the intended design to the product itself. A design defect, on the other hand, arises from the failure to adopt a reasonable alternative design that would have made the product reasonably safe—a traditional negligence analysis.

Accordingly, in applying product liability law to insecure software defects, it is necessary to determine first whether the software insecurity is due to a design defect or a manufacturing defect.

Software development generally goes through a number of phases before reaching the user. These steps can be classified as (i) the design phase, (ii) the coding phase, (iii) the testing phase, and (iv) the replication and distribution phase. There is no argument that a defect introduced into the product during the design phase would be deemed a design defect. And likewise there is no debate that a defect introduced into the product at the replication and distribution phase would be deemed a manufacturing defect. However, the most critical issue left open to debate is the coding phase (and to a lesser extent the testing phase). Should these phases be considered part of the design process or the manufacturing process of a software product?

Vendors would generally argue that everything before the replication and distribution phase is part of the product design process, hence, a negligence standard should apply to insecure software, except in the rare case where the defect occurred in the replication process.

Licensees would argue that the design defect standard should apply only to defects introduced in the design phase, and that everything thereafter should be deemed part of the manufacturing phase—and subject to a strict liability standard.

The licensee's position is more in line with the commonly understood stages involved in software development—that software design is generally completed before software coding begins. The training and duties of software designers and coders are usually different, particularly among those working for the larger software vendors that are most likely to be developing operating systems and major security-related software products.

[. . .]

B. Insecure Software as a Design Defect

Under the Third Restatement, a negligence standard is to be applied in design defect claims. The Third Restatement adopts the "risk utility" analysis as the sole test for determining design defectiveness. This test is based on the Learned Hand formula (B < PL) set forth in United States v. Carroll Towing Co. Under that formula, the court will look at the burden (cost) to the vendor of making its product less defective, and balance that burden against the probability of injury to the user from using that defective product multiplied by the magnitude of the injury that the user may suffer as a result of the defect.

It does not take an expert to understand that defects in software can and often do lead to massive damages to software users and third parties as a result of hackers, system crashes, and other manifestations of those defects. This is particularly true in the area of system security, where the potential injury may be incalculable. How do you put a price tag on the damage caused by a hacker shutting down an air traffic control system during a blizzard, or a terrorist causing a water treatment plant to over-chlorinate the drinking supply of a major city and poisoning its citizens? These doomsday scenarios (and countless others) are all too real when you consider how much companies, government agencies, and individuals rely on software-controlled devices to protect and assist them in their daily duties.

With regard to a product's design, negligence law requires a manufacturer to "exercise reasonable care in a variety of different functions." With security-related software, the vendor's responsibilities would include carefully formulating the design of the software to prevent vulnerabilities that can be exploited by hackers and other third parties, properly implementing the design in code, thoroughly testing the code to expose any vulnerabilities, and revising the code to remove the vulnerabilities before releasing the software to the public.

Under the Third Restatement, the analysis focuses on whether there was a "reasonable alternative design" available. It does not require the vendor to rid its software of every vulnerability. Whether a "reasonable alternative design" for any given operating system or security application is available is a fact-specific inquiry and will differ for each software product at issue. But experience has shown that what is often needed for software containing security-related flaws is not an extensive redesign of the entire software package, but merely the rewriting of a small portion of the code to remove the vulnerability.

C. Insecure Software as a Manufacturing Defect

Under the Third Restatement, strict liability continues to apply to cases involving manufacturing defects. Manufacturers are "obliged to keep abreast of any scientific discoveries and are presumed to know the results of all such advances." Further, they "bear the duty to fully test their products to uncover all scientifically discoverable dangers before the products are sold."

Those supporting the application of strict liability to defective software argue that the vendor should be held liable because (i) the vendor is in the best position to prevent software vulnerabilities; (ii) the vendor will be motivated to develop secure software; (iii) the vendor can spread the cost of providing secure software by increasing the price of its products; and (iv) the vendor will "treat the burden of . . . injury as a cost of production to be covered by liability insurance."

Over the last twenty years, there have been calls to impose strict product liability on software vendors for defects in their products, but to no avail. To date, there are no reported decisions in the United States holding a software vendor liable under a strict liability theory.

Opponents of strict liability for software vulnerabilities argue that the spectre of potentially massive damage awards would inhibit innovation and cause vendors to avoid developing products in these areas. They also point out that the user of their software is in a better position to evaluate the risks it faces if there is a business interruption—whether due to software vulnerabilities or other causes—and to insure against such eventualities. Vendors also point out that in complex software products defects are inevitable and cannot be prevented even by using today's software development "best practices."

The issue of whether the vendor, for any given software package, should be held strictly liable for a manufacturing defect should not depend on generalized public policy arguments, but instead should result from an analysis of the vendor's coding and testing methodologies and whether they comport with the general legal rules applicable to product liability law.

———

The concept of strict liability is a powerful one and, as Professor Scott has described, can be a useful legal approach when one party is in a position of knowledge and power in relation to another, as software vendors are with respect to users. Professor Hurwitz echoes this approach, describing the effects of strict liability approach for firm behavior.

GUS HURWITZ, *CYBERENSURING SECURITY*

49 U. CONN. L. REV. 1495 (2017)

III. STRICT CYBERLIABILITY

Section II explained that the law, when working well, can create powerful incentives that align individual conduct with socially-optimal goals, but that, in the case of cybersecurity, various factors confound the law's utility. This Section argues that a transition to strict liability for cybersecurity related harms would remedy the majority of these concerns, thereby allowing standard private law institutions to function and bring about dramatic improvements to the state of the cybersecurity ecosystem.

[. . .]

A. Defining Strict Liability

The primary private law mechanism that has been used—or attempted, as described above—to address cybersecurity concerns is negligence. Under this model, parties are only liable for harms that they cause to others through their own negligence. In the classic formulation, a party engaging in an action that causes harm to someone else has acted negligently if the party failed to take precautions against such harms commensurate with the reasonably foreseeable likelihood and magnitude of those harms. In other words, we expect people to take at least $50 worth of precaution to avoid a one in ten chance of causing $500 in harm to others.

The central idea behind the negligence model is that risk is unavoidable. Parties may be able to invest in mitigating risk, but cannot eliminate the possibility of risk entirely. If we were to hold parties responsible for any harm that they may cause to others, we are concerned that parties will over-invest in precaution or avoid risky but socially valuable activity. For instance, driving is inherently risky—on any given drive there is a chance that you will get into a costly accident. If we put too high a burden on drivers to avoid such accidents, they may over-invest in safety or avoid driving. But by only holding parties responsible for taking reasonable precautions—that is, those commensurate with foreseeable harms—we do not dissuade any socially beneficial activities. In other words, modern negligence liability is designed to ensure that parties engage in the socially optimal level of activities.

But negligence is not the only approach to assigning liability. Starting in the 1960s, courts began to impose so-called strict liability in some cases.

Under a strict-liability regime, a given party is always responsible for the harm incurred by its counterparties, no matter how careful that party was to avoid such harm. The underlying theory is that one party may be in a better position to prevent or assess the likelihood of certain harms than the other. An important situation where this is the case is where assigning liability to one party allows for risk pooling. For example, parties on one side of a transaction systematically may not be able to absorb costs, or the expected costs may be distributed too thinly to justify taking precautions. It is also the case where one party is in a better informational position than the other, or is in a better position to gather or disseminate information.

Counterintuitively, as will be considered further in Section V, strict liability does not affect the level of care that a party will take. One intuitively expects that if we impose strict liability on a party, that party will take greater precautions to avoid such harms than if it would only be liable in the event of its own negligence. This is not the case. Under either model, parties will only invest in avoiding harms up to the point that the cost of such investment is commensurate with the expected magnitude and likelihood of harm. In other words, it never makes sense to spend $75 to mitigate a one in ten chance of causing $500 in harm. Rather, under strict liability, one will spend $50 in precaution and simply pay the balance of $450 if that $500 in harm happens to occur. The key difference between negligence and strict liability is how the $450 loss that results when the harm does occur. Both negligence and strict liability accept that bad things happen and that no amount of precaution can prevent every risk. In fact, we do not want people to invest in inefficient levels of precaution. The difference between the two systems is that in a negligence regime, the harmed party bears the cost of the harm. Contrastingly, in a strict-liability regime, it is borne by the other party. While the strict liability model may seem grossly unfair, we will see in Section IV that it turns out to function much like an insurance system and that it can be a very positive model in some circumstances.

B. No Strict Cyberliability Today?

At this juncture, the point must be clearly made that software and computer systems historically have not been subject to strict liability and, absent statutory intervention, are not likely to be made subject to strict liability. In the modern tort setting, strict liability applies almost exclusively in the context of products liability. Over the past several decades, courts have struggled to fit computer software within the ambit of products liability. They have struggled to determine whether software is a "product"; they have struggled over whether inadvertent software errors rise to the level of defective design; and they have struggled with whether software released without sufficient testing to avoid errors is defectively manufactured. Indeed, because software is generally not viewed as a "product," and because it is generally licensed under copyright law, courts have generally found any contractual and license terms pertaining to the sale or license of software to be enforceable—and these terms almost always include disclaimers and waivers of liability.

Even if we view software as a product and software defects as design or manufacturing defects, there are still challenges to applying strict liability for software. For instance, we still face difficulties in establishing damages and recovery may be limited by the economic loss doctrine. And an even greater challenge to bringing a "strict" products liability claim is that courts have increasingly embraced what is known as the risk-utility test to determine products liability. Under this approach, products liability takes on a very negligence-like characteristic. Given the near impossibility of designing defect-free software, many commentators believe that it will be exceptionally difficult to successfully bring a products liability claim.

Over the years, there have been frequent calls for the application of strict products liability principles to computer software. Nonetheless, the status quo today is that defective software today is only subject to liability under principles of ordinary negligence, if at all.

C. Cybersecurity is a Classic Case for Strict Liability

Despite the discussion above, cybersecurity presents a near textbook case for strict liability. The policy rationales for strict liability—the challenges that strict liability evolved to address—match the challenges created by cybersecurity. Indeed, even the historical challenges that gave rise to modern strict liability map onto the issues faced today in the cybersecurity setting. And while there are a number of common concerns about strict liability—concerns that militate against its use in various settings—they are largely inapposite to the cybersecurity setting. The discussion below turns away from the application of the legal rules that surround strict liability today and focuses instead on the historical development of the doctrine and the economic understanding of how it functions.

1. The Origins of Strict Liability

The origins of modern strict liability in the American legal tradition are generally traced to Judge Cardozo's famous opinion in MacPherson v. Buick Motor Company, which eliminated the privity requirements for suits brought in tort. Prior to MacPherson, individuals could only bring suit against those with whom they shared some direct connection (that is, with whom they had privity). In other words, if a driver were injured in an automobile accident caused when a component of her car failed, she could only sue the person who sold her the car—she could not sue either the car manufacturer or a third-party manufacturer of the component that failed (for instance, if the component that failed had been bought by the manufacturer and integrated into the final component, as is often the case with many automotive components, such as tires). All of these parties only have an indirect relationship with the driver, so are said to lack privity. Under the pre-MacPherson model, the driver would be expected to sue to person who sold her the car and that person could then countersue other third parties, either under separate legal theories or seeking indemnification.

MacPherson changed all of this, opening the door to direct suits by drivers (or other end-users) against manufacturers (or other responsible parties in the supply chain). The underlying rationales were intended to address the same sort of challenges that we see in the cybersecurity context. The multiplicity of parties in a supply chain make it difficult to figure out who to sue and make it difficult to establish or apportion liability. In both the case of MacPherson and the modern cybersecurity setting, this effectively externalizes risk onto consumers, and creates perverse incentives for how the various entities through the relevant product ecosystems design their products and services.

MacPherson was only the first step towards the modern understanding of strict liability. While it allowed parties to bring suits in the absence of privity, those suits were still brought under a negligence standard. Starting in the 1960s, some courts began developing the modern understanding of strict liability in cases involving consumers harmed by (arguably) defectively designed or manufactured products. The canonical case is Greenman v. Yuba Power Products, which involved a wonderfully monstrous power tool sold by Yuba, the "Shopsmith, a combination power tool that could be used as a saw, drill, and wood lathe." Mr. Greenman was injured a year or so after his wife purchased Shopsmith for him as a Christmas present, and brought suit for breach of warranty and negligence. The trial court determined that the manufacturer had not been negligent, and that Mr. Greenman's harms were not covered by any express or implied warranty.

On appeal, the Supreme Court of California found the manufacturer strictly liable for Mr. Greenman's injuries, explaining that the question of "liability is not one governed by the law of contract warranties but by the law of strict liability in tort." As explained by the court, "[a] manufacturer is strictly liable in tort when an article he places on the market, knowing that it is to be used without inspection for defects, proves to have a defect that causes injury to a human being. "The purpose of such liability is to insure that the costs of injuries resulting from defective products are borne by the manufacturers that put such products on the market rather than by the injured persons who are powerless to protect themselves." Critically, under a strict liability model, parties are not free to assign risk of harm by contract—any contract or warranty attempting to do so is a legal nullity.

2. Strict Liability and Negligence

Strict liability is an exception to the ordinary rule of negligence—it is only used in certain cases. The traditional examples are products liability, such as was the case in Greenman, and so-called ultrahazardous activities, such as keeping dangerous animals as pets or the use of explosives. It is clear why we only turn to strict liability in cases like these—and why cybersecurity is a similar case—when we look to the core policy rationale underlying strict liability: ensuring that liability for harms be assigned to parties best able to bear it. Both negligence and strict liability accept that some amount of harm naturally occurs in the world. Under a negligence model, we assume that parties bear, and are able to bear, comparable responsibility for preventing or accepting the risk of harm. Under strict liability, we assume that the parties—especially in their abilities to prevent or accept risk—are asymmetric. In terms of preventing risk, we are generally concerned about risks that would be unreasonably, or impossibly, costly for individuals to detect. For instance, if a consumer could not determine whether a saw blade contained manufacturing defects without engaging in destructive testing of the blade, the law may hold the blade's manufacturer strictly liable for manufacturing defects. Similarly with ultrahazardous activities, where it is unreasonable, for instance, to expect individuals to take precautions against the use of explosives in construction operations or pet tigers that may be roaming the streets, we place a strict burden on the party engaging in the atypical activity. We see the same in terms of accepting risk. In this case, the concern relates to the parties' relative abilities to bear the costs of a risk should harm come to pass. Again, the example of an injury related to power tools is illustrative: such an injury could be physically or economically devastating to an ordinary consumer, and many consumers do not have the knowledge or wherewithal to insure against such losses. The manufacturer, on the other hand, is in a much better position to assess the possible risks, and to insure consumers against those risks.

This rationale for strict scrutiny is not without criticism or nuance. Many of the criticisms of, and concerns raised by, strict-liability regimes will be considered shortly below—and the idea that strict liability acts as a form of insurance will be considered in greater depth in Section V.

3. Strict Liability and Cybersecurity

Before considering these issues, we can outline the case for applying strict liability in the cybersecurity context. We already saw that the rationale for the first steps towards strict liability—MacPherson's abandonment of privity requirements—mirrored concerns similar to those we see in the cybersecurity context: the difficulty of attributing liability and recovering damages that results from the multiplicity of actors and the complexity of their interconnected relationships. So, too, do the concerns about parties' relative abilities to prevent and accept risk motivate modern principles of strict liability mirror reality of the cybersecurity setting. As discussed in Section I, every entity engaged in conduct online—from individuals, to small businesses, to non-profit and governmental organizations, to large non-tech firms, to large tech firms—is exposed to cybersecurity risks. Mitigating these risks is far beyond the expertise of the vast majority of these entities. And, even if it were not beyond their expertise, most defects in third-party systems are latent. Even if these third parties open their systems up for inspection, it is functionally impossible to expect even sophisticated parties to audit them for defects at reasonable costs.

This is largely descriptive of the situation that exists in the business-to-business landscape. Even among sophisticated parties, few are in a position to meaningfully understand, let alone prevent, cybersecurity risks. But this is even more dramatically the case in the consumer-to-business relationship. Here, consumers are almost entirely at the mercy of the firms they interact with online to keep data that they disclose to those firms secure. Consumers have no visibility into those firms' systems, into what data those firms retain, how they manage that data or use it, or to whom it is disclosed (intentionally or unintentionally). Once their data has been shared with a firm, consumers have literally no ability to monitor its subsequent use or handling, to take precautions to prevent harm, to detect its misuse, or to take action in response to those harms.

Indeed, the cybersecurity context arguably presents a more "textbook case" for the use of strict liability than seen in most "textbook cases." Strict-liability regimes have two basic effects: they increase the price of products and services and they encourage risk-taking by consumers. They increase the cost faced by providers of products and services because those providers bear the risk of any liability. But these costs are almost always passed on to consumers. The net effect, discussed in more detail in Section IV, is that firms subject to strict liability act as insurers: they spread the cost of risk across the entire pool of consumers, collecting a premium for that risk through the price they charge, and they use those premiums to pay out damages as they occur on a stochastic basis. Importantly, the concern about increasing prices has an important, potentially pernicious, secondary effect: more price sensitive consumers, or those who are less exposed to risk, may select themselves out of the market. This has the effect of spreading the cost of risk across smaller pool of consumers, each of whom therefore has to pay proportionally more. Taken to the extreme, this can make some products unviable in the market—as was indeed observed in the [insurance crisis of the] 1980s. In proposing a strict-liability regime, we need to be very cautious about this concern, as it could be devastating to the market. The second concern is similarly important: if consumers are aware (implicitly or explicitly) that another party is liable for any harm that befalls them, consumers may have an incentive to opportunistically engage in riskier behavior. For instance, consumers may shirk on routine maintenance of potentially dangerous products, or fail to read manuals or otherwise educate themselves to the safe operation of potentially dangerous products, if they know that they will receive compensation despite their own negligence.

QUESTIONS

1. Scott's article gets into a greater level of doctrinal detail than we have previously seen (some of these issues will be returned to in Chapter 10). What is the "negligence" (what are the legal requirements to establish a negligence claim)? What is strict liability? Products liability? How do these relate to one another? (Different readers may want to spend more or less time on this level of detail, some of which goes beyond what is covered in this book).

2. Why is it difficult to establish a negligence claim relating to defective software? For more detail on this issue, see the discussion of the economic loss doctrine in Chapter 10.

3. Scott is arguing that products liability law should apply to defective software. Why is it difficult to establish products liability claim for defective software? Why does he argues that products liability law should apply?

4. Hurwitz argues for the application of strict liability in the cybersecurity context. (His argument is somewhat more complicated than this: he argues in the rest of this article that the Federal Trade Commission should apply a strict liability-like rule to firms for cybersecurity incidents unless they have insurance coverage that covers the incident.) What is strict liability, and how does it relate to negligence?

5. Hurwitz argues that strict liability has insurance-like features. Why is this? (See Chapter 12 for further discussion of insurance.) This idea of tort law acting as a form of insurance has actually been present throughout this chapter. See, for instance, the end of the Holmes excerpt. Can you see this idea reflected, directly or indirectly in the materials on Coase or Calabresi and Melamed?

C. SUBSTANTIVE CATEGORIES OF LAW (PRIVATE LAW, CRIMINAL LAW, AND PUBLIC LAW)

The criminal and civil law are the primary vehicles through which society sets expectations regarding the behavior of individuals in society generally (the criminal law) and the behavior of individuals and entities among each other (the civil or "private" law).

The criminal law focuses exclusively on the behavior of individuals. It sets standards of conduct through a series of commands, primarily negative prohibitions against action (e.g., "you will not murder") but occasionally through affirmative requirements for action (e.g., "you must support your minor children"). Unlike other areas of law, these commands concern topics where society has decided the requirement is so important that disobedience should be the subject of "moral condemnation" by society (e.g., the status of becoming a "criminal") and the availability of "physical pain" (usually confinement or compelled public service) as punishment. In the context of cybersecurity, the criminal law focuses on using the threat of criminal sanction as a deterrent to certain activities.

Other areas of private law include torts (negligence and other forms of direct liability), contract law, and property law. These areas of law primarily focus on transactions and interactions among private individuals and set guidelines for those interactions which are enforced by state action. For example, if a party to a contract violates a term of that contract, a court of law may compel the party to comply with that term and/or face payment in the form of a remedy or injunctive relief. Violations of private law most commonly involve financial compensation or *financial remedy*, but in extraordinary cases may involve courts issuing orders of compliance or *injunctive relief* (violations of which are considered criminal acts). In the context of cybersecurity, this area of law is largely undeveloped and untested, except inasmuch as courts have been reluctant to hold data custodians liable to individual consumers for data breaches under a theory that actual harm is too difficult to establish.

Although this chapter has been organized to provide you with a brief introduction to the way the U.S. legal system works, additional chapters in this book will provide more specific examples of how these types of law work in practice. For example, we will go into more detail about contract law and tort, as they apply to recent cybersecurity decisions and landmark cases.

CHAPTER 7

BUSINESS FOUNDATIONS

■ ■ ■

A. INTRODUCTION TO THE ORGANIZATION

A variety of organizations operate and function in different ways that influence how cybersecurity decisions are made and to what extent the law regulates these organizations. This section and the rest of this chapter is intended to serve as a brief introduction to various types of organizations and the underlying concepts and processes that influence how organizations make decisions.

1. ORGANIZATIONAL TYPE

The term "organizations" encompasses all varieties of purposefully organized groups centered around a common mission, vision, goal, or charge. Organizations loosely can be considered organized groups of people that, in their common charge, become something altogether different. For example, businesses are one type of organization. Businesses are usually defined as for-profit, or in existence to make money, though the rules that apply to different types of legal entities restrict what businesses must or must not do in relation to their for-profit status. Businesses may be involved in selling goods, offering services, or fulfilling a role in furtherance of these activities.

Although the majority of our focus is on variations of for-profit businesses, it is worth noting that "businesses" and "companies" (as you may know them colloquially) are not the only types of organizations. Organizations may be non-profit, such as charitable, advocacy, and political organizations. Organizations may also be related to the government, such as the U.S. Postal Service (a government corporation) or some state universities (which may be organized as non-profits but partially funded and supervised by the state), and certain types of quasi-governmental organizations like the United Nations. Lastly, it is important to remember that governments themselves—and their constituent agencies—are organizations as well.

Organizations and Business Associations is, quite literally, an entire semester-long law school or business school course. For the purposes of understanding organizations' role in cybersecurity, we focus this Chapter primarily on for-profit organizations. This is for two reasons: (1) the structure of many non-profit and quasi-governmental organizations is often quite similar to for-profit organizations, differing only in that excess revenue neither is the goal nor can it be distributed to owners as profits; and (2) many of the aspects of public administration—the question of how government organizations operate—are covered in part in Chapter 6. Yet for-profit organizations play both a key role (from a technological standpoint) and a substantial role (from a percentage standpoint) in the cybersecurity ecosystem. Thus understanding their purpose, operation, and structure is important to understanding cybersecurity.

A primary, if not the primary, activity of for-profit businesses is the sale of goods and services.

a. Businesses Selling Goods

Businesses involved in the sales of goods are described in relation to the supply chain, or the process by which goods are produced and eventually sold. As you may have learned in Uniform Commercial Code (UCC) courses like Sales and Leases or even in contract law courses, businesses involved in the goods supply chain are governed heavily by the UCC, which primarily focuses on contractual relationships between organizational entities in the supply chain. The UCC is a model code that informs state law. These state laws set forth the rules by which the common law, as described in Chapter 6, operates in the judicial system, at least in defining the creation of, and interpretation of, contracts between businesses and their customers. Usually the orientation of sales of goods are described as B2B (Business-to-Business) or B2C (Business-to-Consumer).

The laws that apply to these transactions often depend on these designations. B2B transactions in goods are usually governed heavily by private ordering, or negotiations and contracts between sophisticated business entities. For example, robotic manufacturing equipment used to manufacture high technology devices will likely be subject to a great deal of scrutiny by the purchasing business entity due to the cost of the equipment and the potential for manufacturing defects. For these types of transactions, the law usually operates more permissively and gives a great deal of power to sophisticated entities to determine the terms of their agreements.

B2C transactions are often subject to more involvement from administrative agencies and certain behaviors are more directly regulated by state and federal statutes. For example, the Consumer Financial Protection Bureau (CFPB) of the Federal Trade Commission is specifically charged with protecting consumers from "unfair or deceptive trade practices," under Section 5 of the FTC Act. These practices include: false or misleading labeling practices, claims related to common household products, the contents of consumer terms of use agreements and privacy notices (amongst others). When consumers are involved, many states have passed similar laws, and judges have engaged in common law determinations regarding what can, for example, qualify as a contract regarding purchase of certain goods online. The Consumer Product Safety Commission (CPSC) is also concerned with the safety of products sold to consumers.

Both B2B and B2C transactions, due to their involvement in supply chain activities, are heavily regulated by federal import and exports laws that restrict the manner goods may enter or leave the United States to those that are reasonably safe and do not pose some risk to U.S.. Goods produced by these entities must also meet certain safety and environmental requirements, which are established both at the federal and state level. For example, cars must meet both federal emissions requirements and state requirements. Some sectors, like health goods production, are also regulated by government administrative agencies like the Food and Drug Administration, which is a division of the Department of Health and Human Services. Under the Food Drug and Cosmetics Act (and its subsequent updates), tobacco products, medical devices, veterinary products and foods, food production and manufacturing, cosmetics, and pharmaceuticals are regulated by the Food and Drug Administration.

Consider, for example, a food manufacturer that produces frozen entrees. The food manufacturer sources raw materials in China and ships them to a food manufacturer in China to manufacture according to a recipe. That product is packaged using plastic containers produced by another manufacturer in the United States, and these food containers are shipped to the Chinese manufacturer to be used in the manufacturing process. Once the containers are filled with the product and sealed, they are boxed and loaded onto trucks, which drop the product at a warehouse, where they are loaded onto pallets to await shipping. These pallets are then loaded onto a shipping vessel that ships the product to a U.S. port over four weeks or more. The product shipping labels are checked, and the U.S. import inspection process begins.

Once the products are cleared by inspectors, they are picked up from the shipyard and transported to distribution centers for further distribution. For example, these centers could be managed by retailers that will distribute the food product to their stores, or the centers could be a distributor that is employed by the manufacturer to distribute to grocery chains. When the grocery chains or retail locations receive the products, these entities must then ensure the product is stored properly and then preserved according to certain conditions until a consumer then purchases the frozen product. As you can see from Figure 1, the number of individual parties involved in a supply chain process are numerous.[1]

---

[1] Supply chain is one of the new and emerging areas of cybersecurity attention, as the food supply chain is both critically important and also has greater potential for vulnerabilities.

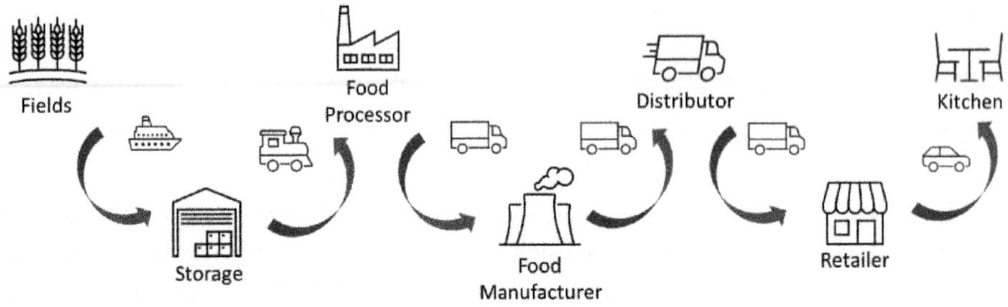

Figure 1: Food Supply Chain

Each of the businesses included in this supply chain must be regulated in some way to ensure that the food is safe and that it is manufactured according to what the manufacturer has specified. Although the business-to-business relationships are generally governed by private contract, the food supply, like other consumer products, is heavily regulated by an administrative agency, the FDA. The FDA is primarily concerned with the manufacturing entity of record, so the primary manufacturer often needs to ensure via contract that the other entities doing work on the manufacturer's behalf, or third parties, are adhering to the agency's requirements. Often, third parties are either 1) not regulated by the same law as the primary organization or 2) not regulated in the United States, so outsourcing these requirements via contract is an important legal practice that applies to business law in general and specifically in cybersecurity practices.

b. Services Businesses

Businesses involved in the sales of services are comparatively less regulated than consumer goods manufacturers, but the same distinction between B2B and B2C applies in that B2B relationships are often subject to private ordering via contract, whereas B2C relationships often are more regulated. Services are often discussed more frequently in cybersecurity because they are "virtual," or not physical goods. Services can include activities performed by people or computers. Many businesses, for example, require janitorial or HVAC services to keep physical premises clean and comfortable, or they may employ security guards to monitor the premises. Businesses may hire external recruiting firms to find new employees or may contract with personnel consulting companies to temporarily fill certain positions.

Services businesses, however, may also provide services through technology. For example, organizations of all kinds often do not want to invest a great deal of resources in creating their own technologies, or "home grown" solutions. For one, building new software or applications can require hiring new employees or providing new training. It may also require computing resources, such as servers or a large data center, that may be cost-prohibitive to maintain. In other cases, organizations do not have the expertise to build or effectively maintain solutions. Cost and expertise are the two reasons organizations often "outsource" technology services.

For example, a non-profit organization, such as a hospital, must store patient records in a common physical location or system so that hospital personnel can access critical information, such as allergy information or previous treatments and conditions. However, hospitals are not usually well-positioned to create their own common systems. After all, hospitals know about treating people, not creating software. Hospitals frequently work with technology service providers, such as those who have an interface for creating and storing electronic Health Records (EMR). Furthermore, often hospital *systems*, or a number of different hospitals, may want to provide service to a specific patient. This means that each hospital will need to access the same records. Storing this data at each individual hospital location will likely mean some information is not updated in one or more of the records, creating a risk for the individual patient.

Consider a banking institution. Although a portion of the population does not have a bank account, the "underbanked," a large proportion of the population is dependent on access to bank account funds on a regular basis. After all, how many of us keep thousands of dollars under our mattress or in a safety deposit box? The bank account is a key part of the equation for payment and money transfer, as is required for transactions facilitated by Venmo, Zelle, or similar online transactions. For individuals who prefer to draw directly on a bank account, debit cards may be used like a credit card. Although some banks do manage their own card brands, most banks are part of a complex card-based ecosystem where payment processors, card brands, banks, and other technology service providers are a key part of the payment process. Without technology service providers, capabilities like money transfer via Venmo would be nearly impossible unless all participants were part of the same bank. In fact, inter-regional and international wire transfers would not be possible.

Technology services are regulated directly and indirectly. They are regulated directly through statute and indirectly, as through the FTC's enforcement against unfair and deceptive trade practices. Most technology services must follow state and federal requirements when such services have greater attendant risks of harm. Although we will be discussing more statutory details later in this book, some examples of areas where state and federal laws apply to technology services are: health, including protected health information data used in patient care or billing and medical device manufacturing; and financial, including banking customer data, investment customer data, and internal corporate financials. These laws have been passed specifically because these areas have been considered either a) more highly targeted by attackers or b) pose more risk to individuals. This is the area where privacy law and cybersecurity law often overlap.

Although all services pose some cybersecurity risk to organizations, frequently information technology services receive the most attention in terms of potential risk. Why might this be? Well, when organizations use information technology services, these services are used for one of two purposes: 1) to collect, manage, transfer, or store organizational information or 2) to collect, manage, transfer, or store customer information. In both of these circumstances, if data are compromised, operational, financial, reputational, or legal repercussions will likely result. Furthermore, regulation usually applies the primary organization, not the technology service provider. As a result, often technology service providers are assessed, audited, or reviewed by the primary organization before and after forming a business relationship with them.

c. Third Parties

All organizations use service and goods businesses to varying extents. As you might have gathered from the descriptions of the food production supply chain earlier in this chapter, organizations very rarely, if ever, rely only on themselves. Each organization, regardless of its status or type, relies on other organizations to complete its overall purpose.

In the risk management context, organizations that are not the primary customer contact, data collector, or creator of information are considered "third parties" with respect to the first organization. The terminology refers mainly to the idea that this organization is not subject to (or has rights with respect to) primary contractual relationships, such as between a retailer and their customer, or a business service provider and another organization. It is important to acknowledge here that the terminology "third party" means with respect to data and relationship, not necessarily with respect to contract. You may have heard the term "third party" related to contracts disputes wherein someone may have an interest in the outcome of litigation. As you may recall, not anyone can sue someone for breach of contract, even if they have an interest in the result. Rather, usually these actions are between the parties of a contract, or those in privity. In risk management, the concept of third party is a practical, rather than a legal designation: third parties are those performing services on behalf of a primary party.

These third parties may be vulnerable to attackers because of their 1) personnel or 2) systems. Just like a primary organization, third parties must implement appropriate security controls to protect their assets. However, third parties are often not directly regulated by the same entities that regulate a primary organization, both due to how the law is written and where the third party is geographically located. For example, a U.S.

financial institution may work with a third-party technology consulting company in India to build financial products, such as online bill pay or financial apps for the banking business.

The Indian technology consulting company may also have third parties that manage server farms for cloud computing services in China. In this example, the primary financial services company engages a third party, which is using a different third party. The primary relationship for purposes of cybersecurity is the relationship between the consulting company and the financial services company. However, the only entity regulated in this situation is the financial institution. The consulting company is still a third party with respect to the financial institution. And the cloud computing services company is a third party to the consulting company. These attenuated relationships in technology can make it highly difficult to regulate cybersecurity activities directly, as in statute. As a result, many statutes require a primary, regulated organization to facilitate a contract to bind these third parties, as well as their third parties.

In this case, the financial institution is required to follow the Gramm-Leach-Bliley Act (GLBA), which requires certain security practices when dealing with non-public customer information. Because ultimately the financial institution is responsible for complying with GLBA with respect to customer data, it must ensure that its third parties will meet the same requirements. To ensure compliance, the financial institution may do any of the following: 1) conduct risk assessments to ascertain potential non-compliance or other risks before signing a contract or agreeing on a particular third party, 2) include security terms in the contract that "outsource" U.S. law by specifying compliance requirements in the contract, 3) periodically monitor compliance through risk assessments or audits, conducted by itself or an external auditor, or 4) request other indicia of compliance, such as certifications or alternative expert determinations. However, it may be substantially more difficult for a financial institution to perform any of the options above for the third party's third parties, such as the cloud provider.

The most challenging aspect of third parties is the lack of functional control: whereas an organization can hold itself accountable through internal policy and monitoring of implementation of attendant cybersecurity controls, a direct third party may only be controlled through assessment and contract. A third party's third party (sometimes called a 'subcontractor') may only be controlled by the third party with which it has a relationship. Later in this book, we will address the contractual challenges of these relationships and what organizations might do to better contractually manage these relationships, but for now it is important to remember that technology systems are based on the actions of multiple organizations, and some of these organizations may be difficult if not impossible to control.

2. ORGANIZATIONS AND THEIR REGULATORS

Cybersecurity issues affect every type of organization. Non-profit organizations may be as exposed to attackers as well as for-profit businesses and government entities. However, some non-profit organizations are not as heavily regulated as other organizations. Government entities are often regulated by other government entities. The regulators for cybersecurity are usually related to: 1) the nature of the organization, specifically inherent risks for a type of organization, broadly construed and 2) the inherent risk of a compromise in a particular sector.

For example, the U.S. Securities and Exchange Commission (SEC) regulates publicly traded companies, or those for which stock is sold on the public market to individuals located in various geographies (in the U.S. and outside the U.S.). Stock is sold primarily to raise capital for an organization to function (e.g., the stock sold at the New York Stock Exchange, for example). Publicly traded companies are owned by their shareholders; therefore, corporate leadership of a publicly traded companies owe certain duties to shareholders. For this reason, the SEC has recently been interested in how publicly traded companies invest in cybersecurity solutions to protect valuable assets, which influences the effective value of the company. Practically speaking, repeat data breaches could affect overall company valuation and stock price, causing shareholders to lose money.

As you may be aware, publicly traded companies are just one type of for-profit business. Most small businesses are in the categories of Limited Liability Companies (LLC), Limited Liability Partnerships (LLP), and General Partnerships, yet their shares are not sold in the public marketplace. The types of businesses and how they are defined are creatures of state law. The distinctions between these types of companies relates to how profits are shared, how the company will function, and how the company will be taxed. For example, limited liability companies provide some protection to the owners from each other's actions. Privately held corporations usually carry stock, but there are only a few stock holders, and these stocks are not sold on the public marketplace. Although these companies are not subject to heavy SEC oversight, state laws related to data breach notification and state Attorneys General actions for unfair or deceptive trade practices may still apply. Furthermore, if these companies provide services across state lines, they may also be subject to Federal Trade Commission purview related to unfair or deceptive trade practices.

Non-profit organizations are usually defined by their income statements and tax structure: they are required not to "make" money in the same way a company does and ultimately receive tax relief in exchange for this status. Non-profit organizations may include private universities, religiously affiliated organizations, or public services organizations that do are not directly managed by government entities. However, although non-profit organizations frequently do not have large numbers of personnel, under most laws, non-profit organizations still must adhere to the same laws regarding data collection, use, and security. For example, many health care organizations are non-profit in tax status and organization, yet they must still follow HIPAA requirements and are regulated by the Department of Health and Human Services, both at state and federal levels.

Type of Organization	**General Description**	**For-Profit**	**Non-Profit**
(Stock) Corporation	Entity the ownership of which is determined by the issuance of fraction ownership (i.e., "shares") pursuant to state law. Allows for flexible capital and management structures.	Subject to state and/or federal corporate taxation.	Permitted for non-profits, not generally subject to corporate taxation.
Limited Liability Company (LLC)	Entity the ownership of which is determined by allocation of percentage ownership among members, but which does not require complex accounting for ownership allocation and does permit non-managing owners who have limited liability.	Allows for "partnership" (pass-through) taxation, avoiding tradition corporate tax, but cannot be publicly traded.	Permitted for non-profits, no tax advantage over stock corporations and no liability advantage over LLPs, however annual reporting requirements may be lessened.

Limited Liability Partnership (LLP)	Entity the ownership of which is determined by allocation of ownership among partners, which allows for limited liability, but requires more complex accounting for ownership allocation.	Allows for "partnership" (pass-through) taxation and provides liability limits, but requires more complex accounting.	Technically permissible for non-profits, but uncommon.
General/Limited Partnerships	Entity the ownership of which is allocated among partners, some/all of whom may be managers, but with few (if any) liability limitations.	Allows for "partnership" (pass-through" taxation, but provides little to no liability limits for members.	Technically permissible for non-profits, but uncommon.
(Nonstock) Corporation	An entity that is treated as a corporation under the laws of a jurisdiction, which may be subject to less annual reporting requirements and does not issue fractional shares in a traditional fashion.	Uncommon in for-profit businesses, with the exception that some single- or family-owned small businesses may make use of this form.	Sometimes used for non-profits, depending on state law.
Unincorporated Entities	An entity that is none of the above forms, but is recognized under state law as a legal entity distinct from its owners. May, but does not always, require registration under state law.	Generally not permitted in for-profit businesses, with the limited exception of some sole proprietorships and unregistered partnerships being treated this way in some states.	Sometimes used for smaller non-profits.

Table 1: Entity Definitions

Government entities are usually regulated under specific statutes related to government activities and data use or collection of resident data. For example, government entities usually have a lot of highly confidential and sensitive data, not only about their personnel and U.S. residents, but also potentially store data pertaining to military and other defense information, clandestine intelligence efforts, or diplomatic policy information. For this reason, federal government entities are subject to the Federal Information Systems Management Act (FISMA), which requires these entities to also follow the National Institute of Standards and Technology (NIST) requirements. NIST was established via congressional action to be a source for national technology standards, though these standards generally are not compulsory for organizations other than government entities. Furthermore, NIST does not have any regulatory function: its sole purpose is to establish standards, not to ensure government entities follow them. Rather, the top-level regulator for government entities is usually the Office of the Inspector General which is an independent office within most government entities. The Inspector General Act of 1978 created the requirement to have an independent oversight office, and these offices consider broad issues, sometimes including cybersecurity considerations.[2]

In addition to the internal OIG, administrative government agencies receive direction and are largely co-regulated by both Congress and the Executive Branch. Because administrative agencies receive, to varying extents, direction from the Executive, Executive Orders are one method by which the President of the United States may direct administrative agencies to do certain things, so long as that direction is not statutorily limited. For example, the President may sign an Executive Order requiring that the Office of the Comptroller of Currency, the regulator of financial services organizations under the Gramm-Leach-Bliley Act (GLBA), ensure that banks use multi-factor authentication processes (such as log-in, password, and a one-time code sent to a bank customer's mobile device). However, multi-factor authentication is not specified under GLBA, so this requirement would extend beyond what the law demands. However, Executive Orders can regulate how government agencies work with respect to their own operations and give some direction to how agencies regulate organizations where congressional direction is open-ended or unclear.

Some entities operate at the intersection of government function and business, due to the nature of their services. These entities usually are central to how humans live, providing essential services. These services are usually framed in cybersecurity parlance as "critical infrastructure." Although for most countries, critical infrastructure is operated extensively by government entities, in the United States, these organizations differ

---

[2] For example, in 2018, the Department of Health and Human Services Office of the Inspector General found that the Food and Drug Administration did not have sufficient cybersecurity rules established for medical device manufacturers.

greatly depending on the municipality, state, or federal function. Common examples of critical infrastructure include: water treatment, dam or other water mechanics operations, nuclear power plants, oil or other fossil fuel extraction and refinement, solar grids and air turbine operation, electrical grids, transportation (e.g., from air traffic to trains), and emergency services. For example, it is common for the electrical grid and airlines to be heavily regulated and subsidized by the government while remaining private business entities. However, water treatment is typically managed by a specific municipality.

As noted throughout the beginning chapters of this book, non-government entities, or for-profit businesses and non-profit organizations are usually regulated, at least at the federal level, based on a particular sector or specific activities. See Table 1, below, for a sampling of the types of organizations and their regulators.

Regulation/ Sector	Applicable Laws (Privacy laws are included where they specify security activities)	Administrative Agency	Regulation Method
Banking/ Financial	Gramm-Leach-Bliley Act (GLBA), Cybersecurity Law (NY)	Office of the Comptroller of Currency (OCC)	Bank examination protocol (periodic assessment)
Investment	Regulation S-P (Reg S-P) (federal), FINRA (not precise law, co-regulated industry standards), Cybersecurity Law (NY)	Securities and Exchange Commission (SEC), FINRA, New York State Dept. of Financial Services (DFS)	Examination protocol
Insurance	Health Insurance Portability and Accountability Act (HIPAA) (federal), Cybersecurity Law (NY)	Department of Health and Human Services (DHHS) (enforcement arm: Office for Civil Rights [OCR]), New York State Dept. of Financial Services (DFS)	Self-reporting
Payment card use	Washington, Nevada, Minnesota state laws, encourage Payment Card Industry (industry standard compliance)	State Attorneys General	N/A, usually offer liability defense if compliance is proven
Health	HIPAA	DHHS, OCR	Complaint investigations
Medical Device	Food, Drug, and Cosmetics Act (FDCA)	Food and Drug Administration (FDA)	Clearance processes, security through guidance documents
Consumer Products	Federal Trade Commission Act Section 5, California IoT Law	Federal Trade Commission (FTC), California Attorney General	Complaint investigations
Government	Federal Information Systems Management Act (FISMA)	OIG, Executive	N/A
Critical Infrastructure	Executive orders	Executive	N/A
Publicly Traded	Sarbanes-Oxley Act (SOX), SEC Rules	Securities and Exchange Commission rules	Examination, Disclosure to shareholders
European Personal Data	Privacy Shield	Department of Commerce (DOC)	Self-certification w/DOC review
All Business	Executive orders, California Consumer Protection Act	Executive, California Attorney General	Federal liability defense in exchange for incident disclosure

Table 2: Example Regulation/Statute and Regulators

As you review this sample list of regulations and regulators, one important takeaway is that most organizations implement more than the minimum specified in these regulations. As previously described, most risk management programs include both compliance requirements, or efforts used to demonstrate and manage compliance with legal requirements, and industry or risk-based requirements designed to protect the organization. For example, a healthcare organization regulated under HIPAA may implement more requirements than are mandated by the Department of Health and Human Services to comply with HIPAA, which could include NIST requirements or other industry requirements.

Recall our discussion about risk categories: operational, financial, reputational, and legal risk. Although an organization may be compliant with respect to legal risk, three other risk types may inform whether or not that organization implements more than the bare minimum. For example, an organization may be a manufacturer, which (as you can see above) is not likely subject to many regulations. However, what if the supply chain is interrupted for a lengthy period of time due to a ransomware attack? What if data in the system are changed and you receive the incorrect volume of raw materials? Likely, this kind of an unauthorized change, whether from an adversary or not, could cost millions of dollars. As a result, most organizations integrate industry best practices with legal requirements in their risk management programs.

QUESTIONS

1. The term "sub-privity," coined by Professor Tschider, refers to contract obligations that expand past the four corners of the contract. For example, a third-party technology provider may be bound by an organization to adhere to specific cybersecurity requirements. Also included is a contract term that obligates the technology provider to execute contract terms at least as strict as the terms to which it just agreed. What practical problems might arise?

2. International cybersecurity laws, including those of the United States, frequently require an organization directly regulated by the law to execute a contract with its third parties binding the third parties to the requirements under the law. Why might policy makers prefer to do this? Can you think of any reasons why it might be impractical to directly regulate a third party?

B. A BIT MORE ABOUT TRANSACTION COSTS

One question you might ask yourself—if organizations are so much work to maintain and require so much regulatory compliance, why do we have them? The short answer is something called "transaction costs."[3] For those not familiar, transaction costs are—quite literally—self-descriptive, in the sense that the describe the amount of value lost (i.e., the "cost") in executing a given transaction. So, for example, if you need to go buy groceries, you are incurring (at least) two transaction costs: (1) the *time, energy, and resources* you spend going to/from and at the store; and (2) any fees associated with the payment of the bill at the store. *Notice that the cost of the groceries is not included.*

The concept of transaction costs doesn't refer to the elements of the transaction itself, so much as the *attendant costs* associated with the transaction. In this case, the primary elements of the transaction are exchanging money for food/supplies. The *cost of the exchange* is the transaction cost.

Organizations exist because, to build complex things, lots of people and lots of things need to be involved. Of course, technically, one could build a skyscraper by having a whole bunch of individual contracts with suppliers, workers, and all the other people needed to supply materials and build the building. That would (remember our discussion of complexity?) result in the number of contracts required growing at least exponentially. This is deeply inefficient and would create enormous transaction costs, because each contract includes the transaction cost of negotiating that contract.

Organizations simplify complex tasks by allowing some degree of hierarchical organization under a "general" contract, so to speak. Employees can be given assignments without the need to negotiate a new contract for each assignment, and one entity—the organization—can negotiate with all outside entities that cannot be "swept up" into it (e.g., suppliers, vendors, contractors, and other kinds of third parties). While this is not a book on transaction cost economics, it is important to understand the general principle, because this will affect how organizations make decisions about the effective allocation of resources in cybersecurity.

C. AGENCY AND RESPONSIBILITIES

Of course, organizations cannot make decisions or operate on their own—they require leadership. Even for publicly traded companies, the shareholders themselves do not often get involved in the day-to-day operations of the company, or even attempt to influence overall strategic

[3] The concept of transaction costs was also discussed in the Hurwitz excerpt in Chapter 6.B. That excerpt reflected the development of the concept by Nobel laureate Ronald Coase in *The Problem of Social Cost* (1960) as a way to understand the design of legal rules. Coase developed the concept of transaction costs initially in a 1937 paper, *The Nature of the Firm*. It is for this work that Coase was awarded the Nobel prize. Coase argued that transaction costs—and, in particular avoiding or economizing upon them—is the reason that firms exist.

direction.[4] Organizations usually have one individual who is directly responsible for making operational decisions on behalf of the organization. This individual may be called a Chief Executive Officer (CEO) for a publicly traded company, a President for non-publicly traded companies, or a Director for a government entity or non-profit organization. Each of these leaders for non-governmental organizations, at least in larger organizations, answers to a Board of Directors.

The Board of Directors is a group of individuals that represent different stakeholders within the organization. For example, a non-profit organization may wish to include a representative on the board that is well-versed in non-profit fundraising. For publicly traded companies, sometimes members of the executive team, such as the Chief Financial Officer (CFO), the Chief Technology Officer (CTO), or the CEO may be members of the board, as well. For larger companies, usually board members consist of non-active members of the larger business community, such as retired CEOs from well-known or similarly sized businesses. For family-owned businesses, frequently members of the family (the main shareholders) are on the board, when the president is not a shareholder.

The purpose of any board is to shape the overall direction of the organization and to make decisions about leadership with respect to the organization. A Board's essential functions include first ensuring that organizational leaders are well-positioned to make the organization successful and that these leaders will continue to perform effectively. The board is the only decision-making entity that has the power to make decisions regarding the organization's leader. The executive leader owes many duties to the organization as the ultimate decision-maker, such as a duty of loyalty. This means that executive leaders should not act unilaterally to primarily benefits themselves; rather, executive leaders owe a duty to improve results for the organization.

1. AGENCY COST

The actions of executive leadership on behalf of an organization are not always considered to be in the best interest of the organization, especially considering that humans usually act to further their own interests. For companies, shareholders or investors (principals) may have different interests or perspectives than executive leaders, and executives may not have the right combination of abilities needed to make competent decisions for a specific area of expertise.[5]

---

[4] One exception to this are shareholder activists, who acquire enough shares of a particular designation for purposes of shifting company priorities in some way, usually through replacement of key members of the company's board of directors.

[5] We distinguish here between investors and shareholders because shareholders have specific rights in relation to the activity of publicly traded companies. Investors may, under some circumstances, have more power in relation to the activities of an organization.

Although hypothetically shareholders and investors have some rights with respect to members of the board of directors, usually shareholders do not hold enough shares to have the ability to provide direction to a company. Furthermore, even when shareholders have some ability to influence company decisions, usually those decisions are more reflective of a directional influence rather than specific decisions. When an organization's executive leadership team is not competent, or when conflicts arise between what principals want and what agents want, inefficiency may result.

As you read the following excerpt, consider how cybersecurity issues might arise as potential challenges between investors or shareholders and executive leadership.

ZOHAR GOSHEN & RICHARD SQUIRE, *PRINCIPAL COSTS: A NEW THEORY FOR CORPORATE LAW AND GOVERNANCE*

117 COLUM. L. REV. 767 (2017)

To produce firm value—meaning the value of the goods or services that a firm produces minus the cost of the resources it consumes in producing them—someone must exercise control over the firm. Regardless of whether that someone is an investor, a hired manager, or both, the creation of firm value requires that someone select the business strategy and then execute it by hiring (and, when necessary, firing) employees, timing product launches, and so on. Both components—strategy and execution—require control. Therefore, the main benefit of control in business firms, exercised through the efficient use of effort, expertise, and talent, is the creation of firm value. [. . .]

Our distinction between principals and agents requires a note of clarification. We generally use the term principal to refer to an investor and agent to refer to a manager. In many firms, however, this distinction is blurred by the presence of managers who have also contributed capital. One solution would be to define degrees of "principalness" and "agentness," but this would probably introduce more complexity than it is worth. To keep things simple, we define agents as parties whose share of the discretionary control rights exceeds their share of the cash-flow rights, and principals as parties whose share of the cash-flow rights equals or exceeds their share of the discretionary control rights. As applied to most corporate-governance structures, these definitions are workable and accord with common usage. Thus, although a principal-agent relationship exists between a corporation's board of directors and its officers, this Essay treats them as a unified agent. If the corporation is widely held, the shareholders are the principals; if instead the firm has a controlling shareholder (holding a control block either of common shares or of the vote-controlling shares in a dual-class share structure), the controller is the agent along with the directors and officers, and the noncontrolling shareholders are the principals. [. . .]

A . . . compelling explanation for the separation of ownership and control—the font of all conflict costs—is competence. Investors hire managers who can run a business more competently than they can, thereby increasing firm value. Therefore, competence costs—or, more specifically, principal competence costs—are the problem that all governance structures are ultimately designed to solve. [. . .]

Models concerned with the problem of agency costs tend to assume that the only reason managers ever harm their firms is the misalignment of incentives caused by the separation of ownership and control. But of course managers also make honest mistakes, generating agent competence costs. The magnitude of the costs will vary with the manager: Intelligent, informed, and unbiased managers make fewer mistakes than dull, ignorant, and biased managers. If overconfident corporate managers are too optimistic about a proposed project, their decision to devote corporate funds to the project will also generate agent competence costs. [. . .]

Competence can be activity specific. A hedge fund manager might be good at picking stocks and managing a portfolio but bad at running a company. Similarly, an entrepreneur might be good at identifying business opportunities but bad at managing people. We can expect organizations to allocate control accordingly.

A firm's overall competence in decisionmaking might also depend on the type of business the firm is engaged in. Mistakes are more likely in firms that are complex in terms of size, technology, or geographic scope of operations. Complexity makes honest mistakes more likely and challenges investors by impeding the evaluation of managerial performance. Therefore, when a firm is in a complex industry, its investors are more likely to make mistakes when evaluating managers and deciding whether to replace them. Similarly, when investors use a firm's public stock price as a performance proxy, market imperfections can lead investors to misevaluate managerial competence and loyalty.

Besides differing in probability, control mistakes can differ in magnitude. Important determinants of a mistake's magnitude include the levels of competition in the firm's product market and in the input markets where the firm acquires capital, materials, and employees. A mistake could either bankrupt a firm or barely dent its earnings, depending on whether the markets in which it operates are competitive or monopolistic.

As the expected cost (the magnitude multiplied by the probability) of a mistake increases, parties will be willing to expend more effort to prevent it, such as by acquiring more expertise and information. Some mistakes will, however, be unavoidable, in the sense that their expected costs are less than the costs of avoiding them. Because mistakes can result from managers' intellectual and emotional endowments, the mistakes might be tolerable if the manager is otherwise competent or is especially good at an aspect of management that is important to the firm. But if the mistakes are unendurable, their prevention might necessitate curtailing the manager's control or hiring a replacement. [. . .]

But how likely is it that Direct Democracy Company would succeed?[6] Because its shares are widely held, its shareholders would have dispersed views, conflicting interests, and differing investment horizons. They also would face collective-action and coordination problems because most shareholders would own only a small fraction of the corporation, which each shareholder would view in the context of a diversified portfolio.[7] Further, the shareholders would not be privy to most of the relevant information possessed by the firm's managers, as posting all inside information on the company's website would compromise the firm's competitive position. Under such conditions, the two sources of principal costs—competence costs and conflict costs—would most likely consume all of the firm's potential value. It is thus unsurprising that widely held firms never adopt this governance structure. Rather, structures that give equity investors direct control over strategic decisions are found only in sole proprietorships, small partnerships, and some closely held corporations. State law recognizes the costs of direct democracy in business corporations by vesting management of a corporation's business and affairs in the board of directors, and federal law follows suit by permitting public firms to exclude from annual proxy statements shareholder proposals related to the company's ordinary business operations, even if the proposals are framed in precatory terms.

2. MANAGEMENT ROLES/RESPONSIBILITIES

Most organizations divide responsibilities into key focus areas that require different skill sets. Large organizations offer a good model for management division of labor; for smaller organizations, many of these responsibilities are combined for each leader. The executive team reports to the CEO or President of a company, and the Executive Committee typically consists of the Chief Financial Officer (CFO), who manages the financial decisions of the company, the Chief Technology Officer (CTO), who manages technology decisions for the company, General Counsel, who is responsible for giving legal advice to the CEO and other leaders of the company, and a variety of other specific leaders depending on the company. For example, a Chief Marketing Officer (CMO) is responsible for marketing

[6] Book author's note: "Direct democracy" would be shareholders making every decision without delegation to executives.

[7] Book author's note: Most shareholders have what is called a diversified portfolio, in that they hold stock from any number of different businesses to spread financial risk across a variety of sectors and businesses. This would make it complicated for most shareholders to exert direct control over the decisions of each business in which they own some stake.

decisions, while a Chief Operating Officer (COO) is responsible for managing any key operations activities for the organization.

Some additional roles pertinent to cybersecurity include the Chief Communications Officer (CCO), who manages all internal and often external communications, including publicity and public relations, and the Chief Risk Officer (CRO) and Chief Compliance Officer, who manage enterprise risk programs, including overall compliance activities. Technology companies may also have a Chief Innovation Officer, who is responsible for cutting edge technology investments. These positions all play an important role in supporting various cybersecurity activities. See Figure 2 for an example organizational chart, which is a chart representing reporting relationships across an organization.

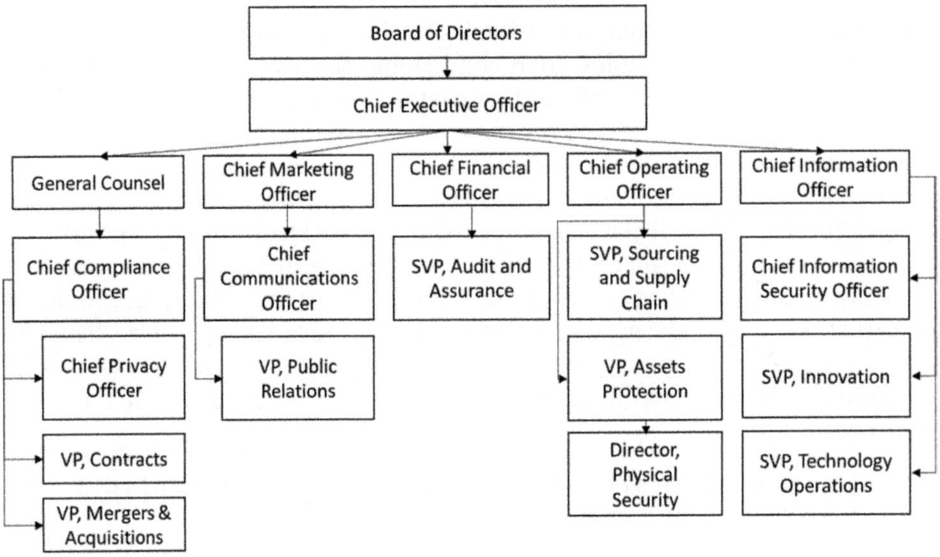

Figure 2: Sample Org Chart of Roles Pertinent to Cybersecurity

Many large companies have a Chief Information Security Officer (CISO), who is directly responsible for managing a company's cybersecurity program. Although the CISO is directly accountable, all personnel are responsible for ensuring security controls, from executives to individual contributors, and including everyone from contact center agents to engineers. The CISO, sometimes called a Chief Security Officer (CSO), usually has a team of technical and non-technical experts aligned to key aspects of an information security risk management program, as described below.

3. THE BUSINESS JUDGMENT RULE

Executive leadership is directly responsible for making decisions in the best interest of any organization, subject to direction of the board of directors. Executive leadership teams owe a fiduciary duty, for example a duty of loyalty and a duty of care, to the organizations they serve. For publicly traded companies, this duty is of particular importance when determining whether executive leadership has acted appropriately in a shareholder derivative lawsuit, which we will discuss in more detail later in this text. Generally, the behavior of executives is subject to the business judgment rule (BJR), which creates a presumption that executives will act in the best interest of the company. The BJR affords individuals a great deal of discretion in fulfilling their role, including appropriate decisions regarding technology investments.

CHARLES CRESSON WOOD, *SOLVING THE INFORMATION SECURITY & PRIVACY CRISIS BY EXPANDING THE SCOPE OF TOP MANAGEMENT PERSONAL LIABILITY*

43 NOTRE DAME J. LEG. 65 (2016)

Like all people in America today, top managers are operating in the midst of a complex modern social system, and are thus subject to influence from a variety of objectives, incentives, and constraints. Beyond their own personal objectives and personalities, the behavior of top management can be predicted to be a function of those same objectives, incentives, and constraints. For example, if (thanks to limited corporate liability laws) top management at a high-tech venture-capital funded firm is playing with other people's money, and their own net worth will not be adversely impacted if a serious security or privacy problem were to occur, top management will be encouraged to take on an excessive level of risk in the hope that they might hit it big with the new firm. So if the budget allocation for information security and privacy is insufficient, and a serious loss does later result, top management does not generally personally pay the price. The price is instead paid by the organization, and/or third parties such as suppliers and in some instances, investors, customers, and the general public. Since top managers personally enjoy the benefits of a restricted budget for information security and privacy, via higher quarterly bonuses, more promotions, etc., and because top management can spread the costs across third parties (economists call the effects of this spreading "externalities"), top management is now economically encouraged to keep information security and privacy budgets dangerously low [. . .]

At the same time, computer systems and networks are some of the most complex things that humans have ever created. To manage them adequately, notably to keep them properly secure and private, top management must establish and maintain exceedingly complex control systems. The development and use of these control systems requires a long-term effort that requires an incredible amount of both management attention and resources. The computer systems and networks that our society is now so dependent upon are the result of decades of compounded growth, where the older technologies have been augmented by newer technologies. As a result of this adding-on process, various problems are introduced, including gaps in knowledge, lapses in controls, inconsistencies, irregularities, and incompatibilities, and these problems in turn have often led to security and privacy losses. The many layers of inconsistent technological systems that now exist are revealed by the plugs and jacks used to connect various types of computers and mobile computing devices. In this environment, even a layperson can get a sense for the irregularity, non-standardization, inconsistency, and lack of coherence in many information systems today.

Since top management is now rewarded primarily based upon short-term financial performance, they have a disincentive against investing in the long-term control systems necessary to bring coherence, consistency, organization, security, and privacy to these information systems. As a consequence, top management helps to create long-term information security and privacy risks of immense proportion that only get more dangerous, pervasive, and more systemic as time goes on. In order to stop these risks from growing still more disastrous and pervasive, a change in the legal system that recognizes top management personal liability for harms done to third parties is now required.

The pervasive use of stock options, as a part of a typical private sector top management compensation package, creates many of the same dysfunctional results as bonuses based on quarterly financial results. The ensuing focus on stock price brings a short-term viewpoint that encourages short-term thinking, and short-term strategies. This focus will hopefully hold up at least until the top-level manager instituting them has retired, has taken a job at another organization, or has died. Since information security and privacy requires a significant dedicated long-term investment in order to be done successfully, to the extent that chief executives are paid with stock options, this arrangement further supports their focus on short-term financial results, which can and often does have dysfunctional impacts on the necessary long-term investment in technological infrastructure, such as in information security and privacy. [. . .]

One additional employment-market-oriented incentive system that motivates top management is the chance to significantly advance one's career by taking a higher-paying or more prestigious position with another organization. In past decades, many top managers would have been with their company for their entire working careers. Today, frequent job changes are the norm, and along with that higher job change frequency goes the focus on short-term thinking, short-term financial results, and, not surprisingly, an undue acceptance of short-term risks in the information security and privacy areas. [. . .]

In terms of losses caused to third parties resulting from corporate activity, there is convincing economic justification for having corporations bear the risk for unintentional harms in order to encourage both entrepreneurial risk taking and an expanded level of economic activity. But that same justification is not relevant to knowing and intentional harms caused by actions taken by top management. In support of this claim of inapplicability is ample evidence for the "deflection hypothesis" by which top management of corporations has the involved corporation bear a disproportional amount of the risk of knowing and intentional misdeeds for which they are responsible. For example, empirical research shows that when increased directors' and officers' insurance shields top management from personal liability related to mergers and acquisitions, the results are detrimental to shareholder returns.

If corporations are not able to shift some of this risk bearing for intentional and knowing acts back to top management personally, then socially undesirable results are likely to ensue. For purposes of the following discussion about information security and privacy related harms caused to third parties, it is critical that we as a society come to appreciate that inadequate investment in information security and privacy be clearly seen as an intentional and knowing act, an act for which top management should be held personally liable.

At the current time, insufficient top management investment in information security is a vague and often inadequately explored area when it comes to assigning liability for the harms caused to third parties. As will be explained further below, it is now possible to clearly delineate what is an adequate level of investment in information security and privacy, and thus a court can now readily determine whether there has been such an intentional and knowing act on top management's part. Top management personal liability is thus suggested as an appropriate penalty when intentional and knowingly inadequate investment in information security and privacy takes place.

Sanctions imposed on corporations will typically be increased when top management is shown to have been involved through intentional and knowing acts, for example via the "alter ego theory," whereby top management uses the corporation as its own alter ego to pursue personal purposes. Sanctions will also typically be increased if top management can be shown to have directed certain misdeeds, as can be found in the organizational sentencing guidelines found in the Model Penal Code. Of particular concern are those cases where top management takes the corporation down a knowing or reckless path, leading to significant damage to third parties, not just investors, but also customers, prospective customers, business partners, and members of the general public. Recent examples of such knowing or reckless behavior have included firms like Enron, Worldcom, and Global Crossing.

Corporate officers have a variety of duties to their company and to shareholders, including the duty of care, the duty of good faith, the duty of loyalty, the duty of disclosure, the duty of oversight, the duty not to violate the law, and the duty of reasonable reliance and delegation. Corporate officers may face personal liability if they breach these fiduciary duties, but the standard is quite high, as evidenced by the Caremark decision. In general, only the most egregious cases result in either director or officer personal liability. The types of lawsuits now possible for the breach of these duties are either direct or derivate suits and are brought by shareholders or, in some cases, by creditors. There are generally no legally recognized duties of corporate officers to third parties. As discussed later in this article, in addition to other affirmative defenses, there is most prominently the business judgment rule, which generally protects both directors and officers against personal liability.

For businesses, the interplay between the shareholders, the board, and executive leadership is known as corporate governance. The duties that executive leadership has with respect to the company and shareholders inform decisions, such as which investments to make and the priority for those investments, may be effective or ineffective, depending on the competency of leadership and their ability to accurately calculate risks, costs, and benefits. Later in this book, we will be discussing the types of actions shareholders may have against executive leadership in the event leaders have not honored these duties with respect to appropriate cybersecurity measures.

CHAPTER 8

WHY CYBERSECURITY IS HARD

■ ■ ■

In the first chapters of this textbook, you have learned the basics of cybersecurity, including information about threats and threat sources, risk management, technology basics, and a few of the underlying economic and practical issues facing cybersecurity as a function, practice, and legal area. This chapter is intended to reflect on these issues within the context of several examples and a full case study. If you have not yet done so in class, this is an opportunity to apply the concepts you are learning to actual scenarios.

In this chapter we tackle the question of why it is so difficult to implement effective cybersecurity solutions. As a preliminary note, it is important to recognize that cybersecurity problems (and therefore solutions) vary widely. From a strictly technical standpoint, why one given problem is hard is almost certainly different than why another problem is hard. Such a detailed treatment of complex systems software engineering and secure design and implementation practices is not the purpose of this chapter or this text. Rather, what we explore is a set of generally applicable themes that make almost every cybersecurity problem "hard."

This concept of "almost every problem being hard" is—to a degree—novel and unique to cybersecurity. It is certainly unlikely that, with the exception of some readers who previously studied cybersecurity, you likely have not been told "all problems in this field are necessarily hard." Furthermore, there are few such fields where this claim can be made and where the nature of the field constantly is changing and evolving (the study of infectious diseases may be one other example). In this sense, it is a "novel" and "unique" problem.

In another sense, however, the problem neither is novel or unique. There *are* other problems for which we can demonstrate that no "perfect" (or even 'good') solution exists. Transportation is a classic example: a drive down Broadway in New York City, or around the Capitol Beltway near Washington, DC would serve as an effective experiential learning tool. The design of systems of democratic governance is another. Winston Churchill is famously quoted in a speech to the United Kingdom's House of Commons as saying that "it has been said that democracy is the worst form of government except all those other forms that have been tried from time to time . . ."[1] Churchill's observation regarding public sentiment about democracy is hardly accidental; scarcely a week goes by where one does not hear a complaint about the failings of government or elected officials. But that does not lessen the Framers' concerns that neither "angels governed [people]" nor "were [people] angels." Some problems just are hard.

So what makes cybersecurity different? Think back to what we have covered thus far. Cybersecurity is difficult to define precisely, and easily confused. It is necessarily interdisciplinary, so that confusion is worsened. It involves a complex ecosystem for which we do not yet have adequate modeling, particularly given the constantly changing nature and motivations of the actors in that ecosystem. It necessarily involves computing and information systems, which provably have limitations on their own ability to detect problems in their design (e.g., the Halting Problem). Those computing and information systems are very complex, and their complexity grows at least exponentially as computers are used to perform more tasks. Yet humans are the ultimate users of the system, and humans are governed by laws.

This set of interactions from many different disciplines—engineering, law, economics, psychology, etc.—in an incredibly complex system is what makes cybersecurity *necessarily* "hard" in the general case. While all cybersecurity problems have different aspects to them, all cybersecurity problems also share a common thread of this complex, interdisciplinary nature. In this chapter, we encourage you to think through why this is the case, what to do in the presence of such challenges, and how traditional ways of thinking about solving problems must adapt when applied to cybersecurity's.

A. THE PROBLEM OF COMPLEXITY, OR THE "HALTING" PROBLEM

One of the biggest problems in cybersecurity is that problems are highly complex to solve. Technology systems are highly complex and only are becoming more complex. With the advent of artificial intelligence (AI), a computational model where systems can self-learn based on the data input, as well as changing interrelationships and weightings between those data, systems have become increasingly more complex than ever before. AI is a great example of complexity because it leverages, fully, computing resources by identifying relationships between data points in furtherance of a specific codified goal or goals.

For example, if you wanted to design an AI interview scanner to determine who to hire, you might want to measure the length of responses,

---

[1] It is worth noting that, in this speech, Churchill was actually speaking quite favorably of democratic forms of government, and some have argued that his speech was in fact deriding this quoted text as unfair to the successes of democratic governance.

and whether such responses included certain words or phrases you wanted to hear. However, you might not think to consider other things like the length of pauses or the rate of speech. By training AI on successful interviewees, the AI over time might identify other data elements that affect the success of an interviewee across hundreds or thousands of data points. The output of an AI system is an algorithm or collection of algorithms. For unlocked algorithms, or those that are permitted to self-learn after a training phase ('in the wild'), the algorithm should continuously become more effective and refined, enhancing its predictions.

A great example of this use case is the most common form of AI, machine learning. Machine learning systems may be supervised or unsupervised, which simply reflects the degree to which human design limits how the system may develop, including the selection of data on which machine learning will make its calculations. From a cybersecurity perspective, however, how might you know if an attacker has changed the data on which machine learning algorithms have been created, rendering an ineffective or dangerous algorithm? Further, can you be certain that the direction coming from an algorithm has not been altered in transmission (a common cybersecurity attack)?

A significant challenge in cybersecurity is protecting large data stores from unauthorized access or change in *big data* databases. The terminology "big data" is used to describe databases that can accommodate extremely large data volumes. As you might imagine, big data databases require use of several database servers, or computers that are specially configured to handle data organization and storage. The cost of managing many servers can be very high for most organizations, so organizations often contract with big data server providers that are geographically distributed, or *cloud providers*. Although the terms "big data" and "cloud" seem like unique concepts in technology, big data is simply a large data store, and the cloud is just an Internet-connected, geographically distributed set of servers performing some function. There are a variety of configurations of these servers that have a bearing on the potential security and privacy of data contained therein. We will discuss cloud providers and their services later in this book.

As you can see, modern systems span organizations (primary and third parties), geographies (both within countries and globally), and technology types. Furthermore, there are still technologies, such as neural networking in AI or quantum computing, of which humans have limited understanding, despite creating them. So, practically speaking, how might an organization protect systems that are extremely complex? For those of you with a computer science background, you may have read to some degree about the father of modern computers, Alan Turing's "halting" problem related to solving larger complexity problems.

JEFFREY M. LIPSHAW, *HALTING, INTUITION, HEURISTICS, AND ACTION: ALAN TURING AND THE THEORETICAL CONSTRAINTS OF AI LAWYERING*

5 SAVANNAH L. REV. 133 (2018)

To answer the question, we need to go back to some history and basics about machine thinking. Today's digitally connected world has its roots in an exercise in abstract mathematics. In the early 1900s, the mathematician David Hilbert famously set forth the view that the goal of all mathematics was to show that it could be expressed "in the form of a complete, consistent, decidable formal system—a system expressing 'the whole thought content of mathematics in a uniform way.' " In 1900, at the International Congress of Mathematicians in Paris, Hilbert set out a list of the twenty-three most important problems in mathematics yet to be solved.

Three of the problems were as follows:

- Can every mathematical statement be proved formally from a given set of axioms? This is the issue of completeness.
- Can only true statements be proved? This is the issue of consistency. For example, if we could prove that sometimes ten plus ten equals twenty and sometimes it equals thirty, the mathematical system would have a problem.
- Is there always a definite procedure (i.e., one that follows a series of logical rules of inference) that can determine in a finite amount of time whether a mathematical statement is true or false? Take the following assertion: there are no three positive integers, x, y, and z, for which xn + yn = zn for any integer n greater than 2. Is there a set of logical steps one could always perform to prove that these formulae would always be true? This issue is known in German as the *Entscheidungsproblem*, or, in English, the decision problem.

As to the first two problems, the mathematician Kurt Gödel published a paper in 1930 demonstrating that if a formal mathematical system is consistent, it cannot also be complete. In other words, the first statement and the second statement cannot be true at the same time. [. . .]

To introduce even greater rigor to the concept of computability, Turing imagined just such a computing machine (now referred as a "Turing machine" even though it is a thought experiment, not a physical machine). A Turing machine consists of a scanner that contains a finite set of "states". States (or as Turing called them "m-configurations") are discrete sets of instructions for the scanner. An imaginary and infinitely long tape runs past the scanner. The tape is divided into squares. Each square of the tape may contain a symbol, usually either 0 or 1, or may be blank. The scanner only "reads" one square at a time. The machine works by being in a particular "state," "seeing" what symbol is or is not in the square, and then acting on the state instructions that tell the machine what to do based on what it "sees" in the square. The scanner has two possible physical operations. It can print or erase symbols in the scanned square, and it can move right or left to a different square. The machine can also remember what it has already printed or erased on the tape.

A complete and discrete instruction for the machine would include the following four elements: (1) its current state; (2) the symbol (or lack of one) in the scanned square; (3) the operations (printing, erasing, or moving) to be performed in that state, given the symbol appearing in the scanned square; and (4) the state to which the machine changes after completion of the operation. Moreover, the machine is automatic in the sense that all it can do is act on the information it has on the tape and the instructions within any given state.

The reason the concept of the Turing machine was useful theoretically was because its combination of symbols on the tape and instructions within the scanner could compute any computable number. The point of all this was to create a definite, or algorithmic, procedure of computation to satisfy Hilbert's articulation of the *Entscheidungsproblem*. To distinguish between a computable number and one that was not computable, Turing distinguished between a machine that was "circular" and one that was "circle-free." That is, a circular machine goes into a loop. It reaches a configuration (i.e., a combination of tape symbol and state) from which there is no next move, or an inability to write any more symbols. A sequence is computable if it can be computed by a circle-free machine. In other words, the machine continues the computation and does not loop.

Turing's next step was to reduce the entire machine M to something expressible as a string of numbers. In modern terminology, this would be the exercise of translating a series of steps understandable in English to machine readable binary code consisting of nothing but 0s and 1s. As discussed above, any computation algorithm would be expressible as a table in which each line of the table showed the four elements of that step: current state, symbol, operation given the symbol, and new state. It turns out that each line of the table could be reduced by convention to a series of symbols separated by semicolons. Turing called this the machine's "standard description." Each symbol in the standard description, i.e., letters and semicolons, could be replaced by Arabic numbers, called "description numbers." These would always be in the form of a (long) string of integers. Thus, the algorithm for the computation of any computable sequence can be reduced to a description number that has a complete meaning because segments of the number represent, in turn, current states, symbols, operations, and new states. Hence, a (very long) description number represents machine M. If the description number represented a circle-free machine (i.e., one that would satisfactorily perform the calculation rather than going into a loop), in Turing's terminology, it was a "satisfactory" number. To repeat, the point of this entire exercise was to prove "that there can be no general process for determining whether a given number is satisfactory or not." In other words, there is no way of *always* determining conclusively that a particular algorithm will continue the desired computation to the desired halting point without looping. [. . .]

Nevertheless, Turing's own work provides the basis for thinking about overcoming the constraints. "[I]f a machine is expected to be infallible, it cannot also be intelligent. There are several mathematical theorems which say almost exactly that. But these theorems say nothing about how much intelligence may be displayed if a machine makes no pretense at infallibility." Turing's position was not that machines could learn to think perfectly or even like humans, but that the positives of machines would outweigh the limitations. Human experts had the luxury of using common sense, learning from mistakes, applying short-cut rules of thumb, and making the occasional blunder. Wrote Turing, "Against it I would say that fair play must be given to the machine . . . No man adds very much to the body of knowledge, why should we expect more of a machine?"

The practical impact of Turing's halting problem in cybersecurity is related to the complexity and changeability of modern computer programming. If we were to ensure appropriate security, we would need to know before the machine functions, exactly how it will function to ensure that such functions are protected from adversaries. A fairly clear example of this is the application of malware detection software. The purpose of such software is to scan individual terminals or computers, as well as servers, peripherals (devices that only function when connected to computers, like a printer), and the network itself to determine whether malware has been installed. The software function by having definitions, similar to the way a vaccine works by emulating a virus and causing cells that defend the body from sickness to have a definition of the virus before encountering it again. If you feed a malware detection program the definitions of known malware, such as computer viruses, the malware detection program knows what to identify as a virus, alert a security team, and, where possible, quarantine the virus. The security is then able to review what has been quarantined or take other actions, such as stopping connectivity with an individual computer that is spreading a virus and re-installing a previous version of the computer (pre-virus) if needed.

However, the entire function of malware detection, or, indeed, vaccines, is based on historical knowledge that a particular virus or other malware exists and that we have a definition for it. For this reason, malware detection is inherently backwards facing. Although security teams often work with a third-party software provider to update definitions frequently, sometimes a virus or other malware will spread before there is a definition for it. A similar problem exists in vulnerability management. You will learn more about vulnerability management in Chapter 9, but like malware definitions, employing certain tactics to avoid vulnerabilities means that vulnerabilities must be known prior to an organization doing something to remediate it. And from a security perspective, this means that teams are perpetually trying to keep up with adversaries' new threat vectors. Ultimately, it is both the reality of cybersecurity operations *and* the increasing complexity of computer functions that makes it very difficult to perform cybersecurity functions perfectly. The only real method to make something completely secure is to disconnect it from the Internet and power it down. Neither of these steps does anything to support real and necessary organizational operations.

In the example that follows, consider the degree to which the integration of basic technologies with more advanced AI systems might intensify the halting problem from a cybersecurity perspective.

1. AI DISTRIBUTED RISK EXAMPLE

JeanMe is a personalized jean retailer and manufacturer that creates jeans for individuals based solely on uploaded pictures, social media preferences, and sizing details. JeanMe has been successful in anticipating the desires of jean wearers, including their personal style and styles that will fit the body of each wearer. JeanMe takes orders, which require a potential wearer to connect their social media accounts to JeanMe's systems, in a primary system. These data points, including image data and other data to a third-party provider, AI Analytics, Inc., that conducts data analysis on the data using an advanced AI system. It is not known to JeanMe or to AI Analytics exactly which data points are used in the images or social media accounts to inform the recommendations. Rather, the AI system has been built based on user feedback: potential users receive recommendations on jean fit, color, cut, and flourishes, and these users accept or reject recommendations and provide detailed feedback.

The system implementation is pictured (in limited form), as follows in Figure 1:

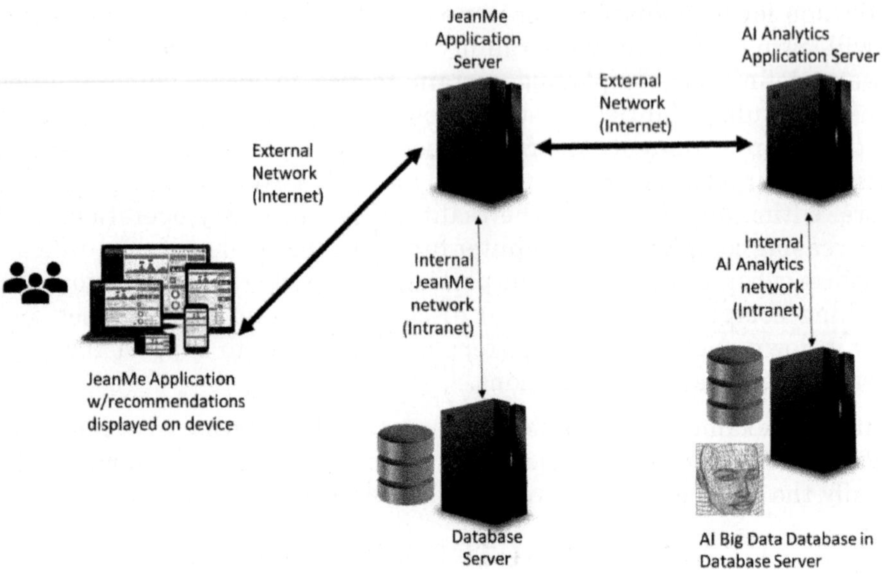

Figure 1: Example technology diagram for JeanMe Application Infrastructure (JeanMe Application asset)

Considering the issues described above:

1. Reviewing the basic infrastructure diagram above, how might you hack this system?
2. How might the complexity or halting problem affect how your organization, as a target (or focus of an adversary), decide to invest capital to protect this system?
3. What do you think, from the perspective of a CEO or other organization leader, would be a "reasonable" business decision with regard to cybersecurity controls? How might complexity play into this determination?
4. If an adversary attacked the AI database, scrambled the data, and replaced some data elements, and the algorithm resulted in some injury (economic or otherwise) to JeanMe customers, what do you think courts would find "reasonable" in a negligence tort action?

B. THE PROBLEM OF CHANGING, EVOLVING ENVIRONMENTS

In the JeanMe example above, the algorithm changes regularly as it updates to be more effective, but all technology environments, regardless of whether they include AI technologies, are constantly evolving. Evidence of the constantly changing technology environment is anticipated, even standardized in technology management. One common management approach is called ITSM, or Information Technology Service Management. ITSM is the model for handling any and all technology operational procedures necessary for an organization to run effectively.

For example, common processes that need management include incident, problem, service request, and change. Incident in the ITSM context is separate from incident in the cybersecurity context: incident for technology management is simply anything that is not working as designed. For example, an *incident* could be a log-in problem, or it could be that data is not displayed as designed or that a technology is not connecting properly. A *problem* is a more complex incident, or an issue that is not easily resolved by technology support personnel, such as the IT Help Desk. A service request is any request that is not an incident or a problem. The ITSM also manages technology changes. In a technology environment, any unauthorized change can result in instability of technology resources. As we discussed at the beginning of the book, two of the key considerations for any IT systems are data integrity and data availability. When changes occur without appropriate planning, they can cause major service disruptions, risking significant operational impacts.

Despite the potential risks, technology changes occur frequently for a few different reasons. First, organizations are constantly growing and changing. A business area may find a new, more efficient way to manage vendors and purchases associated vendor management software or a new customer app might be offered to distribute coupons and offer incentives to shop at a specific retailer. Second, organizations spend an incredible proportion of their expenses on technology infrastructure. As a result, organizations often look for better ways to manage technology, which can mean sunsetting, or retiring, older systems in favor of newer ones. Third, all business organizations must compete for business, which could mean making changes for purposes of improving performance or simply because a new technology might attract more customers. Fourth, as previously mentioned, incidents and problems may trigger technology changes.

Protecting an asset is not a matter of identifying one discrete technology and building a virtual wall around it. Rather, security measures must consider the entire infrastructure from the user interface (what an individual user sees) all the way back across network connection to individual servers and the data or instructions they contain. Furthermore, each node in the network or each discrete technology often needs more than one method of protection. Security practitioners call this "defense in depth," or the idea that more than one security control is usually needed to protect against a variety of different attack vectors, or methods of attack.

The challenge of protecting assets in a system from cyberattack is that every time something in the system changes, the strategy of protecting the asset could change. Recall the house metaphor from earlier in this book. Imagine that as one of your security controls, you have installed a security system in your house that includes magnetic pairs that will signal when the pairs are not aligned. When your front door is closed, the security system does not send an alert message to you. However, when the front door opens, the magnetic connection is severed, and the security system sends a message to you. Imagine hiring a contractor to replace your front door, and you depend on the contractor to reinstall the magnetic pair on your door. What if the contractor forgets to install the magnetic pair or installs the pair incorrectly? You will not receive your security alerts, and potentially an intruder could enter the house without notifying the police. To ensure that they are installed properly, you may need to require the security company to come out and verify their installation, or perhaps you will want to be part of the installation process.

In an organization, changes happen all day, every day. To ensure that these changes do not affect system performance or functionality, every change that will likely impact a system in a more than nominal way must go through a change management process. In this process, technology leaders or experts for the affected technologies discuss the potential change with other technology leaders, the Change or Architecture Review Board. This review ensures that whoever has requested the change has appropriately planned to avoid any issues. Usually change management processes also have a backout or reversion plan. For example, you likely have a mobile device. Many organizations that permit their personnel to use their personal mobile devices for business purposes will request that personnel do not update to the newest updates until they permit such an update.

The purpose of such rule seems counterintuitive: shouldn't the update be installed immediately to reduce security issues? Unfortunately, some companies generating updates do not provide any notification to organizations dependent on their technologies in advance of the general public. For example, Apple is famous for releasing updates without notifying anyone, which sometimes causes non-Apple apps to fail. Moreover, the change in the technology itself may actually result in potential security issues, since the security experts built the security system based on the previous operating system version.

1. RISKS OF OUTSOURCING TO THE CLOUD EXAMPLE

GreenAcre is a municipality in Dakotasota. In order to manage municipal functions, the GreenAcre government uses a variety of computer programs, including its Department of Motor Vehicles (DMV) ticketing software. The software that runs on GreenAcre's terminals at the DMV connects to a common database server. That database server is also connected to an application server that runs a Web application so that residents can look up the updated version of their ticket record. For example, if someone comes into the DMV and pays their ticket, the online ticket record should be updated. GreenAcre received some funding from Dakotasota intended to improve state security, and now GreenAcre intends to upgrade all of its technology to the newest version, which tout the latest security features. See Figure 2 for a simple diagram that describes the current infrastructure:

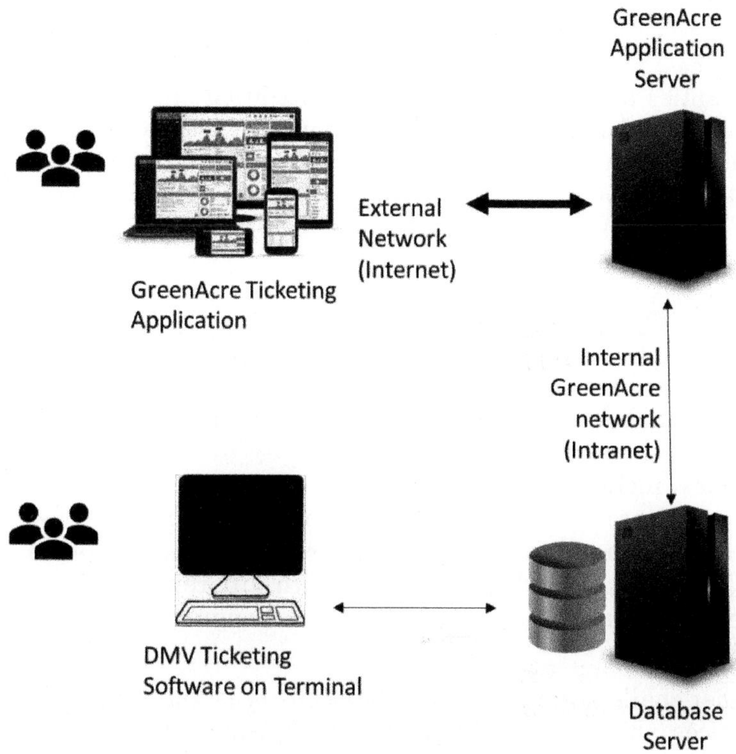

Figure 2: GreenAcre Ticketing Application

As you review Figure 2, consider what controls may have previously been implemented or not implemented on these legacy, or original (not updated) systems and reflect on the following:

QUESTIONS

1. If you had designed the original systems, how might you have protected them?

2. The DMV Ticketing Software currently is installed on each terminal, which is connected via ethernet cable to the internal network. The current log-in is specific to each user but only requires a user ID and basic password. The new ticketing approach for DMV users is to use a Web app for both DMV tellers and GreenAcre residents, which has been designed and will be hosted at a third-party site. The GreenAcre CIO has stated that the current security

approach for the existing system has not resulted in any real security issues, and that the new system should duplicate that approach. Do you agree?

3. Thinking like an adversary, what new vulnerabilities might the new application, hosted by a third-party, pose to DMV operations and GreenAcre residents? What questions might you ask to ascertain what new risks are posed by this change?

4. The DMV has decided to combine the DMV licensing system with the DMV ticketing system in one system. The third party that has designed and currently is hosting the ticketing application has an additional module it sells to municipalities to also manage vehicle registration, including cars, trucks, motorcycles, RVs, boats, and other recreational vehicles. GreenAcre believes that this is a good financial strategy to combine and upgrade these systems at the same time. Do you think the existing system, as designed will work for both purposes? What issues might you face in combining these systems on one platform?

C. THE PROBLEM OF FIT-FOR-PURPOSE SECURITY

As you saw above in Section 8.B, the ever-changing nature of IT makes it difficult to ensure a high degree of security at any given time. Some organizations include a member of the security team on the change management board or require disclosure of their plan to review and test security controls as part of their preparation for executing a change. However, installing brand new systems with different architectures and, sometimes, infrastructures, may make it challenging to maintain a basic level of security.

Another challenging aspect of cybersecurity is that although there are best practices and industry standards for cybersecurity that serve as a starting point for designing security into systems, the security of a given asset requires someone versed in security to evaluate a system's overall architecture and infrastructure from the perspective of an adversary. That is, to effectively design a secure system, a qualified security expert must develop a series of threat models to understand what the target might be and consider how an adversary might attack the system. This can be tremendously difficult when the architecture does not yet exist. However, it does explain why cybersecurity is not necessarily a matter of writing some requirements into law and mandating companies to follow them. Ultimately, organizations can spend millions of dollars implementing security controls into their systems, but if they are not the correct controls, they will have spent substantial funds with very little additional security.

Once again, let's use the house metaphor to discuss differences in cybersecurity approaches. An apartment in Manhattan might be subject to very different attacks than a farmhouse in rural Wyoming. The Manhattanite likely will have deadbolts and locks on their doors, but the likelihood of someone breaking in through the window is unlikely if they are on the 35th floor. Instead, the building will likely have some form of desk security, use of a passcode or scan key to get in the door after certain hours, and closed-circuit TV (CCTV) cameras in the entrance, elevators, and parking garage may be monitored by security. The farmhouse in Wyoming may have window locks and door locks, but it may also block off the gravel road to the home with a gate, chains, and a deadbolt with barbed wire along the property line. The farmhouse may include some motion-activated lights or cameras in areas where the owners keep high-value livestock or product. Although both require locks and monitoring of some kind, as you can see the exact type of solution is highly dependent on the setting, the assets of value, and the likely attack vectors.

Without considering the actual risks from the perspective of potential threat sources, the farmhouse will have desk security and the apartment will rely on barbed wire. Of course, this is ridiculous. But it is exactly the type of conversation that happens in the technical realm, as well. Appropriate security solutions take into account at least three considerations: 1) the asset's technology capabilities, including its technical affordances or constraints (what it can or can't do), 2) the system architecture and infrastructure, including how data are transmitted and where data are stored, and 3) the value of the asset and the corresponding threat models that would target this asset. Below, you will read two separate examples with a few questions related to technology controls. Although we have not explained many types of security controls, you will see some basic controls described in the questions following these examples.

1. INDUSTRIAL MANUFACTURING EXAMPLE 1

Flavorfav is a chemical manufacturing company that creates artificial flavors that are guaranteed to taste as close to the real thing as something artificial can taste. They are a supplier to some of the biggest food manufacturers, such as Kraft Heinz and General Mills. Flavorfav's most critical system is the system running their chemical production facility. Flavorfav has one primary factory and a smaller factory that is only used for emergencies. Both use the same system set-up and software. Flavorfav uses a traditional industrial control system (ICS). This means that all servers running the manufacturing equipment are housed onsite. In this case, the factory can only be given instructions by terminals operated by employees who have gained access to the physical premises, but the terminals have the ability to connect to the Internet, and employees can receive company email there. When asked, the CEO of Flavorfav has said that their biggest concern is that the factory would shut down, causing them, on average, $3 MM in weekly losses through non-productivity of workers and inability to sell product.

2. INDUSTRIAL MANUFACTURING EXAMPLE 2

Flavorfav engineers have created an internal, "homegrown" online ordering system through which its customers place orders for product. This system allows customers to place orders in the ICS' queue for production at the manufacturing facility. The homegrown system consists of the application server used to host the online ordering system, as well as a database in a database server and an internal application that is hosted within Flavorfav's data center. The database can only be updated only by Flavorfav personnel using Flavorfav computers through the internal application. The data submitted in the ordering process includes purchase order (P.O.) numbers, which are tied to account numbers and billing information for their customers. This enables Flavorfav to track purchase orders from request through billing and even shipping to ensure the product is correct, completed on time, and delivered as requested.

Now that you have reviewed both examples, answer the following questions. Please note: there is no right or wrong answer; rather, we would like you to think through how different assets and different business scenarios might influence your selection of controls.

QUESTIONS

1. For the two FlavorFav examples, what are the assets being evaluated?

2. Sketch each FlavorFav infrastructure including the main application or software, the type of connection it has to servers (internet or intranet), and the type of servers used. Be sure to notate who is controlling each of the pieces of infrastructure.

3. List out the types of threats that might affect each of the assets described. Mark each of the threats as attacker or non-attacker. For those marked "attacker," what do you think their motivation would be? Of all threats listed, underline or highlight which you think, given your limited knowledge, would be most likely to occur.

4. For each of the two examples, do you think that encryption is necessary for the data collected? Why or why not?

5. For each of the two examples, how do you think an attacker might make use of poor access controls, such as granting, changing, or terminating access?

6. For each of the two examples, do you think malware is a concern? Why or why not?

D. THE PROBLEM OF TECHNICAL DEBT AND COMPLEXITY AS-IMPLEMENTED

In Chapter 9, we will introduce a concept known as "technical debt" in more detail. For now, think back to our examination of complexity in Chapter 5. When building a complex system, frequently tradeoffs must be made not just between features, but between the time required to implement a feature and the time by which the project or organization demands the overall system be available. Business decisions often, if not almost always, govern how many resources are available for a given project, and time is often the most limiting resource in software and related systems development. The contest between the complexity and effort of adding a new security feature versus adding a new feature that might appeal directly to prospective customers is frequently decided in favor of the marketable feature; security rarely "sells", but flashy features do. Remember, from complexity theory, adding in that "one more" feature not only increases the overall risk of a security issue, but it also makes implementing other security features that more complex!

The result is that organizations often push off certain types of decisions until later in their development cycle. Sometimes called "move fast and break things," this culture of software development follows the "minimum viable product" model of business development, in which organizations focus on producing something sufficient to gain traction, with the assumption that defects will be worked out later. The flexible nature of software, in theory, allows such updates to be pushed out in a way not available in traditional physical manufactured products (which, generally, once produced, are not easily updateable).

The problem is that this theory of "deferred maintenance" ignores the basic principles of complexity, system design, and exponentially increasing costs. It may be true that the digital nature of software allows updates to be applied without the *physical* costs of manufacturing. But it is deeply false that such updates are costless. In fact, as we will discuss in Chapter 9, those updates often are far *more costly* than might be the case with traditional manufactured goods—so much so that organizations may avoid them entirely. When such "bad" design choices become baked into a system, and subsequent features are built on top of those choices—becoming dependent on them—the result is a system which has "baked in" a series of problems into its foundational elements, the cost of repairing which only grows as the system develops. This is the concept of technical debt—and it accrues interest as a nasty rate!

Perhaps the most famous example of "technical debt" is that of the preponderance of operating systems, which only supported two-digit year fields. When an operating system is first developed, most commonly it is dealing with providing a limited set of computational features running on a limited set of hardware. For example, operating systems developed in the early 1980s were designed to run on computers that had memory sizes measured (at most) in kilobytes, meaning the entire memory of the computer was *less than the data stored in the average email!* In an environment like this, the idea of "wasting" extra space on things like unnecessary numbers seemed foolish. Why would one store a calendar date, for example, in 8 digits (MM-DD-YYYY) when a two-digit year can perfectly distinguish one year from the next? Those first two digits in the year haven't changed *since before computers were invented!*

You can, mostly likely, see where this story is headed. Decisions were built on top of those early choices, software and applications built on operating platforms that provided two-digit abstraction of the year, and so on . . . and then the late 1990s came around. The designers of the early 1980s generally had never imagined their systems still would be in use in that form almost 15 years later and, if so, certainly they assumed that the systems would have been updated by then. But they weren't, and an enormous amount of time and effort was spent on correcting software problems before the (Gregorian) calendar year 2000.

E. THE PROBLEM OF INTRANSIGENCE AND WRITING LAWS FOR CYBERSECURITY

You may have begun to observe some of the challenges in writing laws in this area. The biggest challenges involve *who* and *what* is being regulated. As we discussed in Chapter 7, organizations are small and large, complex and simple, to say nothing of specific sector norms and behaviors. Although good security practices exist, a good security architecture is often implementation-specific. Furthermore, organizations implementing a risk-based approach cannot invest in security solutions at the same level, regardless of the potential risk to the organization or to individual people, for it would cost far too much. Consider the following example from the perspective of risk-based decision-making.

1. MAKING RISK-BASED CHOICES EXAMPLE

Intertrust Financial Management is a company that manages trusts for (largely wealthy) families. They ensure that trust accounts are adequately managed through financial oversight, such as targeted investments in mutual funds to grow account values over time as the money is held and that withdrawing funds from such account follow strict standards for verification. As part of their offerings, Intertrust holds these accounts on behalf of traditional banks as a service to bank customers. Customers who work with their banks know that Intertrust is holding these funds and managing their accounts, but their primary relationship is with their bank. Intertrust permits access to trust account summaries, including account transactions, through a secure connection between the customer's bank applications and their internal application server. The customer logs into their bank system and clicks on "Trust Accounts," which displays their trust account without the customer having to log in again (single-sign-on, or SSO). Intertrust has been asked by its customer banks to implement reasonable security controls consistent with the Gramm-Leach Bliley Act, which mandates organizations to implement and ensure reasonable security controls with respect to the size and complexity of the organization.

Intertrust conducts regular security assessments by which it prioritizes its remediation efforts and financial commitments. Recently, one of its bank customers, during a third-party audit, demanded Intertrust demonstrate that it has met a series of security requirements for all of its internal systems. Although Intertrust has implemented most of these controls to comply with GLBA for its banking customers' customers, it has not implemented the same controls for some of its other systems, such as the human resources (HR) system that manages employee information and performance appraisals or its internal e-mail system. Based on risk assessments it has conducted, although risks exist for these other systems, Intertrust has prioritized remediation efforts related to its banking customers.

Based on the information above:

1. Do you think that Intertrust is right in its assessment to not implement the same security controls for its internal HR system as it would implement for its bank customer sites?
2. If you were writing a law that would provide a floor, or base-level requirements for all organizations, what would you select?
3. If you were writing a law that incorporate some variability, what language might you use or which variables might change which type of controls might need to be implemented?
4. Frequently, laws that are intended to establish cybersecurity expectations use language like "reasonable security requirements," "administrative, technical, and physical controls," and "risk management" or "risk assessment." What are the positives and negatives of broad language like this? If you were writing a law do you think you would draft it to be more general or more specific, taking into account different organizations with different sizes and complexities?

2. WHY CYBERSECURITY LAWS ARE WRITTEN BROADLY

To date, most cybersecurity laws are written broadly for three primary reasons: 1) market impact, 2) lack of technical knowledge, and 3) technical changeability and variability. First, any laws that are written will likely impact the marketplace in some way by increasing costs for producers, who then may pass along costs to the marketplace. The challenge in regulating the marketplace generally is considering the degree to which different sized organizations might be affected by certain requirements. For example, a small corner grocer may not pose the same risk to consumers as a social media site, and yet we would likely prefer that the corner grocer have some security protections when we provide personal information to them. Being able to have confidence in a system is big part of enabling the commercial marketplace. However, too stringent requirements would likely put the grocer out of business. From a market perspective, it is tremendously difficult to balance both consumer interests and relevant behavior with costs to these organizations.

Next, the individuals who write bills are typically those with experience writing laws, rather than writing technical requirements. For this reason, many laws use general terminology due to the challenge of "getting it right." Finally, the law does not change that rapidly. Often, we live by laws that have been eclipsed and never reviewed or reworked due to alternative priorities. For this reason, laws that *do* have some specificity often become obsolete as new technical standards evolve. If drafters were to write requirements in too much detail, complying with new, yet different, technical standards could hypothetically force an organization out of compliance. The likelihood of an administrative agency actually enforcing a lesser standard seems unlikely, but the possibility of this demonstrates the challenge of writing any specific requirements into law.

The challenge of course, is that laws perform a notice function as well as a regulatory function. Sometimes, organizations that are less sophisticated may not know which areas to address or that they need to implement certain security controls at all. For these organizations, it can be useful to have some legal incentive to implement cybersecurity programs. At least for data breaches where personal information is exfiltrated, it is tremendously difficult to prove injury as a plaintiff against an organization. For this reason, some of the usual incentives for change, such as market demand and cost avoidance, are not present for cybersecurity. For example, the average person does not usually know the details of any organization's security practices, unless they are part of that organization (and even then, usually not). Therefore, assuming the market will incentivize strong security practices is not a useful assumption. Furthermore, if the law does not punish organizations for poor security practices, the organization may not have the incentive to change, absent other impacts, like broad media coverage that hurts an organization's reputation.

One important note as it relates to cybersecurity laws is that cybersecurity laws do not protect organizations against their own poor judgment. For example, cybersecurity laws do not establish cybersecurity standards for activities that do not include either personal information or critical infrastructure, such as energy, water, transportation, and other important public services that could cause catastrophic impacts if they fail. In short, where laws are written they are written to protect people. This means that frequently, with the exception of critical infrastructure, most cybersecurity laws perform both privacy and cybersecurity functions.

Some laws do exist which, even if drafters were intending to effectively regulate cybersecurity, the categories do not represent appropriate corresponding programmatic areas of focus. One example of this is the Health Insurance Portability and Accountability Act (HIPAA). HIPAA is unique in that it actually establishes some granularity of specific categories of focus, but some categories that are integral to a security program are not actually listed. However, given the challenge of keeping up with technological change, under some circumstances it may be preferable to be general rather than specific. Because HIPAA's Security Rule was in effect as of 2003, the changes in the security ecosystem make some parts of HIPAA seem obsolete. The excerpt following does not endorse HIPAA or a model of increased specificity but rather criticizes the lack of breadth for technical programmatic capabilities.

CHARLOTTE A. TSCHIDER, *ENHANCING CYBERSECURITY FOR THE DIGITAL HEALTH MARKETPLACE*

26 ANNALS HEALTH L. 1 (2017)

In contrast to the HIPAA Privacy Rule, which relies on standard privacy principles and clear rules, the HIPAA Security Rule applies risk management techniques to manage data confidentiality, integrity and availability for PHI. Risk management techniques typically offer more overall flexibility for an organization to choose a particular solution to comply with the HIPAA Security Rule.

The HIPAA Security Rule organizes implementation specifications into two categories: addressable and required. In contrast with a required implementation specification, an addressable specification permits a Covered Entity (CE) or Business Associate (BA) (two specific types of organizations regulated under HIPAA) to choose how it satisfies the objective of the requirement. Satisfying the objective may include meeting the specification, finding an alternative solution, or not meeting the specification with additional documented substantiation. In all cases, the CE or BA must document its decision. When determining security measures to include, organizations must evaluate the size, complexity, and capabilities of the organization; the technical infrastructure, hardware, and software security capabilities; the costs of security measures; and the probability and criticality of potential risks to electronic PHI (ePHI).

The HIPAA Security Rule, which preceded many modern developments in digital health, requires compliance with a smattering of program-level specifications, yet does not explicitly require many cybersecurity controls. Ultimately, twenty-one specifications of thirty-nine relate purely to security rather than broad IT practices, and of those twenty-one specifications, six describe high-level identity and access management procedures, four relate to higher-level risk management specifications, and three relate to an incident response process. Although these focus areas are important to protect PHI from unauthorized disclosure or change and ensure availability of PHI, only eight specifications in some way describe technical cybersecurity controls, none of them required.

In an effort to evolve cybersecurity maturity for CEs and BAs, the OCR has mapped applicable National Institute of Standards and Technology (NIST) specifications to the HIPAA Security Rule, a so-called "crosswalk." Unfortunately, this mapping and other NIST guidance do not establish mandatory requirements for CEs or BAs, and many still mistakenly believe that HIPAA compliance sufficiently protects against cybersecurity risk.

In 2011 and 2012, the OCR developed, pursuant to new HITECH responsibilities, an audit framework transitioning HIPAA specifications into an audit control set and worked with 115 CEs to test the audit process. In 2015, the OCR selected and initiated its first candidate pool for audits, notifying CEs in July of 2016, with planned (at the time of writing) notification of BAs in the fall of 2016. The audit protocol matched HIPAA statutory requirements and was written similarly to the HIPAA privacy, security, and data breach notification rules. Overall, HIPAA coupled with OCR oversight has set a standard for organizational privacy and security. However, the limited application via narrow statutory entity definitions and lack of comprehensive required technical security controls illustrate a need for more comprehensive regulation of the digital health marketplace. [. . .]

Passed in 2012, the Food and Drug Administration Safety and Innovation Act (FDASIA) required the Food and Drug Administration (FDA), the National Coordinator for Health Information Technology (ONC), and the Federal Communications Commission to create a report on a proposed strategy for a risk-based framework involving mobile applications.[2] The 2014 FDASIA Health IT Report recognized four significant conclusions with respect to health information technology that apply to the digital health cybersecurity landscape and shape expectations regarding the FDA's involvement in cybersecurity management: 1) that existing FDA functionality is effective, within a culture of safety and quality, including voluntary and non-punitive reporting; 2) health IT should use recognized standards; 3) agency roles should be clarified and

[2] It should be noted here that FDA requirements only apply to technologies properly identified as "medical devices," which may include software, applications, or apps when such technologies are used for diagnostic purposes, as well as physical medical devices.

avoid overlap; and 4) the FDA will not regulate general, non-health-specific use of IT infrastructure or devices. Further, the FDASIA report clearly illustrated a continuing focus for regulatory agencies on security principles, not applicable technical standards.

In 2014, the FDA began issuing pre- and post-release cybersecurity guidelines and issued device vulnerability notices to assist device manufacturers in producing and managing devices less likely to adversely impact consumers. The 2014 Pre-Release Cybersecurity Guidelines addressed incorporating cybersecurity considerations in the design and development of medical devices as part of "software validation and risk analysis . . . [in] 21 CFR 820.30(g)." The FDA recommended incorporating asset identification, threat analysis, and vulnerability reviews into an organization's device development process, including risk assessment and analysis, to determine residual risk and apply mitigation strategies. Such processes should take into consideration the intended use and implementation of a device, such as home use. Moreover, medical device manufacturers are encouraged to specify "cybersecurity safeguards" in premarket submission processes, such as "hazard analysis" and "design considerations" for a medical device, and risks like device cybersecurity controls considered or implemented.

The premarket cybersecurity safeguards recommending asset identification, threat analysis, and vulnerability reviews, reflect a level of standardization in cybersecurity practice. These standards incorporate best practice cybersecurity capabilities, such as access and identity management—the capability that bars unauthorized users from accessing a system, code validation and management, cybersecurity incident response capabilities, and business continuity—continuing function of devices even when compromised. These standards have been established by the International Electrotechnical Commission (IEC), the "world's leading organization" for electrical technologies.

The FDA's Guidance for Industry-Cybersecurity for Networked Medical Devices Containing Off-the-Shelf (OTS) Software explicitly allocated responsibility for new cybersecurity activities under existing FDCA laws governing technology validation processes. The Guidance further explained that manufacturers should work with vendors to timely receive cybersecurity updates, such as patches, and develop a "cybersecurity maintenance plan."

In January 2016, the FDA distributed the Postmarket Management of Cybersecurity in Medical Devices for comment purposes. This guidance document reiterated the responsibility of manufacturers to include cybersecurity considerations throughout product development and to continuously monitor for device vulnerabilities throughout each device's lifecycle. Specifically, the FDA recommends following the NIST Framework for Improving Critical Infrastructure Cybersecurity, a risk management framework, and also sharing identified cybersecurity risks and security incident data via the National Health Information Sharing & Analysis Center.

The FDA also recommends monitoring for cybersecurity vulnerabilities, assessing potential vulnerability impact, and developing mitigation strategies, including deploying patches or remediating code to neutralize vulnerabilities. These recommendations represent industry standard vulnerability management practices, and very thoroughly explain the relationship between vulnerabilities and essential clinical performance. Although the Postmarket Guidelines do not establish binding rules for manufacturers, the details expressed a relatively comprehensive understanding of vulnerability management practices, which significantly affect the ability of a manufacturer to manage medical device risk.

In 2015, the FDA directly communicated its intention to regulate only mobile applications classified as "medical devices" where their function(s) could pose a risk to patient safety, though it began communicating its overall reluctance to regulate mobile health applications in 2014. In January of 2016, the FDA first reiterated and solidified its intention to minimize its involvement in mobile application regulation, in particular general wellness products. This recent, non-binding direction effectively focuses attention on implanted and physically invasive connected devices and Classes II and III, which the FDA deems not "low risk," and it neglects Class I devices.

In the FDA's Mobile Medical Apps Guidance, issued in February 2015, the FDA gave specific examples of mobile medical apps where the FDA may exercise enforcement and reiterated the FDA's sole focus on patient safety. These examples include medical devices providing technology to monitor patients, conduct data analysis, or for controlling the medical device via a mobile application; mobile applications connecting to sensors, displays, or attachments of existing medical devices; and mobile apps that perform the functions of existing diagnostic or therapeutic software, most likely Class II and Class III devices. Reinforcing the FDA's focus on patient safety, the FDA also listed mobile apps for which the FDA will exercise enforcement discretion or choose not to regulate. The FDA will not actively regulate the majority of these apps that may be vulnerable to information loss, including apps that help patients manage disease, track health information, provide remote medical care, provide access to health information, or transfer data from a medical device. In short, the FDA has demonstrated it will regulate direct physical safety, not data loss or disclosure.

The existing statutory framework regulating the digital health marketplace is not sufficient to reduce and manage cybersecurity risk. FDA guidelines do not effectively manage a market heavily driven by compliance-oriented activities, and entities required to follow HIPAA only covers a subsection of organizations involved in creating digital health products and services. Unlike internal confidential data loss affecting an organization only, parties affected by insufficient cybersecurity controls can be patients or consumers, often individuals in a compromised health position. Many patients assume, given the FDA's involvement in device safety matters and HIPAA's coverage of PHI, that health safety and confidentiality meet existing industry best practices. Others may not be able to effectively advocate their interests, either because of health status or comparatively less bargaining power.

Because the market cannot effectively guarantee this protection and patients often expect a basic level of safety for digital health products, a regulatory framework provides the best option for managing cybersecurity risk. However, achieving a level of specificity in the law that actually reduces risk requires knowledge and regulation of technology as it actually works. Although computer systems collect, compile, process, transfer, display, or store data, specific implementations may use different variations of security controls to meet a security principle, for example, methods for managing password resets. Frameworks should balance specificity with flexibility to ensure adequate adherence without stifling cybersecurity innovation.

Although a framework could improve cybersecurity for the digital health marketplace, no clear and comprehensive regulatory responsibility currently exists. Overlapping administrative agency responsibilities between the FDA, the Office for Civil Rights (the regulatory enforcement body for HIPAA), the National Coordinator for Health Information Technology (ONC), and the Federal Trade Commission (FTC) results in a lack of clear cybersecurity direction and accountability for digital health providers. Both part of the Department of Health and Human Services (DHHS), the OCR monitors HIPAA compliance for CEs and BAs while the FDA evaluates FDCA compliance for medical devices. Meanwhile, the ONC, also part of DHHS, creates high-level standards for cybersecurity and privacy and the FTC establishes rules and holds organizations accountable for unfair or deceptive trade practices under Section 5 of the FTC Act, increasingly for privacy and cybersecurity concerns. This mélange of guidance exists, yet no clear stance has emerged that provides a level of specificity, leaving organizations with few options aside from inventing rules inconsistently and independently.

An alternative viewpoint on HIPAA and the Security Rule is that the generality encoded in the Rule's "areas of focus" is beneficial to heterogeneous regulatory environments like healthcare. Consider the following excerpts which describe HIPAA, evaluate its efficacy at reducing reportable data breaches, and evaluate the comparative efficacy of flexible styles of regulation like that found in HIPAA used for cybersecurity:

DAVID THAW, *THE EFFICACY OF CYBERSECURITY REGULATION*

30 GA. ST. U. L. REV. 287 (2014)[3]

Management-based regulatory delegation is a mode of regulation under which administrative agencies, through legislative-mandated collaboration with regulatory stakeholders, promulgate regulations requiring regulated entities to develop plans designed to achieve certain aspirational goals laid out by the legislature. The regulatory goal in this case is the development of the compliance plan itself (and possible adherence to that plan), rather than the necessary achievement of stated goals or usage of certain means to achieve those goals, as is the case with directive regulation.

This category of regulation is a combination of two threads of discussion in the current literature: 1) Coglianese and Lazer's management-based regulation; and 2) Bamberger's regulatory delegation. Management-based regulation relies on a concept of administrative agencies promulgating requirements that regulated entities develop (and possibly adhere to) compliance plans. The application of this paradigm, once decoupled from issues of timing, to information security regulation is relatively straightforward. It is, however, incomplete for two reasons. First, Coglianese and Lazer's conception fails to capture the concept of legislatively-mandated involvement of private parties (regulatory capture). Second, management-based regulation alone fails to capture the degree to which organizations may be subject to other incentives not directly enshrined in but resulting from the structure of the regulation.

As Bamberger (and later Bamberger and Mulligan) discuss, in certain contexts regulators lack the experience or resources necessary to understand and/or keep pace with the myriad different challenges facing regulated entities (particularly in heterogeneous industries) or to promulgate regulations lacking relevance to guide business decision-makers (particularly in privacy matters). The result is a circumstance in which, to move forward effectively, regulators must rely increasingly on input from regulated entities. Management-based regulation provides a solid foundation for such an approach but requires greater input from stakeholders than envisioned by Coglianese and Lazer to ensure the promulgated regulations setting forth compliance plan requirements are sufficiently robust to avoid a compliance "race to the bottom." This is particularly true in the context of information security, where regulators rely heavily on a concept of "reasonableness"—a concept traditionally understood in law, but lacking operational meaning in the context of information security due to a lack of an appropriate "reasonable person"

[3] This was originally published with the Georgia State University Law Review. The original text can be found at 30 GA. ST. U. L. REV. 287 (2014).

standard and a lack of a well-agreed upon *licensed* professional standard upon which to rely for expert advice.

By extending the concept of management-based regulation to include a concept of regulatory delegation to private entities (particularly with substantial involvement of private parties in the rulemaking process, as described above), the model proposed here addresses the concomitant challenges of a rapidly evolving regulatory climate, substantial heterogeneity among regulated entities, and a need for sufficiently well-defined regulations so as to avoid a regulatory "race to the bottom" in an environment relying heavily upon but lacking good definition of "reasonableness."

Thus, merging the concepts of management-based regulation and regulatory delegation provides a category into which to group information security laws and regulations for the purposes of comparison. The sections that follow examine this combination of principles in the context of the Health Insurance Portability and Accountability Act of 1996 (HIPAA), the Gramm-Leach-Bliley Financial Modernization Act (GLBA), and the regulatory jurisprudence of the Federal Trade Commission (FTC) through its Enforcement Actions and Consent Decrees on information security matters. The combination of these two themes in regulation allows these three core areas of information security regulation to be understood together. Understanding them together is important because of the degree to which their evolution relied upon one another and as a result the degree to which they share common characteristics as a class of regulation.

1. Health Insurance Portability and Accountability Act Security and Privacy Rules (HIPAA)

HIPAA was passed in 1996 as part of broad effort to reform various aspects of the healthcare and health insurance systems in the United States. As part of the legislation, Congress included provisions with respect to the information security of certain information describing the identity, medical conditions, and finances of individuals. This information is collectively termed Protected Health Information ("PHI") and includes information created or received by entities involved in the healthcare process relating to the health condition or care of an individual.

The provisions pertaining to information security apply to any organization which is a Covered Entity or (under certain circumstances) a Business Associate of a Covered Entity. Covered Entities generally include health (insurance) plans, healthcare information clearinghouses, and healthcare providers. Business Associates generally include any organization that works with a Covered Entity and handles PHI on behalf of or to provide services to the Covered Entity. Although there has been some discussion as to the applicability of various aspects of the term Business Associate, these definitions generally mean that the HIPAA Security Rule applies to all healthcare insurance organizations, processing organizations that support healthcare insurance organizations, medical providers (if they use electronic records), and any other entities that engage in business with them if that business transaction involves the exchange or handling of PHI.

The HIPAA Security Rule comprises two key elements: (1) a statutory instruction by Congress for the Department of Health and Human Services to promulgate regulations establishing information security standards for the handling of PHI and (2) a general instruction to organizations covered by the Rule that they maintain appropriate administrative, technical, and physical safeguards. The first element is the key provision under which specific information security regulations part of HIPAA are promulgated. It generally requires that the regulations take into account available technologies, costs of security measures, training needs, the value of various security measures, and the varying sizes of healthcare organizations and providers.

The regulations promulgated by the Secretary of Health and Human Services pursuant to this provision are too numerous to list here in a comprehensive fashion, and doing so would not substantially illuminate the discussion of characterizing HIPAA's Security Rule as a regulatory device. Rather, it is worth examining the method by which the regulations are promulgated and the substantive breadth of resultant regulations in the context of the ISPL.

HIPAA is a hybrid form of management-based regulation. It exhibits the classic characteristics of management-based regulation, requiring firms to conduct risk assessments and develop plans to address the identified risks. The HIPAA regulations also specify certain protection measures that regulated organizations must undertake, similar to means-based regulation. Unlike traditional means-based regulation, however, the regulations do not specify the implementation details for those measures. Rather, such regulations explicitly leave those implementation details to the regulated entities.

HIPAA involves a notice-and-comment process with legislative direction to give deference to key stakeholders. Specifically, it requires the Department of Health and Human Services to consult with the National Committee on Vital and Health Statistics, which comprises key stakeholders from industry, government, and academia.

The regulations promulgated under the HIPAA Security Rule bear many aspects of traditional management-based regulation under Coglianese and Lazer's typology. The general requirements and flexibility of approach specified in the general rules for security standards require organizations to ensure the confidentiality, integrity, and availability of electronic medical records, protect against reasonably anticipated threats, and ensure workforce compliance.

This general requirement that organizations engage in comprehensive activities to protect their information assets typifies management-based regulation. The "flexibility of approach" provision effectively delegates the responsibility for planning these activities to the regulated entity, thereby exhibiting the classic form of management-based regulation. This provision provides that covered entities may use any security measures reasonably and appropriately capable of achieving the specific security goals and requires that the entity take into account its size, scope, complexity, current technical infrastructure, costs, and levels of risk in making such determinations as to reasonableness.

Furthermore, in addition to this flexibility of approach, the regulations specifically require regulated entities to "[c]onduct an accurate and thorough assessment of the potential risks and vulnerabilities to the confidentiality, integrity, and availability of electronic protected health information held by the covered entity . . . ." and to "[i]mplement security measures sufficient to reduce risks and vulnerabilities to a reasonable and appropriate level to comply with § 164.306(a)." These directives to conduct risk assessments and implement security measures consistent with those risk assessments are perfect examples of traditional management-based regulation.

The HIPAA Security Rule is far more expansive, however, than the assessment and planning requirements outlined above. Unlike traditional management-based regulation, it goes on to detail highly-specific elements the plan must contain—almost taking it to the degree of means-based regulation, but stopping short by leaving the details of implementation to the discretion of the regulated entity consistent with the flexibility of approach provisions outlined above. Consider the following four provisions of the HIPAA Security Rule regulations:

> (i) Unique user identification (Required). Assign a unique name and/or number for identifying and tracking user identity.
>
> (ii) Emergency access procedure (Required). Establish (and implement as needed) procedures for obtaining necessary electronic protected health information during an emergency.
>
> (iii) Automatic logoff (Addressable). Implement electronic procedures that terminate an electronic session after a predetermined time of inactivity.
>
> (iv) Encryption and decryption (Addressable). Implement a mechanism to encrypt and decrypt electronic protected health information.

The four provisions are the "implementation specifications" for the "standard" specified in 45 C.F.R. § 164.312(a)(2) governing access control, which states that regulated organizations must "[i]mplement technical policies and procedures for electronic information systems that maintain electronic protected health information to allow access only to those persons or software programs that have been granted access rights as specified in § 164.308(a)(4)." The standard clearly resembles management-based regulation, but the implementation specifications diverge from traditional management-based regulation by clearly targeting the Implementation/Maintenance Stage of the ISPL. This bifurcated approach is replicated in nearly all sections of the regulations implementing the HIPAA Security Rule, thus suggesting that HIPAA is also management-based regulation that targets the Implementation/Maintenance Stage of the ISPL. This bifurcation has implications for the relationship between senior managers and information security professionals at regulated organizations.

[. . .]

B. Blended Regulation is Optimal at Preventing Breaches

Based on the trend periods established through the above methods, I conducted analysis comparing PREs and PUEs during these periods. The results suggest that a blend combining both directive regulation and Management-Based Regulatory Delegation is optimal for incentivizing organizations to employ security measures to prevent security breaches involving sensitive personal information.

The two sections that follow explain the implications of these trends [visuals omitted] for the regulatory efficacy and suggest why a blended regulation model is optimal at preventing breaches of personal information.

1. Blended Regulation Compared to Directive Regulation Alone

The effects of blended regulation, or a combination of directive regulation and Management-Based Regulatory Delegation, are measured by the decreasing trend in breach incidence after t_2 for PREs. After t_2, PREs—generally healthcare and finance organizations—were subject not only to their respective forms of Management-Based Regulatory Delegation (HIPAA or GLBA), but also to the state SBNs. Like all organizations, they have an incentive to reduce their reportable incidents by implementing security measures to prevent reportable breaches. Thus, the downward trend (represented by the blue linear regression line in Figure 3) represents how rapidly PREs reduced their reportable incidents.

The rate at which PREs reduced their reportable incidents was nearly four times less than the rate at which PUEs (represented by the red linear regression line in Figure 3) decreased their reportable incidents. At first glance, this might appear as though Management-Based Regulatory Delegation was detrimental, as PREs reduced incidents at a slower rate than did PUEs. Paradoxically, however, the opposite is true.

There is no evidence that organizations' incentives to reduce security breach incidents vary by industrial sector. If there were such variance, however, it would likely indicate that the finance and healthcare sectors had higher incentives than the collective remainder of industry as those sectors traditionally handle more sensitive information. Additionally, there is no control data against which to compare breach incidence—thus there is no method to determine whether certain sectors were subject to more attacks than were other sectors. The compliance saturation point (t_2), however, provides a method by which to infer comparative competency.

If incentives and available resources to reduce breaches are equal, and there is a limited total reduction in breaches that can be achieved (perfect security is, as discussed above, impossible), then the rate of decrease after t_2 will be inversely proportional to organizations' *prior* effectiveness at preventing breaches. In other words, organizations already possessing information security competencies will experience a *less rapid* drop-off in breach incidence reporting after t_2 *because they had less far to improve* (i.e., they were already some percentage of the way there). By contrast, organizations that had none or minimal information security measures in place prior to the influence of SBNs (at time t_2), will experience a more rapid decrease (i.e., because they had "further to go").

Thus the results reported here suggest that the combination of directive regulation and Management-Based Regulatory Delegation, at least over the short term, may be as much as four times more effective at preventing breaches of personal information as is directive regulation alone. Over the longer term, the trends may suggest that both organizations will develop sufficient competencies (assuming the regulatory penalties are sufficient), however this finding has strong implications for any new subject of regulation seeking shorter-term efficacy.

This analysis, and the implications it has for the *style of compliance* present in the HIPAA Security Rule is summarized in the following excerpt:

DAVID THAW, *CYBERSECURITY STOVEPIPING*

96 NEB. L. REV. 339 (2017)[4]

C. Risk-Analytic Framework for Cybersecurity

The analysis in this section suggests the need for cybersecurity research, practice, and policy making to employ a risk-analytic framework.

[4] Reprinted with permission from the *Nebraska Law Review*. This article was previously published in the *Nebraska Law Review*. See David Thaw, Cybersecurity Stovepiping, 96 NEB. L. REV. 339 (2017).

Stated more simply, each security measure needs to be examined in the context of an overall system in empirical practice to determine whether given measures produce a net positive or net negative effect when implemented. Current approaches variously define cybersecurity through mathematical modeling or enumerated compliance, with few exceptions. Of particular import, these notable exceptions—applicable to the healthcare and finance industries in the United States—performed nearly four times more effectively at preventing data breaches reportable under U.S. law during the period from January 2000 through December 2010. Collectively, this evidence and the analysis in this Article suggest an alternate, risk-analytic-based definition for cybersecurity. This definition can be phrased as a simple question: Do the risk-mitigation techniques for a given information system match the risk-tolerance level appropriate to that system's goals and functions? This question, while perhaps apparently simple, is quite complex to unpack and translate to a workable definition. A regulatory approach I call Federated Regulation, which describes a unique approach to cybersecurity regulation used in U.S. federal health-care-cybersecurity regulation, has shown substantial promise in this regard.

Federated Regulation (also known as Management-Based Regulatory Delegation) is a theory for engaging private expertise in regulation both on the front end (rulemaking) and on the back end (compliance). It replaces the direct (or "checklist") style of regulation with one based on a risk-analytic framework, transforming the regulatory requirement to a four-part process: (1) regulatory authorities define general or "aspirational" areas of concern to be addressed; (2) regulated entities must conduct risk assessments of those areas and develop compliance plans consistent with reasonable management of those risks; (3) regulated entities must follow their own compliance plans; and (4) the plans must be "reasonable" and be updated periodically and with changes in the organization's risk profile. As described by Perri and Thaw:

> This process has been very successful in engaging private expertise to manage healthcare privacy and cybersecurity in the United States. Under this model, legislatures establish an organic statutory framework that calls upon an administrative agency to develop regulations in conjunction with the entities subject to that regulation (and other relevant stakeholders). The regulations then promulgated by the agency, rather than defining strict standards for compliance, instead, lay out general or aspirational goals for regulated entities to achieve. Entities then are required to develop compliance plans which reasonably achieve those goals, and to follow their own plans. This last step becomes the primary compliance objective, subject to regulatory agency oversight for reasonableness of the plans and entities' adherence to those plans.

The comparative-efficacy points discussed earlier in this Article are based primarily on a comparison of Federated Regulation and de facto directive regulation at preventing certain cybersecurity breaches of statutorily identified "personal information" during the years 2000 through 2010. That preliminary work showed substantially improved capacity at preventing such breaches, controlling for various factors such as attractiveness of target; size, scope, and complexity of organizations; defensive capabilities of organizations; and the different time periods during which organizations first became aware of the threats facing their data in an internetworked Information Age. While preliminary, the results are pronounced and suggest the promise of Federated Regulation and similar models at addressing the types of technologically and scientifically complex problems considered in this Article.

As you can see in the excerpts above, part of the challenge in writing laws for cybersecurity, in addition to a lack of technical knowledge, is the need to clarify exactly who will regulate and under what circumstances. Choosing the appropriate regulator is often a challenge for areas where multiple agencies have some stake. Likewise, choosing the appropriate form of regulation can have substantial impact on its efficacy at achieving the normative goals motivating the regulation. In the context of cybersecurity, these are complex questions which rarely have simple answers. As you think about these varying approaches and varying observations regarding them, consider why drafting cybersecurity regulations may be difficult.

QUESTIONS

1. The excerpts above did not go into this detail, but the FDA only regulates cybersecurity for purpose of device safety (in a non-binding form), while the OCR regulates HIPAA cybersecurity requirements in connection with protected health information (PHI) and specific HIPAA requirements. Under some circumstances, cybersecurity may be regulated by both regulators. If you were a digital health company that had to comply with FDA rules and HIPAA, how would you decide how to comply?

2. Considering the excerpts from this chapter and the limited information about HIPAA we've presented so far, how might you improve the security rule? Would you take a more general and flexible approach or a strict requirements approach? Why or why not?

3. We will be discussing the role of industry or outside standards for organizations. Do you see any benefit or drawback of linking to these types of external requirements in law? Why or why not?

CHAPTER 9

ENGINEERING FOR RISK

■ ■ ■

What can organizations actually do to prevent attacks in the first place. As you may recall from Chapter 3, there are different risk types, stochastic and adversarial risks. When engineers implement appropriate controls, both risk types can be addressed. However, challenges arise when innovation mindsets and competing priorities exist with respect to development. Organizations do not just engineer products and systems for the purpose of reducing risk. Rather, organizations engineer products and systems for what they can *do*, whether they build a coupon app that will encourage customers to shop at their retail location or a new data analytics tool that promises to improve operational efficiency. In short, organizations usually build or procure technology for other organizational benefits, usually related to financial gains either through savings or accrual. It is important to consider risk from this perspective because to most organizational leaders, cybersecurity is a *cost*, not an investment.

Often your role as an advisor to these leaders is to help them reconceptualize cybersecurity as an integral part of every step of any technology lifecycle, rather than one adjacent and costly step. There are a number of organizational dynamics that lead to the non-prioritization of security built into products and systems. In this chapter, we will discuss some of the dynamics that result in poorly designed or engineered systems that create risk to an organization and individuals, as well as strategies more successful organizations use to integrate security into products and systems to reduce overall downstream cost. But first, it is important to understand why cybersecurity is not always built into products and systems.

A. UNDERSTANDING THE DEVELOPMENT AND ENGINEERING MENTALITIES

You may have heard the phrase "move fast and break things," a motto that has motivated countless new technology representing the golden age of software development. Since the beginning of the 2000s, this motto, which is discussed in greater detail in section C, below, motivated a development mindset of getting solutions to a point of working versus getting solutions to a more perfect form. The goal of this development mentality was to create more innovative products as quickly as possible. As we will describe later in this chapter, there are divisions of organizations and specific organizational types that operate heavily in this mindset, for example, start-ups. However, even for larger organizations, modern development teams have embraced this concept. Also called "fail fast," this approach enables organizations to try new or innovative strategies with less risk or expectations. Consider the following excerpt from Clayton Christensen describing the impetus to innovate that originated the famous phrase.

CLAYTON M. CHRISTENSEN, *INNOVATOR'S DILEMMA: WHEN NEW TECHNOLOGIES CAUSE GREAT FIRMS TO FAIL*

Harvard Bus. School Press (1997)

1. The context, or value network, in which a firm competes has a profound influence on its ability to marshal and focus the necessary resources and capabilities to overcome the technological and organizational hurdles that impede innovation. The boundaries of a value network are determined by a unique definition of product performance—a rank-ordering of the importance of various performance attributes differing markedly from that employed in other systems-of-use in a broadly defined industry. Value networks are also defined by particular cost structures inherent in addressing customers' needs within the network.

2. A key determinant of the probability of an innovative effort's commercial success is the degree to which it addresses the well-understood needs of known actors within the value network. Incumbent firms are likely to lead their industries in innovations of all sorts—architecture and components—that address needs within their value network, regardless of intrinsic technological character or difficulty. These are straightforward innovations; their value and application are clear. Conversely, incumbent firms are likely to lag in the development of technologies—even those in which the technology involved is intrinsically simple—that only address customers' needs in emerging value networks. Disruptive innovations are complex because their value and application are uncertain, according to the criteria used by incumbent firms.

3. Established firms' decisions to ignore technologies that do not address their customers' needs become fatal when two distinct trajectories interact. The first defines the performance demanded over time within a given value network, and the second traces the performance that technologists are able to provide within a given technological paradigm. The trajectory of performance improvement that technology is able to provide may have a distinctly different slope from the trajectory of performance improvement demanded in the system-of-use by downstream customers within any given value network. When the slopes of these two trajectories are similar, we expect the technology to remain relatively contained within its initial value network. But when the slopes differ, new technologies that are initially performance-competitive only within

emerging or commercially remote value networks may migrate into other networks, providing a vehicle for innovators in new networks to attack established ones. When such an attack occurs, it is because technological progress has diminished the relevance of differences in the rank-ordering of performance attributes across different value networks. For example, the disk drive attributes of size and weight were far more important in the desktop computing value network than they were in the mainframe and minicomputer value networks. When technological progress in 5.25-inch drives enabled manufacturers to satisfy the attribute prioritization in the mainframe and minicomputer networks, which prized total capacity and high speed, as well as that in the desktop network, the boundaries between the value networks ceased to be barriers to entry for 5.25-inch drive makers.

4. Entrant firms have an attacker's advantage over established firms in those innovations—generally new product architectures involving little new technology per se—that disrupt or redefine the level, rate, and direction of progress in an established technological trajectory. This is so because such technologies generate no value within the established network. The only way established firms can lead in commercializing such technologies is to enter the value network in which they create value. As Richard Tedlow noted in his history of retailing in America (in which supermarkets and discount retailing play the role of disruptive technologies), "the most formidable barrier the established firms faced is that they did not want to do this."

5. In these instances, although this "attacker's advantage" is associated with a disruptive technology change, the essence of the attacker's advantage is in the ease with which entrants, relative to incumbents, can identify and make strategic commitments to attack and develop emerging market applications, or value networks. At its core, therefore, the issue may be the relative flexibility of successful established firms versus entrant firms to change strategies and cost structures, not technologies.

These propositions provide new dimensions for analyzing technological innovation. In addition to the required capabilities inherent in new technologies and in the innovating organization, firms faced with disruptive technologies must examine the implications of innovation for their relevant value networks. The key considerations are whether the performance attributes implicit in the innovation will be valued within the networks already served by the innovator; whether other networks must be addressed or new ones created in order to realize value for the innovation; and whether market and technological trajectories may eventually intersect, carrying technologies that do not address customers' needs today to squarely address their needs in the future.

This mindset dominated much of the early 2000s. Mark Zuckerberg, CEO of Facebook, a company he and a friend conceptualized and created in a Harvard dorm room, is famously quoted saying "Move fast and break things. Unless you are breaking stuff, you are not moving fast enough," which became a Facebook motto until fairly recently.[1] Bill Gates famously wrote a memo to his employees in 1995, outlining many of these concepts.

BILL GATES, *'INTERNET TIDAL WAVE' MEMO*

E-MAIL TO MICROSOFT EMPLOYEES (May 26, 1995)

Our vision for the last 20 years can be summarized in a succinct way. We saw that exponential improvements in computer capabilities would make great software quite valuable. Our response was to build an organization to deliver the best software products. In the next 20 years the improvement in computer power will be outpaced by the exponential improvements in communications networks. The combination of these elements will have a fundamental impact on work, learning and play. Great software products will be crucial to delivering the benefits of these advances. Both the variety and volume of the software will increase. Most users of communications have not yet seen the price of communications come down significantly. Cable and phone networks are still depreciating networks built with old technology. Universal service monopolies and other government involvement around the world have kept communications costs high. Private networks and the Internet which are built using state of the art equipment have been the primary beneficiaries of the improved communications technology. The PC is just now starting to create additional demand that will drive a new wave of investment. A combination of expanded access to the Internet, ISDN, new broadband networks justified by video based applications and interconnections between each of these will bring low cost communication to most businesses and homes within the next decade.

The Internet is at the forefront of all of this and developments on the Internet over the next several years will set the course of our industry for a long time to come. Perhaps you have already seen memos from me or others here about the importance of the Internet. I have gone through several stages of increasing my views of its importance. Now I assign the Internet the highest level of importance. In this memo I want to make clear that our focus on the Internet is crucial to every part of our business. The Internet is the most important single development to come along since the IBM PC was introduced in 1981. It is even more important than the arrival of the graphical user interface (GUI). The PC analogy is apt for many reasons. The PC wasn't perfect. Aspects of the PC were arbitrary or even poor. However a phenomena grew up around the IBM PC that made it a

---

1 Mark Zuckerberg, *Mark Zuckerberg, Moving Fast and Breaking Things*, BUSINESS INSIDER (Oct. 14, 2010), https://www.businessinsider.com/mark-zuckerberg-2010-10.

key element of everything that would happen for the next 15 years. Companies that tried to fight the PC standard often had good reasons for doing so but they failed because the phenomena overcame any weaknesses that resisters identified.

The Internet Today

The Internet's unique position arises from a number of elements. TCP/IP protocols that define its transport level support distributed computing and scale incredibly well . . . The HTTP protocols that define HTML Web browsing are extremely simple and have allowed servers to handle incredible traffic reasonably well. All of the predictions about hypertext—made decades ago by pioneers like Ted Nelson—are coming true on the Web. Although other protocols on the Internet will continue to be used (FTP, Gopher, IRC, Telnet, SMTP, NNTP). HTML with extensions will be the standard that defines how information will be presented. Various extensions to HTML, including content enhancements like tables, and functionality enhancements like secure transactions, will be widely adopted in the near future. There will also be enhanced 3D presentations providing for virtual reality type shopping and socialization.

Another unique aspect of the Internet is that because it buys communications lines on a commodity bid basis and because it is growing so fast, it is the only "public" network whose economics reflect the latest advances in communications technology. The price paid for corporations to connect to the Internet is determined by the size of your "on-ramp" to the Internet and not by how much you actually use your connection. Usage isn't even metered. It doesn't matter if you connect nearby or half way around the globe. This makes the marginal cost of extra usage essentially zero encouraging heavy usage.

Most important is that the Internet has bootstrapped itself as a place to publish content. It has enough users that it is benefiting from the positive feedback loop of the more users it gets, the more content it gets, and the more content it gets, the more users it gets. I encourage everyone on the executive staff and their direct reports to use the Internet. I've attached an appendix, which Brian Flemming helped me pull together that shows some hot sites to try out. You can do this by either using the .HTM enclosure with any Internet browser or, if you have Word set up properly, you can navigate right from within this document. Of particular interest are the sites such as "YAHOO" which provide subject catalogs and searching. Also of interest are the ways our competitors are using their Websites to present their products. I think SUN, Netscape and Lotus do some things very well.

Amazingly it is easier to find information on the Web than it is to find information on the Microsoft Corporate Network. This inversion where a public network solves a problem better than a private network is quite stunning. This inversion points out an opportunity for us in the corporate market. An important goal for the Office and Systems products is to focus on how our customers can create and publish information on their LANs. All work we do here can be leveraged into the HTTP/Web world. The strength of the Office and Windows businesses today gives us a chance to superset the Web. One critical issue is runtime/browser size and performance. Only when our Office-Windows solution has comparable performance to the Web will our extensions be worthwhile. I view this as the most important element of Office 96 and the next major release of Windows.

One technical challenge facing the Internet is how to handle "real-time" content—specifically audio and video. The underlying technology of the Internet is a packet network which does not guarantee that data will move from one point to another at a guaranteed rate. The congestion on the network determines how quickly packets are sent. Audio can be delivered on the Internet today using several approaches. The classic approach is to simply transmit the audio file in its entirety before it is played. A second approach is to send enough of it to be fairly sure that you can keeping playing without having to pause. . .Only with this improvement and an incredible amount of additional bandwidth and local connections will the Internet infrastructure deliver all of the promises of the full blown Information Highway. However, it is in the process of happening and all we can do is get involved and take advantage.

I think that virtually every PC will be used to connect to the Internet and that the Internet will help keep PC purchasing very healthy for many years to come. PCs will connect to the Internet a variety of ways. . .Eventually you will be able to find the name of someone or a service you want to connect to on the Internet and rerouting your call to temporarily be a point-to-point connection will happen automatically. For example when you are browsing travel possibilities if you want to talk to someone with expertise on the area you are considering, you simply click on a button and the request will be sent to a server that keeps a list of available agents who can be working anywhere they like as long as they have a PC with ISDN. You will be reconnected and the agent will get all of the context of what you are looking at and your previous history of travel if the agency has a database. The reconnection approach will not be necessary once the network has quality of service guarantees.

Another way to connect a PC will be to use a cable-modem that uses the coaxial cable normally used for analog TV transmission. Early cable systems will essentially turn the coax into an Ethernet so that everyone in the same neighborhood will share a LAN. . .The On-line services business and the Internet have merged. What I mean by this is that every On-line service has to simply be a place on the Internet with extra value added. . .The amount of free information available today on the Internet is quite amazing. Although there is room to use brand names and quality to differentiate from free content, this will not be easy and it puts a lot of pressure to figure out how to get advertiser funding [. . .]

Next Steps

In highlighting the importance of the Internet to our future I don't want to suggest that I am alone in seeing this. There is excellent work going on in many product groups. Over the last year, a number of people have championed embracing TCP/IP, hyperlinking, HTML, and building client, tools and servers that compete on the Internet. However, we still have a lot to do. I want every product plan to try and go overboard on Internet features. One element that will be crucial is coordinating our various activities. The challenge/opportunity of the Internet is a key reason behind the recent organization.

File sharing/Window sharing/Multi-user. We need to give away client code that encourages Windows specific protocols to be used across the Internet. It should be very easy to set up a server for file sharing across the Internet. . .By giving away the client code to support all of these scenarios, we can start to show that a Windows machine on the Internet is more valuable than an arbitrary machine on the net.

Forms/Languages. We need to make it very easy to design a form that presents itself as an HTML page[. . .]

Formats. We need to make sure we output information from all of our products in both vanilla HTML form and in the extended forms that we promote. For example, any database reports should be navigable as hypertext documents[. . .]

Electronic commerce. Key elements of electronic commerce including security and billing need to be integrated into our platform strategy. . .Perhaps it makes sense to do a tax business that only operates on on-line. Perhaps we can establish the lowest cost way for people to do electronic bill paying. . .All the financial institutions will find it very easy to buy the best Internet technology tools from us and others and get into this world without much technical expertise.

The Future

We enter this new era with some considerable strengths. Among them are our people and the broad acceptance of Windows and Office. Since the Internet is changing so rapidly we will have to revise our strategies from time to time and have better inter-group communication than ever before.

Our products will not be the only things changing. The way we distribute information and software as well as the way we communicate with and support customers will be changing. We have an opportunity to do a lot more with our resources. Information will be disseminated efficiently between us and our customers with less chance that the press miscommunicates our plans. Customers will come to our "home page" in unbelievable numbers and find out everything we want them to know.

The next few years are going to be very exciting as we tackle these challenges are opportunities. The Internet is a tidal wave. It changes the rules. It is an incredible opportunity as well as incredible challenge I am looking forward to your input on how we can improve our strategy to continue our track record of incredible success.

Perhaps the most critical lines from this excerpt is Gates's exhortation that "we still have a lot to do. I want every product plan to try and go overboard on Internet features," and his conclusion that "The Internet is a tidal wave. It changes the rules." In making these observations, Gates was responding to a largely new development mindset that had been ushered in over the course of the development of the early modern Internet in the 1980s and, in particular, the mantra of "rough consensus and running code." During this same period, Microsoft had followed more a traditional software and product development lifecycle. But as the Internet was commercialized and rapidly grew in use and importance in the early 1990s, the marketplace and approach to software development rapidly shifted.

It is useful to look at the origin and meaning of the phrase "rough consensus and running code," along with the sentence that came alongside its first utterance by Internet pioneer David Clark: ""We reject: kings, presidents, and voting."

ANDREW RUSSELL, *'ROUGH CONSENSUS AND RUNNING CODE' AND THE INTERNET-OSI STANDARDS WAR*

28 IEEE ANNALS HIST. OF COMPUTING 48 (2006)

Historians interested in conflict and consensus in technological systems stand much to gain from examining standardization—the processes of creating and implementing technical standards. Standardization requires sophisticated technical work as well as organizational and strategic coordination. In the late 1970s, it was reasonable to assume that formal standards-setting institutions, such as the International Telecommunication Union (ITU) and the International Organization for Standardization (ISO), would lead the coordination and standardization of information services, much as they did for international telecommunications. Beginning in 1977, ISO oversaw a large, ambitious attempt to define a network architecture called Open Systems Interconnection (OSI). Between the late 1970s and the early 1990s, the OSI seven-layer model became enshrined in computer science curricula and endorsed by governments around the world. Competing networks—including experimental TCP/IP networks [which are the basis of the

Internet]—were expected to fade away once OSI protocols were standardized and implemented by users and manufacturers.

By the mid-1990s, however, ISO's slow standardization process had failed to keep up with alternative, informal mechanisms that were more effective at coordinating rapid technological change. These informal mechanisms—the focus of this article—provided vital institutional support for the eventual success and global deployment of the Internet architecture and Internet standards such as TCP/IP.

In most existing histories of the Internet, leaders such as Vinton Cerf and Robert Kahn receive plaudits for their technical work, especially for their roles in the creation of the core Internet standards TCP and IP. What is often overlooked, however, is the extent to which the success of the Internet depended on organizational innovations directed by Cerf, Kahn, and other Internet pioneers such as Jon Postel and David Clark. Starting in the 1970s, researchers in groups such as the Internet Configuration Control Board (ICCB), the Internet Activities Board (IAB), and the Internet Engineering Task Force (IETF) coordinated Internet standards and architectural development. These institutions deserve special attention not only for their technical achievements, but also because they fostered a voluntary international consensus during a period of intense technical and institutional change in computing and telecommunications.

[. . .]

'OSI Bigots' and 'IP Bigots': Cultural dimensions of a standards war

A spirited rivalry between respective advocates of OSI and TCP/IP networks emerged as they fought for jurisdiction over standards for computer internetworks. Richard des Jardins—an early contributor to the ISO Reference Model and president of the GOSIP Institute [a group working to publish OSI standards for adoption by US government agencies through NIST]—captured the intensity of this rivalry when, in a 1992 article, he compared the "OSI Bigots" and the "IP Bigots" to people who objected to "the convergence of cultures and races in the world at large."

Tensions between the OSI and Internet communities became apparent in the early 1980s, well before GOSIP came into being. For example, in their 1983 paper describing the similarities between the ARPA and ISO protocol architectures, Danny Cohen and Jon Postel painted the ISO model as an abstraction, far too rigid in its reliance on seven interrelated levels, and inappropriate to be used "as a model for all seasons." In an unusually colorful paper, Cohen and Postel—both of whom were instrumental in the early history of TCP/IP—mockingly speculated that "mystical" traditions such as Early Zoroastrianism, New Testament celestial beings, and the Christian seven deadly sins might have "shaped the choice of Seven." Another Internet advocate, in his 1991 "technical travelogue" of networking in 21 countries across the world, suggested that trying to implement OSI over slow, low-quality lines was "akin to looking for a hippopotamus capable of doing the limbo."

The resentment of Cohen, Postel, and their Internet colleagues stemmed from their frustration with the technical aspects of OSI as well as with ISO as a bureaucratic entity. Where TCP/IP was developed through continual experimentation in a fluid organizational setting, Internet engineers viewed OSI committees as overly bureaucratic and out of touch with existing networks and computers. OSI's political and formal process did not endear the TCP/IP Internet community—who were accustomed to a decentralized division of labor throughout the standards process—to the ISO Reference Model. In a scathing 1985 critique of OSI and its advocates, one veteran of the Arpanet and Internet community, Mike A. Padlipsky, characterized the ARPA Internet Reference Model as "Descriptive" and ISO Reference Model as "Prescriptive." Another networking pioneer, David Mills, agreed in a 2004 interview: "Internet standards tended to be those written for implementers. International standards were written as documents to be obeyed." "Another way of putting it," Padlipsky wrote, "is that whereas the Descriptive approach is suitable for technology, the Prescriptive approach is suitable for theology."

Internet's constitutional crisis

[At a June 1992 meeting of the Internet Architecture Board, the Board announced that it was considering a technology developed as part of the OSI model to address a significant architectural shortcoming of the Internet's TCP/IP protocol (the limitation on the number of IP addresses possible in IP's 32-bit address space). The idea that that IAB would adopt the OSI model's approach to address this problem—and even more, that it would do so by announcing, in a top-down manner, an architectural change to the network's protocols—did not sit well with members of the IETF or newly-formed Internet Society.]

At the July 1992 IETF meeting in Cambridge, Massachusetts, irate IETF participants protested to the Internet Society about what they perceived as a unilateral decision by the IAB. Approximately 700 IETF participants demanded that the newborn Internet Society intervene and ensure that the IETF would remain in control of the standards process. In the face of a massive "palace revolt," the IAB, with Vint Cerf prominent among them, relented. As Cerf addressed the IETF, he slowly removed the layers of his signature three-piece suit, performing a striptease that revealed a T-shirt: "IP on Everything." The T-shirt, according to Cerf, was to reiterate a goal of the IAB: to run IP on every underlying transmission medium. Like Cerf, David Clark turned his plenary presentation into a memorable occasion, one that would "rally the troops" and reaffirm the values of the Internet community.

'We reject: kings, presidents, and voting'

Clark framed his talk in terms of architectural choices the IETF would have to make. After spending several minutes urging the audience to focus on network security and the basic assumptions of the protocol architecture, Clark considered how the IETF should "manage the process of change and growth." As he reminded the IETF audience of the vital importance of the values of the process by which they made standards, Clark punctuated his discussion with his summary of the IETF approach: "We reject: kings, presidents, and voting. We believe in: rough consensus and running code." The IETF community responded with overwhelming approval. "Rough consensus and running code" was so popular that Marshall Rose, a vocal participant in the IETF "palace revolt," created the ultimate form of computer geek approval: T-shirts with the phrase emblazoned across the front. [. . .]

"Rough consensus and running code" generated and sustained this level of enthusiasm because of the way it framed the successful aspects of the IETF process in opposition to the ISO process. The rough-consensus component of this motto refers to the decision-making process within IETF working groups. Since its inception, the IETF never had members, only participants, and hence it could not have a formal voting structure. In the tradition of Cerf's ICCB discussions, IETF leaders encouraged newcomers to contribute their expertise, and approved proposals that enjoyed broad support within the group. IETF veterans place an acceptable level of agreement at around 80 to 90 percent: a level high enough to demonstrate strong support, but flexible enough to work in the absence of unanimity. In short, rough consensus was an apt description of this informal process in which a proposal must answer to criticisms, but need not be held up if supported by a vast majority of the group. To IETF participants, this process was vastly superior to the bureaucratic and political approach of ISO.

[. . .]

Conclusion

By the time National Institute of Standards and Technology (NIST) abandoned GOSIP in favor of TCP/IP in 1994, the grand future planned for OSI was on the rapid decline. The market for network protocols had tipped in favor of TCP/IP, epitomized by the popularity of a new application—the World Wide Web—that was designed to take advantage of the Internet's end-to-end architecture. The veterans of the Internet-OSI standards war were no doubt wiser from the experience, but the millions of users who got on the Internet in the mid-1990s were oblivious to the fact that their new toy was the product of a protracted international struggle. For those who read the last issue of *Telecommunications Policy* in 1993, William Drake provided an insightful summary:

> The debate is not merely about the comparative efficacy of two sets of standards, but it is rather between two competing visions of how international standardization processes and network development should be organized and controlled.

The religious, political, and military metaphors that participants used to describe the competition between the Internet and OSI confirm that this was no mere technical dispute. At the height of the "religious war" between TCP/IP and OSI, tensions within the IETF and IAB over architecture and organizational power created a "constitutional crisis." This crisis, a divisive force in a community that had always prided itself on its attention to due process and consensus, forced engineers in the IETF and IAB to examine their core procedural beliefs. In other words, strains in the technical architecture—the address space—prompted strains in the organizational architecture. Forged in the face of this crisis, the credo "rough consensus and running code" articulated a political philosophy, a style of network architecture and of engineering. While it is now common to see participants in the Internet standards community refer to the "rough consensus and running code" ideal, Clark's rejection of alternative forms of decision making—kings, presidents, and voting—reminds us of the close links between network standards and international politics.

As you can see from the excerpts above, the mid-1990s was a turning point for innovation, especially as that innovation involved the development of the internet. The market saw massive investment and growth, especially in the underlying networks but also the early Internet economy in the late 1990s, before a major market correction starting in March of 2000 (the bursting of the "dot-com bubble"). Growth resumed in the early 2000s and has generally been strong—generally leading the market—other than a brief waning period surrounding the economic crash of 2008. The 2007 invention of the first smartphone, Apple's iPhone, reinvigorated the online marketplace and ushered in the era of mobile Internet access. This new access model complemented the traditional Internet model with mobile accessibility. The invention of the "app," which is simply a program ("application") designed for mobile devices, complemented to Apple's development of the "app store" as an easy and convenient way to install new apps on its smartphones, also drove substantial interest for, engagement with, and investment in this market. The influence of the fast development cycle created new expectations for fast turnaround in other development areas, as well.

There are a few dynamics that have further entrenched this way of thinking. First, organizations have increasingly begun to invest in information technology solutions as market differentiators and value-add services. Consider, for example, the medical device sector: a medical device company might manufacture insulin pumps, but it may also provide a diet and exercise app to support good health management practices to those with Type-1 diabetes. The prevalence of mobile devices, the increasing demand for e-commerce (online purchasing), and the ease of application and app design also prompted the creation of quick and fast general consumer applications.

A classic turn of phrase for any Information Technology (IT) consulting company reflects on the self-limiting conditions of any IT project: "fast, good, cheap." This phrase references the constraints of any project: any project cannot satisfy all three conditions—fast, good, and cheap. Usually organizations must instead choose one or two of these conditions. To do something quickly, the cost is usually higher, and the quality of the product is usually not as high. To do something cheaply, usually the speed is slower and the quality is also not as high. Finally, to do something well, usually it is not cheap or fast. And yet, the mindset for most technology development is that all three should be satisfied. The reality is that, to create systems quickly with a high degree of quality, the cost will usually be higher.

QUESTIONS

1. Why do you think many technology companies embrace the "move fast, break things" mentality? Why do you think this might complicate cybersecurity goals?

2. How might you convince a group of innovative technologists to plan for cybersecurity? Do you think arguing that there may be a legal impact will be persuasive? Why or why not?

3. What are the tradeoffs between "rough consensus and running code" and "kings, presidents, and voting" as ways of developing software in different environments? Are these the only alternatives? What do these different approaches tell us about the attitudes of different types of developers, their approach to development, and the software (and other innovations) they are likely to produce?

4. Consider the following statement: "The IETF's bottom-up 'rough consensus and running code' model represents an engineering viewpoint, while the OSI's top-down model represents a legalistic viewpoint." Is this a fair or accurate characterization?

5. Think back to the discussion of hackers and their motivations in Chapter 4. Do you see echoes of The Mentor or TheHackerGiraffe in Gates's Internet Tidal Wave memo or the relationship between IETF engineers and the OSI initiative? In the Hacker Manifesto, The Mentor declared of the early Internet that "This is our world now. . . the world of the electron and the switch." In declaring that the IETF "rejects kings," was Clark asserting the same thing as The Mentor?

B. BUSINESS INFLUENCE ON TECHNOLOGY SPEND

So why has the "go fast" mindset dominated development and engineering conversations? At least one answer lies in the prioritization of features over responsible function. Businesses know that new features and capabilities attract the attention of customers are part of an organization's overall value proposition. Security controls are enabling in large part: although controls are a key part of the technology, they are not usually standalone features or capabilities, which are usually the reason a technology product or system can be sold or marketed. The first phase of most product development is a Proof of Concept (PoC). The goal of a PoC is to demonstrate viability—that a product or system can be developed to fulfill some business goal or solve a problem. A *prototype* is the step after a PoC where a usable, functional product or system is created for use.

The innovation business dynamic is crucially important to understand the engineering mindset. One of the most common business models is where a start-up, or very small business (consisting of usually 1–20 employees), creates a technology product or system. This product or system is usually at the PoC or prototype phase, where the goal of development is to simply make something work and demonstrate that it does work. For most start-ups and very small businesses, the next business step is to determine the appropriate intellectual property protection, such as submitting a patent or identifying potential trade secrets. After determining this approach, business leaders then begin to identify the strategic direction for the technology, including whether to license it to business customers or position the business for acquisition by a larger organization. At this stage, usually the priority for both the start-up and the acquiring or licensing company is to validate the functionality and viability of the technology.

Smaller innovation centers within organizations similarly develop products and systems in this way. When something new is created, the focus is often on functional capabilities rather than nonfunctional capabilities. In development and engineering, functional capabilities are capabilities that are interaction-based, meaning that a user would observe or interact with these capabilities. For example, on a banking application, the functional capabilities would be the account summary page, the ability to transfer funds, or the ability to pay bills. However, functional capabilities also require nonfunctional capabilities to function in a system. For example, to transfer funds, the system would need to validate in a backend database that the account has enough available funds to transfer to another account. Further, we may want this process to be validated quickly, with some requisite level of performance.

The purpose of describing the difference between functional and nonfunctional capabilities is that often cybersecurity capabilities are nonfunctional in nature, and nonfunctional capabilities are usually not developed until later in the process. The process by which both types of capabilities are defined, in detail, is requirements articulation. And the software development lifecycle includes requirements articulation and management as a core part of overall product and system development at full-scale, rather than PoC or prototype stages.

C. THE SOFTWARE DEVELOPMENT LIFECYCLE

The software development lifecycle is a process by which technology products are built. This process usually involves four key phases: Design, Build, Test, Production. It is these phases that usually define what will be built and ensure that it is built. Consider how you might build a house. Before you start building, you will need to know how many rooms you might want, how much square footage is appropriate for your lifestyle, and how much money you have to spend. This broad-scale planning is usually done in an upfront strategic conversation before the details of the house have been drawn. Similarly, in development processes, these upfront discussions occur before you decide what style of faucet you plan to install in the bathroom. Usually a member of the development team is a technical architect, or someone who understands how all of the pieces should fit together, including what must be built to support the type of product or system to be created.

After the large-scale plans have been developed, an architect may draw or build a miniature replica of a prototype for purposes of validating your broad-scale goals for this home. Once you have a general sense of what you want, the detailed requirements process begins. You will likely work with an architect and maybe a designer to determine other types of requirements, such as the size of your windows, the type of flooring, or countertops you might need. An architect or designer will usually record these specifics to ensure that what is built is to your precise requirements. But often these requirements are what you as a future homeowner would observe by living in the house. Usually there are other types of requirements that you might not even consider. These requirements are things like the amount of insulation needed for the climate in which you live, the specific padding needed under your flooring to minimize sound in a lower level, or flashing on the roof that is needed to prevent moisture intrusion. These types of requirements are not usually articulated but are nonetheless necessary for a quality home.

In a traditional software development lifecycle, usually business contacts partner with technology business analysts to articulate functional requirements. This process usually is repeated multiple times as questions arise from the business analyst or the developers and engineers. Functional blueprints may be "mocked up" or drawn, such as how screens in a process should look. For example, for a developer to code a particular screen, the developer needs to know how it will look and how interactive features will function, for example whether a drop-down box should be used and what will appear when an option is selected. You may have heard of the fields user experience (UX), user design, or usability. These fields specifically focus on these functional capabilities from the perspective of the products audience, or users, by examining the *user interface*, the part of the technology with which the user interacts.

After the functional requirements have been finalized and the user interface has been designed, usually engineers turn to nonfunctional requirements. Nonfunctional requirements consist of the actual backend infrastructure needed to support functional requirements, such as the size and preferred version of database, the location of data storage, performance speeds for the system overall, and system redundancy. Although we do not discuss business continuity in depth in this text, business continuity is the technology function that focuses on performance and system uptime. Usually business continuity is managed by a team other than the security team, and this function is primarily concerned with ascertaining system requirements and testing such requirements to ensure that, for example, the highest priority systems do not experience any prolonged downtime. Redundant systems are those that enable an organization to function when one system is not available, due to technical issues or, for example, a cybersecurity attack.

Although there may be some limited functional requirements that pertain to security like displaying a dialogue window that displays the text "creating a secure connection," most security requirements will be nonfunctional in nature (unless the software being created is *for* security purposes). For example, a security requirement could be a detective control, such as the conditions under which a system will send alerts to a Security Operations Center (SOC). Frequently, alerts are designed to communicate unusual behavior, such as logging into a system from an IP address in an unusual geographic location and from an unusual or uncharacteristic time for that user. These alerts are then sent to a central operations center to determine whether the behavior signals some security issue or not. As we will explain in more detail, the SOC is a critical aspect of an effective incident response program.

After functional and nonfunctional requirements are defined for a product or service, engineers and developers start to build to the specs. Throughout the build phase, engineers and developers communicate back to the business analyst to clarity certain requirements. A project manager will review resources to determine whether the financial spend is near to what was estimated after requirements articulation. Often, the build phase is when certain requirements are reworked or removed entirely to manage project cost and complexity.

Many technology experts are required in the build phase. For example, a database architect may be needed to define how the data are organized in a particular database. An expert in middleware may be needed to fit certain technologies together. An expert in a particular third-party system might be needed when integrating technologies, such as SAP, a common technology used for ordering, customer, and financial management.

After the product or system has been built, it must be tested to ensure it will work effectively. Just prior to formal testing or upon completion of a testable segment of code, developers conduct code reviews. The value of a code review is to bring in an objective developer to ensure the developers who created the product or system didn't miss anything, including duplicative or problematic code, or even inefficient code. If the code used to run these products or systems is problematic, it can open up the system to security vulnerabilities or create performance issues downstream. For example, poorly written code can mean the product or system can experience significant downtime or fail for some tasks. It is important for organizations to validate that the code will work appropriately before formal testing begins.

The first step of formal testing is called User Acceptance. User Acceptance Testing (UAT) is the process of validating functional requirements. This is usually completed by testing analysts and business contacts to ensure that what is built meets the original requirements. When any requirement is not satisfied, it is registered as a "bug" which needs to be closed prior to a product or system going live. You may have heard the term "bug bounty," which is simply an incentive for outsiders to find certain issues within a given product or system.

Bugs can be any issues, and frequently bug bounties may be oriented towards security issues. As you may recall from your own use of mobile devices, frequently "updates" are focused on closing known bugs to improve performance. For example, a new OS version for a product might be called "OS 15" but the subsequent updates may be called "OS 15.1" or similar. This connotes that the update is an update on the previous version to close bugs discovered in the OS after the update has gone live. In this example, the change was already made, and bugs were later discovered. For formal testing, bugs are discovered *prior* to go-live. But the discovery of bugs does not usually end even when the system goes live.

In the following excerpt, Jukka Ruohonen and Luca Allodi examine the emergence of bug bounties related to vulnerabilities for Web-based applications.

JUKKA RUOHONEN & LUCA ALLODI, *A BUG BOUNTY PERSPECTIVE ON THE DISCLOSURE OF WEB VULNERABILITIES*

WEIS 2018 (2018)

The history of bug bounties traces to the early 2000s emergence of commercial vulnerability disclosure programs and different security alerting services. The perhaps most memorable example is the TippingPoint's Zero Day Initiative that was launched already in 2005. This still active program relies on a business model that compensates hackers for their vulnerability discoveries on one hand, and helps the opt-in customers to patch their products on the other [4]. When reflected against the history of vulnerability disclosure practices, the new element brought forward by ZDI and related programs was the monetary compensations paid for the vulnerabilities disseminated through the programs. These monetary compensations were also a key element in the emergence of crowd-sourced bug bounty programs in the early 2010s.

Direct bug bounty programs are nowadays orchestrated by many vendors themselves. In fact, the concept of a (direct) bug bounty is older than ZDI and related programs; Netscape introduced the first known bug bounty already in 1995. Although also the Mozilla Foundation later adopted the same approach, these early initiatives did not gain widespread traction in the software industry. It was much later in the early 2010s when direct bug bounties became commonplace through the initiation of programs by many technology giants, including Google, Microsoft, Facebook, and Yahoo, among others. These bug finding contests directly orchestrated by technology companies themselves were also quickly adopted for initiating different platforms (see [17] for the concept of platform and related theory). HackerOne is currently the perhaps most famous case of these bug bounty platforms. [. . .]

The paper's main empirical findings, theoretical points, and contributions can be summarized and generalized as follows:

- Bug bounty platforms in general align well with the theories about network effects and platform economy.
- However, when excluding the crowd-sourcing elements, innovation seems limited from a business perspective; most current bug bounties mimic the business models that have been used already in the older vulnerability markets.
- In terms of the mere volume of software vulnerabilities disseminated, bug bounties can be successful without monetary compensations, although the lack of compensations tends to intensify the focus on quantity over quality.
- Only a relatively few participants disclose most of the web vulnerabilities disseminated through bug bounties.

- Automated tools for web vulnerability discovery are used also in the bug bounty context, and this automation presumably influences the websites targeted and affected.
- In addition to the productivity gap between participants, the use of automated tools can create knowledge gaps even with respect to a single type of web vulnerabilities.

As you can see from the excerpt above, the term "bug" is appropriate in any type of testing, whether it is specific to products or systems before full release or in the wild. Like security vulnerabilities, many bugs related to how the infrastructure functions, and are discovered via other types of system testing, such as stress testing or performance testing. For example, stress testing could find that when 10,000 concurrent users are using a product, the product fails. These testing protocols enable testers to find problems before they manifest in the live version of the product or system.

After testing has been completed, the process is still not done. As previously discussed, change management processes must be satisfied. This ensures that 1) no significant issues will occur when the product or system goes live and 2) that there are no collisions in the release. This can result when organizations use shared resources, such as common databases or other infrastructure, and two changes are executed at the same time. Once the change management process has been satisfied, the product or system can go live and the code is in the wild. See Figure 1 for a sample flow of the overall development stages and associated activities.

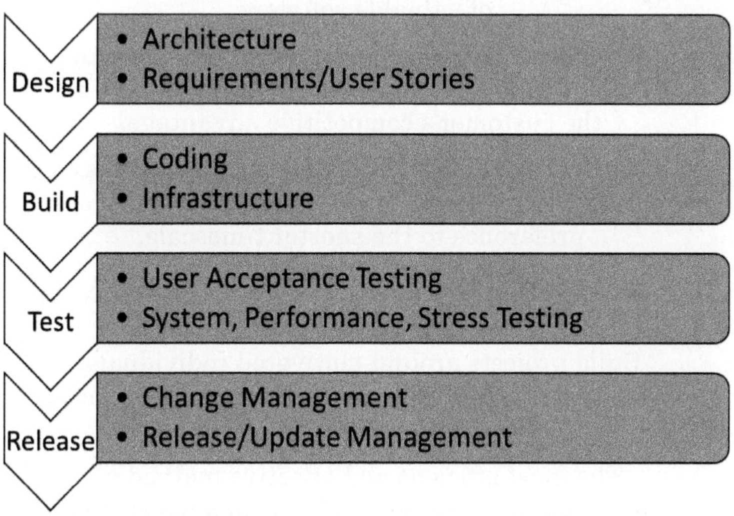

Figure 1: Software Development Flow

1. ALTERNATIVE DEVELOPMENT MODELS

The software development lifecycle described above is a formalistic and long version of development processes, commonly called *waterfall* methodology. Waterfall methodologies are used when the organization has a very clear idea of what should be built or when doing development related to infrastructure only, rather than user interface development.

The two most common development methodologies used today are *iterative* and *Agile* methodologies. Both of these methodologies are designed to provide more back and forth between development teams and their business partners. In an iterative methodology, the waterfall approach is conducted in smaller cycles, for example building a portion of the technology at a time, usually repeating the requirements gathering and build phases multiple times before moving to the testing phase. The Agile methodology is frequently used for more innovative technologies where a portion of the system is built and tested for a particular module. Instead of detailed requirements articulation, Agile focuses on user stories, or a description of what a user is trying to accomplish. The principles of the agile methodology were set forth in the *Agile Manifesto*:

PRINCIPLES BEHIND THE AGILE MANIFESTO

(2001)

We follow these principles:

Our highest priority is to satisfy the customer through early and continuous delivery of valuable software.

Welcome changing requirements, even late in development. Agile processes harness change for the customer's competitive advantage.

Deliver working software frequently, from a couple of weeks to a couple of months, with a preference to the shorter timescale.

Business people and developers must work together daily throughout the project.

Build projects around motivated individuals. Give them the environment and support they need, and trust them to get the job done.

The most efficient and effective method of conveying information to and within a development team is face-to-face conversation.

Working software is the primary measure of progress.

Agile processes promote sustainable development.
The sponsors, developers, and users should be able
to maintain a constant pace indefinitely.

Continuous attention to technical excellence
and good design enhances agility.

Simplicity—the art of maximizing the amount
of work not done—is essential.

The best architectures, requirements, and designs
emerge from self-organizing teams.

At regular intervals, the team reflects on how
to become more effective, then tunes and adjusts
its behavior accordingly.

One concept that is closely related to the agile methodology, and is often attributed to it, is that of "failing fast." This is sometimes paired with the ideas of "and fail often" or "and iterate." The idea behind this concept is twofold. First, if a project or design is going to fail, it is better that this be discovered quickly, while problems can be more easily corrected and before substantial investment in flawed designs has been made. And second, that lessons can—and must—be learned from these failures (so failing often is actually a positive learning outcome) and incorporated into future designs (such that we should iterate to new designs based upon past failures).

It is interesting and illustrative to note Mark Zuckerberg's famous invocation of these ideas in his moto for Facebook and to consider how it compares to the Agile Manifesto.

LETTER FROM MARK ZUCKERBERG

SEC FORM S-1, REGISTRATION STATEMENT FOR FACEBOOK, INC.
INITIAL PUBLIC OFFERING (Feb 1, 2012)

Facebook was not originally created to be a company. It was built to accomplish a social mission—to make the world more open and connected.

We think it's important that everyone who invests in Facebook understands what this mission means to us, how we make decisions and why we do the things we do. I will try to outline our approach in this letter.

At Facebook, we're inspired by technologies that have revolutionized how people spread and consume information. We often talk about inventions like the printing press and the television—by simply making communication more efficient, they led to a complete transformation of many important parts of society. They gave more people a voice. They encouraged progress. They changed the way society was organized. They brought us closer together.

Today, our society has reached another tipping point. We live at a moment when the majority of people in the world have access to the internet or mobile phones—the raw tools necessary to start sharing what they're thinking, feeling and doing with whomever they want. Facebook aspires to build the services that give people the power to share and help them once again transform many of our core institutions and industries.

There is a huge need and a huge opportunity to get everyone in the world connected, to give everyone a voice and to help transform society for the future. The scale of the technology and infrastructure that must be built is unprecedented, and we believe this is the most important problem we can focus on.

[. . .]

The Hacker Way

As part of building a strong company, we work hard at making Facebook the best place for great people to have a big impact on the world and learn from other great people. We have cultivated a unique culture and management approach that we call the Hacker Way.

The word "hacker" has an unfairly negative connotation from being portrayed in the media as people who break into computers. In reality, hacking just means building something quickly or testing the boundaries of what can be done. Like most things, it can be used for good or bad, but the vast majority of hackers I've met tend to be idealistic people who want to have a positive impact on the world.

The Hacker Way is an approach to building that involves continuous improvement and iteration. Hackers believe that something can always be better, and that nothing is ever complete. They just have to go fix it—often in the face of people who say it's impossible or are content with the status quo.

Hackers try to build the best services over the long term by quickly releasing and learning from smaller iterations rather than trying to get everything right all at once. To support this, we have built a testing framework that at any given time can try out thousands of versions of Facebook. We have the words "Done is better than perfect" painted on our walls to remind ourselves to always keep shipping.

Hacking is also an inherently hands-on and active discipline. Instead of debating for days whether a new idea is possible or what the best way to build something is, hackers would rather just prototype something and see what works. There's a hacker mantra that you'll hear a lot around Facebook offices: "Code wins arguments."

Hacker culture is also extremely open and meritocratic. Hackers believe that the best idea and implementation should always win—not the person who is best at lobbying for an idea or the person who manages the most people.

To encourage this approach, every few months we have a hackathon, where everyone builds prototypes for new ideas they have. At the end, the whole team gets together and looks at everything that has been built. Many of our most successful products came out of hackathons, including Timeline, chat, video, our mobile development framework and some of our most important infrastructure like the HipHop compiler.

To make sure all our engineers share this approach, we require all new engineers—even managers whose primary job will not be to write code—to go through a program called Bootcamp where they learn our codebase, our tools and our approach. There are a lot of folks in the industry who manage engineers and don't want to code themselves, but the type of hands-on people we're looking for are willing and able to go through Bootcamp.

———

The examples above all relate to engineering, but we have distilled these principles into five core values for how we run Facebook:

Focus on Impact

If we want to have the biggest impact, the best way to do this is to make sure we always focus on solving the most important problems. It sounds simple, but we think most companies do this poorly and waste a lot of time. We expect everyone at Facebook to be good at finding the biggest problems to work on.

Move Fast

Moving fast enables us to build more things and learn faster. However, as most companies grow, they slow down too much because they're more afraid of making mistakes than they are of losing opportunities by moving too slowly. We have a saying: "Move fast and break things." The idea is that if you never break anything, you're probably not moving fast enough.

Be Bold

Building great things means taking risks. This can be scary and prevents most companies from doing the bold things they should. However, in a world that's changing so quickly, you're guaranteed to fail if you don't take any risks. We have another saying: "The riskiest thing is to take no risks." We encourage everyone to make bold decisions, even if that means being wrong some of the time.

Be Open

We believe that a more open world is a better world because people with more information can make better decisions and have a greater impact. That goes for running our company as well. We work hard to make sure everyone at Facebook has access to as much information as possible about every part of the company so they can make the best decisions and have the greatest impact.

Build Social Value

Once again, Facebook exists to make the world more open and connected, and not just to build a company. We expect everyone at Facebook to focus every day on how to build real value for the world in everything they do. Thanks for taking the time to read this letter. We believe that we have an opportunity to have an important impact on the world and build a lasting company in the process. I look forward to building something great together.

These stories then require the entire development and engineering team to identify what is needed both functionally and nonfunctionally to accomplish the story. Because the module is described in this way, underlying nonfunctional requirements must be identified for the entire user story to be able to "go live" and be deployed to production (another way of saying 'go live'). The effect, in theory, is that a fully working module is available for broader testing after it is in the wild. This process, then, is repeated for all user stories until the business has determined its needs are met. The benefit of such an approach is that more stories can be added if there is still funding available, and the most crucial stories are usually identified first, which ensures accurate prioritization.

It is important to understand the basics of project development because security, if it is built in the most cost-effective way (more below on technical debt), will be part of the project development lifecycle, whether part of nonfunctional requirements elicitation or user story planning. In the best product or service implementations, a security architect has also been part of the initial design processes before any detailed requirements or user stories have been determined. In the next section, we will talk about the ways in which security can be effectively included in this process.

2. SECURITY BY DESIGN

Security by design, often called Secure Development Lifecycle (SDLC) is the process by which organizations effectively integrate security within a standardized development process. But how does one know exactly how to design a secure system? The combination includes both knowns, or common vulnerabilities specific to a technology and modeling, or anticipating what adversaries may target the system. In this chapter, we will be discussing the first, known issues, and how to implement security in the lifecycle. However, later in this book, we will discuss threat modeling, or the approach by which we can to some degree) anticipate threat vectors, or the path by which a threat source may "pwn"[2] a system.

Let's return to the house metaphor from earlier in this book. The average homeowner will know that putting locks on any points of entry for a home is a good idea to generally prevent unauthorized access to your home, whether by a burglar, a drunk person who mistakenly thinks it's their home, or the curious teenager down the street. However, knowing who might specifically try to access your home depends a lot on what assets you plan to store in your home. If you have million-dollar art pieces, for example, your threat pool expands significantly, and you may want to include additional security. SDLC usually focuses on the former, or known issues present in all technologies of a certain type.[3]

In order to have an initial conversation about security, a security architect needs to know generally what the architecture will be. For example, if there is a user interface that will contain sensitive data, and the interface connects over the open internet, it is likely that the connection will need to be encrypted when data are transmitted between the interface entry point and the destination application server. And if data pass through the application server and are sent to a database server over an internal connection, perhaps access to both servers should be restricted to least user access, or only those users who have a demonstrated business need to access them, such as those providing support, ensuring that the system is working as designed. Often, developers who create the product or system don't even have access to the production (live) version. This is because those developers no longer have a need to access such systems, at least in most implementations,[4] and even trusted developers could potentially make a mistake or become an adversary. Remember, all humans are hackable!

These general determinations reveal basic information about the requirements of the architecture that will be built, and the high-level network connections and hardware are usually detailed in an architecture diagram. Architecture diagrams are tremendously useful for anyone trying

---

[2] "pwn" is a colloquialism, particular in online gaming, expressing one's dominance over another. It has associations with the same meaning within hacking community. *See Words We're Watching, 'What Does 'Pwn' Mean?' (And how do you say it?)"*, Merriam-Webster, https://www.merriam-webster.com/words-at-play/pwn-what-it-means-and-how-you-say-it.

[3] A corollary to the SDLC is privacy by design, or the process of including privacy controls in the product or system, as well. We will not be discussing this in detail, but it is important to remember that additional controls may be needed that will impact design and may influence which security controls are implemented.

[4] Many organizations increasingly embrace a "DevOps" model, in which the development and operational sides of the software and systems development lifecycle are increasingly integrated, to ensure that fixes are identified and deployed quickly for high priority systems. This model is generally used for higher-priority products, systems, and customers. More recently, developers also deploy a "DevSecOps" model, which attempts to better integrate security considerations—code quality and reliability on the development side, for instance, and auditing and implementation of fixes on the operations side—into the development life cycle.

to determine which cybersecurity controls should apply and where, enabling someone to ask the right questions, assuming the diagrams have been recently updated. For example, you might ask what data is transferred over which connections and where those data are stored, which will enable you to ask whether appropriate access controls have been designed for each of the locations identified. Frequently, you will find that security controls may be planned for some, but not all of the locations.

A good source of requirements for technologies starts with the policies in place for an organization and the corresponding controls or requirements in the controls framework. Organizations that have guidelines or procedures in place have already made efforts to solve problems that are likely to arise in the systems they build. We will discuss more about the controls framework and risk management programs in Chapter 11.

There are many challenges inherent in designing security into products and systems, but it helps to think of the activity as a starting point, rather than a complete solution for building secure systems. For example, in any user interface, you would want to ensure that malicious code is not entered in open text fields. In one of the casebook author's experiences, an incident resulted when a "reviews" portion of an online retailer had open text fields that did not validate the content. As a result, attackers were able to post malicious code in a review, which was then passed through the system and resulted in attackers being able to access the database. This is precisely why one of the security requirements for a system is usually data validation, or when input fields are limited to certain characters and length, or when a drop-down box is used instead of an open text field.

Consider Web applications you have accessed in the past: have you noticed that only numbers are permitted for a phone number field? Have you noticed that a state or country field requires you to select something from a drop-down menu? Data validation has the important function not only of standardizing database entries to improve data analysis, but it also has an important security function. This is an example of security requirements that are both functional (the drop-down) and nonfunctional (validation requirements). Similarly, have you noticed that if you enter your credit card number or social security number in a field once, usually on the next screen if it's displayed, it blocks out most of the numbers, such as the last four digits of your social security number? This is an example of masking or covering and obscuring digits to improve overall security. It is the same reason someone validating your account when you call the help desk only asks for the last four digits of your social security number: it protects your entire number from being used by someone operating the helpline.

Of course, this seems straightforward: take the controls for a specific technology from the controls or requirements library and implement them.

However, there are at least two major challenges that arise when trying to integrate security requirements: 1) the software development lifecycle itself and 2) competing demands and limited funding. First, the software development lifecycle, when using a traditional waterfall methodology, may be straightforward, but it requires enough knowledge of the system at the requirements stage to ensure that security controls are built into both functional and nonfunctional requirements. Frequently, the business, developers, and engineers do not have detailed knowledge in security to ensure the correct requirements are included. This means that they will not likely be able to integrate appropriate security requirements without additional training.

Furthermore, the type of development process used could make identifying broad security requirements more challenging. With Agile, for example, the focus on specific and discrete user stories can often mean that broader security requirements are not included when such user stories are drawn to the user experience. Many security controls are designed both based on the entire system and designed to be used in conjunction with one-another. This "security in depth" means that holistically achieving a high degree of security for an entire product or system may be difficult when designing individual modules separately. As you will see in 9.D, competing demands and limited funding may have even more of an impact on security, when organizations do not dedicate resources to build security into the software development lifecycle.

QUESTIONS

1. Now that you understand a bit more about the technology development process, at what point in the process do you think it is most likely for security risks to be created?

2. For each of the project lifecycle phases, how should security be considered as part of the process?

3. Are there tensions in these different lifecycle practices? Is the process described in Zuckerberg's IPO letter the same as that described in the Agile Manifesto?

4. Whose interests do these different approaches serve? Note in particular the extent to which both Zuckerberg's IPO letter and the Agile Manifesto emphasize the importance of serving interests other than the engineers (the customer in the case of the Agile Manifesto and building social value in the case of Facebook). Are these documents about serving those interests? About constraining "hackers" and engineers? About facilitating the work that hackers and engineers want to undertake?

5. Think back to the discussion of "rough consensus and running code" in Section A, above, about the competing attitudes towards engineering and standards development reflected by the OSI and IAB and IETF approaches to

Internet standards development. How does that discussion the development of Internet standards relate to this discussion of the development of software?

6. What aspects of cybersecurity's adversarial nature will make anticipatory cybersecurity work (as in the technology development process) less effective? Hint: what do we know about adversaries?

7. Think back to the discussion of hackers and their motivations in Chapter 4 and the discussion of Gates's Internet Tidal Wave memo and the relationship between the IETF engineers and the OSI discussed in Section A, above. Do you see echoes those discussions in the materials discussed above?

D. TECHNICAL DEBT AND DEFERRED COSTS

The term "technical debt" was coined by American software pioneer Ward Cunningham, who famously said that "some problems with code are like financial debt. It's OK to borrow against the future, as long as you pay it off."[5] The concept of technical debt is, in some ways, no different than financial debt. When security controls are expensive to implement or budgets are tight (and they almost always are for IT), usually organizations prefer to spend money on functional features rather than security. The result, sadly, is that security if often an afterthought: organizations do not invest until they are forced to do it—usually responding to results of an assessment, audit, or even legal action. Dan Geer and Gunnar Peterson have advanced the concept of Security Book Value, or rather what they call the "Margin of Safety" or the ratio of security investment versus assets,[6] for purposes of estimating whether greater security investment is needed in relation to project investment. Ariadi Nugroho, Joost Visser & Tobias Kuipers have created an empirical model for technical debt long-term costs, which clearly demonstrates significant cost increases over time (see Figure 2, below).

---

5 Charl van der Walt, Understanding and Assessing Technical Debt for Improved Cybersecurity, COMPUTER BUSINESS REVIEW (SEPT. 2018), https://www.cbronline.com/opinion/technical-debt-cybersecurity.

6 *Id.* (referencing the article 'Margin of Safety or Speculation? Measuring Security Book Value' at https://www.usenix.org/system/files/login/articles/12_geer.pdf).

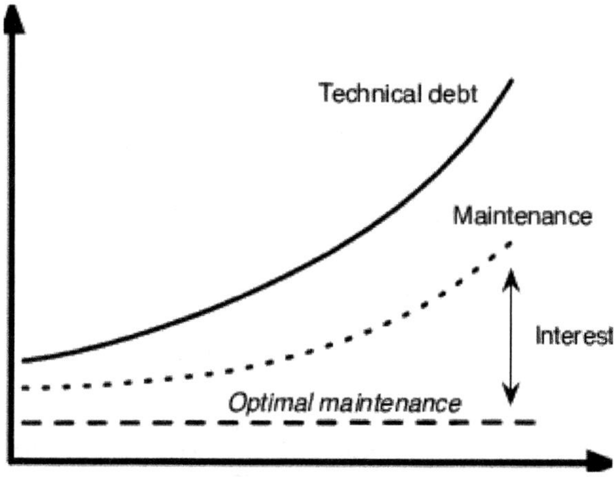

Figure 2: Empirical Model of Technical Debt[7]

The impact of security as an afterthought is significant both from security risk perspective and from a financial perspective. First, not having effective security controls in place from the start introduces a period of time where it is more likely for a security incident to occur, usually at a time the organization would least like to see an incident occur, such as a product launch. Second, the cost of adding security later is often significantly more costly when a system is already built.

How might this be? Recall the descriptions above about the software development lifecycle and our previous description of the change management process. To implement security controls, a team doesn't just need to implement the controls and deploy them, a team will need to complete the entire development lifecycle, including testing and change processes, which require resources and time. Although some controls might be relatively easy to implement and fairly modularized, other controls might affect all parts of the system as a whole, making it more difficult to implement a change. The complexity of downstream security changes is directly tied to the type of control that needs to be implemented. For example, conducting regular access control review is a procedural process involving managers or a system owner reviewing who as access to a particular asset on a regular basis. This usually doesn't include direct changes to a system. However, a system that must integrate in single sign-on (SSO), a technology that permits authentication across "permitted" systems so that a user only needs to authenticate once to access all systems, would be significantly more difficult to implement.

The challenges of moving too quickly resulting in downstream cost is properly known as technical debt. Technical debt results from inadequate upfront planning, causing much larger costs in the future. In a sense,

[7] Nugroho et al., An Empirical Model of Technical Debt and Interest, MTD '11 (201) [needs approval to use], https://www.researchgate.net/publication/228684782_An_Empirical_Model_of_Technical_Debt_and_Interest.

organizations build products that work ("rough consensus and running code") but require additional costs to scale, perform, or secure. Technical debt is not just a security problem, but it disproportionately affects security, as often security is an afterthought in part because of a lack of security knowledge in technical experts and also because security is not required for a system to function at a very basic level.

CRAIG TIMBERG, *THE LONG LIFE OF A QUICK 'FIX': INTERNET PROTOCOL FROM 1989 LEAVES DATA VULNERABLE TO HIJACKERS*

WASHINGTON POST (May 31, 2015)

By the time a pair of engineers sat down for lunch together in Austin, the Internet's growing pains had become dire. Once a novelty for computer scientists, the network was now exploding in size, lurching ever closer to a hard mathematical wall built into one of the Internet's most basic protocols.

As the prospect of system meltdown loomed, the men began scribbling ideas for a solution onto the back of a ketchup-stained napkin. Then a second. Then a third. The "three-napkins protocol," as its inventors jokingly dubbed it, would soon revolutionize the Internet. And though there were lingering issues, the engineers saw their creation as a "hack" or "kludge," slang for a short-term fix to be replaced as soon as a better alternative arrived.

That was 1989.

More than a quarter-century later—a span that has seen the fall of the Berlin Wall, the rise of the smartphone and an explosion of hacking—the "three-napkins protocol" still directs most long-haul traffic on the global network despite years of increasingly strenuous warnings about critical security problems. The three-napkins protocol has become the kludge that never died.

"Short-term solutions tend to stay with us for a very long time. And long-term solutions tend to never happen," said Yakov Rekhter, one of the engineers who invented the "three-napkins protocol." "That's what I learned from this experience."

The Internet can appear as elegantly designed as a race car as it immerses us in consuming worlds of sight and sound. But it's closer to an assemblage of kludges—more Frankenstein than Ferrari—that endure because they work, or at least work well enough.

The consequences play out across cyberspace every second of every day, as hackers exploit old, poorly protected systems to scam, steal and spy on a scale never before possible. The flaws they exploit often are well-known and ancient in technological terms, surviving only because of an industry-wide penchant for patching over problems rather than replacing the rot.

"You're in Hackerville here on the Internet. Period," said Randy Bush, a computer scientist who specializes in routing security. "All of this stuff lacks formal discipline. . . . It's paint and spackle."

Such is the story of the "three-napkins protocol," more formally known as Border Gateway Protocol, or BGP.

At its most basic level, BGP helps routers decide how to send giant flows of data across the vast mesh of connections that make up the Internet. With infinite numbers of possible paths—some slow and meandering, others quick and direct—BGP gives routers the information they need to pick one, even though there is no overall map of the Internet and no authority charged with directing its traffic.

The creation of BGP, which relies on individual networks continuously sharing information about available data links, helped the Internet continue its growth into a worldwide network. But BGP also allows huge swaths of data to be "hijacked" by almost anyone with the necessary skills and access.

The main reason is that BGP, like many key systems on the Internet, is built to automatically trust users—something that may work on smaller networks but leaves a global one ripe for attack.

The honor system

Hijackings have become routine events that even experts struggle to explain: What made traffic between two computers in Denver take a 7,000-mile detour through Iceland? How could a single Pakistani company crash YouTube? Why did potentially sensitive Pentagon data once flow through Beijing?

To these questions, there are technical answers. But they all boil down to this fact: BGP runs on the honor system, allowing data to get pushed and pulled across the planet in curious ways, at the behest of mysterious masters.

Warnings about the risks inherent in BGP are almost as old as the protocol itself. "I knew that routing security was a problem," Columbia University computer scientist Steven M. Bellovin said. "Seeing this conceptually is fairly easy and straightforward. Sorting it out in terms of the engineering is fiendishly difficult."

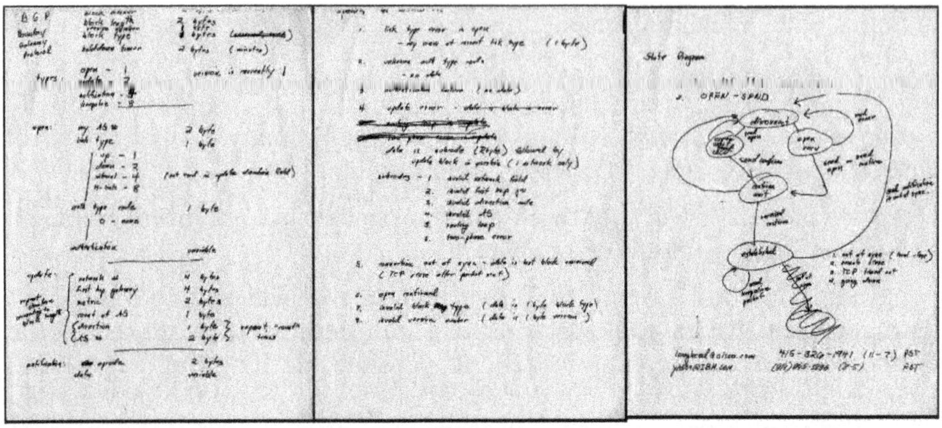

Figure 3: A scanned copy of the "three napkins" outline of the Border Gateway Protocol (Cisco Archive Collection, 2014-57-001)

Rekhter, an immigrant to the United States who once played in an underground rock band in the Soviet Union, said security "wasn't even on the table" when he sat down with his soft-spoken co-inventor, Kirk Lougheed, for lunch during an engineering conference in January 1989.

This was an era when hacks were rare and the toll modest. Lougheed recalled: "In the early days of the Internet, getting stuff to work was the primary goal. There was no concept that people would use this to do malicious things. . . . Security was not a big issue."

The big issue of the day was the possibility that the Internet might break down. A halt in its furious expansion would have hurt the network's users and the profits of companies supplying gear and services. Rekhter at the time worked for computing giant IBM; Lougheed was a founding employee of Cisco, maker of networking hardware.

"We needed to sell routers. And we had a strong economic motive to make sure this party would continue," Lougheed said. "When Yakov and I showed up with a solution and it seemed to work, people were quite willing to accept it because they didn't have anything else."

There were other efforts underway to build routing protocols. BGP won out because it was simple, solved the problem at hand and proved versatile enough to keep data flowing as the Internet doubled in size, again and again and again. Networks across the world embraced the protocol, giving it an edge it has never relinquished.

Once technologies are widely deployed, they become almost impossible to replace because many users—including paying customers of technology companies—rely on them and resist buying costly new hardware or software. The result can be a steady buildup of outdated technology, one layer on top of another. It's as if today's most important bank vaults sit on foundations of straw and mud. [. . .]

'Knee-deep in alligators'

The creators of BGP were hardly the first inventors to sketch out their initial ideas quickly and crudely, only to refine them later through real-world testing. Speed, nimbleness and pragmatism were hallmarks of Internet development in its early decades, fueling both its exponential growth and its ability to outcompete rival technologies whose development was more formal and—perhaps inevitably—more ponderous as well.

David D. Clark, an MIT scientist who oversaw Internet protocol development for years, captured the idea in a widely quoted 1992 presentation, saying: "We reject kings, presidents and voting. We believe in rough consensus and running code"—meaning solutions that work and have been widely embraced.

This approach did not always encourage long-term planning for eventual security threats as the Internet attracted a growing universe of users, including many whose motives were quite different from those of the academics who first embraced modern computer networking technology in the 1970s and '80s.

In the following excerpt, Banker, Liang & Ramasubbu analyze the effect of technical debt more generally, finding a substantial cost associated with deferred technical investment.

RAJIV BANKER, YI LIANG & NARAYAN RAMASUBBU, *TECHNICAL DEBT AND FIRM PERFORMANCE*

MANAGEMENT SCIENCE (forthcoming)

Firms invest considerable resources to acquire, customize, and maintain enterprise information systems that orchestrate their business processes and day-to-day workflows. An emerging research stream in the information systems and software engineering literatures highlights that "quick and dirty" customizations of enterprise systems need to be considered as "technical debt" because they reduce system reliability and create long-term maintenance obligations. Poor reliability of enterprise systems may cause disruptions to a firm's business processes, which further undermine the performance of the firm. At the same time, case studies have revealed that such actions that cause noncompliance with established design standards have benefited some firms, at least in the short term, by accelerating systems deployment and/or by aiding the quick roll out of new business features after initial adoption. Therefore, the net effect of technical debt on firm performance remains an open empirical question.

It is well known that in competitive industries, teams tend to accelerate their pace of system development and deployment of functionality demanded by businesses to respond to competitor strategies. Specifically, because information systems can help enhance business process functionalities that create competitive advantages, firms in competitive industries and turbulent environments often seek early and/or even partial adoption of new IT-enabled functionalities. The chance of early and/or partial adopters of new IT-enabled functionalities incurring technical debt is high, especially in the context of packaged software systems, because vendors' design standards and product roadmaps are volatile during the early phase of their product lifecycles. Similarly, firms operating in R&D-intensive industries may also be prone to accumulating higher levels of technical debt because such industries often operate at a higher "clock speed", which requires firms to correspondingly accelerate their development and deployment processes.

Our main findings can be summarized as follows. First, we find that technical debt is negatively associated with a variety of future performance metrics including GROA, asset turnover ratio, gross margin, sales growth, and operating income. The magnitude of the negative impact of technical debt on firm performance is economically significant. For example, we estimate that a 10 percent increase in technical debt reduces GROA by 16 percent. Second, we find that the negative impact of technical debt becomes stronger over time, both statistically and economically. Our results indicate that for a firm with a median level of technical debt, the net benefit of the system to the firm turns negative after five years of system operation. These results are robust to several alternative model specifications including lead-lag regressions, rank regressions, median regressions, and a semi-parametric smoothing spline estimation.

As you can see in the above excerpt, there is specific evidence that technical debt reduces other positive business attributes.

Another big problem in the "move fast" mentality is that organizations may also build products or systems as a POC or prototype, then assume that it is possible to operationalize those products or systems are built to implement with very few changes. For this reason, mature organizations conduct a risk assessment on products that will be licensed (as a third-party risk assessment) and fully evaluate any businesses positioned for acquisition from a risk perspective, as well.

The following excerpts capture some of the business and technical realities of dealing with the costs of technical debt. The first excerpt is a 2002 letter from Bill Gates to all Microsoft employees, in which he announces the company's refocus on "Trustworthy Computing." This is, in effect, a recission of his prior "Internet Tidal Wave" memo. Importantly, it is useful to note that this refocus came after both Microsoft's rise to dominance in the Internet browser market and completion of the United

States Department of Justice antitrust suit against Microsoft. The general understanding of these are that they are related: that Microsoft violated the antitrust laws in order to displace Netscape as the dominant web browser with Microsoft's own Internet Explorer. The second excerpt suggests that that story may not be entirely accurate: Netscape's decision to rewrite its codebase between versions 4.0 and 5.0 of its software may have dealt a fatal self-own to the Netscape platform. Why, one may ask (and the except discusses), did Netscape feel that such a rewrite was necessary? Because it felt it was necessary to pay down the technical debts that had been incurred in developing its software through version 4.0. But, as the excerpt makes clear, the decision to pay down these debts can be quite costly. The final excerpt presents the same issue in a slightly different context, exploring the difficulty of patching production systems, and suggesting that sometimes patching systems, even to address known concerns, may not be the right thing to do.

BILL GATES, '*TRUSTWORTHY COMPUTING*' *MEMO*

E-mail to Microsoft Employees (JAN 15, 2002)

Every few years I have sent out a memo talking about the highest priority for Microsoft. Two years ago, it was the kickoff of our .NET strategy. Before that, it was several memos about the importance of the Internet to our future and the ways we could make the Internet truly useful for people. Over the last year it has become clear that ensuring .NET is a platform for Trustworthy Computing is more important than any other part of our work. If we don't do this, people simply won't be willing—or able—to take advantage of all the other great work we do. Trustworthy Computing is the highest priority for all the work we are doing. We must lead the industry to a whole new level of Trustworthiness in computing. [. . .]

Computing is already an important part of many people's lives. Within 10 years, it will be an integral and indispensable part of almost everything we do. Microsoft and the computer industry will only succeed in that world if CIOs, consumers and everyone else sees that Microsoft has created a platform for Trustworthy Computing.

Every week there are reports of newly discovered security problems in all kinds of software, from individual applications and services to Windows, Linux, Unix and other platforms. We have done a great job of having teams work around the clock to deliver security fixes for any problems that arise. Our responsiveness has been unmatched—but as an industry leader we can and must do better. Our new design approaches need to dramatically reduce the number of such issues that come up in the software that Microsoft, its partners and its customers create. We need to make it automatic for customers to get the benefits of these fixes. Eventually, our software should be so fundamentally secure that customers never even worry about it. [. . .]

Trustworthiness is a much broader concept than security, and winning our customers' trust involves more than just fixing bugs and achieving "five-nines" availability. It's a fundamental challenge that spans the entire computing ecosystem, from individual chips all the way to global Internet services. It's about smart software, services and industry-wide cooperation.

There are many changes Microsoft needs to make as a company to ensure and keep our customers' trust at every level—from the way we develop software, to our support efforts, to our operational and business practices. As software has become ever more complex, interdependent and interconnected, our reputation as a company has in turn become more vulnerable. Flaws in a single Microsoft product, service or policy not only affect the quality of our platform and services overall, but also our customers' view of us as a company. [. . .]

But we need to go much further.

In the past, we've made our software and services more compelling for users by adding new features and functionality, and by making our platform richly extensible. We've done a terrific job at that, but all those great features won't matter unless customers trust our software.

So now, when we face a choice between adding features and resolving security issues, we need to choose security. Our products should emphasize security right out of the box, and we must constantly refine and improve that security as threats evolve. [. . .]

Bill

JOEL SPOLSKY, *THINGS YOU SHOULD NEVER DO, PART I*

JEOL ON SOFTWARE (April 6, 2000)

Netscape 6.0 is finally going into its first public beta. There never was a version 5.0. The last major release, version 4.0, was released almost three years ago. Three years is an awfully long time in the Internet world. During this time, Netscape sat by, helplessly, as their market share plummeted.

It's a bit smarmy of me to criticize them for waiting so long between releases. They didn't do it on purpose, now, did they?

Well, yes. They did. They did it by making the single worst strategic mistake that any software company can make:

They decided to rewrite the code from scratch.

Netscape wasn't the first company to make this mistake. Borland made the same mistake when they bought Arago and tried to make it into dBase for Windows, a doomed project that took so long that Microsoft Access ate their lunch, then they made it again in rewriting Quattro Pro from scratch and astonishing people with how few features it had. Microsoft almost made the same mistake, trying to rewrite Word for Windows from scratch in a doomed project called Pyramid which was shut down, thrown away, and swept under the rug. Lucky for Microsoft, they had never stopped working on the old code base, so they had something to ship, making it merely a financial disaster, not a strategic one.

We're programmers. Programmers are, in their hearts, architects, and the first thing they want to do when they get to a site is to bulldoze the place flat and build something grand. We're not excited by incremental renovation: tinkering, improving, planting flower beds.

There's a subtle reason that programmers always want to throw away the code and start over. The reason is that they think the old code is a mess. And here is the interesting observation: they are probably wrong. The reason that they think the old code is a mess is because of a cardinal, fundamental law of programming:

It's harder to read code than to write it.

This is why code reuse is so hard. This is why everybody on your team has a different function they like to use for splitting strings into arrays of strings. They write their own function because it's easier and more fun than figuring out how the old function works.

As a corollary of this axiom, you can ask almost any programmer today about the code they are working on. "It's a big hairy mess," they will tell you. "I'd like nothing better than to throw it out and start over."

Why is it a mess?

"Well," they say, "look at this function. It is two pages long! None of this stuff belongs in there! I don't know what half of these API calls are for."

Before Borland's new spreadsheet for Windows shipped, Philippe Kahn, the colorful founder of Borland, was quoted a lot in the press bragging about how Quattro Pro would be much better than Microsoft Excel, because it was written from scratch. All new source code! As if source code rusted.

The idea that new code is better than old is patently absurd. Old code has been used. It has been tested. Lots of bugs have been found, and they've been fixed. There's nothing wrong with it. It doesn't acquire bugs just by sitting around on your hard drive. Au contraire, baby! Is software supposed to be like an old Dodge Dart, that rusts just sitting in the garage? Is software like a teddy bear that's kind of gross if it's not made out of all new material?

Back to that two page function. Yes, I know, it's just a simple function to display a window, but it has grown little hairs and stuff on it and nobody knows why. Well, I'll tell you why: those are bug fixes. One of them fixes that bug that Nancy had when she tried to install the thing on a computer that didn't have Internet Explorer. Another one fixes that bug that occurs in low memory conditions. Another one fixes that bug that occurred when the file is on a floppy disk and the user yanks out the disk in the middle. That LoadLibrary call is ugly but it makes the code work on old versions of Windows 95.

Each of these bugs took weeks of real-world usage before they were found. The programmer might have spent a couple of days reproducing the bug in the lab and fixing it. If it's like a lot of bugs, the fix might be one line of code, or it might even be a couple of characters, but a lot of work and time went into those two characters.

When you throw away code and start from scratch, you are throwing away all that knowledge. All those collected bug fixes. Years of programming work.

You are throwing away your market leadership. You are giving a gift of two or three years to your competitors, and believe me, that is a long time in software years.

You are putting yourself in an extremely dangerous position where you will be shipping an old version of the code for several years, completely unable to make any strategic changes or react to new features that the market demands, because you don't have shippable code. You might as well just close for business for the duration.

You are wasting an outlandish amount of money writing code that already exists.

Is there an alternative? The consensus seems to be that the old Netscape code base was really bad. Well, it might have been bad, but, you know what? It worked pretty darn well on an awful lot of real world computer systems. [. . .]

STEVEN M. BELLOVIN, *PATCHING IS HARD*

SMBLOG (May 12, 2017)

There are many news reports of a ransomware worm. Much of the National Health Service in the UK has been hit; so has FedEx. The patch for the flaw exploited by this malware has been out for a while, but many companies haven't installed it. Naturally, this has prompted a lot of victim-blaming: they should have patched their systems. Yes, they should have, but many didn't. Why not? Because patching is very hard and very risk, and the more complex your systems are, the harder and riskier it is.

Patching is hard? Yes—and every major tech player, no matter how sophisticated they are, has had catastrophic failures when they tried to change something. Google once bricked Chromebooks with an update. A Facebook configuration change took the site offline for 2.5 hours. Microsoft ruined network configuration and partially bricked some computers; even their newest patch isn't trouble-free. An iOS update from Apple bricked some iPad Pros. Even Amazon knocked AWS off the air.

There are lots of reasons for any of these, but let's focus on OS patches. Microsoft—and they're probably the best in the business at this—devotes a lot of resources to testing patches. But they can't test every possible user device configuration, nor can they test against every software package, especially if it's locally written. An amazing amount of software inadvertently relies on OS bugs; sometimes, a vendor deliberately relies on non-standard APIs because there appears to be no other way to accomplish something. The inevitable result is that on occasion, these well-tested patches will break some computers. Enterprises know this, so they're generally slow to patch. I learned the phrase "never install .0 of anything" in 1971, but while software today is much better, it's not perfect and never will be. Enterprises often face a stark choice with security patches: take the risk of being knocked of the air by hackers, or take the risk of knocking yourself off the air. The result is that there is often an inverse correlation between the size of an organization and how rapidly it installs patches. This isn't good, but with the very best technical people, both at the OS vendor and on site, it may be inevitable. [. . .]

Today's attack [the ransomware attack references at the start of this excerpt] is blocked by the MS17-010 patch, which was released March 14. . . . Two months seems like plenty of time to test, and it probably is enough—but is it enough time for remediation if you find a problem? Imagine the possible conversation between FedEx's CSO and its CIO:

"We've got to install MS17-010; these are serious holes."

"We can't just yet. We've been testing it for the last two weeks; it breaks the shipping label software in 25% of our stores."

"How long will a fix take?"

"About three months—we have to get updated database software from a vendor, and to install it we have to update the API the billing software uses."

"OK, but hurry—these flaws have gotten lots of attention. I don't think we have much time."

So—if you're the CIO, what do you do? Break the company, or risk an attack? (Again, this is an imaginary conversation.)

That patching is so hard is very unfortunate. Solving it is a research question. Vendors are doing what they can to improve the reliability of patches, but it's a really, really difficult problem.

QUESTIONS

1. Look back over the materials discussed earlier in this chapter and consider how they related to the material in this section. Are the "rough consensus and running code" and "move fast and break things" models, which drove the innovation that built most of the technological infrastructure of modern society worth all of the technical debt that it incurs? Does this approach lead us to a point where all of our innovative energy will be focused on incremental fixes to address newly discover bugs and security flaws, refactoring pieces of software one by one?

2. Who should bear the cost of technical debt? The Bellovin excerpt suggests that firms incur substantial costs testing and deploying patches to fix buggy software. Does it make sense that these costs should be borne by customers instead of the developers of the buggy software? If the costs were borne by the developers, would any software be developed? How should this affect how we think about liability for buggy or defective software?

3. How would you describe the concept of technical debt to executive leaders to convince them to invest in cybersecurity?

4. A recent Ponemon Institute study on the cost of data breaches estimates the cost of a data breach at around $3.6 million per 20,000 records, at an occurrence of once every two years. How might this information help you make a persuasive case to implement a $50,000 security solution for a strategic system?

5. Remediation, or corrective action, after a system has been built can be as much as three times as expensive as building it correctly the first time. Although logically it might make more sense to spend less money at the outset, there may be business reasons why an organization may opt not to invest. What might some of those legitimate reasons be?

6. Think back to the discussion of hackers and their motivations in Chapter 4, as well as the materials from Sections A and C of this chapter. Is technical debt something that is necessarily incurred as part of a responsible engineering strategy? Does it reflect a juvenile, or perhaps merely adolescent (in a non-pejorative, "in the process of growing up"), aspect of software development? Is technical debt incurred as a necessary but unfortunate aspect of competitive markets and business forces?

E. CONSIDERING THE INTERDISCIPLINARY STRUGGLES OF CYBERSECURITY

One of the key issues in cybersecurity—indeed, a defining theme of this book—relates to the different perspectives experts bring to policy discussions. Much like the perspectives described in this text, when technologists, lawyers, and business leaders discuss potential policy choices, often they do not speak the same language. Bruce Schneier describes this challenge in the following excerpt.

BRUCE SCHNEIER, *TECHNOLOGISTS VS. POLICY MAKERS*

18 IEEE 72 (Jan. 21, 2020)

Sometime around 1993 or 1994, during the first Crypto Wars, I was part of a group of cryptography experts that went to Washington to advocate for strong encryption. Matt Blaze and Ron Rivest were with me; I don't remember who else. We met with then Massachusetts Representative Ed Markey. (He didn't become a senator until 2013.) Back then, he and Vermont Senator Patrick Leahy were the most knowledgeable on this issue and our biggest supporters against government backdoors. They still are.

Markey was against forcing encrypted phone providers to implement the NSA's Clipper Chip in their devices, but wanted us to reach a compromise with the FBI regardless. This completely startled us techies, who thought having the right answer was enough. It was at that moment that I learned an important difference between technologists and policy makers. Technologists want solutions; policy makers want consensus[. . .]

Over that time, I have observed many other differences between technologists and policy makers—differences that we in cybersecurity need to understand if we are to translate our technological solutions into viable policy outcomes.

Technologists don't try to consider all of the use cases of a given technology. We tend to build something for the uses we envision, and hope that others can figure out new and innovative ways to extend what we created. We love it when there is a new use for a technology that we never considered and that changes the world. And while we might be good at security around the use cases we envision, we are regularly blindsided when it comes to new uses or edge cases. (Authentication risks surrounding someone's intimate partner is a good example.)

Policy doesn't work that way; it's specifically focused on use. It focuses on people and what they do. Policy makers can't create policy around a piece of technology without understanding how it is used—how all of it's used.

Policy is often driven by exceptional events, like the FBI's desire to break the encryption on the San Bernardino shooter's iPhone. (The PATRIOT Act is the most egregious example I can think of.) Technologists tend to look at more general use cases, like the overall value of strong encryption to societal security. Policy tends to focus on the past, making existing systems work or correcting wrongs that have happened. It's hard to imagine policy makers creating laws around VR systems, because they don't yet exist in any meaningful way. Technology is inherently future focused. Technologists try to imagine better systems, or future flaws in present systems, and work to improve things.

As technologists, we iterate. It's how we write software. It's how we field products. We know we can't get it right the first time, so we have developed all sorts of agile systems to deal with that fact. Policy making is often the opposite. U.S. federal laws take months or years to negotiate and pass, and after that the issue doesn't get addressed again for a decade or more. It is much more critical to get it right the first time, because the effects of getting it wrong are long lasting. (See, for example, parts of the GDPR.) Sometimes regulatory agencies can be more agile. The courts can also iterate policy, but it's slower.

Along similar lines, the two groups work in very different time frames. Engineers, conditioned by Moore's law, have long thought of 18 months as the maximum time to roll out a new product, and now think in terms of continuous deployment of new features. As I said previously, policy makers tend to think in terms of multiple years to get a law or regulation in place, and then more years as the case law builds up around it so everyone knows what it really means. It's like tortoises and hummingbirds.

Technology is inherently global. It is often developed with local sensibilities according to local laws, but it necessarily has global reach. Policy is always jurisdictional. This difference is causing all sorts of problems for the global cloud services we use every day. The providers are unable to operate their global systems in compliance with more than 200 different—and sometimes conflicting—national requirements. Policy makers are often unimpressed with claims of inability; laws are laws, they say, and if Facebook can translate its website into French for the French, it can also implement their national laws.

Technology and policy both use concepts of trust, but differently. Technologists tend to think of trust in terms of controls on behavior. We're getting better—NIST's recent work on trust is a good example—but we have a long way to go. For example, Google's Trust and Safety Department does a lot of AI and ethics work largely focused on technological controls. Policy makers think of trust in more holistic societal terms: trust in institutions, trust as the ability not to worry about adverse outcomes, consumer confidence. This dichotomy explains how techies can claim bitcoin is trusted because of the strong cryptography, but policy makers can't imagine calling a system trustworthy when you lose all your money if you forget your encryption key.

Policy is how society mediates how individuals interact with society. Technology has the potential to change how individuals interact with society. The conflict between these two causes considerable friction, as technologists want policy makers to get out of the way and not stifle innovation, and policy maker s want technologists to stop moving fast and breaking so many things.

Finally, techies know that code is law that the restrictions and limitations of a technology are more fundamental than any human-created legal anything. Policy makers know that law is law, and tech is just tech. We can see this in the tension between applying existing law to new technologies and creating new law specifically for those new technologies.

Yes, these are all generalizations and there are exceptions. It's also not all either/or. Great technologists and policy makers can see the other perspectives. The best policy makers know that for all their work toward consensus, they won't make progress by redefining pi as three. Thoughtful technologists look beyond the immediate user demands to the ways attackers might abuse their systems, and design against those adversaries as well. These aren't two alien species engaging in first contact, but cohorts who can each learn and borrow tools from the other. Too often, though, neither party tries.

In October, I attended the first ACM Symposium on Computer Science and the Law. Google counsel Brian Carver talked about his experience with the few computer science grad students who would attend his Intellectual Property and Cyberlaw classes every year at UC Berkeley. One of the first things he would do was give the students two different cases to read. The cases had nearly identical facts, and the judges who'd ruled on them came to exactly opposite conclusions. The law students took this in stride; it's the way the legal system works when it's wrestling with a new concept or idea. But it shook the computer science students. They were appalled that there wasn't a single correct answer.

But that's not how law works, and that's not how policy works. As the technologies we're creating become more central to society, and as we in technology continue to move into the public sphere and become part of the increasingly important policy debates, it is essential that we learn these lessons. Gone are the days when we were creating purely technical systems and our work ended at the keyboard and screen. Now we're building complex socio-technical systems that are literally creating a new world. And while it's easy to dismiss policy makers as doing it wrong, it's important to understand that they're not. Policy making has been around a lot longer than the Internet or computers or any technology. And the essential challenges of this century will require both groups to work together.

CHAPTER 10

RISK AND THE LAW

■ ■ ■

As we began to discuss in Chapter 6, cybersecurity as a legal theme applies to a variety of legal focus areas as well as, in a coextensive government of state and federal jurisdiction, both state and federal courts. Cybersecurity triggers state common law (specifically tort, contract, and shareholder derivative actions), state statutes, federal statutes, constitutional issues, and administrative government behavior. In this chapter, we will explore the current state and potential issues of these specific subject matter areas.

As you may recall, the common law develops through judicial decision-making on cases. The common law (such as real property law, torts contracts, and a few others), consists of two aspects: 1) state law that specifies what a plaintiff must successfully argue to carry their case, which is informed by common legal frameworks and code,[1] and 2) judicial interpretation of the present case in the context of state law.

For example, for a plaintiff to successfully argue a case, they must satisfy *prima facie* (prime-ah fae-shuh or prime-ah fae-zha) case requirements. Prima facie case requirements are specified in the state law, but whether or not the actual evidence supports these requirements is usually a question of judicial determination or determination by a jury.

Consider this negligence case: the plaintiff was walking on the sidewalk and begins to pass the defendant's home. The plaintiff slips and breaks her arm. The plaintiff would like to recover her medical fees as well as the lost income directly resulting from not being able to work as a server at a popular restaurant (which requires use of both of her arms). A negligence case, under the state of Yorkfornia, requires the following prima facie case "prongs" or requirements be satisfied: 1) the reasonable defendant, from the perspective of a similarly situated party, has some duty to do or refrain from doing something, 2) the defendant did or failed to do something that resulted in breaching that duty, 3) the defendant's

---

[1] For example, state law usually is built, at least in part, from restatements and uniform codes. The Uniform Commercial Code (UCC) is a common code that informs some commercial transactions, such as sales of good, leases of goods, and secured interests (such as what must be secured and how) for loans. Restatements are similarly discussed and developed by legal experts on specific subjects, such as torts or contracts. These restatements and codes are considered directly by legislatures reviewing and potentially making changes to state law. For this reason, the UCC and restatements are not binding on states to actually pass. Instead, they give some consistency from state to state.

breach of duty is the but-for (causal reason) cause of the plaintiff breaking her arm and also the legal cause of the plaintiff breaking her arm, 4) the plaintiff sustains an injury that is the cause of the defendant.

These prima facie case requirements are established via state law. However, how the actions of the defendant are evaluated is a matter of common law. For example, at some point in the law's history, a court determined that a reasonable duty for a homeowner was to keep a sidewalk in front of the home clear of ice. Although the prima facie case requirements do not change if the plaintiff is claiming negligence on the part of the defendant (duty, breach of duty, causation, injury), the way these prongs are interpreted might be. For example, what if the defendant had cleaned some of the ice off the sidewalk and applied salt to the rest, but it wasn't quite enough to fully remove the ice from the sidewalk? What if the sidewalk was under construction and blocked? Each of these scenarios could potentially change the outcome of the case. However, determining that a defendant has a general duty to clear ice from a common sidewalk in front of the defendant's home then becomes precedent for later cases. The next time the court determines a similar case, the defendant will need to overcome this precedent within that same court, which may be difficult.

The same concept of the common law's development applies to other common law cases. Similarly, even though contract law has a long history and state laws that establish a prima facie case for breach of contract, as discussed in more detail in section B.1, below, the question of whether a terms of use (TOU) document is considered enforceable as a contract between a platform user and the platform (e.g., an Instagram user and Instagram) is a question of the common law. Once resolved, the decision becomes precedent in that jurisdiction.

Cybersecurity complicates traditional notions of tort, contract, and principles of business law (such as shareholder actions).[2] As you might imagine, the biggest challenge is the virtual nature of nearly all issues that might give rise to a cause of action; the loss of something that is not tangible, like data, is hard to determine as an injury in many circumstances. However, as you now know, data also has tremendous value, especially if it is used to conduct business operations or if it is identifiable with respect to an individual. Unfortunately, the law has simply not caught up with this new world yet. But it will, either through the common law, one decision and one jurisdiction at a time, or by statute.

Rather than taking the common law approach, states and the federal government have tried to adapt quickly to new technology by creating specific statutes with respect to data. Further, administrative agencies

---

[2] The creation of a business entity, such as an LLC or Corporation, is a question of state law—usually the state government's secretary of state is responsible for business registration. For this reason, much of the law related to business conduct is at the state law level, although the federal government also regulates business (as we will see later in this chapter).

have clamored to be involved in regulating these behaviors. As you navigate the remainder of this chapter, ask yourself whether the current state of cybersecurity law is as it should be. Do you think this cornucopia of laws is the appropriate way to regulate this type of behavior? How might the law improve with respect to what you already know about cybersecurity and organizational behavior?

A. THE COMMON LAW OF TORT

Although we discuss cybersecurity as a distinct field from privacy law, data breach liability is one area where there is considerable cross-over. For tort, usually cybersecurity issues will fall into one of three categories: 1) negligence, 2) negligence per se, or 3) products liability.[3] Negligence is the common law version of "fault" and injury as described in the introduction to this chapter. We pursue negligence actions when someone does something that hurts us and we believe they are at fault. Negligence does not mean that someone has intended to harm us; rather negligence is a question of burden, asking: when someone is injured, was a defendant in a position do or not do something that would have prevented the injury, so much so that we would determine that the defendant (a person or an organization) has a duty? Is this even a tort (wrong) the law will recognize?

If this wrong is one that logically extends from previous definitions of tort, the underlying legal perspective for tort is that the law enables a plaintiff, assuming a prima facie case is proven, to return to the position they were in *before* the tort occurred. From this perspective, any compensation provided to the plaintiff is tied to returning the plaintiff to the position prior to the tort, what is called compensatory damages (or damages to compensate, directly, the plaintiff due to direct injuries). However, for tort, courts also have the ability to award punitive damages, or damages designed to curb future "bad" or egregious behavior. These damages are at the discretion of the court, and these can result in plaintiffs receiving more than they requested and defendants paying more than expected. In response to significant monetary judgments, especially with class action lawsuits (where multiple plaintiffs sue due to similarities in circumstances and injuries, including the same defendant, in cases), legislatures have sought to cap overall tort awards, so-called tort reform.

Many of these issues and ideas were introduced in Chapter 6. The discussion below further builds on them and considers the application of several specific legal doctrines that affect the availability of legal claims relating to cybersecurity incidents.

---

[3] Other torts include, for example, intentional harms, such as battery and trespass (to both land and personal property), infliction of emotional distress (IEED, and dignitary torts such as defamation and privacy-related torts (e.g., intrusion upon inclusion).

1. TYPES OF TORT: NEGLIGENCE VS. PRODUCTS LIABILITY

Although most legal commentators acknowledge that the tort system operates for important purposes, often scholars debate the merits of what are called *ex ante* and *ex post* systems in encouraging "good" behavior. For example, it is acknowledged that when plaintiffs must experience some injury to recover, *ex post*, or in a court of law, the damage has already been done. Although some plaintiffs can recover, even those who receive some award are not really "made whole." Rather, they are offered financial compensation for something that cannot really be taken back. Legal systems focused on *ex ante* solutions to problems establish requirements upfront and often rely on administrative agencies to ensure these requirements are met so that downstream injuries are less likely to occur.

Some systems include both *ex ante* and *ex post* approaches. These are usually statutes that permit a private right of action, or the ability of an individual to enforce the statute in a court of law against a defendant. These statutes usually relate to negligence actions, making a *negligence per se* cause of action, rather than just negligence. As described above, negligence requires the plaintiff to establish, as part of the prima facie case requirements, that the defendant had some duty and breached that duty. The benefit of a negligence per se action is that the plaintiff does not need to establish duty because the duty is established in statute and that, according to the evidence, the defendant did not fulfill that duty.

A third and common tort option is a products liability lawsuit. Products liability is distinctly different than negligence in that the prima facie case primarily requires establishing: 1) the organization manufactures a specific product, 2) the product had a defect in from design or manufacture, and 3) the defect caused the plaintiff's injury, whether a defect resulted from the defendant's design or manufacturing processes.

The fourth tort option often described in relation to cybersecurity and data is strict liability. Strict liability is often used when there is an inherent asymmetry in knowledge that causes individuals to have significantly more risk of real injury. Often, strict liability is also used in situations where the result of engaging in certain activities is unknown. Usually, strict liability is used for ultrahazardous activities, such as large-scale building demolitions involving explosive material.

Consider the following descriptions of these tort prima facie case requirements in Table 1 for a comparison:

	Negligence	Negligence per se	Products Liability	Strict Liability
Duty	Established from the "reasonable person/organization" perspective, except where there is some special duty, e.g., doctors to their patients	Established by statute. The legislature establishes what negligence means under the law, usually not doing something prescribed	Manufacturers have a general duty to reasonably design and manufacture products free from defect (absent other special requirements for specific products)	None. Facts demonstrate organization is involved in certain types of activities defined by statute
Plaintiff's Responsibility	To generally avoid known and obvious dangers, signage, etc.	Within the class of people intended to be protected by the law	To use product as designed, pursuant to labeling and associated documentation	None
Causation	But-for (factual) causation—breach of duty causes injury AND proximate causation (defendant actually responsible—e.g., no intervening, unforeseeable cause)	But-for (factual) causation—breach of duty causes injury AND proximate causation (defendant actually responsible—e.g., no intervening, unforeseeable cause)	Product was but-for cause of injury AND proximate causation (defendant actually responsible—e.g., no intervening, unforeseeable cause)	Defendant was engaged in statutorily defined or ultrahazardous activities and plaintiff was injured (defendant actually responsible—e.g., no intervening, unforeseeable cause)
Injury	Meets Article III standing requirements, state injury requirements	Meets standing requirements, may be relaxed per *Spokeo, Inc. v. Robbins*, 578 U.S. (2016)	Meets Article III standing requirements, state injury requirements	Meets Article III standing requirements, state injury requirements

Table 1: Common Tort Actions

For cybersecurity, each of these torts is challenging for a variety of reasons. In most contexts where torts occur (that is, where a potential plaintiff has been injured), the hardest questions what duty the defendant may have owed to the plaintiff and whether that duty was breached by the defendant. The injury in most cases is relatively obvious, as is the fact that the defendant's conduct caused that injury. For instance, where a driver injures a pedestrian, a consumer is injured by a poorly designed power tool, or a contractor damages a client's property, there is little question of what whether there are damages or how they were caused—the hard question is who is responsible for them (that is, who had a duty to avoid them, or assumed the liability should they come to pass).

For reasons that will become clear in the materials below, questions of injury and causation can predominate in cases relating to cybersecurity. As a result, we start our discussion with questions of injury (under the heading of "standing," which is a legal inquiry that asks whether a party was injured in a way that the law is able to remedy), and then turn to questions of causation and other related topics. The issue of duty is addressed later in this chapter in the context of the FTC's *LabMD* litigation, which involves questions over the meaning of "reasonable" security precautions.

Felix Wu discusses questions of standing in the excerpt below.

2. STANDING

FELIX WU, *HOW PRIVACY DISTORTED STANDING LAW*

66 DEPAUL L. REV. 440 (2017)

The Supreme Court[, in *Spokeo, Inc. v. Robbins*, 136 S.Ct. 1540 (2016),] has held that under Article III, the judicial power of the federal courts extends only to cases and controversies in which the plaintiff can establish an "irreducible constitutional minimum of standing." Article III standing requires the plaintiff to demonstrate the following:

First, the plaintiff must have suffered an "injury in fact"—an invasion of a legally protected interest which is (a) concrete and particularized, and (b) "actual or imminent, not 'conjectural' or 'hypothetical.' " Second, there must be a causal connection between the injury and the conduct complained of—the injury has to be "fairly . . . trace[able] to the challenged action of the defendant, and not . . . th[e] result [of] the independent action of some third party not before the court." Third, it must be "likely," as opposed to merely "speculative," that the injury will be "redressed by a favorable decision."

The Supreme Court has treated Article III standing as a trans-substantive requirement that must be met in every case. Defenders of this view see the doctrine of standing as indispensable to an appropriate separation of powers. Standing keeps the federal courts in check, ensuring that the courts are used only to protect individual rights and not to decide broad issues that are better left to the legislative and executive branches.

Other commentators have argued that standing should be properly understood as a determination on the merits of whether a particular plaintiff has a valid cause of action under a particular law. [. . .]

In analyzing standing in a privacy case, the Supreme Court had, until recently, continued this pattern of focusing on whether the plaintiff was affected, rather than on the nature of the effects. In Clapper v. Amnesty International USA, the Court denied standing to a group of plaintiffs seeking to challenge the constitutionality of surveillance authorized under section 702 of the Foreign Intelligence Surveillance Act (FISA). The crux of the problem for the plaintiffs was that they were unable to show that their particular communications would actually be acquired by the government through a section 702 order. In the absence of any information about who the government targets under this program (information that the government obviously tries to keep secret), the Court deemed the plaintiffs' assertions that their communications would be targeted to be "highly speculative."

Implicit in the Court's reasoning in Clapper is that if the plaintiffs had been able to show that their communications had been acquired, then that acquisition would have been a sufficient injury for standing purposes. The Court traced a chain of inferences that underlie the plaintiffs' argument for standing, starting with the government "decid[ing] to target the communications of non-U.S. persons with whom [the plaintiffs] communicate" and ending with the plaintiffs being "parties to the particular communications that the Government intercepts." At no point did the Court suggest that perhaps even the interception would not be enough.

It is true that the Court in Clapper did find one kind of harm not to be cognizable—namely, the plaintiffs' "fear of surveillance" and the steps the plaintiffs took in response to that fear. In the absence of information about how the government chooses surveillance targets, however, that fear arises from the existence of the program itself, rather than anything the government has actually done under the program. In theory that fear could be equally applicable to anyone. Thus, as in Laird, the Court's refusal to recognize such fears can be understood as a version of its refusal to recognize generalized harms. To be sure, perhaps the Court should have been more willing to acknowledge what everyone knows: Government surveillance programs are more likely to target some kinds of communications than others. Moreover, perhaps the unique dangers of surveillance warrant a rule in which broadly shared chilling effects ought to suffice to establish standing. The point here is that even if Clapper was wrongly decided, it did not represent a sharp departure from the Court's prior standing law.

In contrast, lower courts deciding privacy cases began to shift the standing inquiry in a more substantial way, toward an evaluation of whether certain harms are cognizable and away from primarily determining whether those harms have occurred or will occur to the plaintiff. For example, in Reilly v. Ceridian Corp., an unknown hacker infiltrated the defendant's computer systems and potentially gained access to the plaintiffs' personal information, including social security numbers, dates of birth, and bank account information. The plaintiffs sued, asserting a number of state common law and statutory causes of action. The Third Circuit held that the plaintiffs lacked Article III standing because they had made only "allegations of hypothetical, future injury," which were "insufficient."

In justifying its conclusion, the court in Reilly cited Lyons and Lujan and described a chain of inappropriately speculative inferences that plaintiffs needed to make in order to allege harm, much as in Clapper. But whereas the Clapper chain ended with the government's acquisition of the plaintiffs' communications, the chain in Reilly started with the unauthorized acquisition and ended with the use of "such information to the detriment of Appellants by making unauthorized transactions in Appellants' names." In other words, the court assumed that the mere acquisition of personal information was not a cognizable injury and that instead, unauthorized use was required to establish Article III standing.

The Third Circuit in Reilly further asserted that "[i]n data breach cases where no misuse is alleged, . . . there has been no injury—indeed, no change in the status quo." The court then used this assertion to distinguish cases involving medical malpractice or toxic torts. If intended as a factual claim, the assertion is surely false. The status quo has changed because some unauthorized individual now has access to information that he or she previously did not have access to. To make sense of the assertion, one must read it as a legal conclusion: There has been no change in any status quo that the law recognizes. The opinion in Reilly, however, did little to defend such a novel conclusion.

Nor does a case like Reilly fit into the paradigm of courts rejecting harms as too generalized. The plaintiffs in data breach cases are the ones whose data has been breached. They are suing because they are directly affected by whatever unlawful actions led to the breach and not merely because they are citizens asserting a right to live in a society free of unlawful actions. The harms they are asserting are individual harms, not societal ones. This remains true even in contexts in which large databases are amassed or breached, and thus many individuals are affected. [. . .]

To be sure, reversing the trend and broadly recognizing injuries for standing purposes may not make much difference to the outcomes of many privacy cases. This is because a showing of damages is required as an element of many of the substantive claims brought in privacy and security cases, and "injury-in-fact" sufficient for standing may not be sufficient to show "damages" in the underlying claim. Thus, for example, in the Ninth Circuit, which has often adopted relatively permissive standing rules, data breach plaintiffs have just as often failed on the merits, even after surpassing the standing hurdle.

Nevertheless, it is important to distinguish properly between rejecting the plaintiff's claim on the merits and rejecting it for want of Article III standing. The former is a legislative matter, while the latter is a judicial one. When the underlying cause of action is based in state common law, the merits question is ultimately one for the state common law courts.

Similarly, when the cause of action is a statutory one, the merits question is a matter of statutory interpretation. Article III standing is a constitutional question on which the federal courts have the last say and which is ultimately not a matter of statutory interpretation, at least as the Supreme Court has conceived of the doctrine. Thus, plaintiffs whose state law claims fail on the merits can seek to change the law through state courts or through legislatures, while plaintiffs whose claims fail on Article III standing grounds cannot seek to change the law in the same way. Using Article III standing as a substitute for a merits determination shifts the locus of control over the development of the law. [. . .]

Courts have not been clear about precisely what they mean in saying that standing serves the goal of separation of powers, but the basic idea seems to be to distinguish between resolving individual disputes—the province of courts—and resolving social policy questions—the province of the political branches. In *Lujan*, for example, the court wrote:

Whether the courts were to act on their own, or at the invitation of Congress, in ignoring the concrete injury requirement described in our cases, they would be discarding a principle fundamental to the separate and distinct constitutional role of the Third Branch—one of the essential elements that identifies those "Cases" and "Controversies" that are the business of the courts rather than of the political branches. "The province of the court," as Chief Justice Marshall said in *Marbury v. Madison*, "is, solely, to decide on the rights of individuals." Vindicating the public interest (including the public interest in Government observance of the Constitution and laws) is the function of Congress and the Chief Executive.

The vast majority of privacy and security cases, though, are indeed ones involving individual rights, not merely broad questions of public interest. Almost invariably, privacy plaintiffs are specific individuals who claim that their own personal information has been mishandled in some way. That mishandling then provides the factual basis for their legal claims under statutory or common law.

When courts deny standing in these cases on the basis of the injuries being insufficiently concrete, they are not deciding whether the cases are ones that concern individual rights, but rather deciding the substantive content of those rights. Far from supporting an appropriate separation of powers, this move amounts to a usurpation of legislative power by the federal judiciary.

Consider again the Seventh Circuit's decision in *Gubala*, finding the unlawful retention of data to be an insufficiently concrete injury. The court supported its holding by claiming that "otherwise the federal courts would be flooded with cases based not on proof of harm but on an implausible and at worst trivial risk of harm." But where did the court get the authority to reject the case for fear of being "flooded"? Such a judgment is a quintessentially legislative one. Surely the federal courts could not, on their own accord, decide that they were being flooded with trivial class action cases and thereby impose some additional requirements on class actions, something that Congress of course can do (and has done). Similarly, common law courts often take into account the potential for a flood of cases in deciding whether to recognize new causes of action or how far to extend certain duties. But the federal courts are not common law courts. Under the Constitution, Congress gets to decide whether or not to flood the federal courts. For the federal courts to make this decision is to upend the constitutional order.

The reality of standing is that it, along with pleading standards (or the content of the claims brought when a plaintiff begins a lawsuit), are the initial barriers to successfully bringing a case. If a plaintiff cannot successfully clear these two barriers, the merits of a case cannot be heard in court. The overall effect is that standing has created a near-impossible barrier for consumer plaintiffs to bring cases following data breaches. What is standing in the way of demonstrating injury? First, a federal statute caps credit card damages for fraud, and usually credit card issuers and banks do not collect for fraudulent charges because they can write them off for tax credit and are a usual part of business. Historically, credit card fraud schemes have been the most frequent result of data breaches.

However, data breaches are not only a question of credit card data. Under some circumstances, data breaches result in loss of other personal information, such as social security numbers, health data, or employment information. They may also result in loss of critical business information from a third party. In the latest case, it may be much easier to put a dollar amount of the specific loss. Courts have largely resisted a direct loss of information as injury in and of itself for personal information. Often, this is because courts identify injury related to economic compensability, which is established by common law losses over time.

However, injury isn't necessarily impossible to identify in terms of compensation: we can put a cost on losing a limb in a car accident or a missing organ due to medical malpractice, and yet the courts are unwilling to identify a cost associated with data loss in and of itself. When injury is sufficient to demonstrate standing, typically this is in relation to secondary impacts—for example, loss of employment or direct economic losses. Despite these challenges, another significant challenge relates to causation as a common prong across all four tort actions previously discussed.

3. CAUSATION

The nature of cybersecurity complicates causation, as well. Causation requires two steps: first, the plaintiff must prove that the breach of duty was the "but-for" cause of the plaintiff's injury. But-for causation is factual causation, or whether or not factually the breach of duty caused the plaintiff's injury. Legal causation, or proximate cause, is a bit more complicated. It requires a court to determine whether, despite the breach of duty causing the plaintiff's injury, the defendant can be held legally responsible for the plaintiff's injury. Consider a simple example: a car is driving down the road, and a cyclist hits a sizable pothole the city has not filled, throwing the cyclist into the car's path. The car strikes the cyclist. In this example, it is undisputed that the car is the but-for cause of the cyclist's injuries. It is clear: the car hit the cyclist. However, legally, we want to ask more questions: was the cyclist in a bicycle lane? Was the cyclist cycling appropriately and wasn't under the influence? Did the cyclist reasonably avoid the pothole?

The car didn't just hit a cyclist in the normal course of driving down the street. The car was driving, the cyclist hit the pothole, then the car struck the cyclist. These other factors complicate legal causation. Now imagine a more complex version of the facts: the driver is continuing down the street, not paying attention to the street lights, which have turned red. The driver hits another car that properly enters the intersection. The driver then hits the car that entered the intersection legally, which pushes the car into the bike lane, hitting the cyclist. In this case, the cyclist is suing the first driver, the driver that entered the intersection illegally, for his injuries. Although the driver is the but-for cause of his injuries, there is some question as to the causative chain. The driver did not actually hit the cyclist. The car legally entering the intersection was an *intervening cause* that caused the cyclist to be hit. In this case, can we still hold the first driver liable for setting this process in motion?

Certainly, we may feel the first driver is blameworthy for engaging in dangerous driving—in this case, not abiding by traffic lights. Yet, the question of whether the first driver should be held accountable in a tort action when an intervening cause actually causes the injury is a question of foreseeability. The court must ask: was the intervening cause (here, the second car) reasonably foreseeable from the perspective of the defendant? Here, in running a red light, it likely would be foreseeable that another car would enter the intersection, and that likely some injury or accident would result. The plaintiff does not need to prove that his specific injuries and the specific events were foreseeable, only that some injury was reasonably foreseeable.

For the time being, let's set aside any legal challenges related to injury and what is or is not injury related to data. One of the main issues with cybersecurity-related legal actions is related to causation evidence. Adversaries are usually good at covering their tracks, which means that it may be tremendously difficult, even in the event of an incident or data breach, to determine the exact cause. Usually some of the threat vectors used to attack a system may be discovered, while others might not. Why might this be? Generally, newer technologies have the ability to store and, if properly secured, prevent deletion of historical records, including who, when, and from where a system might have been accessed. However, legacy technologies often do not include such records; one of your casebook authors recalls a specific system that relied only on shared IDs and passwords, used to store sensitive data. For these reasons, it may be difficult to put together the specific events that resulted in the incident.

The second issue is related to the nature of foreseeability. In all, the biggest challenge is that although the defendant did collect, store, retain, transmit, duplicate, or erase plaintiff data, the defendant did not breach its own systems. Rather, an intervening cause in nearly any cyberattack scenario is the cyberattacker! If a plaintiff is arguing negligence or another tort, it is premised on the belief that the defendant is both the but-for and proximate cause of the plaintiff's injury.

One of the most interesting areas for tort is the Internet of Things (IoT). IoT are consumer devices that connect to the Internet, and these devices have a variety of inherent risks related to privacy or discriminatory impact as well as cybersecurity risk. They are unique from a tort perspective specifically because they blend both the intangible aspects of data transmission across the Internet, including, for example data valuable to an adversary, with a physical device that could cause a physical manifestation of a virtual attack.

IoT, unlike online services, have an inherent physicality, meaning that *cyberkinetic* attacks are possible. Cyberkinetic attacks are cyberattacks that have a physical outcome. For example, a Nest home thermostat, if hacked, could potentially lower the temperature of a home, causing the pipes to freeze and explode, costing tens of thousands or more of damage. The hacker of an Internet-connected oven could exceed the temperature beyond its normal limits by instructing the ovens computer system to keep heating even after the oven has hit a desired temperature, causing a fire that could injure people or damage property.

And IoT do not just include household goods, as described in the earlier excerpt. IoT include IoHT, the Internet of Health Things,[4] including medical devices.[5] We refer to Internet-enabled devices within critical industrial infrastructure as the IIoT, the Industrial Internet of Things, which include distributed computerized nuclear power plants, wind turbine farms, dams, and electrical grids.[6]

Sometimes, the statutory legal definition i of critical infrastructure actually includes health services, such as pervasively connected medical

---

[4] Nicolas P. Terry, *Will the Internet of Things Transform Healthcare?* 19 VAND. J. ENT. & TECH. L. 327, 333–34, http://www.jetlaw.org/wp-content/uploads/2017/02/Terry-Final.pdf.

[5] Charlotte A. Tschider, Annals Health Law

[6] GE DIGITAL, *Everything you need to know about the Industrial Internet of Things* (2020), https://www.ge.com/digital/blog/everything-you-need-know-about-industrial-internet-things.

devices. In both of these important areas, physicality is everything. In fact, frequently the adversarial threat source's motivation is *precisely* to affect some physical function of the target device(s). It is for these specific areas that the concepts of data integrity and availability have even more importance: if a dam's control is severed completely, how will the dam be managed appropriately? If the message delivered to a patient's neurostimulation implant directs the implant to increase the electrical pulse frequency at a higher dosage, the patient will likely be injured.

The purpose of describing the current state of the IoT, especially for consumer devices, is two-fold. First, although frequently legal commentators focus on the role of terms of use and discuss online services in relation to cybersecurity, Internet-connected physical machines may pose more risk of physical injury or property damage. Second, security employed in these devices is not disclosed in specifications or similar paperwork included in the box upon purchase, so a consumer is not able to effectively evaluate potential cybersecurity safety issues.

REBECCA CROOTOF, *THE INTERNET OF TORTS*

69 DUKE L. J. 583 (2019)

While there is no agreed-upon definition for the "Internet of Things," everyone can agree there are a lot of them. And the already mind-boggling number of internet-connected devices is expected to skyrocket as companies slap sensors and wireless capabilities onto more and more items. A 2015 McKinsey Report estimated that "there are more than nine billion connected devices around the world, including smartphones and computers," and that by 2025 there may be somewhere between twenty-five to fifty billion such devices. Others predict that there will be more than one trillion IoT devices by 2025. As this Article considers the problem of consumer harm, it focuses on the millions of IoT devices marketed for individual or household use rather than public or industrial IoT systems, such as smart city or factory logistical, monitoring, or maintenance systems. This subset of IoT devices represents a significant percentage of the IoT ecosystem: it is estimated to have an economic impact of $370 billion to $1.9 trillion per year by 2025.

An IoT device's distinctive fusion of traits—its ability to collect personal data, its capacity for ongoing communication with an IoT company, and its physicality—combine to form a product that is simultaneously an object and a service. An IoT speaker might double as a smart-home hub or link with a voice-activated, cloud-based service to provide requested content. A smart thermostat develops customized energy-saving heating plans and a monthly energy report. An internet-connected vehicle offers built-in navigation, roadside assistance, or real-time alerts regarding engine, emission, or airbag status. Water bottles can track your daily water intake, egg monitors can send reminders that eggs are going bad, and tires can alert you if they become deflated. Medical wearables and implantables allow for better drug management and the early identification of a need for intervention.

As a result . . . when you engage with an IoT device, you do more than just use an item; you enter into an ongoing and surprisingly intimate relationship with an IoT company, characterized by a new power dynamic—and a new risk of property and bodily harm. [. . .]

IoT devices are "embodied": they have a presence in and ability to interact with the physical world. And with physicality comes the possibility of physical harm. Consider the relatively innocuous Roomba, an autonomous vacuum-cleaning robot. In addition to cleaning untold numbers of floors, one Roomba caused the Pooptastrophe; another "attacked" its sleeping owner; and a third destroyed itself on a hot plate and, due to the resulting smoke damage, left its owner homeless. While there might be disagreement about where fault lies in each of these scenarios, the overarching point is that IoT devices' physicality alters and magnifies the harm potential of remote interference. The remote deletion of your music file or e-book might frustrate you; the remote disabling of your security alarm, car, or implantable medical device could kill you.

The possibilities for potential injuries are limited only by the item's damage potential. A disabled smart thermostat could allow a house to become so hot or cold that plumbing, pets, and potentially even people could be harmed. Pacemakers, insulin pumps, drug administration devices, and other wearable or implanted medical devices could affect someone's physical health, while IoT vehicles could injure or kill drivers, passengers, other drivers, and pedestrians . . .

To fully conceptualize the scope of potential harms posed by connected devices that affect our bodies and environment, however, it is worth discussing the potential physical threats posed by hacked devices. In the mad rush to be first to market, companies unaccustomed to considering cybersecurity issues are slapping sensors and transmitters on everything from Barbie dolls to Buddhist prayer beads, resulting in the neologism that "[t]he 'S' in 'IoT' stands for 'security.' " Even reputable and experienced tech companies are producing insecure products. One team of researchers was able to remotely take control of a Jeep SUV while it was being driven; another team identified flaws in Apple's HomeKit smart-home system that would have permitted hackers to unlock front doors. The insecurity of the "Internet of Things Inside Our Body" risks deadly hacks, as highlighted by Vice President Dick Cheney's decision to disable his heart implant's wireless connectivity while he was in office and the FDA-mandated recall of more than four hundred thousand pacemakers due to a cybersecurity vulnerability. Other hackers have demonstrated that it is possible to take control of smart lights and use them to induce epileptic seizures. Further, the more electrical grids, transportation services, health and medical systems, and other critical infrastructure are incorporated into the IoT ecosystem, the more likely it is that disruption of those systems will threaten human safety and national security. In June 2017, for example, the NotPetya malware attack rendered data on compromised systems completely inaccessible, forcing banks to close, hospitals to cancel operations, and the radiation monitoring system at Ukraine's Chernobyl Nuclear Power Plant to go offline.

While hackable cars, home-security systems, pacemakers, and other IoT devices certainly create problems worth addressing, the current focus on the physical risks of criminal hacks distracts from the physical risks of corporate remote interference. [. . .]

Unsurprisingly, IoT-device terms of service agreements attempt to minimize industry liability for the harms resulting from their remote interference through liability disclaimers or caps on the costs of breaches. Specific- and exclusive-remedy clauses allow companies to predetermine customer rights. For example, Nest's terms of service note that, should someone not want the company's over-the-air updates, "[their] remedy is to stop using [the Services and] the Product[s]." Meanwhile, monetary ceilings on direct damages and exclusions of special, incidental, or consequential damages also limit corporate liability.

These terms purportedly reflect the informed agreement of the contracting parties; in reality, most of these "agreements" are contracts of adhesion where unsophisticated consumers have limited information about the risks of remote interference and no opportunity to bargain, effectively allowing companies to unilaterally price harms. Given that many IoT devices are used by individuals who are not in privity of contract with the IoT company, IoT companies are reasonably trying to "find ways to 'bake' or incorporate 'the equivalent of a click-wrap' agreement into the functionality of their device," to limit corporate liability with regard to all device users. Ultimately, these contracts "launder injustice" insofar as they legitimize otherwise unfair allocations of liability.

Granted, the ability to contractually limit liability is not unbounded. While we are far from the days when courts would strike down any contractual limitation on liability for negligence, most states circumscribe a limit's application. Exculpatory clauses that limit future liability for physical injury are invalid in three states. Other states invalidate exculpatory clauses that are overly broad, are presented in complex or unclear language, attempt to waive liability for intentional acts or gross negligence, or are otherwise unconscionable or contrary to public policy. Further, under the U.C.C., clauses limiting liability for bodily harms caused by consumer goods are prima facie unconscionable, and—when litigated—courts rarely uphold such clauses.

Given the variability of these rules and many consumers' lack of access to justice, however, companies often purport to waive all claims to the extent legally possible—and then some. For instance, Tesla's warranty states that its "limitations and exclusions shall apply whether your claim is in contract, tort (including negligence and gross negligence), breach of warranty or condition, misrepresentation (whether negligent or otherwise) or otherwise at law or in equity." Some IoT contracts attempt to waive liability even for "reasonably foreseeable" harm; others induce reliance on a risk-avoidance service and then claim to waive liability when corporate remote interference results in a failure to provide that service. . .

Nor will modern courts likely find exculpatory clauses void as unconscionable in cases involving IoT devices marketed for individual or household use. As has been frequently bemoaned, "the doctrine [of unconscionability] offers little hope in the consumer goods realm." While the U.C.C. creates a strong presumption of unconscionability for IoT devices that cause bodily harm, it does not create a similar one for property damage; nor will it easily be applied when IoT devices cause bodily harm indirectly. Further, courts are generally unwilling to find commercial contracts procedurally unconscionable, particularly—as will be the case for most IoT items—where the consumer has options regarding which product to buy or where the contract circumscribes corporate liability for a recreational or frivolous activity. And even though IoT-device terms of service are often "take-it-or-leave-it" contracts, this is insufficient to establish procedural unconscionability. Meanwhile, for a provision to be found substantively unconscionable, the terms must be "shocking to the conscience," "monstrously harsh," or "exceedingly calloused"—and exculpatory clauses rarely meet this high bar. In addition to these familiar limits, remote interference introduces an additional snarl: because the unconscionability doctrine applies to the sale of goods, courts may not apply it to sales of IoT devices that bundle a good with one or more services, especially where the injury results from the cessation of a service. [. . .]

When purchased items do not operate as expected, consumers can bring breach of warranty claims grounded in express or implied warranties. Assuming an IoT company does not explicitly state that it will not remotely alter or deactivate the IoT device—indeed, most terms of service have statements to the opposite, expressly reserving the right to engage in such activities—a consumer's only possible warranty claim for harms arising from remote interference would be a violation of an implied warranty of merchantability. This generally means that the goods are "fit for the ordinary purposes for which such goods are used," are of a fair quality, and "conform to the promise or affirmations of fact made on the container or label." But breach of warranty claims for consumer harms resulting from remote interference will likely fail, either because the IoT device will be deemed incidental to the provision of a service, such that U.C.C. implied warranties will not attach, or because they are barred by contractual provisions.

Courts rarely find that devices that exist primarily to provide a service have an implied warranty of merchantability. Where a product bundles a good with a service, as is often the case for IoT devices, courts employ the predominance test to evaluate whether an implied warranty attaches; if the product's primary purpose "is the rendition of service, with goods incidentally involved," courts will generally find that there is no implied warranty of merchantability. An Amazon Echo, which "connects to Alexa to play music, make calls, set music alarms and timers, ask questions, [and] control smart home devices" might fail this test.

IoT devices that are primarily goods, like a "smart" scale, will have an implied warranty of merchantability. But savvy companies can include various provisions in their terms of service contracts to preclude breach of warranty claims for harms resulting from remote interference. This implied warranty only represents a promise about the condition of the product at the time it is sold; it does not guarantee that a product will last or operate consistently for any specific length of time, and sellers can contractually modify the warranty's time period. Furthermore, implied warranties do not address problems arising from failure to follow directions or improper maintenance; an IoT company could certainly argue that contractually prohibited tinkering or failure to install an update would constitute a failure to follow directions or engage in proper maintenance, voiding any express or implied warranty. Finally, IoT companies can include disclaimers and express warranties that circumscribe implied consumer rights. Courts tend to uphold implied warranty disclaimers and find that express warranties displace implied ones. [. . .]

Modern products liability law considers how best to allocate liability for harms arising from consumer use of a product, based on what the seller can, does, or should know about the product being sold and the foreseeable uses, misuses, and extraneous harms that might arise. Corporations cannot contract out of products liability claims, and these claims create a route of recourse for those not in privity with a company to bring suit, which will often be relevant in the IoT context. But while it is natural to look to products liability law to remedy harms caused by corporate remote interference, none of the three main products liability claims—that there is a manufacturing defect, design defect, or informational defect—map well onto these situations.

Certainly, existing products liability law can be applied to IoT devices. As with any other product, "smart" devices can be poorly designed, improperly manufactured, or inadequately labeled. When harm is caused by a design defect, manufacturing defect, or insufficient warning, it can be addressed under the appropriate standard. Further, sellers' growing information about, access to, and control over their products could significantly expand their obligations, as sellers' increased knowledge could increase their liability for design or informational defects, postsale failures to warn, and even postsale failures to update.

For claims to succeed under the consumer-expectations test, a jury must find that the product did not function as safely as a reasonable consumer might expect. Automobiles, coffee makers, and many other IoT devices do not obviously depend on the remote provision of services, and so a jury today might decide that a reasonable consumer could find certain kinds of remote interference unreasonably dangerous. However, this claim's strength depends in part on how the social norms and relevant law evolve. Even today, contractual notice of remote interference will undermine claims that the consumer did not know it was a possibility. In the longer term, it may become more commonplace for companies to affect items in our homes, which in turn may make the possibility of harmful remote interference less and less surprising—or more and more "expected."

The risk-utility test weighs a product's risk of causing harm against its expected usefulness. While this sounds objective and useful in the abstract, it is unpredictable in application when the value and damage potential of an item are both low or both high. For example, certain IoT devices, like smart fidget spinners, are neither useful nor dangerous. What would the test proscribe? Alternatively, connected automobiles, smart-home hubs, and medical devices can increase convenience or even be life-saving, but they also have a greater damage potential. Is the risk of harm worth the item's utility? Unsurprisingly, courts have tended to apply the test arbitrarily, and would likely continue to do so when evaluating harms caused by corporate remote interference.

In an attempt to increase predictability, the Restatement (Third) [of Torts] endorsed the reasonable-alternative-design test. To succeed, plaintiffs need to identify a design flaw and prove that a reasonable alternative design exists that would have reduced or eliminated the resulting harm, without increasing other kinds of harm. Whether an alternative design is reasonable requires an assessment of a host of factors, including its economic feasibility, its technological feasibility, and its effect on the product's longevity, maintenance, repair, and aesthetic. Further, a plaintiff must show that the alternative design is an actual alternative, rather than an entirely different product, as "[g]enerally, courts are unwilling to hold manufacturers liable for a defective design when the only means of making the product safer is to alter the defining characteristic of the product." For example, plaintiffs arguing that ionization smoke alarms did not provide sufficient warnings compared with smoke alarms that incorporated both ionization and photoelectric technology lost their suit; the court held that the plaintiffs' proposal was essentially a design for a different product. Nor will a product be considered defective just because it was not designed as safely as possible if the proposed alternative design requires changing a fundamental characteristic . . .

Finally, all three of the design-defect tests face a similar problem: they assume a static product design, not something that can be unilaterally altered postsale. Although courts have recognized postsale duties, they have been largely limited to a narrow duty to warn. However, the Restatement does suggest that sellers and distributers may be liable for an unreasonable failure to provide appropriate postsale warnings when they learn of a new potential risk. Accordingly, a plaintiff might argue that a company that remotely alters or curtails a device's capabilities in ways that foreseeably increase the likelihood of harm has a renewed duty to issue an updated warning. [. . .]

Would-be plaintiffs can also bring negligence claims, notwithstanding contractual terms purporting to limit them. To succeed, the plaintiff would need to show that the IoT company breached a duty of care—that it had an obligation to do or not to do something, and it did not satisfy this obligation. Depending on the case-specific facts and the analogies used, this standard may be difficult to meet in cases involving corporate remote interference.

The existence of a duty and its scope will necessarily depend on the scenario. The easiest case for finding a duty will be where an IoT device purports to reduce or mitigate the possibility of a physical harm, such as an IoT fire alarm or security system, and the device fails to render that service because of some act of remote interference. It is less clear what duty an IoT company owes a consumer who breaches a contract—say, by attempting to jailbreak a device or failing to make a required payment. It is also unclear what duty IoT companies owe consumers to ensure that their remote interference does not enable intervening sources of harms. [. . .]

The doctrine of intervening causes applies in situations where an unforeseeable act occurs and breaks the chain of causation. In *Stahlecker v. Ford Motor Company*, a woman's car failed in a remote area, and a man found, raped, and murdered her. Her parents sued the car company, alleging that the car's inoperability had caused their daughter's death. The court dismissed the case, reasoning that the murderer's actions were "independent and intervening" and that the car company "had no reason to expect intentional tortious or criminal acts by a third person." Similarly, IoT companies could argue that intervening events break the chain of causation linking their possibly negligent actions to the consumers' injuries. A company may have bricked your car while you were in an intersection, but it is the other driver that hit you. They may have deactivated your door lock, but it was the burglar who assaulted you.

The fact that there may be an intervening cause of harm, however, does not necessarily imply that the harm was unforeseeable—or that the entity that enabled it should not be held liable. In *Addis v. Steele*, for example, the court held that an inn was liable for the injuries residents suffered in a fire set by an arsonist. Although there was an intervening criminal cause of harm, the lack of an escape route created a situation where injury from a fire was foreseeable. Similarly, landlords have a duty to take measures within their power to protect tenants from intervening criminal actors and business owners have a duty to take reasonable measures to minimize the risk of foreseeable criminal acts.

These are all examples of what torts scholar Robert Rabin has termed "enabling torts": situations where, in addition to an immediate perpetrator of harm, a plaintiff has a claim against "the individual, or more often, the enterprise, that set the stage for the suffering that unfolded. The Enabler." Rabin argues that enabled torts do not depend on a relationship between the enabling defendant and the injured plaintiff; however, the existence of a relationship between IoT companies and users makes the case for liability "at least as strong if not stronger."

Ultimately, if the intervening source of harm is sufficiently foreseeable, the causation requirement linking corporate remote interference to an individual's injury is satisfied; if not, the intervening source of harm breaks the chain . . .

Not only do IoT devices enable corporate remote interference, they also mask the role of IoT companies in enabling the resulting injuries. Technology can shift responsibility from those who make decisions at a distance to those more temporally and physically close to an accident, even when the distant decision-makers had more power to minimize its likelihood or impact. This occurs in part because remote decisions are obscured by later actions and in part because courts tend to find that early users of new technology assume the risks and should shoulder the resulting harms. Sometimes this attribution is sensible, as when individuals involved in an accident are able to take steps to minimize a risk of harm; sometimes it is not, as when those immediate actors are presumed to have more power than they do. [. . .]

But won't the market solve this problem? Either consumers will purchase less safe but cheaper devices, demonstrating that the cost savings is worth the added risk, or they will forego unsafe ones, incentivizing companies to invest in developing and advertising safer products.

Unfortunately, the market for IoT devices has significant information asymmetries and failures that will prevent the invisible hand from perfecting it. First, there are the usual critiques regarding the reasonableness of assuming consumers are actually making informed purchasing decisions based on contractual terms. Also, reputational harms only attach if the company name is tied to an accident, but as noted above, technology's ability to deflect responsibility from remote decision-makers can make it difficult to link an accident to a company. Further, one technology can sometimes shield another. For example, many are aware that the first autonomous vehicle to kill a pedestrian was an Uber car; far fewer know that it was a Volvo. Additionally, rather than creating a market for safer products, the damage potential of some IoT devices might encourage industries to collectively downplay the risk of harm. Just as airlines have little incentive to market their respective safety scores to a populace with an irrational fear of crashes, autonomous vehicle companies attempting to lure skeptical buyers have little incentive to highlight their comparatively low accident rates.

IoT companies' ability to evade the reputational costs that might otherwise attend accidents has two consequences, both of which encourage a market for lemons. First, consumers cannot accurately judge which IoT devices and contracts are safer and therefore cannot make informed choices when selecting among products. Second, and consequentially, IoT companies that act with due care are unable to pass the costs of doing so onto consumers, which will discourage them from shouldering those costs in the absence of other legal incentives. Ultimately, the market disincentivizes corporate investment in designing and manufacturing safer IoT devices.

Granted, reputational costs will attach when an egregious act or spectacular accident can be tied to a particular IoT company. For example, Sonos is facing popular backlash and losing customers after announcing that customers who do not agree to policy changes that allow more intensive data gathering would not receive necessary software updates; Tesla's stock crashed following an investigation into a fatal accident.

But even a sensational story may have relatively little impact, as companies are increasingly attempting to lock consumers in proprietary ecosystems. Company X's smart toaster may receive terrible reviews, but that might not be sufficient for someone enmeshed in Company X's network to switch to Company Y's smart toaster, given that the latter could not interact with the other items in their smart kitchen. Further, "in addition to traditional forms of lock-in, personal data introduces a form of monopoly power that deepens the connection between buyer and seller. Switching opportunities are not 'just a click away' when the competitor lacks the advantages gained from years of developing personalization and knowledge about the user." These ecosystems create significant barriers to entry for market newcomers, minimizing competition that might foster the development of safer IoT devices. Ultimately, in a situation defined by power and information asymmetries and high switching costs, we cannot rely on the market to produce safe IoT devices.

Regardless of one's theory of tort law, the current situation is problematic. Under a fairness theory, IoT companies are knowingly creating nonreciprocal and therefore "unfair" risks of harm. IoT companies are also not required to make their users whole, despite the fact they bear at least partial moral responsibility for the resulting harms. And, as the costs of accidents are not being appropriately allocated, the resulting harms will not be efficiently deterred. How, then, should civil liability standards be changed to better achieve fairness, justice, and efficiency?

Now that you have thought a little more about the context of tort for Internet-connected devices and services, let's examine two scenarios to determine how causation issues might surface in cybersecurity matters.

Example 1: DataScale, Inc., offers a data aggregation service for organizations. As a third party, DataScale was providing data aggregation services to Shotwell, a national hockey retailer looking to aggregate all of its sales and merchandising data. DataScale provides access to its aggregated reporting application over the Web, and credentials are assigned to Shotwell personnel. DataScale did not require multi-factor authentication and did not have any password requirements, so Shotwell employees used easy-to-remember passwords.

Shotwell employees also had the ability to read AND modify reports, including deleting or changing data upon which the reports were based. A cyberattacker guessed the password using a dictionary attack, where common words are tested against the password, accessed the site and changed both data and reports to make them unusable. DataScale did not have any event alerts that would have tipped them off to the cyberattack, and they discovered it nearly a year later when making routine updates. Relying upon the accuracy of these reports, Shotwell made a number of business decisions that impacted their company's performance, such as overextending on certain purchases. In the contract between Shotwell and DataScale, Shotwell specified that DataScale must employ "reasonable security controls."

Shotwell will sue DataScale under one of two different approaches: for breach of contract and for negligence. The breach of contract action is likely a better option in part because typically contracts will specifically document an organization's expectations with respect to its third parties, including activities that are not objectively reasonable but nevertheless were specified under the contract. For example, Shotwell might have required DataScale to implement multi-factor authentication under the terms of the agreement. However, from a negligence perspective, multi-factor authentication may not have been reasonable (since MFA is not used in every type of application today).

However, there may be other issues: contracts often set the value of a breach of contract,[7] and the evaluation is one of conduct versus what the contract demands. For this reason, it is important for parties forming a contract to be aware of what the recovery could be, should a data breach or incident result. For example, Ponemon Institute has approximated the

[7] Contracts often include a maximum cost for breach of contract—a common factor is two times the value of the contract. This reins in potential costs that could be higher and gives some reliability for what kinds of losses the parties might face.

average data breach, which is 20,000 records, at a frequency of 20% over two years, and the average cost per record is $162 [need citation]. This puts the average breach at just over $3.2 MM. Most contracts, especially where software or hosting is involved, would not meet this number if a liability ceiling is in place, creating significant costs for the first party when the cause is the first party's fault.

Where a contract is not in place, or where a contract overtly caps damages at a very small value, it may make more sense for Shotwell to pursue a tort action, though usually negligence is reserved for personal injury type cases between a customer and a business. If Shotwell were to sue under negligence, Shotwell will need to demonstrate that DataScale breached its duty to perform reasonably. Here, it could be possible to introduce evidence of reasonable behavior as described in the contract, but usually reasonable duty will be a common law bar (or what a similarly situated company like DataScale would do in this position). Although injury may be less of a challenge, Shotwell will likely end up in a fight over causation: was the data breach reasonably foreseeable from DataScale's perspective so that avoiding the breach amounts to breach of duty? This might be a comparatively harder case to make.

Example 2: A variety of personal information was included in Shotwell's data set, including some sensitive biometric data. Shotwell had recently invested in custom hand grips that improve the angle at which hockey players hold their sticks. To make these hand grips, Shotwell uses a computer system to measure the hand angles and contours of player hands. It became known that this biometric information was included in the data breach, and now these players' families are trying to decide whether to sue as a breach of contract action based on the terms of use the players and their parents signed to use the data to create the grips, or whether negligence is more appropriate.

First, assuming players and their parents overtly signed a document or clicked on a button to accept terms at the time of data collection, courts will likely find that the terms of use/terms of service) document describing treatment of the data collected will be an enforceable contract. This is important, because at least some TOU/TOS documents require binding arbitration to resolve any disputes related to the relationship created between the parties in the TOU/TOS [would this apply to tort?]. Further, it's likely that the TOU/TOS did not include any specific guarantees of this kind. Likely, the TOU/TOS instead used language like "Shotwell will use reasonable security practices to protect your data." This generalized language may be difficult to interpret within a contract, causing difficulty in litigation.

These plaintiffs might also have a difficult time for each negligence prong: first, was the cyberattack so foreseeable that Shotwell had a duty to monitor its third parties and ensure MFA was implemented? Or was

Shotwell's conduct appropriate given how primary parties usually work with third parties? What injury did these plaintiffs truly suffer? Certainly, there is no evidence, yet, that this biometric data was anything more than simply access as a casualty of the real target of the data breach. However, there is no way to know if it could be used for something else. Unfortunately, apprehension of injury (or anticipation, or worry) is not enough to demonstrate injury. Rather, injury must be concrete, particularized, and non-speculative.

You can see in both of these examples how there are different nuances at work between contract and tort, as well as within a B2B relationship and a B2C relationship.

4. LIABILITY ASSIGNMENT

Liability assignment is the act of transferring risk or transferring liability to a third party. Risk or liability transfer is usually completed via insurance. For example, all physical premises usually have some insurance that will pay in case of property damage or personal injury. If someone falls at my home and hurts themselves, they will sue me, and I will notify my insurance company, which may pay out the judgment. Part of why I have an insurance policy is because I can't obsess over every detail of my property and what could happen. What if a friend simply trips on their own?

The purpose of liability assignment is to spread risk around to cover circumstances that are difficult to anticipate and may happen from time to time less frequently, and to divert liability to those most effectively positioned to share the costs for the liability. Of course, insurance companies are for-profit entities, as well, so they will not hurry to pay out insurance coverage amounts unless the loss is legitimate. If the insurance company investigates and finds that I did not maintain the property as required under my policy, it is possible the policy will not cover my losses; insurance companies always inspect what they plan to cover. Who wants to insure a person's home when the occupant operates a non-insulated wood fireplace that could cause a major fire? In order to receive insurance, a less desirable insurance candidate may have to pay a higher premium to offset a greater probability of loss.

Cyberrisk or cyberliability insurance works in a similar way. When an organization adopts one of these policies, an organization provides some financial support to hedge against some unknown probability of cyberattack. *Cyberrisk* is often adopted in modern insurance discussions instead of *cyberliability* because of its applicability to a broader set of business operations and potential impacts. In some circumstances, for example, cyberrisk insurance may apply to events involving service interruption or compromise by non-malicious individuals (e.g., not a hacker or malicious insider, like a disgruntled employee) that nevertheless require funding to recover.

Examples of such interruptions could stem from an IT employee's mistake in a production version of a software application or a natural disaster. In contrast, cyberliability is often used to describe activities leading to or probable to invoke liability, whether it includes failure to meet contractual obligations for a customer resulting in breach of contract or an actual legal action following a consumer data breach. Other names for this type of insurance include privacy or information security liability insurance. Despite these distinctions, insurance providers intermix these terms; *cyberliability* insurance will be used here, as insurers most frequently use this name to describe this product.

Cyberliability coverage may include a variety of activities necessary in the event of a data breach, such as immediate recovery for business operation, engagement of third party experts, setting up call centers to handle inquiries, data breach notification, credit monitoring offerings, litigation expenses, acts and omissions of third parties, and sometimes remediation activities. Most cyberliability policies, like any other insurance policy, include events limiting claim payout and may restrict payout for certain types of data breach effects, but not others. For example, most cyberliability policies do not extend coverage to physical injury or property damage, even though cybersecurity attacks could harm the physical operation of machinery. Increasingly, cyberliability insurers have found opportunities to deny claims for organizations suffering data breaches.

Some insurers require an organization to provide evidence of risk mitigation strategies and program formalities prior to underwriting a policy, such as distributing a questionnaire or requiring submission of documentation. In other circumstances, insurers may not require such evidence, but may be amenable to organizations demonstrating improved security maturity to negotiate a lower deductible. Developing and continuously improving an information security program enables an organization to demonstrate its security maturity.

A cybersecurity risk management program includes processes needed to submit cyberliability claims and manage later claim payments. For example, without intrusion detection systems (IDS), which identify when an intrusion has occurred and alert a security team, or a security incident and event monitoring (SIEM) tool, which helps a security team manage and monitor systems, an organization might not know that a data breach has occurred. Similarly, an incident response plan and associated procedures help an organization manage what could be a crisis situation. During an incident, security personnel will follow procedures for maintaining accurate copies of affected systems, conducting early investigations, and understanding when the business legitimately needs third party services like an external forensic investigator to draft a court-admissible report.

This illustrates but one example of where an organization's information security program can ensure cyberliability insurance policies work effectively, ensure insurance companies demand an acceptable premium and deductible, and prevent reasonable claim denial.

5. ECONOMIC LOSS DOCTRINE

Insurance plans will cover liability expenses resulting from court actions to an extent. Although these plans may cover these expenses, including adverse judgments, one significant barrier for organizations successfully bringing actions in tort is the economic loss doctrine. The economic loss doctrine bars certain tort actions when the injury is solely economic as the result of a contractual relationship. Consider the following example: Organization B, organization A's third party, caused a cybersecurity incident when organization B fails to implement reasonable security controls.

Organization B's failures resulted in direct economic losses: a manufacturing plant shut down, causing a loss of productivity for 30 days. Under the economic loss doctrine, which is a court-developed doctrine adopted by the majority of states, organization A will be barred for recovering purely economic losses. The economic loss doctrine is part of the reason why organizations typically favor forming a contract in B2B relationships and specifying damages and litigating for breach of contract, rather than seeking economic recovery in tort. The following excerpt examines the complexities of the economic loss doctrine as it applies to credit card processing.

DAVID W. OPDERBECK, *CYBERSECURITY, DATA BREACHES, AND THE ECONOMIC LOSS DOCTRINE*

75 MD. L. REV. 935 (2016)

It is not a question of if you will suffer a data breach; it is a question of when. That is the warning cybersecurity experts regularly provide to enterprises of every sort in every segment of the economy. This warning is more than an effort by high-priced consultants to spread FUD in the hope that their clients will purchase expensive cybersecurity services. It is a reality of the digital age. Your cybersecurity may be good, but the hackers are better. Your data security policies may be comprehensive, but it takes only one tired, lazy, stupid, or malicious employee to release your native data irretrievably into the wild.

Most analysts agree that the cost of data breaches are significant. The most recent Verizon Data Breach Report suggests that the average cost to breached entities is 58¢ per record, while the most recent Ponemon Institute report suggests an average cost of over $200 per record. A breach involving a major retailer may encompass tens of millions of individual records. A recent study suggests that data breaches will cost the U.S. economy $2 trillion by 2019.

The size and scale of these estimates suggests that the data breach problem is not only poorly contained—it is out of control. The enormous disparity between the cost to the breached entity (which already is sizable) and the overall economic costs (which could represent a meaningful percentage of GDP) suggests that the problem entails significant externalities. An externalities problem of this scope ordinarily indicates a need for some kind of governmental regulation. Where the problem entails a need to exercise care against harms that impose externalities, tort law naturally presents itself as an option in the regulatory mix. But even as the U.S. Congress has failed to pass significant cybersecurity legislation, the tort system has proven largely incapable of exercising much discipline over cybersecurity standards.

Claims in civil data breach cases have fallen into two broad categories: (1) claims by consumers of the breached entity—usually a retailer, bank, or consumer service provider—whose credit card information, social security numbers, or other personally identifying information has been disclosed; and (2) claims by entities in the financial services chain who have incurred reimbursement, remediation, and other costs as a result of a data breach suffered by another party in the chain—again, usually a retailer, bank or consumer service provider.

Most of these cases have failed at the pleading stage. On the consumer side, the problem is that any direct losses usually are reimbursed by the credit card issuer and any potential future losses are speculative. Tort claims in most consumer cases are resolved, or can be resolved, through Article III standing requirements. On the business side, however, plaintiffs often are able to prove unreimbursed economic damages caused by the data breach. The issue in these cases is that the direct losses are solely economic, and it is often unclear whether, or to what extent, there might be a contractual remedy for those losses. In business-to-business data breach cases, in other words, the deeper question is whether tort claims are barred by the "economic loss doctrine."

[Disagreement over the economic loss doctrine] is particularly acute in the data breach context because the economic risks are so pervasive and wide-ranging. Today's global economy cannot function without the Internet, the "cloud," email, networked computer automation, and other components of "cyberspace," including the global consumer credit card payment networks. When everything is connected, a breach at one node of the network potentially affects all nodes, or a multiplicity of nodes, in unpredictable, non-linear ways. Can tort law play any principled role in managing this risk? Or is it more likely that tort claims will provide windfalls to lawyers and some individual plaintiffs without improving the system over private ordering—or worse, while making the system more rigid and vulnerable? [. . .]

An individual card customer acquires a branded card (such as a Visa card) from an issuer bank. Merchants are set up to receive credit card payments for goods and services by acquirer banks. The issuer and acquirer banks each have contractual relationships with the card network. The card network supplies to the banks the right to use the brand and access to the networks payment processing services. The banks each pay membership dues and per-transaction fees to the networks. When a cardholder makes a purchase using his or her card, the merchant transmits the purchase information to the acquirer bank, which, through the card brand network, inquires about the cardholder's credit status at the issuer bank. If the cardholder possesses adequate credit, the approval of the transaction is communicated from the issuer bank to the acquirer bank through the card network. The acquirer bank reimburses the merchant for the purchase price of the goods or services supplied to the customer, like a "discount fee," which is a percentage of the transaction price. The issuer bank reimburses the acquirer bank for the purchase price, less an "interchange" fee. The customer is responsible to repay the purchase amount to the issuer bank, usually with interest, if the amount is not paid in full within the first billing cycle.

The largest networks worldwide are Visa and Mastercard. The Visa and Mastercard networks are "four-party" networks, which involve an issuer bank, the cardholder, an acquirer bank, and the merchant. Other substantial networks include American Express, Discover Card, and Diners Club. These are three-party networks in which the issuer bank is the same as the acquirer bank.

Both three- and four-party networks require the issuer and acquirer banks to agree to detailed sets of policies that govern the parties' relationships. These policies typically include data security provisions. The VISA Core Rules, for example, state that all Visa network members must "[m]aintain all materials or records in any form that contains account or Transaction Information in a safe and secure manner with access limited to authorized personnel, as specified in the Payment Card Industry Data Security Standard ("PCI DSS")" and further must "[e]nsure that all agents and Merchants with access to account or Transaction Information comply with the . . . PCI DSS." The VISA Core Rules also require members to ensure that agents and merchants do not store certain information, including the "[f]ull contents of any data taken from the Magnetic Stripe," subsequent to a transaction authorization.

The Fair Credit Billing Act ("FCBA") limits the cardholder's liability for unauthorized use of his or her credit card to $50 and provides for zero liability if the card number was stolen without the physical card. The Electronic Fund Transfer Act ("EFTA") limits the card holder's liability for unauthorized use of his or her card to $50 if the loss is reported within two business days after it is discovered or to $500 if the loss is reported between two business days and sixty calendar days after it is discovered.

In practice, the major card networks have adopted "zero liability" policies in cases of data theft. Under the VISA Core Rules, for example, an issuer is required to credit the cardholder's account for any electronic commerce transaction that involves fraud where the card was physically absent. Further, in the U.S., "an [i]ssuer must limit the [c]ardholder's liability to zero upon receipt of notification from its [c]ardholder of an unauthorized Visa Consumer Card or Visa Business Card Transaction." The VISA Core Rules further purport to "assign liability" between the issuer and acquirer for certain counterfeit transactions and provide an arbitration and compliance mechanism for disputes between members.

As noted above, cardholder information stolen in a data breach is fully reimbursed for any charges or debits made as a result of the theft. For this reason, most courts have found that consumers lack standing to sue and/or have no ascertainable damages under various common law theories.

Some consumers have sought to recover costs of future credit monitoring, akin to claims for medical monitoring expenses in personal injury cases. Prior to the Supreme Court's decision in *Clapper v. Amnesty International USA*, there was a circuit split concerning whether such claims satisfy Article III standing requirements. In *Clapper*, a case involving the NSA's surveillance programs authorized by the FISA Court, the Supreme Court held that Article III standing requires at least "certainly impending" or "substantial" risk of future harm. It is unclear whether *Clapper* implicitly abrogates the holdings in cases that had previously allowed future credit monitoring claims to proceed in data breach cases.

Consumers have also filed claims under state consumer fraud and data breach reporting statutes, with varying degrees of success depending on the particular standing and out-of-pocket loss requirements of the statutes. These cases generally do not implicate the economic loss doctrine because they are statutory and not common law tort claims.

The second broad category of data breach cases is comprised of claims by commercial entities for losses caused by breaches of other commercial entities. These cases involve quantifiable, unreimbursed out-of-pocket losses, so they do not usually fail on threshold Article III standing grounds.

An important question that arises in connection with this web of relationships is why civil litigation would ever ensue in the first place. The card networks and banks obviously are engaged in a highly lucrative enterprise that is designed to be self-policing . . . some courts and regulators have found that aspects of the credit card networks can violate the antitrust laws. It would seem exceedingly strange for an issuing or acquiring bank that has suffered some loss as the result of a credit card data breach to air this dirty laundry in court. The answer to this question may lie in several existing and emerging aspects of consumer credit and data security.

First, many of the high-profile commercial cases have been filed by credit unions associated with pension funds and labor unions. The credit unions often issue Visa or MasterCard credit and debit cards to their members, but the credit unions usually do not function as issuing or acquiring banks because they are not regulated as banks. Nevertheless, the credit unions may be charged by the credit card network or the issuing bank with the costs of reimbursing cardholders for losses after a data breach. If the party that was breached was the acquiring bank or the merchant, the credit union may not have any leverage or recourse under the card network agreements. [. . .]

The litigation resulting from one of the first major retail data breaches, involving BJ's Wholesale Club, provides an excellent example of the economic loss doctrine as applied in a data breach case. In *Sovereign Bank v. BJ's*, plaintiffs alleged that BJ's had stored electronic credit card information in violation of the Visa Operating Regulations and that Fifth Third Bank, the merchant bank that processed the BJ's transactions, failed to ensure BJ's compliance with the Regulations. One of the plaintiffs, Sovereign Bank, was an issuer bank that was required to reimburse its cardholders for losses incurred as a result of the breach in accordance with the Visa cardholder agreement. The other plaintiff, Pennsylvania State Employees Credit Union ("PSECU"), also functioned as an issuer of Visa cards to its members and claimed that it had incurred approximately $98,000 in out-of-pocket expenses when it canceled and reissued its members' cards that were compromised by the breach.

Both Fifth Third and PSECU suffered direct, ascertainable losses as a result of the breach. Nevertheless, the Court of Appeals for the Third Circuit, applying Pennsylvania law, held that the plaintiffs' negligence claims were barred under the economic loss doctrine. According to the Third Circuit, Pennsylvania had adopted a relatively straightforward version of the economic loss doctrine: "The Economic Loss Doctrine provides that no cause of action exists for negligence that results solely in economic damages unaccompanied by physical or property damage."

The court rejected Sovereign Bank's argument that Pennsylvania law in fact was more nuanced than this bald rule statement suggests. The Third Circuit quoted at length from a Pennsylvania Superior Court decision: "To allow a cause of action for negligent cause of purely economic loss would be to open the door to every person or business to bring a cause of action. Such an outstanding burden is clearly inappropriate and a danger to our economic system."

Similarly, the Third Circuit rejected PSECU's argument that Pennsylvania had modified its economic loss doctrine in later case law. In addition, the court waived off PSECU's argument that there was, in fact, physical property damage because its consumers' compromised credit cards were canceled. According to the court, "PSECU deemed the cards useless not because they were damaged, but because PSECU was exposed to liability for unauthorized charges."

The BJ's data breach also spawned litigation that reached the Massachusetts Supreme Judicial Court in *Cumis Insurance Society v. BJ's Wholesale Club, Inc.* In *Cumis*, claims were asserted against Fifth Third and BJ's by a group of credit unions that had issued MasterCard and Visa cards to their members and by an insurer of the credit unions that had reimbursed credit union card members for fraudulent charges. The court rejected the plaintiffs' negligence claims under the economic loss doctrine. Like the court in Sovereign Bank, the Massachusetts high court stated the economic loss doctrine, under Massachusetts law, in stark terms: "In addition, the economic loss doctrine bars recovery unless the plaintiffs can establish that the injuries they suffered due to the defendants' negligence involved physical harm or property damage, and not solely economic loss."

The court in *Cumis* was even less sanguine than the Third Circuit, however, about third-party beneficiary claims. The Massachusetts court noted that the agreement between BJ's and Fifth Third contained a clause expressly disclaiming any intent to benefit third-parties. The court further concluded that the security provisions in the Visa and MasterCard operating regulations did not override this express disclaimer of third-party liability. Rather, the court said, "nothing in the Visa and MasterCard operating regulations prohibits [the merchant bank and the merchant from] entering into agreements that explicitly exclude enforcement by third parties." Unlike the Third Circuit, the Massachusetts Supreme Judicial Court had no qualms about foreclosing the sort of contract remedy that could provide an alternative to a tort claim for economic losses.

As you can see, at least for purely economic injury resulting from cyberattacks, or injury not including property damage or personal injury, tort is an unlikely means of recovery, even when a plaintiff successfully argues the prima facie tort requirements for negligence or products liability. Courts have usually seen the economic loss doctrine as a means to prevent double-dipping in litigation: when purely economic losses result from a contractual relationship, courts prefer parties litigate under breach of contract. In the next section, we will be discussing the likelihood of recovering under this model and the potential challenges therein.

QUESTIONS

1. State the prima facie case for a tort action. For each of the prongs of the prima facie case, what are the relevant challenges in establishing a case?

2. Thinking back to our discussion of technical debt and the software development life cycle in the last chapter, how does it make sense to allocate liability between developers and users? How would changing the allocation of liability affect the development process? Can these liabilities be assigned by contract?

3. Why do you think the economic loss doctrine complicate cybersecurity cases? What would have to be true about the nature of the injury to survive the economic loss doctrine?

B. THE COMMON LAW OF CONTRACTS

As described earlier in this chapter, the common law of contracts is related to 1) the nature of the relationship (B2B or B2C) and 2) what is being sold (goods or services). Due to the relative primacy of the economic loss doctrine, most contractual relationships will be subject to the contents of the contract. For example, if a contract mandates arbitration to resolve a dispute, the parties will likely resolve any legal issues in arbitration, or a non-court decision-making process that is enforceable by courts and final. Except where contractual provisions are void (illegal) or voidable (unfair to one party, allowing the party to revoke the contract), contractual provisions govern every aspect of a contractual relationship, including how the contract will be interpreted and what options exist for resolving issues. These issues can include the amount of damages awarded or what law will apply if the matter is adjudicated.

Of course, the enforcement of contractual obligations is evaluated, at least when such issues are before a court rather than an arbitral plurality, under the laws applicable to the court. However, often the laws used for interpreting the contract are based on what is selected in the contract, regardless of where an action is brought. For example, typically Delaware is thought to be more solicitous to business interests, and for this reason courts there may resist reaching too far outside the text of the contract to interpret its terms. When two parties execute a contract, the parties may select Delaware as the choice of law designation in the contract, which under most circumstances will mean that even a court in New Mexico will apply Delaware contract law, including precedent and common law interpretations, in their legal determination.

State laws do, however, usually designate between goods-specific contracts law, as integrated in statute, and services contract law, as integrated in statute. For example, the statute of frauds requirements in most states require that any transactions in goods over $500 must be in writing to be enforceable. In these states, if contracts are not executed, courts will have to invent some type of contract, because there is nothing in writing to interpret, in *equity*. Determinations in equity are distinct from legal holdings—they exist to avoid unfairness.

For example, two kinds of equity determinations are *quantum meruit* (unjust enrichment) and contract implied in fact (constructive or quasi contract). Unjust enrichment exists when someone receives something of value and does not compensate the other party for enjoying the thing of value. For example, if someone starts painting your house, and instead of interrupting them and saying they are painting the wrong house you just let them paint it, they have relied on you paying them. The painter will be out of some money, and you will have the benefit of a newly painted home. If you do not interrupt and correct the problem, courts will likely find that you have unjustly been enriched by the service. Contracts implied in fact look at the collection of overall actions in a scenario to determine whether a contract has been formed. For example, even if a contract was not executed between the painter and you, but the painter painted and you paid them, likely a court will find a contract was formed for purpose of not leaving either party without what they expected in the contract.

However, strictly speaking, contracts are not enforceable if they are not in writing, and the benefit of contract law is that the courts, as much as possible, prefer for individual agreements to govern any issues that arise from them. For example, can you imagine a court looking at a breach of contract action and deciding that the value of the contract, which was $5,000, was too much and instead awarding a payment of $3,000? Courts do not look into the reasonableness of contractual terms, especially between organizational entities, because the courts expect sophisticated parties to know the difference between a good deal and a bad deal. Often, courts look to the contract itself to find answers and compel parties through legal determinations to follow the contract. If the contract states that the defendant must pay the plaintiff 2x the cost of the contract if the contract is breached, and the court finds that, based on the facts, the contract has been breached, usually the court will require the defendant to pay the cost specified.

It is important to understand the power of the written contract because this is where most organizations have a great deal of power to control certain outcomes with respect to risk mitigation and management, as well as allocate costs after a cyberattack. Of course, there are some challenges in crafting the appropriate language that will do both, and potential pitfalls common in these types of agreements.

1. B2C CONTRACTS

a. Service Contracts—Terms of Use

Service contracts are usually formed between consumers and organizations at the point of install or use. You may have heard the terms "terms of use," which are the contracts that usually govern these relationships. The degree to which these contracts may be enforced as a contract is a broader conversation, but usually the enforceability is related to the degree the consumer has manifested their agreement. For example, if a terms of use agreement is followed by the button "I agree," likely that terms of use will be enforced as a matter of contract. Terms of use that just happen to be on a site passively without any forced or opportunity to review coupled with a means of assent likely will be less enforceable.

Terms of use can be important if a cyberattack occurs. For example, if an organization promised "industry standard security" yet did not employ industry standard security controls, it may be found in breach of the terms of use. Similarly, terms of use could be used as an affirmative defense to such claims: if an organization only promised "reasonable effort to protect data," the organization may argue that they did perform such a reasonable effort by employing some, although not all, security controls. You can see how security language in a terms of use document could cut both ways, depending on what is promised. And there is more than just a potential contracts action at stake: terms of use are often reviewed by the Federal Trade Commission as part of investigations into unfair or deceptive trade practices.

Organizations, then, should first ensure that terms of use do not include anything deceptive or misleading, either by manufacture or mistake. For example, it is frequently the case that organization simply forget they have a terms of use document posted on an application. Often, engineers expect the terms of use will not change, business contacts don't think about the terms of use at all, and lawyers are not involved much in system or process updates, unless called upon. This collective lack of attention often means that terms of use stay the same, sometimes over five or more years, while the practices an organization uses with respect to cybersecurity may change.

b. Goods Contracts—"Wrapped" Agreements

For consumer goods, including those that are connected to the Internet, nearly all terms related to the product's function and the consumer's rights are included in the box. In a landmark case, *Pro CD v. Zeidenberg*, the Seventh Circuit held that even when a consumer is not able to assent to terms prior to purchasing a product, the terms are still enforceable. Practically speaking, these agreements, or the paper in a box that comes with a product, are called shrink-wrap agreements.

Typically, in contract formation, courts look to specific actions that signify offer and acceptance, or mutuality of assent to the terms of the agreement. Only with offer, acceptance, and consideration (the actual stuff exchanged, like money or products) is a contract formed. However, for most products, including products purchased at a retailer or online, the terms are included in the box, including warranties and other guarantees as to the product's performance and specifications. This could put consumers in a fairly compromising space when purchasing Internet-connected products, such as Internet of Things (IoT) devices.

For devices sold to consumers, requirements of the Uniform Commercial Code, the common code governing transactions in goods, as passed by each state, will apply to the packaged terms. For example, the UCC requires that if a manufacturer chooses to not make any promises of general warranties of merchantability (i.e., that the device works), the UCC requires that this disclaimer be prominent, such as in larger, bold print, or capital letters. However, courts will uphold the terms as included in the box, so long as the consumer has an opportunity to read the terms and return the device, if the consumer so chooses. Courts rationalize that for a contract's terms to be binding in this scenario, enough time needs to have passed where if consumers objected to the terms, they could reject the offer by simply returning the device.

We expect two parties to negotiate a contract under the average scenario, why might courts enforce terms stuffed in a box after sale when a consumer does not have an opportunity to read? The economic reality of negotiating terms related to the same device for every individual consumer would be untenable in the modern realities of retail distribution and sale. Practically, negotiating at the point of sale (such as a cash register) would not likely be easy to do. Even negotiating online would become arduous and time-consuming. Furthermore, in the stream of commerce, it is not practical for manufacturers to have to maintain hundreds of thousands or millions of different contract terms simultaneously.

For IoT manufacturers, the inefficiencies of private ordering, or individual consumers negotiating contracts with manufacturers, is magnified. The most compelling reason why negotiating agreements in this space is untenable is actually related to technical efficiency, rather than purely economic efficiency. For example, consider the technical realities of differentiated contractual terms as they might relate to an IoT weight scale. The IoT weight scale is usually connected to diet, fitness, or diabetes management apps so that users can manage health information in one place. Weight values are automatically updated when the scale is connected via Bluetooth to a mobile device, tracking weight over time in the app.

In this case, if the manufacturer's terms of use enclosed in the scale's box included specific technical commitments, and the consumer could individually negotiate the terms, the manufacturer would have to maintain multiple implementations of the same service or manufacture different devices altogether. It's hard to imagine this type of a scenario because it conflicts with our concept of modern manufacturing. If consumers want a different version of the device, for example a device with more comprehensive technical measures, we expect that manufacturers will advertise the relative benefits of a different version. Or, consumers may select a different scale altogether.

As you can see from a goods and services perspective, it is not practical for companies to manage multiple versions of terms of use, browse wrap, click wrap, or shrink wrap contracts.[8] There are many reasons why these types of contracts are legitimate from a stream of commerce perspective. However, there are some accompanying dangers related to unfairness for these types of contracts, commonly called *contracts of adhesion*. The law defines contracts of adhesion as contracts that are inherently one-sided, or "take it or leave it." The thought is that a contract of adhesion is one where a consumer cannot bargain and therefore must select a completely different product if they disagree with the terms presented.

Contracts of adhesion are not, in and of themselves, voidable. Contracts of adhesion perform important functions in terms of modern commercial behavior and general efficiency, and we also know that contracts of adhesion are generally enforced by courts under most circumstances, even if consumers read them after purchase, so long as they keep the products. There are, however, some limited circumstances when contracts of adhesion are not enforceable: when such contracts are deemed unconscionable.

Most courts require that to declare a contract unconscionable and therefore voidable, the party seeking the contract not be enforced (usually the plaintiff) must demonstrate that the contract's terms as well as the method for soliciting assent were both unconscionable: substantive and procedural unconscionable. Contracts of adhesion, due to their one-sided nature, may be considered procedurally unconscionable. However, to actually find a contract unconscionable, it must also mean that the terms themselves are unconscionable and fundamentally unfair. For example, arbitration terms may be considered substantively unconscionable, such as

---

[8] Browse wrap contracts are usually those that govern Web site or app usage but do not require consent. Usually browse wrap contracts are not enforceable against a user but may be enforceable against the organization providing them. Click wrap contracts usually involve some manifestation of assent on the part of a user, and click wrap contracts can apply to applications or other online usage or can extend to IoT device use. The enforceability of click wrap contracts depends on the method by which a user assents. Shrink wrap contracts are packaged in the box of a manufactured good. Online services coupled with IoT devices may either use a shrink-wrap contract or a click-wrap contract as the basis for the relationship between a manufacturer and a customer.

when binding arbitration must occur in a forum very far away from the plaintiff or at a substantial cost to the plaintiff.[9]

Why might unconscionability be a relevant factor for cybersecurity terms in a contract? For IoT devices, for example, having language that declares no warranties with respect to cybersecurity features on the device could potentially be considered substantively unconscionable. General warranties usually are included for all consumer devices under the UCC, even when a manufacturer doesn't include them in the written terms. For example, an implied warranty of merchantability guarantees consumers that the product is free of substantial defects for a given time period, usually four years.

This means that a consumer *could* potentially make a number of arguments with respect to an Internet-connected device that cause physical injury or property damage: 1) if unconscionable, the courts could find in equity (essentially rewriting the contract) that the consumer recovers due to a security defect, 2) if not unconscionable, the courts could find that an implied warranty of merchantability guarantees the consumer some protection from a security defect, or 3) the consumer could recover under a tort with the duty element informed in part by the contract. In fact, it is this implied warranty of merchantability that often gives rise to products liability actions in tort.

2. SPECIAL PROBLEMS

In addition to challenges in establishing a prima facie case, there are additional challenges that make recovery under the common law more difficult.

a. Common Law Problems

The most significant remaining questions for contracts include whether courts will recognize a security defect as being covered under an implied warranty of merchantability, or as a "defect" with respect to a consumer good. Historically, most functionality claims (as in pure implied warranty of merchantability, where the product doesn't work as specified) or products liability claims (as in safety issues causing injury or property damage) are based on non-IoT products that are not Internet-connected. For example, it will be far easier to recover damages by an oven that overheats and burns down a house due to design or manufacturing issues

[9] For those new to arbitration, arbitration is a private remedy that is enforced by the courts: the arbitral body examines the evidence and allegations and makes a binding determination. It is a little like a court, without the typical Constitutional protections, such as the ability to appeal a decision. Arbitration can have benefits, such as using arbitral "judges" that have more knowledge of the subject matter, and the speed of hearings/determination. However, some organizations may be able to stack arbitral judges in favor of their position, unless endorsed by an arbitration body that requires a "neutral" judge. Arbitration is a type of "alternative dispute resolution" that is designed to reduce time for courts and speed results to parties.

with electric shielding and insulation than a smart oven where an attacker remotely exceeds the oven's temperature limits or disables a sensor, causing an otherwise safe oven to cause damage.

The benefit of the common law for contracts and torts actions is that court determinations encode a level of predictability and consistency through the principles of precedent. Courts seek to resolve legal issues in light of previous legal reasoning, rules, and holdings, at least within binding precedent. Whether or not courts extend existing rationales related to warranties, torts, or even injury depend in large part upon a court's ability and willingness to analogize and build upon historical rulings. Is a cyberattack similar to a manufacturing defect? Is a cyberattack foreseeable? Is pure information loss an injury? Each of these questions will need to be resolved in courts of law within each jurisdiction, as well as federally. Due to our federal system of state and federal courts, even the Supreme Court of the United States of America is not binding on purely state systems.

3. B2B CONTRACTS

Business to business contracts are interpreted by courts slightly differently than consumer agreements. Generally speaking, courts expect that organizations doing business have a level of sophistication and bargaining that individual consumers do not. For this reason, the concept of a contract of adhesion does not typically apply to the business context, even when one entity has less bargaining power than another. Most of the issues related to dominating behavior, such as anti-competitive behaviors are saved, to some extent, for Antitrust Law and these issues are largely are focused on impacts to consumer buying behavior rather than individual transactions.

Economic perspectives of contract also apply in B2B agreements. One area is in service contracts: substantial performance. Substantial performance also applies to consumer agreements, but it is more dominantly enforced in B2B contracts. As previously discussed, courts often believe that organizations create contracts with open eyes. They understand what could go wrong and guard against these possibilities using contractual terms. Courts also dislike economic waste. Substantial performance is when one of the parties of a contract does not perform the specific terms of an agreement, but what has been performed is very close to what was promised. Substantial performance is usually positioned as an affirmative defense to allegations of breach of contract. Consider the following example including cybersecurity terms to explain this concept a bit more.

GuardETC is a software product that blocks malware, including viruses on individual client machines, such as laptops and PCs, at a purchaser's organization. In GuardETC's contracts with customer organizations, it commits to update virus and malware definitions in its product at least monthly, so that organizations may timely block new viruses or malware launched by cyberattackers. Six months ago, GuardETC updated its definitions and sent the update to its customer organizations two days before the end of the month. In the two days after their update, a new virus was created by attackers and deployed via phishing emails. One of the customer organizations, Pharmaqual, a mailorder pharmaceutical company, updated its systems as required by the contract with GuardETC as soon as it received the updates. Two days later, some of Pharmaqual's employees clicked on a phishing link, which launched the new virus on its systems. The virus spread quickly through the Pharmaqual intranet, shutting down some of Pharmaqual's key operational systems. The overall impact is that Pharmaqual could not send pharmaceuticals for two weeks, causing some people dependent on receiving these pharmaceuticals to not receive their medications. Likely some of Pharmaqual's customers had issues filling prescriptions or had to go to other pharmacies to fill them. Some of these customers then cancelled their subscriptions and went with a Pharmaqual competitor instead. Pharmaqual is seeking to recover for damages a direct cause of GuardETC not deploying its monthly update on time.

A court hearing this case might come out one of two ways: first, a court might find that the monthly timeframe for deploying updates was sufficiently explicit and crucial to the performance of the contract that any deviation from the specified timeframe would amount to a breach of contract. Alternatively, the court could determine that two days is a fairly small deviation from the contract, and that it does not amount to a breach of contract. For the average contract, this would likely amount to substantial performance, and yet for a malware service like this, timing certainly matters. How the court decides a case like this will likely be a matter of how the parties contextualize the importance of adhering to the timeframe specified.

In breach of contract actions, a plaintiff must prove the following:

- A valid contract existed
- The plaintiff performed its required actions under the contract (such as paying)
- The defendant did not perform one or more required actions under the contract
- Non-performance resulted in some injury to the plaintiff.

Substantial performance is one way that a defendant might demonstrate that the defendant did perform the required actions. Another argument the defendant might make is that the term in contest was not a material term of the agreement, or a term that was important enough to the entire agreement. In the example above, GuardETC might argue that deploying the monthly update was a material term but the time specification was not, meaning that the nonfulfillment would not constitute a material breach of contract.

For B2B agreements, often the biggest challenge is the variation in cybersecurity terms and their specificity. Contract terms put the other party on notice of their expected performance and will be used later to enforce the contract. Instead of including detailed cybersecurity terms in an agreement, many organizations use broader language, such as "reasonable administrative and technical controls," or broad confidentiality language that applies to private or proprietary organizational data. There are benefits to broader language like this, for example permitting more advanced security to be implemented or security expectations to evolve over time. With the right court, broad language like this could also allow for better argumentation related to "reasonableness."

However, it is possible that less specific cybersecurity terms might also complicate a court's ability to determine when breach of contract has occurred. For example, if the selling business commits to reasonable security requirements in the contract with the customer business, but conversations about the product or service include a commitment that the selling business will encrypt the customer's data, usually those conversations will not be enforced outside what is specified in the agreement per the parol evidence rule.

Courts will usually look to what is in the agreement rather than external conversations, alternative documents, or oral commitments, except when the term itself is intrinsically unclear. If data are then exposed because they were not encrypted, it may be difficult for the customer business to effectively sue the selling business for breach of contract. And, as we have discussed, a purely economic loss will most likely be barred in tort, as well. For these reasons, most sophisticated organizations will include at least some specific cybersecurity terms in their agreements with service or product providers. We will discuss more details related to the types of terms found in these agreements in Chapter 11.

QUESTIONS

1. Access management is the process of provisioning and terminating access subject to specific activities, like provisioning access to systems upon hire. Effectively managing access is a key tenet of a cybersecurity practices. Draft a sample contractual provision related to access management, and feel free to research before you do so.

2. Now that you've drafted a sample contractual provision, did you take a more flexible or a more specific approach?

3. The economic loss doctrine often bars purely economic tort actions, but the economic loss doctrine does not bar contracts actions. Economic loss

doctrine aside, why might a breach of contract claim be a better strategy than a negligence claim?

C. SHAREHOLDER DERIVATIVE LAWSUITS

The final type of common law action that may affect organizations related to cybersecurity are shareholder derivative lawsuits. In Chapter 8, you learned about directors' duties related to the organizations they serve. Shareholder derivative lawsuits occur when the shareholders who own a publicly traded company collectively sue directors of a company on behalf of the company for breaching one or more of the directors' duties. Publicly traded companies are both subject to state law (because they are organized and given status according to state law) and federal law (because they are traded in markets regulated by federal agencies like the Securities and Exchange Commission). Most shareholder derivative lawsuits are subject to state law and are filed in state court (for example California, New York, and Delaware); in limited cases, they can be filed in federal courts.

Shareholder derivative lawsuits are usually most successful when there is a prolonged and measurable reduction in stock value and where substantial evidence illustrates that directors ignored a known problem, which counters the strong affirmative defense of the business judgment rule. In the following excerpt, Professors Trautman and Ormerod examine one of the biggest prolonged cybersecurity catastrophes, involving at least three breaches, at Yahoo.

LAWRENCE J. TRAUTMAN & PETER ORMEROD, *CORPORATE DIRECTORS' AND OFFICERS' CYBERSECURITY STANDARD OF CARE: THE YAHOO DATA BREACH*

66 AMER. U. L. REV. 1233 (2017)

Yahoo! Inc. ("Yahoo" or the "Company") announced on September 22, 2016, that a state-sponsored hacker had breached the Company's digital systems in 2014 and had stolen personal information from over 500 million user accounts. The information stolen likely included names, birthdays, telephone numbers, email addresses, "hashed passwords (the vast majority with bcrypt), and, in some cases, encrypted or unencrypted security questions and answers." At the time it was announced, this 2014 theft represented the largest data breach ever. This record would only later be surpassed by another Yahoo breach: a 2013 breach affecting 1 billion user accounts that the Company announced in December 2016. Yahoo further disclosed its belief that the stolen data "did not include unprotected passwords, payment card data, or bank account information." Just two months before Yahoo disclosed its 2014 data breach, it announced a proposed sale of the Company's core business to Verizon Communications, Inc. ("Verizon"). During mid-December 2016, Yahoo announced that another 1 billion customer accounts had been compromised during 2013, establishing a new record for the largest data breach ever.

Almost all corporations—from technology companies like Yahoo to brick-and-mortar sales companies that use electronic commerce services—face a significant risk from data breaches, and mergers and acquisitions may result in cyber liability and vulnerabilities for the acquirer. This announced acquisition raises a number of important corporate governance issues: whether Yahoo breached its duty to provide data security, its duty to monitor, its duty to disclose, or some combination thereof; the impact on Verizon shareholders of a renegotiated deal for the two companies to share the cost of liability; and whether more severe and wide-ranging compensation clawbacks would be appropriate. [. . .]

Corporate directors and officers have a duty to behave reasonably. This duty of care applies across directors' and officers' myriad responsibilities, including handling the corporation's digital data. There is, therefore, an emerging specific application of the duty of care as related to information technology: the duty to secure data. The applicable standard of care requires directors "to provide 'reasonable' or 'appropriate' physical, technical, and administrative security measures to ensure the confidentiality, integrity, and availability of corporate data."

There is not, however, a single source—such as a comprehensive federal statute or regulation—that imposes a duty to provide data security. Rather, corporate legal obligations to implement data security systems are "set forth in an ever-expanding patchwork of state, federal, and international laws, regulations, and enforcement actions, as well as in common law duties, contractual commitments, and other expressed and implied obligations to provide 'reasonable' or 'appropriate' security for corporate data." [. . .]

Of the [myriad statutory] authorities . . . that impose a data security duty, most simply state that there is "an obligation to implement 'reasonable' or 'appropriate' security measures," but they "provide little or no guidance as to what is required for legal compliance." While there is little question that the legal standard for what constitutes reasonable security is still emerging, much progress has been made in recent years.

Thomas J. Smedinghoff, a leading expert on this emerging cybersecurity standard, explains that the emerging digital security standard is particularized and case specific. Unlike prior specific requirements, such as passwords or firewalls, the new corporate security obligation is fact-specific, requiring companies to go through a "process" and determine what security measures are most appropriate for the company's security needs. The emerging legal standard follows suit by allowing companies to create their own specific security measures so long as the companies conduct ongoing reviews of their security mechanisms. This repetitive review process includes detecting and evaluating risks, implementing specific security responses to those risks, verifying the effective implementation of those security responses, and updating the measures as needed in reaction to developing security concerns.

Specifically, Mr. Smedinghoff's process-oriented approach to satisfying a "reasonable" or "appropriate" standard of care for a duty to provide security is composed of the following seven provisions:

Assign Responsibility: A corporation should expressly designate one or more employees to be responsible for maintaining the data security program.

Identify Information Assets: A corporation should identify its information assets that require protection, which include both the data itself (i.e., records containing personal information) and the computing systems that store the personal information (e.g., servers, laptops, and portable devices).

Conduct Risk Assessment: A corporation should perform a risk assessment to identify both internal and external risks to its data security, and it should evaluate the effectiveness of the company's current practices for safeguarding and minimizing the risks identified.

Select and Implement Responsive Security Controls: A corporation should implement physical, administrative, and technical security controls it considers appropriate to minimize the risks it identified in its risk assessment.

Monitor Effectiveness: A corporation should regularly monitor, test, and reassess the security controls it has chosen to implement in order to ensure its security program is operating in a manner reasonably calculated to protect personal information. Relatedly, a corporation should regularly upgrade its security controls as necessary to limit emerging risks.

Regularly Review the Security Program: A corporation should review and adjust its data security program no less than once per year. A corporation should also perform security program reviews whenever there is a material change in business practices that could affect personal information or after any incident involving a breach of its data security.

Address Third Party Issues: A corporation should take all reasonable steps to verify that every third-party service provider that has access to the company's data assets and personal information has the capacity to protect that information.

An ever-increasing number of authorities are expressly adopting this process-oriented approach to data security, which is referred to as a Written Information Security Program ("WISP"). The FTC is the most important of the authorities that have adopted the WISP standard. According to the FTC, businesses in all industries should comply with the process-oriented approach to information security as it demonstrates the "best practice" for legal compliance. The FTC has demonstrated this view by requiring any company resolving FTC complaints about failure to provide adequate information security through consent decrees to implement and comply with this process oriented approach. The FTC's adherence to the WISP standard is particularly important in light of the agency's post-2005 theory of liability that sanctions a duty to protect data. [. . .]

The Duty to Monitor

Among other duties, corporate directors and officers owe the corporation and its shareholders a duty of care. The duty of care is a concept adapted from tort law, and it requires an actor to behave reasonably. Director liability for a breach of the duty of care may arise in two distinct contexts. First, liability may "follow from a board decision that results in a loss because that decision was ill advised or 'negligent.'" Second, liability may "arise from an unconsidered failure of the board to act in circumstances in which due attention would, arguably, have prevented the loss."

In *In re Caremark International Inc. Derivative Litigation*, a seminal 1996 Delaware Chancery Court decision on the duty of care, the court took pains to emphasize that judicial inquiries into a director's affirmative actions center on the adequacy of the *process* that gave rise to the shareholders' derivative action, not the *content* of the decision itself. Therefore, a director will not be found liable for a decision after-the-fact if the decision making process used was in good faith or rational in promoting the corporation's interest. The overwhelming majority of a director's affirmative acts are evaluated under the deferential business judgment rule. But the business judgment rule applies differently in situations where a director's lax oversight—a failure to monitor and be informed—results in corporate losses.

At its core, a breach of the duty to monitor arises when "a loss eventuates not from a decision but, from unconsidered inaction." Noting that "[m]ost of the decisions that a corporation, acting through its human agents, makes are . . . not the subject of director attention," the *Caremark* court nonetheless recognized that "ordinary business decisions that are made by officers and employees deeper in the interior of the organization can . . . vitally affect the welfare of the corporation and its ability to achieve its various strategic and financial goals." At a minimum, corporate boards fail to satisfy their obligation to be reasonably informed about the corporation if they do not "assur[e] themselves that information and reporting systems exist in the organization that are reasonably designed to provide . . . timely, accurate information sufficient to allow management and the board . . . to reach informed judgments concerning . . . the corporation's compliance with law." This is not to say, however, that there is a universal, one-size-fits-all solution to the duty to monitor—"the level of detail that is appropriate for such an information system is a question of business judgment." Nor does the existence of an adequate monitoring system eliminate the risk "that the corporation will violate laws or regulations, or that senior officers or directors may nevertheless sometimes be misled or otherwise fail reasonably to detect acts material to the corporation's compliance with the law."

Thus, the duty to monitor requires "the board [to] exercise a good faith judgment that the corporation's information and reporting system is in concept and design adequate to assure the board that appropriate information will come to its attention in a timely manner." To avoid liability and conform to relevant legal norms, a director should attempt in good faith to ensure the company has a "corporate information and reporting system" that the board finds satisfactory. Accordingly, the corporate law duty of care centers on whether corporate directors and officers employed a "good faith effort" to remain reasonably informed sufficient to "exercise good judgment."

The Duty to Disclose

A publicly traded corporation's duty to disclose the existence of a data breach stems from at least two distinct authorities: Delaware state corporate common law and the SEC's 2011 corporate finance disclosure guidance, which identifies material data security risks that companies must disclose under securities law disclosure requirements and accounting standards. Companies that know about a data breach but fail to disclose it to shareholders, regulators, and consumers risk liability under potentially corporate, breach notification, and securities laws.

Directors' and officers' fiduciary duty to shareholders and the corporation imposes a duty to disclose—sometimes referred to as a duty of complete candor—that is well established in Delaware common law.

Two decades ago, Professor Lawrence A. Hamermesh noted that Delaware courts have recognized "that a fiduciary duty to disclose all material information arises when directors approve any public statement, such as a press release, regardless of whether any specific stockholder action is sought." Director negligence is irrelevant in assessing the duty to disclose. The duty serves two purposes: (1) to "afford stockholders a remedy," regardless of whether they relied upon a misstatement or omission, and (2) "to afford a 'virtual per se rule' of damages," awarding stockholders a monetary award "without having to establish actual loss."

The Delaware Supreme Court later confirmed Professor Hamermesh's interpretation. In *Malone v. Brincat*, the Delaware Supreme Court clarified that directors and officers owe a duty of honesty to shareholders in both communications seeking shareholder action and "[w]henever directors communicate publicly or directly with shareholders about the corporation's affairs, with or without a request for shareholder action." The court held that "directors who knowingly disseminate false information that results in corporate injury or damage to an individual stockholder violate their fiduciary duty, and may be held accountable in a manner appropriate to the circumstances." In sum, the duty to disclose in Delaware requires that directors provide shareholders with "all material information" about the corporation whenever they communicate with the shareholder or market, even if the shareholder did not request it.

Additionally, the SEC's 2011 Guidance notes that "federal securities laws, in part, are designed to elicit disclosure of timely, comprehensive, and accurate information about risks and events that a reasonable investor would consider important to an investment decision." Although the Guidance acknowledges that "no existing disclosure requirement explicitly refers to cybersecurity risks and cyber incidents," the SEC nonetheless required the disclosure of "material information regarding cybersecurity risks and cyber incidents" to prevent misleading the public.

The Guidance provides examples of situations in which disclosure is mandatory—several of which are likely implicated here. First, the Guidance provides that the SEC "expect[s] registrants to evaluate their cybersecurity risks and take into account all available relevant information, including prior cyber incidents and the severity and frequency of those incidents." Second, the Guidance advises that: "[r]egistrants should address cybersecurity risks and cyber incidents . . . if the costs or other consequences associated with one or more known incidents or the risk of potential incidents represent a material event, trend, or uncertainty that is reasonably likely to have a material effect on the registrant's results of operations, liquidity, or financial condition."

Consequently, some commentators—like Jacob Olcott, former Senate Commerce Committee counsel—believe that the "Yahoo hack could become a test case of the SEC's [2011] guidelines . . . due to the size of the breach, intense public scrutiny and uncertainty over the timing of Yahoo's discovery." [. . .]

[Omitted: description of Yahoo's attempts to find bidders amongst multiple years of reduced stock prices, no mention of security breaches, and eventually Verizon's decision to purchase Yahoo. After this time, another data breach occurs.]

The Verizon Acquisition

On July 23, 2016, the parties entered into a Stock Purchase Agreement, providing that Verizon purchase all of Yahoo's outstanding shares of Yahoo Holdings for a cash purchase price of $4,825,800,000, subject to certain adjustments as provided for within the contract for sale.

As renegotiations stemming from the data breach disclosures continued in early 2017, Yahoo announced on January 10, 2017, that when the Company completes the Verizon deal, Yahoo will "whittle down its board" by six members, with several longtime directors—including CEO Marissa Mayer and co-founder David Filo—stepping down from the board. Upon sale of its core internet business to Verizon, the remaining entity will rename itself Altaba, Inc., and Altaba's remaining assets will include Yahoo's stake in Alibaba Group Holdings Ltd. and Yahoo Japan.

On February 15, 2017, news of a renegotiated deal between Verizon and Yahoo leaked, and the leak asserted that the two companies had agreed on a new price $250 million lower than their initial agreement. But on February 21, 2017, when Verizon disclosed the renegotiated deal to acquire Yahoo's core Internet business, Verizon announced a $350 million discount. The renegotiated price brings the original $4.8 billion price down to $4.48 billion. Further, "Verizon and the entity that remains of Yahoo after the deal, . . . Altaba Inc., are expected to share any ongoing legal responsibilities related to the breaches." The deal closed on June 8, 2017.

On September 22, 2016, Yahoo announced (what was at that time) "the largest data breach in history—affecting at least 500 million user accounts." Yahoo's statement on the breach disclosed that user information—which included names, email addresses, telephone numbers, birth dates, encrypted passwords and, in some cases, security questions—was compromised in late 2014. Further, Yahoo's statement alleged that an unnamed "state-sponsored actor" was responsible for the breach. In March 2017, the U.S. Department of Justice indicted two Russian intelligence officers for "directing a sweeping criminal conspiracy" to hack Yahoo in 2014 and steal more than 500 million Yahoo users' personal information.

Then, on December 14, 2016, Yahoo disclosed an earlier and even larger data breach than the 2014 breach disclosed in September 2016. This attack occurred in 2013 and exposed more than one billion accounts, which "involved sensitive user information, including names, telephone numbers, dates of birth, encrypted passwords and unencrypted security questions that could be used to reset a password." It is, however, unclear how many of the same user accounts were compromised in the 2013 and 2014 data breaches; Yahoo has more than one billion active users, but there is lingering uncertainty about the number of inactive accounts that were hacked.

Notwithstanding the magnitude of the security breaches, considerable controversy surrounds the timing of when Yahoo employees learned of the 2014 breach. Despite representing in a September 9, 2016 SEC filing that Yahoo was not aware of any security breaches—and a recent disclosure that at least some Yahoo employees were aware of the breach in 2014—most current accounts of internal knowledge of the breach maintain that CEO Marissa Mayer was aware of it in late July 2016. [. . .]

Four specific examples of Yahoo's seemingly lax commitment to corporate cybersecurity from the New York Times report illustrate the shortcomings of Yahoo's security. First, Yahoo did not begin compensating hackers for providing the Company with information on digital vulnerabilities until 2013—three years after Google adopted the same policy—and Yahoo adopted the policy only "after it lost countless security engineers to competitors and experienced a breach of more than 450,000 Yahoo accounts in 2012 and a series of humiliating spam attacks in 2013."

Second, even after it took Yahoo a year to hire a new chief information security officer ("CISO") following former U.S. National Security Agency contractor Edward Snowden's disclosure of damaging information—which revealed that Yahoo was a constant target for nation-state spies—Yahoo failed to empower, and denied requested resources to, its new CISO.

Outsiders initially hailed the 2014 hiring of CISO Alex Stamos, who left the Company in 2015, as potentially signaling a renewed corporate commitment to cybersecurity. But Mr. Stamos frequently clashed with Mayer and Yahoo's senior vice president, Jeff Bonforte, who oversaw Yahoo's email and messaging services. For example, Mr. Bonforte revealed in a December 2015 interview that Mr. Stamos had quickly pressed senior management to adopt end-to-end encryption for the Company's entire digital infrastructure, which would prevent Yahoo from being able to read the content of users' communications. Mr. Bonforte resisted the recommendation because doing so would hinder the Company's ability to index and search message data, precluding it from tailoring new, additional user services.

Third, Ms. Mayer repeatedly refused to invest meaningful resources to secure Yahoo's security infrastructure—to the chagrin of Mr. Stamos and his team. According to the half-dozen insiders, Ms. Mayer "denied Yahoo's security team financial resources and put off proactive security defenses, including intrusion-detection mechanisms for Yahoo's production systems." Some commentators have deemed Ms. Mayer's refusal to invest in Mr. Stamos's team and follow their recommendations a major contributor to a mass exodus from the Company's cybersecurity team that Mr. Stamos assembled. According to the publication Recode, "[o]ne executive close to the situation said that former Yahoo information security head Alex Stamos had tried aggressively to get management to act more strongly at the time, but he had not been successful," which ultimately led to Mr. Stamos' resignation from Yahoo and move to Facebook as chief security officer in mid-2015.

Fourth and finally, Ms. Mayer rejected the suggested implementation of one of the most basic security measures: automatically resetting all users' passwords, "a step security experts consider standard after a breach." Ms. Mayer's rationale for rejecting such a fundamental staple of data breach response derived from a "fear that even something as simple as a password change would drive Yahoo's shrinking email users to other services." Indeed, a Yahoo spokesperson confirmed this continues to be the Company's policy: "Yahoo's policy is that if we believe a user's password has been compromised, we lock the account until the user resets the password."

As you can see from the excerpt above, the Yahoo breach, taking all accounts from the *New York Times* at face value, appears to evidence some failure of directors to fulfill their duties.

QUESTIONS

1. From the account described in this excerpt, do you think that Yahoo shareholders might be able to argue a successful shareholder derivative action against Yahoo for the reduced sales price of the company? For a company that has a limited drop in share values that ultimately bounce back, do you think the same arguments might be as successful?

2. One of the most powerful affirmative defenses in a shareholder derivative lawsuit is the business judgement rule, or that may executive business decisions, judged from information available at the time (rather than in hindsight), were reasonable. If you were Ms. Mayer, what arguments might you make? What facts do you think would be most relevant to establish Ms. Mayer was within her reasonable decision-making under the business judgment rule?

D. STATE STATUTES & STATE ATTORNEYS GENERAL

In the previous section, we discussed a variety of common-law actions related to cybersecurity measures. However, we also described several situations in which these actions may not be successful, in part due to courts unwillingness to extend common law doctrine to new situations involving cybersecurity. For this reason, some states have passed explicit statutes related to cybersecurity, including data breach notification statutes (as referenced earlier in this book), direct requirements to create security programs, and limitations on liability when organizations do implement security programs that meet specific requirements.

Furthermore, many states have broad unfair or deceptive trade practices statutes that permit state attorneys general to take action when organizations have engaged in unfair or deceptive trade practices related to cybersecurity program development. These statutes largely emulate the Federal Trade Commission's (FTC's) Section 5 of the FTC Act and permit broad enforcement by state attorneys general.

Statutes, including unfair or deceptive trade practice statutes, vary widely and are specific to states and vary whether private rights of actions can be brought by consumers. For example, some unfair or deceptive trade practices statutes permit a consumer to bring the action and even receive attorney's fees if they are successful! Conversely, some data breach notification statutes do not permit a private right of action but do permit state attorneys general to prosecute. At the time of writing, there is no one dominant model of private rights with respect to these actions.

In this section, we will profile a few of the state laws that reference cybersecurity. [Please note: this is a sampling rather than a comprehensive list of all state statutes related to cybersecurity, and your professor may opt to present more statutes relevant to your state or a specific organizational sector.]

THE NEW YORK DEPARTMENT OF FINANCIAL SERVICES CYBERSECURITY REGULATION

23 NYCRR 500 (2017)

Section 500.01 Definitions. For purposes of this Part only, the following definitions shall apply:

(a) Affiliate means any Person that controls, is controlled by or is under common control with another Person. For purposes of this subsection, control means the possession, direct or indirect, of the power to direct or cause the direction of the management and policies of a Person, whether through the ownership of stock of such Person or otherwise.

(c) Covered Entity means any Person operating under or required to operate under a license, registration, charter, certificate, permit, accreditation or similar authorization under the Banking Law, the Insurance Law or the Financial Services Law. . . .

(g) Nonpublic Information shall mean all electronic information that is not Publicly Available Information and is:

(1) Business related information of a Covered Entity the tampering with which, or unauthorized disclosure, access or use of which, would cause a material adverse impact to the business, operations or security of the Covered Entity;

(2) Any information concerning an individual which because of name, number, personal mark, or other identifier can be used to identify such individual, in combination with any one or more of the following data elements: (i) social security number, (ii) drivers' license number or non-driver identification card number, (iii) account number, credit or debit card number, (iv) any security code, access code or password that would permit access to an individual's financial account, or (v) biometric records;

(3) Any information or data, except age or gender, in any form or medium created by or derived from a health care provider or an individual and that relates to (i) the past, present or future physical, mental or behavioral health or condition of any individual or a member

of the individual's family, (ii) the provision of health care to any individual, or (iii) payment for the provision of health care to any individual.

Section 500.02 Cybersecurity Program.

(a) Cybersecurity Program. Each Covered Entity shall maintain a cybersecurity program designed to protect the confidentiality, integrity and availability of the Covered Entity's Information Systems.

(b) The cybersecurity program shall be based on the Covered Entity's Risk Assessment and designed to perform the following core cybersecurity functions:

(1) identify and assess internal and external cybersecurity risks that may threaten the security or integrity of Nonpublic Information stored on the Covered Entity's Information Systems;

(2) use defensive infrastructure and the implementation of policies and procedures to protect the Covered Entity's Information Systems, and the Nonpublic Information stored on those Information Systems, from unauthorized access, use or other malicious acts;

(3) detect Cybersecurity Events;

(4) respond to identified or detected Cybersecurity Events to mitigate any negative effects;

(5) recover from Cybersecurity Events and restore normal operations and services; and

(6) fulfill applicable regulatory reporting obligations.

Section 500.03 Cybersecurity Policy.

Cybersecurity Policy. Each Covered Entity shall implement and maintain a written policy or policies, approved by a Senior Officer or the Covered Entity's board of directors (or an appropriate committee thereof) or equivalent governing body, setting forth the Covered Entity's policies and procedures for the protection of its Information Systems and Nonpublic Information stored on those Information Systems. The cybersecurity policy shall be based on the Covered Entity's Risk Assessment and address the following areas to the extent applicable to the Covered Entity's operations: (a) information security; (b) data governance and classification; (c) asset inventory and device management; (d) access controls and identity management; (e) business continuity and disaster recovery planning and resources; (f) systems operations and availability concerns; (g) systems and network security; (h) systems and network monitoring; (i) systems and application development and quality assurance; (j) physical security and environmental controls; (k) customer data privacy; (*l*) vendor and Third Party Service Provider management; (m) risk assessment; and (n) incident response.

Section 500.04 Chief Information Security Officer.

(a) Chief Information Security Officer. Each Covered Entity shall designate a qualified individual responsible for overseeing and implementing the Covered Entity's cybersecurity program and enforcing its cybersecurity policy (for purposes of this Part, "Chief Information Security Officer" or "CISO"). The CISO may be employed by the Covered Entity, one of its Affiliates or a Third Party Service Provider. To the extent this requirement is met using a Third Party Service Provider or an Affiliate, the Covered Entity shall: (1) retain responsibility for compliance with this Part; (2) designate a senior member of the Covered Entity's personnel responsible for direction and oversight of the Third Party Service Provider; and (3) require the Third Party Service Provider to maintain a cybersecurity program that protects the Covered Entity in accordance with the requirements of this Part.

(b) Report. The CISO of each Covered Entity shall report in writing at least annually to the Covered Entity's board of directors or equivalent governing body. If no such board of directors or equivalent governing body exists, such report shall be timely presented to a Senior Officer of the Covered Entity responsible for the Covered Entity's cybersecurity program. The CISO shall report on the Covered Entity's cybersecurity program and material cybersecurity risks. The CISO shall consider to the extent applicable: (1) the confidentiality of Nonpublic Information and the integrity and security of the Covered Entity's Information Systems; (2) the Covered Entity's cybersecurity policies and procedures; (3) material cybersecurity risks to the Covered Entity; (4) overall effectiveness of the Covered Entity's cybersecurity program; and (5) material Cybersecurity Events involving the Covered Entity during the time period addressed by the report.

Section 500.05 Penetration Testing and Vulnerability Assessments.

The cybersecurity program for each Covered Entity shall include monitoring and testing, developed in accordance with the Covered Entity's Risk Assessment, designed to assess the effectiveness of the Covered Entity's cybersecurity program. The monitoring and testing shall include continuous monitoring or periodic Penetration Testing and vulnerability assessments. Absent effective continuous monitoring, or other systems to detect, on an ongoing basis, changes in Information Systems that may create or indicate vulnerabilities, Covered Entities shall conduct:

(a) annual Penetration Testing of the Covered Entity's Information Systems determined each given year based on relevant identified risks in accordance with the Risk Assessment; and

(b) bi-annual vulnerability assessments, including any systematic scans or reviews of Information Systems reasonably designed to identify publicly known cybersecurity vulnerabilities in the Covered Entity's Information Systems based on the Risk Assessment.

Section 500.06 Audit Trail.

(a) Each Covered Entity shall securely maintain systems that, to the extent applicable and based on its Risk Assessment: (1) are designed to reconstruct material financial transactions sufficient to support normal operations and obligations of the Covered Entity; and (2) include audit trails designed to detect and respond to Cybersecurity Events that have a reasonable likelihood of materially harming any material part of the normal operations of the Covered Entity. (b) Each Covered Entity shall maintain records required by section 500.06(a)(1) of this Part for not fewer than five years and shall maintain records required by section 500.06(a)(2) of this Part for not fewer than three years.

Section 500.07 Access Privileges.

As part of its cybersecurity program, based on the Covered Entity's Risk Assessment each Covered Entity shall limit user access privileges to Information Systems that provide access to Nonpublic Information and shall periodically review such access privileges.

Section 500.08 Application Security.

(a) Each Covered Entity's cybersecurity program shall include written procedures, guidelines and standards designed to ensure the use of secure development practices for in-house developed applications utilized by the Covered Entity, and procedures for evaluating, assessing or testing the security of externally developed applications utilized by the Covered Entity within the context of the Covered Entity's technology environment.

(b) All such procedures, guidelines and standards shall be periodically reviewed, assessed and updated as necessary by the CISO (or a qualified designee) of the Covered Entity.

Section 500.09 Risk Assessment.

(a) Each Covered Entity shall conduct a periodic Risk Assessment of the Covered Entity's Information Systems sufficient to inform the design of the cybersecurity program as required by this Part. Such Risk Assessment shall be updated as reasonably necessary to address changes to the Covered Entity's Information Systems, Nonpublic Information or business operations. The Covered Entity's Risk Assessment shall allow for revision of controls to respond to technological developments and evolving threats and shall consider the particular risks of the Covered Entity's business operations related to cybersecurity, Nonpublic Information collected or stored, Information Systems utilized and the availability and effectiveness of controls to protect Nonpublic Information and Information Systems.

(b) The Risk Assessment shall be carried out in accordance with written policies and procedures and shall be documented. Such policies and procedures shall include: (1) criteria for the evaluation and categorization of identified cybersecurity risks or threats facing the Covered Entity; (2) criteria for the assessment of the confidentiality, integrity, security and availability of the Covered Entity's Information Systems and Nonpublic Information, including the adequacy of existing controls in the context of identified risks; and (3) requirements describing how identified risks will be mitigated or accepted based on the Risk Assessment and how the cybersecurity program will address the risks.

Section 500.10 Cybersecurity Personnel and Intelligence.

(a) Cybersecurity Personnel and Intelligence. In addition to the requirements set forth in section 500.04(a) of this Part, each Covered Entity shall: (1) utilize qualified cybersecurity personnel of the Covered Entity, an Affiliate or a Third Party Service Provider sufficient to manage the Covered Entity's cybersecurity risks and to perform or oversee the performance of the core cybersecurity functions specified in section 500.02(b)(1)–(6) of this Part; (2) provide cybersecurity personnel with cybersecurity updates and training sufficient to address relevant cybersecurity risks; and (3) verify that key cybersecurity personnel take steps to maintain current knowledge of changing cybersecurity threats and countermeasures. (b) A Covered Entity may choose to utilize an Affiliate or qualified Third Party Service Provider to assist in complying with the requirements set forth in this Part, subject to the requirements set forth in section 500.11 of this Part.

Section 500.11 Third Party Service Provider Security Policy.

(a) Third Party Service Provider Policy. Each Covered Entity shall implement written policies and procedures designed to ensure the security of Information Systems and Nonpublic Information that are accessible to, or held by, Third Party Service Providers. Such policies and procedures shall be based on the Risk Assessment of the Covered Entity and shall address to the extent applicable: (1) the identification and risk assessment of Third Party Service Providers; (2) minimum cybersecurity practices required to be met by such Third Party Service Providers in order for them to do business with the Covered Entity; (3) due diligence processes used to evaluate the adequacy of cybersecurity practices of such Third Party Service Providers; and (4) periodic assessment of such Third Party Service Providers based on the risk they present and the continued adequacy of their cybersecurity practices.

(b) Such policies and procedures shall include relevant guidelines for due diligence and/or contractual protections relating to Third Party Service Providers including to the extent applicable guidelines addressing: (1) the Third Party Service Provider's policies and procedures for access controls, including its use of Multi-Factor Authentication as required by section 500.12 of this Part, to limit access to relevant Information Systems and Nonpublic Information; (2) the Third Party Service Provider's policies and procedures for use of encryption as required by section 500.15 of this Part to protect Nonpublic Information in transit and at rest; (3) notice to be provided to the Covered Entity in the event of a Cybersecurity Event directly impacting the Covered Entity's Information Systems or the Covered Entity's Nonpublic Information being held by the Third Party Service Provider; and (4) representations and warranties addressing the Third Party Service Provider's cybersecurity policies and procedures that relate to the security of the Covered Entity's Information Systems or Nonpublic Information.

(c) Limited Exception. An agent, employee, representative or designee of a Covered Entity who is itself a Covered Entity need not develop its own Third Party Information Security Policy pursuant to this section if the agent, employee, representative or designee follows the policy of the Covered Entity that is required to comply with this Part.

Section 500.12 Multi-Factor Authentication.

(a) Multi-Factor Authentication. Based on its Risk Assessment, each Covered Entity shall use effective controls, which may include Multi-Factor Authentication or Risk-Based Authentication, to protect against unauthorized access to Nonpublic Information or Information Systems.

(b) Multi-Factor Authentication shall be utilized for any individual accessing the Covered Entity's internal networks from an external network, unless the Covered Entity's CISO has approved in writing the use of reasonably equivalent or more secure access controls.

Section 500.13 Limitations on Data Retention.

As part of its cybersecurity program, each Covered Entity shall include policies and procedures for the secure disposal on a periodic basis of any Nonpublic Information identified in section 500.01(g)(2)–(3) of this Part that is no longer necessary for business operations or for other legitimate business purposes of the Covered Entity, except where such information is otherwise required to be retained by law or regulation, or where targeted disposal is not reasonably feasible due to the manner in which the information is maintained.

Section 500.14 Training and Monitoring.

As part of its cybersecurity program, each Covered Entity shall:

(a) implement risk-based policies, procedures and controls designed to monitor the activity of Authorized Users and detect unauthorized access or use of, or tampering with, Nonpublic Information by such Authorized Users; and

(b) provide regular cybersecurity awareness training for all personnel that is updated to reflect risks identified by the Covered Entity in its Risk Assessment.

Section 500.15 Encryption of Nonpublic Information.

(a) As part of its cybersecurity program, based on its Risk Assessment, each Covered Entity shall implement controls, including encryption, to protect Nonpublic Information held or transmitted by the Covered Entity both in transit over external networks and at rest. (1) To the extent a Covered Entity determines that encryption of Nonpublic Information in transit over external networks is infeasible, the Covered Entity may instead secure such Nonpublic Information using effective alternative compensating controls reviewed and approved by the Covered Entity's CISO. (2) To the extent a Covered Entity determines that encryption of Nonpublic Information at rest is infeasible, the Covered Entity may instead secure such Nonpublic Information using effective alternative compensating controls reviewed and approved by the Covered Entity's CISO.

(b) To the extent that a Covered Entity is utilizing compensating controls under (a) above, the feasibility of encryption and effectiveness of the compensating controls shall be reviewed by the CISO at least annually.

Section 500.16 Incident Response Plan.

(a) As part of its cybersecurity program, each Covered Entity shall establish a written incident response plan designed to promptly respond to, and recover from, any Cybersecurity Event materially affecting the confidentiality, integrity or availability of the Covered Entity's Information Systems or the continuing functionality of any aspect of the Covered Entity's business or operations.

(b) Such incident response plan shall address the following areas: (1) the internal processes for responding to a Cybersecurity Event; (2) the goals of the incident response plan; (3) the definition of clear roles, responsibilities and levels of decision-making authority; (4) external and internal communications and information sharing; (5) identification of requirements for the remediation of any identified weaknesses in Information Systems and associated controls; (6) documentation and reporting regarding Cybersecurity Events and related incident response activities; and (7) the evaluation and revision as necessary of the incident response plan following a Cybersecurity Event.

Section 500.17 Notices to Superintendent.

(a) Notice of Cybersecurity Event. Each Covered Entity shall notify the superintendent as promptly as possible but in no event later than 72 hours from a determination that a Cybersecurity Event has occurred that is either of the following: (1) Cybersecurity Events impacting the Covered Entity of which notice is required to be provided to any government body, self-regulatory agency or any other supervisory body; or (2) Cybersecurity Events that have a reasonable likelihood of materially harming any material part of the normal operation(s) of the Covered Entity.

(b) Annually each Covered Entity shall submit to the superintendent a written statement covering the prior calendar year. This statement shall be submitted by February 15 in such form set forth as Appendix A, certifying that the Covered Entity is in compliance with the requirements set forth in this Part. Each Covered Entity shall maintain for examination by the Department all records, schedules and data supporting this certificate for a period of five years. To the extent a Covered Entity has identified areas, systems or processes that require material improvement, updating or redesign, the Covered Entity shall document the identification and the remedial efforts planned and underway to address such areas, systems or processes. Such documentation must be available for inspection by the superintendent. [. . .]

Section 500.20 Enforcement.

This regulation will be enforced by the superintendent pursuant to, and is not intended to limit, the superintendent's authority under any applicable laws.

The above regulation, as you can see, is specific to only the covered entities specified and is enforced by New York state's Department of Financial Services Superintendent. At the time of writing, NYDFS has built a state cybersecurity regulatory program, but no organizations have been sanctioned. Although specific to limited organizations over a certain financial revenue base or overall size, this statute is by far the most comprehensive cybersecurity statute in the United States.

Other states, such as California, have passed cybersecurity laws focused on consumer safety and privacy. The IoT cybersecurity law, also known as SB-127, focuses on consumer personal information privacy as its core goal in specifying requirements. This statute came into effect January 1, 2020.

STATE OF CALIFORNIA INFORMATION PRIVACY OF CONNECTED DEVICES

SB-127 (2020)

TITLE 1.81.26. Security of Connected Devices

1798.91.04. (a) A manufacturer of a connected device shall equip the device with a reasonable security feature or features that are all of the following: (1) Appropriate to the nature and function of the device. (2) Appropriate to the information it may collect, contain, or transmit. (3) Designed to protect the device and any information contained therein from unauthorized access, destruction, use, modification, or disclosure.

(b) Subject to all of the requirements of subdivision (a), if a connected device is equipped with a means for authentication outside a local area network, it shall be deemed a reasonable security feature under subdivision (a) if either of the following requirements are met: (1) The preprogrammed password is unique to each device manufactured. (2) The device contains a security feature that requires a user to generate a new means of authentication before access is granted to the device for the first time.

1798.91.05. For the purposes of this title, the following terms have the following meanings:

(a) "Authentication" means a method of verifying the authority of a user, process, or device to access resources in an information system.

(b) "Connected device" means any device, or other physical object that is capable of connecting to the Internet, directly or indirectly, and that is assigned an Internet Protocol address or Bluetooth address.

(c) "Manufacturer" means the person who manufactures, or contracts with another person to manufacture on the person's behalf, connected devices that are sold or offered for sale in California. For the purposes of this subdivision, a contract with another person to manufacture on the person's behalf does not include a contract only to purchase a connected device, or only to purchase and brand a connected device.

(d) "Security feature" means a feature of a device designed to provide security for that device.

(e) "Unauthorized access, destruction, use, modification, or disclosure" means access, destruction, use, modification, or disclosure that is not authorized by the consumer.

1798.91.06. (a) This title shall not be construed to impose any duty upon the manufacturer of a connected device related to unaffiliated third-party software or applications that a user chooses to add to a connected device.

(b) This title shall not be construed to impose any duty upon a provider of an electronic store, gateway, marketplace, or other means of purchasing or downloading software or applications, to review or enforce compliance with this title.

(c) This title shall not be construed to impose any duty upon the manufacturer of a connected device to prevent a user from having full control over a connected device, including the ability to modify the software or firmware running on the device at the user's discretion.

(d) This title shall not apply to any connected device the functionality of which is subject to security requirements under federal law, regulations, or guidance promulgated by a federal agency pursuant to its regulatory enforcement authority.

(e) This title shall not be construed to provide a basis for a private right of action. The Attorney General, a city attorney, a county counsel, or a district attorney shall have the exclusive authority to enforce this title.

(f) The duties and obligations imposed by this title are cumulative with any other duties or obligations imposed under other law, and shall not be construed to relieve any party from any duties or obligations imposed under other law.

(g) This title shall not be construed to limit the authority of a law enforcement agency to obtain connected device information from a manufacturer as authorized by law or pursuant to an order of a court of competent jurisdiction.

(h) A covered entity, provider of health care, business associate, health care service plan, contractor, employer, or any other person subject to the federal Health Insurance Portability and Accountability Act of 1996 (HIPAA) (Public Law 104–191) or the Confidentiality of Medical Information Act (Part 2.6 (commencing with Section 56) of Division 1) shall not be subject to this title with respect to any activity regulated by those acts.

In the above regulation, you can see that it does not confer any rights to consumers for recovery, and that it is specifically oriented towards devices not otherwise regulated under federal laws like HIPAA. Next, we will examine a law that specifically focuses on payment card transactions and applies generally to retailers. This law works in a bit of a different way, once again conferring no rights to consumers but protecting organizations that do comply. This law, passed in Minnesota in 2007 and prior to the Target Corporation data breach, attempted to incorporate some of the Payment Card Industry Data Security Standards (PCI-DSS) as an incentive mechanism to avoid liability with financial institutions. States including Nevada and Washington state have passed similar laws. PCI-DSS is a professional standard, required compliance with which is a condition of accepting the major card brands at a retailer.

MINNESOTA PLASTIC CARD SECURITY ACT

325E.64 (2007)

325E.64 Access Devices; Breach of Security.

Subdivision 1. Definitions.

(a) For purposes of this section, the terms defined in this subdivision have the meanings given them.

(b) "Access device" means a card issued by a financial institution that contains a magnetic stripe, microprocessor chip, or other means for storage of information which includes, but is not limited to, a credit card, debit card, or stored value card.

(c) "Breach of the security of the system" has the meaning given in section 325E.61, subdivision 1, paragraph (d).

(d) "Card security code" means the three-digit or four-digit value printed on an access device or contained in the microprocessor chip or magnetic stripe of an access device which is used to validate access device information during the authorization process.

(e) "Financial institution" means any office of a bank, bank and trust, trust company with banking powers, savings bank, industrial loan company, savings association, credit union, or regulated lender.

(f) "Microprocessor chip data" means the data contained in the microprocessor chip of an access device.

(g) "Magnetic stripe data" means the data contained in the magnetic stripe of an access device.

(h) "PIN" means a personal identification code that identifies the cardholder.

(i) "PIN verification code number" means the data used to verify cardholder identity when a PIN is used in a transaction.

(j) "Service provider" means a person or entity that stores, processes, or transmits access device data on behalf of another person or entity.

Subd. 2. Security or identification information; retention prohibited.

No person or entity conducting business in Minnesota that accepts an access device in connection with a transaction shall retain the card security code data, the PIN verification code number, or the full contents of any track of magnetic stripe data, subsequent to the authorization of the transaction or in the case of a PIN debit transaction, subsequent to 48 hours after authorization of the transaction. A person or entity is in violation of this section if its service provider retains such data subsequent to the authorization of the transaction or in the case of a PIN debit transaction, subsequent to 48 hours after authorization of the transaction.

Subd. 3. Liability.

Whenever there is a breach of the security of the system of a person or entity that has violated this section, or that person's or entity's service provider, that person or entity shall reimburse the financial institution that issued any access devices affected by the breach for the costs of reasonable actions undertaken by the financial institution as a result of the breach in order to protect the information of its cardholders or to continue to provide services to cardholders, including but not limited to, any cost incurred in connection with:

(1) the cancellation or reissuance of any access device affected by the breach;

(2) the closure of any deposit, transaction, share draft, or other accounts affected by the breach and any action to stop payments or block transactions with respect to the accounts;

(3) the opening or reopening of any deposit, transaction, share draft, or other accounts affected by the breach;

(4) any refund or credit made to a cardholder to cover the cost of any unauthorized transaction relating to the breach; and

(5) the notification of cardholders affected by the breach.

The financial institution is also entitled to recover costs for damages paid by the financial institution to cardholders injured by a breach of the security of the system of a person or entity that has violated this section. Costs do not include any amounts recovered from a credit card company by a financial institution. The remedies under this subdivision are cumulative and do not restrict any other right or remedy otherwise available to the financial institution.

Each of these statutes has illustrated a different model of regulation related to cybersecurity. First, you examined a law that incorporates specific cybersecurity requirements and has a specially appointed government authority to enforce it. Next, you reviewed a law that includes broad cybersecurity requirements for a specific type of technology. Finally, you reviewed a law that incorporates an industry standard to incentivize good behavior through a liability defense. In most states, however, cybersecurity requirements are incorporated to some degree with either a) privacy laws or b) data breach notification laws. We encourage you to look up the data breach notification and privacy laws for your specific jurisdiction to review whether there are any references to security, cybersecurity, or "administrative and technical" controls.

QUESTIONS

1. Most cybersecurity statutes do not afford a private right of action for an injured consumer or business. What are the positives and negatives to a private right of action for these types of injuries?

2. If you were crafting a cybersecurity statute, would it be applicable to one industry (sectoral) or applicable to all industries (omnibus)? Would you write it more generally or more specifically?

3. From the excerpts above, which statute did you prefer and why?

E. GENERAL REGULATORY REGIMES

At the federal level, as we have previously described, most laws are specific to particular sectors or types organizations, usually because these sectors or organizations pose more risk to consumers. HIPAA, GLBA (financial institutions), Regulation S-P (investment institutions), and the Federal Information Security Modernization Act (FISMA) (government agencies), for example, focus on protecting personal information. For purposes of this chapter, we will include excerpts from HIPAA and FISMA. In addition to these federal laws, as we have discussed, there are other types of administrative models for incentivizing good security behavior. The executive branch, including both the President of the United States of America via executive orders and administrative agencies via rule-making authority, have created additional models of regulation, including direct rules and incentivizing models.

1. SECTOR-SPECIFIC FEDERAL STATUTES

In this section, we will include specific requirements for HIPAA. HIPAA is the most comprehensive sector-specific statute currently in place. As you will see, HIPAA requires covered entities and their business associates to implement the HIPAA Security Rule.

a. HIPAA Security Rules (1996, Security Rule Adopted in 2003, Updated in 2007)

As you read the HIPAA security rules, keep in mind that a covered entity (CE) is the primary organization that is being regulated by HIPAA. A business associate (BA) is a third party of a covered entity that, by virtue of its relationship, is also regulated under HIPAA. Some organizations may be *hybrid entities*, or organizations that may be a covered entity for some services and a business associate for others. An organization may only be one or the other with respect to a given service, but many organizations have many different services they provide. For example, many medical device manufacturers will be CEs or BAs, depending on the role they are fulfilling with respect to patients and other organizations. As you can see in the below definitions, many more organizations, including technology service providers and law firms, are BAs. Covered entities are a much more limited list. Although other requirements under HIPAA may be specific to CEs, the security rule applies to both organizations.

In this excerpt you will see some language that may be new to you. First, you will see a description of the security controls with the notation "addressable" or "required" in parentheses. Addressable requirements under HIPAA are those that are required but may be negotiable depending on other controls that are present and the size/complexity of the organization. Basically, addressable requirements may not be fulfilled if an organization documents the justification and the justification is reasonable. Required requirements are generally non-negotiable. Further, you will see the term "audit" in reference to requirements. Audit is a type of control, generally synonymous with detective controls as we described earlier in this book. Audit requirements are requirements that enable downstream investigation, such as after a data breach or other security incident.

Importantly, HIPAA does not permit any private right of action, and any enforcement is fulfilled by the Office for Civil Rights (OCR), the enforcement arm of the Department of Health and Human Services for HIPAA. OCR has the ability to engage in any administrative enforcement activities, such as investigations, fines, or administrative actions. For more information on previous enforcement actions, visit the HHS website and search for consent orders or consent decrees.

THE HEALTH INSURANCE PORTABILITY AND ACCOUNTABILITY ACT OF 1996

(updated 2003, 2009, 2013)

§ 160.103 Definitions.

Except as otherwise provided, the following definitions apply to this subchapter:

Business associate:

(1) Except as provided in paragraph (4) of this definition, business associate means, with respect to a covered entity, a person who: (i) On behalf of such covered entity or of an organized health care arrangement (as defined in this section) in which the covered entity participates, but other than in the capacity of a member of the workforce of such covered entity or arrangement, creates, receives, maintains, or transmits protected health information for a function or activity regulated by this subchapter, including claims processing or

administration, data analysis, processing or administration, utilization review, quality assurance, patient safety activities listed at 42 CFR 3.20, billing, benefit management, practice management, and repricing; or (ii) Provides, other than in the capacity of a member of the workforce of such covered entity, legal, actuarial, accounting, consulting, data aggregation (as defined in § 164.501 of this subchapter), management, administrative, accreditation, or financial services to or for such covered entity, or to or for an organized health care arrangement in which the covered entity participates, where the provision of the service involves the disclosure of protected health information from such covered entity or arrangement, or from another business associate of such covered entity or arrangement, to the person.

(2) A covered entity may be a business associate of another covered entity.

(3) Business associate includes: (i) A Health Information Organization, E-prescribing Gateway, or other person that provides data transmission services with respect to protected health information to a covered entity and that requires access on a routine basis to such protected health information. (ii) A person that offers a personal health record to one or more individuals on behalf of a covered entity. (iii) A subcontractor that creates, receives, maintains, or transmits protected health information on behalf of the business associate.

(4) Business associate does not include: (i) A health care provider, with respect to disclosures by a covered entity to the health care provider concerning the treatment of the individual. (ii) A plan sponsor, with respect to disclosures by a group health plan (or by a health insurance issuer or HMO with respect to a group health plan) to the plan sponsor, to the extent that the requirements of § 164.504(f) of this subchapter apply and are met. (iii) A government agency, with respect to determining eligibility for, or enrollment in, a government health plan that provides public benefits and is administered by another government agency, or collecting protected health information for such purposes, to the extent such activities are authorized by law. (iv) A covered entity participating in an organized health care arrangement that performs a function or activity as described by paragraph (1)(i) of this definition for or on behalf of such organized health care arrangement, or that provides a service as described in paragraph (1)(ii) of this definition to or for such organized health care arrangement by virtue of such activities or services.

Covered entity means:

(1) A health plan. (2) A health care clearinghouse. (3) A health care provider who transmits any health information in electronic form in connection with a transaction covered by this subchapter.

Protected health information means individually identifiable health information:

(1) Except as provided in paragraph (2) of this definition, that is: (i) Transmitted by electronic media; (ii) Maintained in electronic media; or (iii) Transmitted or maintained in any other form or medium. (2) Protected health information excludes individually identifiable health information: (i) In education records covered by the Family Educational Rights and Privacy Act, as amended, 20 U.S.C. 1232g; (ii) In records described at 20 U.S.C. 1232g(a)(4)(B)(iv); (iii) In employment records held by a covered entity in its role as employer; and (iv) Regarding a person who has been deceased for more than 50 years.

§ 164.306 Security standards: General rules.

(a) General requirements. Covered entities and business associates must do the following: (1) Ensure the confidentiality, integrity, and availability of all electronic protected health information the covered entity or business associate creates, receives, maintains, or transmits. (2) Protect against any reasonably anticipated threats or hazards to the security or integrity of such information. (3) Protect against any reasonably anticipated uses or disclosures of such information that are not permitted or required under subpart E of this part. (4) Ensure compliance with this subpart by its workforce.

(b) Flexibility of approach. (1) Covered entities and business associates may use any security measures that allow the covered entity or business associate to reasonably and appropriately implement the standards and implementation specifications as specified in this subpart. (2) In deciding which security measures to use, a covered entity or business associate must take into account the following factors: (i) The size, complexity, and capabilities of the covered entity or business associate. (ii) The covered entity's or the business associate's technical infrastructure, hardware, and software security capabilities. (iii) The costs of security measures. (iv) The probability and criticality of potential risks to electronic protected health information.

(c) Standards. A covered entity or business associate must comply with the applicable standards as provided in this section and in § 164.308, § 164.310, § 164.312, § 164.314 and § 164.316 with respect to all electronic protected health information. . . .

§ 164.308 Administrative safeguards.

(a) A covered entity or business associate must, in accordance with § 164.306:

(1)(i) Standard: Security management process. Implement policies and procedures to prevent, detect, contain, and correct security violations. (ii) Implementation specifications: (A) Risk analysis (Required). Conduct an accurate and thorough assessment of the potential risks and vulnerabilities to the confidentiality, integrity, and availability of electronic protected health information held by the covered entity or business associate. (B) Risk management (Required). Implement security measures sufficient to reduce risks and vulnerabilities to a reasonable and appropriate level to comply with § 164.306(a). (C) Sanction policy (Required). Apply appropriate sanctions against workforce members who fail to comply with the security policies and procedures of the covered entity or business associate. (D) Information system activity review (Required). Implement procedures to regularly review records of information system activity, such as audit logs, access reports, and security incident tracking reports.

(2) Standard: Assigned security responsibility. Identify the security official who is responsible for the development and implementation of the policies and procedures required by this subpart for the covered entity or business associate.

(3)(i) Standard: Workforce security. Implement policies and procedures to ensure that all members of its workforce have appropriate access to electronic protected health information, as provided under paragraph (a)(4) of this section, and to prevent those workforce members who do not have access under paragraph (a)(4) of this section from obtaining access to electronic protected health information. (ii) Implementation specifications: (A) Authorization and/or supervision (Addressable). Implement procedures for the authorization and/or supervision of workforce members who work with electronic protected health information or in locations where it might be accessed. (B) Workforce clearance procedure (Addressable). Implement procedures to determine that the access of a workforce member to electronic protected health information is appropriate. (C) Termination procedures (Addressable). Implement procedures for terminating access to electronic protected health information when the employment of, or other arrangement with, a workforce member ends or as required by determinations made as specified in paragraph (a)(3)(ii)(B) of this section.

(4)(i) Standard: Information access management. Implement policies and procedures for authorizing access to electronic protected health information that are consistent with the applicable requirements of subpart E of this part. (ii) Implementation specifications: (A) Isolating health care clearinghouse functions (Required). If a health care clearinghouse is part of a larger organization, the clearinghouse must implement policies and procedures that protect the electronic protected health information of the clearinghouse from unauthorized access by the larger organization. (B) Access authorization (Addressable). Implement policies and procedures for granting access to electronic protected health information, for example, through access to a workstation, transaction, program, process, or other mechanism. (C) Access establishment and modification (Addressable). Implement policies and procedures that, based upon the covered entity's or the business associate's access authorization policies, establish, document, review, and modify a user's right of access to a workstation, transaction, program, or process.

(5)(i) Standard: Security awareness and training. Implement a security awareness and training program for all members of its workforce (including management). (ii) Implementation specifications. Implement: (A) Security reminders (Addressable). Periodic security updates. (B) Protection from malicious software (Addressable). Procedures for guarding against, detecting, and reporting malicious software. (C) Log-in monitoring (Addressable). Procedures for monitoring log-in attempts and reporting discrepancies. (D) Password management (Addressable). Procedures for creating, changing, and safeguarding passwords.

(6)(i) Standard: Security incident procedures. Implement policies and procedures to address security incidents. (ii) Implementation specification: Response and reporting (Required). Identify and respond to suspected or known security incidents; mitigate, to the extent practicable, harmful effects of security incidents that are known to the covered entity or business associate; and document security incidents and their outcomes.

(7)(i) Standard: Contingency plan. Establish (and implement as needed) policies and procedures for responding to an emergency or other occurrence (for example, fire, vandalism, system failure, and natural disaster) that damages systems that contain electronic protected health information. (ii) Implementation specifications: (A) Data backup plan (Required). Establish and implement procedures to create and maintain retrievable exact copies of electronic protected health information. (B) Disaster recovery plan (Required). Establish (and implement as needed) procedures to restore any loss of data. (C) Emergency mode operation plan (Required). Establish (and implement as needed) procedures to enable continuation of critical business processes for protection of the security of electronic protected health information while operating in emergency mode. (D) Testing and revision procedures (Addressable). Implement procedures for periodic testing and revision of contingency plans. (E) Applications and data criticality analysis (Addressable). Assess the relative criticality of specific applications and data in support of other contingency plan components.

(8) Standard: Evaluation. Perform a periodic technical and nontechnical evaluation, based initially upon the standards implemented under this rule and, subsequently, in response to environmental or operational changes affecting the security of electronic protected health information, that establishes the extent to which a covered entity's or business associate's security policies and procedures meet the requirements of this subpart. (b)(1) Business associate contracts and other arrangements. A covered entity may permit a business associate to create, receive, maintain, or transmit electronic protected health information on the covered entity's behalf only if the covered entity obtains satisfactory assurances, in accordance with § 164.314(a), that the business associate will appropriately safeguard the information. A covered entity is not required to obtain such satisfactory assurances from a business associate that is a subcontractor. (2) A business associate may permit a business associate that is a subcontractor to create, receive, maintain, or transmit electronic protected health information on its behalf only if the business associate obtains satisfactory assurances, in accordance with § 164.314(a), that the subcontractor will appropriately safeguard the information. (3) Implementation specifications: Written contract or other arrangement (Required). Document the satisfactory assurances required by paragraph (b)(1) or (b)(2) of this section through a written contract or other arrangement with the business associate that meets the applicable requirements of § 164.314(a).

§ 164.310 Physical safeguards.

A covered entity or business associate must, in accordance with § 164.306:

(a)(1) Standard: Facility access controls. Implement policies and procedures to limit physical access to its electronic information systems and the facility or facilities in which they are housed, while ensuring that properly authorized access is allowed. (2) Implementation specifications: (i) Contingency operations (Addressable). Establish (and implement as needed) procedures that allow facility access in support of restoration of lost data under the disaster recovery plan and emergency mode operations plan in the event of an emergency. (ii) Facility security plan (Addressable). Implement policies and procedures to safeguard the facility and the equipment therein from unauthorized physical access, tampering, and theft. (iii) Access control and validation procedures (Addressable). Implement procedures to control and validate a person's access to facilities based on their role or function, including visitor control, and control of access to software programs for testing and revision. (iv)

Maintenance records (Addressable). Implement policies and procedures to document repairs and modifications to the physical components of a facility which are related to security (for example, hardware, walls, doors, and locks).

(b) Standard: Workstation use. Implement policies and procedures that specify the proper functions to be performed, the manner in which those functions are to be performed, and the physical attributes of the surroundings of a specific workstation or class of workstation that can access electronic protected health information.

(c) Standard: Workstation security. Implement physical safeguards for all workstations that access electronic protected health information, to restrict access to authorized users.

(d)(1) Standard: Device and media controls. Implement policies and procedures that govern the receipt and removal of hardware and electronic media that contain electronic protected health information into and out of a facility, and the movement of these items within the facility. (2) Implementation specifications: (i) Disposal (Required). Implement policies and procedures to address the final disposition of electronic protected health information, and/or the hardware or electronic media on which it is stored. (ii) Media re-use (Required). Implement procedures for removal of electronic protected health information from electronic media before the media are made available for reuse. (iii) Accountability (Addressablc). Maintain a record of the movements of hardware and electronic media and any person responsible therefore. (iv) Data backup and storage (Addressable). Create a retrievable, exact copy of electronic protected health information, when needed, before movement of equipment.

§ 164.312 Technical safeguards.

A covered entity or business associate must, in accordance with § 164.306:

(a)(1) Standard: Access control. Implement technical policies and procedures for electronic information systems that maintain electronic protected health information to allow access only to those persons or software programs that have been granted access rights as specified in § 164.308(a)(4). (2) Implementation specifications: (i) Unique user identification (Required). Assign a unique name and/or number for identifying and tracking user identity. (ii) Emergency access procedure (Required). Establish (and implement as needed) procedures for obtaining necessary electronic protected health information during an emergency. (iii) Automatic logoff (Addressable). Implement electronic procedures that terminate an electronic session after a predetermined time of inactivity. (iv) Encryption and decryption (Addressable). Implement a mechanism to encrypt and decrypt electronic protected health information.

(b) Standard: Audit controls. Implement hardware, software, and/or procedural mechanisms that record and examine activity in information systems that contain or use electronic protected health information.

(c)(1) Standard: Integrity. Implement policies and procedures to protect electronic protected health information from improper alteration or destruction. (2) Implementation specification: Mechanism to authenticate electronic protected health information (Addressable). Implement electronic mechanisms to corroborate that electronic protected health information has not been altered or destroyed in an unauthorized manner.

(d) Standard: Person or entity authentication. Implement procedures to verify that a person or entity seeking access to electronic protected health information is the one claimed.

(e)(1) Standard: Transmission security. Implement technical security measures to guard against unauthorized access to electronic protected health information that is being transmitted over an electronic communications network. (2) Implementation specifications: (i) Integrity controls (Addressable). Implement security measures to ensure that electronically transmitted electronic protected health information is not improperly modified without detection until disposed of. (ii) Encryption (Addressable). Implement a mechanism to encrypt electronic protected health information whenever deemed appropriate.

§ 164.314 Organizational requirements.

(a)(1) Standard: Business associate contracts or other arrangements. The contract or other arrangement required by § 164.308(b)(3) must meet the requirements of paragraph (a)(2)(i), (a)(2)(ii), or (a)(2)(iii) of this section, as applicable. (2) Implementation specifications (Required). (i) Business associate contracts. The contract must provide that the business associate will—(A) Comply with the applicable requirements of this subpart; (B) In accordance with § 164.308(b)(2), ensure that any subcontractors that create, receive, maintain, or transmit electronic protected health information on behalf of the business associate agree to comply with the applicable requirements of this subpart by entering into a contract or other arrangement that complies with this section; and (C) Report to the covered entity any security incident of which it becomes aware, including breaches of unsecured protected health information as required by § 164.410. (ii) Other arrangements. The covered entity is in compliance with paragraph (a)(1) of this section if it has another arrangement in place that meets the requirements of § 164.504(e)(3). (iii) Business associate contracts with subcontractors. The requirements of paragraphs (a)(2)(i) and (a)(2)(ii) of this section apply to the contract or other arrangement between a business associate and a subcontractor required by § 164.308(b)(4) in the same manner as such requirements apply to contracts or other arrangements between a covered entity and business associate. [. . .]

§ 164.316 Policies and procedures and documentation requirements.

A covered entity or business associate must, in accordance with § 164.306:

(a) Standard: Policies and procedures. Implement reasonable and appropriate policies and procedures to comply with the standards, implementation specifications, or other requirements of this subpart, taking into account those factors specified in § 164.306(b)(2)(i), (ii), (iii), and (iv). This standard is not to be construed to permit or excuse an action that violates any other standard, implementation specification, or other requirements of this subpart. A covered entity or business associate may change its policies and procedures at any time, provided that the changes are documented and are implemented in accordance with this subpart.

(b)(1) Standard: Documentation. (i) Maintain the policies and procedures implemented to comply with this subpart in written (which may be electronic) form; and (ii) If an action, activity or assessment is required by this subpart to be documented, maintain a written (which may be electronic) record of the action, activity, or assessment. (2) Implementation specifications: (i) Time limit (Required). Retain the documentation required by paragraph (b)(1) of this section for 6 years from the date of its creation or the date when it last was in effect, whichever is later. (ii) Availability (Required). Make documentation available to those persons responsible for implementing the procedures to which the documentation pertains. (iii) Updates (Required). Review documentation periodically, and update as needed, in response to environmental or operational changes affecting the security of the electronic protected health information.

As you read the above excerpt, you likely noticed that HIPAA has defined the Security Rule to include not only technical requirements but also administrative requirements that do not require technology, and physical security requirements. HIPAA also requires organizations to have procedures and plans related to emergencies. When you think about it, this makes sense! Without emergency procedures, how would hospitals continue to run when information systems go down? Strong security programs require all of these areas, even though most cybersecurity teams focus mainly on technical and sometimes administrative controls.

From a risk management perspective, Congress passes statutory requirements when it desires to preventatively control risk rather than waiting until certain events transpire and responding to them. The degree of detail included largely is a matter of determining what the desired behaviors are and how best to balance flexibility with specificity.

2. BROAD FEDERAL STATUTES

Federal Government Requirements—FISMA (2014)

FISMA was first passed in 2002 as part of the E-Government Act, responding to the movement of paper records to increasingly digital systems. And in 2014, amidst a flurry of federal agency breaches and concerns not only about individual U.S. residents but also highly classified and sensitive data the U.S. government collects, uses, and maintains. FISMA was updated to clarify the responsibilities of each federal agency director's cybersecurity obligations. FISMA is comprehensive because it explicitly requires compliance with the National Institute of Standards and Technology requirements, an otherwise non-binding set of requirements established by the primary national standard-bearing institution.[10]

THE FEDERAL INFORMATION SECURITY MANAGEMENT ACT

in THE ELECTRONIC GOVERNMENT ACT OF 2002, PL. No 113–283

Sec. 301. Information Security. [. . .]

(b) Additional Definitions.—As used in this subchapter:

(1) The term 'information security' means protecting information and information systems from unauthorized access, use, disclosure, disruption, modification, or destruction in order to provide—(A) integrity, which means guarding against improper information modification or destruction, and includes ensuring information nonrepudiation and authenticity; (B) confidentiality, which means preserving authorized restrictions on access and disclosure, including means for protecting personal privacy and proprietary information; and (C) availability, which means ensuring timely and reliable access to and use of information.

(2)(A) The term 'national security system' means any information system (including any telecommunications system) used or operated by an agency or by a contractor of an agency, or other organization on behalf of an agency—(i) the function, operation, or use of which—(I) involves intelligence activities; (II) involves cryptologic activities related to national security; (III) involves command and control of military forces; (IV) involves equipment that is an integral part of a weapon or weapons system; or (V) subject to subparagraph (B), is

[10] It should be noted here that NIST does not have any regulatory power specifically. No organizations are required by law to follow NIST, except where NIST is specifically referenced in the text. At the time of writing, only the federal government is required by law to follow NIST requirements.

critical to the direct fulfillment of military or intelligence missions; or (ii) is protected at all times by procedures established for information that have been specifically authorized under criteria established by an Executive order or an Act of Congress to be kept classified in the interest of national defense or foreign policy. (B) Subparagraph (A)(i)(V) does not include a system that is to be used for routine administrative and business applications (including payroll, finance, logistics, and personnel management applications).

§ 3544. Federal agency responsibilities

(a) In General.—The head of each agency shall—

(1) be responsible for—(A) providing information security protections commensurate with the risk and magnitude of the harm resulting from unauthorized access, use, disclosure, disruption, modification, or destruction of—(i) information collected or maintained by or on behalf of the agency; and (ii) information systems used or operated by an agency or by a contractor of an agency or other organization on behalf of an agency; (B) complying with the requirements of this subchapter and related policies, procedures, standards, and guidelines, including—(i) information security standards promulgated under section 11331 of title 40; and (ii) information security standards and guidelines for national security systems issued in accordance with law and as directed by the President; and (C) ensuring that information security management processes are integrated with agency strategic and operational planning processes;

(2) ensure that senior agency officials provide information security for the information and information systems that support the operations and assets under their control, including through—(A) assessing the risk and magnitude of the harm that could result from the unauthorized access, use, disclosure, disruption, modification, or destruction of such information or information systems; (B) determining the levels of information security appropriate to protect such information and information systems in accordance with standards promulgated under section 11331 of title 40, for information security classifications and related requirements; (C) implementing policies and procedures to cost-effectively reduce risks to an acceptable level; and (D) periodically testing and evaluating information security controls and techniques to ensure that they are effectively implemented;

(3) delegate to the agency Chief Information Officer established under section 3506 (or comparable official in an agency not covered by such section) the authority to ensure compliance with the requirements imposed on the agency under this subchapter, including—(A) designating a senior agency information security officer who shall—(i) carry out the Chief Information Officer's responsibilities

under this section; (ii) possess professional qualifications, including training and experience, required to administer the functions described under this section; (iii) have information security duties as that official's primary duty; and (iv) head an office with the mission and resources to assist in ensuring agency compliance with this section; (B) developing and maintaining an agency wide information security program as required by subsection (b); (C) developing and maintaining information security policies, procedures, and control techniques to address all applicable requirements, including those issued under section 3543 of this title, and section 11331 of title 40; (D) training and overseeing personnel with significant responsibilities for information security with respect to such responsibilities; and (E) assisting senior agency officials concerning their responsibilities under paragraph (2);

(4) ensure that the agency has trained personnel sufficient to assist the agency in complying with the requirements of this subchapter and related policies, procedures, standards, and guidelines; and

(5) ensure that the agency Chief Information Officer, in coordination with other senior agency officials, reports annually to the agency head on the effectiveness of the agency information security program, including progress of remedial actions.

(b) Agency Program.—Each agency shall develop, document, and implement an agency-wide information security program, approved by the Director under section 3543(a)(5), to provide information security for the information and information systems that support the operations and assets of the agency, including those provided or managed by another agency, contractor, or other source, that includes—

(1) periodic assessments of the risk and magnitude of the harm that could result from the unauthorized access, use, disclosure, disruption, modification, or destruction of information and information systems that support the operations and assets of the agency;

(2) policies and procedures that—(A) are based on the risk assessments required by paragraph (1); (B) cost-effectively reduce information security risks to an acceptable level; (C) ensure that information security is addressed throughout the life cycle of each agency information system; and (D) ensure compliance with—(i) the requirements of this subchapter; (ii) policies and procedures as may be prescribed by the Director, and information security standards promulgated under section 11331 of title 40; (iii) minimally acceptable system configuration requirements, as determined by the agency; and (iv) any other applicable requirements, including standards and guidelines for national security systems issued in accordance with law and as directed by the President;

(3) subordinate plans for providing adequate information security for networks, facilities, and systems or groups of information systems, as appropriate;

(4) security awareness training to inform personnel, including contractors and other users of information systems that support the operations and assets of the agency, of—(A) information security risks associated with their activities; and (B) their responsibilities in complying with agency policies and procedures designed to reduce these risks;

(5) periodic testing and evaluation of the effectiveness of information security policies, procedures, and practices, to be performed with a frequency depending on risk, but no less than annually, of which such testing—(A) shall include testing of management, operational, and technical controls of every information system identified in the inventory required under section 3505(c); and (B) may include testing relied on in an evaluation under section 3545;

(6) a process for planning, implementing, evaluating, and documenting remedial action to address any deficiencies in the information security policies, procedures, and practices of the agency;

(7) procedures for detecting, reporting, and responding to security incidents, consistent with standards and guidelines issued pursuant to section 3546(b), including—(A) mitigating risks associated with such incidents before substantial damage is done; (B) notifying and consulting with the Federal information security incident center referred to in section 3546; and (C) notifying and consulting with, as appropriate—(i) law enforcement agencies and relevant Offices of Inspector General; (ii) an office designated by the President for any incident involving a national security system; and (iii) any other agency or office, in accordance with law or as directed by the President; and

(8) plans and procedures to ensure continuity of operations for information systems that support the operations and assets of the agency. [. . .]

§ 3545. Annual independent evaluation

(a) In General.—(1) Each year each agency shall have performed an independent evaluation of the information security program and practices of that agency to determine the effectiveness of such program and practices. (2) Each evaluation under this section shall include—(A) testing of the effectiveness of information security policies, procedures, and practices of a representative subset of the agency's information systems; (B) an assessment (made on the basis of the results of the testing) of compliance with—(i) the requirements of this subchapter; and (ii) related information security policies, procedures, standards, and guidelines; and (C) separate presentations, as appropriate, regarding information security relating to national security systems.

(b) Independent Auditor.—Subject to subsection (c)—(1) for each agency with an Inspector General appointed under the Inspector General Act of 1978, the annual evaluation required by this section shall be performed by the Inspector General or by an independent external auditor, as determined by the Inspector General of the agency; and (2) for each agency to which paragraph (1) does not apply, the head of the agency shall engage an independent external auditor to perform the evaluation.

(c) National Security Systems.—For each agency operating or exercising control of a national security system, that portion of the evaluation required by this section directly relating to a national security system shall be performed—(1) only by an entity designated by the agency head; and (2) in such a manner as to ensure appropriate protection for information associated with any information security vulnerability in such system commensurate with the risk and in accordance with all applicable laws. [. . .]

§ 3547. National security systems

The head of each agency operating or exercising control of a national security system shall be responsible for ensuring that the agency—(1) provides information security protections commensurate with the risk and magnitude of the harm resulting from the unauthorized access, use, disclosure, disruption, modification, or destruction of the information contained in such system; (2) implements information security policies and practices as required by standards and guidelines for national security systems, issued in accordance with law and as directed by the President; and (3) complies with the requirements of this subchapter.

SEC. 302. Management Of Information Technology.

(a) In General.—Section 11331 of title 40, United States Code, is amended to read as follows:

§ 11331. Responsibilities for Federal information systems standards

(a) Standards and Guidelines.—(1) Authority To Prescribe.—Except as provided under paragraph (2), the Secretary of Commerce shall, on the basis of standards and guidelines developed by the National Institute of Standards and Technology pursuant to paragraphs (2) and (3) of section 20(a) of the National Institute of Standards and Technology Act (15 U.S.C. 278g–3(a)), prescribe standards and guidelines pertaining to Federal information systems. (2) National Security Systems.—Standards and guidelines for national security systems (as defined under this section) shall be developed, prescribed, enforced, and overseen as otherwise authorized by law and as directed by the President.

(b) Mandatory Requirements.—(1) Authority To Make Mandatory.—Except as provided under paragraph (2), the Secretary shall make standards prescribed under subsection (a)(1) compulsory and binding to the extent determined necessary by the Secretary to improve the efficiency of operation or security of Federal information systems. (2) Required Mandatory Standards.—(A) Standards prescribed under subsection (a)(1) shall include information security standards that—(i) provide minimum information security requirements as determined under section 20(b) of the National Institute of Standards and Technology Act (15 U.S.C. 278g–3(b)); and (ii) are otherwise necessary to improve the security of Federal information and information systems. (B) Information security standards described in subparagraph (A) shall be compulsory and binding.

(c) Authority to Disapprove Or Modify.—The President may disapprove or modify the standards and guidelines referred to in subsection (a)(1) if the President determines such action to be in the public interest. The President's authority to disapprove or modify such standards and guidelines may not be delegated. Notice of such disapproval or modification shall be published promptly in the Federal Register. Upon receiving notice of such disapproval or modification, the Secretary of Commerce shall immediately rescind or modify such standards or guidelines as directed by the President.

(d) Exercise of Authority.—To ensure fiscal and policy consistency, the Secretary shall exercise the authority conferred by this section subject to direction by the President and in coordination with the Director of the Office of Management and Budget.

(e) Application of More Stringent Standards.—The head of an executive agency may employ standards for the cost-effective information security for information systems within or under the supervision of that agency that are more stringent than the standards the Secretary prescribes under this section if the more stringent standards—(1) contain at least the applicable standards made compulsory and binding by the Secretary; and (2) are otherwise consistent with policies and guidelines issued under section 3543 of title 44.

As you can see from the above excerpt, FISMA controls behavior by squarely placing responsibility on the directors of the government agencies. This line of direct responsibility ensures that an individual is responsible for implementing these programs.

a. The U.S. Securities and Exchange Commission

As previously described, the Securities and Exchange Commission regulates publicly traded organizations. With regard to cybersecurity, the SEC has not specified any explicit requirement for preventative security. However, it has developed guidance that specifically interprets what is considered "materiality" with regard to shareholder disclosures. Publicly traded companies have a longstanding obligation to disclose information materially relevant to shareholder decision-making. In the following excerpt, the authors question whether cybersecurity information is materially relevant to shareholder decision-making.

GILLES HILARY, BENJAMIN SEGAL & MAY H. ZHANG, *CYBER-RISK DISCLOSURE: WHO CARES?*

Georgetown McDonough School of Business Research Paper No. 2852519 (2016)

There is increasing interest in cyber-risk among the general public. The number of mentions of this threat in the popular press is high and is growing. Similarly, the number of Google queries regarding cyber-breaches is trending upward and regularly spikes after high profile breaches play out in the media. For example, recent major breaches at Sony and Home Depot have made the headlines for their size. In fact, a Presidential Proclamation of National Cybersecurity Awareness Month was issued by President Barack Obama in October 2009. In contrast, we find that disclosure filings by US listed firms on this topic are limited. Perhaps as a response to this discrepancy, the SEC (starting with guidance issued in 2011) and other regulators have increased pressure on registrants to disclose cyber-risks. We empirically find that this has led to an increase in disclosure but a modest one. We then examine whether this lack of disclosure is warranted or rather reflects a market failure.

We consider data breaches primarily, because the highest profile cases of cyber-crises among US listed firms are tied to this issue (e.g., Sony, Home Depot, Target, Anthem and most recently, Yahoo). We examine the Chronology of Data Breaches database that aims to provide a comprehensive list of privacy data breaches from 2005 to 2014. We observe that the frequency of these events varies over these years but overall, reported data breaches remain relatively rare. Perhaps more relevant for our purpose, the market reaction to the announcement of data breaches is limited. More specifically, the median (mean) three-day period market-adjusted abnormal return is approximately −0.5% (−0.7%). In comparison, the average reaction when a firm announces asset impairment is approximately −1.3%.

Thus, the market reaction to cyber-breaches is statistically significant but economically limited. A qualitative analysis also reveals no significant and persistent negative market reaction when the recent major data breaches at Sony, Target, Home Depot, Anthem and Yahoo were revealed. Consistent with this lack of market reaction, estimates of the costs associated with these breaches to the targeted firms are not material. When we consider the distribution of short window returns, we identify only 3 cases of return below −10% in the ten-year period that encompasses our sample. A cross-sectional analysis indicates that returns upon announcement of a breach are more substantial for more severe breaches and for high book-to-market firms. We do not find that a discussion of cyber-issues in the annual report is associated with the size of the market reaction. Other variables such as a time trend, firm size or being in the financial sector are not statistically associated with short term abnormal returns. Although we find an increase in disclosure after a breach, we find no statistically significant difference between breached firms and a matched sample of firms not affected by a breach. In other words, the increase in disclosure for breached firms cannot be distinguished from a secular trend of a modest increase in disclosure for all firms.

We then consider long term returns a 6- and 12-month periods after the breach announcement. The objective is to evaluate the hypothesis that the market initially under-reacts to the news. Using the methodology proposed by Stafford and Mitchell (2000), we do not find that long-term abnormal returns statistically differ from zero. In addition, we can identify no variable that is statistically associated with these long-term returns. In particular, discussions of cyber-issues in the annual 10-K report are not significantly associated with post-announcement returns. Thus, the evidence does not indicate that the markets over- or under-react to cyber-breach announcements. We also fail to observe significant changes in operational performance measured by the return on assets (ROA). Similarly, we find no significant changes in shareholder clientele. Proportions of transient, dedicated and quasi-indexer investors remain stable after a breach announcement. Finally, we consider the effect of a breach on the likelihood of CEO or other top executive departure (among the five highest compensated at the firm). We do not find any association between the two. Firms that have been breached are similar in terms of propensity of CEO or executive departure before and after the breach, the breach does not increase the probability of a departure, and the difference in differences between the two groups is not significant.

Overall, the lack of disclosure about cyber-risk does not seem to stem from a market or regulatory failure. Although the breach database likely misses some data breaches events, the lack of market reaction in even the most prominent cases suggests that we did not miss many economically significant ones. We acknowledge that our analysis is limited to data breaches and it is possible that other forms of cyber-risks are more problematic. One possibility would be disrupting incidents such as Distributed Denial of Service (DDoS) attacks or ransomware. However, Gordon et al. (2011) find no significant market reaction in a 2002–2007 sample of 31 cyber-incidents disrupting operational capabilities. We also empirically observe that corporate disclosure on these topics is even more limited than on breaches. However, this type of threat may be particularly relevant when it is sponsored by a nation-state. The most prominent case is the major disruption that has affected Aramco in 2012 though, thus far, this type of high-profile incident does not have a publicly known equivalent in the USA or in other large developed economies. The occurrence and consequences of such complex attacks are particularly hard to predict. It is also difficult to imagine what a meaningful corporate disclosure policy should be to address this case.

Another possibility is that we do not capture the effect of cyber-espionage, in particular state-sponsored. This activity may be common. For example, an industry report by Hackmageddon suggests that 10% of cyber-attacks are linked to espionage activities. Interestingly, a Google Trend analysis indicates that the highest density of requests for keywords such as "cyber-security" and "data breaches" comes from cities such as Washington DC, Arlington and Alexandria, locations that are known for their intelligence communities. Indeed, members of intelligence agencies frequently raise this issue as a significant economic threat and this was a major topic of discussion between the US and Chinese presidents at the 2015 G20 Summit. On the one hand, anecdotal evidence provides examples of industrial espionage conducted by all nations that have the technical capabilities to do so, even if most incidents are not publicly revealed. Anecdotal evidence also suggests that firms may have lost business opportunities because of cyber-espionage. For example, it is argued that there is a "growing consensus" that the information hackers seek is "increasingly directed at spying on mergers and acquisitions" and on "any commercial activities related to the trade in oil, gas and other minerals." However, in numerous discussions with practitioners, only one case of corporate demise among large North American firms was brought to our attention (Nortel). People familiar with the case have also suggested that other factors may have played a significant role in this case. In addition, organizations in charge of combatting this threat may have incentives and psychological tendencies to exaggerate its significance. Thus, whether cyber-espionage is a common strategic issue for firms remains an open question. Although financial transparency suggests greater disclosure on this topic, large political and proprietary costs associated with state-sponsored espionage make this unlikely. Empirically, we find little disclosure on this topic.

Our findings have implications for regulators and investors. There is growing interest in cyber-issues among regulatory circles. The main justification for this interest appears to be large economic costs associated with cyber-attacks. Hence, this threat is seen as a material risk for a large cross-section of firms. Our results suggest that, at least historically, senior management nor investors have not considered cyber to be substantial.

Although it is probably prudent to monitor this issue for a change in the environment, our results do not support the notion that regulators with limited resources should focus on this topic for the time being. [. . .]

In 2011, the Securities and Exchange Commission (SEC) issued guidance on disclosure related to cyber risks. It states that "registrants should disclose the risk of cyber incidents in their MD&A if these issues are among the most significant factors that make an investment in the company speculative or risky." The SEC is prescriptive about what companies should take into consideration when assessing cyber-risk: "In determining whether risk factor disclosure is required, we expect registrants to evaluate their cybersecurity risks and take into account all available relevant information, including prior cyber incidents and the severity and frequency of those incidents." The guidance also indicates that: "As part of this evaluation, registrants should consider the probability of cyber incidents occurring and the quantitative and qualitative magnitude of those risks, including the potential costs and other consequences resulting from misappropriation of assets or sensitive information, corruption of data or operational disruption."

In practice, disclosure requirement may be relevant for multiple sections in 10k filings including Risk Factors, MD&A, Description of Business, Legal Proceedings, Financial Statement Disclosures (e.g., material prevention costs, or losses sustained). Masterson (2015) notes that SEC comment letters increasingly encourage or require public companies to enhance disclosures about cyber risks and incidents after the issuance of the guidance.

In a subsequent note, PwC (2015) discussed specific items that are expected to be disclosed by the SEC and the associated potential pitfalls:

- The adequacy of preventative actions taken to reduce cybersecurity risks, in the context of the company's industry. Clients often misjudge adequacy based on the perception that their enterprises are not targeted, and misjudge security requirements based on peer groups.
- Threatened attacks of which the company is aware, including incidents experienced by the registrant that are individually or, in the aggregate, material. This raises the issue not only of what attacks the company is aware of, but of what it is doing to identify attacks.
- Which aspects of business or operations give rise to material cybersecurity risks. Materiality is not always obvious—especially when considering the compromise of intellectual property, trade secrets and other issues which could possibly imperil the brand and, therefore, its value in the market.

- The potential costs and consequences of such material risks. There are many variables here. The loss of personal information in a data breach may involve different costs than, say, the loss of intellectual property and trade secrets.

Apparently, the SEC feels that more needs to be done. For example, Commissioner Luis A. Aguilar opined in 2014 that "[t]here is no doubt that the SEC must play a role in this area. What is less clear is what that role should be." Consistent with this view, the agency recently censured a regional investment company, RT Jones Capital Equities, after a cyber-attack exposed information on 100,000 brokerage clients. The SEC also announced an initiative to review the cyber-security posture of US-registered investment advisers and broker-dealers.

We conduct a systematic analysis of 10-K forms filed with the SEC between the years 2000 and 2015 for cyber related disclosures. Specifically, we download and strip of HTML tags all Form 10-K filings on EDGAR within the period, identify their relevant sections (Item 1A—Risk Factors, Item 7—MD&A). For resulting forms with machine identifiable sections/items, we then run a search that counts all mentions of a wide array of cybersecurity risk related expressions based on language from the SEC disclosure guidance as well as from our readings of practitioner guidance and popular press. The expressions include permutations of cyber or cybersecurity risk or attack and data or information or network breach (hyphenated or spaced and case insensitive). We then aggregate the counts of different expressions across Item 1A and 7 and form a cyber-risk disclosure score (DiscScore). We also create a separate indicator variable (DiscNum) that takes the value of one if the firm makes any mention of cyber-risk, zero otherwise.

We also count the number of words in each section, the average length of the words, and the number of words in a sentence, to gauge the readability of the disclosure. Untabulated correlations between DiscNum or DiscScore and the readability measures in 10K Item 7 are all negative and significant. In other words, firms that disclose information about cyber-risks provide more complete (i.e., longer disclosures with more words and more sentences) and more readable (i.e., shorter words and sentences) discussions in Section 7 (i.e., the MDA). Untabulated results also indicate that these firms provide more complete discussion in 10K Item 1A. However, the results for readability scores are more mixed: they use shorter words but longer sentences.

Cost estimates of cyber breaches vary, depending on the sample and the methodology used by consulting firms. For example, Kaspersky puts the average cost of a cyber-breach at 500,000 US dollars while the estimates from CyberRiskNetwork, IBM and the Ponemon Institute are 675,000, 4 million, and 5 million, respectively. At any rate, the costs associated with a "garden variety" breach do not seem material for a reasonably large listed firm.

Costs associated with catastrophic breaches are more difficult to estimate. For example, an analyst at Mizuho Investors Securities initially estimated the cost of the 2014 Sony breach to be 1.25 billion US dollars. Some media reports indicated that "Credit card data breach estimated to cost Target $3.6 billion." However, the estimates provided by victims of major breaches are much lower. Sony estimated the investigation and remediation costs in the year following the breach to be 35 million dollars. Home Depot indicated in its 10Q filling that "The results for the third quarter and first nine months of fiscal 2014 included $28 million of pretax net expenses related to a breach of our payment data systems." Target estimated the net cost for its breach in 2013 to be 162 million pre-tax for the fiscal years 2013 and 2014. The retailer agreed to pay 10 million dollars to settle a class-action lawsuit in 2015 stemming from its cyberbreach. If the cost estimates provided by these firms are accurate, the effect of high profile breaches is not material for these large firms.

It should also be noted that most large firms have insurance to partially cover their cyberrisk. For example, Home Depot indicates that the company "maintained $100 million of network security and privacy liability insurance coverage in fiscal 2014 [prior to the breach], above a $7.5 million deductible, [. . .]. As of February 1, 2015 [after the breach], we had received an initial payment of $10 million of insurance reimbursements. In fiscal 2015, we entered into a new policy, with $100 million of network security and privacy liability insurance coverage, above a $10 million deductible [. . .]." This suggests that a leak of over 100 million records had a limited impact on Home Depot ability to obtain cyber-insurance (and on the wealth of its insurer). If this case is representative, it suggests that the operational costs of a cyber-breach are more or less equally shared between the company, its insurer and the tax saving.

There is increasing interest in cyber-risk among the general public. In contrast, we find that disclosure by US listed firms on this topic is rare and boiler-plate. Perhaps as a response to this discrepancy, the SEC and other regulators have increased pressure on registrants. We empirically find that this has led to an increase in cyber-risk disclosure but a modest one. We examine whether this relative lack of disclosure is warranted or rather reflects a market or regulatory failure.

To answer this question, we primarily consider data breaches because the highest profile cases of cyber-crises among US listed firms have been tied to this issue. We observe that the number of these events has varied over the years but overall, the phenomenon remains relatively rare. Perhaps more importantly for our purpose, the market reaction to the announcement of data breaches has been limited (approximately −0.5% over a three-day period). A qualitative analysis also reveals no significant persistent negative market reaction when the recent major data breaches at Sony, Target, Home Depot, Anthem and Sony were revealed. Consistent with this lack of market reaction, the estimates of the costs associated with these cases made by the targeted firms are not material. Variables such as prior disclosure, a time trend, size or being in the financial sector are not statistically significant in predicting short term returns. Similarly, we do not find any evidence of longer-term abnormal return. Finally, we do not observe strong reactions after the breaches. A "Diff-in-Diff" analysis reveals that the change in operational performance, in CEO departure likelihood, in shareholder clientele or in the amount of disclosure does not differ from the changes in a matched sample of firms that were not breached.

The excerpt above applies an economic modeling method and quantitative analysis to examine the degree to which actual shareholder decision-making may be influenced by cybersecurity disclosures. The following section describes how administrative agencies may use tools at their disposal to advance the cybersecurity posture of organizations they regulate.

3. REGULATORY TOOLS

Currently, there is no *omnibus*, or generally applicable federal cybersecurity law. Instead, most laws establishing cybersecurity requirements are specific to a particular sector or are for criminal law. For this reason, regulatory agencies have, in some cases, taken an interest in regulating organizations on this topic. Two examples of this interest include the Food and Drug Administration (FDA), a division of the U.S. Department of Health and Human Services, and the Federal Trade Commission (FTC).

The FDA is responsible under the Food, Drug, and Cosmetics Act and its subsequent update, the Medical Devices Amendments Act of 1976, for regulating medical device safety and efficacy. As part of this model, the FDA has, subject to the Administrative Procedure Act (APA), passed certain rules with which organizations must comply. The APA permits regulatory agencies like the FDA to pass legally binding rules that have the effect of law pursuant to a period of time during which the public can offer comments on a proposed rule. During this process, the administrative agency posts a proposed rule in the Federal Register. After the public has had an opportunity to comment for a period of time (at least 30 days), the administrative agency takes the comments into account and passes (or doesn't pass, if disinclined to move forward) a particular rule in the Code of Federal Regulations.

In addition to formally integrated rules, administrative agencies also conduct studies, host workshops, and ultimately develop specific guidelines or guidance that are non-binding. The FDA, for example, has embraced an internal risk management model in the way it establishes requirements. Medical devices that are low risk in terms of potential for bodily injury, such as consumer health apps, are considered exempt from the FDA's review. The FDA has also passed specific rules requiring some consideration of cybersecurity (albeit not specific in nature) for high-risk devices, such as pacemakers. However, the bulk of the FDA's views on cybersecurity have been established through guidance and guidelines both preventative and responsive in nature.

The FTC, as previously discussed earlier in this book, has broad enforcement authority to regulate unfair trade practices and deceptive trade practices under Section 5 of the FTC Act. The FTC also is responsible for antitrust enforcement. These dual responsibilities position the FTC as a guardian of the *consumer* rather than business entities. The FTC considers certain behaviors from the perspective of a consumer, such as whether a consumer would be on reasonable notice as to how their data would be handled, or if providing inaccurate information might induce a consumer to purchase a product they wouldn't have purchased otherwise. The FTC considers these issues broadly and has partnered with the FDA on issues related to over-the-counter drug labels and marketing and with the Computer Fraud Protection Bureau (CFPB) on other product labeling issues.

As you may recall from Chapter 3, the FTC has, in recent years, taken an interest in cybersecurity matters specifically, although this interest has not translated to any binding rules established by the FTC. Rather, most of the FTC's views on cybersecurity are enshrined in consent decrees, instead of formal, legally binding rules. Although the Third Circuit, in *FTC v. Wyndham Worldwide Corp.*, established that the FTC has the ability to regulate cybersecurity under Section 5 of the FTC Act, the recent Eleventh Circuit decision in *LabMD, Inc. v. Federal Trade Commission* has created a higher bar for the FTC's ability to enforce certain cybersecurity activities.

LABMD, INC. V. FEDERAL TRADE COMMISSION

891 F.3d 1286 (2018)

Section 5(a) of the FTC Act authorizes the FTC to protect consumers by "prevent[ing] persons, partnerships, or corporations . . . from using unfair . . . acts or practices in or affecting commerce." The Act does not define the term "unfair." The provision's history, however, elucidates the term's meaning.

The FTC Act, passed in 1914, created the FTC and gave it power to prohibit "unfair methods of competition." Rather than list "the particular practices to which [unfairness] was intended to apply," Congress "intentionally left development of the term 'unfair' to the Commission" through case-by-case litigation—though, at the time of the FTC Act's inception, the FTC's primary mission was understood to be the enforcement of antitrust law. In 1938, the Act was amended to provide that the FTC had authority to prohibit "unfair . . . acts or practices." This amendment sought to clarify that the FTC's authority applied not only to competitors but, importantly, also to consumers. Hence, the FTC possesses "unfairness authority" to prohibit and prosecute unfair acts or practices harmful to consumers.

In 1964, the FTC set forth three factors to consider in deciding whether to wield its unfairness authority. The FTC was to consider whether an act or practice (1) caused consumers, competitors, or other businesses substantial injury; (2) offended public policy as established by statute, the common law, or otherwise; and (3) was immoral, unethical, or unscrupulous. The Supreme Court cited these factors with apparent approval in dicta in the 1972 case FTC v. Sperry & Hutchinson, 405 U.S. 233, 244 n.5, 92 S. Ct. 898, 905 n.5 (1972). [. . .]

Here, the FTC's complaint alleges that LimeWire was installed on the computer used by LabMD's billing manager. This installation was contrary to company policy. The complaint then alleges that LimeWire's installation caused the 1718 File, which consisted of consumers' personal information, to be exposed. The 1718 File's exposure caused consumers injury by infringing upon their right of privacy. Thus, the complaint alleges that LimeWire was installed in defiance of LabMD policy and caused the alleged consumer injury. Had the complaint stopped there, a narrowly drawn and easily enforceable order might have followed, commanding LabMD to eliminate the possibility that employees could install unauthorized programs on their computers.

But the complaint continues past this single allegation of wrongdoing, adding that LimeWire's installation was not the only conduct that caused the 1718 File to be exposed. It also alleges broadly that LabMD "engaged in a number of practices that, taken together, failed to provide reasonable and appropriate security for personal information on its computer networks." The complaint then provides a litany of security measures that LabMD failed to employ, each setting out in general terms a deficiency in LabMD's data-security protocol. Because LabMD failed to employ these measures, the Commission's theory goes, LimeWire was able to be installed on the billing manager's computer. LabMD's policy forbidding employees from installing programs like LimeWire was insufficient.

The FTC's complaint, therefore, uses LimeWire's installation, and the 1718 File's exposure, as an entry point to broadly allege that LabMD's data-security operations are deficient as a whole. Aside from the installation of LimeWire on a company computer, the complaint alleges no specific unfair acts or practices engaged in by LabMD. Rather, it was LabMD's multiple, unspecified failures to act in creating and operating its data-security program that amounted to an unfair act or practice. Given the breadth of these failures, the Commission attached to its complaint a proposed order which would regulate all aspects of LabMD's data-security program—sweeping prophylactic measures to collectively reduce the possibility of employees installing unauthorized programs on their computers and thus exposing consumer information. The proposed cease and desist order, which is identical in all relevant respects to the order the FTC ultimately issued, identifies no specific unfair acts or practices from which LabMD must abstain and instead requires LabMD to implement and maintain a data-security program "reasonably designed" to the Commission's satisfaction.

The decision on which the FTC based its final cease and desist order exhibits more of the same. The FTC found that LabMD "failed to implement reasonable security measures to protect the sensitive consumer information on its computer network" and that the failure caused substantial consumer injury. In effect, the decision held that LabMD's failure to act in various ways to protect consumer data rendered its entire data-security operation an unfair act or practice. The broad cease and desist order now at issue, according to the Commission, was therefore justified.

The first question LabMD's petition for review presents is whether LabMD's failure to implement and maintain a reasonably designed data-security program constituted an unfair act or practice within the ambit of Section 5(a). The FTC declared that it did because such failure caused substantial injury to consumers' right of privacy, and it issued a cease and desist order to avoid further injury.

The Commission must find the standards of unfairness it enforces in "clear and well-established" policies that are expressed in the Constitution, statutes, or the common law. The Commission's decision in this case does not explicitly cite the source of the standard of unfairness it used in holding that LabMD's failure to implement and maintain a reasonably designed data-security program constituted an unfair act or practice. It is apparent to us, though, that the source is the common law of negligence. . .

The gist of the Commission's complaint and its decision is this: The consumers' right of privacy is protected against unintentional invasion. LabMD unintentionally invaded their right, and its deficient data-security program was a legal cause. Section 5(a) empowers the Commission to "prevent persons, partnerships, or corporations . . . from using unfair . . . acts or practices." The law of negligence, the Commission's action implies, is a source that provides standards for determining whether an act or practice is unfair, so a person, partnership, or corporation that negligently infringes a consumer interest protected against unintentional invasion may be held accountable under Section 5(a). We will assume arguendo that the Commission is correct and that LabMD's negligent failure to design and maintain a reasonable data-security program invaded consumers' right of privacy and thus constituted an unfair act or practice.

The second question LabMD's petition for review presents is whether the Commission's cease and desist order, founded upon LabMD's general negligent failure to act, is enforceable. We answer this question in the negative. We illustrate why by first laying out the FTC Act's enforcement and remedial schemes and then by demonstrating the problems that enforcing the order would pose.

The FTC carries out its Section 5(a) mission to prevent unfair acts or practices in two ways: formal rulemaking and case-by-case litigation.

The Commission is authorized under 15 U.S.C. § 57a to prescribe rules "which define with specificity" unfair acts or practices within the meaning of Section 5(a). Once a rule takes effect, it becomes in essence an addendum to Section 5(a)'s phrase "unfair . . . acts or practices"; the rule puts the public on notice that a particular act or practice is unfair. The FTC enforces its rules in the federal district courts. Under 15 U.S.C. § 45(m)(1)(A), the Commission may bring an action to recover a civil penalty against any person, partnership or corporation that knowingly violates a rule. This case does not involve the enforcement of an FTC-promulgated rule.

What is involved here is the FTC's establishment of an unfair act or practice through litigation. Because Congress thought impossible the task of legislating a comprehensive list of unfair acts or practices, it authorized the Commission to establish unfair acts or practices through case-by-case litigation. In the litigation context, once an act or practice is adjudged to be unfair, the act or practice becomes in effect—like an FTC-promulgated rule—an addendum to Section 5(a).

The FTC Act provides two forums for such litigation. The Commission may choose to prosecute its claim that an act or practice is unfair before an ALJ, with appellate review before the full Commission and then in a federal court of appeals. See 15 U.S.C. § 45(b), (c); 16 C.F.R. § 3.1 et seq. Or, under Section 13(b) of the Act, 15 U.S.C. § 53(b), it may prosecute its claim before a federal district judge, with appellate review also in a federal court of appeals. [. . .]

[Details regarding cease and desist order procedures: here, the FTC was seeking a cease and desist against LabMD, Inc.]

The prohibitions contained in cease and desist orders and injunctions must be specific. Otherwise, they may be unenforceable. Both coercive orders are also governed by the same standard of specificity, as the stakes involved for a violation are the same—severe penalties or sanctions.

In the case at hand, the cease and desist order contains no prohibitions. It does not instruct LabMD to stop committing a specific act or practice. Rather, it commands LabMD to overhaul and replace its data-security program to meet an indeterminable standard of reasonableness. This command is unenforceable. Its unenforceability is made clear if we imagine what would take place if the Commission sought the order's enforcement. As we have explained, the standards a district court would apply are essentially the same whether it is entertaining the Commission's action for the imposition of a penalty or the Commission's motion for an order requiring the enjoined defendant to show cause why it should not be adjudicated in contempt. For ease of discussion, we posit a scenario in which the Commission obtained the coercive order it entered in this case from a district court, and now seeks to enforce the order.

The Commission moves the district court for an order requiring LabMD to show cause why it should not be held in contempt for violating the following injunctive provision:

"[T]he respondent shall . . . establish and implement, and thereafter maintain, a comprehensive information security program that is reasonably designed to protect the security, confidentiality, and integrity of personal information collected from or about consumers . . . . Such program . . . shall contain administrative, technical, and physical safeguards appropriate to respondent's size and complexity, the nature and scope of respondent's activities, and the sensitivity of the personal information collected from or about consumers . . ."

The Commission's motion alleges that LabMD's program failed to implement "x" and is therefore not "reasonably designed." The court concludes that the Commission's alleged failure is within the provision's language and orders LabMD to show cause why it should not be held in contempt.

At the show cause hearing, LabMD calls an expert who testifies that the data-security program LabMD implemented complies with the injunctive provision at issue. The expert testifies that "x" is not a necessary component of a reasonably designed data-security program. The Commission, in response, calls an expert who disagrees. At this point, the district court undertakes to determine which of the two equally qualified experts correctly read the injunctive provision. Nothing in the provision, however, indicates which expert is correct. The provision contains no mention of "x" and is devoid of any meaningful standard informing the court of what constitutes a "reasonably designed" data-security program. The court therefore has no choice but to conclude that the Commission has not proven—and indeed cannot prove—LabMD's alleged violation by clear and convincing evidence. See McGregor, 206 F.3d at 1383.

In sum, assuming arguendo that LabMD's negligent failure to implement and maintain a reasonable data-security program constituted an unfair act or practice under Section 5(a), the Commission's cease and desist order is nonetheless unenforceable. It does not enjoin a specific act or practice. Instead, it mandates a complete overhaul of LabMD's data-security program and says precious little about how this is to be accomplished. Moreover, it effectually charges the district court with managing the overhaul. This is a scheme Congress could not have envisioned. We therefore grant LabMD's petition for review and vacate the Commission's order.

As you can see in the above excerpt, the Eleventh Circuit was unwilling to uphold the FTC's demand for LabMD to develop a comprehensive cybersecurity program because the FTC did not establish, via rule-making, a legally binding set of requirements against which LabMD's behaviors might be enforced. The result of this case leaves a murky area for the FTC. The FTC may enforce against unfair or deceptive trade practices related to cybersecurity choice, but the FTC first must establish some specificity in what unfair or deceptive cybersecurity practices actually are, or what is a "reasonable" cybersecurity program with respect to a given company.

This question of "reasonableness" is not unique to the FTC's cybersecurity efforts. To the contrary, it is a theme that runs throughout the law—and perhaps no area of law more than tort law. If you recall from earlier in this chapter the discussion of the prima facie case for a negligence claim in in tort, the first elements of establishing a negligence claim are demonstrating that the defendant had a duty to the plaintiff that was breached.

The duty in at issue in negligence cases is that of "ordinary care." The most canonical statement of what constitutes "ordinary care" tells us that "Negligence is the omission to do something which a reasonable man, guided upon those considerations which ordinarily regulate the conduct of human affairs, would do, or doing something which a prudent and reasonable man would not do."[11]

Importantly, this standard of reasonableness that is used in tort negligence claims is that of an *objectively* reasonable person—that is, did the defendant act as a hypothetical ordinary person would have acted—as opposed to that of a *subjectively* reasonable person—one who subjectively believed their conduct to be reasonable, whether or not it in fact was. This distinction between objective and subjective standards of reasonableness comes up in many areas of law. Tort law's objective standard for negligence, it turns out, is an outlier. Consider the following excerpt:

---

[11] *Blyth v Birmingham Waterworks Company*, 11 Exch. 781, 156 Eng. Rep. 1047 (1856).

JUSTIN (GUS) HURWITZ, *RESPONSE TO MCGEVERAN'S THE DUTY OF DATA SECURITY: NOT THE OBJECTIVE DUTY HE WANTS, MAYBE THE SUBJECTIVE DUTY WE NEED*

103 MN. L. REV. HEADNOTES 139 (2019)

Introduction

William McGeveran's recent article, *The Duty of Data Security*,[12] is a significant contribution to ongoing debates about what duty firms holding electronic information about consumers owe in ensuring the security of that data. It also supports the opposite conclusion from that which McGeveran articulates. McGeveran frames the article as identifying a clear duty of data security. This response argues that in his efforts to locate a clear duty in existing data security law he has identified a standard that, in all meaningful ways, is one of subjective (not objective) reasonableness—and therefore offers no clarity at all. There is likely room for disagreement on both sides of this argument—both that which McGeveran makes and my response to it. The ultimate purpose this this response, however, is to recognize this aspect of the duty that McGeveran has identified and to reframe it in the familiar terms of objective vs. subjective reasonableness. This distinction is both useful and important, and has gone unremarked upon in two decades of discussions about the data security obligations.

McGeveran is responding to arguments that any duty of data security created by the law is "insufficiently specific, concrete, or uniform," and that "there is no way to understand the meaning of 'reasonable' data security measures under consumer protection law." Presumably in the interest of jocular and spirited debate, he calls such claims "balderdash." The purpose of his article is to support his claim of "balderdash"—to argue that many "duties" of data security are found throughout the law and that these "numerous sources of a duty of data security sound together in harmony, not cacophony."

To this end he undertakes the yeoman's task of surveying a large cross-section of American law as it pertains to data security. He looks, in total, at 14 different areas of law—including seven areas of public law and seven areas of private law—and distills from this survey a range of commonalities that exist across this body of law. He then synthesizes from these commonalities the attributes of what he calls a duty of data security. This "duty," however is largely meaningless because it is one of subjective reasonableness. Though it has not been framed in these terms, a significant part of the data security debate over the past decade has been about whether data security is governed by an objective reasonableness standard. By situating the duty of data security in subjective reasonableness, McGeveran effectively torpedoes the arguments of the enforcement advocates to whom he believes he is an ally. [. . .]

---

[12] William McGeveran, *The Duty of Data Security*, 103 MINN. L. REV. 1135 (2019).

McGeveran's Argument, and Where We Agree

McGeveran's article offers a masterful descriptive analysis of vast swaths of current data security law. Roughly the first half of his article is a survey of the dominant public and private law frameworks for regulating data security. This includes, for instance, HIPAA and GLBA, FTC enforcement through its consumer protection authority, state laws and regulations, industry self-regulation, professional certification, and contractual mechanisms. Other than its exclusion of common law mechanisms—a reasonable exclusion given the uncertain and to date largely ineffective status of common law tools in regulating data security practices—this is without a doubt the most comprehensive current survey of data security law.

Part II of McGeveran's article offers his core analysis, synthesizing common characteristics across the regimes surveyed in the first half of the article to identify the core "content" common across all of these regimes. He breaks this analysis down into four parts, the first two of which reflect canonical understandings and the latter two of which are at least very interesting. The central element of the "duty of data security" that he identifies relates to reasonableness and risk. As he describes it, "all the frameworks [considered in Part I] embrace some form of a reasonableness requirement, whether or not using that name." I will return to his discussion of reasonableness as the defining element of the duty of data security in Part II below—for now, it suffices to say that I agree with his identification of reasonableness as central, but believe that it mischaracterizes the nature of reasonableness embodied in this standard.

The second conceptual element that he identifies is that data security is built around what he calls "systems of compliance." This, too, is common understanding within the field—more commonly phrased as security is about process, not state. In other words, good security requires continual identification, assessment, monitoring, responding, and improvement—it is not about achieving a state of being secure, but is about approaching security as on ongoing activity. This is best captured from a regulatory perspective, for instance, by the HHS OCR's general emphasis in HIPAA compliance on whether a firm that may have experienced a security incident had security procedures in place and not whether those procedures were substantively good.

The third conceptual element that McGeveran identifies is interesting, if less compelling. He identifies three architectural components of good data security practices: access controls, encryption, and multi-factor authentication. Substantively he overstates his case. For instance, implementing access controls is better characterized as part of the process that makes up a system of compliance. That this is a process- or system-level element is indicated by the fact that the extent of access control requirements needs to be scoped to the systems or data to be protected (that is, any system that implements absolute access controls would be unusable). Similarly, with multi-factor authentication, which is an aspect of an access control implementation—some system components need no authentication, others may reasonably only need a single factor of authentication, while others may need multiple factors (and even continuous affirmation) of authentication. Encryption is an even more contentious element for McGeveran to identify as a clear architectural element of data security. Not all the frameworks he considers, for instance, require all data to be encrypted in all circumstances, and from a compliance perspective encryption safe harbors (common in many of the frameworks) have been criticized as leading to overall poorer security environments.

The fourth conceptual element McGeveran identifies—"worst practices"—is notably interesting and reflects ongoing discussion within the community about applying concepts such as per se negligence to address overtly problematic conduct that falls below any arguable understanding of reasonable security. This is a developing area of discussion and McGeveran's characterization of these practices is in line with much current thinking.

Importantly, the idea of per se negligence for such clearly problematic "worst practices" is complementary to the standard of reasonableness discussed in the rest of this response. As discussed below, the standard of reasonableness that McGeveran identifies (and discusses as the first conceptual element of data security) is a *subjective* standard, not an *objective* one. This is reflected in the characteristics that define the concept of reasonableness throughout the various frameworks that he surveys and by the centrality of process (or "systems of compliance" in McGeveran's terminology) in understanding the duty of data security. The evolving, and increasingly accepted, norm for good data security is for firms to adhere to an exceptionally low baseline of minimal practices and, beyond that baseline, to engage in reasonable effort to secure their systems (that is, to try to be secure, regardless whether they succeed). This roughly corresponds to a subjective reasonableness standard backed by a per se negligence standard for extremely objectionable conduct. [. . .]

What is the Duty of Data Security Debate?

The animating issue in the debate about the duty of data security is not whether such a duty exists. It is whether that duty is based on an objective or subjective standard that can be applied economy-wide. The focal point of this debate has been the Federal Trade Commission's efforts to develop a "common law" of data security based upon its broad Section 5 "unfairness" authority. This effort was crystalized in the Commission's efforts to act against LabMD, a small medical testing laboratory that allegedly experienced a data breach in 2008. As McGeveran's article was nearing completion, the 11th Circuit court of appeals issued its opinion in LabMD's final appeal of the FTC's efforts in that case, vindicating LabMD's arguments that the FTC's data security standard was unenforceable vague and vacating the FTC's decade-long case against LabMD.

In its efforts to develop these standards, including in litigation against LabMD, the FTC has analogized the standard it applies in data security cases to that of negligence in the tort setting (that is, of objective reasonableness). Critics of the FTC's objectiveness standard, myself included, have argued, in effect, that there is no objective standard or reasonableness in the data security context and that any subjective standard is fundamentally unavailing in a generalized, economy-wide, context. In its opinion the 11th Circuit agreed. The 11th Circuit characterized the central provision of the Commission's order against LabMD as subject to "an indeterminable standard of reasonableness," and characterized five other commands in that order as "equally vague."

In other words, because the FTC's order provides no objective standard by which the court can evaluate the reasonableness of LabMD's data security efforts, the court would be forced to evaluate compliance with that order on an ongoing, case-by-case, basis. In particular, the court explains, the FTC's order "is devoid of any meaningful standard informing the court of what constitutes a 'reasonably designed' data-security program." That is, because there is no objective standard by which the court can evaluate compliance with the order the court cannot enforce the order.

The 11th Circuit was concerned with the judicial enforceability of the FTC's orders. But the same concern trickles down to the firms regulated by the FTC—literally every business in the country. Most businesses are no more expert in data security than a typical judge. Indeed, courts are assisted by expert witnesses and extensive briefing on the specific issues before them. If the standard proffered by the FTC is too indeterminate for a court to objectively evaluate conduct in specific cases, then clearly it is too indeterminate to be applied in the general case. Indeed, this is part of the reason that other judges had raised concerns about the FTC's data security efforts on due process grounds. That is, it is an inherently subjective, not objective, standard.

McGeveran's Compelling Case for a Subjective Standard

The LabMD case, of course, is just one data point. The structure of the 11th Circuit's opinion is fairly characterized as "curious." The 11th Circuit's focus on the judicial enforceability of the Commission's order is an awkward sidestep of a direct evaluation of the Commission's substantive authority.

Fortunately, McGeveran has undertaken the arduous task of comprehensively surveying data security law as it exists across the country. What he overwhelmingly finds is that it is subject to a subjective reasonableness standard. Consistent with the 11th Circuit, such a standard is exceptionally difficult to enforce through the legal system.

Throughout his survey of data security standards, McGeveran comes across myriad examples of reasonableness standards. Importantly, McGeveran does not explicitly distinguish between objective and subjective reasonableness. He does offer a brief discussion of the concept of reasonableness, noting that "Perhaps the most prominent reasonableness standard in law is the general measure of liability for negligence torts," and citing to the Restatement of Torts' definition of reasonableness. Tellingly, while he cites the Restatement comment that discussed the "Qualities of the 'reasonable man,'" he omits the subsequent comment on the "Standard of the 'reasonable man." This subsequent comment explains that:

> Negligence is a departure from a standard of conduct demanded by the community for the protection of others against unreasonable risk. The standard which the community demands must be an objective and external one, rather than that of the individual judgment, good or bad, of the particular individual.

In other words, tort law's negligence objective reasonableness standard is atypical; more often reasonableness is adjudged on a subjective basis.

Curiously, McGeveran takes a moment to chastise the 11th Circuit for importing the tort negligence standard—one based on objective reasonableness—into the LabMD case. McGeveran responds to this concern by distinguishing the tort negligence standard from the reasonableness standard he finds across data security law. As an example of the "reasonableness" standards, he cites examples where reasonable data security is defined, for instance, in terms of requiring "each company to assess its specific risk profile and design a program that addresses its risks in a robust fashion." He then goes on to cite the NIST Cybersecurity Framework as another example:

> With this information, organizations can determine the acceptable level of risk for achieving their organizational objectives and can express this as their risk tolerance. With an understanding of risk tolerance, organizations can prioritize cybersecurity activities, enabling organizations to make informed decisions about cybersecurity expenditures.

McGeveran doesn't cite the FTC's typical language in describing its data security expectations, but they are similar, modeled after the data security requirements in HIPAA and GLBA (which he does cite). The specific language, for instance, from the FTC's LabMD order noted by the 11th Circuit is:

> [T]he respondent shall . . . establish and implement, and thereafter maintain, a comprehensive information security program that is reasonably designed to protect the security, confidentiality, and integrity of personal information collected

> from or about consumers . . . . Such program . . . shall contain administrative, technical, and physical safeguards appropriate to respondent's size and complexity, the nature and scope of respondent's activities, and the sensitivity of the personal information collected from or about consumers . . . .

"Company specific risk profiles"? "Achieving organization objectives," "risk tolerance," and "prioritizing cybersecurity activities"? "Safeguards appropriate to [] size and complexity"? These are requirements that firms tailor their security programs to their specific circumstances, based on firm-specific assessments. This is the language of subjective reasonableness.

Ultimately, it seems likely that McGeveran would agree that the reasonableness standard he finds situated in his survey of data security standards has elements of subjective reasonableness. Indeed his articulation of the duty of data security emphasizes that that duty is rooted in flexible standards and calibrated to the risks faced by and resources available to the firm holding data.

As we have established above, there are multiple challenges in each mode of enforcement: private law for consumers, private ordering and law between organizations, statutory enforcement, and even administrative agency behavior. One of the most unique aspects of cybersecurity law in each of these areas is the role of an individual or individuals, the adversaries in these scenarios, as they are not often part of the liability scheme under any of the previous legal models we have just discussed. Rather, prosecution of cybercriminals is often a matter for criminal law.

QUESTIONS

1. Do you think Section 5 of the FTC Act, "unfair or deceptive acts or practices in or affecting commerce," should apply to cybersecurity matters, as the U.S. Court of Appeals for the Third Circuit did in *FTC v. Wyndham Worldwide Corporation, et al.*, 799 F.3d 236 (3d Cir. 2015)?

2. What are the relevant benefits and drawbacks to the FTC using their discretion to levy fines and prosecute cybersecurity-related unfair or deceptive trade practices under Section 5 without creating specific rules or guidance on the topic?

3. Does the distinction between objective and subjective reasonableness matter in cybersecurity cases? Is there such a thing as objectively reasonable security standards?

4. Earlier in this book (Chapter 2.A), we discussed the idea of "security as process." How does this idea affect how we may evaluate whether a system that has been compromised was sufficiently "secure"? Do the specific security

standards or protocols that a defendant had in place matter? Should we focus instead whether on the defendant was demonstrably making well-intended efforts to have secure systems?

F. CRIMINAL STATUTES

Although up until this point in this chapter we have discussed civil remedies, statutory requirements, and administrative agency behavior, criminal law is a very important part of overall cybersecurity policy at the state and federal levels. State law usually parallels federal criminal statutes so that states can ensure a similar degree of enforcement for digital crimes. In your class, you may discuss criminal statutes specific to your state—many states have passed a state-oriented version of the Computer Fraud and Abuse Act, detailed in this section. For purposes of this chapter, we will discuss only federal laws.

JEFF KOSSEFF, *DEFINING CYBERSECURITY LAW*

103 IOWA L. REV. 985 (2018)

The United States has very few laws that mention cybersecurity by name. The lack of explicit references to cybersecurity is understandable, as "cybersecurity" is a relatively new term. Indeed, the first time that a published U.S. court opinion even used the word "cybersecurity" was in a footnote to a 2007 Seventh Circuit opinion. However, there are a number of U.S. state and federal statutes, regulations, and court opinions regarding data security, hacking, and related issues that address some aspects associated with cybersecurity law. . .

The existing cybersecurity framework focuses largely on protecting the confidentiality of information for the purposes of protecting individual privacy. However, the laws could be improved to focus more other aspects, including: (1) integrity and availability; (2) protecting systems and networks; and (3) promoting economic and national security interests. Moreover, cybersecurity law could benefit from a more forward-looking perspective with the goal of preventing future incidents, rather than the current focus on penalizing companies for failing to safeguard against previous attacks. [. . .]

Computer Hacking Laws

The primary computer hacking laws at the federal level are the Computer Fraud and Abuse Act ("CFAA") and the Economic Espionage Act ("EEA").

The CFAA criminalizes seven different types of activities, which could generally be described as: (1) hacking to commit espionage; (2) hacking to obtain information; (3) hacking a federal government computer; (4) hacking to commit fraud; (5) hacking to commit damage; (6) trafficking in passwords; and (7) threats of hacking. In addition to criminal penalties, the

CFAA allows victims of computer hacking who have suffered damage or loss to sue under certain circumstances.

Companies that have had information stolen or suffered damage to their systems or networks frequently bring civil claims under CFAA. The CFAA defines "damage" as "any impairment to the integrity or availability of data, a program, a system, or information." For instance, in 2011, the United States Court of Appeals for the Sixth Circuit held that the CFAA applied to an email campaign aimed at impairing the ability of a company to send and receive emails. Similarly, in 2012, a federal judge concluded that "damage" under the CFAA broadly includes "the destruction, corruption, or deletion of electronic files, the physical destruction of a hard drive, or any 'diminution in the completeness or usability of the data on a computer system.' " In that respect, it is among the more comprehensive existing cybersecurity laws, as it addresses not only harms to confidentiality, but also integrity and availability. Similarly, the CFAA encompasses more areas of cybersecurity law by covering not merely harms to information, but also damage to systems or networks.

That is not to say that the CFAA is the model for cybersecurity law. For one thing, much of it was drafted more than 30 years ago, and critics argue that it has not kept up with the times. Most notably, courts are deeply divided as to the scope of the CFAA. The seven provisions only apply to acts that are done "without authorization" or that "exceeds authorized access." The courts are deeply divided as to whether an individual who misuses information to which she had lawful access is subject to the CFAA. The United States Court of Appeals for the Ninth Circuit has narrowly interpreted the CFAA, concluding that "[i]f Congress meant to expand the scope of criminal liability to everyone who uses a computer in violation of computer use restrictions—which may well include everyone who uses a computer—we would expect it to use language better suited to that purpose." Other courts, however, have focused not only on whether the initial access was authorized, but on whether that initial access was used to further unauthorized activities. The circuit court split on this issue is one example of the ambiguity of some provisions of the CFAA. Indeed, critics argue that CFAA is overly punitive, potentially exposing defendants to decades in prison. For instance, Aaron Swartz was indicted for 11 counts of CFAA violations arising from allegedly downloading millions of academic articles from a school's access to a proprietary database, exposing him to up to 35 years in prison. Swartz committed suicide before going to trial, and many critics of CFAA have used his case to criticize the "disproportionate" nature of the CFAA and computer crime laws in general.

The CFAA also has attracted criticism from some commentators for its likely—though far from certain—prohibition on the ability of private parties to "hack back" against those that attack them. This is seen as ultimately constraining the ability of the private sector to mitigate and prevent cyberattacks, and some scholars and lawmakers have proposed amending the CFAA to explicitly allow companies to obtain information from and damage the systems of hackers.

Although the CFAA is the primary on-point federal statute for computer hacking, prosecutors and private parties also use the EEA against cyber criminals. This Act prohibits individuals from stealing, copying, receiving, or possessing trade secrets without authorization if the individuals either (1) "intend[ed] or kn[ew] that the offense [would] benefit any foreign government, foreign instrumentality, or foreign agent" or (2) acted for the "benefit of anyone other than the [trade secret's] owner." The statute imposes criminal penalties, and it recently was amended to allow victims of trade secret misappropriation to bring civil actions.

Congress passed the EEA in 1996, recognizing that the proliferation of computers "enables rapid and surreptitious duplications of the information." Since its passage, the government has prosecuted a number of cases in which the defendants allegedly stole trade secrets, often from their former employers, to benefit another company or nation. The recent revisions that allow civil claims arising from trade secret theft likely will increase the Act's use in cyber-theft cases.

Unlike the CFAA, which is more broadly focused on the theft of data and damage to systems and networks, the EEA focuses on the confidentiality of data. In that sense, the EEA addresses the same narrow avenue of cybersecurity law as many of the other protections. Although the EEA is particularly effective at addressing insider threats from employees and others who already have authorized access to trade secrets, it is rare to see the Act be used to prosecute or bring claims against external hackers.

Moreover, the EEA is narrowly focused on protecting the confidentiality of certain types of information. The EEA only applies to trade secrets and therefore would not penalize the theft of personal information that does not qualify for trade secret protection. Likewise, the EEA does not impose criminal or civil penalties on hackers who launch attacks on systems or networks, or who threaten the availability or integrity of information. For instance, a ransomware campaign that shuts down a company's internal servers for a week probably would not violate the EEA, as the campaign would not involve the theft of trade secrets.

Electronic Communications Privacy Act

Restrictions on the ability of the public and private sectors to access electronic data often are associated with cybersecurity, although there is an equally strong argument that they primarily are privacy laws. The Electronic Communications Privacy Act ("ECPA") is the primary federal restriction on electronic surveillance by public and private actors. ECPA consists of three separate statutes: (1) the Wiretap Act (which restricts the surveillance of communications content while it is in transit); (2) the Stored

Communications Act (which restricts the surveillance of communications content while it is in storage); and (3) the Pen Register Act (which restricts the use of devices to collect metadata, such as phone numbers dialed and email addresses in the "to" and "from" headers).

The ECPA is an attempt to codify into statute some of the Fourth Amendment protections against unreasonable searches and seizures of electronic data, though it has faced some criticism for failing to adequately protect certain data—in part due to the failure of Congress to significantly update the statute since 1986. However, the statutes go beyond restrictions on government surveillance. They also restrict the ability of private parties to monitor user data or share it with other parties, including the government.

To be sure, the ECPA contains a number of exceptions that allow service providers to monitor networks and share information with the government. However, even narrow restrictions on monitoring and disclosure may make it more difficult for the government and private sector to work together to combat cyber-threats.

That is not to say that the ECPA's restrictions on access to data are misplaced. Indeed, they are fundamental to protecting privacy and preventing government and corporate overreach. But these privacy protections do, to at least some extent, stifle the potential for cooperation between the government and the private sector in achieving better cybersecurity. As we assess how our existing laws contribute to our new conception of cybersecurity law, we must assess how they encourage or impede such collaboration.

The Cybersecurity Act of 2015

The Cybersecurity Act of 2015 is an attempt to address impediments to such collaboration between the public and private sectors. Although, as discussed in the Introduction to this Article, the statute does not explicitly define "cybersecurity," it covers the field of cybersecurity law better than any other single statute. In that sense, the Cybersecurity Act is the statute that is most closely focused on this Article's conception of cybersecurity law.

Among the many provisions of the Cybersecurity Act are provisions that allow private entities to: (1) monitor information systems for cybersecurity purposes; (2) operate "defensive measures" for cybersecurity purposes; and (3) share information about cyber-threat indicators or defensive measures with other private entities or the federal government. These provisions abrogate some of the ECPA's limits on monitoring and disclosure, described above, though the extent of the abrogation is unclear because no court has yet applied the Cybersecurity Act to privacy claims.

The Cybersecurity Act provides limited protection from liability for companies that monitor information systems under the statute or share or receive cyber-threat indicators. However, this open-ended communication can pose problems. Despite requirements for private entities to take steps to remove personal information before sharing cyber-threat indicators, critics attacked the statute for potentially immunizing companies that violate individuals' privacy rights while not necessarily helping companies improve their cybersecurity. The lengthy and spirited debate over the law demonstrates the tension that is often present between privacy protections and collaborative cybersecurity efforts.

Although the privacy concerns are well-founded, the statute—and the DHS's implementation of the sharing law—provide fairly strong safeguards to reduce the likelihood of privacy violations. It remains to be seen the extent to which the Cybersecurity Act improves cybersecurity, as agencies are still in the process of implementing it.

However, there is a reasonable likelihood that the Cybersecurity Act's broad approach to cybersecurity law will have a positive effect. Importantly—and unlike many of the other laws and regulations discussed in this Article—the Cybersecurity Act provides a cooperative framework for companies to work with the government. For three decades, cybersecurity law in the United States has developed under a primarily coercive regulatory structure, with companies and individuals facing the prospect of huge fines and other enforcement actions arising from their failure to adequately safeguard data. Those coercive statutes play an important role, and this Article in no way suggests that the Cybersecurity Act and similar statutes replace them. Rather, the Cybersecurity Act's proactive and cooperative measures compliment those of the CFAA, data security statutes, and other coercive regulations.

Additionally, the Cybersecurity Act's broad approach contemplates not only threats to confidentiality, but also to integrity and availability, as it focuses on information, systems, and networks. Consider, for instance, the definition of "cyber threat indicators" that companies may share:

"[I]nformation that is necessary to describe or identify—

(A) malicious reconnaissance, including anomalous patterns of communications that appear to be transmitted for the purpose of gathering technical information related to a cybersecurity threat or security vulnerability;

(B) a method of defeating a security control or exploitation of a security vulnerability;

(C) a security vulnerability, including anomalous activity that appears to indicate the existence of a security vulnerability;

(D) a method of causing a user with legitimate access to an information system or information that is stored on, processed by, or transiting an information system to unwittingly enable the defeat of a security control or exploitation of a security vulnerability;

(E) malicious cyber command and control;

(F) the actual or potential harm caused by an incident, including a description of the information exfiltrated as a result of a particular cybersecurity threat;

(G) any other attribute of a cybersecurity threat, if disclosure of such attribute is not otherwise prohibited by law; or

(H) any combination thereof."

This definition contemplates not only threats to the confidentiality of data, but also access that could result in the unauthorized modification or unavailability of data, systems, and networks. More than many of the other prominent cybersecurity laws, this statute broadly addresses a range of modern cybersecurity threats.

Relatedly, while the Cybersecurity Act may encourage companies to improve their cybersecurity to prevent data breaches (and therefore promote individual privacy), the Cybersecurity Act also helps to address threats to companies' business operations (by allowing the sharing of information about DDOS attacks) and to national security (by allowing companies and the government to more agilely cooperate and identify emerging threats).

The excerpt above references four different statutes that perform four distinct functions:

Statute	Applies to	Purpose
Computer Fraud and Abuse Act (CFAA)	Cybercriminals, organizations	• Establishes as a federal crime cyberintrusions (fine + prison) • Provides a right of civil action for organizations against cybercriminals
Economic Espionage Act (EEA)	Organizations, criminal enterprise, cybercriminals, an organization's personnel	• Establishes information stealing and transfer to a foreign entity as a crime • Provides a right of civil action for the Attorney General and injunctive acts
Defend Trade Secrets Act	Organizations, criminal enterprise, cybercriminals, an organization's personnel	• Federal statute for formerly state trade secret misappropriation statute • Criminalizes trade secret misappropriation • Civil trade secret misappropriation actions at the federal level
Electronic Consumer Privacy Act (ECPA)	Digital Services, law enforcement	• Bars unconsented personal information disclosure to third parties • Sets specific requirements for law enforcement to access personal information of subscribers

The Cybersecurity Act	Organizations	• Offers a safe harbor (from liability) for organizations that disclose threat and incident information Establishes information sharing organizations to monitor systems and offer defensive measures Bolsters federal agency cybersecurity practices, implements measures for critical infrastructure

Table 1: Example Security Laws

Although there are multiple approaches to managing risk, organizations today will likely face a myriad of legal challenges. As you begin to contemplate what may occur after a data breach, consider the common law, statutory requirements, and administrative rules that may apply to a given organization. As you have seen in this chapter, organizations of any kind, even organizations that are not highly regulated, likely face a number of different legal actions. See Figure 1 below for an example of the legal ecosystem following a data breach. In this figure, black boxes represent civil actions, gray boxes represent civil and criminal actions, and white boxes represent criminal actions.

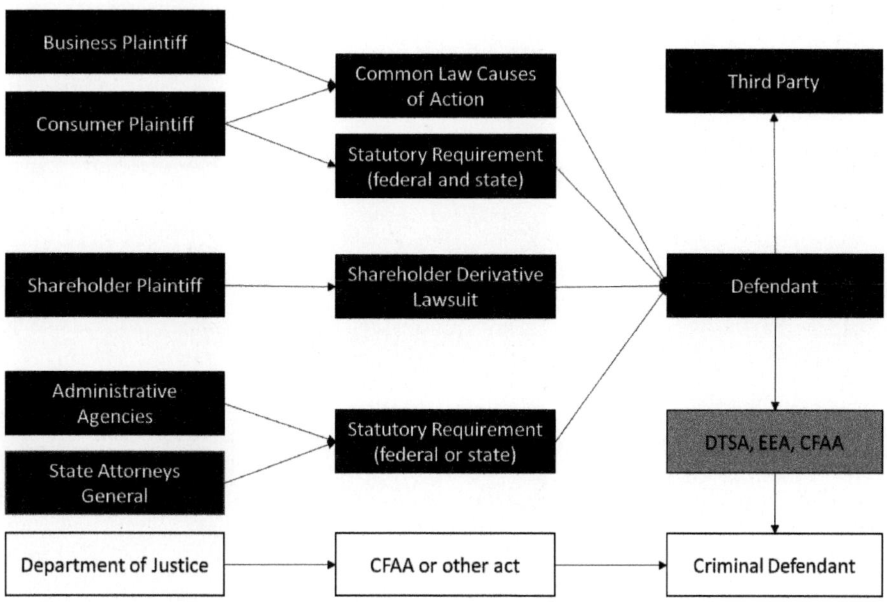

Figure 1: Organizational Legal Actions

Figure 1 illustrates the types of plaintiffs or prosecutors, variety of causes of action, and the potential defendants. As you recall previously discussed breaches, such as the Yahoo and Target breaches, would you have expected this many lawsuits and legal actions to result? Here, you will note that there are also lawsuits the breached organization might bring against a third party responsible for a breach, a cybercriminal, or a former employee that is responsible for the breach or a co-conspirator. The challenging lawsuit ecosystem following a data breach is precisely because aggrieved parties are many: a consumer or business customer, the organization itself that has been breached, and the individual responsible, not to mention third parties that may or may not be partially or fully responsible for some action or inaction related to the breach.

QUESTIONS

1. As you review Figure 1 and consider the reality of cybersecurity issues and particularly data breaches, are you surprised by the multitude and variety of simultaneous lawsuits? Why or why not?

2. Practically, a breached organization has to manage these lawsuits, including communication to internal employees about what to say or not to say, saving internal records, and working with internal and external counsel. If you were General Counsel, Chief Technology Officer, or Chief Executive Officer of this organization, what would be most concerning to you? What would your strategy be specifically in relation to these lawsuits and whether or not to settle them?

CHAPTER 11

BUSINESS APPROACHES TO CYBERSECURITY RISK

■ ■ ■

In Chapter 10, we discussed legal requirements and considerations that organizations must consider when making choices about cybersecurity, and the criminal sanctions that adversaries face when engaging in cyberattacks.

Practically speaking, however, organizations of all kinds, including businesses and governmental entities, need to implement operational capabilities that help them make informed decisions about how to invest resources, like personnel or funding to make changes that will reduce the risk of a cybersecurity breach. As we have discussed earlier in this book, there are at least four types of risk that an organization must consider: operational, financial, reputational, and legal risk. When organizations consider where and whether to invest resources, they must consider the potential risk to the organization. This might mean that decisions are made about potential impacts to an organization's reputation, such as the reputation of an organization to customers or citizens or costs (recovery and legal fees) after a cybersecurity incident has occurred.

A. GOVERNANCE

As we have discussed risk throughout this book, you've learned the various sources and types of risk, but we have not yet discussed the "management" aspect of risk management as it relates to enterprise risk and specifically cybersecurity risk. The central challenges for any organization, regardless of its legal obligations are 1) establishing a common way of "doing" risk management, 2) operationalizing risk management, and 3) making informed decisions about risks. These are separate and distinct aspects of risk management programs, and often organizations will establish the first without investing in the second, making informed decisions nearly impossible. Risk management is not a one-time activity—it is a 24/7 ongoing engagement of a variety of individuals within an organization, from cybersecurity professionals implementing security by design (SDLC) to the CEO or Director of an organization. As one of the casebook's authors recalls from a previous organization, the internal tagline for security was: "Security: It's Everyone's Responsibility." Properly managing risk involves almost every role within an organization.

Making decisions about how to invest resources in cybersecurity is often a question of governance, or managed decision-making within an organization according to a risk management model. Although "corporate governance" is used to reference the interplay between executive leadership, the board, and shareholders, organizations also use the term governance to reflect internal informed decision-making. For example, a multi-million-dollar technical investment likely would be decided in most organizations by the CEO, President, or Director, rather than an engineer. The reason we have governance within organizations is to effectuate the broader corporate governance reality: executive leadership owes a duty of care and duty of loyalty to their shareholders or investors, whereas an engineer likely owes a duty of confidentiality and commits to perform some role under an employment agreement.

However, a duty of care or duty of loyalty, once assumed, cannot be broken without consequence. The damage to shareholders due to a breach of these duties can be catastrophic, as in the infamous accounting scandals at Enron and other companies where executives falsified records to make it appear as though these companies were performing better than they actually were. As a result of widespread injury to shareholders due to this breach of duty, Congress passed the Sarbanes-Oxley Act in 2002, which includes cybersecurity and other administrative steps to ensure that financial accounting records of publicly traded companies are verifiable and cannot be falsified to the detriment of shareholders.

Executive leadership is required to be, as part of their duties, well-informed and inform the board of potential risks that may affect the financial performance and quarterly earnings for that company. For non-public businesses and other organizations, leaders should also consider potential risks and potential benefits of investments that may improve the overall position of the organization with respect to its mission and goals. Enterprise risk management is a function that combines data and inputs from a variety of departments and specialty areas with the primary purpose of improving leadership's knowledge of potential risks to the organization while enabling informed decision-making. Risk inputs include everything from environmental risks to competitor risks, tax law changes and emerging laws, or upcoming large investments, such as the need to replace expensive manufacturing equipment. Enterprise risks like these are identified through common frameworks, given a risk rating, and presented to executive leadership and often the board of directors for awareness and to solicit overall direction.

1. ENTERPRISE RISK MANAGEMENT

As previously discussed in this book, enterprise risk management (ERM), typically led by the Chief Risk Officer (CRO), uses the four risk types (or a variation on these types) to identify and understand the multi-faceted nature of every risk. For example, a new emission standard passed under federal law might dramatically change the design, engineering, and overall cost of manufacturing a car. Perhaps an engine that is highly fuel efficient needs to be reworked for all the cars that will use it. The financial risks of investing in new engines, as well as the operational challenges of building these new engines could be very high. However, the reputational and legal risks of not meeting new emissions requirements could similarly be very costly to the manufacturer's brand or result in large fines. This would undoubtedly be considered an enterprise risk because, although it primarily relates to one area of the business, it carries broad risk that could affect profits or stock price.

ERM may be accompanied or replaced by an assurance team. Assurance teams use repeatable auditing practices, informed by industry standard models like COSO or COBIT, to identify issues throughout the organization. For example, one assurance team could focus only on technology while another could focus only on financial health.[1] In all cases, audit departments are designed to identify risks with respect to specific departments or key initiatives, and their findings are typically reported to the board of directors.

In the most mature organizations, ERM and assurance work together as semi-autonomous business functions to highlight areas where the board of directors needs to advise executive leadership on overall direction to avoid major issues that affect the organization. Although these teams report through the CEO, President, or Director, their semi-autonomous nature means that they answer not just to executive leadership but also to the board. Summaries of key issues may also be communicated to shareholders or investors. See Figure 3 for an explanation of the general enterprise risk management process. This process is used, in varying forms, in any type of risk management process, including information security risk identification.

[1] Historically, assurance teams focused primarily on financial matters. In their role making significant risks visible to leadership, they are focused indirectly on the potential impact of certain organizational situations to overall organizational financial health. For this reason, assurance teams have embraced other types of risk analyses beyond basic financial accounting and tax risks. External third-party accounting firms today also will perform technology audits, despite being an accounting firm.

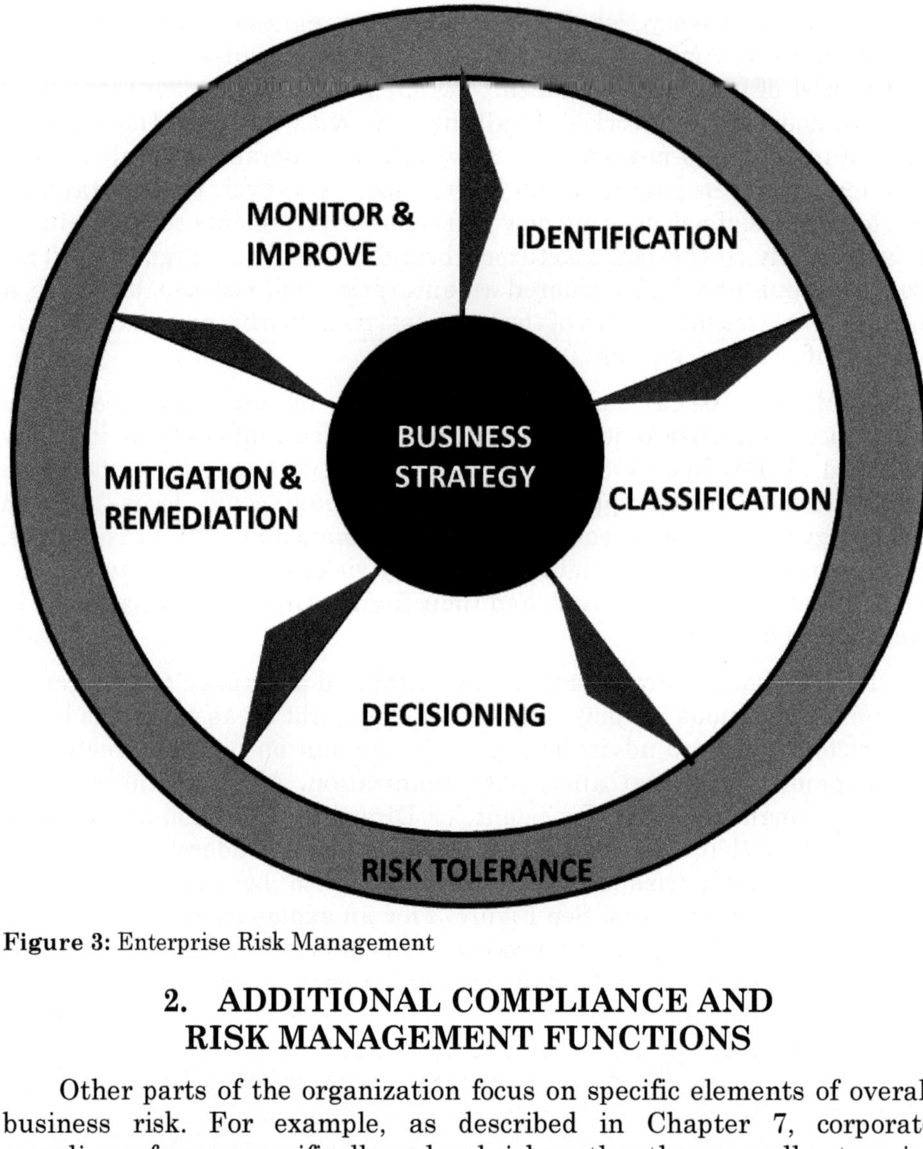

Figure 3: Enterprise Risk Management

2. ADDITIONAL COMPLIANCE AND RISK MANAGEMENT FUNCTIONS

Other parts of the organization focus on specific elements of overall business risk. For example, as described in Chapter 7, corporate compliance focuses specifically on legal risks rather than overall enterprise risks. Although organizations are broadly concerned with risk, compliance is the operational process of complying with applicable laws. However, because legal risks are often difficult to understand, usually a separate team assesses and partners with teams across an organization to ensure that these teams have complied. The separate team ensures internal compliance by establishing and implementing key policies, standards, processes, and procedures to meet legal requirements.

For example, a corporate compliance team for manufacturing might have individuals that are specially focused on import and export law to ensure that materials brought into the United States are permitted and follow the appropriate inspection process and have legally required documentation. Other individuals might focus on the materials themselves, for example if those materials are sourced from countries prohibited from importing into the U.S. due to human rights or environmental toxicity issues. Still others might focus on quality requirements for specific manufacturing processes, such as validating that certain high technology products do not emit excessive electromagnetic radiation. A company that instead provides insurance services would have completely different legal requirements that must be operationalized within an organization. It is this variety that informs the structure and function of a corporate compliance team.

Within the compliance team or legal function, a privacy or data protection team usually focuses on privacy-related legislation, which may or may not also include security requirements.[2] The Health Insurance Portability and Accountability Act (HIPAA), described in Chapter 10, and the Gramm-Leach-Bliley Act (GLBA) and Regulation S-P, which respectively govern banking and investment relationships and transactions, include privacy requirements, such as providing privacy notice and soliciting consent for some data uses, as well as security requirements. Because sensitive personal information, or personal information that is more likely to be identifiable or be misused, is collected in financial and health-related transactions, it makes sense that security requirements would be included. For this reason, often the privacy or data protection teams will work closely with security teams to ensure appropriate policies, standards, processes, and procedures have been implemented.

Despite privacy law's initial focus on privacy *law*, some organizations couple privacy and security together due to their dual focus on the treatment of data. For example, both teams would participate in data classification efforts, or determining which controls apply to certain types of data based on the data element's risk of misuse or misappropriation. It is this relationship, whether structural or collaborative, that is one of the most crucial with respect to technology within an organization.

QUESTIONS

1. Review Figure 3 of this section. How would a multitude of compliance areas, such as environmental compliance, financial compliance, or food safety compliance use the steps described in the chart to create a risk management program?

---

[2] The placement of a privacy or data protection team varies depending on the organization. In some organizations, the privacy team may report to the CISO, while in others the privacy team may report directly to General Counsel or the CEO. At least one of your casebook authors once reported to the CFO!

2. Choose one of the steps in Figure 3. If you were implementing a cybersecurity program, what processes or procedures would be needed to satisfy that step? How would you validate that it had been completed?

3. In Chapter 7, we explored organizational roles that often make decisions about specific types of risks. What are the similarities and differences between how a cybersecurity team, led by a Chief Information Security Officer, and a privacy team, led by a Chief Privacy Officer, might view the step you just analyzed? How might they work productively together when overlap exists?

B. POLICY MANAGEMENT

As referenced above, the key to operationalizing compliance and risk-related activities is building a common framework for reducing overall risk for an organization. Without the ability to identify risk, it is difficult to make decisions about it. There are two techniques that enable effective organizational risk management: policy and process. One is the foundation for a common framework, while the other focuses on the operationalization of the framework.

Although all technology implementations are unique with respect to their potential threats and vulnerabilities, certain strategies are often used to ensure at least a base level of security depending on the potential risk to the organization. Establishing base requirements for an organization usually means creating common policy that all personnel must follow, and these must be tied to formal organizational policy. Organizational policy ensures that all personnel and even third parties clearly understand, what is permitted and what is not. Not just security policies, but policy of all variations, are essential for organizational governance and consistent practices.[3]

Policies have the added benefit of being explicitly referenced in employee and contractor employment agreements, stating that any individuals who do not follow the policy may be disciplined, up to or including termination. Although usually this step is reserved for the most severe cases, it reinforces the seriousness of following common policies. Furthermore, corporate training on any number of subjects usually reinforces key policy areas to ensure that personnel are well-aware of internal policy requirements.

In addition to internal purposes for implementing policy, policies also demonstrate an organization's commitment to external entities. Frequently, organizations such as B2B service providers are requested by

[3] We use the term "security" in this context purposefully: security policies are more than cybersecurity policies and often include things like acceptable use, bring your own device to work policies, or general data classification policy. These policies are essential to effective cybersecurity but are broader, including practices like maintaining a "clean desk," locking file cabinets, or not permitting individuals to "piggy-back" or obtain access to a floor without swiping their key card. As we have described in earlier chapters, physical security is an essential aspect of cybersecurity, and these practices can make or break otherwise effective cybersecurity practices.

their business customers to share their policies as one way to explain their internal practices. When regulators routinely examine, investigate, or audit an organization, often the first thing requested is a copy of all policy documentation. Later in this book, we will be discussing at more length the most common security policies and what they contain.

Standards are more detailed versions of policies. For example, an information security policy may say "encrypt sensitive data." A corresponding encryption standard could require "encrypt sensitive data in transit and in storage." Procedures and processes, then, further explain the details of implementing encryption, such as the appropriate protocols, encryption key rotation or key generation techniques, or how to secure the key database. Policies and standards are usually intended for broader audiences, while procedures are used by specific audiences, such as engineers or developers building a system that uses encryption. Guidelines may be used in some circumstances where multiple options are possible. For example, some encryption models might be preferable, but the implementation might depend on the specific technology.

You might ask "what is the source of requirements of a policy?" Policy requirements are usually found both in legal sources (specific statutes, rules, or legal guidance) and industry standards (common frameworks used in an industry or across industries, which we will discuss more later in this chapter). Together, these sources are considered "authoritative sources," and they are typically mapped to a policy framework in the form of a controls library. A controls library is a common index of requirements from authoritative sources, which is cross-referenced to those sources and used for risk assessments. In cybersecurity, one authoritative source is NIST. The excerpt below examines NIST as a potential baseline for reasonable duty with respect to cybersecurity controls.

SCOTT SHACKLEFORD, ANDREW PROIA, BRENTON MARTELL & AMANDA CRAIG, *TOWARD A GLOBAL CYBERSECURITY STANDARD OF CARE? EXPLORING THE IMPLICATIONS OF THE 2014 NIST CYBERSECURITY FRAMEWORK ON SHAPING REASONABLE NATIONAL AND INTERNATIONAL CYBERSECURITY PRACTICES*

50 TEX. INT'L L.J. 305 (2015)

What constitutes the burgeoning field of "cybersecurity law and policy" is open to debate—but likely encompasses a wide array of topics from cybercrime and privacy to data protection, contracts, torts, intellectual property, and even Internet governance. For the present purposes, cybersecurity refers to the policy field concerned with managing cyber threats, including unauthorized access, disruption, and modification of electronically stored information, software, hardware, services, and networks. The cyber threat matrix itself is always evolving; it consists of activities ranging from cyber economic espionage that targets trade secrets and is carried out by transnational criminal organizations—sometimes at the behest of nation states—to hacktivists out to make a political point. Many firms have begun to proactively invest in cybersecurity best practices to better protect themselves against increasingly sophisticated attackers, but the ever-changing nature of the problem and sheer number of actors involved has made crafting a cybersecurity standard of care difficult.

Yet despite gaps in the legal framework and the ever-changing cyber threat, courts are increasingly willing to hold both organizations and firms liable for not protecting sensitive information. For example, the Michigan Court of Appeals held a union responsible for failing to safeguard the private information of members who became victims of identity theft. Another federal court judge in Michigan ruled that a local bank was at fault for not detecting earlier the losses its customers sustained through a phishing attack. There have also been major class actions filed in invasion of information privacy lawsuits. Two such cases filed in 2003 against several of the largest information brokers in the United States also implicated the state of Florida for not protecting the privacy of its residents. Damages sought were more than $2,500 per violation, adding up to billions under the federal Driver Privacy Protection Act. Ultimately, one of the defendant banks in the case was fined $50 million for purchasing data containing the personal information of hundreds of thousands of Florida residents for just $5,656. In 2006, ChoicePoint, a large data broker that maintains digital dossiers on many adults in the United States, was fined $10 million by the FTC—at that point, "the largest civil penalty in the agency's history." In all, hundreds of millions of personal records have been exposed in thousands of incidents. A single incident in 2006 involving the theft of a laptop owned by the Veterans Administration led to the loss of 26 million social security numbers of retired and active duty military personnel, resulting in a class action lawsuit claiming more than $26.5 billion in damages. Yet litigation is by no means universally successful. In late 2012, for example, a federal judge dismissed a case against Sony resulting from its massive data breach on the grounds that its users signed a privacy policy that contained "clear admonitory language that Sony's security was not 'perfect,' " and, therefore, "no reasonable consumer could have been deceived."

Other courts have considered whether victims of identity theft may bring a claim against financial institutions that have carelessly handled their personal information, sometimes arriving at contradictory rulings. Still other decisions have recognized a broad tort duty of confidentiality, which suggests that banks and other protectors of private information have a fundamental duty to keep their customers' personal information secure and confidential. Some scholars are getting creative, advocating for an independent tort of "negligent enablement of cybercrime" based on principles of premises liability (requiring that landowners who open their land to the public must use reasonable care in ensuring safety for their guests), product liability (holding producers liable for defective products), and warranty. Such a tort is meant to get around mass market license agreements (the "accept" checkbox), which typically include liability waivers for negligent software design, and could help protect consumers against breaches caused by foreseeable software flaws, shifting the burden to the party best able to evaluate cybersecurity. Other lawsuits have been brought under the theory of "negligent enablement of imposter fraud." However, these have so far been unsuccessful because of an absence of the duty element required in a negligence suit.

Negligence, put simply, is conduct that "falls below the standard established by law for the protection of others against unreasonable risk of harm." Avoiding liability for negligence generally requires conforming to a standard of conduct equivalent to that of another that would be considered "reasonable . . . under like circumstances." A legislature or the courts may define this standard of conduct. In all contexts, including cybersecurity, negligence might apply both to an action or omission—that is, failure to act when a duty was owed to do so. In cybersecurity law, there is no explicit or overt "cybersecurity negligence" framework, although attempts have been made to categorize cybersecurity negligence cases that highlight how each of the four negligence prongs have been met, perhaps demonstrating that a standard may be slowly emerging.

The standard of care in negligence is not static but rather evolves over time along with technological advancements. A commonly utilized approach to determining negligence has been the "risk/utility formula" famously articulated by Judge Learned Hand of the Second Circuit Court of Appeals. Suggestions of the formula's use appeared in 1932, when a group of tugboats were hit by a storm and sank, resulting in the loss of their cargos of coal. In the resulting lawsuit, the plaintiffs argued that the tug vessels were "unseaworthy" because they did not have radio receiving sets, which would have warned the tugboats of the storm and prevented the loss of the barges and cargo. The tugboat companies defended themselves on the basis that they were following the prevailing standard practice of the industry; radio receivers were expensive to purchase and maintain, so they were not typically found in tugboats—and therefore the companies should not be liable. However, Judge Learned Hand broke new ground, writing that even though having radios aboard was not yet an established industry custom, "[c]ourts must in the end say what is required; there are precautions so imperative that even their universal disregard will not excuse their omission."

Judge Hand would be faced with a similar opportunity to articulate what should be required in *United States v. Carroll Towing*. In this case, Judge Hand devised a formula for determining negligence, focusing on three primary elements: "(1) The probability that injury will occur; (2) the gravity of the resulting injury, if it occurs; and (3) the burden of adequate precautions." Thus, "liability depends upon whether B [the burden of adequate precautions] is less than L [the gravity of the injury] multiplied by P [the probability of the harm]"—articulated in the algebraic formula B < P*L. Though cybersecurity negligence case law is still in its infancy, a number of scholars have looked to Judge Hand's "risk/utility formula" as a means of determining liability for companies who suffer damage from lax cybersecurity.

An open question extending from this case law, then, is whether judges should exercise similar discretion in requiring companies to better manage cyberattacks by boasting a given set of cybersecurity best practices. For example, cybersecurity surveys regularly rank firewalls and anti-virus software as the security technologies most often used, but fewer companies regularly update such software. After that, percentages drop off. Roughly sixty-five percent of companies use encryption for data in transit, according to 2011 surveys conducted by Computer Science Institute and Verizon. About half use intrusion prevention systems and encryption for data in storage, while approximately one-third use public-key encryption, specialized wireless security systems, or content monitoring systems to prevent data loss. However, these percentages are constantly changing, which raises questions; for example, would a judge be justified in finding a firm negligent that suffered a data breach due to firewalls or spyware that had not been updated, even if many companies do not regularly update? What about not encrypting data at rest and in transit, or failing to do regular penetration testing?

Though the risk/utility formula has yet to be fully analyzed by a court within a cybersecurity context, courts have addressed what constitutes reasonable standards of cybersecurity care through alternative rationales with varying outcomes. Some courts, for example, have looked to established practices to determine whether a trier of fact should be allowed to determine negligence; however, this approach is by no means consistent. Consider Sony, which in May 2011 was attacked with hackers reportedly compromising more than 100 million gamers' names, addresses, emails, usernames, and passwords.

In the ongoing case, *In re Sony Gaming Networks and Customer Data Security Breach Litigation*, the court suggested that Sony's failure to employ industry cryptology standards was enough for plaintiffs to allege that Sony breached its duty to employ reasonable data security measures. In its complaint, victims of the hack allege that Sony had a duty "to design, implement, maintain, and test Sony's security system in order to ensure Plaintiffs' Personal Information was adequately secured and protected," and that "Sony breached this duty by failing to implement proper procedures to protect Plaintiffs' Personal Information." Sony contested, arguing, among other things, that it had no legal duty to provide reasonable security. Based on California and Massachusetts law, the court in this case agreed with the plaintiffs, finding that, "because [p]laintiffs allege that they provided their Personal Information to Sony as part of a commercial transaction, and that Sony failed to employ reasonable security measures to protect their Personal Information, including the utilization of industry-standard encryption, the Court finds [p]laintiffs have sufficiently alleged a legal duty and a corresponding breach."

Beyond particular technologies, other courts have placed considerable weight on industry report recommendations, which may be considered similar to the NIST Framework, in determining whether a reasonable level of data security had been provided by an entity. For instance, in Shames-Yeakel v. Citizens Financial Bank, the U.S. District Court for the Northern District of Illinois found that Citizens' failure to comply with security measures recommended in a report by the Federal Financial Institutions Examination Council (FFIEC) was enough to establish a triable issue of fact as to whether Citizens breached its duty of care. Marsha Shames-Yeakel was the owner of a bookkeeping company, "Best Practices," which had a business checking account with Citizens Financial Bank. According to the court, an "unknown person" gained access to Shames-Yeakel's credentials, stealing upwards of $26,500 on Shames-Yeakel's home equity credit line. Shames-Yeakel argued that Citizens' online banking security "lagged behind industry standards," as Citizens Financial Bank only used "single-factor identification" as opposed to "multifactor identification." Specifically, Shames-Yeakel cited the FFIEC's Report, Authentication in an Internet Banking Environment, which "does not endorse any particular technology" but states: "agencies consider single-factor authentication, as the only control mechanism, to be inadequate for high-risk transactions involving access to customer information or the movement of funds to other parties." Citizens filed a motion for summary judgment, arguing, in part, that though it had a duty to protect its customer data, Shames-Yeakel had not produced sufficient evidence that Citizens had breached its duty of care. The court denied Citizens' motion for summary judgment as to Shames-Yeakel's negligence claim. While an expert retained by Citizens found the bank's use of single-factor authentication to be "reasonable," the court stated that Citizens' "delay" in complying with FFIEC security standards could lead "a reasonable finder of fact . . . [to] conclude that the bank breached its duty to protect Plaintiffs' account against fraudulent access." [. . .]

The Cybersecurity Framework takes a risk-based approach for organizations to detect, mitigate, and respond to cyber threats. Rather than developing new cybersecurity standards and risk management processes, the Cybersecurity Framework "relies on a variety of existing standards, guidelines, and practices to enable critical infrastructure providers to achieve resilience," which allows the Framework to "scale across borders, acknowledge the global nature of cybersecurity risks, and evolve with technological advances and business requirements." The Cybersecurity Framework provides a "common language" for entities to evaluate their current cybersecurity posture; determine their targeted state for cybersecurity; prioritize opportunities for improvement; assess progress toward their targeted state; and establish sufficient methods of communication among internal and external stakeholders about cybersecurity risk. The substance of the Cybersecurity Framework is composed of three parts: (1) The Framework Core, (2) The Framework Implementation Tiers, and (3) The Framework Profile.

1. The Framework Core

The Cybersecurity Framework begins by laying out the Framework Core, which "provides a set of activities to achieve specific cybersecurity outcomes, and references examples of guidance to achieve those outcomes." While neither an exhaustive list nor a checklist, the Framework Core is an organizational map of industry-recognized cybersecurity practices that are helpful in managing cybersecurity risk and provides unified terminology for organizations to understand successful cybersecurity practice outcomes. The Framework Core is broken down into four elements—Functions, Categories, Subcategories, and Informative References—that assist in mapping applicable cybersecurity standards, guidelines, and best practices.

The Core begins by delineating essential cybersecurity activities "at their highest level," referred to as Functions. The Framework recognizes five Functions—Identify, Protect, Detect, Respond, and Recover—that are intended to assist an organization in expressing its management of cybersecurity risk by organizing practices into these key areas. Each Function contains more detailed subsets of overarching practices, referred to as Categories, which are "groups of cybersecurity outcomes, closely tied to programmatic needs and particular activities." Each Category assists an organization's approach to mapping the key Functions underlying the Cybersecurity Framework. Each Category provides a brief description to more efficiently place it within the context of its corresponding Function, as well as to guide further categorization within the remaining Core elements. For example, the "Identify" Function contains within it the "Asset Management" Category, which articulates practice outcomes to identify and manage the "data, personnel, devices, systems, and facilities that enable the organization to achieve business purposes . . . consistent with their relative importance to business objectives and the organization's risk strategy."

The NIST framework not only offers specific requirements, it maps these requirements to a risk assessment process and to common industry frameworks to simplify the creation of a controls library. For example, if you wanted to understand if a mobile app your organization had recently developed met your internal policy, you would need some list of requirements against which to measure it. The controls library would have all the requirements indexed and likely would be written in a questionnaire format. Usually a controls library corresponds to multiple questionnaires depending on what someone would like to assess. If you had a banking app likely regulated under GLBA and expected an examination from the Office of the Comptroller of Currency (OCC), which enforces GLBA, you might choose to conduct an assessment only using GLBA controls. An effective controls library would enable you to ask questions related to GLBA, ask questions specific to a particular industry standard, ask questions related to the data classification, or ask questions related to a geographic area (such as just the U.S. or perhaps the European Union). The most effective controls libraries enable granular assessments while also managing multiple questionnaires, many authoritative sources, and several mappings. For this reason, often organizations choose to implement a Governance Risk Compliance (GRC) tool that performs the role of a risk register, or a database of all identified risks mapped to controls and associated questionnaires. We will discuss the risk register in more detail later in this chapter.

1. THE INFORMATION SECURITY POLICY LIBRARY

As described earlier in this chapter, the information security policy library is crucial for organizational personnel to understand and follow these practices. However, typically organizations only have a few information security policies. Organizations then map these policies to standards, which are mapped to controls in the controls library and procedures. See Figure 4 for an image of the relationships between these documents.

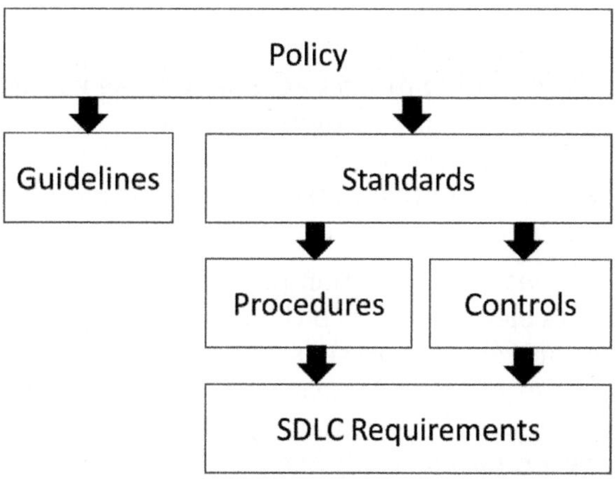

Figure 4: Policy Library, Controls Library, and Requirements

As you can see from Figure 4, Policy is the broadest category, and often policy informs both recommended, but non-compulsory (but recommended) guidelines as well as compulsory standards. However, standards inform required downstream activities, including internal procedures and specific controls used for risk assessment purposes. Both inform requirements to be implemented in all technical products home-grown at an organization or created on behalf of an organization by a contractor.

The number of policies implemented by an organization are largely dependent on how the organization wishes to manage its internal personnel. However, in most mature organization, at least five key policies are routinely used. First, a common information security policy sets out the required activities of an information security program as well as establishing the use of key technologies. An *Information Security Policy* might say something like "the information security program shall conduct regular risk assessments on organizational technologies" or "encrypt data classified as 'sensitive data.' " The goal of an information security policy is to lay out the high-level commitments of technology and internal practices to be a map for the rest of the detailed internal documents and subsequent requirements.

The second policy most organizations implement is called a *Data Classification Policy*. Data classification is essential to interpret any downstream controls. For example, a requirement like "encrypt data in transmission using TLS v1.3" would likely apply to more sensitive, desirable data, rather than public data in transmission. Consider the role of encryption. Symmetric encryption is usually used for purposes of confidentiality of the CIA triad. Without effective encryption protocols, data might be transmitted in plain text or be easy to decrypt. Therefore, the threats to such data might be man-in-the-middle attacks, where an individual siphons off information as it is passed between two entities, or packet-based attacks where only part of the message (or none of the message) is transmitted, in line with an availability attack. However, encryption usually is used to protect against attacks where the contents of the message are independently valuable. For this reason, many controls like encryption only make sense when data is of independent value on the black market, such as sensitive personal information or highly sensitive business data, such as upcoming mergers or acquisitions or trade secrets.

The value of a data classification policy is to establish the category of certain types of data elements, which then enables an organization to apply certain advanced controls to more sensitive types of data and less advanced controls to other types of data. For example, all data might require unique, individual access (or specific user ID and password for all users rather than shared IDs). However, perhaps only sensitive data require quarterly access reviews where all access is reviewed by management periodically. Or, sensitive data may require multiple approvals to grant access whereas less sensitive data requires only one approval.

Data classification policies establish the mapping of data elements to categories. Most organizations have three or four categories. See Figure 5 for an example of two different types of data classification schemes. Keep in mind that organizations are often highly specific as to what is most valuable to each and where the most risk lies. For example, a government organization will likely have a different classification (including certain schemes consistent with government document classification) than a private organization. Organizations that deal mostly in lower data sensitivity may nevertheless classify other data elements as highly sensitive. In short, data classification is *relative* or specific to the ecosystem in which an organization operates.

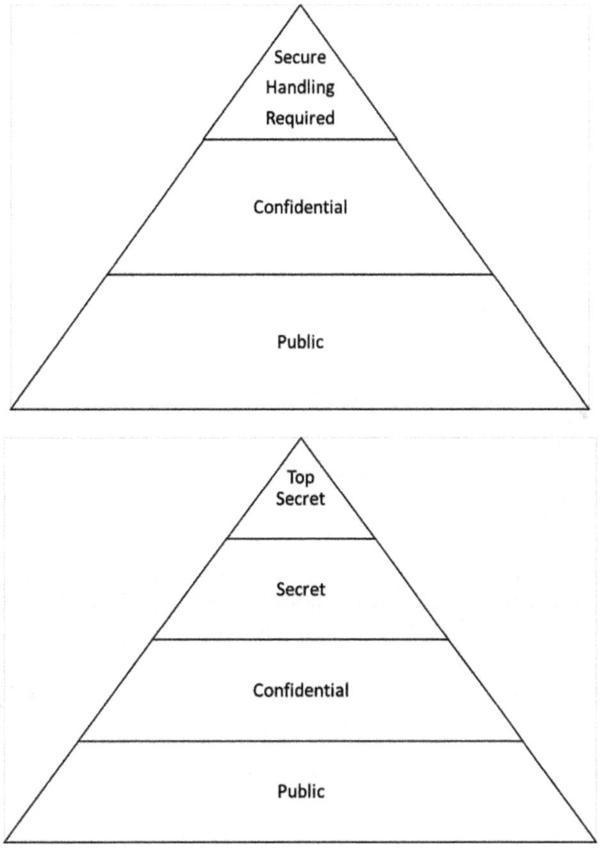

Figure 5: Example Data Classification Schemes

For each of these classifications, data elements are cross-referenced in the Data Classification policy. For example, consider Table 1 below as an example of these categories.

Classification	Data Elements
Secure Handling Required	Personal information, including sensitive personal data and other identifying elements that have not been de-identified. Trade secrets and intellectual property patent information until the patent is granted. Strategic annual plans, quarterly earnings data prior to public disclosure. Identified compliance and other risk findings prior to public disclosure.
Confidential	Departmental strategy, organizational charts, internal business process and procedures, technical system details (when not trade secrets), business customer data (when not personal information), contracts, employment data as job grades and position descriptions (when not personal information), e-mail contents, marketing communications and ads prior to public release, internal security procedures
Public	Published ads, published marketing materials, released quarterly earnings reports, public Website details and architecture, public e-mail addresses and phone numbers

Table 1: Example Data Classification

In addition to the information security policy and the data classification policy, organizations often have at least two other policies related to data management: a data retention policy and an acceptable use policy. The data retention policy provides details related to the length of time an organization must retain certain types of records, usually accompanied by retention schedules for specific departments or types of records. Unlike general data, records are intentionally defined, fixed collections of data that are used for some legal or business purposes. These purposes include record-keeping for compliance purposes, for financial accounting, in healthcare, or for legal reasons, such as e-Discovery purposes.[4] Records require 1) a high degree of accuracy and 2) verifiability, sometimes independent or from a third party.

An acceptable use policy establishes expectations for how an organization's personnel may use certain facilities and resources. For example, most acceptable use policies restrict use of company computer devices or printers for personal matters, prohibit downloading unapproved software to such devices, and may restrict use of USB ports or other

[4] Although e-Discovery is not described in detail in this book, e-Discovery is the process of finding records for the purpose of using as evidence in a legal matter. For example, an organization may place a "hold" on certain records, such as employee e-mails or annual appraisal records for later introduction if a legal matter results.

external media such as external CD-ROMs. Newer policies often include references to using unapproved cloud providers for transmitting internal documents and data.

Some organizations may also have a physical security policy. This policy may establish requirements for access to physical property, such as requiring use of a key card upon entry, the presence of a security guard maintaining a visitor log, employing CCTVs and the length of time recordings must be stored, and requirements personnel must follow when transporting computer equipment or internal records.

Finally, some organizations permit their personnel to use personal computing devices, such as mobile devices, tablets, or laptops to access organizational materials. For example, some apps might be created to be viewed on mobile devices, such as e-mail apps or access to human resources materials. In other cases, an organization might offer personal wireless connectivity for personnel to use in off-hours, such as during lunch or other breaks. Because these devices may introduce viruses or other malware onto the internal network, often the "Bring Your Own Device" (BYOD) or similarly named policy will establish limits, such as an understanding that personnel will not directly connect, via ethernet cord, with the internal network. Newer devices increasingly connect primarily over wireless connections, so many organizations employing these policies instead focus on network segmentation, separating networks with personal device traffic from trusted, comparatively "clean" machines on the trusted internal network.

Although personnel must follow many additional policies for compliance and risk management purposes, such as non-bribery or human resources policies, the policies above are commonly of interest to cybersecurity interests, as they introduce threat vectors that may affect overall organizational cybersecurity.

C. RISK ASSESSMENT

The purpose of using questionnaires for purposes of risk assessment is to identify potential risks to your organization and make decisions about those risks. Risk assessment, or evaluating certain assets (such as an app) with respect to a common set of controls, is one of the most critical parts of having an effective risk management program in any risk area, but especially in cybersecurity. Risk assessment processes often follow these steps:

1. Determine what is of value to your organization.
2. Determine what requirements apply.
3. Assess if the requirements have been applied.
4. Make a decision about what to do and do it.

5. Monitor progress on decisions made.
6. Ensure follow-through.
7. Repeat.

Based on these steps, do you see any similarities between this process and the ERM process described earlier in this chapter?

When a risk assessment is complete, each risk identified must be examined to determine whether any compensating controls have been implemented. Compensating controls are alternative controls than the required control. Although compensating controls are not the required controls in a given situation, they may nevertheless reduce overall risk. For example, you may not encrypt a database of sensitive data, but perhaps you also have limited access to four heavily monitored accounts. This may not completely eliminate the risk of failing to encrypt the database, but you may have reduced the risk of compromise.

As you may recall from the earlier chapters, risk is an extension of impact and likelihood: if the impact is low and the likelihood is high, it is unlikely that the overall risk will be high. Similarly, if the likelihood is low but the impact is high, it is unlikely that the overall risk will be high. It is important to consider both of these, as well as compensating controls in place when giving each identified risk a risk value of, for example, low, medium, high, or critical. Assigning a risk value of some kind, however, is crucial: without any values, organizations are unable to prioritize remediation effectively. This means that organizations may spend money on the wrong investments that overall do not measurably reduce risk.

After a risk rating is assigned to an identified risk, the organization must make a decision about it. There are four primary risk decisions that can be made: 1) mitigate, 2) remediate, 3) avoid, 4) accept. Technically, a fifth option, *transfer*, is available, but this is largely a question of cyberliability or cyberrisk insurance, as transfer accepts or mitigates the risk but assume that remaining risk, if realized, will be compensated via insurance payout. It should be noted that although insurance may provide compensation, other types of losses, such as those related to reputation or legal issues, likely are not completely transferrable.

Risk mitigation is a reduction of risk that still has some residual, or remaining, risk. Risk mitigation works by reducing the overall risk value to a level that may be more acceptable to an organization by applying compensating controls. In contrast, risk remediation completely eliminates any risk to the organization by fixing the issue causing the risk. After a risk has been remediated, there is no longer any risk value.

Risk avoidance is opting to go in another direction from the original plan and is used when evaluating a future strategy. For example, an organization may want to implement a new Web application for managing its supplier contracts, but the number of risks identified during an assessment may encourage the organization to pursue another solution. The main difference between risk remediation and risk avoidance is that risk avoidance applies when technology is in planned but has not been implemented.

Finally, risk acceptance is the activity of accepting the risk as-is either indefinitely, or for a period of time. Usually, risk acceptance triggers an exception process, wherein leadership reviews and signs off on a record that states a risk will not be remediated for a given period of time or indefinitely.

Together, the controls library, questionnaires, a database of assets, the responses to such questionnaires, the identified risks and corresponding risk values, and recorded decisions are contained in a Governance Risk Compliance (GRC) tool, also known as a risk register. The risk register often includes analytical capabilities so that an organization can evaluate its current or past risk posture. See Figure 6: Risk Register for a visual of how these pieces relate to each other in a specific tool.

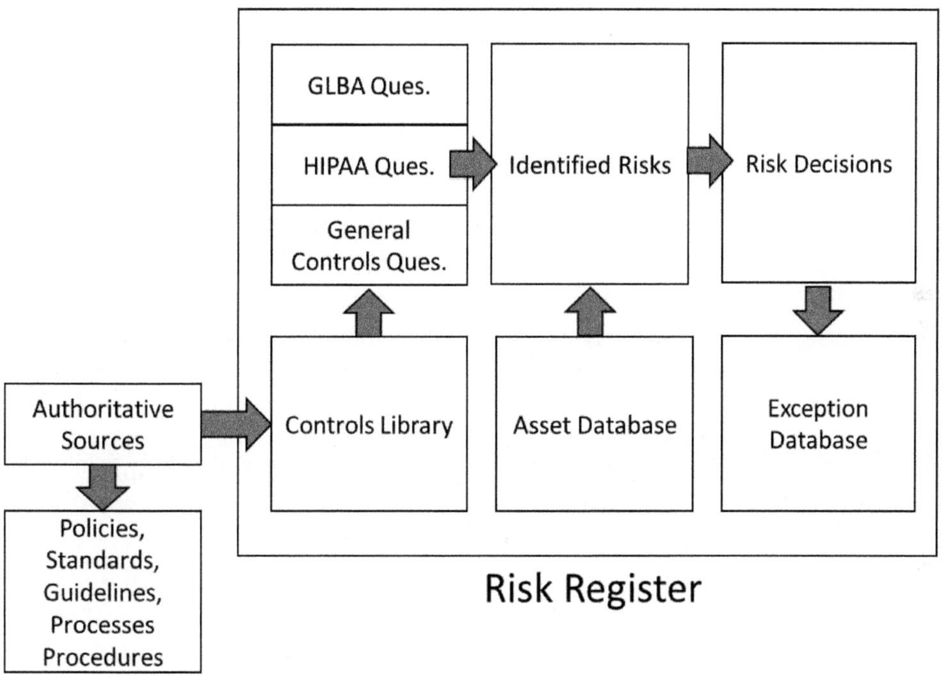

Figure 6: Risk Register

Risk, Impact, and Likelihood all integrate questions of threat and vulnerability, although in general risk management these terms might not exist. For example, the term "hazard" is used in manufacturing and environmental fields instead of threat and vulnerability to illustrate known potential issues that must be guarded against using specific controls. When controls are ineffective or non-existent, it is more likely (though not certain) that a hazard will result in an actual incident. For this reason, a risk that is realized means that there is no probability anymore: a realized risk is an incident.

QUESTIONS

1. You are the new CISO of BoomRound, an events marketing company that provides services to Fortune-150 companies. How would you sell the importance of purchasing a GRC tool to your CEO? What might you need to know to make an effective proposal?

2. A policy library is a set of documents but does not really "do" anything on its own. Why, then, is policy a critical focus area for most cybersecurity statutes?

3. In your opinion, what is the purpose of a risk assessment? How frequently should an organization conduct them? When would a third-party service provider be a good candidate to perform a risk assessment on behalf of the organization?

D. RISK RATING AND DECISIONING

Once a risk has been identified, a decision must be made with respect to that individual risk as distinct from all other risks identified in the risk assessment for that asset. Organizations must take great care to assess each risk separately, rather than grouping all risks together and, for example, "accepting" them. There are a wide variety of quantitative and qualitative methods for assessing risk, but the most important thing is to rate risk consistently.

Rating risk consistently can take a number of forms: for example, the organization should use a common equation for rating risk, or a common group of professionals could discuss risk together and determine a rating. Why might this be? Although some industries might objectively carry more risk than others, the purpose of risk rating is not to compare risks externally. Rather, the purpose of risk rating is to prioritize within the organization and determine how resources should be prioritized.

Take, for example, a car. Cars have all kinds of things that can go wrong with them but determining what to fix often is a question of safety versus comfort. If there is an engine problem, the car likely will not run. If there is a problem with the internal cabin's A/C, likely it will be uncomfortable, but the car will still run. If asked to choose between the two, with limited resources, most car owners will fix the engine first. However, a number of different scenarios could change the calculus. Maybe the car owner doesn't have enough money to fix the engine but does have enough money to fix the A/C now, and owner will have funds to fix the engine in a month. Or imagine a situation where the occupants of the car are especially sensitive to heat, and the car is being driven in a desert. Perhaps the car is used to transport organs for donation. In these cases, the priority of remediating the A/C issue may take precedence over the engine issue in the short term.

The purpose of describing this scenario is to get you thinking about the critical aspects that affect both the actual risk in relation to an enterprise and the priority of remediation. These two steps are often distinct, although the actual risk rating usually influences the priority of remediation. The first step uses the equation we discussed earlier in this book, $R = P \times I$, or risk equals probability (likelihood) times impact. This general equation is the foundation of how risk ratings are determined. For example, say the probability of an asset being compromised is low, but the impact is high, it is likely that the resulting risk will be medium. If the probability is high, but the impact is low, it is also likely that the resulting risk will be medium.

Most organizations often over-rate risk by overemphasizing impact and deemphasizing probability. If the asset is critical to an organization's function, even if the probability of compromise is low, teams will likely rate any risk related to that asset as high. Understanding compensating controls may be in place, as well as which threats are likely to target such an asset, is critical to determining a reasonable risk rating.

For students of statistics and research methodologies, typically such determinations across a body of risk assessments should loosely fit a bell curve. A bell curve is often used to reduce outliers and ensure that data results do not skew too high or too low. This is usually the reason why many classes are graded "on a curve." Considering the shape of a bell curve can be useful when determining both a risk rating framework and rating based on that framework. However, organizations should also use caution. For example, low-maturity organizations may skew high, perhaps because objectively there are more high risks, or maybe because the organization has not rated many risks before. High-maturity organizations may likely skew low, in that practices have been implemented and higher risk issues have already been remediated. Whatever the model an organization uses, it should be used consistently over time so that progress may be measured and reported to management, and so management can effectively make decisions within their risk tolerance.

It should be noted that risk assessment findings remediation should be managed simultaneously with security by design. The purpose of doing both is to reduce risk in live systems while also preventing new issues by designing new systems with security in mind (and avoiding potential risk). In addition, organizations must be careful not to "purchase" risk by implementing or using third-party solutions that have not been assessed and effectively remediated. We will discuss third-party management in more detail later in this chapter.

1. RISK RATING PROCEDURES

As a legal or cybersecurity professional, you will be asked for your advice as to what risk level a particular risk finding should receive. Although many quantitative methods exist, often the easiest way to determine risk is using a basic X/Y diagram. Consider Figure 7 as an example, with white representing low risk, gray representing medium risk, and black representing high risk.

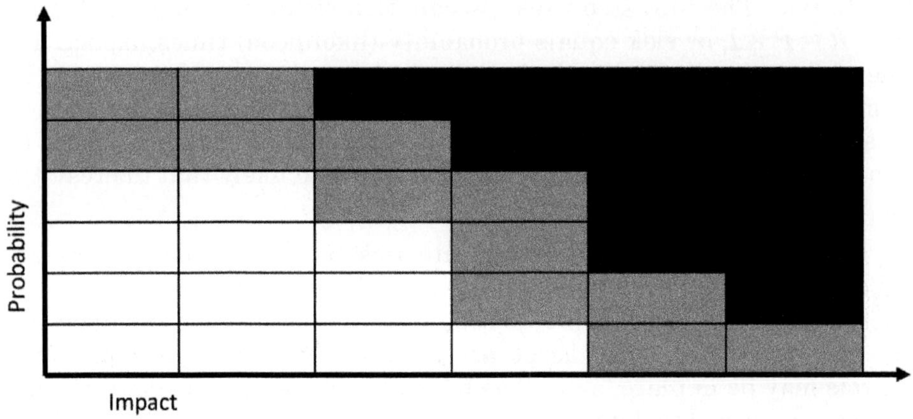

Figure 7: Probability × Impact = Risk Graph

Using the graph above, each risk identified should be evaluated both for its probability of the risk being realized and for the impact once the risk is realized. Furthermore, the risk rating should be considered from operational, legal, reputational, and financial perspectives.

As you might imagine, this exercise feels highly conjectural, which is actually how it should be. How can any one person know, with certainty, whether an individual risk will be realized? Take, for example, a Web application that stores information about individual performance appraisals (employment review), previous raises, desired job, and salary, of fifty employees. It also stores information about the individual's contact information. One of many risks identified with this system. The risk was identified when a control that specified "Assets containing or transmitting secured handling required data must review access to such a system on a quarterly basis" failed in the risk assessment.

In this case, access to the system was reviewed only on an annual basis. In this case, quarterly access reviews (QARs) are in place to ensure that someone who no longer has a need to access the system is not able to do so. And the type of access can have a significant bearing on the attendant risk. For example, the HR asset could reduce access significantly: there might be only two individuals permitted to actually change data in the system. The system might contain different user privileges and conditions for those privileges, wherein only an individual's manager can change data and only within a specific timeframe. Perhaps most employees have only "read" access to most of the applications.

How might you rate this risk? Well, first, you need to examine the asset itself to determine what motivations a threat might have with respect to this asset. Specifically, consider the CIA triad—who might want to impact the confidentiality of the data by exfiltrating it? Who might want to impact the integrity of the system by changing details in it? Who might want to interrupt access to it in an availability attack? Here, it is probably most likely that an employee would want to change data about themselves or others. It may be possible though less likely that the data are valuable from a confidentiality perspective, for example, an outside party trying to discover salary or address information of an individual they are trying to target.

In evaluating the risk here, individuals in a group will largely debate the degree to which non-satisfaction of the control, or the fact that access is reviewed only once per year, introduces risk to the organization. Here, in order to effectuate a confidentiality or integrity attack, the adversary would need to gain access either to read or change the data. If an individual's access has not been removed, it is possible that someone could use that access in an unauthorized manner to attack.

QUESTIONS

1. What might you want to know about the asset before making a risk determination?

2. Which compensating controls, or controls that mitigate the risk of this particular risk, might reduce the overall risk?

3. There are no laws that specifically create security obligations for employees, with the exception of credit checks and monitoring. The FTC does not focus on employee security, only consumer security. Taking this into account, how might an attack on the confidentiality or integrity of employee data impact legal risk, directly or indirectly?

4. If legal risks are more indirect, how might other risk types of financial, operational, and reputational risk be implicated for this risk?

5. What else might you want to know before giving this a risk rating? If you could create your ideal team to discuss risk ratings, who would you include and why?

6. (Optional) As a group, discuss this specific scenario and come to a risk rating on which your group can agree.

2. RISK DECISIONING

In Section 11.D.1, you assessed the risk. After discussing with a variety of different professionals from different parts of the organization, you determined the risk was low. What next?

Making a risk determination, or rating the risk, is only one part of the process. Next, it is important once all risks have been given a rating, that the team discusses the risk ratings with someone who can make decisions about the asset. As previously discussed, there are often many levels of management involved in running a specific asset. For example, you might consult the Information Technology manager who manages that asset to keep it running for the Human Resources team. You might also discuss resulting risks with the Human Resources team whose data is stored within the technology. Both have a vested interest in whether the risk is remediated and what means are employed. And one or both of them will likely have to provide resources to complete remediation of the issue. Who should ultimately decide whether a risk will be remediated?

Answering this question is difficult for two reasons: first, usually technology involves coordination of multiple groups and investment from multiple groups as described above. Second, often the individual who has the initial conversation about risk and reviews the risk assessment findings is not the ultimate decision-maker. This means that often multiple groups and multiple leadership levels are involved in making a risk determination.

One way to think about the first difficulty is to reframe the role of teams with respect to making decisions about risk. Some organizations use what is called an "information ownership" model. This model clarifies, for the organization, who makes the decision about organizational risk and who should be consulted as part of the decision-making. In this model, often the department supplying and using the data is the "information owner."

In the scenario above, the information owner is likely Human Resources. However, IT has a vested interest because they will likely be asked to make some of the changes needed for remediation. Usually, the team that manages the technology asset that contains HR information, is IT. The team that manages the asset is often called the "asset owner" and sometimes "information custodian." The purpose of these titles is to clarify who makes the risk decision and who must be consulted in the process. Usually, who makes the decision is a matter of organizational structure and resources. For some IT-centric organizations, the information owner will not make decisions. In other business-focused organizations, the information owner will give direction to IT.

Next, the question is who can make a decision and under what circumstances based on the roles above. If, for example, the asset owner is permitted to make a decision about whether or not to remediate (and to commit resources to do so), the question is whether a manager is the appropriate leadership level to make such a decision without any awareness on the part of executive managers. Because executives are expected to perform their roles in good faith and with loyalty to the organization, it is in their best interest to be aware of cybersecurity risks within their organization. For example, if Yahoo had made a decision not to fix a known issue, and this information was never shared with executive leaders, ultimately resulting in multiple data breaches, can we really hold executive leaders accountable?

Organizations that implement strong cybersecurity practices also focus on security governance related to risk decision-making. Often decision-making is vested in individuals who have the accountability and ability to commit financial or other resources to remediating an issue, and who, by virtue of their responsibility and position within the organization, should be aware of these risks. This often means that choosing the right individuals to make a decision about risk is both a matter of accountability and expense. For this reason, many organizations create governance models for risk remediation and for risk acceptance. These models may be different or may be the same. For example, risk acceptance, wherein an organization does not plan to remediate a risk for a time period or indefinitely (increasing the organization's overall potential for exposure), may require a higher-level approval than commitment to the financial resources to remediate it.

Risk remediation is largely a question of committing resources and having the accountability to ensure remediation is completed. Larger organizations may permit directors to commit to remediation for low risk items under a given financial threshold, with medium risks at the Vice President level, and high risks at the President/Senior Vice President level. Other organizations may assign thresholds based on remediation cost. However, for risk acceptance, some organizations may decide to require approval a level above the remediation level, requiring CEO approval to overtly decide not to remediate a risk. In addition to financial commitment and responsibility, risk acceptance also requires transparency. Individuals at lower levels of an organization will likely not be held as accountable as senior executives when things go wrong. Consider the following example:

NYTTime Entertainment is a video game company that is known for ultra-violent video games. For some time, anti-violence advocates have been attacking their servers, attempting to interrupt their services. During a routine risk assessment, the primary application database, when receiving routine updates, was not re-encrypting the database containing personal information of NYTTime's subscribers. Due to the recent attacks, the risk rating team determined that this was a high risk to NYTTime. NYTTime does not have a governance model, and the asset owner, a manager at NYTTime, determined that the cost to fix the encryption issue was simply too high given all of the other new applications that needed to be set up and loaded. The manager has proposed an exception for this risk.

QUESTIONS

1. In the example above, what do you think could go wrong?

2. Why or why not do you think escalation to executive leadership is a good idea in this situation?

3. How might you effectively use executive time in a situation like this? How would you describe the potential risks to someone who is not an expert in cybersecurity?

4. Imagine you have been asked to lay out a proposed model for appropriate escalations. How might you determine who makes the decision and when? Try to sketch out a model or table to describe this process.

3. GOVERNANCE REVIEW

Even when the appropriate decision-makers, pre-determined by the organization, make a decision, there may be some circumstances that require broader review. For example, even if an HR Senior Vice President has made the decision, there are many other leaders at the same level who might have a different view on the topic and who might not be comfortable accepting risk that may cause more problems for the organization.

For organizations that are more mature, a committee or escalation process involving multiple departments and capabilities are often involved in approving a particular decision. Especially when such decisions implicate legal or compliance decisions, or when financial commitments are sizeable, this level of review can be instrumental in making a fully informed decision. Consider the following example:

HYPO-Dispose is a company that enables individuals to drop off hypodermic needles and receive clean needles, anonymously, at their facilities. One line of business is taking and disposing of these needles and replacing them to discourage the transmission of AIDS and Hepatitis between drug users. Another line of business involves addiction counseling for individuals who pursue a path to sobriety. As part of the counseling services, HYPO-Dispose may work with individuals' insurers or may transmit data to a health provider when an individual chooses to take a next step. For part of its business, HYPO-Dispose is a HIPAA Covered Entity. Risk assessors recently discovered in a routine risk assessment that one of HYPO's main IT systems containing HIPAA-covered patient data (Protected Health Information) had a number of vulnerabilities that had not been patched in some time, including some zero-day vulnerabilities that were currently being used to gain access to systems. The team managing the asset told the risk assessment team that they had not patched the vulnerabilities because the patching process had resulted in some service interruptions they were trying to avoid.

In this case, imagine that the risk assessment finding had traveled up the chain and the CIO had determined that the system would not be patched and the risk should be accepted, as uptime was of primary concern. In this case, however, the CIO is not in a position to make this determination without consulting with anyone else. Why? Because in this scenario, non-compliance with HIPAA could cause other types of legal and compliance issues beyond a technology concern. By including more decision-makers, it may mean that the CCO, CISO, CPO, and the CIO disagree on a direction. Perhaps the cost to remediate the risk is too high. In some circumstances, risks may even require the CEO or President of an organization to make a decision and commit the resources to fix the issue.

The purpose of having a committee determination and escalation is to ensure that the risk accepted by an organization is visible to leadership and determined by the appropriate level within the organization. Because all organizations are different, this determination, as well as the review process, should be specific to each organization. Organizations will not make decisions in exactly the same way, but decision-making *must* at least be consistent within the organization.

E. THIRD PARTY MANAGEMENT

In the previous sections, we have focused primarily on internal organizational risk assessments and decisions. However, third-party risks are often realized, to an organization's detriment. Because the first party often has a standing relationship with B2B and B2C customers, as well as its own personnel, the first party usually is left answering for the actions of a third party. In this section, we will discuss not only processes for managing third-party risk, but also contractual vehicles to enable a first party to act or collect when a third party does not fulfill its cybersecurity commitments.

1. INTRODUCTION TO THIRD-PARTY RISK

In the following excerpt, West and Zentner describe the prevalence of third-party risks from a cybersecurity perspective.

TOBI A. WEST & AERON ZENTNER, *THREATS AND MAJOR DATA BREACHES: SECURING THIRD-PARTY VENDORS*

SSRN (2019)

Third-party data breaches increased by four times in 2018, putting client provider reputations and their pocketbooks at risk ("Third Party Data Breach", 2019). According to Patterson, Soha Systems reported that 63% of data breaches "can be attributed to third-party vendors" (2017). A third-party threat can include remote workers connecting via virtual private network (VPN), mobile devices connecting to the network, contractors that need temporary access to the Internet or networked systems, and vendors with long standing connections to the network and data (Patterson, 2017). This paper will focus on system threats that exist while working with third-party vendors.

Vendors have an obligation to reduce risk, and at the same time, client providers are obligated to manage and monitor the data relationship between the two parties (Garcia, 2017). This paper covers three major data breaches that occurred due to issues with a third-party vendor, impacting millions of government employees, shoppers, and hotel guests. The breaches have a recurring theme that originates with the third-party vendor systems. The paper also covers how vendors can secure information to reduce the risk of threats to preserve the client provider's reputation and recommendations for other third-party vendors to take.

In recent years, third-party data breaches have crossed multiple industries, including banking, health care, major car manufacturing, credit monitoring services, and event ticket sales (Chickowski, 2018). In some cases the breaches have caused records to be exposed to the Web, making personally identifiable information (PII) about consumers publicly available. In many cases, the breach led to PII and credit card information being sold on the Dark Web. An examination of three major third-party data breaches affecting government systems, a department store, and a hotel chain follows. [. . .]

A third-party threat exists when the client provider's system is not secure, the third-party's system is not secure, or the connection between them is not secure. Generally, there is an exchange of data between the third-party vendor and the client provider to allow the vendor to provide a service or product to the client provider. Sometimes that will also include a connection for the vendor to one or more of the client provider's systems. In 2015, Tender reported the top 5 threats to client providers from third-party vendors were shared credentials, irregular access, the joint cloud, public Internet exposure, and proximity to privileges. These can all be monitored through vendor management services. The attack types for the three third-party breaches are described below. There appears to be a recurring theme for the attacks with no boundaries for industry types or government systems. [. . .]

Cyber hygiene is a key element for vendors' internal culture to help raise awareness about the organization's connections to client providers and how these relationships make the vendor organization a target for cybercriminals. Additional measures include multi-factor authentication and raising awareness about potential email phishing attacks that can lead to malware downloads ("10 Most Important Cyber Security Tips for Your Users", 2018). Vendors should be aware of the network relationship between their system and the client provider's network. The vendor has an extra burden to uphold the reputation of the client provider and the vendor is responsible for maintaining security on the vendor system as well as the network data connections to the client provider. The vendor should be prepared to provide updated vulnerability and risk assessment reports to the client provider to demonstrate the measures taken to secure the vendor network (Wu, 2019).

Vendors should regularly assess their needs from the client provider, including system credentials, data types, and system connections to update them, reducing the risk by limiting access whenever possible ("Five Things To Know About Third Party Risk", 2019). Vendors should also be aware of production data being used in the test environment and ask the client provider not to do so (Sen, 2019). Sen also recommends that vendors avoid sharing any data from the client provider with their third parties which could lead to a fourth party breach for the client provider.

Threat hunting can help organizations find APTs that have a foothold in the network. This is the proactive search for attackers and malware within the system (Byrne, 2018). According to the report on Security Intelligence by Byrne, cybercriminals are inside the network for 191 days before being detected (2018). Threat hunting is for more sophisticated security teams and is intended to catch the 20% of attacks that are not prevented by traditional monitoring systems, such as firewalls, antivirus, and security information and event management (SIEM) tools.

In addition to security planning to prevent a data breach, vendors should also have a response plan in case a breach occurs. The response plan should include communication strategies, a designated team that will assist with the response, and keep all reputations intact by following through on the response plans (Hill, 2019). It is the responsibility of both parties, the client provider and the vendor, to follow through on the response plans to maintain both reputations.

Recommendations from Wu (2019), are that client providers take the following actions to avoid third-party breaches: know your vendors and what systems they have access to within your network, regularly discuss third-party risk with your leadership, be willing to cut ties with the vendor, know who your third-party outsources to, and continuously assess your vendors for security risks. This in-depth awareness and continuous monitoring of the third-party vendor is meant to ensure that changes in the relationship between the client provider and vendor do not result in a data breach or public data exposure.

As described above, many third-party risks result from poor front-end review and ineffective third-party management. Figure 8 illustrates the steps organizations should take to ensure effective third-party management.

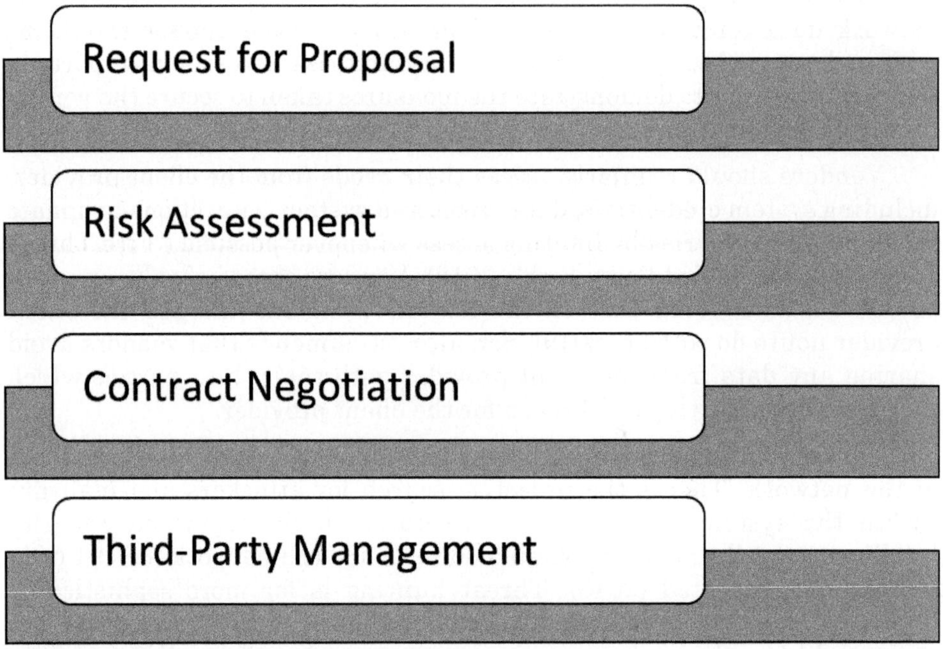

Figure 8: Four phases of Third-Party Cybersecurity Management

Third-party cybersecurity practices are not just a matter of ensuring you know who your third parties are, but rather managing and assessing third parties before they ever are a third party. Once an organization forms a relationship with another entity, it is often difficult to dissolve, especially when a third party stores or handles your organization's information.

The first step organizations should take is to assess whether a third party has the basic cybersecurity capabilities to make it a good service provider for your organization. Many organizations simply choose a third party without considering other providers. For this reason, a standardized process for selecting third parties is often a positive step, whether in a Request for Quote (RFQ), where a third party provides basic information, or in a Request for Proposal (RFP), where a third party provides detailed information in a competitive bid scenario. After the request has been reviewed for cost, services, fit, and security practices, a risk assessment can be conducted.

A third-party risk assessment, described below, considers each third party with respect to the *inherent risk* it poses to an organization. For example, a third-party service provider that provides janitorial support likely will not have the same inherent risk to cybersecurity as a third party that manages a million records in a cloud data store. Based on this inherent risk, an organization may determine whether or not to complete a full risk assessment. After the risk assessment has been completed, or while the assessment is being completed, contract details should be discussed and negotiated. Often the response a third party provides during a risk assessment may differ from those committed in a contract, so cybersecurity professionals, including attorneys, technologists, and business professionals, should be looking for any inconsistencies.

Finally, after outstanding issues have been negotiated, a contract may be signed. After the contract is signed, however, an organization must continue to assess and manage risks introduced by the third party, including responding to incidents reported by the third party or conducting a periodic re-assessment to ensure controls are still in place.

2. THIRD-PARTY RISK ASSESSMENTS

Third-party risk assessments should be conducted for all third parties posing an inherent risk level to the organization. Depending on the organization's risk tolerance and available security personnel to conduct such assessments, these assessments should be conducted on at least third parties whose assets or operations pose high risk to an organization.

Third parties are usually triaged (prioritized) before assessment, based on certain categories of inherent risk, usually: data classification of data provided to, transferred through, or stored by the third party; the number of data elements or records involved; overall contract spend or strategic significance of the third party; overall maturity of the third party; and criticality of operations performed by the third party. The thresholds for these categories are specific to an organization. For example, the number of records implicating a high inherent risk might be one million at a large company or one thousand for a small municipality. The goal is to manage risk that is high with respect to the organization itself. See Figure 9 for a simplified example of inputs for assessment triage and frequency.

	Tier 1	Tier 2	Tier 3
Data Type	• Sensitive data	• Sensitive data	• Conf. data
Vendor/Supplier Status	• Strategic or high availability vendor	• Moderate use vendor	• Low-medium use vendor
Number of records	• 100K + records	• 10K-100K records	• Up to 10K records
Assess. Freq.	1 year	2 year	3 year

Figure 9: Third-Party Assessment Triage Example

Third-party risk assessments use the same controls as any other risk assessment, and this makes perfect sense! If a third party is doing business on behalf of your organization, wouldn't you want the third party to hold itself to your standards? Of course, risks identified and attendant decision-making, including risk acceptance, is still part of the risk assessment process. Some third parties, such as start-ups or small businesses may not have the ability to meet the same requirements as a large organization. However, in these circumstances, it is still valuable to be aware of these risks and conduct a cost/benefit analysis with respect to choosing this vendor. Sometimes, an organization will choose a lower-cost vendor with poorer cybersecurity practices when the inherent risk is not very high.

One difference in how third-party risk assessments are conducted is in the method of responding to the questions. For internal risk assessments, often an internal contact is available and other knowledgeable team members are available for additional questions. For third-party risk assessments, a cybersecurity contact inside the company usually sends the assessment questions to a contact at the third party's organization and waits for a response.

Receiving a response quickly can be a bit difficult because third parties often fill out questionnaires for multiple potential customers at one time, so the delay can be significant. If the contract is already in the process of being negotiated, sometimes the results of the third-party assessment cannot be reviewed before the contract has been signed. This creates some obvious issues, usually in terms of what is included in the contract. If a third party has open risks after the risk assessment, the organization has the opportunity to walk away before the contract is signed. Alternatively, an organization can include specific terms related to remediating any identified issues, or the organization can offer to pay for these changes or negotiate a reduction in price for services. Overall, having more information prior to finalizing the contract is crucial if an organization hopes to use its leverage to protect its cybersecurity interests.

Well-written cybersecurity contract terms usually include two provisions for ongoing third-party management: the commitment to fill out periodic repeat third-party assessments and the right for an organization to audit the third party in the event of a serious incident or data breach. Ensuring appropriate third-party contract language effectively enables ongoing third-party management.

3. THIRD-PARTY CONTRACTS

It should be noted before describing the details of third-party contracts that such contracts are not always between a true third-party vendor or supplier and an organization. There are a wide variety of different third parties, and the contracts that are signed usually reflect these differences. However, each type should merit inclusion of some cybersecurity terms, regardless of the third party's status. Figure 10 describes some of the variations of third-party status.

Vendors	Suppliers	Partners	Affiliates
• Provide services to organization • Provide contractors • Sometimes used interchangeably with "Supplier"	• Provide products to an organization • Provide both physical and virtual technology	• Legally binding relationship • Partial ownership/ operation (not 100%)	• Legally binding relationship • Often have information sharing agreements

Figure 10: Variations of Third Parties

Although we are not discussing the details of contracts for mergers, acquisition, or divestiture in this book, it should be noted that due diligence proceedings and associated contracts should similarly contemplate cybersecurity issues and ensure that in the event of mergers and acquisitions, organizations are selecting candidates that have employed adequate cybersecurity measures, including an information security program. For start-up acquisitions, organizations must at least ensure that the technology or services purchased as part of acquisition have appropriate cybersecurity controls included and that the cybersecurity programmatic practices between entities are a good fit.

For most of the third parties detailed above, it is useful to understand the general anatomy of most agreements, as well as where it is imperative for organizations to negotiate or otherwise pay attention to potential cybersecurity pitfalls. Why is it so important to have a contract that contemplates cybersecurity issues? The biggest issue is related to money. Imagine a situation where a cybersecurity issue occurs that is expensive for your organization but is the third party's fault? How might you recover? Recall the economic loss doctrine from Chapter 10.

Unfortunately, a B2B relationship likely will not result in economic recovery when it is brought in tort. For that reason, the only hope of recouping lost money, for example the costs of forensic investigations, external legal counsel, or public relations firms, data breach notification, consumer payouts, or identity monitoring, is to have a contract in place. As a note, often cyberliability and cyberrisk insurance policies only cover the primary, not the third, party. And small businesses often do not have these insurance policies themselves.

Beyond financial reasons, contracts put into sharp focus the requirements of a relationship. It is precisely the purpose of negotiating terms to figure out what limits an organization's program might have, especially when coupled with third-party assessment findings. The following example was actually experienced by one of your casebook authors when negotiating with a third party.

A technology service provider was going to license an application to a travel organization. The engineering plan was to integrate the application with the licensee's environment via an Application Programming Interface (API), which would securely send data back to the organization. The organization would market this new application to its customers and it would be branded per the organization's colors and styles but be operated by the service provider. The service provider could not return a third-party assessment on time, and the contract negotiation had already begun. The service provider continued to redline (delete) language in the contract related to encryption of the data, and the contract negotiators asked why. The third party did not meaningfully respond to the question but reiterated that they do encrypt the application data. Finally, the third-party assessment response indicated that the company did not encrypt the application data. When this response was raised in the contract negotiation, the third party stated that they did not encrypt the data in the database. Rather, they only encrypted data sent via the API. Ultimately, after protracted negotiation, the organization opted to consider another service provider instead.

So which contract terms should actually be included in third party contracts? To effectively answer this question, it is important to understand the general framework of most contracts of this type. Figure 11 describes the main areas of a contract with which cybersecurity professionals should be familiar.

Applicable Law	Definitions Section	Relevant Terms	Indemnity	Termination	Breach
What law applies to this contract?	How do we interpret "data breach?"	What must each of us do?	Who pays during legal action?	When can we terminate?	What is considered breach of contract?
What laws apply to our activities?	How is personal information defined?	What rights does each party elect to use?	When must you cover me?	What is the payout if you terminate?	What is the penalty for breach (ceiling for recovery)?

Figure 11: Primary Contract Sections

First, applicable law may matter a lot for cybersecurity. Some countries outside of the U.S., particularly in relation to personal information, may have higher legal standards. Applicable law can mean either where the contract will be interpreted *or* what law applies to provisioning the contract. For an organization, it is important to document the region and specific laws that will apply to the third party. For example, if an organization is dealing in banking data, the organization will want to include a reference to the Gramm-Leach-Bliley Act specifically.

The definitions section often seems like a less important section of the contract, but it is critical to interpretation of the agreement. A couple definitions to pay attention to in particular are terms like "personal information" or "confidential information," as they are often referenced in the more comprehensive sections. For example, a third party may describe personal information very narrowly, then only require data breach disclosure when it involves personal information. This would overly narrow obligations that reference "personal information."

Indemnification determines overall allocation of legal liability according to the details of the contract. Usually the purpose of indemnification is to allocate costs if any legal issue arises. For example, if a third party does or does not do something in the contract (usually listed in relation to the indemnification provision) that results in the organization experiencing legal costs, the organization may recoup the loss from the third party.

Termination can also be an important section of the contract. Usually, termination is only permitted due to breach of certain terms of the agreement. However, if cybersecurity-related terms are not referenced in the termination section, and these terms are breached, an organization may be required to continue to pay or continue a professional relationship with a service provider anyway. For example, if an expensive data breach occurs, the termination section of the contract may not permit termination.

Finally, contracts usually define what a "breach of contract" actually is. Defining certain actions as breach of contract means that an organization can quickly pursue legal action if a supplier acts or fails to act in a specified way. For an organization, it is often best to have the ability to claim breach as well as trigger termination, depending on what most benefits the organization. Some contract breach terms establish a ceiling for breach of contract damages. Challenges arise when such damage ceilings include costs related to an incident or data breach, which often are much more expensive than damage ceilings. For example, a common term is that the damage ceiling cannot be more than the cost of the contract. However, the cost of a data breach could be in the millions of dollars. If terms related to a data breach or incident are not specifically exempted from the damage ceiling, an organization might have to pay for any additional costs beyond the ceiling, even if the third party caused the incident or data breach.

Other relevant terms are specific privacy and cybersecurity terms that establish limitations and requirements of what a third party can do with the information used, accessed, transferred, or stored at the direction of the first party. In the past, most organizations included general commitments to confidentiality, without much more detail. Today, mature organizations draft security contractual terms from five up to fifty additional pages as a "Security Addendum." The best addendums are written in contractual language but establish high-level requirements in alignment with internal organizational policy. Figure 12 lists the specific types of terms most organizations should consider when writing boilerplate language.

Security Requirements	Policies/standards, security program, security contact, incident response, data breach disclosure, audit/assessment rights, vulnerability management, secure architecture/development practices, virus/malware scanning, secure network, remote access, identity and access management, physical security, data destruction, business continuity/disaster recovery, independent certifications, background checks, data breach cost allocation, credit monitoring cost
Privacy Requirements	Compliance requirements, other requirements (e.g. PCI specific terms), definitions of sensitive or personal information (use statutory language too), explicit privacy requirements (notice, consent, choice, collection/proportionality, use, transfer, processing, retention, deletion), data breach public notice rights, notice and approval of new third party use prior to contracting
Other Legal	General confidentiality clause, applicability to affiliates or other legally connected parties, sub-contractors or processor responsibilities, insurance coverage (e.g. cyberliability limits), financial viability/solvency requirements, liability limitations/allocation, third party beneficiaries (who can sue), applicability after service (continuing obligations), severability and modification clauses, rights to data upon sale/data use restrictions, localization requirements

Figure 12: Common Boilerplate Terms

Of course, some third parties may not agree to these terms, or even an organization's boilerplate. Large technology service providers, for example, may insist that their boilerplate is used, which likely is far less comprehensive than an organization may desire. However, the organization may also know the third party well or receive some indicia of their overall security competence and maturity. For example, companies like Microsoft, Apple, and Amazon have met any number of industry cybersecurity standards, and they often carry certifications to demonstrate this. Although they may not agree to an organization's boilerplate terms, they may nevertheless demonstrate appropriate maturity by sharing certifications and compliance reports.

F. INDUSTRY STANDARDS

One model for organizations to comply with many legal requirements while also managing internal risk is by adhering to one or more industry frameworks. Industry frameworks include both frameworks created by the United States and frameworks established through certification bodies for specific industries or across industries Although there may be many sources of industry requirements, also considered "authoritative sources," for purpose of a controls library, organizations often have to choose which framework or frameworks to use. For some industries, not complying with a seemingly voluntary framework may raise additional organizational risks, such as not being able to do business. Organizations operating in, for example, generally high-risk sectors will usually have additional industry standards with which to comply.

Of course, this does not mean that legally an organization has any direct obligation, but rather that in order to attract a business or retain certain business capabilities, it may have to comply nonetheless. The frameworks described in this section are only examples of potential frameworks an organization may choose to follow; it is not an exhaustive list on the topic, and a variety of new frameworks continue to emerge in this area. This list includes that are most long-standing and well-recognized.

1. NIST CYBERSECURITY FRAMEWORK[5]

The most popular, generally applicable framework today was created by the National Institute of Standards and Technology (NIST) in 2014. This framework is not binding for any organizations except for those that must follow FISMA, or federal government agencies pursuant to a 2017 executive order.[6] However, the NIST Cybersecurity Framework (Cybersecurity Framework) has usefully mapped all controls within the framework to many other industry standards, which makes it a useful tool for any organization looking for common controls to include in the controls library. For example, the International Standards Organization, the most well-known standards body in the world, has, for nearly two decades, established information security controls in its ISO-27001 framework. Many global organizations, therefore, follow ISO-27001, at least for its controls library if not for specific certification.[7]

NIST has, in relatively short time, established a substantial following for U.S. businesses as well. One of its benefits is that its controls library cross-references ISO-27001, and also covers these requirements. Therefore, if an organization implements the Cybersecurity Framework fully, it will likely also be compliant withISO-27001. Actual certification takes a separate step, where an external certification body actually tests the controls and provides a report of the organization's compliance. Notably, NIST does not provide any such service for NIST controls.

Separate from but connected to the Cybersecurity Framework, NIST has also established a wide variety of specific processes, procedures, white papers, and other documentation on a variety of cybersecurity practices. One of the most compelling aspects of the Cybersecurity Framework is its

---

[5] For detailed documents, see: https://www.nist.gov/cyberframework/framework. This framework is also discussed in Chapter 2.B.

[6] Executive Order 13800: Strengthening the Cybersecurity of Federal Networks and Critical Infrastructure (May 11, 2017), https://www.whitehouse.gov/presidential-actions/presidential-executive-order-strengthening-cybersecurity-federal-networks-critical-infrastructure/.

[7] Although this book focuses on the United States, ISO-27001 certification has become one of the gold standards for international regulatory bodies to review security practices. For example, ASIP Santé, the regulatory body reviewing medical device compliance, now requires ISO-27001 certification for medical device safety clearance. Increasingly, for privacy regulations around the world, ISO-27001 has been positioned as a type of rebuttable presumption: if the asset in question demonstrably complies, the regulatory agencies have a strong likelihood of not bringing a specific case against an organization.

description of required programmatic processes. See Figure 14 for a general picture of the Cybersecurity Framework.

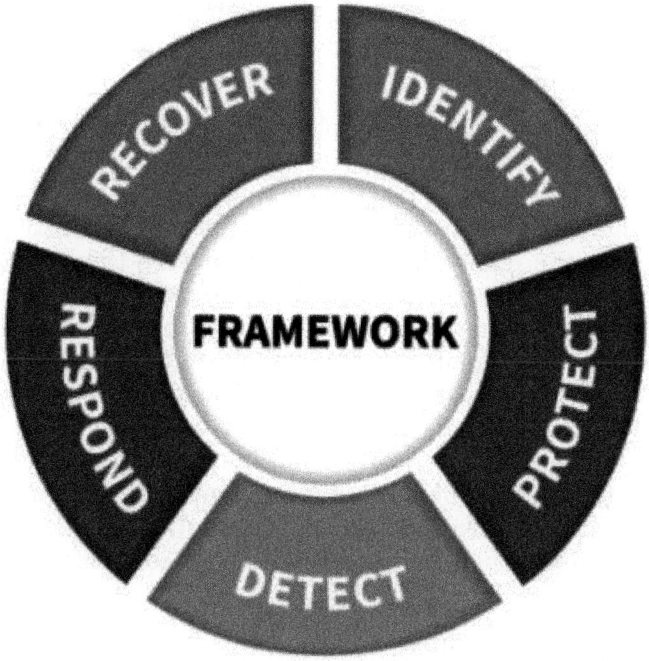

Figure 14: Cybersecurity Framework Functions

The functions described in the Cybersecurity Framework represent the layered nature of security and appropriate functions for a cybersecurity risk management program. For each of these five functions, NIST has established specific controls to ensure security in depth. For example, you may remember the difference between preventative controls and detective controls. The former type of control is used to prevent an issue from occurring, while the latter is used to enable forensic measures, or to enable an organization to figure out what has happened and either immediately respond or conduct investigations.

Identify is the step of identifying assets and data flows between assets (e.g., where data are collected, transmitted, and stored across multiple assets).

Protect is the step of employing preventative controls to stop intrusion and exfiltration.

Detect involves steps of both employing appropriate technology settings, such as event flags, to determine when a cyberattack is occurring or has occurred. Events are predetermined occurrences that do not fit the typical use of a system. For example, if all of the users for a particular system do their work between 7 AM and 10 PM in United States time zones, an event might be flagged by the system when log-ins occur between 10 PM and 7 AM, or when a user logs in from another geographic location, according to their IP address. Events enable an organization to determine if an adversary is attacking a system, then employ appropriate practices to thwart the attempt or identify the adversary for purposes of involving law enforcement involvement.

Respond is the practice of taking action after a cyberattack has been identified. Of course, an organization cannot respond if it cannot detect. The practice of responding is usually conducted by two groups: a security operations center (SOC) and an incident response team. The SOC is usually very involved in the detection step, which enables them to capture and immediately act when necessary, including beginning investigations and saving valuable evidence. The Incident Response Team (IRT) will be discussed later in this chapter in greater detail, but the IRT acts once an incident has been confirmed, which could include a cybersecurity incident that does not result in actual exfiltration, such as an attempt to gain access to the organization's intranet, or an incident that does involve viewing, accessing, or exfiltrating non-public organizational information (a data breach). The activities involved in respond largely depend on the nature of the situation, and whether the incident has been confirmed.

Recover involves processes to return to normal operation, which might include reestablishing access to a system that suffered a ransomware attack or Distributed Denial of Service attack (DDoS), implementing specific remediation activities to fix the vulnerability that enabled the successful cyberattack, and completing a root cause analysis to identify what went wrong and ensure it doesn't happen again. Recover involves all of the steps an organization must take to begin successful operations again, with less risk of experiencing another incident of the same type.

Each of these functions is mapped to a category and sub-category. See Figure 14 for an example of how NIST maps controls ('subcategory') to overall grouping ('category') and informative references (what we might call in a GRC tool an 'authoritative source'). The Informative References are mappings against common frameworks—for example as you can see, ISO/IEC is one of those references, in addition to ISA and COBIT, two models used for auditing programs.

Function	Category	Subcategory	Informative References
PROTECT (PR)	**Identity Management, Authentication and Access Control (PR.AC):** Access to physical and logical assets and associated facilities is limited to authorized users, processes, and devices, and is managed consistent with the assessed risk of unauthorized access to authorized activities and transactions.	**PR.AC-6:** Identities are proofed and bound to credentials and asserted in interactions	**CIS CSC**, 16 **COBIT 5** DSS05.04, DSS05.05, DSS05.07, DSS06.03 **ISA 62443-2-1:2009** 4.3.3.2.2, 4.3.3.5.2, 4.3.3.7.2, 4.3.3.7.4 **ISA 62443-3-3:2013** SR 1.1, SR 1.2, SR 1.4, SR 1.5, SR 1.9, SR 2.1 **ISO/IEC 27001:2013**, A.7.1.1, A.9.2.1 **NIST SP 800-53 Rev. 4** AC-1, AC-2, AC-3, AC-16, AC-19, AC-24, IA-1, IA-2, IA-4, IA-5, IA-8, PE-2, PS-3
		PR.AC-7: Users, devices, and other assets are authenticated (e.g., single-factor, multi-factor) commensurate with the risk of the transaction (e.g., individuals' security and privacy risks and other organizational risks)	**CIS CSC** 1, 12, 15, 16 **COBIT 5** DSS05.04, DSS05.10, DSS06.10 **ISA 62443-2-1:2009** 4.3.3.6.1, 4.3.3.6.2, 4.3.3.6.3, 4.3.3.6.4, 4.3.3.6.5, 4.3.3.6.6, 4.3.3.6.7, 4.3.3.6.8, 4.3.3.6.9 **ISA 62443-3-3:2013** SR 1.1, SR 1.2, SR 1.5, SR 1.7, SR 1.8, SR 1.9, SR 1.10 **ISO/IEC 27001:2013** A.9.2.1, A.9.2.4, A.9.3.1, A.9.4.2, A.9.4.3, A.18.1.4 **NIST SP 800-53 Rev. 4** AC-7, AC-8, AC-9, AC-11, AC-12, AC-14, IA-1, IA-2, IA-3, IA-4, IA-5, IA-8, IA-9, IA-10, IA-11
5 Functions	23 Categories	108 Subcategories	6 Informative References

Figure 14: NIST Industry Framework Mapping[8]

NIST also has helpfully established implementation tiers, or specific tiers depending on the size, complexity, and maturity of an organization. This has permitted some organizations to begin implementing some security practices, while continuing to improve maturity of cybersecurity risk management activities over time. Figure 15 shows that each capability (process, program, and participation) are evaluated based on an organization's level of maturity.

	1 Partial	2 Risk Informed	3 Repeatable	4 Adaptive
Risk Management Process	The functionality and repeatability of cybersecurity risk management			
Integrated Risk Management Program	The extent to which cybersecurity is considered in broader risk management decisions			
External Participation	The degree to which the organization: • **monitors and manages supply chain risk[1.1]** • benefits my sharing or receiving information from outside parties			

Figure 15: Maturity scale for Cybersecurity Framework Mapping[9]

For most organizations, the Cybersecurity Framework is an excellent way to begin a program or to ensure common controls are implemented

---

[8] *See* supra note 146.

[9] *See* supra note 146.

across a program. However, for some organizations, additional industry frameworks may be desirable.

2. PCI-DSS

The Payment Card Industry Data Security Standards (PCI-DSS or PCI) apply to organizations that process card payments as part of their operations, which could include any consumer-facing purchasing, such as retail or healthcare. PCI was originally created by the major credit card brands—American Express, Discover Financial Services, JCB International, Mastercard, and Visa—to establish a common security framework and reduce fraud in transactions. Depending on an organization's merchant tier, organizations have to implement any combination of different PCI controls, with organizations processing the most transactions having to not only implement the controls but also to have a Qualified Security Assessor (QSA) certify their compliance. Interestingly, although the PCI Data Security Standards Council is not a legal entity, it has the ability to fine organizations significant amounts or not permit the organization to process these card brands. For example, one casebook author recalls a large organization that would need to pay $10 million dollars for a first finding of non-compliance, with monthly fines of $1 million for each additional month in which it was not in compliance. PCI data security standards tend to be more prescriptive and rigorous than, for example, the relative flexibility of the HIPAA security rule, though many security experts dislike the PCI-DSS.

As part of an external review for larger organizations, a QSA provides a Report on Compliance (ROC), which details the controls an organization has implemented and any additional steps an organization must take to ensure PCI-DSS compliance. Sometimes, to minimize cost, organizations consult with a QSA in a pre-assessment prior to the formal assessment beginning, in order to identify and resolve issues prior to the formal assessment being conducted.

3. HITRUST

HITRUST is a private organization that, in 2007, committed to help healthcare organizations and technology providers establish a common security framework (CSF) to comply with the HIPAA security rule. Although HITRUST is not directly endorsed by the Department of Health and Human Services and does not establish a rebuttable presumption as to an organization's compliance with the HIPAA Security Rule, it helpfully translates the HIPAA Security Rule into specific controls an organization can implement. Accordingly, many organizations operating in the healthcare sector have certified to HITRUST requirements to demonstrate their compliance with the HIPAA Security Rule. Like PCI-DSS, HITRUST is relatively specific as to controls, aiming to take the guesswork out of more general HIPAA categories and requirements.

4. THIRD-PARTY CERTIFICATION

In addition to industry-specific certifications like those described above, many third parties wish to circumvent the laborious contract negotiation and assessment processes by demonstrating their security practices via a certification. For organizations that routinely negotiate B2B relationships, often having one or many third-party certifications is an advantage. There are a variety of certifications specific to, for example, cloud providers, but one third-party certification seems to be used with the greatest frequency for general third parties.

The SSAE18 audit controls, created by the American Institute of Certified Public Accountants, provide some degree of confidence, via an external assessor, that organizations possessing SSAE18 certified reports have implemented appropriate cybersecurity controls. However, the type of audit conducted often informs what types of controls actually implemented by the vendor being evaluated. Usually, organizations seeking SSAE18 audit reports are those working with technology service providers, such as those licensing applications, providing software, or hosting at cloud facilities.

The SSAE18 Service Organization Controls (SOC) 1 report is usually used for cloud facilities, to demonstrate both physical and technical controls requirements and is suited specifically for these uses. For example, controls implemented in a physical facility like this might include cooling or fire-detection controls that ensure the provider will be able to provide uninterrupted services. However, the SOC II Type 1 and SOC II Type 2 reports demonstrate broader technology service control compliance with SSAE18 standards.

The SOC II Type 1 and SOC II Type 2 do not differentiate on the basis of controls. Rather, the SOC II is designed to evaluate technology services, and the types differentiate based on initial versus repeat testing. For this reason, the Type 1 is conducted one time and gives a point-in-time view of compliance whereas the Type 2 is more comprehensive, demonstrating point-in-time and continuous testing of the same controls. The SOC II Type 2, therefore, is the gold standard for third-party service providers but is also significantly more expensive to conduct. Many organizations providing services in a B2B environment find the SOC II, in at least one of its forms, to be nearly required in order to demonstrate a degree of cybersecurity maturity to a business customer.

5. INDUSTRY FRAMEWORKS AND CERTIFICATIONS

A few words of note on industry frameworks and certifications. The NIST cybersecurity framework, like ISO-27001, is truly designed to inform what an organization does internally to implement a strong cybersecurity risk management program. As with most frameworks, the goal is to simplify the process of creating a controls library and ensure due diligence as to an organization's programmatic capability. However, a framework is only useful when an organization uses it to perform effective risk management. For example, if an organization simply implements the controls but accepts all the risks identified in internal and third-party risk assessments, it is no better off.

Specific industry certifications perform a different purpose: to ensure the appropriate audience has a degree of confidence and reassurance as to the organization's cybersecurity practices. PCI-DSS does this so that card brands will enable credit transactions. HITRUST provides the appearance of effective HIPAA compliance. And the SSAE18 certifications similarly demonstrate external certification of practices for third-party providers.

With regard to these industry certifications, organizations working with third parties that provide these indicia of compliance should take great care, however. Simply possessing these certifications does not guarantee maturity or effectiveness. Rather, these are part of the equation in evaluating an organization's practices while assessing the organization. One potential pitfall is related to the scope of such certifications. Often, to save money, organizations will not certify for all systems, but rather only to a subset of systems. This means that when a third party specifies that they hold, for example, an SSAE18 SOC II Type 2 report, an organization looking to sign a contract with them should ask about the scope of the assessment and whether it covers the system or asset currently being negotiated. If you are working for an organization pursuing a certification, it certainly can be a good strategy to give potential customers some reassurance of your cybersecurity practices, but it certainly is not a replacement for a strong risk management program.

G. THE INCIDENT RESPONSE PROCESS

In the previous sections, we discussed how an organization can prevent potential cybersecurity risks from being realized, in part by identifying assets and potential issues, and by building a cybersecurity risk management program with appropriate governance and decision-making. But what happens when, despite all this preparation, an incident occurs anyway?

Before we go into detail about the incident response process, it is important to reiterate a distinction and provide some definitions. Events are activities that do not match expected activities on a system. Some events, when properly configured, will send alert to a SOC to be evaluated. Events could be non-issues or they could indicate something bigger, the potential for an incident. An incident is an *attempted or successful* unauthorized access, use, disclosure, modification, or destruction of information or interference with system operations in an information system. Incidents may involve an electronic computer system or be physical in nature. For example, someone disclosing a trade secret to a foreign entity would still be considered an incident. A data breach is a specific type of incident where data is used, misused, read, accessed, or otherwise exfiltrated. The whole point of a data breach is that data are compromised. Based on these definitions, not all events are incidents, and not all incidents are data breaches.

The analysts in a SOC provide first-level triage of events to determine if they indicate an incident and verify that an incident is likely real. Once an incident is deemed likely to be real, usually a senior analyst begins investigating to get more information, after notifying the incident response manager (or someone in a similar role on the security team). Once the incident response manager gets involved, usually the Incident Response Team, a team of a variety of organizational leaders, begins to discuss the incident, its ramifications, and next steps. The phases of responding to an incident are described in Figure 16.

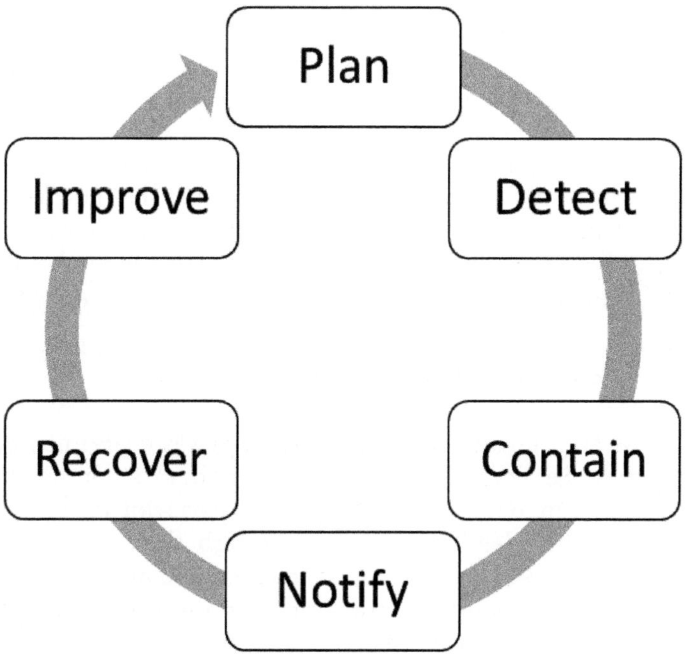

Figure 16: Incident Response Process

1. INCIDENT RESPONSE PLANNING

An incident response process should include upfront planning before an incident ever occurs. Usually this planning process includes three or four activities. First, the organization must develop an incident response plan (IRP), which lays out specifics for operation and roles within the organization. Often, the incident response plan is accompanied by an incident response policy, which is a high-level policy creating the incident response team (IRT), the SOC, and any required activities the organization must do to effectively manage incidents. After the policy is created, the incident response manager or similar role must create an IRP which adds additional detail. The manager must determine who are core members of the incident response team (IRT), who are associate members of the IRT, and what activities the organization commits to do as a manner of preparing for a potential incident.

The IRT usually includes the incident response manager, the head of the SOC, if not the same person, legal counsel, the CISO (or another leader over the incident response manager), and a representative from the communications team. Additional members usually include a technology expert for the associated technology, such as a server technology expert if the server has been attacked, as well as other members for other types of incidents, such as an HR leader if an employee has been involved in the incident. Similarly, an organization must determine who in the organization is permitted to know about the incident, and when. Specifically, leaders in an organization often want to know when such a situation has occurred. For some organizations, this means the CIO and General Counsel should be aware, and even the CEO under some circumstances. An IRP usually includes appropriate procedures for who to notify and when. An incident response manager should have a list of telephone numbers for all individuals who must be notified. With an incident, often time is of the essence, so individuals on the IRT and those who will receive escalations must be prepared to respond quickly. This often means that backups should be named in case an individual is unreachable.

However, planning does not just include creation of the IRT and the IRP. More mature organizations often practice the process of using the IRP through various simulations and with specialized pre-planned documents. Simulations may be completely based on paper, such as a "tabletop exercise." A tabletop exercise creates a realistic situation that is not actually live, enabling leaders to work through the IRP and act out an incident. The conclusion of a tabletop is to look back on the simulation and determine how the IRP might be fine-tuned to improve response the next time. Some organizations also create specific scenario-based responses for the most common or serious incidents.

Organizations that are highly mature may have created blue teams or red teams, and these organizations. Although these definitions may be slightly different depending on the organization, generally, blue teams are teams that, with upfront notification to the organization, seek to ensure compliance with internal systems, which may include conducting penetration tests, conducting vulnerability assessments, or participating in security by design activities. Red teams are teams that attack internal systems, sometimes without notification to the organization. In some cases, organizations may have blue team v. red team exercises, where red teams attack the system, while the blue team defends it. Through these activities, these teams can find issues that may not be covered by implemented controls, and they may also be a source for real-time and actual scenarios for practicing incident response. Often, these live demonstrations can most effectively simulate response and identify issues with the IRP or scenarios. It should be noted, though, that executives usually do not prefer "surprise" internal attacks, as it can result in spending organizational resources to respond to fake attacks.

Regardless of the degree of planning, upfront activities enable effective downstream operations. Without appropriate planning, organizational leadership may overreact to potential incidents, and steps may be missed. For this reason, the most important step in the incident response process is planning.

2. DETECT AND CONTAIN

As we described, detection is dependent on appropriate event monitoring. To monitor events, organizations need to have set up events in necessary systems. For example, mature organizations commonly have network monitoring tools, such as intrusion detection systems (IDS) and intrusion prevention systems (IPS). IPS is a preventative control, defending the network, but the IDS is a responsive system wherein alerts are sent directly to the SOC when activity appears abnormal or malicious. Additional detection focus areas are related to malware detection, a system that detects and contains viruses or other malware of specific definitions that may be present on connected devices or over the intranet.

Further, a vulnerability management team may routinely monitor for third-party patches or known vulnerabilities identified by the Online Web Application Security Project (OWASP) or other sources. This team may become aware of incidents before they occur or alert the SOC to potential zero-day vulnerabilities that may already have been compromised.

In less mature organizations, the incident response manager may be the only individual who becomes aware of an issue. In some organizations, a SOC does not exist. For all organizations and especially for organizations with fewer individuals attempting to detect potential incidents, incident response becomes everyone's responsibility, and therefore education on identifying potential incidents is central to both planning and detecting potential issues. Sometimes incidents are not obvious, but individual people may grow suspicious of certain situations. For example, an individual may see a phishing e-mail and report it, or someone may mistakenly give out important information to an outsider, thinking they are legitimate, and later feel like something just wasn't right. In other cases, an individual may log onto a system and notice that something has changed. It is crucial to detection that not only is the technology able to detect potential incidents, but personnel are adequately trained and reminded to report potential incidents, as well.

Once an incident has been identified and seems reasonably credible, the incident response manager and associated technology experts should take great care to record any details associated with the incident, both documenting the details and retaining a copy of the system as they found it. Then, the experts can investigate whether the incident has actually occurred or is likely to have occurred. If the experts believe it is likely to have occurred and that the impact could be reasonably high or otherwise implicate legal responsibilities, an external forensic service and law enforcement should be notified. Most organizations will contact local law enforcement initially, who will contact the Federal Bureau of Investigation. Of course, not all situations will merit this level of communication. For some, the suspected incident, once examined, is not actually an incident. Others may be relatively low in impact and not necessitate law enforcement involvement.

However, a critical step in the incident response process is to contain the issue. This means that evidence related to the incident must be retained not only to determine forensically what occurred but also in case the evidence is needed in court at a later time, for example in a CFAA case. Most organizations are not well-prepared to retain this information, which is why law enforcement, especially the FBI, or a trusted forensic partner should be brought in at the time that an incident is likely to have occurred. Furthermore, if an incident is still live, the FBI may be able to trace the attacker and gain more information about them, which is valuable in preventing new cyberattacks.

It should be noted that all organizations encounter incidents. It is very common for adversaries to attack and find certain vulnerabilities. However, what matters is how an organization responds to these incidents. Did the organization identify the incident quickly? Did the organization contain the incident quickly? Did the organization partner with the right government and specialized organizations to appropriately respond and collect important information? Did the organization actually close the vulnerability that enabled the incident to occur, not just on this system but on systems like it? If an organization has effectively planned and implemented appropriate responsive or detective controls that are actually monitored, usually the organization will be able to detect a malicious act quickly and respond.

3. NOTIFICATION

In the fourth step, the IRT must determine, based on the incident itself, whether notification is required. As we have previously discussed, not all incidents are data breaches prompting notification to individual consumers, credit monitoring businesses, attorneys general, or administrative agencies. In fact, most incidents are considered highly confidential, and only on a need-to-know basis. This is why individuals on the IRT are often higher-level personnel and the expectations of a high degree of confidentiality are communicated during the process of creating the IRT. Incidents are not usually disclosed even to internal personnel outside the IRT, let alone business customers, unless the law requires it.

Notification is usually required in two situations: 1) per law, to specific parties named in the law, depending on who and what was affected and 2) per contract, to specific business partners where the contract requires notification for certain incidents within a specified period of time. In the first situation, often the triggering factor is that personal information has been compromised, and the law that applies is the law where the individual resides. It is important to have a legal representative as part of the IRT, because the law where the individual resides will define what personal information actually triggers notification. Most state laws specifically enumerate the types of personal information requiring notification, including conditions where notification is not required, such as for encrypted personal information or when risk to the individual is very low (e.g., in most, but not all states). These laws specify the contents of such notifications, and usually require notification to consumers by certified mail.

Federal laws such as HIPAA require notification timing based on the size of the breach. If the data breach compromises PHI, then what matters is how big the breach was: data breaches over 500 individuals must be reported to HHS within 60 days and a covered entity must notify affected individuals within the same time period. The FTC's healthcare data breach rule extends this to organizations with health data that are not regulated under HIPAA, as well, requiring notification to the FTC and to the consumer. If data breaches are under 500 individuals, they must be reported within 60 days of the end of the calendar year via an online portal.

In the second case, private ordering will establish when and under what circumstances third parties must notify organizations of incidents or data breaches. Because organizations may have state or federal obligations to notify as primary parties when the third party is managing individual consumer data, usually contracts include a specified time period for notification of the third party to the organization, commonly 48–72 hours after discovery. These organizations may also have included language about being part of the investigation, receiving regular reports, or being permitted to audit the system after the fact.

Of course, one of the biggest challenges in both business relationships management and in communication to individuals is how to appropriately provide information while also minimizing reputational damage and retaining a customer relationship. After notification, often the trust in such relationships is harmed. For this reason, having internal communications and a public relations firm on retainer is incredibly useful. These IRT members can help to shape appropriate communications that manage the crisis (and indeed, it is a crisis!). Some cyberrisk and cyberliability policies will include coverage of such services, as well. In the event organizations make a public statement or send out notification, organizations also need to prepare personnel to respond to potential inquiries and send a unified message.

Often, the question is one of timing. Because most public notifications involve a description of the incident or data breach, the organization will want a sense of the size and impact of the incident. However, this must be balanced with timely communication. Many notable bloggers and security researchers or journalists, like Brian Krebs, often break news of data breaches and incidents quickly, due to their relationships with cyberattackers. This means that frequently these incidents will be publicized before an organization can determine the size of the incident and create its message. For this reason, often it is useful to draft holding statements in advance of an incident so that the organization can send something to media outlets without being forced to provide information the organization does not yet have. Once a story breaks on a blog or news site, an organization must quickly provide some information or risk looking like they were not prepared.

Further, in the event of consumer data breaches, organizations will need to weigh the potential benefits of additional steps to repair consumer relationships. This means organizations will need to discuss the costs and potential benefits of services like identity or credit monitoring, or financial incentives like coupons or settlement. Usually financial incentives do not work well: they can run the risk of making it look like the organization did something wrong or had inadequate security controls. Identity or credit monitoring is often very expensive, but it usually reduces the potential for real financial impacts that could result in consumers proving injury in tort litigation.

Overall, notification is the most public of steps, and the step on which most organizations will be judged. Handle notification poorly, and the organization will likely experience the brunt of criticism and loss of trust. Handle it well, and the organization will recover faster.

4. RECOVER AND IMPROVE

In recover, organizations must determine how to return to business as usual. Specifically, this means getting the systems operational and working as designed as soon as possible. However, it also means the organization returning to normal operations. During a large-scale data breach, for example, usually teams are deployed to handle the breach in various ways, taking personnel away from other tasks. It is important that recovery is timely while also measured and effective. This means identifying other vulnerabilities like the one that caused the incident and effectively preventing the same issue from happening again. Sometimes recovery takes a very long time, depending on the complexity of the incident. For example, in a ransomware attack, an organization may seek to recreate a system and develop a hot site or other backup site to prevent the issue from happening again. This is not an easy effort.

Improving pertains to both improving security and improving the incident response process. Immediately after handling an incident, organizations should use awareness and energy about the incident to evaluate similar systems to determine where cybersecurity controls may be inadequate. After an incident has occurred, previously identified risks of the same type may actually be higher rated than before. Why? Because now the probability (or likelihood) of the risk being realized is very high! When an incident has occurred, a risk by definition has been realized. The probability is 100%. For similar risks, the risk will be higher and demand prioritization.

Improving the incident response process is a lot like going through a tabletop or similar exercise in that issues with the procedure or process, or even membership of the IRT, will be fresh in everyone's mind. It is an excellent opportunity to figure out what changes need to be made to the IRP and how to best respond in the event of another incident.

QUESTIONS

1. Summarize the incident response process. What are the critical success factors of an effective incident response process?

2. If you were creating an Incident Response Team that must support the incident from beginning to end, who would you include (think back to the chapters introducing business roles as well as technology roles)?

3. Why is it important to distinguish between an event, suspected incident, incident, and data breach?

H. IN CONCLUSION

In this Chapter, we have covered a lot of territory about the practices and frameworks organizations use to manage risk and respond to incidents. Risk management, as you have seen, is more than simply knowing the law and implementing a control. Rather, it is a system of identifying what matters to an organization and determining the appropriate controls to protect these assets. Without an effective risk management program, organizations will likely implement programs that are not actually secure. Legal requirements are but one part of an effective risk management program.

CHAPTER 12

ALTERNATIVE MODALITIES OF RISK REGULATION

■ ■ ■

Technological processes, legal processes, and business processes all have mechanisms for managing risk. Often, particularly with more focused problems (e.g., quality control in consumer products manufacturing), each type of risk can be managed respectively by each of these processes. Certainly they will be *informed* by the other processes, but "creative" approaches may not be necessary. Cybersecurity, by contrast, is quite the opposite.

As we discussed in Chapter 8, doing cybersecurity well is difficult. Cybersecurity is complex, interdisciplinary, and has non-deterministic aspects. Moreover, the risk space can change rapidly. In Chapters 9–11, we discussed the various traditional technological, legal, and business methods of managing risk. In this Chapter, we explore alternate, hybrid, and innovative methods of managing risk. While these are not *substitutes* for the key roles traditional risk management (and the law) plays, as you read through this Chapter consider the degree to which these tools may *complement* traditional risk management approaches and "fill the gaps" created in those approaches by the cybersecurity problem.

A. REGULATING PROCESS, NOT OUTCOMES

Risk management approaches focus on measuring success through outcomes. This can take the form of regulating "performance" (i.e., how well an entity achieves a metric) or regulating "technology" (i.e., which specific tools/processes an entity employs). Performance-based and technology-based regulation has been thoroughly examined by scholars and scientists,[1] and their function is well understood. In more recent decades, however, the concept of regulating *processes* rather than outcomes or tools has advanced cybersecurity thinking as a system-based modality. Similarly, process-based regulation[2] is an approach in which regulatory directives and

[1] David Bernard Thaw, Characterizing, Classifying, and Understanding Information Security Laws and Regulations: Considerations for Policymakers and Organizations Protecting Sensitive Information Assets 8, n. 16 (Spring 2011) (Ph.D. dissertation, University of California, Berkeley) (on file with Georgia State University Law Review).

[2] This has been referred to by many different names in the literature, including but not limited to, 'enforced self-regulation' (Braithwaite 1982), 'mandated self-regulation' (Bardach & Kagan 1982; Rees 1988), 'reflexive' regulation (Orts 1995), or 'process-based standards'

compliance evaluation focus on the methods by which an organization develops and maintains its risk management procedures, rather than the specific tools used or specific performance outcomes achieved. In cybersecurity, this approach often takes the following form:

1. Conduct a risk assessment
2. Develop a risk management plan or decide on identified risks *(responsive to that assessment)*
3. Follow the plan
4. Update the plan *(loop back through step 1)*

By now, this type of reasoning should not surprise you. Notice, however, that this abstract framework neither includes a specific outcome requirement, nor a specific set of technologies which must be employed. What *may* surprise you is that this method of regulation has been in use in cybersecurity for approximately two decades! We discussed this to some extent in Chapter 10, but now will take a deeper look at the concept both in cybersecurity and elsewhere.

We begin with some quick reminders on performance-based and technology-based regulation. These are the most common forms of regulation you likely have encountered in daily life—for example, a highway speed limit is a performance-based regulation—your liability for a "speeding violation" depends on whether or not you have exceeded a specific performance standard (the speed limit). Likewise, a common example of a technology-based regulation is the format of a telephone number—the ten-digit format ensures interoperability not by requiring a specific level of connectivity *performance*, but rather by requiring a specific *tool*. In this case, a ten-digit number comprising a 3-digit area code, a 3-digit local exchange, and a four-digit local number (e.g., 202-456-1414 for the White House switchboard) enable a number to be connected. When international calling was added to the Public Switched Telephone Network (PSTN), the "+" notation was added in front of this as another form of technology-based regulation—any call placed on the PSTN beginning with a "+" treats the next 1–2 digits as a "country code," after which the following digits are passed to that nation's switching system and interpreted accordingly. *What other examples of performance-based and technology-based regulation can you think of?*

What makes process-based regulation different? Process-based regulation specifies neither a specific performance goal to be met nor a specific technology to be used. This may strike you as strange—if neither goals nor tools are specified, how can we be sure the desired result is achieved or a bad outcome is avoided? The idea behind a process-based

---

(Gunningham & Grabosky 1998), 'systems-based standards' (Gunningham 1996; Gunningham & Johnstone 1999), 'management-based regulation' (Coglianese & Lazer 2003), and 'Management-Based Regulatory Delegation' or 'Federated Regulation' (Thaw 2014, 2017).

regulation is that by forcing organizations to perform a set of processes, and evaluate and respond to the results of those processes, the organizations will generate better standards and select better tools *for their specific case* than under any "one-size-fits-all" regulation. In the following excerpt, Professors Cary Coglianese and David Lazer describe this type of regulation (which they refer to as 'management-based regulation', *see* supra fn. 153) and when it may be effective:

CARY COGLIANESE AND DAVID LAZER, *MANAGEMENT-BASED REGULATION: PRESCRIBING PRIVATE MANAGEMENT GOALS TO ACHIEVE PUBLIC GOALS*

37 LAW & SOC'Y REV. 691 (2003)

We analyze a little-studied regulatory approach that we call management-based regulation. Management-based regulation directs regulated organizations to engage in a planning process that aims toward the achievement of public goals, offering firms flexibility in how they achieve public goals. In this article, we develop a framework for assessing conditions for using management-based regulation as opposed to the more traditional technology-based or performance-based regulation. Drawing on case studies of management-based regulation in the areas of food safety, industrial safety, and environmental protection, we show how management-based regulation can be an effective strategy when regulated entities are heterogeneous and regulatory outputs are relatively difficult to monitor. In addition to analyzing conditions for the use of management-based regulation, we assess the range of choices regulators confront in designing management-based regulations. We conclude that management-based regulation requires a far more complex intertwining of the public and private sectors than is typical of other forms of regulation, owing to regulators' need to intervene at multiple stages of the production process as well as to the degree of ambiguity over what constitutes "good management."

The problem of regulatory instrument choice has typically been framed as a choice between technology-based or performance-based regulation (Breyer 1982; Viscusi 1983). Regulators can craft rules that either mandate specific technologies or behaviors (technology-based regulation) or require that certain outcomes will be achieved or avoided (performance-based regulation). Even market-based regulatory instruments, around which an important literature has emerged (Ackerman & Stewart 1985; Hahn & Hester 1989; Stavins 2002), are still linked either to technologies or, more frequently, to the outcomes of firm behavior. Market-based instruments do provide distinctive incentives to firms, but nevertheless regulators enforcing market-based regulation still measure firms' performance for the purpose of either assessing taxes or determining if firms possess an adequate number of tradeable permits.

The treatment of both conventional and market-based instruments in the academic literature has revealed important lessons about the effectiveness of different regulatory standards in advancing social goals. Yet missing from the traditional emphasis on technology-based and performance-based regulation has been much systematic attention to a third type of regulatory instrument that we call "management-based regulation." Management-based regulation does not specify the technologies to be used to achieve socially desirable behavior, nor does it require specific outputs in terms of social goals. Rather, a management-based approach requires firms to engage in their own planning and internal rulemaking efforts that are supposed to aim toward the achievement of specific public goals (Bardach & Kagan 1982:224).

[. . .]

I. What Is Management-Based Regulation?

Regulation may intervene at one of three stages of any organization's activities: the planning, acting, or output stages. Outputs include both private and social goods, that is, saleable products or services (private goods) as well as the positive and negative externalities (social goods and bads) that affect society. The social outputs of an organization's production include the traditional notion of public goods (e.g., a clean environment) as well other cases of "market failure" (e.g., worker safety). The challenge for regulation arises because private actors tend to underproduce social goods (or overproduce social bads), thus creating a need for the regulator to intervene (Viscusi, Vernon, & Harrington 2000).

[. . .]

The ultimate goal of all regulation is therefore to change the production of social outputs, but regulatory intervention targeted at any of the three stages will potentially affect outputs. We therefore distinguish between different types of regulatory instruments based on the organizational stage that they target. Technology-based approaches intervene in the acting stage, specifying technologies to be used or steps to be followed. Performance-based approaches intervene at the output stage, specifying social outputs that must (or must not) be attained. By contrast, management-based approaches intervene at the planning stage, compelling regulated organizations to improve their internal management so as to increase the achievement of public goals.

Under management-based regulatory strategies, firms are expected to produce plans that comply with general criteria designed to promote the targeted social goal. Regulatory criteria for management planning specify elements that each plan should have, such as the identification of hazards, risk mitigation actions, procedures for monitoring and correcting problems, employee training policies, and measures for evaluating and refining the firm's management with respect to the stated social objective. These plans sometimes are made subject to approval or ratification by government regulators, but as we discuss in Part III, they need not be under all types of management-based regulation. Similarly, under some management-based regulations (but not others), firms are required to produce documentation of subsequent compliance or are subjected to reviews by regulators or third-party auditors to certify compliance.

[. . .]

II. The Role for Management-Based Regulation

Having defined and illustrated what we mean by management-based regulation, we turn next to the circumstances under which a management-based regulatory strategy will likely prove effective, especially relative to technology-based and performance-based options. Our theoretical analysis begins with the assumption that government should choose the regulatory option that minimizes the costs of achieving a set of regulatory objectives (such as environmental, safety, or distributive goals). The choice between adopting a technology-based, performance-based, or management-based regulation will therefore depend on the relative overall net social gain each alternative would provide, given a specified regulatory objective.

[. . .]

Whether market-based or uniform, all performance standards require that government effectively monitor and assess the regulated outputs. When this requirement is met, performance-based regulations will generally prove more cost effective than technology-based standards, for the former allow firms the option of selecting the lowest-cost control or prevention options or innovating to find such lower-cost options. Yet it is often difficult or prohibitively expensive to assess critical outputs (Ayres & Braithwaite 1992), and when this is the case the advantages of performance-based standards will be weaker.

Management-based regulation shares some of the advantages of performance-based regulation in that it allows firms the flexibility to choose their own control or prevention strategies. But it is distinguished from performance-based regulation in that management-based regulation mandates specific, and sometimes extensive, planning and management activities. Since management quality is often an important component to achieving regulatory goals (Kagan, Gunningham, & Thornton 2002), management-based regulation requires firms to engage in internal actions that the regulator hopes will lead to improved private management of issues with social ramifications. Clear planning, monitoring, and procedures within a firm can be an important factor in preventing or reducing the social harms that motivate regulation in the first place, especially with respect to problems that arise from breakdowns in complex systems or that require coordination among a large number of interactive human and technological processes.

[. . .]

We have presented the regulators' choice as one among three basic types of instruments that roughly correspond to three stages of an organization's process: technology-based, performance-based, and management-based regulation.

When should a regulator use one type of instrument over another? In a world where government faced no transaction costs in identifying and enforcing an effective response, any regulatory instrument would be optimal (Coase 1960). By transaction costs, we mean the costs involved in selecting and implementing an effective rule, such as the costs of research, analysis, monitoring, and enforcement. For example, in the absence of these transaction costs, the government could craft an infinitely detailed technology-based regulation, where each technological requirement was delicately balanced as to the benefits and burdens imposed on society and where regulatory change was appropriately elastic in the face of new technological developments. If government used a performance-based rule, it could precisely determine the social costs of particular outputs and impose the appropriate tax (or industry-wide quota for a trading system), and in the absence of transaction costs businesses would effortlessly adjust internal processes to internalize these costs. Finally, if management-based tools were used, government would easily evaluate the planning and subsequent implementation of controls on the production of social externalities by private actors.

Yet we live in a world with transaction costs (Komesar 1994; Williamson 1981), and government must invest its limited resources in deciding to encourage some behaviors and deter others. The question therefore becomes one of selecting the regulatory instrument that, under given conditions, achieves the greatest net social gain or that minimizes both the regulated entities' compliance costs and the government's costs of selecting and implementing a standard that achieves a given regulatory objective. For some problems, it will be clearly worthwhile for government to invest large resources to find an optimal technological solution or to devise an appropriate and effective measure of performance. Yet for other problems, the technological solutions or the performance measures might be too costly for government to devise, and they might be more effectively identified by the firms themselves. Indeed, in many situations, the costs will be lower for market actors relative to government to understand the linkages between their behavior and particular outputs.

[. . .]

A. Mandating Planning, Implementation, or Both

As we noted in Part I, management-based regulation is distinctive in that it aims to direct action at the planning stage of the production process. Government seeks to direct such action by backing up a management-based regulation with sanctions. The question for the government decision maker becomes whether, given finite enforcement resources, it should mandate planning by itself, implementation of planning by itself, or both planning and implementation. To address this question, we develop a two-stage model of sanctioning using parameters that capture the regulator's capacity to alter a firm's incentives so as to incorporate public goals into its planning and subsequent implementation process.

We begin by assuming that from the firm's perspective, management-based regulation has two stages: planning and implementation. Government possesses some capacity to monitor whether a firm plans according to stated criteria, as well as some capacity to monitor whether the firm has implemented its plan. We further assume the following: the expected value of the penalty for not planning (and not implementing) is *P1* (> 0); the expected penalty for planning and not implementing is *P2* (> 0); the cost of planning, known at Stage I, is *Cp* (> 0); and *M* is a payoff to the firm from implementation of its plans. Note that *M* is a function of both the costs and benefits of implementing the planning at Stage II. Since *M* is not known by the firm until Stage II, we refer to the expected value of this payoff, *E(M)*, which represents what, at Stage I, the firm expects its payoff will be at Stage II. In the absence of government intervention, *E(M)* is the product of the probability that *M* will be positive and the potential positive value of *M*. In the presence of government intervention, *E(M)* is a function of the values of the alternative plans that the firm produces and the probability for each plan that the government would force the firm to implement that plan. Taking all of these factors together, the firm makes a decision at Stage I based on *P1, P2, Cp*, and *E(M)*, and at Stage II based on *P2* and *M*.

What implications can be derived from these assumptions for regulatory design? Using a model of optimal deterrence for purposes of analysis (Becker 1968; Polinsky & Shavell 1984), four scenarios are possible under the decision framework, ranging from no mandate needed to a mandate needed for both the firm's planning and its implementation of its plan.

1. Scenario A: No mandate necessary

[. . .]

2. Scenario B: Mandate necessary at planning stage only

[. . .]

3. Scenario C: Mandate necessary at implementation stage

[. . .]

4. Scenario D: Mandate necessary at planning and implementation stage

Management-based regulation, even when it is a better option than performance-based or technology-based regulation, will succeed only if government is capable of sufficiently increasing the magnitude of *P1* or *P2*, either by increasing the probability of detecting noncompliance or by increasing the adverse consequences for noncompliance. In Scenario B, the regulator will need to focus its efforts toward increasing the expected penalties at the planning stage rather than at the implementation stage. It may be satisfactory for the regulator simply to possess the capacity to evaluate the expense and effort that the firm took in examining certain processes. Thus, for example, if the firm hires individuals with particular training and demonstrates that it has studied the causes of certain types of hazards in its production process, then an improved set of outcomes is likely to follow.

By contrast, in Scenarios C and D such a regulatory approach would fail. In Scenario C, the firm will invest in the planning regardless of government intervention. A regulatory regime aimed just at the planning stage would fail to improve private behavior. The regulator must focus on the implementation stage. Of course, this does not mean that the planning stage may be disregarded, because government enforcement of implementation gives firms an incentive to obfuscate the conclusions that result from their plans. However, in contrast to Scenario B, the regulator can assume that the firm will invest enough in a rigorous planning process. The regulator therefore needs (1) the planning process to be transparent enough so that the regulator can independently evaluate the data, (2) the technical capacity to evaluate the data and determine whether the plan the firm proposes is consistent with the data, and (3) the capacity to evaluate implementation of the plan.

Scenario D, which is a combination of Scenarios B and C, is the most demanding scenario for the regulator, requiring an evaluation of firms' planning and implementation. An inability to monitor and enforce either planning or implementation will likely compromise policy objectives. If the regulator is unable to evaluate the planning process, then the resulting plans that the firm implements will likely be plans that minimize the firms' costs rather than maximize net societal benefits. If the regulator is only able to evaluate the planning process, firms cannot be expected to implement costly plans, even if such plans would deliver substantial social benefits.

In summary, designing an effective management-based regulation will depend in the first instance on the types of mandates the regulation imposes. A key consideration in deciding whether to mandate (and enforce) planning, implementation, or both will be the degree of overlap between firms' private interests and society's needs. Where there is substantial overlap, all that government may need to do is to require firms to engage in a planning process, since firms can be expected to implement their own plans to serve their own interests even if not to advance public goals. In other (and perhaps most) cases, this overlap will not be sufficient to ensure that firms implement their own plans. In these cases, government will need to mandate planning and implementation and to develop appropriate methods for monitoring and enforcing both.

B. Meta-Management Design Choices

In addition to deciding what to mandate, regulators face other choices when designing management-based regulations. One of these relates to how prescriptive government should be in directing firms' management practices. Another choice is whether to require firms to submit plans for government review and approval before implementation. A final choice concerns methods for monitoring implementation, with options ranging from record-keeping provisions to requirements for third-party auditing and certification. These choices arise in order to address what is effectively a principal-agent problem between the government and the regulated entity.

With management-based regulation, the government takes on the role of what might be considered a "meta-manager," seeking to guide and motivate firms to order their own economic activity in a way that is more aligned with social interests. Yet because regulated firms can be expected to have interests at odds with the government's goals, and because they have an informational advantage, the regulator finds it necessary to develop ways to induce and control firms so that they manage themselves in ways more aligned with social goals. These ways include the degree of specificity in the regulator's prescribed management practices, the degree to which the regulator shares in the development and approval of firms' management plans, and the type and stringency of the regulator's monitoring of firm compliance.

1. Specificity of required management practices

A critical issue in the design of a management-based regulation program is the specificity of the requirements for the planning process dictated by the regulator. Management-based regulations can range from simple requirements calling on firms to develop plans to highly detailed requirements specifying criteria for adequate planning, as well as requirements for firms to monitor their performance and correct departures from their plans. For example, the Massachusetts pollution prevention statute is quite general in its core provision. It requires that firms simply include in their plans "a comprehensive economic and technical evaluation of appropriate technologies, procedures and training programs for potentially achieving toxics use reduction" (TURA 1994 § 11(3)(a)). The state regulations implementing TURA do not get much more specific either, requiring regulated firms to "demonstrate a good faith and reasonable effort to identify and evaluate toxics use reduction options" (310 C.M.R. 50.42(11) 2003).

By contrast, the EPA's risk management regulation is both longer and more specific, providing detailed steps for scenario planning and hazards assessment. Rather than simply requiring firms to identify "appropriate" procedures, EPA is detailed about what kinds of actions should be contained in a firm's operating procedures. For each regulated chemical process, the firm must prepare "clear instructions or steps" that address:

> (1) Initial startup; (2) Normal operations; (3) Temporary operations; (4) Emergency shutdown and operations; (5) Normal shutdown; (6) Startup following a normal or emergency shutdown or a major change that requires a hazard review; (7) Consequences of deviations and steps required to correct or avoid deviations; and (8) Equipment inspections. (Chemical Accident Prevention Provisions 2002, 40 C.F.R. § 68.52.)

The EPA regulations also mandate that firms train their employees in these operating procedures and that "[r]efresher training shall be provided at least every three years, and more often if necessary" (Chemical Accident Prevention Provisions 2002, 40 C.F.R. § 68.54).

[. . .]

2. *Plan Approvals*

Another design issue is the extent and type of involvement by the government at the planning stage. In particular, how are plans negotiated between the regulator and regulated? One might imagine several alternatives: (1) the regulator reviews all management plans in advance and the regulated firm must receive preapproval of its plan before implementing it, (2) the regulated firm must submit a management plan to the regulator which the regulator keeps on file but does not preapprove, or (3) the regulator checks to see if the firm has completed the appropriate plan ex post, either during periodic inspections of the firm's facilities or following an accident or incident. For example, with respect to the application of HACCP to the processing of fish, regulators in the United States do not have a preapproval process, but in Canada they do (Canadian Fish Inspection Regulations 2003, 802 C.R.C. §§ 14(1) & 15(6)). We highlight four key factors that are likely to affect how actively the regulator should be involved during the planning process:

- *Clarity of criteria for planning.* If there is substantial ambiguity over what an acceptable planning process is, or if it is difficult to specify criteria ex ante for what makes a management plan acceptable, then the regulator may find it advantageous to be involved earlier in the process.

- *Need for transparency at planning process.* As noted above, firms can have an incentive to obfuscate data or to treat the planning process as a paper exercise to avoid the implementation of costly, but effective plans. Early and active involvement by the regulator may increase the chances that firms would engage in meaningful planning and accurate record-keeping.
- *Mechanism to subsidize the planning process.* Regulators will often develop an expertise in the generic management challenges that regulated parties face. In particular, in Scenario B above, it may be more efficient and effective for the regulator to take on the role of quasi-consultant, effectively giving away its expertise in return for improved management of public goals by the private sector. Such a role may be better served by early involvement in the planning process, such as through a preapproval requirement.
- *Government resources.* Preapproval of planning does not eliminate the need for subsequent inspections by regulatory agencies and can instead place additional resource burdens on the government. By contrast, reviewing plans only periodically at the time of a regular inspection minimizes the demand on government resources. The number of facilities covered by the regulation will also undoubtedly matter. Where there are many sites relative to the regulator's resources, the costs associated with a pre-approval process will make that option prohibitive. This appears to explain why the resource-starved FDA evaluates plans ex post, whereas the better endowed Canadian counterpart is able to require preapproval.

In short, there are multiple ways to enforce a planning mandate, ranging from preapproval at the time of the planning or enforcement at some time (potentially a long time) after planning has taken place. The desirability of early involvement depends in part on the needs of the regulated firms for feedback and de facto planning subsidies, as well as the informational needs and capacity of the regulator.

3. *Record-Keeping, Inspections, and Third-Party Auditing*

Beyond requiring preapproval, there is the question of how to monitor and enforce planning and implementation mandates. To facilitate such monitoring, management-based regulation will typically be accompanied by record-keeping requirements. For example, the FDA requires juice-processing facilities to maintain onsite documentation of their entire HACCP plans, including hazards analysis, testing, and documentation of implementation of procedures, so that the FDA inspectors can "determine whether the HACCP system or systems are properly implemented and effective" (FDA 2001a:6163).

Regulatory agencies also need to decide how frequently to inspect facilities governed by management-based regulation. They can require a continuous or occasional presence at processing locations. For example, USDA inspectors are onsite continuously at meat processing plants, whereas the FDA visits fish processors only once a year. The key variables underlying the choice of how frequently to inspect include (1) the size of the processors (e.g., meat processors are much larger than fish processors, making it much more economical to have a presence there), and (2) the types of actions the regulator is attempting to observe. If the regulatory problem is such that the regulator needs to observe routine practices, such as how clean processing surfaces are kept, an almost continuous presence may be necessary because firms may only implement these practices when the regulator is present. However, if the regulator is trying to observe implementation of costly technologies, such as installation of refrigeration equipment, occasional visits may be more than adequate.

[. . .]

C. Summary: Designing Management-Based Regulations

The main sets of choices in designing management-based regulation are of two types. The first type is reflected in the choice of whether to mandate planning, implementation, or both. The second type revolves around how the regulator seeks to overcome the principal-agent problems inherent in directing and overseeing firms' management practices. These two types of choices are interrelated. The decision about what to mandate depends on the nature of the incentives firms already have to plan or implement actions directed at addressing issues of social concern. Yet the nature of these incentives also affects regulators' choices about how to direct and oversee firms' management.

To the extent that firms lack adequate incentives on their own to create plans and implement them, they may resist—even in subtle ways—complying with the letter and spirit of any management-based mandate imposed by government. When it comes to planning, some firms will undoubtedly devote as few resources as they can to analysis and will have the incentive to produce plans that minimize the firms' implementation costs rather than maximize social benefits. The regulator therefore needs to be able to assess whether firms' planning processes and resulting plans have been appropriately rigorous. When it comes to implementing these plans, firms may have the incentive to avoid costly and effective implementation, so regulators must be able to assess whether firms have made adequate capital investments and are regularly acting in a way that is consistent with their plans.

The options available to the regulator include the development of specific—and more difficult to evade—mandates embedded within the management-based regulation. In addition, the regulator may be better able to ensure the adequacy of planning by requiring government approval of firms' plans. Finally, the regulator will be better able to ensure effective implementation by imposing suitably detailed record-keeping requirements and instituting inspections or third-party audits. Even so, what makes for "good management" will generally be somewhat open-ended or case-specific, and the greater discretion afforded to firms under a management-based approach to regulation will also inevitably add to the regulator's enforcement challenges.

[. . .]

Conclusion

Our analysis indicates that the preferred point of regulatory intervention in the production process—that is, at planning, action, or output—will be driven by the relative transaction costs the regulator confronts in achieving public goals at each of these stages. Performance-based regulation, while attractive for the flexibility it permits regulated firms, will likely be appropriate only where the regulator can cheaply measure output and evaluate its social impact. Similarly, technology-based regulation will likely be appropriate only where the regulator can cheaply evaluate the relationship between action and output—especially unlikely in heterogeneous or dynamic settings.

Management-based regulation appears to be a strategy for government to use, if nowhere else, when performance-based and technology-based standards are not feasible. Management-based approaches seek to take advantage of private actors' understanding of the relationships between behaviors and their outputs, compelling regulated parties to conduct their own evaluations, find their own control solutions, and document all the steps they take.

Characterized this way, management-based regulation appears to be a promising strategy available when regulation is needed to address some of the most intractable public policy problems. Problems such as worker fatigue, accident prevention, ergonomic injuries, and contamination of food are ones for which government often lacks clear performance measures, at least short of the dire consequences regulators seek to prevent in the first place. These are also problems for which government is often unable to prescribe uniform technological fixes. Management-based regulation may be the best available regulatory approach for problems that require fine-grained analysis of local circumstances too costly, if not undesirable for other reasons, for government to undertake.

What do these models of regulation tell us about cybersecurity? Recall from Chapter 10 how we discussed the HIPAA Security Rule, which follows this model of regulation. The Department of the Treasury's Interagency Guidelines promulgated pursuant to the Gramm-Leach-Bliley Act (GLBA) pertaining cybersecurity of regulated financial institutions operate similarly. While providing less implementation detail than HIPAA, the GLBA-regulated entities nonetheless experienced a lower rate of enforcement action than did HIPAA-regulated entities. This could, of course, be for a variety of different reasons—distinctions between industries, historical experience, etc.—but there is no evidence that there was variation in enforcement. What other factors might explain industrial sector variation?

QUESTIONS

1. How would you describe the differences between performance-based regulation, technology-based regulation, and process (or management)-based regulation?

2. What are the relevant benefits to each of these regulation types?

B. ALTERNATIVE GOVERNMENTAL REGULATION

Process-based regulation is not the only alternate regulatory style available. Another common style is known as "disclosure-based" regulation, where rather than directly penalizing performance, the regulatory requirement compels violators who fail to meet performance standards to disclose (usually publicly) the fact that they failed. Although often viewed as a newer regulatory approach in cybersecurity, this style of regulation has been around for decades. The U.S. Securities and Exchange Commission, for example, requires publicly traded entities to make certain disclosures to investors regarding risks their companies face.

In Chapter 10, we talked about the most prevalent example of disclosure-based regulation in cybersecurity: data breach notification statutes. As a reminder, these laws require organizations to notify affected consumers in the event of certain types of cybersecurity breaches involving the sensitive information of those consumers. Perhaps unintentionally, these laws have had a substantial technology-based regulatory effect—they have massively driven organizations to encrypt sensitive data both in transit and at risk.[3] This is because virtually all such laws provide an exemption from disclosure in the event the compromised data was encrypted. Even more curiously, the statutes provide very little, if any,

---

[3] Historically, state laws have exempted encrypted data from personal information requiring breach notification. *See* Charlotte A. Tschider, *Experimenting with Privacy: Driving Efficiency through a State-Informed Federal Data Breach Notification and Data Protection Law*, 18 TUL. J. TECH. & INTELL. PROP. 45 (2015) for a survey of state data breach laws and common requirements.

functionally useful definition of "encryption" for the purposes of statutory interpretation. Why do you think these outcomes occurred? What are the limits of this type of disclosure-based regulation? As you think about these questions, consider the following excerpt from one of your casebook authors:

DAVID THAW, *DATA BREACH (REGULATORY) EFFECTS*

2015 CARDOZO L. REV. *DE NOVO* 151 (2015)

Comprehensive Regulatory Frameworks

Legislatures often consider data breach notification regulation distinctly from other elements of cybersecurity regulation. Of the 51 U.S. jurisdictions to have adopted such regulations, nearly all (except Massachusetts) did so originally as a free-standing statute, and only a few additional jurisdictions (e.g., California, Nevada) have later amended their regulations to expand the scope beyond breach notification.

This Essay proposes two reasons why breach notification should not continue to be adopted in this standalone, piecemeal fashion. First, doing so creates the risk of unanticipated consequences and "definitional lock-in." Second, empirical research demonstrates that comprehensive cybersecurity regulation is nearly four times more effective at preventing reportable breaches than are breach notification regulations alone.

A. "Definitional Lock-In": The Risks of Standalone Breach Notification

Standalone regulation is attractive to legislatures. It reduces technical complexity, eases the burden of legislative drafting, and may be more politically feasible than comprehensive approaches. Piecemeal regulation, however, ignores the general concern that when later regulations must be adopted, such adoption does not occur in a vacuum—and may interact in unexpected ways with previous regulations. Breach notification should be considered as part of overall, comprehensive cybersecurity regulation to avoid unexpected results from such piecemeal approaches.

Adopting standards for breach notification in the absence of comprehensive cybersecurity regulation will create "definitional lock-in" for categories defined to serve the purpose of breach notification but not well suited for later adoption to broader, comprehensive cybersecurity regulation. Key definitions in regulations will be determined at an early stage, based on a limited scope of purpose not well-suited for the broader purposes later envisioned. Specifically, key definitions, such as the subject of information to be protected (often referred to as "Personal Information"), will be defined for the purposes of consumer breach notification. These purposes are likely very different than those appropriate to comprehensive cybersecurity regulation. Lock-in occurs as a result of the substantial cost to organizations of later "re-classifying" information based on additional categories established by new regulation. This process, when applied to existing data, is often cost-prohibitive and may raise regulatory burdens too high for effective compliance, thus pressuring legislators and regulators to retain existing definitions.

To be specific, consider the example of the types of information that should be subject to protection. In the case of breach notification, this information is most commonly referred to as "personal information" or "personally identifiable information." These terms have widely varying definitions. At the state level, a least common denominator exists: the combinations of an identifying item, most commonly an individual's name, with one of three categories of more sensitive information:

- The individual's Social Security Number;
- The individual's financial account numbers, along with any identification code necessary to access the account; or
- The individual's government-issued identification number (usually driver's license or state identification).

The stated purpose of most jurisdictions' breach notification statutes is to enable consumers to take steps to protect themselves by requiring custodians of this information to inform consumers when those custodians have lost control of this information. Yet many other types of information may pose a great harm to consumers. For example:

- Medical records;
- Wills;
- Diaries;
- Private correspondence (including e-mail);
- Financial records;
- Photographs of a sensitive or private nature; and
- Similar information.

These are all categories of information federal criminal law considers sufficient to warrant substantial criminal sentence enhancements for individuals convicted of computer crimes involving identity theft. The Department of Health and Human Services, the Department of the Treasury, and the Federal Trade Commission each have offered additional definitions of information they consider to be "sensitive" to consumers. All of this information should be the subject of consumer protection. Additionally, consumers should be informed whenever this information is subject to unauthorized disclosure as is necessary to take steps to protect themselves.

These categories are hardly comprehensive of the types of information that need to be protected by comprehensive cybersecurity regulations.

Corporate trade secrets, including sensitive data about products not yet available outside the United States; sensitive business development plans; information about critical infrastructure systems, such as water, electric, or telecommunications grids; and cybersecurity plans are all sensitive information that are not the province of the general consumer. Yet a failure to secure this information may have costly effects, and not just to the organization experiencing the breach. If a business partner of a new pharmaceutical company fails properly to secure its information systems or the information technology services provider to a major financial institution or exchange fails to implement appropriate controls on administrative accounts, substantial negative effects to the broad economy may result if those systems are compromised. None of these eventualities necessarily involves consumer information, but each clearly demonstrates a public interest in collective security.

If a definition of information to be protected is developed based solely on consumer breach notification, the downstream cybersecurity implications will be costly. Either organizations must engage in expensive reclassification of information and redesign of their cybersecurity programs when new regulations are subsequently implemented, or large areas of information may be left vulnerable if the regulations fail to expand the definition of information to be protected. In either case, the cost of considering breach notification separate from comprehensive cybersecurity measures would be high.

B. Comparative Efficacy: Comprehensive Regulation is More Effective

In prior work, I examined the efficacy of existing cybersecurity regulations, specifically including the breach notification statutes present in most U.S. jurisdictions, and compared the effectiveness of breach notification statutes and comprehensive cybersecurity regimes. I combined qualitative, semi-structured interviews of Chief Information Security Officers (CISO) at key U.S. organizations with quantitative analysis of data breach incidence from 2000 through 2010. The results described the effects of each regime at driving cybersecurity practices within organizations, based primarily on the CISO interviews.

The interviewees reported that a primary effect of breach notification laws was to focus intensive effort on encryption of portable devices and media containing personal information. While effective at reducing the number of reportable breaches, some respondents reported that this resulted in focusing *too* much on only one area of security—effectively leaving other venues vulnerable to attack. These attacks affect not only potential compromise of personal information as defined in existing breach notification statutes, but also the ability of outside attackers to compromise the integrity of critical infrastructure systems.

Such attacks are not hypothetical—in 1983, for example, a hacker group compromised the security of Memorial Sloan-Kettering Cancer Center in New York and gained access that effectively would have allowed them to alter the radiation treatment protocols of patients. This compromise led to the addition in 1986 of a felony enhancement to the Computer Fraud and Abuse Act for damaging computer systems relating to medical care.

As noted by the CISOs interviewed from the health care sector, breach notification statutes forced them to focus increased resources on encryption—without receiving additional resources to maintain existing programs. The resultant reallocation of security budgets directed resources away from the areas those CISOs believed were most in need. I describe this phenomenon as "Locking the Bank or Vault Door and Leaving the Back Window Open." Focusing *solely* on consumer breach notification may have detrimental effects to other, critical areas of information security.

The quantitative analysis conducted as part of this project confirms the comparative efficacy of comprehensive cybersecurity regulation. By analyzing periodic breach incidence data from January 1, 2000, through December 31, 2010, I determined that the combination of consumer breach notification and comprehensive cybersecurity regulation was as much as four times more effective at preventing reportable breaches of consumers' personal information than was breach notification alone.

Piecemeal regulation certainly has political and practical advantages. Likewise, standalone breach notification regulation does have certain advantages, most notably including highlighting the presence of cybersecurity concerns by requiring organizations to report certain breaches of security. However, these advantages are substantially outweighed by the risks of unanticipated consequences and definitional lock-in. When these risks are considered together with the comparative efficacy of preventing reportable breaches, a comprehensive approach to cybersecurity regulation is clearly appropriate.

III. Affirmative Presumption Favoring Investigation

The conclusions in Part II do not, of course, suggest that breach notification should be ignored. Quite the contrary—it is an essential component of a comprehensive cybersecurity regulatory framework. In considering the structure of this framework, however, it is crucial to examine the incentives created by various presumptions within the possible regulatory approaches. Any legal presumptions should favor incentives that encourage better security practices, such as the conduct of more thorough post-incident investigations.

When considering the issue of consumer breach notification, legislators and regulators frequently confront the issue of *when* to require notification. Among existing law, some jurisdictions require notification in all cases of loss-of-control (subject to the "encryption exception"), whereas others adopt what is known as a "risk-of-harm" threshold. The empirical data on the comparative efficacy of strict liability versus "risk-of-harm" notification thresholds is incomplete. The focus of this Part, therefore, addresses the cybersecurity implications of certain formulations of the risk-of-harm threshold. Specifically, for those jurisdictions adopting such a threshold, it is important to recognize that some formulations of the threshold negatively impact cybersecurity procedures and outcomes.

Risk-of-harm thresholds may have many forms but generally can be categorized according to the *affirmative* or *negative* presumption of notification. An *affirmative* presumption of notification requires a data custodian who experiences a breach to affirmatively demonstrate that the specified risk of harm threshold *is not satisfied* before they are exempted from consumer notification requirements. A *negative* presumption of notification *does not* require a data custodian who experiences a breach to notify consumers *unless* an investigation reveals that the specified risk of harm threshold has been satisfied.

A negative presumption of notification carries substantial, worrisome implications for cybersecurity procedures and outcomes. Specifically, this presumption disincentivizes organizations from conducting thorough security investigations.

Organizations have incentives to limit the scope and scale of investigations that may uncover information potentially exposing the organization to liability. For example, when conducting comprehensive cybersecurity assessments, auditing and consulting firms often work together with law firms so that the results of these assessments will be privileged as attorney-client work product and thus not subject to discovery in civil litigation or regulatory investigations. Clients of such firms often desire to learn about the risks they face, but do not want to incur liability for failure to remediate security vulnerabilities identified in the assessment. This problem is particularly compounded when faced with low-probability/high-risk vulnerabilities for which the cost of remediation is high. While generally protected by the business judgment rule, executives of publicly traded organizations still bear a fiduciary duty to act in the best interests of their shareholders. A risk analysis might well reveal that the probability is sufficiently low not to justify the direct costs of remediation when combined with the cost of business disruption and other indirect cost. While I do not suggest that organizations engage in willful ignorance of their legal or regulatory obligations, my research data and professional experience support the conclusion that organizations can have substantial incentive not to pursue a comprehensive investigation if it might trigger additional regulatory compliance requirements. Conversely, if pursuing that investigation might alleviate the organization of regulatory compliance requirements (e.g., exempt the organization from consumer notification), my research and professional experience support the conclusion that organizations can have substantial incentive to thoroughly pursue that investigation.

Thus, an *affirmative* presumption of notification is superior from a cybersecurity perspective. Such a presumption avoids disincentivizing thorough cybersecurity investigations, which are one of the most important tools in protecting consumers against future data breaches and securing existing information systems.

Conclusion

The primary goal of this Essay is to apply existing empirical analysis and analytical modeling to describe characteristics and suggest predictions about the function and effects of data breach notification laws. It suggests three primary conclusions in this regard. First, that a well-defined definition of cybersecurity, including the unit of analysis of protection, is critical to any discussion of data breach notification regulation. Second, that data breach notification regulation is more appropriate as part of a comprehensive cybersecurity regulatory regime. Third, that when using a risk-of-harm threshold for when notification is required, that threshold should employ an affirmative presumption requiring notification.

Notwithstanding this primary goal, these conclusions suggest some modest policy prescriptions. These suggestions build on similar regimes found in states such as New York, Massachusetts, and Virginia, each of which require notification to central state regulatory authorities in addition to notification to consumers in the event of a reportable data breach. Such a bifurcated notification regime could be adopted at a federal level and in other nations currently without data breach notification regulations.

Under such a bifurcated notification regime, organizations experiencing a loss-of-control of any covered data would be required to report that incident to a centralized reporting authority, most likely a federal regulator such as the United States Federal Trade Commission. Consumer reporting would be triggered in certain cases deemed appropriate to when consumers can take steps to protect themselves and/or when consumers have an interest in awareness that their sensitive information was subject to unauthorized disclosure.

This bifurcated notification regime, if properly implemented, could achieve many of the goals of consumer breach notification while mitigating the risks of "over-notification" often raised by critics of strict loss-of-control regimes. Specifically, consumers would receive appropriate notification, while all incidents would nonetheless be reported. Thorough information security investigations would be a requirement under this regime as part of the centralized reporting requirement. Additionally, the regulatory agency receiving the reports would have the ability to follow up in cases where they suspect consumer notification should have occurred but did not, to follow up if there is evidence a broader pattern of information security deficiencies may be present, or to follow up and provide support if it believes the organization requires additional information security and/or law enforcement support.

I stress that this proposal is *preliminary*, and I lay out the basic characteristics as guidelines.

QUESTIONS

1. Why might data breach notification statutes help organizations avoid undesirable outcomes?

2. When and why might such regulation be more effective than traditional "direct-penalty" performance-based regulation?

C. SELF-REGULATION

Another approach to regulation is the concept of "self-regulation." Self-regulation is a market condition under which industry sectors or major industry actors voluntarily elect to establish standards by which they agree to operate. This can take many forms, ranging from fully-voluntary industry "evaluation" groups (e.g., the Better Business Bureau) to quasi-compulsory standards bodies (e.g., Underwriters' Laboratories, FINRA). Many options implement a combination of various tools. It is important to remember that, with limited exceptions,[147] self-regulatory mechanisms do not carry the force of law.

The PCI-DSS standard and FINRA's cybersecurity regulations are two of the most common examples of industry self-regulation. To a lesser extent, some view the International Organization for Standardization's publications (the "ISO" series) as a form of industry self-regulation, however it is important to note that ISO standards both: (1) sometimes are incorporated by reference into various formal regulations (e.g., FDA manufacturing requirements); and (2) ISO standards are not the same type of "self-directed" action by industry as are the other examples we study in this chapter. ISO, for example, operates much more as an independent, international organization for the publication of standard—of which many national standards bodies are members—that it does as a body with direct influence on a specific industrial sector. While this may sound like a description of theoretical layers of abstraction not relevant to "on the ground" implementation, in terms of understanding the degree of influence and pragmatic effect a given publication can have on the behavior of private actors, these distinctions matter.

QUESTIONS

1. Recall the discussion of ISO, PCI-DSS, SSAE18, HITECH, and other security standards in previous chapters. Why might an organization voluntarily comply with such standards?

2. Can you imagine other ways in which the law and voluntary standards might intersect?

D. PUBLIC-PRIVATE PARTNERSHIPS

Public-private partnerships are regulatory mechanisms in which regulatory authorities (usually government agencies) work collaboratively with the entities they regulate (usually private organizations) to produce, maintain, and enforce regulatory goals. At first glance, this might seem odd—those subject to regulation are writing their own regulations! This is an understandable response, but the reasoning behind such approaches requires deeper examination of the challenges involved with regulating highly technical, heterogeneous industrial sectors like cybersecurity.

Section A of this chapter discussed the concept of process-based regulation. One argument in favor of process-based regulation is that different organizations may need to use different tools, or achieve different performance goals, in order to achieve the overall regulatory outcomes that facilitate public goals.

The HIPAA Security Rule is a classic example of this. A single-physician, "small family practice," will operate differently, have different capacities to purchase and utilize cybersecurity tools, and face different threats than would a large institutional hospital system spanning across many major metropolitan areas. Likewise, a large nationwide medical insurer would differ in their capabilities. And thus, as we discuss earlier, HIPAA uses a process-based regulatory framework to accommodate these differences.

But there is more to the story. Just as these varied entities use different tools and face different threats, likewise they have different knowledge sets relevant to understanding the regulatory challenge. Process-based approaches help capture that knowledge in part but fail to provide formal mechanisms for the sharing of that knowledge among other entities or government regulators who may benefit from it. Put more simply, Company A may know something about cybersecurity threats that Company B and Regulator 1 do not, and sharing that information might improve overall regulatory outcomes for all parties involved.

This is one example of why involving regulated entities in the process of developing, maintaining, and enforcing regulation may be beneficial. While the regulator must, of course, be mindful of the various potential crossing incentives among the parties, this approach nonetheless can bring important knowledge into the regulatory process which otherwise might not be available.

Professor Hurwitz provides an overview of the general concepts involved with public-private partnerships in the following excerpt:

JUSTIN (GUS) HURWITZ, *REGULATION AS PARTNERSHIP*

3 J. LAW & INNOVATION 117 (2020)

Introduction

The story of regulation over the course of the 20th century, and continuing through today, can be understood as one of oscillation between two competing poles: primary reliance on market-based forces and primary reliance on prescriptive regulatory oversight. Neither of these approaches to regulation, especially in dynamic or fast-moving industries, has proven to be an entirely satisfactory approach to facilitating the growth of socially important industries while maximizing the social benefits of those industries. This article uses the growth of a different mechanism for coordinating control of private enterprise that has grown in prominence in recent decades—the Public-Private Partnership (P3)—as a lens to examine these traditional modalities of regulation.

We see the traditional modalities of regulation play out in the broad legal-political arc of the 20th century, from the *Lochner* era to the New Deal, to post-war stagnation and growth of the regulatory state, to the deregulatory push that ushered Carter out of office and Reagan into office, to the dot-com boom-then-bust and the Great Recession. We see this in the arc of antitrust and industrial organization, from the origins of public interest regulation in *Munn v. Illinois* through *Nebbia v. New York*, and from the original, literal, anti-trust antitrust act to rise of antitrust law's rule of reason, through the embrace of the Structure-Conduct-Performance paradigm and its rejection in favor of the consumer welfare standard, to contemporary discussions across the world arguing for a more regulatory antitrust policy. And we see this in more overtly regulatory contexts. Telecommunications regulation, for instance, went back and forth from the primacy of market-based principles in prior to the 1913 Kingsbury Commitment, to command-and-control regulation following World War I, to reliance on antitrust in the government's 1956 suit against AT&T, to regulation during the *Computer Inquiries* and through the introduction of microwave-based long-distance, to antitrust with the 1984 break-up of AT&T, to regulation designed to fade into competition in the 1996 Telecom Act, to the net neutrality debates of the past decade-plus.

More recently, governments have occasionally embraced a new regulatory paradigm: the public-private partnership (P3). P3s have been embraced in a variety of contexts, and generally involve a governmental entity contracting with private industry to co-provide a service or amenity more traditionally provided by the government. There are several models of P3s, along with several explanatory theories for them—but they generally involve some transfer of risk from the government to the private entity paired with some promise of long-term benefit for the private entity. For instance, in the 1980s HUD used P3s to encourage the development of urban housing by awarding management of housing projects to the companies contracted to build them. Over the course of the 1990s, P3s grew exponentially in popularity in both the United States and globally, with governments turning to private industry to capitalize and build all sorts of infrastructure projects in exchange for ongoing operating rights. And more recently, P3s are an important part of the cybersecurity toolkit—where governments lack the resources to secure their network infrastructure so partner with private industry to provide secured infrastructure, typically in exchange for long-term service contracts of some form of liability protection.

Public-private partnerships initially developed organically largely as an evolution of more traditional government contracting and procurement needs. They were not designed as a form of regulation. But as they have grown in use and sophistication, P3s have developed their own governance practices and norms—they are a form of regulation.

The story of AT&T and government regulation of the telephone industry invoked above presents a curious example of the at-times partnership-like nature of regulation. The history of AT&T is checkered with collaborations—both implicit and explicit—with its regulators. It was instrumental to the war effort during World War II, and its researchers and leadership moved frequently between high-level government and corporate positions. And many of the company's excesses and failures were tolerated so long as it kept regulators and the public satisfied that it was providing an overall satisfactory service to the communities it served. In both examples, it was tacitly understood that the fate of the company was intertwined with the fate of the country and, so long as its operation was beneficial to its regulatory overseers, those regulators would focus their attentions on maintaining the relationship over managing the affairs of the company.

In other words, throughout much of the 20th century the telephone network was operated as public-private partnership of sorts—albeit an implicit on with undefined terms governing the relationship. AT&T presents a possibly extreme example—but once you start looking for elements of partnership in the history of regulation examples abound. This paper considers the lessons that can be learned from governments' recent embrace of the P3 model and what insights from that model can be translated to how we think about regulation more generally.

This question isn't of merely historical importance. Regulators have experimented with various types of more cooperative, partnership-like, regulation in recent decades. In the environmental setting, for instance, the EPA experimented with "negotiated rulemaking" in the 1980s and 1990s, where industry and regulators collaborate on the drafting of regulations. Over the past decade, cybersecurity regulation has widely embraced public-private partnership models. And there is discussion of more collaborative forms of regulation in other areas, such as the regulation of online platforms and online speech. Lessons from experience with P3s yields valuable insights as regulators explore increasingly collaborative regulatory modalities.

In an abstract sense this article is about theories of regulation—whether regulation is necessarily adversarial or whether it can be thought of in more collaborative terms, in terms of partnership between regulators and those they regulate.

But this paper is really about how we regulate the technology industry, and how that industry approaches its regulators. It is prompted by the observation that regulation of AT&T over the course of the 20th century—in many ways a paradigm of, and precursor to today's, technology firms—had many characteristics of a partnership between AT&T and the government. To be sure, AT&T was no paragon of corporate virtue and its history is a case study in traditional modalities of regulation. At the same time, AT&T was an incredibly important firm that made great contributions to our nation—and often did so in collaboration with regulators and with the public interest in mind.

This stands in stark contrast to regulation of today's technology industry. The relationship is fraught on both sides. Regulators approach the industry adversarially, and the industry approaches regulation transactionally. The industry has no sense of corporate "noblesse oblige"—no sense of duty to the public interest; and regulators view the industry's private interests not merely as not aligned with, but actively antagonistic to, those of the public interests.

[. . .]

II. The Partnership Model

Public-private partnerships are of more recent vintage than more traditional regulatory structures.[4] Modern P3s find their origins in complex government development projects—projects where the completion of government undertakings depended significantly upon private industry. In the 1960s and 1970s, many of these projects had an air of industrial

[4] Some scholars argue that we can find examples of P3s throughout much of modern history—dating at least back to the 16th century. There is, indeed, an argument to be made that the original understandings of government patents or corporate charters met some element of public private partnership. And historical examples of public-private arrangements with some characteristics of P3s can be found dating back millennia. Such structures, however, were generally one-off examples that were not widely embraced or lack enough of the defining characteristics of modern P3s that that should be considered as a different structure.

policy, with the government directing (or channeling) private resources to mass-scale government infrastructure or development initiatives. Starting in the 1980s, these partnerships began to take a more routinized, and smaller scale, structure. Urban housing, and related urban development, projects, for instance were increasingly undertaken as P3s. In these projects, the government would fund, and help to facilitate, the development of new housing projects; then those projects would be turned over to the private partners to administer day-to-day operations (including earning market-rate profits—as opposed, for instance, to regulated rates of return).

One important theme in the literature on P3s is that the term "public-private partnership" is used to describe a wide range of relationships between public and private entities, from arrangements that are little more than well-specified procurement contracts to far more ambitious initiatives. That said, P3s do have several common features, even If they have no universally accepted defining characteristics. Part II.A will describe examples of P3s to help orient the discussion.

Economists started studying P3s in earnest in the late 1990s, with key analytical works published around the turn of the century. Perhaps the defining work is Oliver Hart's analysis of them as a solution to the challenges of specifying contingency-complete procurement contracts for either the development or operation of infrastructure or similar projects. One of the most common forms of P3 bundles the development and operation of a project, such that the entity contracted for its development has strong incentives to perform that part of its contract well in anticipation of having an ongoing obligation to operate and maintain the project.

This difference between P3s and traditional procurement contracts is the most defining feature of P3s: they attempt to align the incentives of the public and private parties, such that the contract takes on a more relational character than a transactional one. So long as both parties are committed to maintaining the value of that relationship, such contracts can be relied on as self-enforcing. If implemented correctly, this allows the parties to avoid the most complex parts of negotiating such contracts: specifying detailed contingencies, and monitoring and enforcing breaches of those requirements.

P3s have other notable characteristics or justifications. They are often discussed as a form of risk- and capital-pooling, where government and private actors come together, pooling resources, in a common enterprise. They are viewed as an efficient way to leverage comparative advantages of governmental and private actors in a single enterprise—relying, for instance, on private enterprise to structure capital, develop and implement innovative design, and manage the development process, but on government to implement compliance and regulatory obligations, scope the project to ensure it services necessary constituencies, and the like. And they are viewed as form of regulation, channeling private enterprise to serve public needs and to ensure ongoing democratic oversight of and satisfaction with ongoing provision of privately-managed services. Part II.B will dive more into the economic literature on P3s and consider the different economic explanations of them.

Part II.C will then describe the environments in which P3s succeed and contrast that to situations where they fail.

II.A. Examples of P3s

The most talked-about examples in the literature of P3 are infrastructure projects. Transportation projects like toll roads have been popular around the United States.

For instance, the Texas Department of Transportation entered into a P3 with the LBJ Infrastructure Group in 2010 to construct the "IH 635 Managed Lanes Project," which was designed to "relieve congestion north of Dallas, Texas" on 13 miles of public highway. The total investment in that project was $2.8B. LBJ was given the contract to both design and build the roadway, as well as to operate and maintain it for 52 years. In 2009, the Regional Transportation District of Denver, Colorado entered into a P3 agreement with Denver Transit Partners to design, build and operate the "Eagle Commuter Rail" project which would consolidate and extend a number of commuter rail lines. Denver Transit Partners was given a 30 year commitment for operation of the completed project.

Other infrastructure projects are undertaken as P3s, including in the areas of waste management, water provision, energy, broadband, government buildings, and schools and universities. Kentucky launched an ambitious statewide broadband construction P3 with Macquerie Capital in 2015. The goal of that project is to construct a large middle-mile network that private companies and public bodies could use to connect to for last-mile Internet access. Macquerie Capital was given the right to build and maintain the network for a period of 30 years. [. . .]

Hospitals are frequently built using P3s as well. In the UK, the use of P3s to construct and operate hospitals for the National Health Service began in the 1990s (and was called "Private Finance Initiatives"). Canada also uses the P3 model for its hospital system. For example, the Brampton Civic Hospital in Ontario was begun under a P3 in 2003, with the contractual right to operate non-clinical services by the winning vendor for 28 years.

Cybersecurity presents a different, but no less important, area where P3s can have good effect. Most of the important information systems exposed to cyberthreats are owned by private firms. Exposure to legal liability and an interest in service customer demand (including the demand not to put customers at risk), provides strong incentives for private firms to mitigate risk as best they can. Nonetheless, obtaining the necessary intelligence to effectively combat cyberthreats is difficult for any one firm acting alone. Consortia exist that track bugs and exploits, but their reach into particular incidents are limited by an affected firm's own disclosures. Law enforcement and government agencies are better positioned to understand when and where incidents occur, and to obtain useful information from affected systems. The roles of public officials and private firms is, therefore, likely to be mutually beneficial.

The federal government has long involved private firms in cybersecurity P3s in the form of "Information Sharing and Analysis Centers" ("ISAC"). The first such ISAC, the Financial Services ISAC, began in 1999, and "leverages its intelligence platform, resiliency resources and a trusted peer-to-peer network of experts to anticipate, mitigate and respond to cyberthreats." In 2015, President Obama signed Executive Order 13691, which declared that

> Organizations engaged in the sharing of information related to cybersecurity risks and incidents play an invaluable role in the collective cybersecurity of the United States. The purpose of this order is to encourage the voluntary formation of such organizations, to establish mechanisms to continually improve the capabilities and functions of these organizations, and to better allow these organizations to partner with the Federal Government on a voluntary basis.

Currently, all 50 states have a Chief Information Security Officer responsible for ensuring that government information is kept secure. Some states leverage this office to interface with private industry of security and other IT-related topics. Michigan's CISP, for example, uses a "kitchen cabinet" of IT advisors to receive input on, among other topics, "ways to defend critical information, coordinate access and identity management, and embrace new and emerging technologies."

II.B. Theories of P3s

As introduced above, the literature on P3s has focused a great deal on cost savings, efficiency, finance, and risk assignment. However, the literature has grown to include more robust economic explanations. Below in this section, each theory is surveyed.

II.B.1. Efficiency and Comparative Advantage

The most common benefits touted in the trade literature and by policymakers of P3 projects have to do with cost savings, efficiency, superior financing, and risk assignment. However, it isn't clear why fundraising or risk assignment explain why government chooses to use P3s rather than traditional procurement or building its own capability.

Comparative advantage is the economic explanation for many of the observations about cost savings and efficiency in the trade literature. The private sector is often better than the public sector at delivering on infrastructure projects at lower cost, incentivized by the need for profit. There are also incentives to deliver higher quality in order to win future contracts with government as well. On top of that, the private sector may have superior technical know-how and ability to take advantage of dispersed, tacit knowledge than a centralized authority. However, a private company subject to the need for profit could also cut corners and deliver lower quality to keep costs down.

The example of cybersecurity described above may fit the comparative advantage explanation best. The dispersed knowledge of cyber-threats is much more likely to be known by private companies. Incentivizing the sharing of this information amongst affected industry and with proper authorities in order to protect consumers and citizens is to the benefit of society.

II.B.2. Incomplete Contracts and Agency Costs

Nobel prize-winning economist Oliver Hart identifies a better explanation for P3s: their purpose is to align incentives between parties whose interests to not necessarily align. In his framing, they are a form of incomplete contracting.

With complete contracts, the entire relationship between parties is specified, such that no discretion or autonomy between the parties remains. Thus, there would be no need for P3 projects as the government could just directly procure from the private sector and manage the projects themselves.

In practice, however, no contract is complete. In incomplete contracts, the relationship isn't completely specified. Rather, each party retains autonomy over some portions of how it performs under the contract. Hart's model "suggests that the choice between PPPs and conventional provision turns on whether it is easier to write contracts on service provision than on building provision. . . One of the (modest) benefits [of the model] is that it may shift attention from what seem to be secondary financing issues to what seems to be the central issue: (relative) contracting costs."

As Hart explains, the choice of between a P3 (which he describes as bundling service with building) and "conventional provision" (described as unbundling) depends on relative contracting costs.

Conventional provision ('unbundling') is good if the quality of the building can be well specified, whereas the quality of the service cannot be. . . In contrast, PPP is good if the quality of the service can be well specified in the initial contract (or, more generally, there are good performance measures which can be used to reward or penalize the service provider), whereas the quality of the building cannot be. . . Arguably, prisons and schools fall into the first category: contracting on the building is relatively simple, while contracting on the service may not be. On the other hand, hospitals may fall into the second category: although specifying service quality is far from straightforward, it may be easier to come up with reasonable performance measures concerning how patients are treated than it is to specify what may be a very complex building.

Similarly, P3s can be used to reduce agency costs between the private participants and the government. This is effectively a variation on the incomplete contract perspective above. Agency costs arise when the interests of a principal, one who engages another to perform some service on their behalf, diverge from the interests of the agent, the person engaged to do a service. Scholars have identified agency costs as including the monitoring expenditures by the principal (to make sure the agent is doing what he or she is supposed to), the bonding costs borne by the agent (limitations on agent agreed to as part of deal), and residual loss (the costs due to divergent interests even despite monitoring and bonding).

The agency problem arises due to the fact that the private firms and the government may not always have aligned interests throughout the entirety of a project. As described above, private firms may wish to cut corners in order to hold down costs and maximize profits. Government agents may also have self-interest in being re-elected and can act opportunistically vis-à-vis private firms in refusing price flexibility, especially around elections. This has led many scholars to doubt whether P3s have actually solved agency problems in practice.

The agency cost approach looks at the contracting process for P3s to efficiently allocate risks and responsibilities. A well-designed P3 aligns interests of the principal and agent by limiting the opportunities for moral hazard and adverse selection compared to regular procurement.

II.B.3. Relational Contracting, Norms, and Self-Governance

Relational contracting has been explored by both legal and economic scholars. Legal scholar Ian Macniel pioneered an analysis of a subset of contracts not as discrete one-time events, but as relationships with built-in norms. Scholars like Benjamin Klein have also studied relational contracts from an economic point of view, emphasizing the importance of reputation to participants in long-term incomplete contracts. These two views diverge in important ways, but they share one important overlap in noticing that all exchanges are to some degree relational.

As Hart anticipated, his model on incomplete contracts for P3s can be extended if the time limitation is removed. In a relational contract, norms that unite two parties over an extended period of time are very important for overcoming the agency problems identified above, in an incomplete contract world.

Relational norms refer to "behavioral expectations that are partially shared by a group of decision makers and directed toward collective or group goals." Relational norms include flexibility, information exchange, and solidarity. Flexibility is the notion that two parties are willing to make adaptations because of circumstances changing. Information exchange is the idea that two parties are willing to share useful information with each other. Solidarity refers to the idea that two parties are willing to maintain a bilateral relationship.

These relational norms are especially important due to the long-term nature of P3 projects.

One important characteristic of relational contracts is that they can be self-enforcing. With such a contract, parties value the ongoing relationship created by the contract—or, less romantically, the expected stream of future benefits from ongoing performance of the contract—more than performance or any particular part of the contract itself. As such, parties are unlikely to breach the contract, even when it may be efficient for them to do so at any given point in time.

This gives rise to another important characteristic of relational contracts. Because they are self-enforcing, they do not rely on any external enforcement mechanism to ensure their ongoing performance. That is, they do not rely on the law—or even on the existence on a government to enforce that law—to ensure ongoing performance. Among other things, this is an example of the self-regulation or self-governance envisioned by Elinor Ostrom.

Professor Hurwitz's article touches on a few cybersecurity examples, such as the information sharing arrangements facilitated through Information Sharing and Analysis Centers (ISACs). Cybersecurity is a particularly challenging space to regulate effectively, in large part because both: (1) a substantial amount of critical technical information is held by regulated entities (and no other parties); and (2) regulated entities—mostly organizations—are extraordinarily heterogeneous from a technical perspective. While cybersecurity is not the only regulated space with these characteristics, it is important to remember that there are few examples of a challenge that spans multiple (if not all) industrial verticals and that has heterogeneous risk profiles across nearly all industries.

In the following excerpt, Professor Thaw discusses these challenges in the context of regulating healthcare cybersecurity. As you read, consider the degree to which cybersecurity fits the characteristics described by Professor Hurwitz and to what extent this type of public-private partnership approach might be necessary for regulating cybersecurity effectively:

DAVID THAW, *ENLIGHTENED REGULATORY CAPTURE*

89 WASH. L. REV. 329 (2014)

What is the "Public Interest?"

Debate over what constitutes the "public interest" enjoys a rich history both in political theory and in political action. This Article does not engage in a debate as to what substantively constitutes the public interest. To the contrary, the hypothesis advanced in this Article suggests that the concept of the public interest need not be fully defined a priori the regulatory process. Rather, it proposes that under certain circumstances, the incentives of private parties involved in the regulatory process can be aligned such that those private parties' goals are consistent with the hypothetical legislative process which purports to act in the public interest. This Article does not opine as to whether the legislative process in a representative republic such as the United States can, or whether the U.S. federal legislature actually does, act in such a fashion. Rather, it only takes the position that regulatory interests can be aligned to act similarly to a legislature, thereby increasing the legitimacy and efficacy of the regulatory process.

Of course, being a process of regulation, the legislature will have provided some preliminary guidance as to subject matter and goals. This is precisely consistent with a concept of the public interest that is agnostic respecting the hypothesis of this Article—the assumption is that whatever guidance the legislature provides *must* be in the public interest, and whatever details and discretion are delegated to the administrative agency should operate consistent with that public interest. This Article proposes a hypothesis for improving the process by which the agency exercises that discretion and fills in the details. By structuring the process to function as a miniature or "proxy" legislature, the agency's regulatory outcomes retain greater legitimacy while still fulfilling their task of engaging subject matter expertise and leveraging that portion of the expertise held by private entities.

[. . .]

Cybersecurity Regulation: A Curious Counter-Example

While negotiated rulemaking has produced some successes since its inception, there have been notable failures. Negotiated rulemaking developed in part as a response to social or cultural capture stemming from dissatisfaction with agency action at the time. Ironically, it experienced notable failures in circumstances when the agency employing it failed to yield sufficient control to the interested parties in negotiations. Regrettably, notwithstanding Harter's suggestions, agencies or their enabling statutes, or both, often fail to accomplish this goal and leave agencies with too much control over the process. Negotiated rulemaking may have promise when implemented properly, but its current structure alone appears insufficient.

Nonetheless, in recent years several scholars have suggested—contrary to classic scholarship—that regulatory capture may be used in ways beneficial to the public good. This work is an important step forward in understanding how to engage private expertise to serve the two core goals discussed in this paper: efficacy and legitimacy. As noted by Reiss, however, there is a dearth of empirical data presenting examples of regulatory capture working in the public interest.

This Part presents, to the author's knowledge, the first verifiable example discussed in scholarly literature of legislatively encoded regulatory capture functioning clearly in the public interest. When Congress passed the Health Insurance Portability and Accountability Act of 1996 (HIPAA), it included an information security requirement for entities managing individuals' sensitive health data. The rulemaking authority for that requirement, which ultimately resulted in the HIPAA Security Rule, delegated substantial authority to the National Committee on Vital Health Statistics (NCVHS), a FACA committee composed entirely of representatives of private interests and private experts.

NCVHS, while having substantial statutory capture authority, nevertheless acted neither in the private interests of its membership nor in a least-common-denominator fashion that often plagued negotiated rulemaking committees. Rather, in a fashion rarely seen even in negotiated rulemaking, the committee members brought all their private expertise to the table—*and checked their private agendas at the door.*

[. . .]

A. HIPAA: An Experiment in Negotiated Rulemaking Alternatives

When HIPAA was passed, Congress had decided it wanted to address the privacy of individuals' health information, but had not yet reached agreement on any specifics. The Act had many other important provisions, including requirements for security standards, so instead of delaying its adoption, Congress added a provision to the law that if they failed to revisit the privacy question within thirty-six months, the Department of Health and Human Services (HHS) would be directed to promulgate regulations consistent with basic "broad stroke" aspirational goals laid out in the Act. This direction to HHS also contained the capture-like consultation requirement discussed above. The provisions of the Act granting HHS immediate authority to promulgate regulations governing the security of health information were subject to a similar capture-like consultation requirement.

1. Statutory Framework

HIPAA provided general authority to the Secretary of Health and Human Services to adopt information security standards respecting the transmission and maintenance of health information by health (insurance) plans, healthcare clearinghouses, and healthcare providers who transmit health information electronically. It further provided, as noted above, that if Congress failed to revisit the issue of privacy protections for health information within thirty-six months, the Secretary would be directed to promulgate regulations no later than forty-two months after HIPAA was enacted. Additionally, the Secretary was required within twelve months of HIPAA's enactment to submit a report to Congress containing "detailed recommendations on standards with respect to the privacy of individually identifiable health information."

Privacy and security are often viewed as separate regulatory questions, and sometimes even as being in tension with one another. While this separation was technically true in the case of HIPAA—the authority described above resulted in a Privacy Rule and a Security Rule—the examination of the authority for both bears merit for two reasons. First, the statutory command for both is substantially similar (which I discuss in further detail below), and second, security and privacy are inextricably linked. Many colloquial views of privacy and security place them in tension—for example, the recent debates over government surveillance programs and long-standing disagreement over airport security measures frame privacy and security as opponents in a zero-sum game.

This approach mischaracterizes the relationship between privacy and security. As noted by Derek Bambauer, privacy is a normative exercise in making "decisions about competing claims to legitimate access to, use of, and alteration of information." Security, by contrast, is an objective exercise that "implements those choices . . . mediat[ing] between information and [normative] privacy selections" about the use of/access to that information. The fact that security *implements* privacy is a critical point often lost in legal (and other) scholarship and policy debate, but one important to the context of this paper. Specifically, it explains why consideration of the legislative authority under which HHS promulgated the Security Rule and the Privacy Rule should be considered together, and why both aspects of the rulemaking process are relevant. While this Article focuses on the Security Rule, the statutory authority under HIPAA and the timeline under which HHS acted consider the implication of both privacy and security. Additionally, the importance of this relationship was *not* lost on the members of the NCVHS:

> The security and privacy [sic] are very closely linked. The security is what enables privacy to be implemented and enforced. The security scope is larger in that it addresses not just confidentiality of data, but the standards also address integrity and availability

> of data, is the data there when you need it, is the data correct or have we made sure that it can't be inappropriately altered. Those are things that are outside of the scope of the privacy provisions. But the privacy scope is larger because it addresses paper and oral protected health information and security is only looking at electronic.

Both the language in HIPAA providing authority for the Security Rule and the language providing authority for the Privacy Rule (if Congress failed to act, which was the case) had consultation requirements for the promulgation of those rules. These requirements included the pre-rulemaking engagement of a committee comprising private interests and subject matter experts outside the Department—but, curiously, not only failing to engage the negotiated rulemaking statute but likely excluding the possibility of its application. The language applicable to the Security Rule was:

> In complying with the requirements of this part [which includes § 1173(d)], *the Secretary shall rely on the recommendations of the National Committee on Vital and Health Statistics* established under section 306(k) of the Public Health Service Act (42 U.S.C. [§] 242k(k)), and shall consult with appropriate Federal and State agencies and private organizations. The *Secretary shall publish in the Federal Register any recommendation* of the National Committee on Vital and Health Statistics regarding the adoption of a standard under this part.

Below, I discuss the NCVHS in greater detail. It is sufficient to note for this analysis that the NCVHS comprised entirely private individuals, and the only federal regulators on the Committee—unlike in negotiated rulemaking committees—were assigned "staff to the committee." This distinction is particularly important in light of the emphasized language above—the Secretary was required to rely on the Committee's recommendations, and doing otherwise would likely result in an invalid rulemaking. This language provides substantial regulatory capture to a committee whose voting membership comprises entirely private individuals. Additionally, the statutory language requires further consultation with "private organizations." While affording a lesser degree of capture to non-NCVHS members, this statutory consultation requirement is a far higher threshold than that afforded interested parties during a traditional notice-and-comment rulemaking. Additionally, the requirement that any recommendation put forth by the NCVHS be published in the Federal Register (as a recommendation) supports the proposition that the Committee has capture authority in that its proposals must be published in a fashion similar to Proposed Rules. Finally, it appears from the Committee's transcripts that the members treated their authority in this manner.

Although somewhat less strong than the language directly referencing the enabling authority for the Security Rule, a similar application of the consultation requirement was applicable to the Privacy Rule:

> CONSULTATION. In carrying out this section, the Secretary of Health and Human Services *shall consult with* (1) *the National Committee on Vital and Health Statistics* established under section 306(k) of the Public Health Service Act (42 U.S.C. [§] 242k(k)); and the Attorney General.

This application further emphasizes the degree to which regulatory capture was encoded into the statutory design and the authority placed by Congressional directive in the hands of private individuals.

2. The National Committee on Vital and Health Statistics

The NCVHS was established by the Public Health Service Act to advise and assist the Secretary of Health and Human Services on a variety of policymaking issues. The Full Committee comprises eighteen members, sixteen of which are appointed by the Secretary, one of which is appointed by the Speaker of the House after consultation with the House Minority Leader, and one of which is appointed by the President pro tempore of the Senate after consultation with the Senate Minority Leader. The members of the Committee are experts who have distinguished themselves in various areas related to healthcare provision, statistics, healthcare information systems (specifically including privacy and security), consumer interests in healthcare, and other related areas. The *NCVHS Charter* contemplates the possibility that federal employees may be members of the Committee. Since 1996, however, the membership overwhelmingly comprised representatives of private industry, with additional members who were leading experts (usually academics) and limited representation of State agencies.

The Committee's primary function is to advise the Secretary and the Department on a variety of matters. This specifically includes "[s]tudy[ing] and identify[ing] privacy, security, and access measures to protect individually identifiable health information in an environment of electronic networking and multiple uses of data." The Committee also comprises several subcommittees, which are designated to focus on specific issues. The modern NCVHS has a Subcommittee on Privacy, Confidentiality, and Security, which advises the Secretary on issues related to the Privacy Rule and the Security Rule. When HIPAA was enacted in 1996, however, the Subcommittee on Standards and Security had responsibility for the Security Rule, but not the Privacy Rule.

In addition to the statutory requirements in HIPAA requiring publication of the Committee's activities respecting information security, the NCVHS is subject to the FACA. The FACA requires certain standardized procedures for federal advisory committees, including the creation of a formal charter governing the committee's activities, that committee meetings be open with opportunity for public participation, that detailed minutes and transcripts are kept and made available for public inspection, and other requirements designed to facilitate public participation and provide democratic legitimacy to such committees.

The Committee (and to the extent they acted formally, the subcommittees) had a notably different voting procedure than did negotiated rulemaking committees. Although the FACA does not prescribe a specific voting procedure for committee action, the NCVHS operated by majority vote—*not by required consensus*. While they strove for consensus, one or a few parties could not hold the process hostage to a threat of breaking consensus. Additionally, only fifty-one percent of the membership was required for quorum. This lack of mandatory consensus is one key factor that contributed to the continued success, described below, of the NCVHS in providing regulatory assistance to HHS. Unlike negotiated rulemaking, where members could have "internal" capture over the committee, NCVHS members could not as easily advance their own private viewpoints because they lacked the procedural ability to unilaterally derail committee progress.

The NCVHS is one of the longest-operating federal advisory committees, originally formed in the 1950s and pre-dating FACA. Membership is generally looked upon as an honor within the healthcare field, and members take their duties very seriously. These factors, combined with the effective regulatory capture described above and the FACA openness requirements contribute to the effectiveness of the NCVHS focusing on advancing public interest goals over the private interests represented by a majority of its members. Among the factors listed here, the longstanding nature of NCVHS and the degrees both of autonomy and legitimacy it is afforded by and within HHS appear most prevalent to its success at advancing public interest goals.

3. Creation of the HIPAA Security Rule

HIPAA granted HHS authority to promulgate information security regulations governing the transmission and maintenance of health information by covered entities, and contingent authority to promulgate related privacy regulations should Congress fail to revisit the issue within a specified time period. While now considered substantially interrelated issues, at the time the separation of the regulatory authority and the structure of the NCVHS led HHS to begin moving on the Security Rule shortly after HIPAA's adoption.

HIPAA was enacted on August 21, 1996. The NCVHS Subcommittee on Standards and Security (S&S) began work the following January to investigate the issues surrounding the rules they were required advise on pursuant to HIPAA's consultation requirement. At the time, the S&S subcommittee comprised seven individuals, three of whom were independent experts and four of whom represented private industry. From January through September 1997, the S&S subcommittee met and held hearings on the adoption of security standards consistent with the requirements of HIPAA section 1173(d). In September 1998, the S&S subcommittee sent its first recommendations to the Secretary. Based on these recommendations, HHS promulgated the first Proposed Rule pursuant to HIPAA section 1773(d) in August 1998.

The Proposed Rule received approximately 2350 public comments. NCVHS was responsible for responding to most of these comments, with the S&S subcommittee addressing much of the technical details. During the period when S&S addressed these comments, the Congressional deadline passed, which triggered HHS's authority to promulgate regulations respecting privacy pursuant to HIPAA section 264(c). While, as noted above, separate subcommittees of the NCVHS worked on privacy and on security, these subcommittees had overlapping membership and often considered related questions. As discussed above, the consultation requirement in section 264(d) lent further support to the NCVHS's role and authority in the rulemaking process.

Over the next several years, the NCVHS and the S&S held several hearings and considered the extensive comments received. Based on these actions, the S&S recommended revisions (through the full NCVHS) to the Security Rule and HHS promulgated the Final Rule based on the NCVHS's recommendations in February 2003. The Final Rule was substantially the work of the NCVHS, which essentially "ran the show" on behalf of HHS throughout the rulemaking process.

4. Management-Based Regulatory Delegation and Security Rule Compliance

As discussed above, HIPAA employs a relatively unique regulatory framework both in the front-end rulemaking procedures described in this Part and in the back-end compliance and enforcement procedures adopted in the Security Rule. I examine these procedures in greater detail in earlier work, but highlight here a few points relevant to this Article's proposition regarding the engagement of private expertise to serve public interest goals.

Unlike many regulations, HIPAA adopts a flexible form of regulation I describe as Management-Based Regulatory Delegation, in which the compliance and enforcement aspects are based upon regulated entities' obligation to develop compliance plans conforming to certain aspirations and some specific goals, and then adhere to those goals. The compliance plans are based on requirements laid out in the Security Rule, and the Rule specifies that the degree to which an entity's compliance plan must cover certain items varies with the size, complexity, and capabilities of the organization and the health information it manages.

Although not required by the statute, HIPAA certainly leaves room for this type of compliance, which has been discussed elsewhere in the literature and variously described as Management-Based Regulation. The approach is highly flexible, well-suited to heterogeneous industries (of which healthcare is a prime example), and requires the substantial engagement of private expertise on the compliance "back-end" as each entity develops, self-enforces, and updates its information security compliance plan. It further engages private expertise by requiring individual regulated entities to determine, on a continuing basis, what are the most salient threats facing their organizations. It increases efficacy by shifting the cost of such decisions from the regulators to the individual entities and by allowing the individual entities to use their expertise to make such decisions, but subjecting them to regulatory penalty for deficiencies in so doing. This approach increases legitimacy by allowing organizations a degree of input into their methods of compliance, thus increasing their input into the regulatory compliance process.

B. The Security Rule: Regulatory Capture Used for the Public Interest

In previous work, I explored the nature of information security regulations and their effect on driving security practices in private organizations. That work examined the effects on organizations' security practices using empirical data, including in-depth, semi-structured interviews of Chief Information Security Officers (CISOs) at key U.S. organizations. These included CISOs at several healthcare organizations.

In the course of that work, I discovered that healthcare organizations—as substantially different than organizations in any other industrial sector—reported a stronger "buy-in" respecting the information security regulations to which they were subject. They reported working with the NCVHS in developing the HIPAA Security Rule, and generally evinced positive experiences in that regard. While negotiated rulemaking experienced some successes at increasing interested parties' perceived legitimacy of the process, regulatory agencies generally are not looked upon favorably by the industries they regulate. This sentiment generally was also true of information security regulations, other than HIPAA, applicable to the organizations represented by my interviewees.

[. . .]

1. Literal Accounts "On the Ground"—HIPAA Security Rulemaking in Action

As discussed above, membership on the NCVHS generally is viewed as a notable honor and members take their responsibilities to the public interest seriously. For example, in a July 1997 discussion regarding the role of the NCVHS in implementing the provisions of HIPAA (including the Security Rule), Don Detmer, acting Chairman of the NCVHS, described how the committee needed to act in the public interest, and while that might entail burdens for the organizations they represented, it was the committee's responsibility to develop the rule according to public goals:

> The committee calls on everyone to work together on this in good faith. This is not an easy challenge for us. . . . [W]e are one of the nation's few industrially developed countries that does not have anything like this. . . . [W]e ought to do it because it is the right thing to do. The point is though, health information becomes available for other uses. So unless we get this in place, and get it in fairly soon, we see both risk to patients as well as risks to the record keepers themselves will grow. We believe that everyone will benefit by a well-crafted set of fair information practices. It will impose constraints and restrictions on industry, but I think those are just part of what it is going to appropriately take to be right by this, to the society at large and individual patients.

On its face, this language might appear to be superficial. However, both the outcome of the Final Rule itself and the comments of other members of the committee suggest otherwise, that in fact the members were focused on the public good notwithstanding their private interests. Consider the statement of one individual representing a major health insurance carrier:

> On behalf of the management of United HealthCare, I'm happy to be a part of this session and to assist in any way I can. . . . United HealthCare has consistently supported the incremental market reform principles underlying [HIPAA]. . . . In general, the Federal reforms espoused by the Act will help stabilize and sustain the private market by ensuring that all market players compete under the same high standards. United HealthCare views protecting our member's confidential information to be of the utmost importance. We have explicit information security policies and standards that are mandated by executive management and widely disseminated for compliance within the corporation.

This response is particularly notable in the context of this Article because it demonstrates how the structure of HIPAA and the function of the NCVHS appear to have aligned private incentives with the public interest.

In addition to a general commitment to the process, the members of the S&S subcommittee also demonstrated a belief that if they failed to act, other regulators or legislators would, and that would be a sub-optimal outcome because the NCVHS was the most appropriate entity and a patchwork of inconsistent local rules would both be inefficient and possibly otherwise inferior:

> I think that we really do believe that that is as important for the implementation side of this, as well as obviously the fact that if we do not do it, states will continue to do their own approach to this. . . . [T]o have a thousand or 50 different experiments going on in the country really is not necessarily in the best interests. First of all, people cross state lines a lot for health care and employment and such. A lot of the population, about 50 percent, is near a state border, so that becomes very problematic if people have different policies in all these jurisdictions.

The minutes and transcripts of the NCVHS meetings suggest a general feeling that if they failed to advise the Secretary and suggest a rule, someone else would—and the outcome would be less than desirable. My CISO interviews support this viewpoint, and recent informal interviews with knowledgeable parties concur.

Additionally, the committee members viewed their work not just as "merely advisory," but also as having the opportunity to make rules with the force of law:

> The committee calls on everyone to work together on this in good faith. This is not an easy challenge for us. The probability candidly that *we can pass a law* that will be perfect is very unlikely. I think the issue is, *can we in fact pass solid legislation* that will at least get us benchmarked and on the right track . . . . None of these benefits will be achieved unless *everyone approaches the legislative process* with a spirit of compromise.

As discussed further in Part 0, this belief that the committee had effective rulemaking authority was an important component structuring the incentives for participants to put forth their best effort toward public goals. The committee members appear to view their activities with the responsibility of being a miniature legislature, as noted by the language used and their commitment to (their opinion of what is in) the public interest discussed earlier in this part.

2. Structural Explanations: Statutory, Regulatory, and Incentives Analysis

The preceding sections discuss the structure of negotiated rulemaking proceedings and of HIPAA and the NCVHS. The analysis in those portions suggests substantial differences between HIPAA and other consensual rulemaking proceedings, differences that may suggest improvements for consensual rulemaking and means by which regulatory capture may be harnessed to leverage private expertise to act in the public good.

As discussed above, the HIPAA consultation requirement for the Security Rule gave strong capture authority to the NCVHS. The NCVHS statute requires committee composition including both private industry interests and experts in the relevant fields. The committee procedures were by majority vote, although consensus was desirable. The combination of these limitations creates an uncommon incentive structure for participants. While the committee itself does have effective strong capture over the rulemaking process, unlike negotiated rulemaking no single member has veto authority. Thus rather than driving toward a least-common-denominator rule, individual parties are incentivized to cooperate with one another as much as possible.

At a minimum, they must cooperate sufficiently to achieve a majority interest. The inclusion of subject matter experts, who usually are university faculty or similar researchers, adds an interesting dimension to this process. While in the S&S committee example, industry technically held a 4–3 majority vote, were they to exercise this power to advance private interests such action would be as clear and apparent as a lightning strike at midnight. Given the mission of the NCVHS, and the cultural norm that it operates in the public interest, such activities would likely not result in the Secretary adopting the recommendations particularly over the objections of relevant experts. Under these circumstances, a departure by HHS from the NCVHS recommendations would likely survive judicial review of the consultation requirement—a condition unlikely to be the case in the absence of dissent by experts. Thus, representatives of private industry have statutorily created incentives to work with subject matter experts, placing meaningful limitations on their ability to advance their own private agendas. Furthermore, with most of the subject matter experts being university faculty holding tenure, those experts' job security provides an additional layer of protection against influence.

3. Technological Explanations

A core component of HIPAA and its Administrative Simplification requirements was to promote the safe and efficient interchange of health information among healthcare providers, insurers, and other related entities. Promoting this type of information interchange remains a primary goal of the industry and the current Executive Branch. In a networked information exchange, however, the choices of one bad actor have implications far beyond the boundaries of that single actor. Much like a series of security guards protecting a facility, if one guard turns out to be in collusion with a gang of thieves and lets them in a back door, the activities of the other guards successfully protecting their doors will not make up for the "weak link in the chain."

Information security is precisely similar. When health information is shared among many entities, any single one of those entities could be the "weak link" through which that information is compromised. From the perspective of an attacker, it does not matter where they obtain the information—the value is the same whether they get it from a hospital, an insurance company, or the dumpster behind a local doctor's medical offices. From the perspective of the patient-consumer, it reflects badly upon the entire system any time there is such a compromise, because that patient-consumer likely only provided the information once—at the point-of-care.

The result is a situation in which the potential negative externalities from one organization having deficient information security measures are sufficient to incentivize other organizations to seek regulatory enforcement of reasonable levels of security for all participants in the system. For example, while United HealthCare might take the privacy and security of its consumers' data very seriously, a failure by one of its vendors or providers could cause that information to be compromised. Thus even though information security regulations might not be to United's specific competitive advantage, and may even impose additional regulatory compliance costs, United may nonetheless be incentivized to support such regulation so that they may have confidence in the business partners with whom they exchange information.

The result is a circumstance in which the risk of negative externalities suggests that regulated entities will accept a higher level of constraint of their private interests than otherwise might be the case. Stated differently, the nature of an interconnected information system aligns certain incentives—particularly those pertaining information security—such that private entities' interests coincide with the public interest.

C. Is Cybersecurity Different?

These technological explanations beg the question whether information security is, by nature, *also* unique, thus suggesting that private actors working for the public good may be an exception not applicable to other circumstances. Before considering what lessons cybersecurity regulation may teach, therefore, I consider whether the cybersecurity example should be generalized.

There are two particularly obvious objections to generalizing from cybersecurity: (1) that it is highly technical; and (2) that cybersecurity's interconnected nature renders the negative externalities of one actor's failure disproportionately costly. While both objections bear merit, neither is dispositive and at most both serve to limit, rather than exclude, applicability of lessons learned from cybersecurity regulation.

The idea that a highly technical subject would distinguish cybersecurity regulation from other regulation overlooks one of the core purposes of administrative agencies. In a highly complex society, agencies develop and maintain the necessary expertise to fill in the technical details that legislatures simply lack the time to address. As noted by the United States Supreme Court in *United States v. Mistretta*, the creation of non-binding guidelines for judges sentencing convicted criminals under federal law is a highly technical topic. Industries such as education, environmental protection, and aviation are also highly technical in nature. Nothing about the technical nature cybersecurity suggests that it is any different than other highly technical subjects from a regulatory standpoint. Thus, this objection does not suggest a limit on the applicability of lessons learned from cybersecurity regulation.

The comparatively higher cost of negative externalities from individual deficient actors in cybersecurity may suggest a limitation on the industries to which lessons learned from cybersecurity regulation are applicable. The potential impact on all actors of a single actor's deficiency may be substantial. The resultant incentives for actors to override their individual interests and seek more stringent regulations for all could thus be different than in industries where such potential negative externalities from deficient compliance are not present. In considering the degree to which regulatory capture in healthcare cybersecurity may be replicable for other rulemaking, therefore, the presence of increased cost from negative externalities of individually deficient actors should be considered.

III. The General Case: Harnessing Private Expertise for Public Interest Goals

When Philip Harter first proposed the concept of negotiated rulemaking and laid out the nine factors suggesting circumstances for which it was appropriate, his approach was speculative—a proposal he viewed as addressing the then-current "malaise." As mentioned in the Introduction, in recent years some scholars have revisited this style of speculation—looking for solutions to engage private expertise and improve the legitimacy and efficacy of the regulatory process through various degrees of capture. Alternatively stated, such approaches engage a form of what Kenneth Bamberger describes as regulatory delegation, in which agencies entrust certain of their decision-making powers to private parties through various mechanisms.

These approaches, however, lack empirical validation. This paper provides that validation—the healthcare cybersecurity example demonstrates a clear case where an administrative agency engaged private expertise through legislatively imposed regulatory capture. Notwithstanding this capture, the private interests at the table utilized their private expertise not only primarily to serve public interests, but also sometimes even at the expense of their own private interests.

Building on that example, and preceding analysis that the healthcare cybersecurity example is not an isolated circumstance inapplicable to other cases, this Part proposes two conclusions representing important steps forward in our understanding of the interaction between regulation and private expertise. First, it proposes a set of characteristics about a regulatory problem suggestive that the healthcare cybersecurity style of capture may be effective at engaging private expertise for public goals. Second, it proposes a list of industries best suited to those characteristics—an effective research agenda for future empirical work investigating the applicability of such a "capture process" in practice. Finally, it concludes by suggesting a description of what that capture process might look like in the generic case. I describe this process as Enlightened Regulatory Capture.

A. Enlightened Regulatory Capture: Characteristics When Regulatory Capture Can Be Used to Engage Private Expertise for Public Goals

The healthcare cybersecurity example describes a circumstance when regulatory capture engaged private expertise to advance public goals. Though they were representatives of private interests—with legislatively mandated capture over the rulemaking process—the individuals involved in writing the HIPAA Security Rule nonetheless used their private expertise in the public interest. Their activities thus constitute a form of enlightened self-interest, suggesting the descriptive title Enlightened Regulatory Capture.

Five general characteristics of Enlightened Regulatory Capture (ERC) are present in the healthcare cybersecurity example: (1) the capture function is enforced by rule; (2) there is a perceived detriment to the participants and their industry as a whole if the process fails; (3) procedural constraints are relaxed, requiring only majority approval to act; (4) "reduced-bias" subject matter experts are mandated by rule as participants; and (5) the participants have incentives creating a commitment to the process other than the opportunity to advance their private interests.

The most critical aspect of ERC is that the capture function is enforced by rule. The participants must believe that their work will necessarily become part of the rule that is adopted. This is similar to, but more expansive than, Harter's "inevitability of decision" factor. In previous parts, I considered two cases of regulation regarding the NCLB—one by the DOI, and one by the DOE. The organic statute differs notably between these two cases—both specify the use of negotiated rulemaking, but the DOI has no exemption for it, whereas the DOE has an exemption. As discussed in the analysis of those examples, the "weaker" version of capture is likely one of the reasons the DOI example is noted as a negotiated rulemaking "success" whereas the DOE example is regarded by the literature as a negotiated rulemaking failure. The consultation requirement that effectively caused HHS to turn over the rulemaking process to the NCVHS contributed both to the committee members' perception of their authority and their willingness to act in the public interest—rather than fighting with competitors to advance their own interests.

The second characteristic is that the participants must believe they have a stake in the game—that some negative consequence will result for their individual interests or for the interests of the industry they represent as a whole, or both, should they fail. In the case of healthcare cybersecurity, a failure could exacerbate the negative externalities problem, allow the patchwork of inconsistent state laws to continue, and possibly result in a perceived loss of the prestige members felt at being nominated to serve on the NCVHS for failing to fulfill the responsibilities of their appointment. This is not dissimilar from Harter's "opportunity for gain" factor, but is far more expansive and contemplates a countervailing opportunity for loss as well.

Third, procedural constraints must be far more relaxed than the consensus requirement present in negotiated rulemaking. As discussed throughout this Article, the consensus requirement often results in a minimization effect—where the unilateral veto power held by each participant on a negotiated rulemaking committee results in that outcome which is the least-common-denominator to all interests at the table. While this process may be desirable for certain circumstances, it seems ill-suited to many rulemakings and is often the source of substantial criticism of negotiated rulemaking. In the healthcare cybersecurity example, only a majority was required for NCVHS action. As discussed, this majority requirement was a key component to forcing participants that might otherwise have private agendas to work collaboratively and to preventing any participants from gaining "internal capture" through unilateral veto power.

The fourth requirement, that there be mandatory "reduced-bias" subject matter experts as participants, strongly integrates with the third requirement of relaxed procedural rules. In the healthcare cybersecurity example, the presence of and general characteristics of these experts were mandated by statute. The concept of a "reduced-bias" expert is an individual who is less susceptible to influence as a function of their employment than is an at-will employee of a private organization or a professional whose primary compensation depends upon providing services to private organizations. The most prevalent example of this type of expert is a tenured member of a university faculty, which, as discussed above, was the case in the healthcare cybersecurity example. As discussed in more detail, the relaxed procedural rules work together with this requirement by forcing private interests to work together with these reduced-bias experts, thereby in turn reducing their ability to advance private agendas at the expense of the public interest.

The third and fourth characteristics together describe an essential component of the function and character of ERC. ERC is well-suited when interested parties, at minimum, *can* be capable of working collaboratively toward resolution. By contrast, if fundamental differences that *cannot* be overcome by restrictions on unilateral veto power that render collaboration impossible, then ERC's suitability substantially decreases. Ironically, as discussed above, negotiated rulemaking—which Harter claims is *not* well-suited to fundamental differences—may in fact be better suited to such circumstances.

Finally, consistent with this collaborative function, the fifth characteristic requires that the participants have a commitment to the process beyond the mere opportunity to advance their private interests. Harter describes the participants as needing to have the "opportunity to gain." But the mere opportunity to gain is not sufficient, as evidenced by the DOE example discussed above. The parties must have some other factors that incentivize them to participate in the process not just for personal gain, or private interests may ultimately take over even the best-intentioned of individuals. Several such factors were present in the healthcare cybersecurity example. As discussed in detail in Part II, committee membership on the NCVHS was considered an honor to which obligation to act in the public interest attached. Members accordingly took this responsibility quite seriously, even at times to the possible expense of the private interests they represented. The risk of negative externalities described also contributed to members' incentives in this regard. Additionally, the possibility of "getting it right" so that the continued patchwork of inefficient (and possibly technologically inferior) state-level regulations would not continue presented an opportunity for *positive* externalities to be realized by the process.

The characteristics presented here are neither an exhaustive list nor are they necessarily required for ERC to be an effective approach. They represent preliminary suggestions, generalizing characteristics from the first instance presented in the literature of a verifiable example of regulatory capture working clearly in the public interest. As noted above, other scholars' writing suggests they are conducting similar empirical analysis, and such work should serve as an opportunity to refine the characteristics presented here.

QUESTIONS

1. What does the HIPAA Security Rule example teach about the engagement of private expertise?

2. Do you think that this is unique to *healthcare* cybersecurity? What would make industries more likely to function similarly, and what would make an industry be different from the healthcare example?

3. If you were designing a public-private partnership, how would you begin? Describe three scenarios where you think a public-private partnership would be especially effective.

E. INSURANCE

An often-overlooked method of regulation is the use of insurance. Nearly all organizations carry at least some form of insurance. One of the most common types of business insurance is general commercial liability, which covers organizations against tort claims arising in the ordinary conduct of their business. Modern insurance policies almost always some application process, which allows insurers to price policies relative to their assessment of the insured's risk (or to refuse coverage). They also include various exclusions—conditions under which the insurance policy will not provide coverage—and implied or express affirmative requirements—conditions which must be met for coverage to apply. For example, many general commercial liability policies have exclusions that limit or preclude coverage in the case of intention torts, limiting or restricting coverage only to those cases of negligence or other unintentional error or omission. Some policies also have general maintenance requirements, for example, that an insured party meet at least basic health, safety, and building codes imposed by governmental authorities for coverage to apply.

Commercial insurance policies increasingly provide cybersecurity-related coverage, either as a standalone policy or as part of a general commercial liability policy. At the same time, these policies are often substantially limited, carrying exclusions that substantially limit the types of incidents that the policy will cover.

It is worth noting the relationship between insurance and tort law. As discussed in Chapter 6, tort law largely serves the function of allocating risks that may occur in day-to-day life. As Oliver Wendel Holmes noted in 1897, when tort law places the burden of accidental and negligent injuries on businesses, that liability "sooner or later goes into the price paid by the public. The public really pays the damages, and the question of liability, if pressed far enough, is really the question how far it is desirable that the public should insure the safety of those whose work it uses." Insurance operates in much the same way, albeit more narrowly spreading the burden of this liability across the insured's firm's customers, as opposed to more broadly across the whole of society.

What effects might systematic implementation of such exclusions, limitations or affirmative requirements have? This has been the subject of much scholarship, a non-trivial portion of which suggests that it works to drive behavior. Consider, for example, auto insurance, under which accidents and traffic violations can result in higher premiums. If you get two speeding tickets, which might concern you more? The price of the tickets or the increase in your automobile insurance premiums over the next few years? (This example is a bit trickier with accidents, as they vary in degree of cost and injury.)

How might this scenario apply to cybersecurity? Generally speaking, prior to the late 2010's, existing types of insurance policies were not designed to cover cybersecurity incidents. Actuarial tables were not in place to price the types of risk involved. Often times, however, the *harms* were similar to those resulting from other types of risks. For example, business interruption insurance, which provides coverage in the event an event like a major storm temporarily disrupts the operations of a business, may deal with similar *harms* in terms of the "disruption" that might be caused by a storm as could be caused by a major cybersecurity compromise.

However, risk *pricing* for a storm is fundamentally different than that for a cybersecurity event. Thus, insurers have been reluctant to pay based on cybersecurity events, and, in recent years, some insurers have updated their policies to provide express exclusions.[5] At the same time, insurers have also begun to attempt to develop cyberrisk or cyberliability insurance policies or added coverage options to physical premises and business policies. In many respects, this still is a nascent market, as we lack the longitudinal data to determine confidence risk pricing models. In particular, unlike with most other events, there has yet to be a major, systemic, worldwide "cyber" event. This leaves open a number of questions, including the degree to which cybersecurity insurance can serve a regulatory function. In the following excerpt, Professor Hurwitz explores these questions. We have seen other excerpts from this article in previous chapters, discussing both the cybersecurity ecosystem and the concept of strict liability—this excerpt builds on those discussions.

GUS HURWITZ, *CYBERENSURING SECURITY*

49 U. CONN. L. REV. 1495 (2017)

IV. CYBERINSURING LIABILITY

Section III of this Article [excerpted in Chapter 6B] argued the merits of using strict liability to address harms that result from cyber incidents. Use of strict liability in this context would correct many of the challenges that parties face in establishing liability for harmful conduct discussed in Section II [excerpted in Chapter 4C]. In particular, the failures of existing private and public law mechanisms to assign liability for cyber-incidents creates incentives for those who would otherwise bear the cost of mitigating or the costs of harms caused by such incidents—generally the same parties who are in the best position to take precautions against them—to externalize the risk of cyber-incidents on to third parties—generally those least able to mitigate or afford to bear such risk. In effect, the current model is a no-(third-party)-liability model, which creates pervasive, harmful incentives. Adopting a strict liability model would go far to align public and private incentives to reduce cyber-incident risks to a more efficient level.

It turns out that there is a nexus between strict liability and the sort of insurance that would improve the state of cybersecurity. Academics have been discussing the value of cyber insurance as a mechanism for improving the overall state of cybersecurity for over a decade, but in more recent years have lamented the insurance marketplace's failure thus far to realize this

---

[5] NB: as of the time of this writing, a new class of "excluded" events litigation—global pandemic—likely will arise as well. *To what extent do you think there are comparisons between a "global pandemic" and a "major cybersecurity event"?* See Deirdre K. Mulligan and Fred B. Schneider, Doctrine for Cybersecurity, 140 Daedalus 70–92 (2011).

possibility. Indeed, while the cyber-insurance marketplace has grown substantially in recent years, the policies that are being written are largely structured in ways that limit the broader impact of insurance on the state of cybersecurity. In order to improve the quality of cybersecurity, insurance needs to provide more complete coverage—in particular, insurers (and, through them, the rest of the ecosystem) need to internalize the risks that are systematically externalized due to the diffuse nature of the cybersecurity ecosystem. It turns out that strict liability, in economic terms, actually is a form of insurance, and as a form of insurance it is particularly sensitive to these externalized third-party effects.

This relationship between strict liability and insurance, and potential effects on cybersecurity, is discussed in Section V. Before turning to that discussion, this Section provides a background discussion of insurance generally and of cyber insurance in particular. It starts by providing a general overview of what insurance is, its potential applicability in the cybersecurity context, and its limitations.

A. Defining Insurance

1. Risk Pooling

Insurance is tool for pooling risk. It allows parties that face predictable but uncertain risks to reduce the variance in costs that they face as a result of the risks. It is driving by the statistical "law of large numbers," which tells us that if we take a large number of parties that face similar risks, on average each party will incur the average costs of these risks. In other words, if 100 parties face a 10% chance of a $1,000 loss and a 90% chance of a $0 loss, each of those parties will experience an average loss of $100.

Without insurance, a party subject to this risk will either incur no loss or a $1,000 loss—it will never incur the average, $100 loss. Such a party is said to self-insure: it will face a $1,000 liability should the risk of loss materialize and so must be in a position to pay out that much. Such a party is also said to face a large variance in expected outcomes: it will pay out either $0 or $1,000.

With insurance, the insured party will pay an insurer the average expected loss amount ($100, plus some administrative fee to cover the insurer's costs). Should the risk materialize, the insurer will pay out $1,000; should it not materialize, the insurer keeps the $100. A party buying such an insurance policy faces small variance: it knows that it will pay exactly $100 in all circumstances. This provides the insured with predictable and stable flow of costs.

Insurance does not necessarily reduce or eliminate risk. Rather, it transfers it from the insured party to the insurer. By pooling risk from a large number of insureds, insurers are in a better position to absorb the costs of risk. When a risk materializes into an actual liability, the costs on a self-insuring party can be substantial. This is immediately intuitive to most people: the sudden imposition of tens or hundreds of thousands of dollars that can result from even a non-catastrophic car accident could easily bankrupt most drivers. But, thanks to the law of large numbers, an insurer who insures a sufficiently large number of parties can anticipate and manage its cash flow to accommodate such losses.

2. The Actuarial Process: First- and Third-Party Insurance

The heart of the insurance businesses is the actuarial and underwriting process. This is the process by which insurers identify and estimate the likely costs of the risks that a party wants to insure against. For instance, a driver will provide insurers with demographic information, information about her car and driving record, her driving patterns, and the like. A successful insurer will accurately estimate these risks and their associated costs and charge its insureds a concomitant amount.

On the other side of this process, the party seeking insurance needs to identify what risks it wants to insure against. There are a number of standard risks for which we use insurance: automobiles, unemployment, health care, loss or damage to houses or businesses, and the like. In principle, insurers are generally willing to sell insurance against any risk, provided that they can reasonably estimate the likely risks and costs of loss—though, in cases of indeterminate or particularly costly, likely losses, premiums for such policies can be substantial.

A particularly important distinction in types of insurable risks is that between first-party and third-party liabilities. Most insurance is first-party, meaning that when the insured party experiences a loss, insurance compensates it for those losses. In third party insurance, the party purchasing the insurance is doing so to insure a third-party against loss. For instance, a firm seeking to do business that may cause risk to third parties may agree to purchase insurance to insure those parties against that risk—sometimes even without those third-parties' knowledge.

3. Insurance as Regulation

Most insurers are not passive entities. They make money by reducing the actual rate of loss compared to the actuarially anticipated rate of loss. There are a number of ways that this can be accomplished. A primary function of the underwriting process is not only to assess the actuarial risks of a potential insured, but to educate and instruct the insured on how to reduce those risks. In some cases, this is an entirely passive process. For instance, an automobile insurer is likely to indicate to potential customers that there are discounts for drivers of cars with airbags, anti-lock brakes, or other safety devices; and drivers who have completed driving safety courses are also likely to pay lower premiums. The primary purpose of these discounts is to determine a driver's actuarial risk—but by announcing them, drivers are also educated about ways to reduce their risk. In other cases, this process is more active. For instance, a business seeking insurance against theft is likely to go through a more intensive underwriting process that will involve an actual inspection or in-depth checklist of the business's security practices and that will identify egregious risks (and likely insist that they be addressed prospectively) and will include express directive guidance on best practices.

In other cases, insurers may attempt to improve actuarial risks for all of their actual or prospective clients—instead of focusing on individual customers in the underwriting process. Perhaps the best example of this is the lawsuits filed by automobile insurers in the 1980s to challenge the decision by the National Highway Traffic Safety Administration (NHTSA) to stop requiring cars to come standard with seat belts. Of course, insurers do not do this out of the goodness of their hearts; they do so because it is likely to increase their profitability. This is particularly likely to be the case where the use of insurance is required (expressly or implicitly) by law, where parties subject to the insured risk are unlikely to appreciate the potential costs of the risk, or where the actuarial costs of insurance are high enough to push a significant number of firms out of the market. As we will see below, all three of these are likely to be the case with cyber insurance.

B. The Virtues of Cyber-insurance

Insurance can have a broad regulatory effect on a market, improving both the conduct of those using insurance and the overall state of a given market. Insurers have unique abilities and incentives to inform firms of their legal obligations, to develop best-practices, to audit and educate firms as to those practices, and to lobby for improvements to the overall state of the cybersecurity ecosystem. For this reason, widespread adoption of cyber insurance would potentially spur dramatic improvements in quality of the cybersecurity ecosystem.

Section I of this Article made the case that, stated simply, cybersecurity is hard. Participants throughout the cybersecurity ecosystem have surprisingly little understanding of the pervasive risks and challenges associated with cybersecurity, let alone an understanding of best (or even merely good) practices. At the user level, individuals rarely have familiarity with principles of security "hygiene," as it is referred to in the literature—concepts like how to identify and respond to risks, how to manage passwords, e-mail accounts, and other sensitive information, and with whom to share or not share information. Going up a level in the food chain, small businesses frequently lack all of this knowledge as well but are also tasked with bigger, more complicated challenges: how to design and secure basic IT systems, how to monitor, identify, mitigate, and respond to cyber-incidents, how to design and implement an incident response plan. For most small- and even mid-sized businesses, it is enough of a challenge (and expense) just to get a basic IT infrastructure in place. Especially outside of the tech sector, most firms don't even know what issues they face, let alone how to address them. The same basic story can be told at nearly every level of participation and sophistication in the cybersecurity ecosystem; even those who are implementing systems often lack information about the needs and sophistication of their customers, making it difficult to design systems that promote good security hygiene.

Insurance—and insurers—are uniquely situated to address these system- and ecosystem-level concerns. The basic business of insurance is the collection of data relating to risk, the quantification of that risk, the evaluation of individual insureds' risk profiles, and the minimization of both their insureds' exposure to and the overall market's creation of risk.

An insurer's first job is to build its actuarial tables—to collect data that will allow it to evaluate an individual insured's exposure to risk in a given industry. This is a process that, in the context of cybersecurity, we will return to in Section V.

Once an insurer has a sense of the factors that go into determining an individual insured's exposure to risk, it can begin underwriting new clients. This is the process by which insurers evaluate possible clients' risk profiles to determine their insurability and the premiums to be charged for insurance. In the cybersecurity context, for instance, an insurer is likely to conduct an audit of a firm's systems and procedures: what is the architecture of the firm's network, what data is stored and used, how is access controlled, what incident response plans are in place, how are employees trained and monitored, how is third-party access to the firm's systems (e.g., by contractors) assigned and monitored, and the like. This process alone offers—or would offer—most firms a more in-depth evaluation of their cybersecurity systems than they would ever otherwise receive, except possibly in the case of a serious security incident. Even more important, it would offer these firms the most in-depth education regarding security best-practices that they are likely to ever receive. Moreover, insurers have an incentive to monitor their insured's ongoing performance, providing ongoing updates and training regarding best practices and responses to newly discovered security problems

It is difficult to imagine a more effective approach to educating and evaluating the bottommost layers of the security pyramid. And this leads to a second powerful benefit of widespread adoption of cyber-insurance policies, effective push-back against the pervasive externalization of risks from sophisticated parties onto unsophisticated parties. There are two sources of this push-back. First, as consumers and firms are informed by insurers about their exposure to risk, they will have greater demand for more secure products. This means both that they will be willing to pay more for more secure products (which would lower their insurance premiums), and they will put greater pressure on vendors and service providers to provide more secure products and services. And second, the insurance industry itself will serve as a powerful lobby to push for better designed and more secure products and services. The software and tech industries are powerful interests that have largely been successful in shielding themselves from liability for the quality of their wares—for good reasons and bad. There is no concerted interest group on the other side of this balance—consumers are too diffuse a group with too little an understanding of the relevant harms to which they are exposed to effectively lobby against Silicon Valley or the Business Software Alliance to demand risk be shifted back to those who have built the insecure infrastructure on which we have come to depend.

C. Limitations of Cyber-insurance: Damages, Data, Exposure, Externalities

Despite the positive story about cyber insurance told above, the reality of the cyber-insurance market is less rosy. The cyber-insurance market faces a number of challenges. While it has been growing at a substantial pace in recent years, it is still "just a drop in the bucket" compared to the scale of the cybersecurity problem. As recently noted by Peter Singer, less than half of Fortune 500 firms have cyber insurance; 18,000 mid-size firms do not have cyber insurance; and only 5% of manufacturing firms have cyber insurance. Overall, only about a third of US firms carry cyber insurance policies.

In recent years, academics have extensively studied the incentives that insurers have to offer cyber insurance. The particular focus of these studies has been to determine whether insurers are likely to offer policies that will improve the overall quality of the cybersecurity ecosystem. The general conclusion has been that they do not. Except in the case of a monopoly insurance provider or mandatory insurance, models of the insurance industry predict that insurers will limit the policies that they offer to first-party contracts that only insure firms against their direct losses in the event of a cyber-incident. Indeed, the literature predicts that such policies can worsen the overall cybersecurity ecosystem by reducing firms' incentives to take precautions to avoid third-party harms that could result from compromise of their systems.

The cyber-insurance market has, in fact, proceeded along these lines. Insurers are generally willing to underwrite first-party policies that protect firms against the direct costs that they incur from a security incident—costs that include investigating and recovering from a cyber-incident, and business losses associated with that incident. And, for that matter, insurers are also happy to underwrite third-party risks.

Although insurers are increasingly underwriting these policies, their breadth of coverage remains substantially unclear. Many of the terms, both in Commercial General Liability (CGL) policies that offer cyber-incident coverage and standalone cyber-insurance policies, remain untested in court. Tellingly, "the ratio of premiums to the coverage limit for cyber insurance is triple the ratio of other liability policies and six times higher than the ratio for property insurance"—a circumstance that both speaks to the uncertainty in the scope of these policies' coverage and that likely makes these policies unattractive to many potential insureds.

What is more, and unsurprisingly, insurers are pushing against broad interpretation of their policies' coverage—or, conversely, for broad construction of these policies' exclusions—at every turn. This is, of course, to be expected. But given the multiplicity of actors in the cybersecurity ecosystem, insurers' efforts to cabin the breadth of their policies limits the regulatory effect of their policies.

Another reason that these policies are often limited is that there is dramatic uncertainty as to the actual risk exposure associated with cyber-incidents. In the context of data breaches, for instance, estimates for the per-record cost of a data breach range from several dollars per record breached to several hundred dollars per record breached. Such a potential range of liability makes it difficult for insurers to construct useful actuarial tables—and therefore limits the range of risks that insurers are willing to underwrite.

This is further compounded by the uncertain legal liability faced as a result of a cyber-incident. As discussed in Section II.B, legal institutions have struggled to adapt to the cybersecurity context. Courts routinely dismiss cases for lack of standing or articulable harm, and where losses are clear the economic loss doctrine often limits recovery. These issues are compounded by adding in insurance contracts, where the terms of these contracts need to be interpreted and given meaning in a new setting—a task with which courts have struggled in recent years. The law, however, continues to evolve, and it is entirely possible that, in any given case, a court may break from the short-lived history of cases in this area and find—potentially substantial—liability. This, again, limits the accuracy of insurers' actuarial tables, and therefore the policies that insurers are willing to underwrite.

A final limitation on the cybersecurity risks that insurers are willing to underwrite is that many risks relating to cybersecurity are correlated. This means that that if one insured is likely to experience a loss, other insureds are similarly likely. This results from the interconnected nature of the Internet and the nature of many cyber-incidents. Any given security vulnerability is likely to affect a large number of insured and exploitation of these vulnerabilities often targets many potential targets simultaneously. A contemporary example is ransomware, which is generally distributed widely by e-mail. A year ago, insurers may not have experienced any ransomware related losses, but today those losses may be widespread across a large number of insureds. A fundamental principle of risk pooling is that risks cannot be correlated—the fact that one party experiences a loss cannot suggest that others are more likely to experience the same loss. Because many cybersecurity risks are correlated, insurers are, once again, cautious to write broad policies.

QUESTIONS

1. How might organizations use insurance as a strategy to offset risk?

2. As described briefly in Chapter 11, insurance is often used to *transfer* risk as an alternative decision to accepting, mitigating, or remediating risk. In what scenarios might insurance be the best option?

3. Some policy analysts have considered requiring the purchase of cybersecurity policies in laws. Why do you think this may or may not be a good idea?

4. Private contracts may include minimum cyberliability or cyberrisk insurance requirements (including minimum policy limits). Why might this strategically be a good choice for organizations doing business with a third party?

F. CONCLUDING THOUGHTS AND QUESTIONS

Regulating cybersecurity practices and outcome is deeply complex. Throughout this book, you have seen variations on a theme of "cybersecurity is hard because cybersecurity is complex." What does this tell us about the selection of methods of regulation?

To be sure, no simple regulatory approach is likely to work. By now you have learned that there is no technological silver bullet to protect against cybersecurity harms or deter adversaries from engaging in attacks. Likewise, the past few Chapters endeavor to demonstrate why the same is true for legal and regulatory systems—no simple solution exists to "just make people do 'good' cybersecurity." That's the bad news, and the frustrating part of studying the cybersecurity problem.

The proverbial good news, however, is that by now you also hopefully have seen that there are a lot of potential tools in the toolbox, both on the legal and on the technological side. This chapter explored alternative modes of regulation precisely to see how various tools can be used together, to give you some insight into which tools tend to work under what situations, and to expose you to the idea of more complex, integrated solutions involving many tools working together. We close the book by asking you to consider a few questions about how these tools can work together:

QUESTIONS

1. What are the differences between regulating outcomes, tools, and processes? Why do these differences matter?

2. What does traditional (directive) governmental regulation miss? How can alternative forms of governmental regulation address these shortcomings/gaps?

3. At which situations or activities does government regulation excel, and at which does it fail? Why and when do traditional forms of governmental regulation fall sort?

4. Why does self-regulation exist? What gaps can it fill? What are the risks of self-regulation?

5. What can public-private partnerships do to fill some of the gaps referenced in the preceding questions?

6. What is the role of insurance in directing or driving behavior? Against what harms does insurance protect? *Who* does insurance protect?

7. As you consider the various tactics, especially legal, that this book describes, how would you create an *effective* cybersecurity program? What approach might you use?

8. What might inform whether an organization should follow legal requirements or employ industry standards? What might some incentives be for following more restrictive self-regulation?

9. If you were establishing a cybersecurity program for your organization, what do you believe will be your critical success factor? How do you know you have succeeded?

INDEX

References are to Pages